To four outstanding teachers and great human beings:

With your guidance, inspiration, and patience, you showed me
that everything is possible.

Dr. Sidney H. Englander (1900–1980)
and Mildred K. Englander (1906–2008),
in memoriam my father and mother

Albert L. Daugherty, in memoriam
teacher of Science in Cleveland Heights, Ohio
from 1927 to 1970

Edith B. Malin, in memoriam
teacher of English in Cleveland Heights, Ohio
from 1924 to 1958

BRIEF CONTENTS

PART ONE

AN OVERVIEW OF COMPUTER SYSTEMS   2

   CHAPTER 1   Computers and Systems   4

   CHAPTER 2   An Introduction to System Concepts and Systems Architecture   38

PART TWO

DATA IN THE COMPUTER   66

   CHAPTER 3   Number Systems   68

   CHAPTER 4   Data Formats   96

   CHAPTER 5   Representing Numerical Data   136

PART THREE

COMPUTER ARCHITECTURE
AND HARDWARE OPERATION   178

   CHAPTER 6   The Little Man Computer   180

   CHAPTER 7   The CPU and Memory   198

   CHAPTER 8   CPU and Memory: Design, Enhancement, and Implementation   240

   CHAPTER 9   Input/Output   276

■ CHAPTER 10   Computer Peripherals   306

■ CHAPTER 11   Modern Computer Systems   342

PART FOUR

NETWORKS AND DATA COMMUNICATIONS   368

■ CHAPTER 12   Networks and Data Communications   370

■ CHAPTER 13   Ethernet and TCP/IP Networking   422

■ CHAPTER 14   Communication Channel Technology   446

PART FIVE

THE SOFTWARE COMPONENT   476

■ CHAPTER 15   Operating Systems: An Overview   478

■ CHAPTER 16   The User View of Operating Systems   514

■ CHAPTER 17   File Management   548

■ CHAPTER 18   The Internal Operating System   592

SUPPLEMENTARY CHAPTERS

On the Web at www.wiley.com/go/global/englander

■ SUPPLEMENTARY CHAPTER 1   An Introduction to Digital Computer Logic

■ SUPPLEMENTARY CHAPTER 2   System Examples

■ SUPPLEMENTARY CHAPTER 3   Instruction Addressing Modes

■ SUPPLEMENTARY CHAPTER 4   Programming Tools

CONTENTS

Preface   xxi

About the Author   xxvii

PART ONE

AN OVERVIEW OF COMPUTER SYSTEMS   2

■ **CHAPTER 1**   **Computers and Systems   4**

1.0   **Introduction   5**
1.1   **The Starting Point   9**
1.2   **Components of the Computer System   12**
    The Hardware Component   13
    The Software Component   16
    The Communication Component   18
    The Computer System   18
1.3   **The Concept of Virtualization   20**
1.4   **Protocols and Standards   20**
1.5   **Overview of This Book   22**
1.6   **A Brief Architectural History of the Computer   23**
    Early Work   24
    Computer Hardware   25
    Operating Systems   28
    Communication, Networks, and the Internet   33
Summary and Review   34   For Further Reading   34
Key Concepts and Terms   35   Reading Review Questions   35
Exercises   36

■ **CHAPTER 2**   **An Introduction to System Concepts and Systems Architecture   38**

2.0   **Introduction   39**
2.1   **The General Concept of Systems   40**
2.2   **IT System Architectures   48**
    Distributed Processing Systems   49

The Role of the System Architect   57
Google: A System Architecture Example   58

Summary and Review   62   For Further Reading   63
Key Concepts and Terms   63   Reading Review Questions   63
Exercises   64

PART TWO

DATA IN THE COMPUTER   66

■ CHAPTER 3   Number Systems   68

3.0   Introduction   69
3.1   Numbers as a Physical Representation   70
3.2   Counting in Different Bases   70
3.3   Performing Arithmetic in Different Number Bases   74
3.4   Numeric Conversion between Number Bases   77
An Alternative Conversion Method   79
3.5   Hexadecimal Numbers and Arithmetic   81
3.6   A Special Conversion Case—Number Bases that are
**   Related   81**
3.7   Fractions   83
Fractional Conversion Methods   86
3.8   Mixed Number Conversions   89
Summary and Review   89   For Further Reading   90
Key Concepts and Terms   90   Reading Review Questions   90
Exercises   91

■ CHAPTER 4   Data Formats   96

4.0   Introduction   97
4.1   General Considerations   97
4.2   Alphanumeric Character Data   100
Keyboard Input   106
Alternative Sources of Alphanumeric Input   107
4.3   Image Data   109
Bitmap Images   110
Object Images   114
Representing Characters as Images   117
Video Images   117
Image and Video Input   118
4.4   Audio Data   119
4.5   Data Compression   123

4.6   **Page Description Languages**   124

4.7   **Internal Computer Data Format**   125

       Numerical Character to Integer Conversion   127

Summary and Review   128   **For Further Reading**   129

Key Concepts and Terms   130   **Reading Review Questions**   130

Exercises   131

■ CHAPTER 5   Representing Numerical Data   136

5.0   **Introduction**   137

5.1   **Unsigned Binary and Binary-Coded Decimal Representations**   138

5.2   **Representations for Signed Integers**   141

       Sign-and-magnitude Representation   142

       Nine's Decimal and 1's Binary Complementary Representations   143

       Ten's Complement and 2's Complement   150

       Overflow and Carry Conditions   153

       Other Bases   153

       Summary of Rules for Complementary Numbers   154

5.3   **Real Numbers**   155

       A Review of Exponential Notation   155

       Floating Point Format   157

       Normalization and Formatting of Floating Point Numbers   159

       A Programming Example   162

       Floating Point Calculations   163

       Floating Point in the Computer   165

       Conversion between Base 10 and Base 2   167

5.4   **Programming Considerations**   168

Summary and Review   169   **For Further Reading**   170

Key Concepts and Terms   171   **Reading Review Questions**   171

Exercises   172

PART THREE

COMPUTER ARCHITECTURE AND HARDWARE OPERATION   178

■ CHAPTER 6   The Little Man Computer   180

6.0   **Introduction**   181

6.1   **Layout of the Little Man Computer**   181

6.2   Operation of the LMC   183

6.3   A Simple Program   185

6.4   An Extended Instruction Set   186

6.5   The Instruction Cycle   189

6.6   A Note Regarding Computer Architectures   192

Summary and Review   192   Key Concepts and Terms   193

Reading Review Questions   193   Exercises   194

■ CHAPTER 7   The CPU and Memory   198

7.0   Introduction   199

7.1   The Components of the CPU   200

7.2   The Concept of Registers   201

7.3   The Memory Unit   204

        The Operation of Memory   204

        Memory Capacity   208

        Primary Memory Characteristics and Implementation   209

7.4   The Fetch-Execute Instruction Cycle   211

7.5   Buses   214

        Bus Characteristics   214

7.6   Classification of Instructions   218

        Data Movement Instructions (LOAD, STORE, and Other
          Moves)   219

        Arithmetic Instructions   221

        Boolean Logic Instructions   222

        Single Operand Manipulation Instructions   222

        Bit Manipulation Instructions   222

        Shift and Rotate Instructions   223

        Program Control Instructions   224

        Stack Instructions   225

        Multiple Data Instructions   228

        Other Instructions   229

7.7   Instruction Word Formats   229

7.8   Instruction Word Requirements and Constraints   230

Summary and Review   234   For Further Reading   234

Key Concepts and Terms   235   Reading Review Questions   235

Exercises   237

■ **CHAPTER 8** **CPU and Memory: Design, Enhancement, and Implementation** 240

8.0 **Introduction** 241

8.1 **CPU Architectures** 242
  Overview 242
  Traditional Modern Architectures 243
  VLIW and EPIC Architectures 244

8.2 **CPU Features and Enhancements** 246
  Introduction 246
  Fetch-Execute Cycle Timing Issues 247
  A Model for Improved CPU Performance 249
  Scalar and Superscalar Processor Organization 253

8.3 **Memory Enhancements** 256
  Wide Path Memory Access 257
  Memory Interleaving 258
  Cache Memory 259

8.4 **The Compleat Modern Superscalar CPU** 263

8.5 **Multiprocessing** 265

8.6 **A Few Comments on Implementation** 269

Summary and Review 269　For Further Reading 270
Key Concepts and Terms 271　Reading Review Questions 271
Exercises 272

■ **CHAPTER 9** **Input/Output** 276

9.0 **Introduction** 277

9.1 **Characteristics of Typical I/O Devices** 278

9.2 **Programmed I/O** 284

9.3 **Interrupts** 285
  Servicing Interrupts 286
  The Uses of Interrupts 288
  Multiple Interrupts and Prioritization 293

9.4 **Direct Memory Access** 297

9.5 **I/O Modules** 300

Summary and Review 302　For Further Reading 303
Key Concepts and Terms 303　Reading Review Questions 304
Exercises 304

■ **CHAPTER 10** **Computer Peripherals 306**

10.0 **Introduction** 307
10.1 **The Hierarchy of Storage** 308
10.2 **Solid State Memory** 310
10.3 **Magnetic Disks** 311
  Disk Arrays 317
10.4 **Optical Disk Storage** 318
10.5 **Magnetic Tape** 321
10.6 **Displays** 322
  Liquid Crystal Display Technology 328
  CRT Display Technology 329
  OLED Display Technology 330
10.7 **Printers** 330
  Laser Printers 331
  Inkjet Printers 332
  Thermal Wax Transfer and Dye Sublimation Printers 333
10.8 **User Input Devices** 333
  Keyboards and Pointing Devices 333
  Scanners 335
  Multimedia Devices 335
10.9 **Network Communication Devices** 335
Summary and Review 336   For Further Reading 337
Key Concepts and Terms 337   Reading Review Questions 338
Exercises 339

■ **CHAPTER 11** **Modern Computer Systems 342**

11.0 **Introduction** 343
11.1 **Putting All the Pieces Together** 345
11.2 **Input/Output System Architectures** 353
  I/O Bus Architecture 354
  Channel Architecture 357
  Blurring the Line 358
11.3 **Computer Interconnection: A Brief Overview** 359
11.4 **Clusters** 360
  Overview 360
  Classification and Configuration 360
  Beowulf Clusters 362

11.5   High-Performance Computing   363
       Grid Computing   364
Summary and Review   364   For Further Reading   365
Key Concepts and Terms   365   Reading Review Questions   366
Exercises   366

PART FOUR

NETWORKS AND DATA COMMUNICATIONS   368

■ CHAPTER 12   Networks and Data Communications   370

12.0   Introduction   371
12.1   The Impact of Networking on Business Processes and User
       Access to Knowledge and Services   372
12.2   A Simple View of Data Communications   373
12.3   Basic Data Communication Concepts   376
       Messages   377
       Packets   377
       General Channel Characteristics   378
       Packet Routing   382
12.4   TCP/IP, OSI, and Other Communication Models   386
       Overview   386
       The TCP/IP Network Model   387
       The OSI Network Model   395
       Addressing   396
12.5   Types of Networks   398
       Network Topology   399
       Local Area Networks   402
       Backbone Networks   407
       Metropolitan Area Networks   409
       Wide Area Networks (WAN)   411
       Internet Backbones and the Internet   412
       Piconets   414
12.6   Standards   415
Summary and Review   416   For Further Reading   417
Key Concepts and Terms   417   Reading Review Questions   418
Exercises   419

■ **CHAPTER 13** **Ethernet and TCP/IP Networking** **422**

13.0 **Introduction** 423
13.1 **Introducing The Process—The Application Layer** 423
13.2 **Domain Names and DNS Services** 424
    Domain Name System Directory Services 424
13.3 **Next Steps—TCP and the Transport Layer** 429
13.4 **The Network Layer, IP Addresses, and ARP** 430
    IP Addresses 431
    Dynamic Host Configuration Protocol (DHCP) 433
    The Operation of IP 434
13.5 **The Data Link Layer** 435
    Hub-Based Ethernet 436
    Switched Ethernet 437
13.6 **Quality of Service** 437
13.7 **Network Security** 438
    Physical and Logical Access Restriction 439
    Encryption 440
13.8 **Alternative Protocols** 440
    MPLS 440
    ATM 441
    SONET/SDH 441
    Frame Relay 441
Summary and Review 442   **For Further Reading** 442
Key Concepts and Terms 443   **Reading Review Questions** 443
Exercises 443

■ **CHAPTER 14** **Communication Channel Technology** **446**

14.0 **Introduction** 447
14.1 **Communication Channel Technology** 447
14.2 **The Fundamentals of Signaling Technology** 450
    Analog Signaling 451
    Digital Signaling 460
    Modems and Codecs 465
14.3 **Transmission Media and Signaling Methods** 466
14.4 **Wireless Networking** 468
    Wi-Fi 469

Summary and Review   471   For Further Reading   471

Key Concepts and Terms   471   Reading Review Questions   472

Exercises   473

PART FIVE

THE SOFTWARE COMPONENT   476

■ **CHAPTER 15   Operating Systems: An Overview   478**

15.0   Introduction   479

15.1   The Barebones Computer System   480

15.2   The Operating Systems Concept: An Introduction   481

15.3   Services and Facilities   488

　　　　User Interface and Command Execution Services   489

　　　　File Management   490

　　　　Input/Output Services   491

　　　　Process Control Management   492

　　　　Memory Management   493

　　　　Scheduling and Dispatch   493

　　　　Secondary Storage Management   496

　　　　Network and Communications Support Services   496

　　　　Security and Protection Services   497

　　　　System Administration Support   498

15.4   Organization   502

15.5   Types of Computer Systems   505

Summary and Review   509   For Further Reading   510

Key Concepts and Terms   510   Reading Review Questions   510

Exercises   511

■ **CHAPTER 16   The User View of Operating Systems   514**

16.0   Introduction   515

16.1   Purpose of the User Interface   516

16.2   User Functions and Program Services   518

　　　　Program Execution   518

　　　　File Commands   519

　　　　Disk and Other I/O Device Commands   520

　　　　Security and Data Integrity Protection   521

　　　　Interuser Communication and Data Sharing Operations   521

　　　　System Status Information   522

　　　　Program Services   523

16.3 **Types of User Interface   524**
  The Command Line Interface   525
  Batch System Commands   527
  Graphical User Interfaces   528
  Trade-offs in the User Interface   533
  Software Considerations   535

16.4 **X Window and Other Graphics Display Methodologies   536**

16.5 **Command and Scripting Languages   539**
  The Elements of a Command Language   541
  The Command Language Start-up Sequence Files   542

16.6 **Services to Programs   542**

Summary and Review   544   For Further Reading   544

Key Concepts and Terms   544   Reading Review Questions   545

Exercises   545

■ **CHAPTER 17   File Management   548**

17.0 **Introduction   549**

17.1 **The Logical and Physical View of Files   549**

17.2 **The Role of the File Management System   554**

17.3 **Logical File Access Methods   560**
  Sequential File Access   560
  Random Access   560
  Indexed Access   561

17.4 **Physical File Storage   562**
  Contiguous Storage Allocation   562
  Noncontiguous Storage Allocation   564
  Indexed Allocation   566
  Free Space Management   568
  Tape Allocation   569
  CD, DVD, and Flash Drive Allocation   570

17.5 **File Systems, Volumes, Disks, Partitions, and Storage Pools   570**

17.6 **The Directory Structure   573**
  Tree-Structured Directories   575
  Acyclic-Graph Directories   577

17.7 **Network File Access   581**

17.8 **Storage Area Networks   582**

17.9 **File Protection   584**

17.10 **Journaling File Systems   585**

Summary and Review   586   For Further Reading   586
Key Concepts and Terms   587   Reading Review Questions   587
Exercises   588

■ **CHAPTER 18** **The Internal Operating System   592**

18.0   **Introduction   593**
18.1   **Fundamental OS Requirements   594**
        Example: A Simple Multitasking Operating System   596
18.2   **Starting the Computer System: The Bootstrap   599**
18.3   **Processes and Threads   601**
        Process Creation   604
        Process States   605
        Threads   606
18.4   **Basic Loading and Execution Operations   607**
18.5   **CPU Scheduling and Dispatching   608**
        High-Level Scheduler   608
        Dispatching   610
        Nonpreemptive Dispatch Algorithms   612
        Preemptive Dispatch Algorithms   613
18.6   **Memory Management   615**
        Memory Partitioning   615
18.7   **Virtual Storage   617**
        Overview   617
        Pages and Frames   618
        The Concept of Virtual Storage   623
        Page Faults   624
        Working Sets and the Concept of Locality   626
        Page Sharing   627
        Page Replacement Algorithms   627
        Thrashing   629
        Page Table Implementation   630
        Segmentation   632
        Process Separation   633
18.8   **Secondary Storage Scheduling   633**
        First-Come, First-Served Scheduling   633
        Shortest Distance First Scheduling   634
        Scan Scheduling   634
        N-STEP C-SCAN Scheduling   635

18.9 **Network Operating System Services   635**
    OS Protocol Support and Other Services   635

18.10 **Other Operating System Issues   638**
    Deadlock   638
    Other Issues   640

18.11 **Virtual Machines   641**

Summary and Review 643   **For Further Reading** 644

Key Concepts and Terms 644   **Reading Review Questions** 645

Exercises 647

Bibliography 653

Index 665

SUPPLEMENTARY CHAPTERS

On the Web at www.wiley.com/go/global/englander

■ SUPPLEMENTARY CHAPTER 1   An Introduction to Digital Computer Logic

S1.0   **Introduction**

S1.1   **Boolean Algebra**

S1.2   **Gates and Combinatorial Logic**

S1.3   **Sequential Logic Circuits**

Summary and Review   **For Further Reading**

Key Concepts and Terms   **Reading Review Questions**

Exercises

■ SUPPLEMENTARY CHAPTER 2   System Examples

S2.0   **Introduction**

S2.1   **Hardware Examples**
    The x86 Family
    The POWER Family
    The IBM System 360/370/390/zSeries Family

S2.2   **Operating System Examples**
    The Microsoft Windows Family
    UNIX and Linux
    The IBM z/OS Operating System

S2.3   **Networking Examples**
    Google

Summary and Review   For Further Reading

Key Concepts and Terms   Reading Review Questions

Exercises

▪ SUPPLEMENTARY CHAPTER 3   Instruction Addressing Modes

S3.0   **Introduction**

S3.1   **Register Addressing**

S3.2   **Alternatives to Absolute Addressing**

S3.3   **Alternatives to Direct Addressing**

    Immediate Addressing

    Indirect Addressing

    Register Indirect Addressing

    Indexed Addressing

    Indirect Indexed and Indirect Indexed Addressing

Summary and Review   For Further Reading

Key Concepts and Terms   Reading Review Questions

Exercises

▪ SUPPLEMENTARY CHAPTER 4   Programming Tools

S4.0   **Introduction**

S4.1   **Program Editing and Entry**

S4.2   **The Concept of Program Translation**

S4.3   **Assembly Language and the Assembler**

    Operation of the Assembler

    Assembly Language Formats

    Features and Extensions

    Relocatability

S4.4   **Program Language Description and Rules**

    A Description of Written English

    Programming Language Rules

    Computer Language Descriptions

    The Compilation Process

    Interpreters

S4.5   **Linking and Loading**

S4.6   **Debuggers**

Summary and Review   For Further Reading

Key Concepts and Terms   Reading Review Questions

Exercises

PREFACE

The modern world offers lots of readily available online resources for learning. Wikipedia, Google, news sources, millions of Web sites and blogs, even YouTube, offer access to information in nearly any subject that triggers your curiosity and interest. Nonetheless, I continue to believe that for deep understanding of something, nothing beats the integrated approach and focus of an old-fashioned printed-on-paper textbook.

When I open a new book, in *any* subject, the first thing I want to know is what the book has to offer that makes it worth my while to read it. I would like to try to help you answer that question for the book that you're holding in your hand.

The information systems and technology fields are wonderfully exciting places to be! It seems as though every day brings new developments that alter the ways we create and work with information. Of course, with this excitement comes a challenge. To be a successful player in IS or IT we have to be adaptable and flexible.

Much of the change occurs around computer system technology. The computer is, after all, at the foundation of information systems. A deep understanding of computer systems is, therefore, an essential element of success. We must be able to understand each new development, assess its value, and place it in the context of our knowledge of computer systems.

The subject of this book is the architecture of computer systems. Computer architecture is about the structure and operation of digital computers. Computer architecture is concerned with the operational methods of the hardware; with the services provided by operating system software; with the acquisition, processing, storage, and output of data; and with the interaction between computers.

There is a tendency for people in information systems and technology to neglect a study of computer architecture. After all, the technology changes so rapidly—is it really worth trying to understand something that may be out of date by the time I finish this book? There is no question that computer technology has evolved rapidly. The computer in a personal computer, or even in a cell phone or MP3 player is far more powerful than the mainframe computer of twenty-five years ago, with memory, disk and flash storage capacity, display and multimedia capability, and ease of use that would have been unthinkable just a few years ago. Even more important, connecting systems to work together is now routine and simple.

Interestingly enough, however, as profound as advances in the technology have been, the concepts of computer architecture that really matter have changed only nominally over the last sixty years. The new technologies are based on a foundation of architectural concepts that were developed many years ago. The architecture of a modern computer system was developed in the 1940s. The instruction set in a modern personal computer is nearly identical to that of computers built in the 1950s and 1960s. Modern operating system techniques were developed in the 1960s. The graphical user interface is based on a 1960s project. The Internet is built from concepts developed more than forty years ago.

So you see that an understanding of computer architecture makes it possible to "ride the wave" of technological change, secure in the feeling that you are equipped to deal with new developments as they occur, and to have fun doing so. When you are done reading this book you will have substantial knowledge about how a computer works and a good understanding of the operating concepts, the hardware, and system software that make up a computer. You will see the interaction between computers and between data and the computer. Plus, you will have learned lots of jargon that you can show off at parties and job interviews.

This textbook is designed for a wide range of readers, both undergraduate and graduate. The material is specifically directed toward IS and IT majors. There are no explicit prerequisites, although the book assumes that the student is familiar with a personal computer. It also assumes (but does not require) some basic programming skills: although there is no programming in the book, program code is occasionally used as an example to clarify an idea, and a knowledge of programming is helpful at understanding instruction set design and program execution concepts. The material in this textbook conforms to the criteria of the IT Infrastructure course as described in the December 2008 draft of the joint IS 2008 standard curriculum. Although the material in this book may be useful as background for system design and implementation project courses, the course can be placed anywhere in the curriculum.

Most instructors will not cover the entire textbook in a single semester. The organization of the book is designed to allow an instructor to cover the major topic areas in different levels of depth, depending on the experience and needs of the students. On the other hand, it is my intention that this book will serve a student as a useful reference long after the formal course is completed. It is designed for use as a book where a professional can look up the basic concepts that clarify new developments as they occur.

This text is the outgrowth of courses that I have taught to IS majors and minors at Bentley University at both the undergraduate and graduate level for thirty years. Student responses to the material and the approach have generally been very enthusiastic. Many students have returned after graduation to tell me that their knowledge in this area has directly contributed to their career development. Along the way, student comments have also been extremely helpful to me in the book's continuing evolution.

Those familiar with previous editions will notice that the organization of the fourth edition has undergone substantial revision to reflect current technological practices and trends. In particular, it is no longer reasonable to discuss computers as individual units without also considering the networks that tie them together; computer networking is now covered thoroughly in its own section, and there is an increased emphasis on the integration and synergy of the various components of the computer system and on the system as a whole. Still, the basic philosophy, organization, and approach remain essentially similar to those of the first edition, reflecting the unchanging nature of the underlying principles.

ORGANIZATION OF THE FOURTH EDITION OF THE BOOK

The biggest challenge for me as the author of this book has been to preserve the guiding principles established in the first edition, while reflecting the major changes in the way computers are used, in the rapid deployment of new technology, and in the resulting evolution of IS/IT curriculum to reflect those changes. The fourth edition is the most substantial revision of this book to date, with a new title, a new chapter on systems, and significantly increased coverage of networking. The case study chapters have been updated and moved to the Web, along with the chapter on programming tools and the supplementary chapters on logic design and instruction addressing. Still, users of previous editions will find much that is familiar; after all, the way in which computers are used in IS/IT may have changed, but the basic guiding principles of computer architecture are essentially the same as they have been for many years.

The book is now organized into five parts totaling eighteen chapters, plus four additional supplementary chapters that are posted on the Web. The first part serves as an introduction and overview of the role of the computer in information systems; it introduces the concept of a system and provides a brief introduction to each of the components that make up a modern computer system. Each of the remaining four parts deals with a single architectural aspect of the computer system.

Part Two discusses the role and representation of data in the computer. Here we consider numbers, text, sound, images, video, and other data forms. Part Three presents the hardware architecture and operational concepts. It introduces the components of a computer and shows how they collaborate to execute computer instructions, discusses the nature of a computer instruction set, and explores the interaction between the CPU, memory, and I/O peripheral devices. Part Four presents a thorough introduction to the basics of computer networking. Part Five discusses the system software, the programs that function to make the resources of the computer system, and other interconnected computer systems and components, accessible to the user and to application programs.

The approach within each group of chapters is layered. Each new layer builds upon the previous material to add depth and understanding to the reader's knowledge. Each topic section consists of a short introduction that places the topic to be discussed into the context of the computer system as a whole and then lays out in detail the organization of the chapters within the section. Each topic area is introduced as gently as possible, using ideas and examples that are already familiar to the student. Successive material is progressive and accumulative. In addition to the numerous examples that are used throughout the text, the supplementary chapters offer substantial case studies that show application of the text material to current examples of importance. Overall, the approach is gentle, progressive, and accumulative. As much as possible, each section is self-contained.

An overview of the organization of each part follows. More details can be found in the introductions to each section.

Part One consists of two chapters that present a short overview of computing, placing architectural concepts into the context of information technology. Chapter 1 introduces the components of a computer system and shows the relationships among the components.

It also presents a simple model of computing and discusses the importance of standards and protocols in the development of computer systems. The chapter concludes with a short history of computers from the architectural point of view. Chapter 2 focuses on the concepts of systems, models, and system architectures, using various types of computer systems as examples.

Chapters 3 through 5 comprise Part Two. Chapter 3 introduces number systems and basic number system operations; it then explores the relationships between numbers in different number bases and the conversion techniques between the different representations. Chapter 4 investigates different types of data formats, including alphanumeric, image, video, and audio formats. It considers the relationship between numerical and character-based representations and briefly introduces various devices and data formats used for data input and output. Chapter 5 studies the various formats that are used to represent and to perform calculations on integer and floating point numbers.

Part Three discusses the hardware architecture and operational aspects of the computer. Chapter 6 begins the study with the introduction of the Little Man Computer, a simple model that provides a surprisingly accurate representation of the CPU and memory. The model is used to develop the concept of an instruction set and to explain the basic principles of the von Neumann architecture. Chapter 7 extends the discussion to a real computer. It introduces the components of the CPU and shows their relationship to the Little Man Computer model. It introduces the bus concept, explains the operation of memory, presents the instruction fetch-execute cycle, and discusses the instruction set. It identifies important classes of instructions and discusses the ways in which instructions can be categorized.

Chapter 8 expands the material in Chapter 7 to consider more advanced features of the CPU and memory. It offers an overview of various CPU architectures. It continues with a discussion of techniques for improving memory access, particularly cache memory, and an introduction to current CPU organization, design, and implementation techniques, including pipelining and superscalar processing. This chapter also introduces multiprocessing (or multicore, in current terminology) concepts.

Chapter 9 presents the principles of I/O operation, and Chapter 10 illustrates how I/O is performed in various I/O devices. Chapter 11 discusses the computer system as a whole. It discusses interconnection techniques and integration of the various hardware components. It also addresses the interconnection of computers to increase computer performance and reliability, with a specific focus on clustering and on grid computing.

Three supplementary chapters on the Web provide additional resources to support the chapters in Part Three. Supplementary Chapter 1 (SC1) offers an introduction to Boolean algebra, combinatorial logic, and sequential logic for those readers that would like a deeper understanding of the computer in its simplest and most elegant form. Supplementary Chapter 2 (SC2) offers three detailed case studies of important architectures: the Intel x86 family, including the Pentium IV architecture and Itanium extensions, the PowerPC, and the IBM zSystem. Supplementary Chapter 3 (SC3) discusses alternative approaches to instruction addressing.

Part Four presents a thorough introduction to networking. Chapter 12 introduces the major features and characteristics of networking, including a careful introduction to communication channels, a detailed discussion of layered network models, with particular emphasis on TCP/IP and Ethernet models, an introduction to network topologies, and finally, a discussion of the different types of networks in use, including LANs, MANs, WANs, and the backbones that form the foundation of the Internet. Chapter 13 expands on the material in Chapter 12 to discuss specific details of various layers, including discussions of DNS, TCP connections, IP and physical address resolution, the operation of Ethernet, alternative protocols, and more. Chapter 14 focuses primarily on communication channel technology, including analog and digital signaling, modulation and data conversion techniques between analog and digital, the characteristics of transmission media, and wireless networking. A portion of Chapter 14 appeared in previous editions as a supplementary chapter.

Part Five is dedicated to a discussion of system software. Chapter 15 provides an overview of the operating system. It explains the different roles played by the operating system and introduces the facilities and services provided. Chapter 16 presents the role of the operating system from the viewpoint of the user of a system. Chapter 17 discusses the all-important topic of file systems. Chapter 18 discusses the operating system as a resource manager, with an in-depth discussion of memory management, scheduling, process control, network services, and other basic operating system services. Chapter 18 includes a detailed introduction to virtual memory technique, and also includes an introduction to virtual machines. In addition to its hardware discussions, Supplementary Chapter 3 also provides current Windows, UNIX/Linux, and z/OS case studies.

A fourth supplementary chapter provides an introduction to the system development software that is used for the preparation and execution of programs.

A detailed list of the changes between the second and third editions of the book can be found at the book Web site, www.wiley.com/go/global/englander.

This book has been a continuing labor of love. My primary goal has been to create and maintain a textbook that explains computer architecture in a way that conveys to you, the reader, the sense of excitement and fun that I believe makes a career in information systems and technology so satisfying. I hope that I have succeeded to some extent.

ADDITIONAL RESOURCES

Additional resources for students and instructors may be found at the textbook Web site, www.wiley.com/go/global/englander. I can also be reached directly by e-mail at ienglander@bentley.edu. Although I am happy to communicate with students, I am unable to supply tutorial help or answers to review questions and exercises in the book.

ACKNOWLEDGMENTS

I've discovered that a major, ongoing textbook project is a formidable task. Many individuals have helped to make the task manageable—and kept me going when, from time to time, I became convinced that textbooks really *do* appear by magic and are *not* written by humans. It is impossible to thank people adequately for all their help and support. First and foremost, a special thank you to my nearest and dearest friends, Wilson Wong, Rich Braun, Luis Fernandez, Jan Harrington, Ray Brackett, and Evan Horn. Their continuing backup through four editions has been amazing! I couldn't have asked for a better support team. The champagne is on ice. *Yet* again!

My continuing thanks, too, to Stuart Madnick. Stuart, your technical inspiration and personal encouragement was invaluable to me when I struggled to get the first edition of this book going. You helped me to believe that this project was actually possible and worthwhile. That support has continued to inspire me through every subsequent edition.

Next, I thank the many colleagues at Bentley University who shared their ideas, experiences, and encouragement. Colleagues Wilson Wong, David Yates, Doug Robertson, Mary Ann Robbert, Lynn Senne, Jim Linderman, Kay Green, and Peggy Beranek have all offered contributions that have substantially improved the book over four editions. A special thank you, David, for your helpful technical discussions and reviews of the new data communications material in the fourth edition, and to you, Wilson, for serving as a technical reviewer for both the third and fourth editions, providing many comments, rewrites, and suggestions for clarification, and for creating many of the ancillary materials for the book. A special thank you also to Linda Cotroneo, our Bentley CIS Department Academic Administrative Assistant, who for the past twenty years has generously offered more empathy and support than any person deserves. From the bottom of my heart, Linda, thank you!

Thanks to the editors, production people, and marketing personnel at John Wiley & Sons and the editors and production people at Laserwords. You hassled me when I needed to be hassled and left me alone when I needed to be left alone. Incredible intuition, that! I consider myself fortunate to have worked with such wonderful people. Particular thanks to Beth Lang Golub, Trish McFadden, and Kate Boilard for your ongoing efforts to make this book perfect, even though we all know it's impossible!

I would like to acknowledge the reviewers who gave of their time and effort to assure that this book was as good as it could be: Dr. Stu Westin, The University of Rhode Island; Alan Pinck, Algonquin College; Mark Jacobi, Programme Director for Undergrad Computing at Sheffield Hallam University; Dr. Dave Protheroe, South Bank University, London; Julius Ilinskas, Kaunas University of Technology; Anthony Richardson, United States Army Informations Systems Engineering Command; Renee A. Weather, Old Dominion University; Jack Claff, Southern Cross University; Jan L. Harrington, Marist College; YoungJoon Byun, California State University, Monterey Bay; William Myers, Belmont Abbey College; Barbara T. Grabowski, Benedictine College; G.E. Strouse, York College of Pennsylvania; Martin J. Doyle, Temple University; Richard Socash, Metropolitan State College of Denver; Fred Cathers, Franklin University. Your comments, suggestions, and constructive criticism have made a real difference in the quality of this book. Thank you.

Many colleagues offered corrections to previous editions that have had important impact on the quality of the current edition. To each and everyone, your assistance in eliminating errors has been much appreciated. Among these, I especially wish to acknowledge David Feinstein and his crew at the University of South Alabama, Gordon Grimsey of AIT in Auckland, New Zealand, and Stu Westin of University of Rhode Island for efforts well above and beyond the call of duty. Stu has also generously made his excellent Little Man Simulator publicly available, for which I am truly grateful. Thanks for everything, Stu.

Numerous students, too many to name you all, also offered corrections, made suggestions, and provided ideas. Please accept my deepest appreciation and thanks.

I hope that I have not forgotten anyone. If I have, I apologize.

I have strived to make this book as technically accurate as is humanly possible. Nonetheless, I know that errors have a way of creeping in when one least expects them. I would greatly appreciate hearing from readers who find errors that need correction. Your comments and suggestions about the book are also welcome.

ABOUT THE AUTHOR

D r. Irv Englander has been involved in many different aspects of the computing field for more than forty-five years. He has designed logic circuits, developed integrated circuits, developed computer architectures, designed computer-controlled systems, designed operating systems, developed application software, created the initial system design for a large water monitoring system, performed software auditing and verification of critical control software, and developed and specified hardware components and application software as a consultant for business systems large and small.

As an educator he has contributed papers and given workshops on end-user computing, e-commerce, and on computer architecture education in the IS curriculum. He was an invited contributor and reviewer for the IS-97 and IS-2002 information systems curricula, and continues to take an interest in the technical infrastructure components of the IS/IT curriculum. He is actively involved in the application of new technology to information systems.

Dr. Englander has a Ph.D. from MIT in Computer Science. His doctoral thesis was based on the design of a large image processing software laboratory. At MIT he won the Supervised Investors Award for outstanding teaching. He holds the rank of Professor of Computer Information Systems at Bentley University, where he has taught full-time for thirty years.

PART ONE

$\mathbf{A}$ computer-based information system is made up of a number of different elements:

- The *data* element. Data is the fundamental representation of facts and observations. Data is processed by a computer system to provide the information that is the very reason for the computer's existence. As you will see, data can take on a number of different forms.

- The *hardware* element. Computer hardware processes the data by executing instructions, storing data, and moving data and information between the various input and output devices that make the system and the information accessible to the users.

- The *software* element. Software consists of the system and application programs that define the instructions that are executed by the hardware. The software determines the work to be performed and controls operation of the system.

- The *communication* element. Modern computer information systems depend on the ability to share processing operations and data among different computers and users, located both locally and remotely. Data communication provides this capability.

The combination of hardware, software, communication, and data make up the *architecture* of a computer system. The architecture of computer systems is remarkably similar whether the system is a playstation, a personal computer that sits on your lap while you work, an embedded computer that controls the functions in your cell phone or in your car, or a large mainframe system that is never actually seen by the hundreds of users who access it every day.

Even more remarkably, the basic architecture of computer systems has changed surprisingly little over the last fifty-five years. The latest IBM mainframe computer executes essentially the same instruction set as the mainframe computer of 1965. The basic communication techniques used in today's systems were developed in the 1970s. As new as it might seem, the Internet will celebrate its fortieth anniversary in 2010. All of

AN OVERVIEW OF
COMPUTER SYSTEMS

this is surprising considering the growth of computing, the rapid change of technology, and the increased performance, functionality, and ease of use of today's systems. This makes the study of computer architecture extremely valuable as a foundation upon which to understand new developments in computing as they occur.

Computer system architecture is the subject of this textbook. Each element of the system is addressed in its own section of the text, always with an eye to the system as a whole.

Part I is made up of two chapters that presents an overview of systems, and of the computer system in particular.

Chapter 1 addresses a number of issues, including

- The ways in which a knowledge of computer architecture enhances our abilities as computer users and professionals
- A simplified view of typical computer system architectures
- The basic components that make up a computer system
- The fundamental operations that are performed by computer systems

Chapter 1 concludes with a brief architectural history of the computer.

An encompassing theme throughout this text is that of systems and system architecture. The words "system" and "architecture" appear throughout this book: we talk about information systems, computer systems, operating systems, file systems, software architecture, I/O architecture, network architecture and more. You will probably take a course in *System Analysis and Design* sometime in your college career.

Although most people have an instinctive understanding of what a system is, it is more important for us as system professionals to understand the concepts of systems and system architecture at a deeper level than the average person. Chapter 2 offers careful definitions and examples of the concept of systems and system architecture, both generally and in the specific context of the computer systems that are the focus of this book.

CHAPTER 1

COMPUTERS AND SYSTEMS

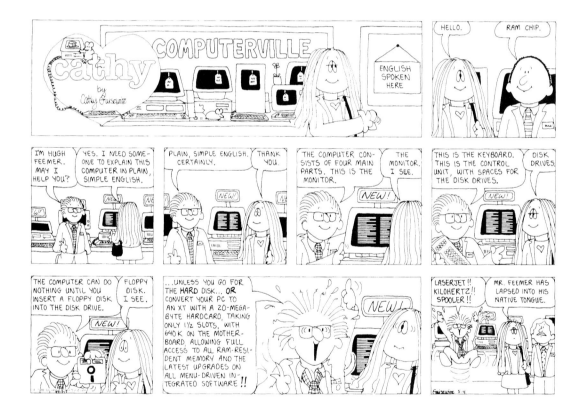

1.0 INTRODUCTION

It is nearly impossible today to escape the immediate reach of computers and computer-based systems. There is probably a cell phone in your pocket or on your desk and, perhaps, an iPod as well. For many of you, your laptop or desktop computer is sitting nearby as you read this paragraph. And that's not all. Your car probably has several embedded computers controlling various functions. Even your microwave oven and the machine that launders your clothes depend on computers to function properly. As you are probably aware, most of these machines can talk to each other, using the Internet or some other networking technology.

Indeed, the jargon of computers has become a part of common daily language. You can open a newspaper and find references to expressions such as "2 GB DDRAM" or "WXGA LCD display" or "2 MB level 2 cache" or "Wi-Fi" in articles and advertisements. (In a way, it's scary!) The ad in Figure 1.1, taken from a Sunday newspaper flier, is typical of recent computer ads.

You'll notice that this computer features a "Core 2 Duo Processor" CPU, 2 GB of DDR2 SDRAM memory, a 16× DVD ±RW Drive, and a 160 GB SATA hard drive. It also contains a 256 MB PCI Express graphics card among other things. But how good a system is this? Are these features important to the user? Is this the right combination of features that you need in your computer to have the computer perform the work that you wish to get done? Are there features missing that we need? Is a Core 2 Duo processor the best CPU for us? Perhaps we are paying too much for the performance that we need. Or maybe we need more. And what does "Core 2 Duo" mean, anyway? What I/O ports might you need to assure a satisfy long-term investment of computers for your organization? Is a 16× DVD ±RW drive adequate for your work? What if you have to burn a lot of disks? What other information about this system would allow you to make a more informed decision? (For example: Hey—where's the networking capability?)

Some of the expressions used in these articles and ads are obvious from the context. Other references may be more obscure. Presumably, everyone today knows what a "display monitor" is. But how many people know the meaning and significance of the terms "cache memory" or "multitasking" or "PCI Express bus"? Yet all these expressions have appeared recently in daily newspaper advertisements with the assumption that people would understand the meaning of the ad.

Despite the jargon, there is obviously no need to understand the inner workings of most modern computer-based systems to operate them adequately. Indeed, in many cases the presence of the computer is hidden from us, or **embedded,** and its operation invisible to us as users.

Even as experienced users, we can run standard software packages on a personal computer without understanding exactly how they work; we can program a computer in a high-level language without understanding the details of how the machine

FIGURE 1.1

A Typical Computer Ad

executes the individual instructions; we can design and implement Web pages without understanding how the Web browser gets its pages from a Web server or how the Web server creates those pages; we can purchase a computer system from a salesperson without understanding the specifications of the system.

And yet, there is something missing. Perhaps the package doesn't do exactly what we want, and we don't understand the machine well enough to risk fooling around with the package's options. Perhaps if we understood the system better we might have written and configured the program to be faster and more efficient. Perhaps we could create Web pages that load faster and work better. Perhaps the salesperson did not sell us the optimum system for our job. Or perhaps it's nothing more than a sense of excitement that's missing. But that's important, too!

You are reading this book because you are a student studying to become a computer professional, or maybe you are simply a user wanting a deeper understanding of what the computer is all about. In either case, you will most likely be interacting with computer systems for the rest of your life. It's nice (as well as useful) to know something about the tools of the trade. More important, understanding the computer system's operations has an immediate benefit: it will allow you to use the machine more effectively.

As a user, you will be aware of the capabilities, strengths, and limitations of the computer system. You will have a better understanding of the commands that you use. You will understand what is taking place during the operation of the programs that you use. You will be able to make informed decisions about your computer equipment and application programs. You will understand more clearly what an operating system is, and how to use it effectively and to your advantage. You will know when it is preferable to do a job manually, and when the computer should be used. You will understand the most efficient way to ''go online,'' and what benefits might be gained from a home network. You will improve your ability to communicate with system analysts, programmers, and other computer specialists.

As a programmer, it will allow you to write better programs. You will be able to use the characteristics of the machine to make your programs operate more effectively. For example, choosing the appropriate data type for a variable can result in significantly faster performance. Soon you will know why this is so, and how to make the appropriate choices.

Computers can perform integer calculations incorrectly if the integers exceed a certain size, but they do not necessarily warn the user of the error. You will learn how this can occur, and what can be done to assure that your programs generate correct results.

You will discover that some computers will process nested loops much more quickly if the index variables are reversed. A rather surprising idea, perhaps, and you'll understand why this is true.

You will understand why programs written in a compiled language like C++ usually run much faster than those written in interpreted program languages like BASIC or scripting languages like JavaScript.

As a systems architect or system analyst, you will be responsible for the design and implementation of systems that meet an organization's information technology (IT) needs, recognizing that the differences in the cost and capabilities of the components that you select may have significant impact on the organization. With the knowledge gained here you will be in a better position to determine and justify the set of computer system components and the system architecture that are appropriate for a particular job and to determine the tradeoffs with other possible system architectures.

You'll be able to assist management in making intelligent decisions about system strategy: should the company adopt a large mainframe/virtual machine system approach for its Web servers, or would a system consisting of a network of off-the-shelf blade servers provide better performance at lower cost? You'll be better prepared to analyze the best way to provide appropriate facilities to meet the needs of your users. In an era of fast-changing technology, you'll be more able to differentiate between simple technological obsolescence that does not affect the organization's requirements significantly and major advances that suggest a real need to replace older equipment.

When selecting computers, you would like to purchase the computer that best meets the needs of the organization's applications and the users. You must be able to read and understand the technical specifications in order to compare different alternatives and to match the system to the users' needs. This book will teach you what you need to know to specify and purchase a system intelligently. You'll know the differences between various CPU technologies and the advantages and disadvantages of each. You will learn what peripheral hardware is appropriate for your organization's files and the trade-offs between different file system formats, what is required to build an intranet, and what the speed and size limitations of a particular system are. You'll be able to compare the features of Windows and Linux knowledgeably and decide which ones are important to you. You'll be able to apply your basic understanding of computers to new technologies such as virtual machines as they appear. You'll learn to understand the jargon used by computer salespeople and judge the validity of their sales claims.

As a system administrator or manager, your job is to maximize the availability and efficiency of your systems. You will need to understand the reports generated by your systems and be able to use the information in those reports to make changes to the systems that will optimize system performance. You will need to know when additional resources are required, and be able to specify appropriate choices. You will need to specify and configure operating system parameters, set up file systems, manage system and user PC upgrades in a fast-changing environment, reconfigure networks, provide and ensure the robustness of system security, and perform many other system management tasks. The configuration of large systems can be very challenging. This text will give you an understanding of operating system tools that is essential to the effective management of systems.

As a Web services designer, you will be able to make intelligent decisions to optimize your Web system configurations, page designs, data formatting and scripting language choices, and operating systems to optimize customer accessibility to your Web services.

In brief, when you complete this book, you will understand what computer hardware and software are and how programs and data interact with the computer system. You will understand the computer hardware, software, and communication components that are required to make up a computer system and what the role of each component in the system is.

You will have a better understanding of what is happening inside the computer when you interact with the computer as a user. You will be able to write programs that are more efficient. You will be able to understand the function of the different components of the computer system and to specify the computer system you need in a meaningful way. You will understand the options that you have as a system administrator or Web services designer.

In an era in which technology changes extremely rapidly, the architecture of the computer system rests on a solid foundation that has changed only slightly and gradually over the last sixty years. Understanding the foundations of computer system architecture makes it possible to flow comfortably with technological change and to understand changes in the context of the improvements that they make and the needs that they meet. In fact, interviews with former students and with IT executives and other IT professionals clearly indicate that a deep understanding of the basic concepts presented here is fundamental to long-term survival and growth in the field of information technology and IT management.

This type of understanding is at the very foundation of being a competent and successful system analyst, system architect, system administrator, or programmer. It may not be necessary to understand the workings of an automobile engine in order to drive a car, but you can bet that a top-notch race car driver knows his or her engine thoroughly and can use it to win races. Like the professional race car driver, it is our intention to help you to use your computer engine effectively to succeed in using your computer in a winning way. The typical end user might not care about how their computer system works, but <u>you</u> do.

. . . These are the goals of this book. So let's get started!

1.1 THE STARTING POINT

Before we begin our detailed study of the architecture of computer systems, let us briefly review some of the fundamental principles and requirements that guide computer system design and operation.

In a simple scenario, you use your laptop or desktop personal computer to word process a document. You probably use a mouse to move around the document and to control the features of the word processor software application, and you use the keyboard to enter and modify the document text data. The word processor application program, together with your document, appears on a screen. Ultimately, you might print the document on a printer. You store the document on a disk or some other storage device.

The fundamentals of a typical computer system are readily exposed in this simple example. Your mouse movements and clicks and your keyboard entry represent input to the system. The computer processes the input and provides output to the screen, and, perhaps, to a printer. The computer system also provides a storage medium of some sort, usually a hard disk, to store the text for future access. In simplest terms, your computer receives input from you, processes it, and outputs results to the screen. Your input takes the form of commands and data. The commands tell the computer how to process the data.

Now consider a second, slightly more complex example. Your task in this example is to access a Web page on the Internet. Again, your input to the computer is via mouse and keyboard. When you type the Web page URL, however, your computer sends a message to another computer that contains Web server software. That computer, in turn, sends a Web page file that is interpreted by the browser on your computer and presented on your screen. You are probably already aware that HyperText Transfer Protocol (HTTP) is used as a standard for Web message exchanges.

The elements of this example differ only slightly from the first example. Your command inputs tell a Web browser software application on your computer what processing is to take place; in this case, your desire to access a Web page. The output from your computer is a message to a Web server on the remote computer requesting the data that represents the Web page. Your computer receives the data as input from the network; the Web browser processes the data and presents the Web page output on the screen. Figure 1.2 illustrates the layout for this example.

The major differences between this and the first example are the source of the input data and the fact that network connectivity is required between the two computers. Instead of the keyboard, the input data to be processed by your Web browser comes from a communication channel. (Note that the exact nature of the channel is not important for this discussion.) In both cases, your computer receives data input to process, and control input that determines how the data is to be processed, performs the processing, and provides output.

These two examples contain all of the key elements found in any IT system, large or small.

- An IT system consists of one or more computer systems; multiple computer systems are connected together using some type of network interconnectivity. As a matter of necessity, network interfaces must conform to standard agreements, known as **protocols,** for messages to be understood by both computers during a message exchange between a pair of computers. The network itself can take on a

FIGURE 1.2

Typical Web Browser Application Use

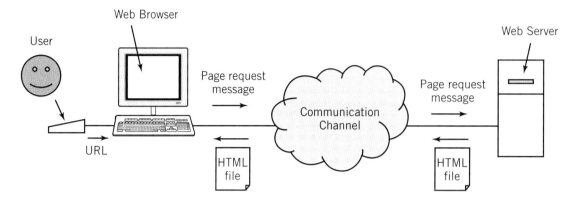

variety of forms, provided that the interface requirements are met, and are determined by such characteristics as performance, convenience, and cost.

■ The work performed by an individual computer system within the IT system can be characterized by input, processing, and output. This characterization is often represented by the **Input-Process-Output (IPO) model** shown in Figure 1.3. Storage is also represented within this model. Alternatively, storage can be interpreted as output to be saved for use as future input. Storage is also used to hold the software programs that determine the processing operations to be performed. The ability to store programs and data on a temporary, short-term, or long-term basis is fundamental to the system. In Chapter 2, Section 2.2, we will show that all IT systems can ultimately be characterized by the same basic IPO model at all levels, from a single computer to a complex aggregation of computers, although the complexity of large systems may obscure the model and make it more difficult to determine the actual inputs, outputs, and processing

FIGURE 1.3

A Computer Process

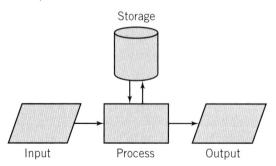

FIGURE 1.4

A simplified IT Computer System Layout

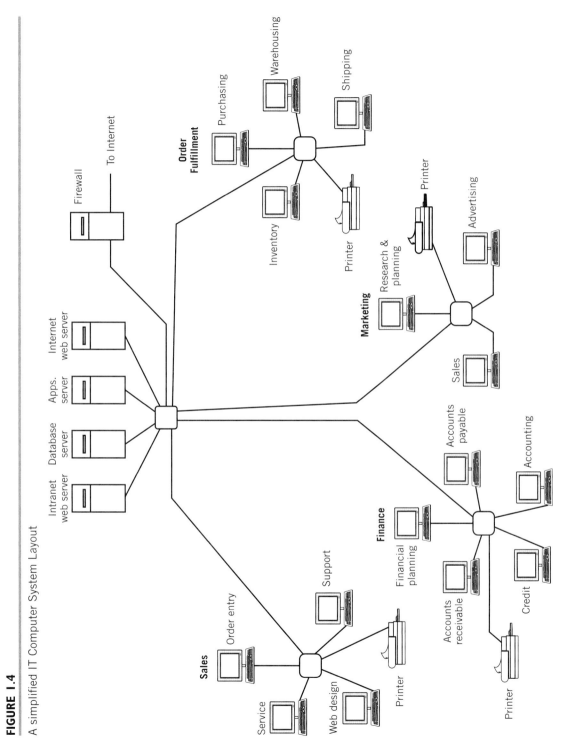

operations. The IPO model provides an important basic tool for system analysis and design practices.

■ The components of an individual computer system consist of processing hardware, input devices, output devices, storage devices, application software, and operating system software. The task of the operating system software is to provide overall control of the individual system, including management of input, output, and file storage functions. The medium of exchange, both with users and between computers within a larger system, is data. (Note that the messages between computers in the second example are a form of data.) Figure 1.4 is a simple illustration of computer systems embedded in a larger IT system.

Figure 1.5 summarizes the basic operations that are performed during computer processing. These operations, in turn, can be reduced to the primitive operations that are also familiar to you from your understanding of programming languages. The primitive processing operations common to high-level programming languages are shown in Figure 1.6.

1.2 COMPONENTS OF THE COMPUTER SYSTEM

As noted in the previous section, there are three components required for the implementation of a computerized input-process-output model:

1. The computer hardware, which provides the physical mechanisms to input and output data, to manipulate and process data, and to electronically control the various input, output, and storage components.

2. The software, both application and system, which provides instructions that tell the hardware exactly what tasks are to be performed and in what order.

3. The data that is being manipulated and processed. This data may be numeric, it may be alphanumeric, it may be graphic, or it may take some other form, but in all cases it must be representable in a form that the computer can manipulate.

In modern systems, input entry, output display, and storage of the data and software used for processing often take place at a location different from the computer where the

FIGURE 1.5

Basic Computer Operations

- Input/output
- Basic arithmetic and logical calculations
- Data transformation or translation (e.g., program compilation, foreign language translation, file updating)
- Data sorting
- Searching for data matches
- Data storage and retrieval
- Data movement (e.g., movement of text or file data to make room for insertion of additional data)

FIGURE 1.6

Basic High-Level Language Constructs

- Input/output (including file storage and retrieval)
- Arithmetic and logical assignment statements
- True/false decision branching (IF-THEN-ELSE or IF-GOTO)
- Loops and/or unconditional branching (WHILE-DO, REPEAT-UNTIL, FOR, GOTO)

actual processing occurs. In many installations, actual processing is distributed among computer systems, with particular results passed to the individual systems that require them. Therefore, we must also consider a fourth component:

4.   The communication component, which consists of hardware and software that transport programs and data between interconnected computer systems.

The hardware and system software components make up the architecture of the computer system. The communication component connects individual computer systems together. The data component, and also the application software, while fundamental to the operation of the computer system, are supplied to the computer system by the user, rather than being a part of the architecture of the computer system itself. (It is useful to note, however, that application software and data structure *are* often considered as part of the overall system architecture when one considers the architecture from the perspective of the organization. We explore this issue briefly in Chapter 2. Note, however, that the focus of this book is primarily on *computer* system architecture, rather than on *organizational* system architecture.)

The Hardware Component

The most visible part of the computer system is obviously the hardware that makes up the system. Consider the computer system upon which you write and execute your programs. You use a keyboard and mouse to provide **input** of your program text and data, as well as for commands to the computer. A display screen is commonly used to observe **output.** A printer is frequently available as an alternative output to the screen. These are all physical components.

Calculations and other operations in your program are performed by a **central processing unit** (**CPU**) inside the computer. **Memory** is provided to hold your programs and data while processing is taking place. Other input and output devices, such as a disk and SD plug-in cards, are used to provide long-term storage of your program and data files. Data and programs are transferred between the various input/output devices and memory for the CPU to use.

The CPU, memory, and all the input, output, and storage devices form the **hardware** part of a computer system. The hardware forms the tangible part of the system. It is physical—you can touch it, which is what the word "tangible" means. A typical hardware

FIGURE 1.7

A Typical Personal Computer System

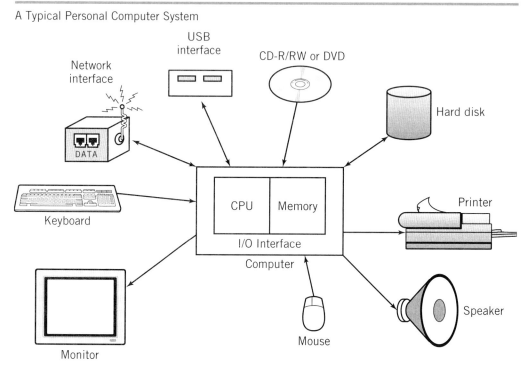

block diagram for a computer is seen in Figure 1.7. In addition to the input and output devices shown in this diagram, Figure 1.8 lists some other input and output devices that are frequently seen as part of computer systems. The diagram in Figure 1.7 actually applies equally well to large mainframe computers, small personal computers, and even devices with computers embedded in them, such as PDAs, iPods, GPSs, and cell phones. Large and small computers differ primarily in speed, capacity, and the selection of peripheral devices provided. The basic hardware components and design are very similar.

Conceptually, the CPU itself is often viewed as a composition of three primary subunits:

1. The **arithmetic/logic unit (ALU)** where arithmetic and Boolean logical calculations are performed.
2. The **control unit (CU)**, which controls the processing of instructions and the movement of internal CPU data from one part of the CPU to another.
3. The **interface unit,** which moves program instructions and data between the CPU and other hardware components.

(In modern CPUs, the actual implementation is usually modified somewhat to achieve higher performance, although the basic concepts are carefully preserved. More about that later, in Chapter 8.)

FIGURE 1.8

Other Common Input/Output Devices

- Bar Code Scanners
- Optical Character Recognition Scanners
- Image Scanners
- RFID Readers
- Video and Audio Capture Devices
- TV Tuners
- Video Cameras
- SD, SmartCard, etc. Card Readers
- Fingerprint and Face Readers
- Touch Screens
- Graphics Tablets
- X-Y Plotters

The interface unit interconnects the CPU with memory and also with the various I/O (input/output) modules. It can also be used to connect multiple CPUs together. In many computer systems, a bus interconnects the CPU, memory, and all of the I/O components. A **bus** is simply a bundle of wires that carry signals and power between different components. In other systems, the I/O modules are connected to the CPU through one or more separate processors known as **channels.**

The main memory, often known as primary storage, working storage, or **RAM** (for **r**andom **a**ccess **m**emory), holds programs and data for access by the CPU. **Primary storage** is made up of a large number of cells, each numbered and individually addressable. Each cell holds a single binary number representing part of a data value or part of an instruction. The smallest addressable size of the cell in most current computers is 8 bits, known as a **byte** of memory. Eight bits of memory can only hold 256 different patterns, so neighboring cells in memory are nearly always combined to form groupings with a larger number of bits. In many systems, for example, 4 bytes of memory combine to form a 32-bit **word.** Modern computers address memory at least 4 bytes (a "32-bit" computer) or 8 bytes (a "64-bit" computer) at a time to take advantage of larger instruction and data groupings.

The amount of primary storage determines the maximum number of instructions and data words that can be loaded into memory from a peripheral device at one time. For example, a computer with 2 gigabytes (GB), actually 2,147,483,648 bytes[1], of memory would not be able to execute a program that requires 2.7 GB for its instructions and data unless some means is provided within the computer to load the program in sections as each section of the program is needed.

The amount of primary storage provided in a typical computer has increased rapidly as computer technology improves. Whereas 64 *kilo*bytes (KB) of memory was considered a large amount in 1980, even the least expensive personal computers today usually have 2 *giga*bytes (GB) of memory or more. Large computers may provide many gigabytes of primary storage. There are programs on the market that require hundreds of megabytes (MB) of memory to execute. The inexpensive availability of increased amounts of memory have allowed the design of very sophisticated programs that would not have been possible just a few years ago.

The same is true for secondary storage. Even small personal computers provide hard disks with storage measured in tens or hundreds of gigabytes. The storage of images and video, in particular, requires tremendous amounts of storage capacity. It is not uncommon to see arrays of hard disks, even on some personal computers, providing trillions of bytes (specified as *terabytes*) of long-term storage.

---

[1] 1 Kilobyte actually equals 1024 bytes. Thus, 1 MB = 1024 × 1024 = 1,048,576 bytes × 2048 = 2,147,483,648 bytes.

The instructions that form a particular program are stored within the primary storage, then brought into the central processing unit and executed. Conceptually, instructions are brought in and executed one at a time, although modern systems overlap the execution of instructions to some extent. Instructions must be in primary storage in order to be executed. The control unit interprets each instruction and determines the appropriate course of action.

Each instruction is designed to perform a simple task. Instructions exist to perform basic arithmetic, to move data from one place in the computer to another, to perform I/O, and to accomplish many other tasks. The computer's power comes from the ability to execute these simple instructions at extremely high speeds, measured in millions or billions or trillions of instructions executed per second. As you are already aware, it is necessary to translate high-level language programs into the language of the machine for execution of the program to take place. It may require tens or even hundreds of individual machine instructions to form the machine language equivalent of a single high-level language statement. Program instructions are normally executed sequentially, unless an instruction itself tells the computer to change the order of processing. The instruction set used with a particular CPU is part of the design of the CPU and cannot normally be executed on a different type of CPU unless the different CPU was designed to be instruction set compatible. However, as you shall see, most instruction sets perform similar types of operations. As a result, it is possible to write programs that will emulate the instruction set from one computer on a computer with a different instruction set, although a program written for the original machine may execute slowly on the machine with the emulator.

The data that is manipulated by these instructions is also stored in memory while being processed. The idea that the program instructions and data are both stored in memory while being processed is known as the **stored program concept.** This important concept is attributed primarily to John von Neumann, a famous computer scientist. It forms the basis for the computer architecture that is standard to nearly every existing computer.

The Software Component

In addition to the hardware requirement, your computer system also requires **software.** Software consists of the programs that tell the computer what to do. To do useful work, your system must execute instructions from some program.

There are two major categories of software: system software and application software. System software helps you to manage your files, to load and execute programs, and to accept your commands from the mouse and keyboard. The system software programs that manage the computer are collectively known as an **operating system,** and differ from the application programs, such as Microsoft Word, or Firefox, or the programs that you write, that you normally run to get your work done. Windows and Linux are the best known examples of an operating system. Others include Unix, Mac OS X, Sun Solaris, and IBM z/OS.

The operating system is an essential part of the computer system. Like the hardware, it is made up of many components. A simplified representation of an operating system is shown in Figure 1.9. The most obvious element is the user interface that allows

FIGURE 1.9

Simplified Operating System
Block Diagram

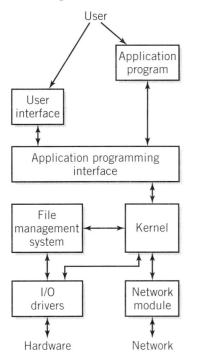

you to execute programs, enter commands, and manipulate files. The user interface accepts input from a keyboard and, in most modern systems, a mouse, touch screen, or other pointing device. The user interface also does output presentation on the display. On some systems, the output display might be simple text, but more likely the display includes a graphical user interface with a windowing system, and various gadgets for manipulating the windows.

The operating system's **application program interface (API),** acts as an interface for application programs and utilities to access the internal services provided by the operating system. These include file services, I/O services, data communication services, user interface services, program execution services, and more.[2]

Many of the internal services are provided by the **kernel** module, which contains the most important operating system processing functions. The remaining services are provided by other modules that are controlled by the kernel. The kernel manages memory by locating and allocating space to programs that need it, schedules time for each application to execute, provides communication between programs that are being executed, manages and arranges services and resources that are provided by other modules, and provides security.

The file management system allocates and manages secondary storage space and translates file requests from their name-based form into specific I/O requests. The actual storage and retrieval of the files is performed by the I/O drivers that comprise the I/O component. Each I/O driver controls one or more hardware devices of similar type.

The network module controls interactions between the computer system and the network(s) to which it is attached.

The operating system software has nearly always been stored on a hard disk, but on some smaller systems, especially lightweight laptops and embedded systems such as cell phones and iPods, a solid state disk or SD card may be used instead. On a few systems the operating system is actually provided as a network service when the system is turned on. In either case, the bootstrap or IPL (Initial Program Load) program in the operating system is stored within the computer using a type of memory known as **ROM,** or **read-only memory.** The bootstrap program provides the tools to test the system and to load the remainder of the operating system from the disk or network. Although the physical medium where the software is stored can be touched, the software itself is considered intangible.

Together, the hardware and system software provide a working computer system environment. Application software, communication support, and user data complete the picture.

---

[2]The same term (API) is also sometimes used to describe the services provided by one application to another. For example, Amazon and Google are among many companies whose application software provides API tools to allow users to extend the functionality of the original software.

The Communication Component

Very few modern computers or computer-based devices (which includes cell phones, iPods, and automobile computers, to name just a few possibilities) operate independently. Instead, they are tied to other computers directly, by modem, or through a network connection of some sort. The computers may be located physically close to each other, or they may be separated, even by thousands of miles. To work together, computers must have means to communicate with each other. The communication component requires both hardware and software to achieve this goal. Additional hardware components physically connect computers together into multiprocessing systems, or clusters, or networks, or, via telephone, satellite, or microwave, to computers at other remote locations. A **communication channel** provides the connection between computers. The channel may be a wire cable, a fiber-optic cable, a telephone line, or a wireless technology, such as infrared light, cellular phone, or radio-based technology such as Wi-Fi or Bluetooth. Special I/O hardware, consisting of a device such as a **modem** or **network interface card** (**NIC**) within the computer, serves as an interface between the computer and the communication channel. There may be additional hardware within the channel itself.

The communication component also requires additional software within the operating system of each computer to make it possible for each computer to understand what the other computers that they are connected with are saying. This software establishes the connections, controls the flow of data, and directs the data to the proper applications for use.

The Computer System

Our general description of the computer is valid for all general-purpose computer systems, and also for most devices with computers embedded in them, regardless of brand name or size. In more general terms, every computer system consists of a CPU, or central processing unit, where all the processing takes place; memory to hold the programs and data while they are being processed; and some form of input and output, usually one or more keyboards and flat-screen display devices plus one or more forms of long-term storage, usually disks, CDs or DVDs, and USB or SD plug-in memory. Most modern computer systems provide more than one CPU (or "core") within the computer system. A single CPU can process only one instruction at a time; the use of multiple CPUs can increase processing speed by allowing instructions that do not affect each other to be executed in parallel.

The validity of our general description is true regardless of how complex or simple the computer system may seem.

As a specific example, the large z10 EC IBM mainframe computer shown in Figure 1.10 can provide complex Web services to thousands of users at a time. IBM mainframes can have dozens of CPUs working together, with up to 1.52 terabytes (TB) of primary storage. They are capable of executing instructions at a rate of tens of billions of instructions per second! The powerful z/OS operating system can keep track of hundreds or thousands of simultaneous users and divides the time among them to satisfy their differing requirements. Even in its smallest configuration, the z10 EC Model S64 system, which is the largest current model at this writing, provides at least 16 GB of memory and processes instructions at

FIGURE 1.10

IBM System z10 EC Mainframe Computer

Courtesy of International Business Machines Corporation.
Unauthorized use not permitted.

FIGURE 1.11

A Laptop Computer

© 2007 Hewlett-Packard Company.

the rate of several billion instructions per second. In addition to the CPU, there are many large I/O devices—including tape drives and high speed printers—and disks that store many billions or trillions of characters. The computer alone weighs over 5000 pounds/2200 kilograms!

In contrast, the laptop PC shown in Figure 1.11 is designed for personal use. Everything is self-contained in one package. This system only has 2 GB of primary RAM storage and operates at a small fraction of the speed of the z10 EC. A hard drive is one of many storage options. The entire system, complete with display screen, built-in webcam, multiple network connections, and battery, weighs about three pounds (1.4 kilograms, if you prefer).

Although these two systems seem very different, the difference is actually one of magnitude, not of concept. The large system operates much faster, can support much more memory, and handles more input and output much faster. It has operating system software that allows many users to share this larger resource. Nonetheless, the fundamental system architecture is remarkably similar in both cases. Even the actual processing performed by the CPU is similar.

In fact, today's CPU operates in the same fundamental way as its CPU counterpart of fifty-five years ago, even though the construction is very different. Since computers all operate so similarly, regardless of size or type, it is not difficult today to transfer data between these different systems, allowing each system to do part of the processing for higher overall efficiency. This concept is known as **distributed computing.** The fact that different types of computers can work together, share files, and communicate successfully is known as **open computing.** Communication technology fulfills the requirements that make open and distributed computing possible.

Computers are sometimes divided into categories: mainframe computers, minicomputers, workstations, and personal computers, but these categories are less significant than they once were. The capability of today's personal computer far exceeds the capabilities of a mainframe computer of just a few years ago.

The Sun Ultra 40 computer is an example of a workstation that is frequently used as though it were a minicomputer, or even a small mainframe. Rather than attempting to categorize a particular computer, it is usually more productive to describe its capabilities in comparison to other systems being discussed or considered.

1.3 THE CONCEPT OF VIRTUALIZATION

The word "**virtual**" appears frequently throughout the computer literature in many different contexts. To name a few applications of the word that appear in this text, there are *virtual* computers, a Java *Virtual* Machine, *virtual* memory, and *virtual* networks. Sometimes, a synonymous word, *logical,* is used instead: in networking we have *logical* connections. *Virtual* storage consists of a relationship between *logical* memory and physical memory.

It is not important at this point that you understand any of the specific concepts mentioned above. (In fact, we realize that you probably don't.) Since the words *virtual* and *logical* represent a number of important concepts, however, we introduce them here.

In optics, a virtual image is the reflection that you see when you stand in front of a regular mirror. (See, for example, the cartoon at the beginning of Chapter 18.) You know that the image isn't real. For one thing, it's behind the wall that the mirror is mounted on. For another, you can't touch it. In early, time-shared computing, a large central computer commonly supplied computing services to users at terminals located remotely from the computer. In a sense, it seemed as though the user had access to a computer that was all her own. Starting in the early 1970s, IBM offered the VM (*virtual machine*) operating system to support this concept.

The *American Heritage Dictionary* offers two applicable definitions of *virtual* that together describe the usage of the word in modern computing:

- Existing or resulting in essence or effect though not in actual fact, form, or name
- Created, simulated, or carried on by means of a computer or computer network

Wikipedia defines *virtualization* as "a broad term that refers to the abstraction of computer resources".

In essence, *virtual* and *logical* are used to refer to something that appears as though it is something different. Thus, the *Java Virtual Machine (JVM)* uses software to simulate a real computer that works well with the Java programming language, even though the actual computer executes a different set of instructions than the JVM. A *logical connection* in networking offers the appearance of a direct communication link for passing data between two computers, even though the actual connection might involve a complex series of interconnections involving many computers and other devices and a variety of software to make it all look simple. The *virtualization* of a computer allows a single computer to appear as a multiplicity of computers, each with its own operating system and hardware resources.

1.4 PROTOCOLS AND STANDARDS

Standards and protocols are of great importance in computer systems. **Standards** are agreements among interested parties, often manufacturers, to assure that various system components will work together interchangeably. Standards make it possible to build a computer with components from different suppliers, for example, knowing that a graphics card will plug properly into a connector on a motherboard and that the image representations will be consistent between the connector, the CPU, memory, and the display monitor.

Standards apply to every aspect of computing: hardware, software, data, and communications, the voltage of a power supply, the physical spacing of pins on a connector, the format of a file, the pulses generated by a mouse. Computer language standards, such as Java and SQL, allow programs written on one type of computer to execute properly and consistently on another, and also make it possible for programmers to work together to create and maintain programs.

Similarly, data format and data presentation standards, such as the GIF and JPEG image format standard, the Unicode text format standard, and the HTML and XML Web presentation standards allow different systems to manipulate and display data in a consistent manner.

Standards can arise in many different ways. Many standards occur naturally: a proprietary data format (PDF) belonging to a single vendor becomes a de facto standard due to the popularity of the product. The PDF print description language is an example of such a standard. The format was designed by Adobe Corporation to provide a way of communicating high-quality printed output between computers and printers. Other standards are created because of a perceived need in an area where no standard exists.

Often a committee will form to investigate the requirements and create the standard. The MPEG-2 and MPEG-4 standards, which establish the means for the transmission and processing of digital video images, occurred in this way. The committee that designed the standard, made up primarily of motion picture engineers and video researchers, continues to develop the standard as improved techniques evolve. The JPEG photographic standard and MP3 sound standard are other examples of standards that were developed formally. Similarly, each version of HTTP has been formalized after many years of discussion by parties interested in Web communication. A nonstandard protocol or data format is limited in use to its supporters and may or may not become a standard, depending on its general acceptance. For example, DVD videos encoded in the proprietary DivX format will play on some DVD players, but not on others.

Protocols define the specific agreed-upon sets of ground rules that make it possible for a communication to take place. Except for special applications, most computers perform their operations such that each hardware or software computer unit will understand what other computer units that they are connected with are saying. Protocols exist for communications between computers, for the communications between various I/O devices and a computer, and for communications between many software programs. A protocol specification defines such communication features as data representation, signaling characteristics, message format, meanings of messages, identification and authentication, and error detection. Protocols in a client-server system assure that requests are understood and fulfilled and that responses are interpreted correctly.

Since the use of a proprietary protocol would be limited to those with permission to use it, protocols are almost always eventually standardized. Although not always the case, protocols that are not standardized tend to die out from lack of use. In fact, international standards are often created to ensure that the protocols are universally compatible. As an example, HTTP, HyperText Transfer Protocol, guides communication between Web servers and Web browsers on the Internet. The movement of data through the Internet is controlled by a **suite** of protocols called TCP/IP (Transmission Control Protocol/Internet Protocol). Storage devices communicate with a computer using a protocol called SATA. There are thousands of such protocols.

New protocols and other standards are proposed and created and standardized as the need arises. XML, RSS, and SIP are all examples of protocols developed recently to meet new demands. Satellite telecasting, near-universal telephone communication, wireless communications, and the Internet all demonstrate powerful and useful technologies made possible by protocols and standards. Indeed, the Internet is a measure of the success to which protocols that govern intercommunication between computer hardware and software have been standardized throughout the world. Discussions of various protocols and standards will occur regularly throughout this book.

1.5 OVERVIEW OF THIS BOOK

The focus of this book is upon the architecture and organization of computers, computer systems, and computer-based IT systems. Technically, there is a slight difference in definition between the terms "computer architecture" and "computer organization." In this book we will usually not attempt to differentiate these terms and will use them interchangeably.

In this book we will be concerned with all four components of computer systems: hardware, software, data, and interconnectivity, and with the interactions between each component. We will also look initially at the larger picture: the organization of computer systems as components, themselves, to form enterprise IT systems. Chapter 2 of this first part is concerned with the system as a whole. The remainder of this book is divided into four additional parts, consisting of discussions of number systems and the representation of data in the computer, the hardware that makes up the computer, the software that the computer uses, and the networks that interconnect computers.

Our first step will be to examine the concept of systems in general. We will look at the characteristics and qualities that define a system. We will then use that basic understanding to look at the characteristics of computer-based IT systems and show how the various elements and requirements of computer systems fit into the system concept. Part 1 illustrates fundamental IT architecture concepts with several examples of IT system architectures.

In Part 2, we will look at the different forms the input data may take, and we will consider the translation processes required to convert data into forms that the computer hardware and software can process. You will see how the various data types that are familiar to you from programming languages are stored and manipulated inside the computer. You'll learn the many different ways in which math calculations can be performed, and the advantages and disadvantages of each. You will see the difference between a number and the alphanumeric representation of a number, and understand why that difference can be critical in whether a program works or not. You will be able to relate the size of a word processing text to the storage capability of the computer's disk.

In Part 3, we will take a detailed look at the various components of the hardware and how they fit together. You will learn how the CPU works, how different I/O devices work, and even how text and graphics manage to appear, seemingly by magic, on the display screen. You will learn what makes some computers faster and more powerful than others, and what that means. You will learn about different ways of connecting I/O devices to the computer and see why you get a fast response from some devices, a slow response from others. You'll learn the difference between a serial port, a USB port, and a parallel port. We'll even explain the difference between PCI and PCI Express buses.

Most important, you will have the opportunity to see what a simple, program-obedient machine the computer really is. You will learn about the limitations of a computer. We all tend to think of the computer as a resource of infinite capacity, speed, and perhaps even intelligence, but of course that's not true. We will consider how these limitations affect your work as a user, and as a means of specifying a system that will your meet your needs and requirements.

Part 4 will provide a careful introduction to the foundational principles of communication and networking. We will consider the basic communication technologies, networking hardware, software, channels and channel media, protocols, and methodologies that are required to support communication between computer systems in an IT system environment.

In the final part, we will consider the software that is used to control the computer's basic processing capabilities. Although computer software falls into two categories, operating system software and application software, we will focus exclusively on the system software. We will be concerned with control and efficient use of the computer hardware, fair and effective allocation of computer resources to different programs, security, storage management and file system structure, system administration, security, user interfaces, and more.

There are also four supplementary chapters covering topics that are somewhat outside the scope of the text, but important and interesting nonetheless. The first supplementary chapter introduces the fundamental logic that makes up a computer. The second supplementary chapter provides case studies that describe the hardware and system software of important real-world computer systems. These examples include the ×86 family of PC hardware, the Microsoft Windows family of operating systems, Linux operating systems, and IBM mainframe hardware and software. The remaining two supplementary chapters, on CPU instruction addressing modes and on programming tools, have been maintained and updated from the 3rd edition. The supplementary chapters can be found on the book's website, www.wiley.com/college/englander.

Additional related topics of current interest may also be found on the book's website. The website also contains numerous links to reference materials, both general to computing as well as specific to individual topics discussed within the book.

1.6 A BRIEF ARCHITECTURAL HISTORY OF THE COMPUTER

Although a study of the history of computing is generally outside the scope of this book, a brief introduction is useful in showing the wide-ranging and quirky path by which IT has arrived to its present position. It is of particular interest to note that nearly all of the revolutionary concepts that define computer systems today were developed between thirty and sixty years ago; today's advances are more evolutionary and incremental in nature. This suggests that an understanding of the basic concepts that we are presenting in this book should serve you, the reader, well in your ability to understand the importance and significance of future developments as they occur.

Early Work

It is not possible, nor particularly useful, to identify the date of the "invention" of the computer. Indeed it has always been the aspiration of humankind to create devices that would simplify people's work. Thus, it is not surprising that people were envisioning mechanical devices to simplify the jobs of routine data processing and calculation even in ancient times. In fact, there is recent evidence of the existence of an ancient computing device used for astronomical calculations. Instead, this discussion covers just a few of the major developments related to computer architecture.

In this context, one could consider the abacus, already in use as early as 500 BC by the ancient Greeks and Romans, to be an early predecessor of the computer. Certainly, the abacus was capable of performing calculations and storing data. Actually, if one were to build a binary numbered abacus, its calculations would very closely resemble those of the computer.

The abacus remained in common use until the 1500s and, in fact, is still considered an effective calculating tool in some cultures today. In the late 1500s, though, European inventors again began to put their minds to the problem of automatic calculation. Blaise Pascal, a noted French mathematician of the 1600s, invented a calculating machine in 1642 at the age of nineteen, although he was never able to construct the machine. In 1801, Joseph Marie Jacquard invented a loom that used punched cards to control the patterns woven into cloth. The program provided by the punched cards controlled rods that raised and lowered different threads in the correct sequence to print a particular pattern. This is the first documented application of the use of some form of storage to hold a program for the use of a semiautomated, programmable machine.

Charles Babbage, an English mathematician who lived in the early 1800s, spent much of his own personal fortune attempting to build a mechanical calculating machine that he called an "analytical engine." The analytical engine resembles the modern computer in many conceptual ways. A photo of an early version of the analytical engine is shown in Figure 1.12. Babbage's machine envisioned the use of Jacquard's punched cards for input data and for the program, provided memory for internal storage, performed calculations as specified by the program using a central processing unit known as a "mill," and printed output. Augusta Ada Byron, Countess of Lovelace and the daughter of the poet Lord Byron, worked closely with Babbage and developed many of the fundamental ideas of programming and program design, including the concepts of branches and loops.

FIGURE 1.12

Babbage's Analytical Engine

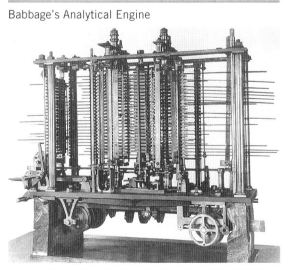

Courtesy of International Business Machines Corporation. Unauthorized use not permitted.

FIGURE 1.13

Block Diagram of Babbage's Analytical Engine

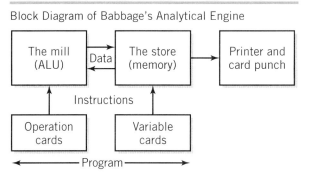

Source: From *Computer Architecture and Organization*, 2nd ed.,
J. Hayes, copyright © 1988, by McGraw-Hill Companies, pg. 14
Reprinted by permission.

A block diagram of the Babbage analytical engine is shown in Figure 1.13. The mill was capable of selecting one of four arithmetic operations, and of testing the sign of a number with a different program branch specified for each result. The sequence of operation was specified by instructions on the operation cards. The operation cards could be advanced or reversed as a means of implementing a sort of "goto" instruction. The second set of cards, known as variable cards, were to be used to specify particular memory locations for the data involved in the calculations.

Babbage envisioned a memory of one thousand 50-digit decimal numbers. Each digit was to be stored using a ten-toothed gear known as a counter wheel. Although the analytical engine was never completed, it should be apparent to you that it contains all the essential elements of today's computers. At approximately the same time, another English mathematician, George Boole, developed the binary theory of logic that bears his name, Boolean logic. He also recognized the relationship between binary arithmetic and Boolean logic that makes possible the circuitry that implements the modern electronic computer.

Computer Hardware

In the late 1930s and early 1940s, several different groups of researchers independently developed versions of the modern electronic computer. The Mark I, built in 1937 by Howard H. Aiken and associates at Harvard University with help and funding from IBM, used thousands of relays; relays are mechanical binary switches controlled by electrical currents, familiar to you perhaps as the clicking devices that control operations in tape cassette players and telephone answering machines. Although binary relays were used for computation, the fundamental design was decimal. Storage consisted of seventy-two 23-digit decimal numbers, stored on counter wheels. An additional counter wheel digit held the sign, using the digit 0 for plus and 9 for minus. The design appears to be based directly on Babbage's original concepts and use of mechanical calculator parts from IBM accounting machines. A similar electromechanical computer was designed and built by Conrad Zuse in Germany at about the same time.

The first totally electronic digital computer was apparently devised by John V. Atanasoff, a physicist at Iowa State College, in 1937. The machine was built in 1939 by Atanasoff and a graduate student, Clifford Berry, using electronic vacuum tubes as the switching components. The machine was known as ABC, for Atanasoff-Berry Computer. It is claimed that Atanasoff worked out the original details as he drove restlessly late one winter night from his house in Iowa to a bar in neighboring Illinois. The machine was not intended as a general-purpose computer, but was built to solve physics equations that Atanasoff was working on at the time. There is some doubt as to whether the machine ever worked completely.

ABC was a binary-based machine, just like today's computers. It consisted of an arithmetic/logic unit with thirty units that could do addition and subtraction, a rotating drum memory that held thirty binary numbers of 50 digits each, and punched card input. Each punched card held five 15-digit decimal numbers. These numbers were converted to binary as they entered the machine. Despite its limitations, ABC was an important pathmark that led to later significant advances in computer design. It is only recently that Atanasoff has begun to receive recognition for his achievement.

Much of the effort that culminated in a successful general-purpose computer architecture resulted from a wartime need for the solution to difficult mathematical formulas related to ballistic missile trajectories and other World War II research. The ENIAC (for Electronic Numerical Integrator and Computer, believe it or not) is generally considered to be the first all-electronic digital computer. It was designed and built between 1943 and 1946 by John W. Mauchly and J. Presper Eckert at the University of Pennsylvania, using the concepts that Mauchly had seen in Atanasoff's machine, although this was not publicly known at the time.

ENIAC had very limited storage capability, with only twenty locations each capable of holding a 10-digit decimal number. An additional one hundred numbers could be stored in read-only memory. Calculations were performed using decimal arithmetic. Ten electronic vacuum tube binary switches were used for each digit, with only one switch in the "ON" position to represent the value of the digit. Input and output used punched cards. The system could also provide printed output.

Programs could not be stored internally, but were hard wired with external "patch panels" and toggle switches. It took many hours to change programs, and, of course, debugging was a nightmare. Nonetheless, ENIAC was an important machine, some say the most important machine, especially since it led directly to the development of the UNIVAC I, the first commercially available computer, in 1951.

ENIAC contained eighteen thousand vacuum tubes, occupied a floor space of more than fifteen thousand square feet, and weighed more than thirty tons. A photograph of ENIAC, taken from *The New York Times* of February 15, 1946, is shown in Figure 1.14. Even in its day, ENIAC was recognized as an important achievement. ENIAC operated successfully until 1955, when it was dismantled, but not destroyed. Parts of the computer can be seen at the Smithsonian Institute, at the U.S. Military Academy at West Point, at the Moore School of the University of Pennsylvania, and at the University of Michigan.

In 1945, John von Neumann, a consultant on the ENIAC project, proposed a computer that included a number of significant improvements over the ENIAC design. The most important of these were

1. A memory that would hold both programs and data, the so-called stored program concept. This solved the difficult problem of rewiring the control panels for changing programs on the ENIAC.
2. Binary processing of data. This simplified the design of the computer and allowed the use of binary memory for both instructions and data. It also recognized the natural relationship between the ON/OFF nature of switches and calculation in the binary number system, using Boolean logic.

The CPU was to include ALU, memory, and CU components. The control unit read instructions from memory and executed them. A method of handling input/output through

FIGURE 1.14

The ENIAC

Courtesy Sperry Univac, Div. of Sperry Corporation.

the control unit was also established. The instruction set contained instructions representing all the essential features of a modern computer. In other words, von Neumann's machine contained every major feature considered essential to modern computer architecture. Modern computer architecture is still referred to as **von Neumann architecture.**

Due to political intrigue and controversy, two different versions of von Neumann's architecture were designed and built, EDVAC at the University of Pennsylvania and IAS at the Princeton University Institute for Advanced Studies (hence the unusual name). Both machines were completed in 1951–1952. The success of EDVAC and IAS led to the development of many offspring, mostly with odd names, and to several commercial computers, including the first IBM computers.

At this point, von Neumann's architecture was firmly established. It remains the prevalent standard to this day and provides the foundation for the remainder of the material in this book. Although there have been significant advances in technology, and improvements in design that have resulted, today's designs still reflect the work done prior to 1951 on ABC, ENIAC, EDVAC, and IAS.

All of these early electronic computers relied on the electronic vacuum tube for their operation. Vacuum tubes were bulky, made of glass, fragile, short-lived, and required large amounts of power to operate. Vacuum tubes require an internal electric heater to function, and the heaters tend to fail quickly, resulting in what was known as a "burned out" tube. Furthermore, the heat generated by the large number of tubes used in a computer required a massive forced-air or water-cooling system. A report reprinted by computer historian James Cortada [CORT87] states that the average error-free operating time for ENIAC was only 5.6 hours. Such bulky, maintenance-requiring systems could not have attained the prevalence that computers have in our society. The technological breakthrough that made possible today's small, sophisticated computers was the invention of the transistor and, subsequently, the integration of transistors and other electronic components with the development of the integrated circuit.

The invention of the integrated circuit led to smaller, faster, more powerful computers as well as a new, compact, inexpensive form of memory, RAM. Although many of these computers played an important role in the evolution of today's computers, two specific developments stand out from the rest: (1) development of the first widely accepted personal computer, by IBM in 1981, and (2) design of the Intel 8008 microprocessor, predecessor to the x86 CPU family, in 1972. The impact of these two developments is felt to this day.

Companies have developed better ways of moving data between different parts of the computer, better ways of handling memory, and methods for increasing the speed of instruction execution. There is a lot more processing power in today's personal computer than there was in the largest mainframe computer in the 1970s. Nonetheless, the basic architecture of today's machines is remarkably similar to that developed in the 1940s.

Operating Systems

Given how easy it is to communicate with computers today, it is hard to picture a time when the user had to do everything by hand, one step at a time. We take it for granted that we can type commands at a keyboard or move a mouse and launch programs, copy files, send text to a printer, and perform myriad other computer tasks. We power up and bootstrap our systems by pressing a switch.

It was not always this way. Early computers had no operating systems. The user, who was also the programmer, entered a program by setting it, one word at a time, with switches on the front panel, one switch per bit, or by plugging wires into a patch panel that resembled a cribbage board. Not a pleasant operation! Needless to say, early computers were single-user systems. Much of the computer's time was tied up with this primitive form of program and data entry. In fact, as late as the mid-1970s, there were still vendors producing computer systems with no operating system and computer hardware that was still bootstrapped by entering the bootstrap program one instruction at a time into switches on the front panel of the computer.

The history of system software, particularly operating systems, is much less well defined than that of hardware. According to Cortada [CORT87],

> Without more sophisticated operating systems, scientists would not have been able to take full advantage of the power of the transistor and later of the [microprocessor] chip in building the computers known today. Yet their contribution to the overall evolution of digital computers has been overlooked by historians of data processing.

Part of the reason, undoubtedly, is that software evolved gradually, rather than as a series of important individually identifiable steps. The first operating systems and high-level programming languages appeared in the early 1950s, particularly associated with IBM and MIT, but with only a few exceptions, these efforts have not been associated with individual people or projects.

The need for operating system software came from the increasing computer power that resulted from the rapid development of new computers in the 1950s. Although the hardware architecture has not changed substantially since that time, improved technology has resulted in a continuum of ever-increasing computer capability that continues to this day. It has been necessary to continually modify and improve operating system architecture to take advantage of that power and make it available to the user. Computing has changed from single-user batch processing (where only a single user, with a single program, could access the machine at one time), to multiple-user batch job submission (where each user's "job" was submitted to the computer by an operator for sequential runs), to multiuser batch job execution (where the computer executed several jobs simultaneously, thereby keeping the CPU busy while I/O took place on another user's job), to multiuser online computing (where each user had direct access to the computer), to single-user interactive personal computing, to today's powerful interactive networked systems, with multitasking, easy-to-use graphical interfaces, the ability to move data between applications, and near-instant access to other computers all over the world.

Each of these developments, plus various hardware developments—minicomputers, PCs, new I/O devices, multimedia—have required additional operating system sophistication; in each case, designers have responded to the need.

The early computers were used primarily by scientists and engineers to solve technical problems. The next generation of computers, in the late 1950s, provided a punched card reader for input and a printer for output. Soon after, magnetic tape systems became available. The first "high-level" languages, primarily assembly language, then FORTRAN, made it possible to write programs in a language other than binary, and offline card punch machines allowed programmers to prepare their programs for entry without tying up the machine. Algol, COBOL, and Lisp followed shortly after. New technology improved the reliability of the computers. All these advances combined to make the computer system practical for business commercial use, especially for large businesses.

Still, these computers were single-user batch systems. Initially, users **submitted** the cards that they had prepared to the computer for execution. Later, separate, offline systems were developed that allowed the cards to be grouped together onto a magnetic tape for processing together. Programs were then submitted to the computer room in the form of *jobs.* A job consisted of one or more program card **decks,** together with the required **data decks** for each program. An output tape could also be used to support printing offline. As an example, Figure 1.15 shows a job that compiles and executes a FORTRAN program.

I/O routines were needed to operate the card readers, tape drives, and printers. The earliest operating systems consisted of just these I/O routines, but gradually operating systems evolved to perform other services. Computer time was very expensive, hundreds of dollars per minute, and in growing demand. To increase availability, control of the computer was placed in the hands of an operator, who fed the punched cards, mounted tapes, and generally tried to keep the system busy and efficient. The operating system provided a monitor that fed jobs to the system and supported the operator by notifying him or her of necessary actions, such as loading a new tape, setting switches on the panel, removing printout, and so on. As system demand increased, the monitor expanded to include accounting and simple, priority-based scheduling of jobs.

It is generally accepted that the first operating system was built by General Motors Research Laboratories in 1953–1954 for their IBM 701 computer. Other early systems included the FORTRAN Monitor System (FMS), IBSYS, and Share Operating System

FIGURE 1.15

Job Card Deck Used to Compile and Execute a FORTRAN Program

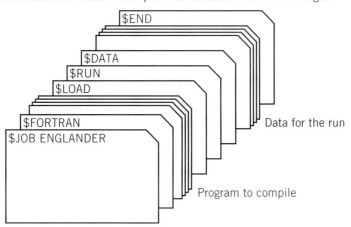

(SOS).[3] Many important breakthroughs in operating system design occurred in the early 1960s. These breakthroughs laid the groundwork for the operating system as we know it today.

- In 1963, Burroughs released its Master Control Program (MCP). MCP contained many of the features of modern systems, including high-level language facilities and support for multiprocessing (with two identical CPUs). Most important, MCP supported virtual storage, as well as powerful multitasking capabilities.

- IBM introduced OS/360 as the operating system for its new System/360 in 1964. OS/360 provided a powerful language to expedite batch processing, JCL, or Job Control Language, and a simple form of multiprogramming that made it possible to load several jobs into memory, so that other jobs could use the CPU when one job was busy with input/output. By this time, disks were also becoming available, and the system was capable of reading cards onto disk while the CPU executed its jobs; thus, when a job completed, the operating system could load another job from disk into memory, ready to run. This improved the OS scheduling capability. JCL is still used for batch processing! The enormous success of the IBM OS/360 and its successors firmly established the basis of an operating system as a fundamental part of the computer.

- In 1962, a group at MIT known as Project MAC introduced the concept of time-sharing with an experimental operating system called CTSS. Project MAC was one of the seminal centers for the development of computer science. Shortly thereafter, MIT, Bell Labs, and GE formed a partnership to develop a major time-sharing system. The system was called MULTICS (Multiplexed

---

[3]Share was a consortium of system programmers who used IBM systems and who met to discuss problems and develop solutions. SOS was produced by a team of consortium members.

Information and Computing Service), and although MULTICS never fully realized its dream of becoming a major computer utility, many of the most important multitasking concepts and algorithms were developed by the MULTICS team. It was supplied for many years as the operating system for Honeywell computer systems.

■   When Bell Labs withdrew from the MULTICS project, Ken Thompson, a MULTICS researcher, turned to the development of a small personal operating system, which he called Unics, later UNIX, to contrast it from MULTICS. He was later joined by Dennis Ritchie. The original UNIX development was performed on a Digital PDP-7 minicomputer and later moved to a PDP-11 minicomputer, the forerunner of the VAX computer. Originally, the system was written in assembly language, but Ritchie developed a new high-level language, which he called C, and the operating system was largely rewritten in C.

UNIX introduced many important OS concepts that are standard today, including the hierarchical file system, the shell concept, redirection, piping, and the use of simple commands that can be combined to perform powerful operations. Thompson and Ritchie included facilities for document production and formatting, including such novelties as a spell checker and a grammar checker. They created many inventive algorithms to improve operating system performance, developed techniques for interprocess communication, and even provided tools for networked and distributed processing. Many facets of operating systems that are taken for granted today were originated in UNIX development.

UNIX earned a reputation for power and flexibility. Because it was written in C, it was also easy to **port** it, that is, convert it for use, to other computers. As a result of these factors, UNIX became an important operating system for universities and was ultimately adopted, in many versions, by the commercial marketplace as well. UNIX continues to be of great importance, particularly due to its flexibility in the area of networks and distributed systems.

■   Another important innovation, some would say the most important development in making the computer accessible to nontechnical users, was the development of the concept of **graphical user interfaces.** Most historians would credit the invention of the windows and mouse interface to Doug Englebart. This work was done, amazingly enough, in the 1960s, at Stanford Research Institute. A practical windowing system was built in the 1970s by Alan Kay and others at Xerox PARC (Palo Alto Research Center), as part of a visionary computer concept known as the Dynabook project. The original intention of Dynabook was to develop a book-sized personal computer with a high-resolution color display and wireless communication that would provide computer capabilities (particularly secretarial), games, e-mail, and a reference library. Although the technology of the time was not sufficient to bring the Dynabook as an entirety to fruition, the engineers at Xerox in the late 1970s built a personal computer workstation with a graphical user interface known as Star. It is believed that a visit to Xerox PARC by Steve Jobs, the founder of Apple, in 1979, inspired the development of the Apple Lisa and, subsequently, the Apple Macintosh.

The next important breakthrough in computer use occurred in 1982, with the introduction of the IBM personal computer. The IBM PC was designed as a stand-alone, single-user computer for the mass market. The IBM PC was supplied with a reasonably easy-to-use operating system, PC-DOS, which was developed and also later marketed by Microsoft as MS-DOS. PC-DOS was actually derived from an earlier personal computer operating system, CP/M (Control Program for Microcomputers), but is important because of the tremendous success of the IBM PC and its derivatives. Gradually, PC-DOS and MS-DOS became the prevalent operating system of the era. With later versions, Microsoft made many improvements, including hierarchical directory file storage, file redirection, better memory management, and an improved and expanded command set. Many of these improvements were derived from UNIX innovations. With the addition of Englebart and Kay's user interface innovations, MS-DOS has gradually evolved into Windows XP and Windows Vista, and most recently, Windows 7.

Even with all these earlier innovations, there continue to be tremendous advances in operating system software. Today's systems, such as Windows XP and Vista, Linux, and Macintosh OS X, combine much more power on one hand with improved user friendliness and ease of use on the other. There are several reasons for this:

- There has been a great increase in computer speed and power. More powerful integrated circuits have allowed the design of faster computers using faster clocks and larger internal data paths, together with techniques for speeding up instruction execution. Even small personal computers can support tens of megabytes of memory and many gigabytes of disk storage. A modern PC may contain as much as one thousand times the memory and execute instructions one thousand times as fast as the 1965 IBM OS/360 mainframe computer. Thus, more capability can be built into the operating system without sacrificing performance.

- There have been fundamental improvements in computer hardware design. Many modern computers are designed as an integrated unit, hardware and operating system software together. Most computer hardware contains special features intended to support a powerful operating system. Such features as special graphics, cache memory, vector processing, and virtual storage memory management hardware are intended primarily for use by the operating system. These features used to be available only on large mainframes. A protected mode of hardware instructions, accessible only to the operating system, provides security and protection to the operating system and allows the operating system to protect the system's resources and users.

- There have been fundamental improvements in operating system software design. Operating system programs have grown in size and complexity. Increased memory capacity has made a larger operating system feasible. Increased speed has made it practical. Gradually, innovative operating system techniques from large computers have drifted down to the PC level. In addition, program design itself has helped the process. New languages, well designed for system programming, and better programming methods such as object-oriented programming have also contributed to the process.

- There has been a shift in focus to creating operating systems that better serve the end user. This has resulted in much current research on human-computer interfaces, and on the ways in which humans work and use the computer. New work paradigms, based on object-oriented programming and communication technologies, and new interfaces continue to extend the role of the operating system. There is a new willingness to include features that were not a part of earlier operating systems and to modularize the operating system in different ways to improve the delivery of services to the user and to the user's application programs.

- Networking has provided the opportunity for innovative research and development in distributed computing, including client-server technology, shared processing, and grid computing. There is a continuing progression of new operating system techniques, developed in response to the changing requirements of modern distributed systems.

- The rapid growth of the Internet, and of e-mail use, the Web, and multimedia in particular, has created opportunities and the need for better methods of accessing, retrieving, and sharing information between different systems. The results have impacted network design, user interface design, distributed processing technology, and open system standardization with corresponding effects in operating system design.

Although today's operating systems are highly complex and sophisticated, with many capabilities made possible by modern technology, particularly fast processors, large amounts of memory, and improved graphical I/O design, it is interesting to note that the major operating system features that we take for granted today are all evolutions based on innovations of more than thirty years ago.

Communication, Networks, and the Internet

With the development of large, multiterminal computer systems in the 1960s and 1970s, it was natural that users would want to use the computer to communicate with each other and to work collaboratively. Data was centrally stored in storage that was available to all, so it was easily shared among users on the same system. It soon occurred to software developers that it would be desirable to allow direct discussion among the users, both in real time and in the form of messages that could be stored on the system and made available to users when they logged in. Since data was centrally stored, the addition of message storage was a minor enhancement. "Talk" facilities that allowed users to communicate in real time were added later. These were similar to today's text messaging, although some had split-screen capability that allowed two users to send messages simultaneously. By 1965, some of these systems supported e-mail, and in 1971, Ray Tomlinson created the standard *username@hostname* format that is still in use today. As modems became available for users to log into their office systems from home and computers became more affordable, software innovators developed bulletin board systems, newsgroups, and discussion boards, where users could dial in and leave and retrieve messages. Gradually, it became possible to support modems on multiple lines, and affordable real-time "chat rooms" became possible.

During the same period, various developments occurred that made it possible to connect different computers together into simple networks. Some were based on direct links between modems on each computer. Others were based on early protocols, notably

X.25, a packet-switching protocol using phone lines. By 1980, these various innovations had evolved into a number of international networks, as well as three companies, Compuserve, AOL, and Prodigy, who offered e-mail, Usenet news, chat rooms, and other services to personal computer users.

All of this activity was, of course, a precursor to the Internet. Much of the modern history of networking and communication can be traced back to two specific developments: (1) a research project, ARPANET, whose goal was to connect computers at various universities and research centers, funded starting in 1969 by the U.S. Defense Department and later by the National Science Foundation and other groups, and (2) the development of the Ethernet by Robert Metcalfe, David Boggs, and others, which started at Xerox PARC in 1973. The ARPANET project was responsible for the design of TCP/IP, which was first tested in 1974, and issued as an international standard in 1981.

Because ARPANET and its successors, CSNet and NSFNet, were funded by the U.S. government, its use was initially limited to noncommercial activities. Gradually, other networks, some of them commercial, joined the network in order to exchange e-mails and other data, while the administrators of NSFNet chose to "look the other way". Ultimately, the government turned over its Internet resources to private interests in 1995; at that point the Internet became commercial and expanded rapidly into the form that we know today.

Although it is only marginally related to the major issues addressed in this book, we would be remiss if we did not complete this discussion with a mention of Sir Tim Berners-Lee, of CERN, the European organization for nuclear research, who in 1991 developed the concepts that became the World Wide Web and Max Andreessen of the University of Illinois, who, in 1993, developed Mosaic, the first graphical Web browser.

SUMMARY AND REVIEW

This chapter has presented a brief review of the basics of computing. We began by recalling the input-process-output model for computing. Next we demonstrated the connection between that model and the components of the computer system. We noted that implementation of the model requires four components: hardware, software, communication, and data. The architecture of the computer system is made up of the hardware and system software. In addition, a communication component exists to enable interconnecting systems. We discussed the general architecture of a computer and noted that the same description applies to CPUs both modern and ancient, both large and small. We introduced the important concepts of virtualization, standards and protocols, noting that these ideas will appear throughout the book. The chapter concluded with a brief history of the computer from an architectural perspective.

FOR FURTHER READING

There are many good general introductory computer texts available for review if you feel you need one. New books appear so rapidly that we are reluctant to recommend any particular one. For alternative coverage of material in this book, you may find recent editions of various books by Stallings [e.g., STAL05] or Tanenbaum [e.g., TANE07] to be useful. Various chapters offer additional suggestions that are specifically applicable to the material in those chapters. The Web is also a rich source of knowledge. Two websites that we have found particularly useful are wikipedia.org and howstuffworks.org. In addition to a wide range of material, these websites also offer numerous references to facilitate further study. Other useful websites include arstechnica.com and realworldtech.com.

The book by Rochester and Gantz [ROCH83] is a fun way to explore the history of computing. Historical facts are blended with other facts, anecdotes, humor, and miscellany about computers. Although the book is (sadly) out of print, it is available in many libraries. You can learn, in this book, about von Neumann's party habits, about movies that became video games, about computer scams and ripoffs, and lots of other interesting stuff. Perhaps the most thorough discussion of computer history is found in the three-volume dictionary by Cortada [CORT87]. Although Cortada is not really designed for casual reading, it provides ready access and solid information on particular topics of interest. Much of the historical discussion in this chapter was obtained from the Cortada volumes.

If you live or vacation in a city with a computer museum, you can enjoy another approach to computer history. Computer museums even allow you to play with some of the older computers. Well-known museums can be found in Washington, D.C., and within the Science Museum in Boston.

KEY CONCEPTS AND TERMS

application programming
   interface (API)
arithmetic/logic unit (ALU)
bus
byte
central processing unit
   (CPU)
channel (I/O)
communication channel
control unit (CU)
data deck
deck (program)
distributed computing
embedded computer
graphical user interface

hardware
input
input-process-output
   (IPO) model
interface unit
kernel
logical
memory
modem
network interface card
   (NIC)
open computing
operating system
output

port (from one computer to
   another)
primary storage
protocol
random access memory
   (RAM)
read-only memory (ROM)
software
standards
stored program concept
submit (a job)
suite (protocol)
virtual
von Neumann architecture
word

READING REVIEW QUESTIONS

1.1   One way to view an information technology system is to consider an IT system as consisting of four major components or building blocks. This book takes this approach by dividing the remainder of the book into parts, with a part devoted to each major type of component. What are the four components of an IT system that you will study in this book?

1.2   Any computer system, large or small, can be represented by the four elements of an IPO model. Draw an IPO model; clearly label each of the four elements in your drawing.

1.3   Explain the differences between primary storage and secondary storage. What is each type used for?

1.4   The book compares a large mainframe computer to a small laptop computer or PDA, and states that the difference between them is one of magnitude, not of concept. Explain the meaning of that statement.

1.5   The book divides the software component of a computer system into two major categories. Identify each category and give an example of each that you are already familiar with. Briefly explain the role of each category.

1.6   What is a protocol? What is a standard? Do all protocols have to be standards? Explain. Are all standards protocols? Explain.

1.7   Virtualization is a concept that has taken on major importance in the early twenty-first century. Explain what is meant by virtualization.

EXERCISES

1.1   For the computer that you normally use, identify which pieces constitute the hardware and which pieces constitute the system software. Now think about the file system of your computer. What part of the file system is hardware, what part software, and what part data?

1.2   Suppose you would like to buy a computer for your own needs. What are the major considerations and factors that would be important in your decision? What technical factors would influence your decision? Now try to lay out a specification for your machine. Consider and justify the features and options that you would like your machine to have.

1.3   Look at the computer ads on the business pages of a large daily newspaper and make a list of all the terms used that you don't understand. Save this list and check it from time to time during the semester. Cross out the items that you now understand and look up the items that have been covered but which you still don't understand.

1.4   Protocols and standards are an important feature of networks. Why is this so?

1.5   Although there is substantial overlap between protocols and standards there are protocols that are not standards and standards that are not protocols. With the help of a dictionary, identify the differences between the definition of protocol and the definition of standard; then, identify a specific example of a standard that is not a protocol; identify a specific example of a protocol that is not a standard.

1.6   Locate a current reference that lists the important protocols that are members of the TCP/IP protocol suite. Explain how each protocol contributes to the operation and use of the Internet.

1.7   Write a small program in your favorite high-level language. Compile your program. What is the ratio of high-level language statements to machine language statements? As a rough estimate, assume that each machine language statement requires approximately four bytes of file storage. Add various statements one at a time to your program and note the change in size of the corresponding machine language program.

CHAPTER 2

AN INTRODUCTION TO SYSTEM CONCEPTS AND SYSTEMS ARCHITECTURE

"Now, this is just a simulation of what the blocks will look like once they're assembled."

2.0 INTRODUCTION

In this book we discuss systems: computer systems, operating systems, file systems, I/O (sub)systems, network systems, and more. Each of these same systems is also an element with a major role in the information technology systems that form the backbone of modern organizations. Indeed, these elements—computer hardware, software, data, and communication—together represent the infrastructure of every IT system. If we are to understand the various types of systems that are the focus of this book, it is important that we first understand the concept of "system" itself, and, then, equally important, the basic architectures of the IT systems that use these elements. Only then is it possible to see clearly the role of the various system elements in the larger IT picture as we visit each in turn.

Use of the word "system" is obviously not unique to IT. In our daily lives, too, we often use the word "system" to describe things in everyday language. Our homes have electrical systems, plumbing systems, heating and air conditioning systems, and maybe for some, even, home theatre systems. There are ignition, braking, fuel, exhaust, and electrical systems in our cars. Our cities have water systems, sewer systems, and transportation systems, to name a few. Philosophers and social scientists talk about social systems and linguistic systems. The economy deals with banking systems, financial systems and trading systems, and, for that matter, economic systems. The word "system" even appears in the names of thousands of companies.

So it seems as though everyone knows what a system is, but what is a system? We use the word "system" intuitively, without thinking about the meaning of the word, so we obviously have an intuitive understanding of what a system is. IT professionals, however, spend their careers analyzing, designing, developing, implementing, upgrading, maintaining, administering, and using systems everyday. It is therefore important that we have a deeper, more formal understanding of system concepts.

In this chapter, we consider the concept of a system from an IT perspective. We investigate the characteristics and composition of systems, explain the meaning of system architecture, and show the fundamental role of systems, particularly various types of IT systems, in business. We offer examples of different types of IT systems, and show how IT systems work together to accomplish tasks and solve problems. We show how systems can themselves be composed of subsystems, where the subsystems also fit the definition of systems.

After you have studied this chapter, you should have a clear understanding of what a system is, what kinds of systems are used in IT, the purpose and goals for each of these systems, and how these systems fit together and interact with each other and with their environment. You'll understand the concept of system architecture. This discussion will set the stage for the remainder of the book, which considers individually and collectively the specific computer-based systems and subsystems that constitute the primary tools and components of business information technology.

2.1 THE GENERAL CONCEPT OF SYSTEMS

The most important characteristic that is shared by all of the systems mentioned above, and, indeed, by all systems, is that each is built up from a set of components that are linked together to form what we think of as a single unit. The house plumbing system, for example, consists of sinks, faucets, toilets, a hot water heater, bathtubs or showers, valves, and more, all connected together by pipes. An IT system consists of groups of computer hardware, various I/O devices, and application and system software, connected together by networks.

Often, the system is intended to serve a purpose or to produce results. The purpose of the house plumbing system is to allow the residents of the home access to water to wash, bathe, and drink. The purpose of an IT system is to allow organizations to process, access, and share information. The results of a successful IT system are documents, information, improved business processes and productivity, profits, strategic plans, and the like. This is, in fact, the "output" of the IPO model described in Chapter 1. In general, though, there is no requirement that a system serve a specific, definable purpose. The fact that the set of components may be considered as a single unit is sufficient to satisfy the concept of a system. The solar system is an example of a system where the purpose is unspecified.

There is also no requirement that the components of a system be physical. The links between components can also be physical or conceptual. In fact, the system itself may be conceptual, rather than physical. The number system is an example of a conceptual system. Computer operating systems are also conceptual, rather than physical. Business systems are also conceptual, although some of the components that they contain may be physical. The words *tangible* and *intangible* are sometimes used in place of physical and conceptual, respectively. Intangible or conceptual components and systems include ideas, methods, principles and policies, processes, software, and other abstractions. If, for example, the components in a system represent steps (intangible) in a multistep process, the links may represent the need to complete one step before the next is begun (also intangible).

Figure 2.1 illustrates a number of different systems to show you some of the possibilities. Figure 2.1(a) is a model of a home plumbing system. This is a physical system. The components are plumbing fixtures, linked by pipes. Figure 2.1(b) is a simplified representation of the solar system. The sun and planets are physical; the links in this system are conceptual, specifically, the distance of each planet from the sun, interplanetary and solar gravity, orbital relationships, the distances between planets at a particular point in time, and other attributes. Figure 2.1(c) is a diagram of a home networking system. The links in this case are a mixture of physical wires and (intangible) wireless connections. Sometimes the nature of the links is important only in terms of providing the proper interface connections to the components. Figure 2.1(d) is a simplified diagram of part of the inventory control portion of a sales system. The relationships between the components in this case are temporal (i.e., related to time). For example, inventory from a previous sale must be deducted from stock before we process the next order; otherwise we can't promise delivery of goods on the new order because we don't know if we still have sufficient goods in stock to fill the order.

With these pictures and ideas about systems in mind, we will define a **system** as follows:

> A system is a collection of components linked together and organized in such a way as to be recognizable as a single unit.

FIGURE 2.1(a)

Plumbing System Diagram

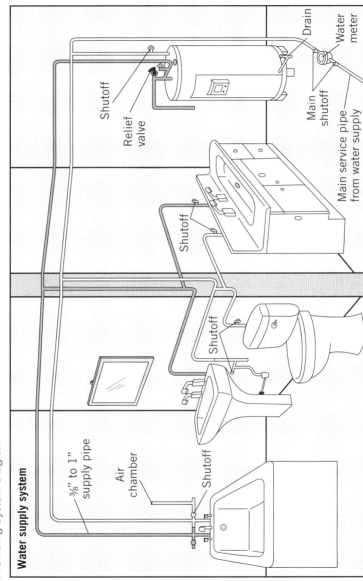

Water supply system

Relief valve

Shutoff

Drain

Water meter

Main shutoff

Main service pipe from water supply

Shutoff

Shutoff

3/8" to 1" supply pipe

Air chamber

Shutoff

FIGURE 2.1(b)

The Solar System

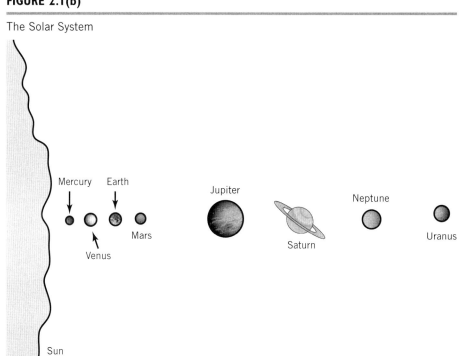

FIGURE 2.1(c)

A Typical Home Network System

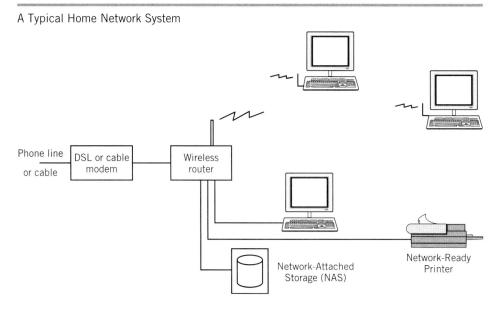

FIGURE 2.1(d)

Flow Diagram for Part of an Inventory Control System

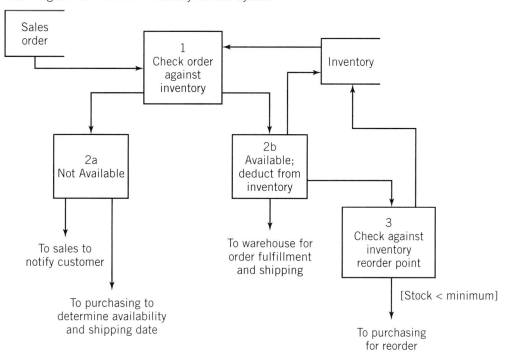

A general representation of a system is shown in Figure 2.2.

The linked components that constitute a system also define a boundary for the system. Anything outside the boundary repesents the **environment** that the system operates or presents itself within. The environment may interact with and affect the system in various ways. The reverse is also true. The **interface** between the system and its environment is an important characteristic of the system. If the interface is well-defined, it is often possible to replace the existing system with a different system, as long as the interface between the system and the environment remains constant. This idea can have important implications when designing IT systems. For example, in a particular IT installation, a single large computer may be functionally the same as a network of small computers. When we define inputs and outputs for a system, the environment is the source of the input and also the receiver of the output.

As an example of the relationship between a system and its environment, consider the rather simplistic view of an e-business system illustrated in Figure 2.3. The organization represented by this illustration purchases goods from suppliers and makes them available for sale. (The value-adding component in the figure consists of various operations that make it worthwhile to buy from this organization, rather than directly from the supplier. For example, Amazon.com makes it possible to buy a wide variety of books from one source, rather than having to place separate orders from a number of different suppliers.) The environment for this system consists of customers who purchase from the system, suppliers

FIGURE 2.2

General Representation of a System

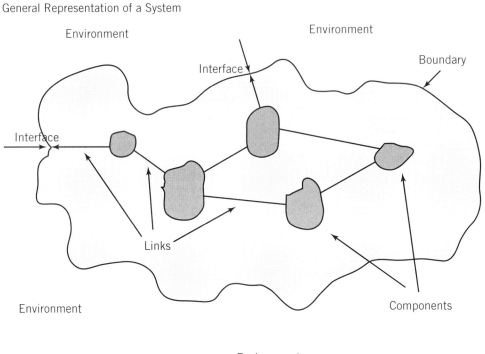

to the system, governments who control the legal aspects of the business and collect taxes, employees and prospective employees, external support personnel (such as repair people), financial resources, and others. The primary interfaces for this system are system input from suppliers and system output to purchasers; however, there are additional, more subtle interfaces to be considered, including legal, cultural, and financial interactions with the system. For example, sensitive cultural and language issues that offend potential customers on a website migh have an important impact on an organization's sales.

When analyzing a system, the components of the system may be treated as irreducible or they may themselves be representable as systems. When considered in the context of a particular system, these components would be viewed more accurately as **subsystems**. A business IT system, for example, might have marketing, manufacturing, purchasing, inventory, finance, and accounting subsystems, among others. Even these components might be expanded. The marketing subsystem might be further broken down into sales, development, and advertising components, as one possibility. The level of detail to be considered depends on the context in which the system is being considered, discussed, evaluated, or used. The division of a system or subsystem into its components and linkages is called **decomposition**. Decomposition is inherently hierarchical. The ability to decompose a system hierarchically into subsequent sets of components and subsytems is an important property of systems.

FIGURE 2.3

A Simple E-Business System

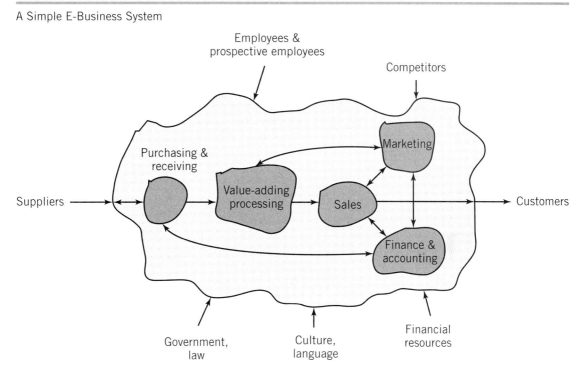

The fundamental properties, and the patterns of relationships, connections, constraints, and linkages among the components and between the system and its environment are known collectively as the **architecture** of the system. Some people choose to differentiate the *architecture* of a system from the *organization* of a system. The assumption is that the architecture is fundamental to the meaning and value of the system whereas the organization is one of possibly many combinations of components and linkages that meets the requirements of the architecture. The difference is subtle and often unimportant.

It is common to represent systems and their components by models or drawings on paper or objects within a computer program. These representations are **abstractions**. They *represent* the real system but are *not actually* the real system. (For example, the solar system does not fit conveniently inside a computer!) It should be obvious to you that all of the illustrations of systems in Figures 2.1, 2.2, and 2.3 are abstractions.

The primary reason for humans to group components into systems and to represent them as abstractions is to simplify understanding and analysis, particularly if the individual components are numerous and complex. We can study the relationships between the different components without the distraction created by the details of individual components. We can decompose, isolate and study individual components when required. We can study the interactions between the environment and the system as a whole. Effectively, our analyses are simplified by eliminating factors that are not relevant in the context of our interests. In a large network of computers, for example, we may be concerned primarily with the flow of data between computers. The details of the individual computers are unimportant. In general, dealing with models at the system level allows us to isolate and focus on the specific elements of interest more easily, by treating other elements collectively.

To escape our fixation on information technology systems for an instant, consider, just for fun, the solar system that we've used previously as an example. If we are studying the Milky Way galaxy, it is convenient and sufficient to treat the solar system as a single irreducible component in the galaxy. We might be interested in the location and movement of our Sun in the galaxy, for example, but the structure of the planets is irrelevant to our study in this case. On the other hand, if we are interested in studying the effects of the tides on a sea shore where we are planning to vacation, we will have to expand the "Earth" component and look at the specific effects of the moon and other nearby objects as part of our analysis.

Consider, too, the role played by decomposition and the ability to isolate and study individual components. A complex system may be divided into relatively independent components and analyzed by different individuals, each a specialist in their own area. Thus a plumber can create a home water system component without concern for the details of the electrician's efforts. They can work together on the linkages that concern both of them, for example, the wiring for the boiler in a hot water heating system. The system architect coordinates the different efforts. The role of an IT system architect is similar: to work with finance experts on the finance component, marketing experts on the marketing component, and so forth.

When the goal of a project is to implement a system of some type, it is sometimes convenient to view the components of a system as modules that can be implemented independently, then linked together to produce the final result. This technique can simplify analysis, design, assembly, upgrading, and even repair. It also supports collaboration during the design process, since individual components can be designed by different individuals using specifications for the interfaces.

For example, a cell phone might consist of a computer control module, a memory module, a display module, an audio input/output module, a radio transmitter/receiver module, a keypad/text input module, and a wireless networking module. Each component might have been developed by a different team. These modules, designed, constructed, and manufactured as individual assemblies, properly interfaced, wired together, and mounted into a case, constitute the design of a typical cell phone. They also represent the components that might appear in the system diagram for a cell phone. The same approach might be taken with a computer system, with a central processor module, a graphics display module, an audio module, a network module, a hard drive controller module, and so on. Figure 2.4, for example, shows the basic system hardware components that make up an iPhone.

It is also important to realize that there may be many different representations for a system, to reflect the various uses of the system model. Returning to our IT roots for an example, the representation of the business system shown in Figure 2.5(a) is a traditional hierarchical oranization chart. The components are departments that perform various functions within the business. In contrast, a partial model of the same business shown in Figure 2.5(b) represents the application architecture of an IT system within this business. Take another look at Figure 1.4 for still another representation of a business. As another simple example, you could represent a house by the physical appearance of its exterior, by the function and layout of its rooms, or by the various subsystems, electrical, plumbing, heating, and so on that the house requires. Presumably, each of these representations would be useful to a different participant. In fact, we would expect an architect to provide all of these for use by the owner, the builder, and the various contractors.

FIGURE 2.4

iPhone Components

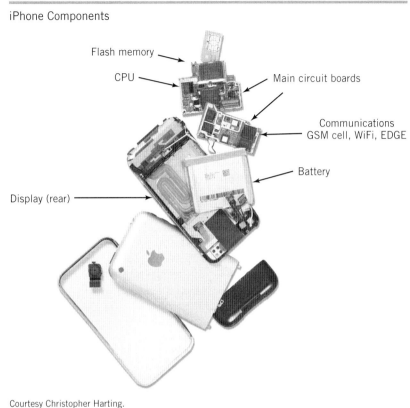

Flash memory

CPU

Main circuit boards

Communications
GSM cell, WiFi, EDGE

Battery

Display (rear)

Courtesy Christopher Harting.

FIGURE 2.5(a)

Business Organization Chart

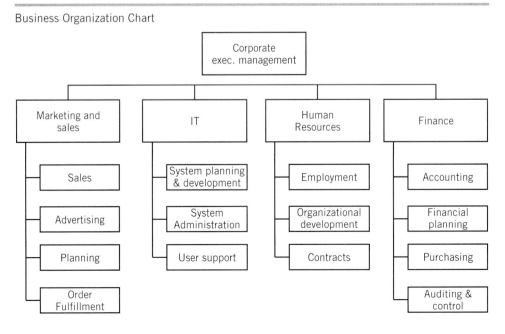

FIGURE 2.5(b)

Partial View of a Business Application Architecture

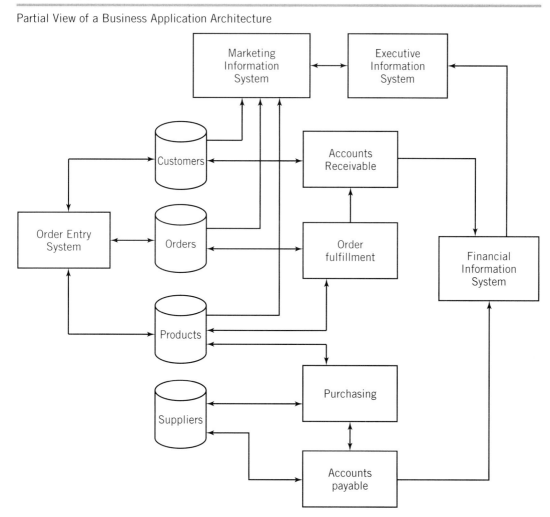

2.2 IT SYSTEM ARCHITECTURES

The use of system concepts is particularly applicable when discussing the various types of IT systems. In general, the goal of IT systems is to assist organizations to meet the strategic needs of the enterprise. Not surprisingly, IT systems are frequently complex, and the ability to separate them naturally into subsystems or components of manageable size simplifies understanding of the system as a whole. The analysis, design, and implementation of IT systems must take place at different levels of detail and frequently require collaboration among many analysts and designers. This corresponds well with the ability to decompose systems into components, hierarchically, which allows us to concentrate at the appropriate levels of detail during each step along the way. This approach is known as a **top-down approach**. The top-down approach allows us to focus on the specific areas of interest without the distraction of details that are irrelevant for the level that we're studying. In this way, a system architect can analyze and study the IT system as a whole, encapsulating the computer systems, software systems, network architecture, and Web architecture that represent components, and focusing instead on the large picture: the purpose of each component and the requirements for the interfaces and linkages that connect and integrate them. With the IT system architecture firmly established, we can consider the individual business functions, computer systems, and networks that will link them together. For IT system analysis, this is often sufficient, at least superficially, assuming that the system architects actually understand the conditions and constraints imposed by details at the lower levels.

Although there are other, equally valid, approaches to IT system analysis and design, and many other important considerations as well, this approach suits the purposes of this book well because it allows us to establish general requirements for IT systems and then to show how the specific capabilities and characteristics of computer hardware, operating systems, networks, and data fulfill those requirements.

With these ideas in mind, let us return to the simple word processing example from Chapter 1 and reconsider it from a system architecture perspective. Recall that in this example you are sitting at your computer typing text into a word processor. We noted that the computer accepted input from your mouse and keyboard, processed it according to rules established by the application software, and produced output, which appeared on a display. From the system perspective, we can, for now, treat the whole computer, keyboard, display, printer, storage, software, and all as a single component. You're the relevant part of the environment for this discussion. Forgetting the issue of control for now, the system has an input and an output. Both of these interface with you, the environment. The data for this interface is alphanumeric text in human-readable form. Other input data to the document might include graphics drawn with the mouse, photographic images from a digital camera, bar codes, or music from an iPod or other audio source. We described this scenario earlier, in Chapter 1, as input-process-output.

A system this simple is unlikely to meet all the needs of even the smallest enterprise or, even, the least computer-literate individual. But it does serve as a starting point to recognizing the value of a system approach to the understanding of information technology.

Distributed Processing Systems

Realistically, modern IT system architectures generally rely on multiple computers connected by networks of communication channels to achieve their goals. In all but the smallest organizations, input data is collected from locations scattered throughout the organization, stored, processed, and distributed to other locations within the organization. Since modern computer hardware and networking equipment is plentiful and inexpensive, it is practical to distribute computing capability to everyone who needs it. Furthermore, the availability of the Internet and alternative structures, such as satellite communications, make global data communication practical. Web access, organization intranets, e-mail capability, analysis tools, such as Microsoft Excel, and document preparation tools are widely available and are considered essential business tools throughout most organizations. Collaboration between different organizations, particularly in the area of automated business-to-business purchasing and sales, is commonplace.

Therefore, when envisioning effective IT systems, designers typically must create system architectures that are capable of supporting large numbers of user workstations who will have ready access to the organizational information that they need. The system must be able to reliably store and protect large amounts of organizational data. For many organizations, customers outside of the organization may also need access to the system to get information and to make purchases.

Consider a few typical simple scenarios:

- A global fast food chain collects data each day from each of its restaurants worldwide to establish sales figures and determine sales trends. This allows the company to determine which locations are most productive and which locations need assistance, which items sell best and which need to be modified or replaced, and so on.

- A large travel organization conducts much of its business online, using travel agents located all over the world. It maintains Web servers that have immediate access to large databases of client information and travel information, as well as continual and instant access to airline and hotel reservation systems to determine current airfares, seat availability, and hotel room availability. All of this information must be immediately accessible to every agent and must be current at every instant. Even brief system failures are very costly.

- A large Web-based retail sales organization sells large quantities of a wide variety of merchandise. (Think Amazon or Wal-Mart.) Orders initially come in to a central facility, where they are billed. Inventory is stored in warehouses in various countries and local regional areas to expedite delivery and reduce delivery costs. The system must be able to distribute orders to the various regional facilities efficiently; it must also maintain appropriate levels of goods at each warehouse to match sales and must be able to locate goods and arrange shipping in response to orders as they come in.

  Inventory replenishment is handled by an automated purchasing IT system component that is integrated with the IT systems of the suppliers. Purchase order data is passed from the retailer to a supplier, which triggers order placement, billing and shipment components in the supplier's systems. Web technology is commonly used to satisfy the need for data and communication compatability between the systems.

- Even conventional business order processing is inherently distributed within an organization. A purchase order, for example, might be entered into the system by a salesperson in the sales department; the order is checked by order fulfillment for inventory, then distributed to the accounting department for a credit check and billing, and sent to the warehousing area for packaging and shipping. Back orders and inventory replenishment are sent to the purchasing department. For planning and marketing purposes, data will be collected into a central location and processed into sales figures, inventory planning and purchase requirements data, and the like. In a large organization, these functions might be widely scattered over a city, country, or even the world.

The emphasis in each of these scenarios is the flow and processing of data within an organization or between organizations or between an organization and its environment. The system architecture representation of such operations is called **application architecture**. Application architecture is primarily concerned with the activities and processing of application programs and the communications between them. Since the application architecture addresses the fundamental business needs of the organization, the application architecture is typically the primary consideration in IT system design. Therefore, the system requirements and constraints set by the application architecture have major impact on the hardware architecture and network architecture requirements for the system. Within the application architecture realm the selection and layout of computer systems and communication networks is of concern primarily to the extent that it adequately supports the application software and its functionality. However, additional factors such as scalability, convenience, information availability, data security, system administration, power and space requirements, and cost may also play important roles in computer and network architectural designs.

CLIENT-SERVER COMPUTING   There are a variety of possible application architectures that can satisfy the requirements of modern organizations. Most, however, are based on different applications of a simple technological concept, the **client-server** model.

In a client-server configuration, a program on a client computer accepts services and resources from a complementary program on a server computer. The services and resources can include application programs, processing services, database services, Web services, file services, print services, directory services, e-mail, remote access services, even computer system initial startup service. In most cases, the client-server relationship is between complementary application programs. In certain cases, particularly for file services and printer sharing, the services are provided by programs in the operating system. Basic communication and network services are also provided by operating system programs.

Basic client-server architecture is illustrated in Figure 2.6. Notice that the link between client and server is essentially irrelevant within the application architecture view of the system. The "cloud" in the figure is intended to indicate only that there is a link of some kind between the client and the server. The link can be a network connection, an intranet

FIGURE 2.6

Basic Client-Server Architecture

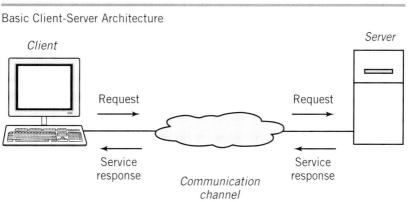

or Internet connection, or some sort of direct connection. In fact, a single computer can act as both client and server, if desired. (A situation where this is the case is described in Chapter 16.)

The client-server model describes the relationship and behavior of programs in one or two computers under particular prescribed circumstances. It is important to understand that the client-server model does not require any special computer hardware. Furthermore, networking software within the operating system of each computer routinely provides basic communication capabilities. The only "special" software required is the software within the complementary application programs that provides the communications between the programs. The requests and responses take the form of data messages between the client and server that are understood by both application programs. As an example, slightly simplified, the HTTP request message sent to a Web server by a Web browser requesting a Web page consists of the word GET followed by a URL. If the request is successful, the message returned by the server contains the HTML text for the page.

From the description and the figure you can see that the Web browser–Web server application described as an example in Chapter 1 fits the description of a client-server application. We will return to this example momentarily.

A typical use of the client-server concept within an organization is shown in Figure 2.7. In this case, a number of clients are sharing a number of servers, showing both the **shared server** nature of client-server computing, as well as to show that there may be multiple servers offering different services on the same network. Notice, also, that the server computer labeled *S2* in the figure is running two different server applications. Since computers are capable of running multiple tasks concurrently, this is a possible scenario. The only limitations to running multiple applications on a single server are the potential slowdowns that may result from the load on the server computer and the traffic on the network to that server. Overall, there is a multiple-multiple relationship between clients and servers: a server can serve multiple clients, and a client can request services from multiple servers.

The use of client-server processing as a basis for IT system architecture has a number of advantages:

- Providing services on a single computer or on a small number of computers in a central location makes the resources and services easy to locate and available to everyone who needs them, but also allows the IT administrators to protect the resources and control and manage their use. The consistency of files and data can be managed and assured.

    For example, client-server technology can ensure that every user requesting a particular program from a server will receive the same version of the program. As another example, suppose a program has a license that limits the number of simultaneous users. The program server can easily limit distribution of the program appropriately.

- The amount of data to be stored, processed, and managed may be extremely large. It is more efficient to equip a small number of computers with the power needed than to require powerful computers at every station.

- Typically, humans request information from knowledgeable sources as they need it. Thus, the client-server approach is naturally consistent with the way humans acquire and use information.

FIGURE 2.7

Clients and Servers on a Network

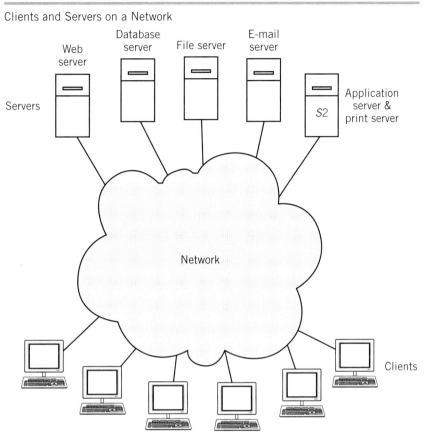

The most familiar example of the use of client-server technology is the Web browser–Web server model used in intranets and on the Internet. In its simplest form, this model is an example of **two-tier architecture**. Two-tier architecture simply means that there are two computers involved in the service. The key features of this architecture are a client computer running the Web browser application, a server computer running the Web server application, a communication link between them, and a set of standard protocols, in this case, HTTP, for the communication between the Web applications, HTML for the data presentation requirements, and, usually, the TCP/IP protocol suite for the networking communcations.

In the simplest case, a Web browser requests a Web page that is stored as a pre-created HTML file on the server. More commonly, the user is seeking specific information, and a custom Web page must be created "on the fly", using an application program that looks up the required data in a database, processes the data as necessary, and formats it to build the desired page dynamically.

Although it is possible to maintain the database and perform the additional database processing and page creation on the same computer as the Web server, the Web server in a large Internet-based business may have to respond to thousands of requests simultaneously. Because response time is considered an important measure by most Web users, it is often more practical to separate the database and page processing into a third computer system. The result, shown in Figure 2.8, is called a **three-tier architecture**. Note that, in this case, the Web server machine is a client to the database application and database server on the third computer. *CGI*, the *Common Gateway Interface*, is a protocol for making communication between the Web server and the database application possible. (In the figure, we have placed the page creation application software on the database machine, but it could be located on the Web server instead if doing so would balance the loads on the two machines better.) In some situations, it is even desirable to extend this idea further. Within reason, separating different applications and processing can result in better overall control, can simplify system upgrades, and can minimize scalability issues. The most general case is known as an *n*-**tier architecture**.

Client-server architecture is a distributed processing methodology, in which some of the processing is performed on the client system and some is performed on the server system. To see this more clearly, consider the distribution of processing between the client and server in a database application, in which the client requests specific information from a database stored on a database server.

At one extreme, the client application provides little more than a request form and a means to display the results. All of the processing is performed on the server. This might be appropriate if there is little computing power in the client. Certain so-called "thin" clients or "end-user" terminals might meet this criterion, but this situation is increasingly rare. Because this extreme case puts the entire processing load on the server, the system designer will have to specify a more powerful computer for the server; additionally, the requirements of the database server may limit the capability of the server computer system to perform other tasks or to scale for increased usage.

At the other extreme, the database server application simply accesses data from the database and passes all of the data to the client. The client application performs all of the processing. This relieves the load on the server, and it is reasonable to assume that modern client computers would be able to handle most database processing tasks relatively easily. However, the potential transfer of large amounts of raw data from the server to

FIGURE 2.8

Three-Tier Database Architecture

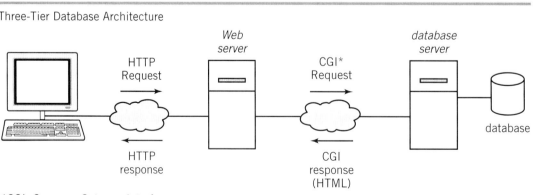

*CGI: Common Gateway Interface

the client for processing may put an extra burden on the network instead, requiring the system designer to specify higher speed network components at potentially higher cost and additional implementation difficulty.

A well-designed system analysis will consider the different factors, the complexity of the applications, expected network traffic, usage patterns, and the like. The optimum solution is likely to fall somewhere in the middle, with some pieces of applications on the server, others on the client.

One of the strengths of client-server architecture is its ability to enable different computer hardware and software to work together. This provides flexibility in the selection of server and client equipment tailored to the needs of both the organization and the individual users. One difficulty that sometimes arises when different computers have to work together is potential incompatibilities between the application software that resides on different equipment. This problem is commonly solved with software called **middleware**. Middleware resides logically between the servers and the clients. Typically, the middleware will reside physically on a server with other applications, but on a large system it might be installed on its own server. Either way, both clients and servers send all request and response messages to the middleware. The middleware resolves problems between incompatible message and data formats before forwarding the messages. It also manages system changes, such as the movement of a server application program from one server to another. In this case, the middleware would forward the message to the new server transparently. The middleware thus assures continued system access and stability. In general, the use of middleware can improve system performance and administration.

WEB-BASED COMPUTING   The widespread success of the World Wide Web has resulted in a large base of computer users familiar with Web techniques, powerful development tools for creating Web sites and Web pages and for linking them with other applications, and protocols and standards that offer a wide and flexible variety of techniques for the collection, manipulation, and display of data and information. In addition, a powerful website is already a critical component in the system strategy of most modern organizations. Much of the data provided for the website is provided by architectural components of the organization's systems that are already in place.

Not surprisingly, these factors have led system designers to retrofit and integrate Web technology into new and existing systems, creating modern systems which take advantage of Web technology to collect, process, and present data more effectively to the users of the system.

The user of a Web-based system interacts with the system using a standard Web browser, enters data into the system by filling out Web-style forms, and accesses data using Web pages created by the system in a manner essentially identical to those used for the Internet. The organization's internal network, commonly called an **intranet**, is implemented using Web technology. To the user, integration between the intranet and the Internet is relatively seamless, limited only by the security measures designed into the system. This system architecture offers a consistent and familiar interface to users; Web-enabled applications offer access to the organization's traditional applications through the Web. Web technology can even extend the reach of these applications to employees in other parts of the world, using the Internet as the communication channel.

Since Web technology is based on a client-server model, it requires only a simple extension of the *n*-tier architecture to implement Web-based applications. As an example, Figure 2.9 shows a possible system architecture to implement Web-based e-mail. Note the similarity between this example and the three-tier database application shown in Figure 2.8.

Many organizations also now find it possible and advantageous to create system architectures that integrate parts of their systems with other organizations using Web technology and Web standards as the medium of communication. For example, an organization can integrate and automate its purchasing system with the order system of its suppliers to automate control of its inventory, leading to reduced inventory costs, as well as to rapid replacement and establishment of reliable stocks of inventory when they are needed. Internet standards such as XML allow the easy identification of relevant data within data streams between interconnected systems, making these applications possible and practical. This type of automation is a fundamental component of modern business-to-business operations.

PEER-TO-PEER COMPUTING An alternative to client-server architecture is **peer-to-peer architecture**. Peer-to-peer architecture treats the computers in a network as equals, with the ability to share files and other resources and to move them between computers. With appropriate permissions, any computer on the network can view the resources of any other computer on the network, and can share those resources. Since every computer is essentially independent, it is difficult or impossible to establish centralized control to restrict inappropriate access and to ensure data integrity. Even where the integrity of the system can be assured, it can be difficult to know where a particular file is located and no assurance that the resource holding that file is actually accessible when the file is needed. (The particular computer that holds the file may be turned off.) The system also may have several versions of the file, each stored on a different computer. Synchronization of different file versions is difficult to control and difficult to maintain. Finally, since

FIGURE 2.9

Three-Tier Web-Based E-Mail Architecture

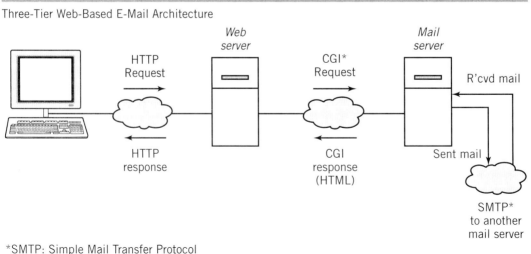

*SMTP: Simple Mail Transfer Protocol
*CGI: Common Gateway Interface

data may pass openly through many different machines, the users of those machines may be able to steal data or inject viruses as the data passes through. All of these reasons are sufficient to eliminate peer-to-peer computing from consideration in any organizational situation where the computers in the network are controlled by more than one individual or group. In other words, nearly always.

There is one exception: peer-to-peer computing is adequate, appropriate, and useful for the movement of files between personal computers or to share a printer in a small office or home network.

Peer-to-peer technology has also proven viable as an Internet file sharing methodology outside the organizational structure, particularly for the downloading of music and video. The perceived advantage is that the heavy loads and network traffic associated with a server are eliminated. (There are legal ramifications, also, for a server that is sharing copyrighted material illegally.) This technique operates on the assumption that the computer searching for a file is able to find another computer somewhere by broadcasting a request across the Internet and establishing a connection with a nearby computer that can supply the file. Presumably, that computer already has established connections with other systems. All of these systems join together into a peer-to-peer network that can then share files. One serious downside to this approach, noted above, is the fact that the computers in an open, essentially random, peer-to-peer network can also be manipulated to spread viruses and steal identities. There are several serious documented cases of both.

An alternative, hybrid model uses client-server technology to locate systems and files that can then participate in peer-to-peer transactions. The hybrid model is used for instant messaging, for Skype and other online phone systems, and for Napster and other legal file download systems.

Although there have been research studies to determine if there is a place for peer-to-peer technology in organizational computing, the security risks are high, the amount of control low, and the overall usefulness limited. The results to date have been disappointing.

The Role of the System Architect

In Section 2.1, we suggested that there are different ways of viewing systems. From the discussion within this section, you can see that the IT system architect must consider the system from the perspectives of application architecture, data architecture, network architecture, and computer architecture. Each of these addresses different aspects of the IT system as a whole. For example, our consideration of different general application architectures—client-server, web-based architecture, peer-to-peer architecture—ignored the networking that links the various computers together. Similarly, we attempted to minimize the effects due to the specifics of individual computer systems when exploring the various requirements of a system from the perspective of application architecture.

Ultimately, it is the responsibility of the system architect to assess the particular needs of an organization and create a system that meets those needs while attempting to achieve an optimum balance of computer power, network capability, user convenience, and budget. To do so, the architect will consider each aspect of the system: application architecture, network requirements, specification of computer systems, and data requirements, just as the architect designing a house considers flow of people through the house, overall use of space and room layout, individual room layouts, mechanical systems, and aesthetic design as different views of the overall architecture of the house.

Although the infrastructure design as defined by the computer hardware, system software, and communication channels is subordinate to the fundamental business requirements that determine a basic IT system architecture, the system architect must understand the features and constraints that establish the feasibility and desirability of a particular infrastructure configuration.

Google: A System Architecture Example

So far, we have considered basic system concepts and simple system architectures as examples. Most IT business systems operate primarily within an organization, with limited collaboration with other, partnered organizations and carefully controlled public access. At the opposite extreme are massive systems that are widely open to the public. Google offers a primary example of such a system.

The primary mission of Google is to provide powerful, fast search capability of material on the Internet for billions of users all over the world. Income to the organization is provided from advertising that is targeted to each user based on the specific nature of the user's search. The design of Google's IT system architecture is obviously fundamental to Google's ability to achieve its mission and to meet reasonable income goals. In keeping with the focus of this book, our primary interest is in the computer and network architectures that Google uses to meet its system requirements; however we will use this example to explore the relationship between the basic system requirements, the IT system architecture created to meet those requirements, and the specific computer and network architectures that evolved from the system architecture.

Some of the basic requirements that the Google IT system must satisfy include the following:

- It must be capable of responding to millions of simultaneous requests from all over the world with pertinent, ranked search results and appropriately targeted advertising. Most desirably, the results and advertising would be matched in language, geographic suitability, and culture as much as possible to the location of the user.

- The system must be able to troll the Internet systematically and thoroughly to retrieve data and to organize the data in such a way as to make it readily available for response to user requests. There must be a processing mechanism to establish a ranking of the results to a request.

- The system must respond to requests with a reliability as near to 100 percent as is technically possible. Individual hardware and software component failures within the system must not affect system performance adversely.

- The system must be easily scalable to handle ever-increasing numbers of requests and must be cost effective.

At the application level, the requirements identify three specific processing tasks that the system must fulfill:

1. The system must accept search requests from users, identify and rank matches, create a Web page, and serve it to the user.

2. The system must collect data—lots of data! This task "crawls the Web", identifies the search terms (every significant word) on every Web page it encounters, and maintains an index database connecting each term to the corresponding page. It likewise stores every Web page in a Web page database and assigns a ranking value to each entry.

3. The system must manage advertisements, identify appropriate advertisements in response to user search requests, and make the advertisements available to the Web page creation application mentioned in 1.

For this discussion we will focus on the processing of search requests. When a user types the Google URL www.google.com into her browser, the Web browser uses a service called *Domain Name Service (DNS)* to identify the IP address of the Web server to which the request is to be sent. Because Google must be able to handle several milllion requests per hour, Google provides a number of alternative IP addresses representing different sites to which the request may be redirected. Based on the approximate location from which the request was sent, the request is routed by DNS to a Google data center near that location. Google maintains more than forty separate data centers around the world to serve user requests.

A simplified system diagram of the application architecture for a Google data center is shown in Figure 2.10. All of the data centers are architecturally identical, differing only in such details as the number of processors and the hardware specifications for each processor. Each data center processes requests independently. Multiple copies of all of the

FIGURE 2.10

Google Data Center Search Application Architecture

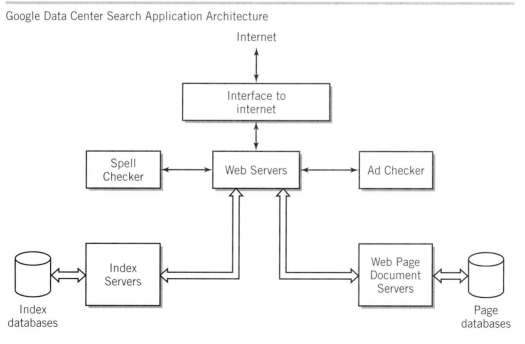

index word data and Web page data are stored locally at every data center, and updated from master data at regular intervals.

A request enters the system from the Internet and is distributed to a Google Web server for processing. A request consists of words and phrases. There are many separate Web servers available so that many requests can be processed in parallel. The words are passed to a spell checker, to an ad server, and to a pool consisting of a large number of index servers.

The spell checker checks each word and considers possible alternatives if it believes that the user may have intended something different. When appropriate, the output of the spell checker will become part of the response sent to the user. ("*Did you mean . . .* " is familiar to most Google users.) The ad checker searches for words in the advertising database that match the user's request and adds the corresponding advertisement(s) to the material that will be used to create the response page.

The index servers look up each word from the request in the index database and compile a list of matching pages for each word. The list is then adjusted for multiple words and phrases and sorted in order of relevance, based on Google's ranking algorithms. This list is then passed back to the Web server.

Next, the Web server calls upon the document servers to look up each matching page in the Web page database. The document servers return a URL, a title, and a short snippet of text for each document to the Web server. Finally, the Web server creates an HTML document from the spelling, ad, and matching page results and returns the page to the user's Web browser.

Although the application processing just described is relatively straightforward, the implementation of this system presented a number of challenges to the system architects, The index and document databases are both massive in size. Many searches will result in a large number of "hits"; each hit must be evaluated and ranked. Each hit requires retrieval and processing of a separate page from the document database. All of this processing must occur very quickly. And the numbers of searches occurring simultaneously may also be extremely large.

Google's system architects responded to these challenges by recognizing that each search could be processed independently on a separate computer, except for certain bottlenecks. For example, each search request arriving from the Internet could be steered by a computer to a different Web browser. They also observed that the major bottleneck was the time required to access the databases on disks, which had to be shared among all the searches taking place. Since the data in the databases never changed as a result of a search, however, they reasoned that the databases could also be replicated and accessed in parallel.

A simplified hardware representation of their solution is shown in Figure 2.11. Groups of up to eighty computers are connected together in a network, then these networks, up to sixty-four of them, are, themselves, connected together to form a larger network, sort of like a miniature Internet of up to 5,120 computers. (There are additional switches and connections built in for reliability that are not shown in the diagram.) Each computer acts as a server, with different computers assigned to different pieces of the application architecture. Each data center is equipped similarly.

Although the computers are manufactured specifically for Google, they are essentially inexpensive commodity PCs, similar to standard, medium power, non-state-of-the-art,

FIGURE 2.11

Simplified Google System Hardware Architecture

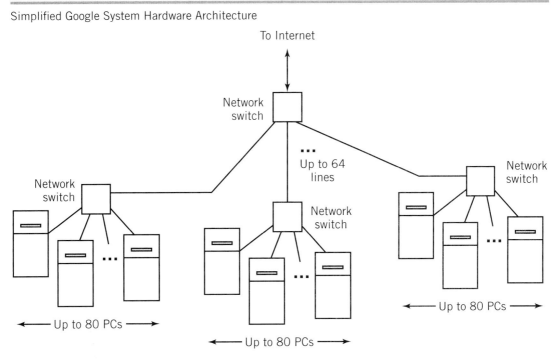

off-the-shelf PCs. Each computer has a fairly large, but still off-the-shelf, hard disk. The index and document databases are divided up among the hard disks on many computers. (Google calls these partial databases *shards.*) This design allows different searches to access different parts of the databases simultaneously. There are multiple copies of each database, so that the failure of a PC or hard disk does not affect the overall ability of the system to conduct searches. Each computer runs standard Linux operating system software, but the application software was specially written by Google programmers.

Overall, this design allows a large number of searches to progress in parallel. The use of inexpensive PC hardware makes the solution cost-effective. The system can be scaled easily by adding more computers. Finally, the failure of a PC does not result in failure and, in fact, has minimal effect on the performance of the system overall. Thus, this solution meets the original requirements admirably. It is worth noting that a fundamental understanding of computer infrastructure was key to the system architects' solution.

This discussion provides a simple overview of the Google system. Hopefully you found even this brief look at the Google system interesting and informative. There are a number of other considerations in the Google system architecture that we have glossed over for now. However, to understand the Google architecture better, it is first necessary to continue our exploration of the hardware, software, and network components that make up the Google system, as well as every other IT system. We will return for a more in-depth discussion of the Google system architecture in Supplementary Chapter 2.

SUMMARY AND REVIEW

When working with large concepts with defined boundaries, it is often easiest to think of them in terms of systems. A system can be defined as a collection of components, linked together and organized in such a way as to be recognizable as a single unit. The components themselves may also be recognized as subsystems, to be further reduced into components, when appropriate. The area outside the boundaries of a system is its environment. The system affects and is affected by various elements of the environment. In many situations, the environment supplies inputs to the system and receives outputs from the system. The patterns of relationships, connections, constraints, and linkages among the components of a system and between a system and its environment are known collectively as the architecture of the system.

Information technology systems are systems that support the strategy and operations of organizations. The technological components of an IT system include computer hardware, application software, operating system software, networks, and data. Other components include personnel, policies, and more.

There are a number of different ways of viewing an IT system, including application architecture, network architecture, software architecture, and hardware architecture. The general architecture for an IT system includes all of these considerations.

Nearly all modern IT systems rely on distributed processing. Data comes from many sources and information is required by users distributed throughout an organization and beyond. The most common application architecture to support distributed processing is client-server architecture, in which server computer systems provide various services—Web, database, file, print, processing—to client computer systems. Client-server systems are convenient for users and offer centralized control for the organization. Client-server architecture is commonly organized in tiers, ranging from two-tier to *n*-tier. The alternative architecture to client-server computing, peer-to-peer computing, is used outside of organizations as a means for sharing files over the Internet, but is of limited use in organizational settings due to difficulties in establishing stable data sources, security risks, and lack of central control. It is also possible to create a hybrid architecture, with features from both client-server and peer-to-peer computing.

A specific type of client-server architecture, Web-based computing, predominates the IT scene, primarily because users are generally familiar with the use of Web browsers, the technology is standardized and already in use in most organizations, and good development tools for designing Web pages and accessing data are readily available. Both intranets and the Internet provide user access.

Protocols are the means used to communicate between computers. IT system protocols of interest to us include network protocols such as TCP/IP, I/O protocols such as USB and PCI-Express, and application protocols such as HTTP. Standards make it possible for different system components to work together. Most modern standards are global. There are standards that are defined by interested groups and de facto standards that arise from common usage.

The first step in IT system analysis and design is about finding an appropriate architecture for a particular business situation. The task can be difficult and challenging. It is easy to see why system architects need a deep understanding of the computer system and network components that comprise the modern IT system to make the appropriate design, selections, and tradeoffs.

Hopefully this short but concentrated chapter has prepared you for the remainder of the book, which considers in detail the data, computer system hardware, operating systems, and networks that make up the technological infrastructure of an IT system.

FOR FURTHER READING

Surprisingly, there are few books that discuss system concepts and system architecture in a truly general way. Most books that claim to be about system architecture are actually specific to a particular field, usually the field of information systems. One general book about systems is by Laszlo [LASZ96]. Some IS systems design and analysis textbooks provide a brief introduction to general system concepts. (Unfortunately, many don't!) One example of a book that provides a good introduction to system concepts is Stampf [STAM05]. Chapter 1 of Stampf covers the topics in this chapter well. Wikipedia offers other references under the topic *system*.

KEY CONCEPTS AND TERMS

abstraction	interface	subsystem
application architecture	intranet	system
architecture	middleware	three-tier architecture
client-server (model)	*n*-tier architecture	top-down approach
decomposition	peer-to-peer architecture	two-tier architecture
environment	shared server	

READING REVIEW QUESTIONS

2.1   What are the most important ideas, keywords, and phrases that are stated in the definition of a system?

2.2   Explain the relationships among the following words: system, environment, boundary, interface.

2.3   Explain the following statement about systems: "Decomposition is inherently hierarchical."

2.4   Explain what is meant by the architecture of a system.

2.5   What is the primary concern of application architecture? Give an example of application architecture, either your own, or one from the examples in the book. Explain how this example fulfills the features and requirements of the concept of application architecture.

2.6   What does the top-down approach allow a system architect to do that might be more difficult otherwise?

2.7   Most modern computing in organizations is based on client-server models. Explain why this tends to be the case. Give an example of client-server computing that you are familiar with and explain the characteristics of your example that fulfill the concept of client-server computing.

2.8   Many system architects base their IT system designs on an *n*-tier architecture, where *n* is a number with value 2 or greater. Explain the difference between a single-tier architecture and an *n*-tier architecture. What are the main advantages claimed for an *n*-tier architecture?

2.9   Web-based system architecture is a popular approach to many organizational systems because it offers a number of advantages to the users and to the organization over other types of systems. Discuss the primary advantages to this approach.

2.10   What are the principal responsibilities of a system architect?

EXERCISES

2.1   Consider a representation of a work organization or school with which you are familiar. Identify the major components that characterize the primary operations within the organization and draw a diagram that represents the system's organization. Show and identify the links that connect the various components. Identify the major environmental factors that impact the organization.

2.2   The human body is an example of an object that can be represented as a system. Consider the various ways in which you could represent the human body as a system. Select a representation and identify the components that constitute the system. Select one component and decompose it to the next subsystem level. Now consider a completely different system representation of the human body and repeat this exercise.

2.3   Thinking in terms of systems allows us to analyze situations that are too complicated for us to understand as a whole. What specific characteristics and features of system thinking make this possible?

2.4   Based on the illustration of an iPhone shown in Figure 2.4, draw a system model for an iPhone.

2.5   Consider this textbook. Using the detailed table of contents as a reference, we can represent this textbook as a hierarchical system. As a first pass, we can define this book by the five component *parts* that make up the body of the text. Identify by general name the objects that constitute the next level of decomposition below the *parts* components. Continue to do this for at least three more levels of the hierarchy.

2.6   Consider a home theatre system consisting of a television set, a receiver, a DVD player, speakers, and any other components you wish to include. Draw a system diagram for this system. Include both components and links. What are the inputs to this system? What are the outputs? (Remember that the DVD player and receiver are both components *within* the system.) Now draw a system diagram for the receiver subsystem. Include both its primary components and the links between them. What are the inputs and outputs for the receiver subsystem? Do these inputs and outputs conform to the links connected to the receiver in your original system diagram?

2.7   Suppose that you have been hired to develop a website-based sales system for a large international retail sales firm. Discuss some environmental issues that are specific to the Web design of your system that you must consider if your system is to be successful at attracting and keeping purchasing customers.

2.8   Figure 2.8 illustrates the basic architecture for a three-tier database system. This system can be viewed as an IPO (input-processing-output) system. What is the input for this system? What environmental element generates the input? (Hint: the Web browser computer is within the system boundary.) What is the expected output from this system? What environmental element receives the output? Briefly describe the processing that takes place in this system.

2.9   It is common to represent network connections in IT systems as a cloud. (See, for example, Figures 2.6, 2.7, 2.8, and 2.9). The cloud is obviously an *abstraction* as we defined abstraction in this chapter. What does the cloud abstraction actually represent?

PART TWO

You are probably aware that all data in a computer is stored in the form of binary numbers, using only 1s and 0s. The situation is more complicated than this, however, because those binary numbers represent both program instructions and data, and they may represent the data in many different forms. Programming languages such as Java, for example, allow a programmer to specify data in primitive form as integer numbers, real numbers, characters, or Booleans. In addition, the files on your computer probably include representations of graphical images, sounds, photo images and video, and who knows what all else!

Each of the myriad different data types and objects uses its own format or formats for storage in the computer. Manipulating data requires keeping track of which format is in use for a particular set of data. Each numerical data format requires a different method for doing arithmetic calculations, and there are a number of different formats for representations of images and the like with different capabilities and manipulation requirements, which complicates data handling even further. Naturally, the computer must be able to perform format conversions between equivalent but different types. Most of this data-type record keeping must be handled within programs; to the computer, the bits all look the same. Only the programs know what the bits actually represent.

Each data type and format has its own uses, advantages, and disadvantages, determined by the context in which it is being used. There is no single "ideal" data type. Knowing when to use each type involves understanding what happens to the data within the computer. When you understand the effect of your data-type choices upon the processing that will be required you can write better, more efficient programs.

Each of the chapters in this section deals with a different aspect of data. We begin in Chapter 3 by reviewing the basics of number systems, to offer you a better understanding of how numbers work, the nature of counting, and how calculations are performed. You

DATA IN THE COMPUTER

will learn how to convert from one number base to another. Although the binary number system is used within computers, we must be able to convert between the system the computer uses and the more familiar decimal system that we use. You will also have a chance to work with the octal and hexadecimal number systems, which are closely related to the binary system. These are frequently used for representing computer data and programs in machine form because they are easy to read and easy to convert to and from binary form.

In Chapter 4 we will explore the ways in which data gets into the computer in the first place and the different forms that it can take inside the computer. We will consider text, sound, and images. You will study the difference between characters and other symbols stored as text and the same symbols stored as images. You will see the different binary codes that are used to represent symbols in text form. We will also consider the difference between numbers stored as groups of numeric characters and those stored in actual numerical form. The chapter also looks at the representations of graphics, photo images, and sound. We present several different formats that are used for the manipulation and storage of image and sound data.

In Chapter 5 we will look at various ways in which numbers are stored and manipulated in computers. We consider various forms of integers and real, or "floating point," number representations and calculations. We discuss the conversion process between real and integer number representations. We look at the strengths and shortcomings of each type from the perspectives of data storage requirements and calculation considerations. The discussion will conclude by considering when the use of each of the different numerical types is appropriate.

CHAPTER 3

NUMBER SYSTEMS

"I call them numbers, you can add them, subtract them, multiply them, divide them ... find their square root..."

3.0 INTRODUCTION

As humans, we generally count and perform arithmetic using the decimal, or base 10, number system. The **base** of a number system is simply the number of different digits, including zero, that exist in the number system. In any particular set of circumstances, a particular base might be chosen for convenience, efficiency, technological, or any other reasons. Historically, it seems that the main reason that we use base 10 is that humans have ten fingers, which is as good a reason as any.

Any number can be represented equivalently in any base, and it is always possible to convert a number from one base to another without changing its meaning.

Computers perform all of their operations using the **binary**, or base 2, **number** system. All program code and data are stored and manipulated in binary form. Calculations are performed using **binary arithmetic**. Each digit in a binary number is known as a **bit** (for binary digit) and can have only one of two values, **0** or **1**. Bits are commonly stored and manipulated in groups of 8 (known as a byte), 16 (usually known as a halfword), 32 (a word), or 64 bits (a doubleword). Sometimes other groupings are used.

The number of bits used in calculations affects the accuracy and size limitations of numbers manipulated by the computer. And, in fact, in some programming languages, the number of bits used can actually be specified by the programmer in declaration statements. In the programming language Java, for example, the programmer can declare a signed integer variable to be *short* (16 bits), *int* (32 bits), or *long* (64 bits) depending on the anticipated size of the number being used and the required accuracy in calculations.

The knowledge of the size limits for calculations in a particular language is sometimes extremely important, since some calculations can cause a numerical result that falls outside the range provided for the number of bits used. In some cases this will produce erroneous results, without warning to the end user of the program.

It is useful to understand how the binary number system is used within the computer. Often, it is necessary to read numbers in the computer in their binary or equivalent hexadecimal form. For example, colors in Visual Basic can be specified as a six-digit hexadecimal number, which represents a 24-bit binary number.

This chapter looks informally at number systems in general and explores the relationship between our commonplace decimal number system and number systems of other bases. Our emphasis, of course, is upon base 2, the binary number system. The discussion is kept more general, however, since it is also possible, and in fact common, to represent computer numbers in base 8 (**octal**) or base 16 (**hexadecimal**). Occasionally we even consider numbers in other bases, just for fun, and also, perhaps, to emphasize the idea that these techniques are completely general.

3.1 NUMBERS AS A PHYSICAL REPRESENTATION

As we embark upon our investigation of number systems, it is important to note that numbers usually represent some physical meaning, for example, the number of dollars in our paycheck or the number of stars in the universe. The different number systems that we use are equivalent. The physical objects can be represented equivalently in any of them. Of course, it is possible to convert between them.

In Figure 3.1, for example, there are a number of oranges, a number that you recognize as 5. In ancient cultures, the number might have been represented as

$$I \quad I \quad I \quad I \quad I$$

or, when in Rome,

$$V$$

Similarly, in base 2, the number of oranges in Figure 3.1 is represented as

$$101_2$$

And in base 3, the representation looks like this:

$$12_3$$

The point we are making is that each of the foregoing examples is simply a different way of *representing* the same number of oranges. You probably already have experience at converting between the standard decimal number system and Roman numerals. (Maybe you even wrote a program to do so!) Once you understand the methods, it is just about as easy to convert between base 10 and the other number bases that we shall use.

FIGURE 3.1

A Number of Oranges

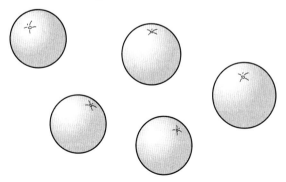

3.2 COUNTING IN DIFFERENT BASES

Let's consider how we count in base 10, and what each digit means. We begin with single digits,

$$0$$
$$1$$
$$2$$
$$3$$
$$.$$
$$.$$
$$.$$
$$9$$

When we reach 9, we have exhausted all possible single digits in the decimal number system; to proceed further, we extend the numbers to the 10's place:

```
10
11
12
 .
 .
 .
```

It is productive to consider what "the 10's place" really means.

The 10's place simply represents a count of the number of times that we have cycled through the entire group of 10 possible digits. Thus, continuing to count, we have

```
1 group of 10 + 0 more
1 group of 10 + 1 more
1 group of 10 + 2
 .
 .
 .
1 group of 10 + 9
2 groups of 10 + 0
 .
 .
 .
9 groups of 10 + 9
```

At this point, we have used all combinations of two digits, and we need to move left another digit. Before we do so, however, we should note that each group shown here represents a count of 10, since there are 10 digits in the group. Thus, the number

```
43
```

really refers to

$$4 \times 10 + 3$$

As we move leftward to the next digit, that is, the hundreds place, we are now counting cycles of the rightmost two digits or, in other words, groups of 10×10, or 10^2, or hundreds. Thus, the number

```
527
```

really represents

```
five groups of (10 × 10) +
two groups of 10 + 7
```

FIGURE 3.2

Counting in Base 2

NUMBER	EQUIVALENT	DECIMAL EQUIVALENT
0	0×2^0	0
1	1×2^0	1
10	$1 \times 2^1 + 0 \times 2^0$	2
11	$1 \times 2^1 + 1 \times 2^0$	3
100	1×2^2	4
101	$1 \times 2^2 \qquad + 1 \times 2^0$	5
110	$1 \times 2^2 + 1 \times 2^1$	6
111	$1 \times 2^2 + 1 \times 2^1 + 1 \times 2^0$	7
1000	1×2^3	8
1001	$1 \times 2^3 \qquad + 1 \times 2^0$	9
1010	$1 \times 2^3 \qquad + 1 \times 2^1$	10

This is also represented as

$$5 \times 10^2 + 2 \times 10^1 + 7 \times 10^0$$

This method can, of course, be extended indefinitely.

The same method, exactly, applies to any number base. The only change is the size of each grouping. For example, in base 8, there are only eight different digits available (0, 1, 2, 3, 4, 5, 6, 7). Thus, each move left represents eight of the next rightmost grouping. The number

$$624_8$$

corresponds to

$$6 \times 8^2 + 2 \times 8^1 + 4 \times 8^0$$

Since $8^2 = 64_{10}$, $8^1 = 8_{10}$, and $8^0 = 1$,

$$624_8 = 6 \times 64 + 2 \times 8 + 4 = 404_{10}$$

Each digit in a number has a *weight*, or importance, relative to its neighbors left and right. The weight of a particular digit in a number is the multiplication factor used to determine the overall value of the particular digit. For example, the weights of the digits in base 8, reading from right to left are 1, 8, 64, 256, . . . , or, if your prefer, $8^0, 8^1, 8^2, 8^3, \dots$. Just as you would expect, the weight of a digit in any base n is n times as large as the digit to its right and $(1/n)$th as large as the digit to its left.

Figure 3.2 shows the corresponding method of counting in base 2. Note that each digit has twice the weight of its next rightmost neighbor, just as in base 10 each digit had ten times the weight of its right neighbor. This is what you would expect if you consider that there are only two different values for digits in the binary cycle. You should spend enough time studying this table until you understand every detail thoroughly.

Note, too, that the steps that we have followed do not really depend on the number base that we are using. We simply go through a complete cycle, exhausting all possible different digits in the base set, and then move to the left one place and count the cycles. We repeat this process as necessary to represent the entire number.

In general, for any number base B, each digit position represents B to a power, where the power is numbered from the rightmost digit, starting with B^0. B^0, of course, is one (known as the units place) for any number base.

Thus, a simple way to determine the decimal equivalent for a number in any number base is to multiply each digit by the weight in the given base that corresponds to the position of the digit for that number.

EXAMPLES

As an example,

$$142305_6 =$$
$$1 \times 6^5 + 4 \times 6^4 + 2 \times 6^3 + 3 \times 6^2 + 0 \times 6 + 5 =$$
$$7776 + 5184 + 432 + 108 + 0 + 5 = 13505_{10}$$

■ ■ ■

Similarly,

$$110010100_2 =$$
$$1 \times 2^8 + 1 \times 2^7 + 0 \times 2^6 + 0 \times 2^5 + 1 \times 2^4 + 0 \times 2^3 + 1 \times 2^2 +$$
$$0 \times 2 + 0 =$$
$$256 + 128 + 16 + 4 = 404_{10}$$

You should probably work out these two examples and check your results against ours.

Often it is useful to be able to estimate quickly the value of a binary number. Since the weight of each place in a binary number doubles as we move to the left, we can generate a rough order-of-magnitude by considering only the weight for the leftmost bit or two. Starting from 1, and doubling for each bit in the number to get the weight, you can see that the most significant bit in the previous example has a value of 256. We can improve the estimate by adding half that again for the next most significant bit, which gives the value of the number in the neighborhood of 384, plus a little more for the additional bits. With a little practice, it is easy to estimate the magnitudes of binary numbers almost instantly. This technique is often sufficient for checking the results of calculations when debugging programs. (You might also want to consider it as a way of doing quick checks on your solutions to exam problems!)

We will discuss number conversion between different bases more carefully later in the chapter.

From the preceding discussion, it is fairly easy to determine the total range of possible numbers—or, equivalently, the smallest and largest integer—for a given number of digits in a particular number base. Since the weight of each digit is one larger than the largest value that can be represented by all the digits to its right, then the range of possible values for n digits is simply the weight of the nth digit, which is represented by the value

$$\mathrm{range} = \mathrm{base}^n$$

Thus, if we want to know how many different numbers can be represented by two decimal digits, the answer is 10^2. We can represent one hundred different numbers ($0 \ldots 99$) with two decimal digits.

It's obviously easier to simply memorize the formula; if you are told that you are working with four digit numbers in base 8, you know from the formula that you can represent 8^4, or 4096 different numbers, ranging from $0 \ldots 7777_8$, or the decimal equivalent ($0 \ldots 4095$).

Just as a pocket calculator stores, manipulates, and displays numbers as a group of digits, so computers store and manipulate numbers as groups of bits. Most computers work with numbers 16 bits, 32 bits, or 64 bits at a time. Applying the preceding formula to a "16-bit" PC, you can represent $2^{16} = 65,536$ different number values in each 16-bit

FIGURE 3.3

Decimal Range for Selected Bit Widths

BITS	DIGITS	RANGE
1	0 +	2 (0 and 1)
4	1 +	16 (0 to 15)
8	2 +	256
10	3	1,024
16	4 +	65,536 (64K)
20	6	1,048,576 (1M)
32	9 +	4,294,967,296 (4G)
64	19 +	approx. 1.6×10^{19}
128	38 +	approx. 2.6×10^{38}

location. If you wish to extend this range, it is necessary to use some technique for increasing the number of bits used to hold your numbers, such as using two 16-bit storage locations together to hold 32 bits. There are other methods used, which are discussed in Chapter 5, but note that, regardless of the technique used, there is *no* way to store more than 65,536 different number values using 16 bits.

A table of base 10 equivalent ranges for several common computer "word lengths" is shown in Figure 3.3. There is a simple way to calculate the approximate range for a given number of bits, since 2^{10} is approximately 1000. To do so, we break up the total number of bits into a sum that consists of values where the range is easily figured out. The overall range is equal to the product of the subranges for each value. This method is best seen with examples.

For example, if you need to know the range for 18 bits, you would break up the number 18 into the sum of 10 and 8, then multiply the range for 10 bits to that for 8 bits. Since the range for 10 bits is approximately 1 K (1024, actually) and 8 bits is 256, the range for 18 bits is approximately 256 K. Similarly, the range for 32 bits would be (10-bit range) $\times$ (10-bit range) $\times$ (10-bit range) $\times$ (2-bit range) $= 1$ K $\times$ 1 K $\times$ 1 K $\times$ 4 $= 4$ gigabytes. This technique becomes easy with a bit of practice.

Notice that it takes 18 bits to represent a little more than five decimal digits. In general, approximately 3.3 bits are required for each equivalent decimal digit. This is true because $2^{3.3}$ is approximately equal to 10.

3.3 PERFORMING ARITHMETIC IN DIFFERENT NUMBER BASES

Next, we consider simple arithmetic operations in various number bases. Let us begin by looking at the simple base 10 addition table shown in Figure 3.4.

FIGURE 3.4

The Base 10 Addition Table

+	0	1	2	3	4	5	6	7	8	9
0	0	1	2	3	4	5	6	7	8	9
1	1	2	3	4	5	6	7	8	9	10
2	2	3	4	5	6	7	8	9	10	11
3	3	4	5	6	7	8	9	10	11	12
4	4	5	6	7	8	9	10	11	12	13

etc.

We add two numbers by finding one in the row and the other in the column. The table entry at the intersection is the result. For example, we have used the table to demonstrate that the sum of 3 and 6 is 9. Note that the extra digit sometimes required becomes a carry that gets added into the next left column during the addition process.

More fundamentally, we are interested in how the addition table is actually created. Each column (or row) represents an increase of 1 from the previous column (or row), which is equivalent to counting. Thus, starting

FIGURE 3.5

The Base 8 Addition Table

+	0	1	2	3	4	5	6	7	
0	0	1	2	3	4	5	6	7	
1	1	2	3	4	5	6	7	10	
2	2	3	4	5	6	7	10	11	
3	3	4	5	6	7	10	11	12	**(no 8 or 9, of course)**
4	4	5	6	7	10	11	12	13	
5	5	6	7	10	11	12	13	14	
6	6	7	10	11	12	13	14	15	
7	7	10	11	12	13	14	15	16	

from the leftmost column in the table, it is only necessary to count up 1 to find the next value. Since $3 + 6 = 9$, the next column will have to carry to the next place, or 10, just as occurred when we demonstrated counting in base 10, earlier. This knowledge should make it easy for you to create a base 8 addition table. Try to create your own table before looking at the one in Figure 3.5.

Of special interest is the base 2 addition table:

+	0	1
0	0	1
1	1	10

Clearly, addition in base 2 is going to be easy!

Addition in base 2 (or any other base, for that matter) then follows the usual methods of addition that you are familiar with, including the handling of carries that you already know. The *only* difference is the particular addition table being used. There are practice problems representing multidigit binary arithmetic and column arithmetic (Exercise 3.8) at the end of the chapter.

EXAMPLE

Add 11100001_2 and 101011_2 (superscripts are carried amounts).

$$
\begin{array}{r}
{}^{1}1 \ \ 1^{1} \ 1 \ \ 0 \ \ 0 \ \ 0^{1} \ 0^{1} \ 1 \\
+ \quad \quad \quad 1 \ \ 0 \ \ 1 \ \ 0 \ \ 1 \ \ 1 \\
\hline
1 \ 0 \ 0 \ 0 \ 0 \ 1 \ 1 \ 0 \ 0
\end{array}
$$

Let's use the estimation technique to see if our result is approximately correct. 11100001 is approximately $128 + 64 + 32$, or 224. 101011 is approximately 32. Thus, the sum should be about 256; 100001100 is indeed approximately 256, so at least we know that our calculation is in the ballpark.

As an aside, it may be of interest to some readers to consider how this addition table can be implemented in the computer using only Boolean logic, without performing any

FIGURE 3.6

The Base 10 Multiplication Table

×	0	1	2	3	4	5	6	7	8	9
0				←	0	→				
1		1	2	3	4	5	6	7	8	9
2		2	4	6	8	10	12	14	16	18
3	↑	3	6	9	12	15	18	21	24	27
4	0	4	8	12	16	20	24	28	32	36
5	↓	5	10	15	20	25	30	35	40	45
6		6	12	18	24	30	36	42	48	54
7		7	14	21	28	35	42	49	56	63
8		8	16	24	32	40	48	56	64	72
9		9	18	27	36	45	54	63	72	81

actual arithmetic: the result bit (the bit in the column that corresponds to the inputs) can be represented by the EXCLUSIVE-OR function of the two input bits. The EXCLUSIVE-OR function has a "1" as output only if either input, but not both inputs, is a "1." Similarly, the carry bit is represented as an AND function on the two input bits. ("1" as output if and only if both inputs are a "1.") This approach is discussed in more detail in Supplementary Chapter 1.

The process of multiplication can be reduced conceptually to multiple addition, so it should not surprise you that multiplication tables in different number bases are also reasonably straightforward. The major difference in appearance results from the fact that the carry occurs at different places.

The easiest way to create a multiplication table is to treat multiplication as multiple addition: each column (or row) represents the addition of the value in the row (or column) being created. Thus, in the following table, you can see that 5×8 is equivalent to $5 \times 7 + 5 = 40$. The familiar decimal multiplication table appears in Figure 3.6, with the example just given indicated.

The same technique can be applied to the base 8 multiplication table (Figure 3.7).

Note in the foregoing table that $3 \times 3 = 3 \times 2 + 3$. Note, though, that counting up 3 from 6 (or adding 3 to 6) results in a carry after 7 is reached: $6 \rightarrow 7 \rightarrow 10 \rightarrow 11$.

The base 2 multiplication table is almost trivial, since 0 times anything is 0 and 1 times 1 is itself:

FIGURE 3.7

The Base 8 Multiplication Table

×	0	1	2	3	4	5	6	7
0			←	0	→			
1		1	2	3	4	5	6	7
2	↑	2	4	6	10	12	14	16
3	0	3	6	11	14	17	22	25
4	↓	4	10	14	20	24	30	34
5		5	12	17	24	31	36	43
6		6	14	22	30	36	44	52
7		7	16	25	34	43	52	61

×	0	1
0	0	0
1	0	1

Because the binary multiplication table is so simple, it turns out that multiplication can be implemented in a computer fairly easily. There are only two possible results: if the multiplier is 0, the answer is 0, even if the multiplicand is a nonzero multidigit number. If the multiplier is 1, the multiplicand is brought down as the result. You might recognize the multiplication table as a Boolean AND function.

If you recall that decimal multidigit multiplication is performed by multiplying the multiplicand by each digit of the multiplier, shifting the result of each multiplication to line up with the multiplier, and adding up the results, then you realize that multidigit binary multiplication can be performed by simply shifting the multiplicand into whatever positions in the multiplier are "1" bits and adding to the result. This is easily illustrated with an example:

EXAMPLE

Multiply

```
        1101101
      × 100110
        1101101    bits shifted to line up with 2's place of multiplier
       1101101     4's place
      1101101      32's place
    1000000101110  result (note the 0 at the end, since the 1's place is
                   not brought down)
```

We note in passing that shifting a binary number one position to the left has the effect of doubling its value. This is a result you would expect, since the shift is equivalent to multiplying the value by a 1 in the 2's place of the multiplier. This result is consistent with the fact that shifting a decimal number to the left by one position will multiply its value by 10. In general, **shifting** a number in any base **left** one digit multiplies its value by the base, and, conversely, **shifting** a number **right** one digit divides its value by the base.

Although we have not mentioned subtraction or division, the methods are similar to those that we have already discussed. In fact, the addition and multiplication tables can be directly used for subtraction and division, respectively.

3.4 NUMERIC CONVERSION BETWEEN NUMBER BASES

Conversions between whole numbers in decimal (base 10) and any other number base are relatively straightforward. With the exception of one special case discussed in Section 3.6, it is impractical to convert directly between two nondecimal number bases. Instead, base 10 would be used as an intermediary conversion base.

The easiest intuitive way to convert between base 10 and another number base is to recognize the weight of each digit in the alternative number base and to multiply that weight by the value of the digit in that position. The sum taken over all digits represents the base 10 value of the number. This is easily seen in an example:

EXAMPLE

Convert the number

$$13754_8$$

to base 10.

From the following diagram we can see the result easily:

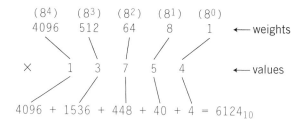

We can use the same method in reverse to convert from base 10 to another base, although the technique is not quite as simple. In this case, it is just a question of finding the value corresponding to the weight of each digit such that the total will add up to the base 10 number that we are trying to convert.

Note that the value for each digit must be the largest value that will not exceed the number being converted. If this were not true, then there would be more than a full grouping of the next less significant digit. This idea is best clarified by example:

EXAMPLE

Suppose that we are reverse converting the preceding example, and we assume that there are six groups of 64 instead of seven. In this case, the 8's place and 1's place combined must add up to more than 64, and we've already seen that is impossible.

This provides a simple methodology for the conversion. Start with the digit whose weight is the largest possible without exceeding the number to be converted. Determine the largest value for that weight that does not exceed the number to be converted. Then, do the same for each successive digit, working from left to right.

EXAMPLE

As an example, let us convert 6124_{10} to base 5. The weights of each digit in base 5 are as follows:

$$15625 \quad 3125 \quad 625 \quad 125 \quad 25 \quad 5 \quad 1$$

Clearly the 15625 digit is too large, so the result will be a six-digit base 5 number. The number 3125 fits into 6124 only once; thus, the first digit is a 1, and the remainder to be converted is 2999. Proceeding to the next digit, 625 goes into 2999 four times with a remainder of 499, 125 into 499 three times with a remainder of 124, 25 into 124 four times, and so on. We get a final result of

$$143444_5$$

It would be useful for you to confirm the answer by converting the result back to base 10.

This method is particularly simple if you are converting from decimal to binary, since the value that corresponds to a particular bit either fits (1) or it doesn't (0). Consider the following example:

EXAMPLE

Convert 3193_{10} to binary. The weights in binary are 4096, 2048, 1024, 512, 256, 128, 64, 32, 16, 8, 4, 2, and 1.

Proceeding as before, the largest bit value in this conversion is the 2048 weight. Subtracting 2048 from 3193 leaves 1145 yet to be converted; thus, there is also a 1 in the 1024 place. Now the remainder is $1145 - 1024 = 121$. This means that there are 0's in the 512, 256, and 128 places. Continuing, you should confirm that the final result is

$$110001111001_2$$

Note that, in general, as the base gets smaller, the representation of a value requires more digits, and looks bigger.

An Alternative Conversion Method

Although the preceding methods are easy to understand, they are computationally difficult and prone to mistakes. In this section we will consider methods that are usually simpler to compute but are less intuitive. It is helpful to understand the reasons that these methods work, since the reasoning adds insight to the entire concept of number manipulation.

BASE 10 TO ANOTHER BASE   Suppose we divide the number to be converted successively by the base, B, that we are converting to, and look at the remainders of each division. We will do this until there is nothing left to divide. Each successive remainder represents the value of a digit in the new base, reading the new value from right to left. Again, let us convert 6124_{10} to base 5:

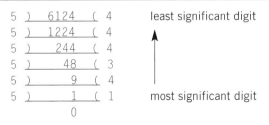

The answer is 143444_5, which agrees with our earlier result.

The first time that we perform the division, we are, in effect, determining how many groups of 5 (or, in the general case, B) fit into the original number. The remainder is the number of single units left over, which is, in other words, the units place of the converted number.

The original number has now been divided by 5, so the second division by 5 determines how many groups of 5^2, or 25, fit into the number. The remainder in this case is the number of 5-groups that are left over, which is the second digit from the right.

Each time we divide by the base, we are increasing the power of the group being tested by one, and we do this until there is no group left. Since the remainders correspond to the part of the number that does not exactly fit the group, we can read the converted number easily by reading the remainders from the bottom up.

Here's another example:

EXAMPLE

Convert 8151_{10} to base 16, also known as hexadecimal:

$$
\begin{array}{rrl}
16 \ ) & 8151 & (\ 7 \\
16 \ ) & 509 & (13 \\
16 \ ) & 31 & (15 \\
& 1 &
\end{array}
$$

in base 16, this is represented by the letter "D"
in base 16, this is represented by the letter "F"

The answer is $1FD7_{16}$. We suggest that you verify this answer by using the technique of digit weight multiplication to convert this answer back to decimal form.

ANOTHER NUMBER BASE TO BASE 10 An alternative method can be used to convert from other number bases to base 10. The technique is also computationally simple: starting from the most significant digit, we multiply by the base, B, and add the next digit to the right. We repeat this process until the least significant digit has been added.

EXAMPLE

Convert 13754_8 to base 10:

$$
\begin{array}{l}
1 \\
\underline{\times\ 8} \\
\quad 8 + 3 = 11 \\
\qquad \underline{\times\ 8} \\
\qquad 88 + 7 = 95 \\
\qquad\quad \underline{\times\ 8} \\
\qquad\quad 760 + 5 = 765 \\
\qquad\qquad \underline{\times\ 8} \\
\qquad\qquad 6120 + 4 = 6124_{10}
\end{array}
$$

If you count the number of times that each digit in the example is multiplied by the base number, in this case 8, you discover that the leftmost digit is multiplied by 8 four times, or 8^4, and that each successive digit is multiplied by 8 one less time, until you arrive at the rightmost digit, which is not multiplied by the base number at all. Thus, each digit is multiplied by its proper weight, and the result is what we would expect. In the next chapter, you will see that this method is also useful for converting a sequence of digits in alphanumeric form to an actual number.

You have now been introduced to two different methods for performing conversions in each direction. You should practice all four methods; then you can use whichever two methods are easiest for you to remember.

3.5 HEXADECIMAL NUMBERS AND ARITHMETIC

The hexadecimal, or base 16, number representation system is important because it is commonly used as a shorthand notation for binary numbers. The conversion technique between hexadecimal and binary notations is particularly simple because there is a direct relationship between the two. Each hexadecimal number represents exactly 4 binary bits. Most computers store and manipulate instructions and data using word sizes that are multiples of 4 bits. Therefore, the hexadecimal notation is a convenient way to represent computer words. Of course, it is also much easier to read and write than binary notation. The technique for converting between binary and hexadecimal is shown later in this chapter.

Although hexadecimal numbers are represented and manipulated in the same way as those of other bases, we must first provide symbols to represent the additional digits beyond 9 that we require to represent sixteen different quantities with a single integer.

By convention, we use the digits 0–9, followed by the first six alphabetical characters A–F. Thus, the digits 0–9 have their familiar meaning; the letters A–F correspond to what in a decimal base would be quantities of 10–15, respectively. To count in hexadecimal we count from 0 to 9, then A to F, and then move left to the next digit. Since there are sixteen digits, each place represents a power of 16. Thus, the number

$$2A4F_{16}$$

is equivalent to

$$2 \times 16^3 + 10 \times 16^2 + 4 \times 16 + 15, \quad \text{or}$$
$$10831_{10}$$

Addition and multiplication tables can be created for the hexadecimal number system. These tables each have sixteen rows and sixteen columns, as you would expect. The addition table is shown in Figure 3.8. Before you look at the figure, you should try to work the hexadecimal addition and multiplication tables out for yourself (see Exercise 3.7).

3.6 A SPECIAL CONVERSION CASE—NUMBER BASES THAT ARE RELATED

A special possibility for conversion exists when one number base is an integer power of another. In this case, a direct conversion can easily be made. In fact, with a bit of practice, the conversion can be done mentally and the answer written down directly. These conversions

FIGURE 3.8

Hexadecimal Addition Table

+	0	1	2	3	4	5	6	7	8	9	A	B	C	D	E	F
0	0	1	2	3	4	5	6	7	8	9	A	B	C	D	E	F
1	1	2	3	4	5	6	7	8	9	A	B	C	D	E	F	10
2	2	3	4	5	6	7	8	9	A	B	C	D	E	F	10	11
3	3	4	5	6	7	8	9	A	B	C	D	E	F	10	11	12
4	4	5	6	7	8	9	A	B	C	D	E	F	10	11	12	13
5	5	6	7	8	9	A	B	C	D	E	F	10	11	12	13	14
6	6	7	8	9	A	B	C	D	E	F	10	11	12	13	14	15
7	7	8	9	A	B	C	D	E	F	10	11	12	13	14	15	16
8	8	9	A	B	C	D	E	F	10	11	12	13	14	15	16	17
9	9	A	B	C	D	E	F	10	11	12	13	14	15	16	17	18
A	A	B	C	D	E	F	10	11	12	13	14	15	16	17	18	19
B	B	C	D	E	F	10	11	12	13	14	15	16	17	18	19	1A
C	C	D	E	F	10	11	12	13	14	15	16	17	18	19	1A	1B
D	D	E	F	10	11	12	13	14	15	16	17	18	19	1A	1B	1C
E	E	F	10	11	12	13	14	15	16	17	18	19	1A	1B	1C	1D
F	F	10	11	12	13	14	15	16	17	18	19	1A	1B	1C	1D	1E

work because a grouping of several digits in the smaller number base corresponds, or maps, exactly to a single digit in the larger number base.

Two particularly useful examples for computer work are the cases of conversion between base 2 and base 8 and conversion between base 2 and base 16. Since $8 = 2^3$, we can represent binary numbers directly in base 8 using one octal digit to correspond to each three binary digits. Similarly, it takes one hexadecimal digit to exactly represent 4 bits.

The advantage of representing binary numbers in hexadecimal or octal is obvious: it is clearly much easier to read and manipulate four-digit hexadecimal numbers than 16-bit binary numbers. Since the conversion between binary and octal and hexadecimal is so simple, it is common to use hexadecimal or octal representation as a shorthand notation for binary. (Note that base 8 and base 16 are not directly related to each other by power, but conversion could be performed easily by using base 2 as an intermediary.)

Since the correspondence of binary and octal or hexadecimal is exact, the conversion process simply consists of breaking the binary number into groups of three or four, starting from the least significant bit (the unit bit), and converting each group independently. It may be necessary to mentally add 0s to the left end of the number to convert the most significant digit. This is most easily illustrated with an example:

EXAMPLE

Let us convert

$$11010111011000$$

to hexadecimal.

Grouping the binary number by fours, we have

$$0011\ 0101\ 1101\ 1000$$

or

$$35D8_{16}$$

Note that we added two zeros at the left end of the binary number to create groups of four.

The conversion in the other direction works identically. Thus,

$$275331_8$$

becomes

$$010\ 111\ 101\ 011\ 011\ 001_2$$

For practice, now convert this value to hexadecimal.

Most computer manufacturers today prefer to use hexadecimal, since a 16-bit or 32-bit number can be represented exactly by a four- or eight-digit hexadecimal number. (How many octal digits would be required?) A few manufacturers still use octal representation for some applications.

You might ask why it is necessary to represent data in binary form at all. After all, the binary form is used within the computer, where it is usually invisible to the user. There are many occasions, however, where the ability to read the binary data is very useful. Remember that the computer stores both instructions and data in binary form. When debugging a program, it may be desirable to be able to read the program's instructions and to determine intermediate data steps that the computer is using. Older computers used to provide binary dumps for this purpose. Binary dumps were complete octal listings of everything stored in memory at the time the dump was requested. Even today it is sometimes important, for example, to be able to read the binary data from a floppy disk to recover a lost or damaged file. Modern computer operating systems and networks present a variety of troubleshooting data in hexadecimal form.

Conversions between binary and hexadecimal notation are used frequently. We strongly recommend that you practice to become proficient at working with hexadecimal notation.

3.7 FRACTIONS

Up to this point we have limited our discussion to whole numbers, or, if you prefer, integers. The representation and conversion of fractional numbers are somewhat more difficult because there is not necessarily an exact relationship between fractional numbers in different number bases. More specifically, fractional numbers that can be represented exactly in one number base may be impossible to represent exactly in another. Thus, exact conversion may be impossible. A couple of simple examples will suffice:

The decimal fraction

$$0.1_{10} \text{ or } 1/10$$

cannot be represented exactly in binary form. There is no combination of bits that will add up exactly to this fraction. The binary equivalent begins

$$0.00011001100011_2...$$

This binary fraction repeats endlessly with a repeat cycle of four. Similarly, the fraction

$$1/3$$

is not representable as a decimal value in base 10. In fact, we represent this fraction decimally as

$$0.3333333...$$

As you will realize shortly, this fraction can be represented exactly in base 3 as

$$0.1_3$$

Recall that the value of each digit to the left of a **decimal point** in base 10 has a weight ten times that of its next right neighbor. This is obvious to you, since you already know that each digit represents a group of ten objects in the next right neighbor. As you have already seen, the same basic relationship holds for any number base: the weight of each digit is B times the weight of its right neighbor. This fact has two important implications:

1. If we move the number point one place to the right in a number, the value of the number will be multiplied by the base. A specific example will make this obvious:

$$1390_{10} \text{ is ten times as large as } 139.0_{10}$$

$$139 \, {}_{\times}0.$$

Moving the point right one space, therefore, multiplies the number by ten. Only a bit less obvious (pun intended),

$$100_2 \text{ is twice as big as } 10_2$$

(Note: We have used the phrase "number point" because the word "decimal" specifically implies base 10. More generally, the number point is known by the name of its base, for example, **binary point** or *hexadecimal point*. It is sometimes also called a **radix point**.)

2. The opposite is also true: if we move the number point to the left one place, the value is divided by the base. Thus, each digit has strength $1/B$ of its left neighbor. This is true on both sides of the number point.

$$246.8_{\times}$$

Moving the point to the left one space divides the value by ten.

Thus, for numbers to the right of the number point, successive digits have values $1/B$, $1/B^2$, $1/B^3$, and so on. In base 10, the digits then have value

$$.D_1 \quad D_2 \quad D_3 \quad D_4$$
$$10^{-1} \quad 10^{-2} \quad 10^{-3} \quad 10^{-4}$$

which is equivalent to

$$1/10 \quad 1/100 \quad 1/1000 \quad 1/10,000$$

This should come as no surprise to you, since $1/10 = 0.1$, $1/100 = 0.01$, and so forth. (Remember from algebra that $B^{-k} = 1/B^k$.)

Then, a decimal number such as

$$0.2589$$

has value

$$2 \times (1/10) + 5 \times (1/100) + 8 \times (1/1000) + 9 \times (1/10,000)$$

Similarly in base 2, each place to the right of the binary point is $1/2$ the weight of its left-hand neighbor. Thus, we have

$$.B_1 \quad B_2 \quad B_3 \quad B_4$$
$$1/2 \quad 1/4 \quad 1/8 \quad 1/16 \quad \text{etc.}$$

As an example,

$$0.101011$$

is equivalent to

$$1/2 + 1/8 + 1/32 + 1/64$$

which has decimal value

$$0.5 + 0.125 + 0.03125 + 0.015625 = 0.671875_{10}$$

Since there is no general relationship between fractions of types $1/10^k$ and $1/2^k$, there is no reason to assume that a number that is representable in base 10 will also be representable in base 2. Commonly, it isn't so. (The converse is not the case; since all fractions of the form $1/2^k$ can be represented in base 10, and since each bit represents a fraction of this form, fractions in base 2 can always be converted exactly to fractions in base 10.) As we have already shown with the value 0.1_{10}, many base 10 fractions result in endless base 2 fractions.

Incidentally, as review, consider the hexadecimal representation of the binary fraction representing 0.1_{10}. Starting from the numeric point, which is the common element of all number bases ($B^0 = 1$ in all bases), you group the bits into groups of four:

$$0.0001\ 1001\ 1001\ 1001 = 0.19999_{16}$$

In this particular case, the repeat cycle of four happens to be the same as the hexadecimal grouping of four, so the digit "9" repeats forever.

When fractional conversions from one base to another are performed, they are simply stopped when the desired accuracy is attained (unless, of course, a rational solution exists).

Fractional Conversion Methods

The intuitive conversion methods previously discussed can be used with fractional numbers. The computational methods have to be modified somewhat to work with fractional numbers.

Consider the intuitive methods first. The easiest way to convert a fractional number from some base B to base 10 is to determine the appropriate weights for each digit, multiply each digit by its weight, and add the values. You will note that this is identical to the method that we introduced previously for integer conversion.

EXAMPLE

Convert 0.12201_3 to base 10.

The weights for base 3 fractions (we remind you that the rules work the same for *any* number base!) are:

$$\frac{1}{3} \qquad \frac{1}{9} \qquad \frac{1}{27} \qquad \frac{1}{81} \qquad \frac{1}{243}$$

Then, the result is

$$1 \times 1/3 + 2 \times 1/9 + 2 \times 1/27 + 1 \times 1/243$$

Two different approaches could be taken at this point. Either we can convert each value to decimal base, multiply, and add,

$$\mathtt{value} = 0.33333 + 0.22222 + 0.07407 + 0.00412 = 0.63374_{10}$$

or, more easily, we can find a common denominator, convert each fraction to the common denominator, add, and then divide by the common denominator. Most easily, we can pick the denominator of the least significant digit, in this case 243:

$$\mathtt{value} = \frac{81 + 2 \times 27 + 2 \times 9 + 1}{243} = \frac{154}{243} = 0.63374$$

If you look at the numerator of the last equation carefully, you might notice that the numerator consists of weighted digits, where the digits correspond to the weights of the fraction as if the ternary point had been shifted five places right to make the fraction into a whole number. (The base 3 number point is called a *ternary* point.) A shift five places to the right multiplies the number by $3 \rightarrow 9 \rightarrow 27 \rightarrow 81 \rightarrow 243$; therefore, we have to divide by 243 to restore the original fraction.

Repeating this exercise with another, perhaps more practical, example should help to solidify this method for you:

EXAMPLE

Convert 0.110011_2 to base 10.

Shifting the binary point six places to the right and converting, we have

$$\mathtt{numerator\ value} = 32 + 16 + 2 + 1 = 51$$

Shifting the binary back is equivalent to dividing by 2^6, or 64. Dividing the numerator 51 by 64 yields

$$\mathtt{value} = 0.796875$$

The intuitive method for converting numbers from base 10 to another base can also be used. This is the method shown earlier where you fit the largest product of weights for each digit without exceeding the original number. In the case of fractions, however, you are working with fractional decimal numbers, and the actual calculation may be time consuming and difficult except in simple cases.

EXAMPLE

Convert the number 0.1_{10} to binary representation. The weights for binary fractions are

$$\frac{1}{2} \qquad \frac{1}{4} \qquad \frac{1}{8} \qquad \frac{1}{16} \qquad \frac{1}{32} \qquad \mathtt{etc.}$$

These are easier to use when converted into decimal form: 0.5, 0.25, 0.125, 0.0625, and 0.03125, respectively. The largest value that fits into 0.1_{10} is 0.0625, which corresponds to a value of 0.0001_2. The remainder to be converted is $0.1 - 0.0625 = 0.0375$. Since 0.03125 fits into this remainder, the next bit is also a 1: 0.00011_2, and so on. As an exercise, you may want to carry this conversion out a few more places.

To convert fractional numbers from base 10 to another base, it is usually easier to use a variation on the division method shown earlier. Recall that for an integer, this involved dividing the number repeatedly by the base value and retaining the remainders. Effectively, this method works by shifting the radix point to the left one place each time we divide by the base value and noticing what drops over the radix point, which is the remainder. The number point is initially assumed to be to the right of the number.

When the value being converted is to the right of the number point, the procedure must work exactly the opposite. We *multiply* the fraction by the base value repeatedly, and record, then drop, the values that move to the left of the radix point. We repeat this procedure until the desired number of digits of accuracy is attained or until the value being multiplied is zero. Each time we multiply, we effectively expose the next digit.

For example, if the value in base 10 is 0.5, multiplying that by 2 would yield 1.0, which says that in base 2 there would have been a 1 in the 1/2-bit location. Similarly, 0.25 would be multiplied by 2, twice, to reach a value of 1.0, indicating a 1 in the 1/4-bit location. An example of the procedure should clarify this explanation:

EXAMPLE

Convert 0.828125_{10} to base 2. Multiplying by 2, we get

```
        .828125
      ×        2
       1.656250    The 1 is saved as result,
      ×        2    then dropped, and the
       1.312500    process repeated
      ×        2
       0.625000
      ×        2
       1.250000
      ×        2
       0.500000
      ×        2
       1.000000
```

The final result, reading the overflow values downward, is 0.110101_2. This is an example of a conversion that reaches closure. You will recall that we stated earlier that 0.1_{10} is an example of a number that does not convert exactly into base 2. The procedure for that case follows.

```
        .100000
      ×        2
       0.200000
      ×        2
       0.400000
      ×        2
       0.800000
      ×        2
       1.600000
      ×        2
       1.200000
      ×        2
       0.400000
```

The repeating nature of this conversion is clear at this point.

Finally, we note that conversion between bases where one base is an integer power of the other can be performed for fractions by grouping the digits in the smaller base as before. For fractions, the grouping must be done from left to right; the method is otherwise identical.

EXAMPLE

To convert 0.1011_2 to base 8, group the digits by threes (since $2^3 = 8$) and convert each group as usual. Note that it is necessary to supplement the second group with 0's. As you would expect, fractional zeros are appended to the right of the fraction.

Therefore,

$$0.101\_100_2 = 0.54_8$$

3.8 MIXED NUMBER CONVERSIONS

The usual arithmetic rules apply to fractional and mixed numbers. When adding and subtracting these numbers, the radix points must line up. During multiplication and division, the radix point is determined in exactly the same way as it would be in base 10. For multiplication in base 8, for example, you would add the number of digits to the right of the radix in the multiplier and the multiplicand; the total would be the number of digits to the right of the radix point in the result.

Extra caution is required when performing base conversions on numbers that contain both integer and fractional parts. The two parts must be converted separately.

The radix point is the fixed reference in a conversion. It does not move, since the digit to its left is a unit digit in every base; that is, B^0 is always 1, regardless of B.

It is possible to shift a mixed number in order to make it an integer. Unfortunately, there is a tendency to forget that the shift takes place in a particular base. A number shifted in base 2, say, cannot be converted and then shifted back in base 10 because the factor used in the shift is 2^k, which obviously has a different value than 10^k. Of course, it is possible to perform the shift and then divide the converted number by the original shift value, but this is usually more trouble than it's worth.

Instead, it's usually easier to remember that each part is converted separately, with the radix point remaining fixed at its original location.

SUMMARY AND REVIEW

Counting in bases other than 10 is essentially similar to the familiar way of counting. Each digit place represents a count of a group of digits from the next less significant digit place. The group is of size B, where B is the base of the number system being used. The least significant digit, of course, represents single units. Addition, subtraction, multiplication, and division for any number base work similarly to base 10, although the arithmetic tables look different.

There are several different methods that can be used to convert whole numbers from base B to base 10. The informal method is to recognize the base 10 values for each digit place and simply to add the weighted values for each digit together. A more formal method converts from base B to base 10 using successive multiplication by the present base and addition of the next digit. The final total represents the base 10 solution to the conversion. Similar methods exist for converting from base 10 to a different number base.

The conversion of number bases in which one base is an integer power of the other may be performed by recognizing that multiple digit places in the smaller base represent a single-digit place in the larger. Conversion is then done by grouping and converting each multiple set of digits individually.

Fractional and mixed numbers must be handled more carefully. The integer and fractional parts must be treated independently of each other. Although the conversion method is the same, the choice of the multiplication or division operation is reversed for the fractional part. Again, directly related bases can be converted by grouping digits in one base and converting each group independently.

FOR FURTHER READING

Working in different number bases was part of a trend in the teaching of mathematics in the 1960s and 1970s known as "the new math". The material is still taught in many elementary schools.

Many libraries carry texts with such titles as "Elementary Math". A good, brief review of arithmetic as it applies to the computer can be found in the Schaum outline series book *Essential Computer Mathematics* [LIPS82]. A funny introduction to "new math" can be found on the recording "That Was the Year That Was" by Tom Lehrer [LEHR65]. In addition, most books on computer arithmetic contain substantial discussions of the topics covered in this chapter. Typical computer arithmetic books include those by Spaniol [SPAN81] and Kulisch and Maranker [KULI81]. A clear and thorough discussion of this material can be found in the computer architecture book by Hennessy and Patterson [HENN06].

KEY CONCEPTS AND TERMS

base	binary-octal conversion	hexadecimal number
binary arithmetic	bit	left shift
binary number	decimal point	mixed number conversion
binary point	decimal-binary conversion	octal number
binary-decimal conversion	fractional conversion	radix point
binary-hexadecimal	hexadecimal-binary	right shift
conversion	conversion	

READING REVIEW QUESTIONS

3.1 How many different digits would you expect to find in base 6? What is the largest digit in base 6? Let z represent that largest digit. What is the next value after 21z if you're counting up by 1's? What is the next value after 4zz if you're counting up by 1's?

3.2 In the book we show that 527_{10} represents $5 \times 10^2 + 2 \times 10^1 + 7 \times 10^0$. What is the representation for 527_8? What would its equivalent base 10 value be?

3.3 Use the table in Figure 3.5 to add 21_8 and 33_8. Use the table in Figure 3.5 to add 46_8 and 43_8.

3.4   What are the first six weights in base 2? Using these weights, convert 100101_2 to base 10.

3.5   Use the base 2 addition table to add 10101_2 and 1110_2. Use the base 2 multiplication table to multiply 10101_2 and 1110_2.

3.6   Using the weights in base 8, convert 212_{10} into base 8. Convert 3212_{10} into base 8.

3.7   What are the first three weights in base 16? Using these weights, convert 359_{16} to base 10. (Notice that the same technique works for *any* base, even if the base is larger than 10.)

3.8   What number in base 10 is equivalent to D in base 16? What number in base 16 is equivalent to the number 10 in base 10? Use the weights method to convert the number $5D_{16}$ to base 10. Use the division method to convert your answer back to base 16.

3.9   Using the weights in base 16, convert 117_{10} into base 16. Convert 1170_{10} into base 16.

3.10   Use the multiplication method to convert 1011_2 to base 10. Verify your answer by using the wieghts method to convert the number back to base 2.

3.11   Use the multiplication method to convert 1357_{16} to base 10. Verify your answer by using the division method to convert your answer back to base 16.

3.12   Use the division conversion method to convert 3212_{10} into base 8. Confirm that your answer is the same as that in question 7, above.

3.13   Use the division method to convert 12345_{10} to base 2. Verify your answer by using the weights method to convert your answer back to base 10.

3.14   Use the division method to convert 1170_{10} to base 16. Confirm that your answer is the same as that in question 8, above.

3.15   Use the division method to convert 12345_{10} to base 16. Verify your answer by using the weights method to convert your answer back to base 10.

3.16   Convert the number 1111001101100_2 *directly* from binary to hexadecimal. Without looking at the original number, convert your answer directly back to binary and compare your final answer with the original number.

3.17   Convert the number 101000101100_2 *directly* from binary to hexadecimal. Without looking at the original number, convert your answer directly back to binary and compare your final answer with the original number.

EXERCISES

3.1   Some older computers used an 18-bit word to store numbers. What is the decimal range for this word size?

3.2   How many bits will it take to represent the decimal number 3,175,000? How many bytes will it take to store this number?

3.3   **a.**   Determine the power of each digit for five-digit numbers in base 6.

   b.   Use your results from part (a) to convert the base 6 number 24531_6 to decimal.

3.4   Determine the power of each digit for four-digit numbers in base 16. Which place digits in base 2 have the same power?

3.5   Add the following binary numbers:

a.

```
    101101101
+    10011011
```

b.

```
    110111111
+  110111111
```

c.

```
    11010011
+   10001010
```

d.

```
  1101
  1010
   111
+  101
```

e.   Repeat the previous additions by converting each number to hexadecimal, adding, and converting the result back to binary.

3.6   Multiply the following binary numbers together:

a.

```
   1101
×   101
```

b.

```
   11011
×   1011
```

3.7   **a.**   Create the hexadecimal multiplication table.

b.   Use the hexadecimal table in Figure 3.8 to perform the following addition:

```
   2AB3
+  35DC
```

c.   Add the following numbers:

```
  1 FF9
+   F7
```

d.   Multiply the following numbers:

```
   2E26
×    4A
```

3.8   **a.**   Create addition and multiplication tables for base 12 arithmetic. Use alphabetic characters to represent digits 10 and larger.

b.   Using your tables from part (a), perform the following addition:

$$25A84_{12}$$
$$+\quad 70396_{12}$$

   c.   Multiply the following numbers together:

$$\begin{array}{r} 2A6_{12} \\ \times\quad B1_{12} \\ \hline \end{array}$$

3.9   Perform the following binary divisions:

   a.

$$110 \overline{)1010001001}$$

   b.

$$1011 \overline{)11000000000}$$

3.10   Using the powers of each digit in base 8, convert the decimal number 6026 to octal.

3.11   Using the powers of each digit in hexadecimal, convert the decimal number 6026 to hexadecimal.

3.12   Convert the following hexadecimal numbers to decimal:

   a.   4E

   b.   3D7

   c.   3D70

3.13   Using the multiplication method, convert the following numbers to decimal:

   a. $110001010010000 1_{2}$

   b. $C521_{16}$

   c. $3ADF_{16}$

   d. 24556_{7}

3.14   Using the division method, convert the following decimal numbers to binary:

   a.   4098

   b.   71269

   c.   37

   In each case, check your work by using the power of each digit to convert back to decimal.

3.15   Using the division method, convert the following decimal numbers:

   a.   13750 to base 12

   b.   6026 to hexadecimal

   c.   3175 to base 5

3.16   Convert the following hexadecimal numbers to binary:

   a.   4F6A

   b.   9902

   c.   A3AB

   d.   1000

3.17   Convert the following binary numbers directly to hexadecimal:

   a.   101101110111010

   b.   1111111111110001

      c.   1111111101111

      d.   110001100011001

3.18   **a.**   Convert the base 4 number 13023031_4 directly tohexadecimal. Check your result by converting both the original number and your answer to decimal.

      b.   Convert the hexadecimal number $9B62_{16}$ directly to base 4; then convert both the original number and your answer to binary to check your result.

3.19   Select a number base that would be suitable for direct conversion from base 3, and convert the number 22011210_3 to that base.

3.20   Convert the octal number 27745_8 to hexadecimal. Do *not* use decimal as an intermediary for your conversion. Why does a direct conversion not work in this case?

3.21   Convert the base 3 number 210102_3 to octal. What process did you use to do this conversion?

3.22   Using whatever programming language is appropriate for you, write a program that converts whole numbers in either direction between binary and hexadecimal.

3.23   Using whatever programming language is appropriate for you, write a program that converts a whole number input from decimal to hexadecimal.

3.24   Using whatever programming language is appropriate for you, write a program that converts a whole number input by the user from base 8 to base 10. Your program should flag as an error any input that contains the digits 8 or 9.

3.25   What is the decimal value of the following binary numbers?

      a.   1100101.1

      b.   1110010.11

      c.   11100101.1

3.26   Convert the following numbers from decimal to binary and then to hexadecimal:

      a.   27.625

      b.   4192.37761

3.27   Convert the following numbers from decimal to hexadecimal. If the answer is irrational, stop at four hexadecimal digits:

      a.   0.6640625

      b.   0.3333

      c.   69/256

3.28   Convert the following numbers from their given base to decimal:

      a. 0.1001001_2

      b. $0.3A2_{16}$

      c. $0.2A1_{12}$

3.29   Draw a flow diagram that shows step by step the process for converting a mixed number in a base other than 10 to decimal.

3.30   Write a computer program in a language appropriate for you that converts mixed numbers between decimal and binary in both directions.

CHAPTER 4

DATA FORMATS

Thomas Sperling, adapted by Benjamin Reece

4.0 INTRODUCTION

In Chapter 3 you had a chance to explore some of the properties of the binary number system. You are already aware that within the computer the binary number system is the system of choice, both for all forms of data storage and for all internal processing of operations. As human beings, we normally don't choose to do our work in binary form. Our communications are made up of language, images, and sounds. For written communications, and for our own data storage, we most frequently use alphanumeric characters and symbols, representing English or some other language. Sometimes we communicate with a photograph, or a chart or diagram, or some other image. Images may be black and white or color; they may be still frames or moving. Sounds often represent a different, spoken, form of written language, but they may also represent other possibilities, such as music, the roar of an engine, or a purr of satisfaction. We perform calculations using numbers made up of a set of numeric characters.

In the past, most business data processing took the form of text and numbers. Today, multimedia, consisting of images and sounds in the form of video conferencing, PowerPoint presentations, VoIP telephony, Web advertising, and more is of at least equal importance. Since data within the computer is limited to binary numbers, it is almost always necessary to convert our words, numbers, images, and sounds into a different form in order to store and process them in the computer.

In this chapter, we consider what it takes to get different types of data into computer-usable form and the different ways in which the data may be represented, stored, and processed.

4.1 GENERAL CONSIDERATIONS

At some point, original data, whether character, image, sound, or some other form, must be brought initially into the computer and converted into an appropriate computer representation so that it can be processed, stored, and used within the computer system. The fundamental process is shown in Figure 4.1.

Different input devices are used for this purpose. The particular choice of input device reflects the original form of the data, and also the desired data representation within the computer. Some devices perform the conversion from external form to internal representation within the input device. At other times, the input device merely serves to transform the data into a raw binary form that the computer can manipulate. Further conversion is then performed by software within the computer.

There are varying degrees of difficulty associated with the input task. Normal keyboard input, for example, is relatively straightforward. Since there are a discrete number of keys on the keyboard, it is only necessary for the keyboard to generate a binary number code for each key, which can then be identified as a simple representation of the desired character. On the other hand, input from a device that

FIGURE 4.1

Data Conversion and Representation

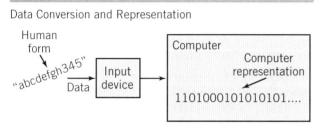

presents a continuous range of data (i.e., analog data) presents a more formidable task, particularly if the data is continuously changing with time, which is the case with a video camera or microphone.

Adequate representation of the sound input from a microphone, for example, will require hardware designed to convert the sound into binary numbers and may require hundreds or even thousands of separate pieces of data, each representing a sample of the sound at a single instant in time. If the sound is to be processed within the computer into the form of words in a document the task becomes even more challenging, since the translation of sounds into character form is very complex and difficult, requiring sophisticated, specialized software.

The internal representation of data within the computer reflects the complexity of the input source, and also the type of processing that is to take place. There is no need to preserve all the individual points that make up a photographic image, for example, if the goal is only to extract and process the characters that are present on the page; it is only necessary to input and represent the entire set of data long enough to extract the actual data that is to be used or kept. On the other hand, if the image is to be used as a figure in an art book, it will be necessary to represent the image, with all its details, as accurately as possible. For input forms that represent a continuum of values, such as photographic images, video, and sound, the quantity of binary numbers and the number of bits in each that are required to represent the input data accurately will grow quite rapidly with increasing accuracy and resolution. In fact, some form of algorithmic data compression will often be necessary to reduce the amount of data to a manageable level, particularly if the data is to be downloaded or streamed over a low-speed transmission device, such as a telephone modem or a network with limited bandwidth.

Of course, once the input data is in computer form it can be stored for future use, or it can be moved between computers through networks or by using portable computer media such as CD-ROM, flash drives, or, perhaps, even iPods. Images and sounds can be downloaded from a website or attached to e-mail, for example. Provided that the receiving computer has the appropriate software, it can store, display, and process a downloaded image just as though the picture had been produced by an image scanner connected directly to its own input.

For storage and transmission of data, a representation different from that used for internal processing is often necessary. In addition to the actual data representing points in an image or characters being displayed, the system must store and pass along information that *describes* or *interprets the meaning* of the data. Such information is known as **metadata**. In some cases, the description is simple: to read a pure text file may require only a single piece of information that indicates the number of characters in the text or marks the end of the text. A graphic image or sound requires a much more detailed description of the data. To reproduce the image, a system must know the type of graphical image, the number of colors represented by each data point, the method used to represent each color, the number of horizontal and vertical data points, the order in which data points are stored, the relative scaling of each axis, the location of the image on the screen, and much more. For a sound, the system must know how long a time period each sample represents, the number of bits in each sample, and even, perhaps, how the sound is to be used and coordinated with other sounds.

Individual programs can store and process data in any format that they want. The format used to process and store text in WordPerfect is different from that used by Microsoft Word, for example. The formats used by individual programs are known as **proprietary formats**. Proprietary formats are often suitable for an individual user or a group of users working on similar computer systems. As noted in Chapter 1, proprietary standards sometimes become de facto standards due to general user acceptance.

Note that it is important to distinguish between the data representation used within an individual piece of software and the data representation used for the input, output, storage, and exchange of data, however. Modern computer systems and networks interconnect many different types of computers, input and output devices, and computer programs. A Web page viewed on a Macintosh computer might contain an image scanned on a Hewlett-Packard image scanner, with HTML created on a Dell PC, and be served by an IBM mainframe, for example.

Thus, it is critical throughout this discussion that *standard* data representations exist to be used as interfaces between different programs, between a program and the I/O devices used by the program, between interconnected hardware, and between systems that share data, using network interconnections or transportable media such as CD-ROMs. These data representations must be recognized by a wide variety of hardware and software so that they can be used by users working within different computer environments.

A well-designed data representation will reflect and simplify the ways in which the data is to be processed and will encompass the widest possible user community. For example, the order of the letters in the alphabet is commonly used for the sorting and selection of alphanumeric business data. It makes sense, then, to choose a computer representation of alphabetic characters that will simplify these operations within the computer. Furthermore, the representation of alphanumeric characters will encompass as many of the world's languages as possible to aid in international communication.

FIGURE 4.2

Some Common Data Representations

Type of data	Standard(s)
Alphanumeric	Unicode, ASCII, EBCDIC
Image (bitmap)	GIF (graphical image format), TIFF (tagged image file format), PNG (portable network graphics), JPEG,
Image (object)	PostScript, SWF (Macromedia Flash), SVG
Outline graphics and fonts	PostScript, TrueType
Sound	WAV, AVI, MP3, MIDI, WMA
Page description	pdf (Adobe Portable Document Format), HTML, XML
Video	Quicktime, MPEG-2 or -4, RealVideo, WMV, DivX

There are many different standards in use for different types of data. A few of the common ones are shown in Figure 4.2. We have not included the standard representations for numerical data; those are discussed in the next chapter.

This section described the general principles that govern the input and representation of data. Next, we consider some of the most important data forms individually.

4.2 ALPHANUMERIC CHARACTER DATA

Much of the data that will be used in a computer are originally provided in human-readable form, specifically in the form of letters of the alphabet, numbers, and punctuation, whether English or some other language. The text of a word processing document, the numbers that we use as input to a calculation, the names and addresses in a database, the transaction data that constitutes a credit card purchase, the keywords, variable names, and formulas that make up a computer program, all are examples of data input that is made up of letters, numbers, and punctuation.

Most of this data is initially input to the computer through a keyboard, although alternative means, such as magnetic card stripes, document image scanning, voice-to-text translation, and bar code scanning are also used. The keyboard may be connected directly to a computer, or it may be part of a separate device, such as a video terminal, an online cash register, or even a bank ATM. The data entered as characters, number digits, and punctuation are known as **alphanumeric data**.

It is tempting to think of **numeric characters** as somehow different from other characters, since **numbers** are often processed differently from text. Also, a number may consist of more than a single digit, and you know from your programming courses that you can store and process a number in numerical form within the computer. There is no processing capability in the keyboard itself, however. Therefore, numbers must be entered into the computer just like other characters, one digit at a time. At the time of entry, the number 1234.5 consists of the alphanumeric characters "1", "2", "3", "4", ".", and "5". Any conversion to numeric form will take place within the computer itself, using software written for this purpose. For display, the number will be converted back to character form.

The conversion between character and number is also not "automatic" within the computer. There are times when we would prefer to keep the data in character form, for example, when the numbers represent a phone number or an address to be stored and processed according to text criteria. Since this choice is dependent on usage within a program, the decision is made by the programmer using rules specified within the program language being used or by a database designer specifying the data type of a particular entity. In simple languages like BASIC, for example, the programmer makes the choice by placing a $ character at the end of a variable name that is to be used to keep data in alphanumeric form. In C++ or Java, the type of variable must be declared before the variable is used. When the data variable being read is numerical, the compiler will build into the program a conversion routine that accepts numerical characters and converts them into the appropriate numerical variable value. In general, numerical characters must be converted into number form when calculations are to be performed.

Since alphanumeric data must be stored and processed within the computer in binary form, each character must be translated to a corresponding binary code representation as it enters the computer. The choice of code used is arbitrary. Since the computer does not "recognize" letters, but only binary numbers, it does not matter to the computer what code is selected.

What *does* matter is consistency. Most data output, including numbers, also exits the computer in alphanumeric form, either through printed output or as output on a video screen. Therefore, the output device must perform the same conversion in reverse. It is obviously important that the input device and the output device recognize the same code. Although it would be theoretically possible to write a program to change the input code so that a different output code would result in the desired alphanumeric output, this is rarely done in practice. Since data is frequently shared between different computers in networks, the use of a code that is standardized among many different types of computers is highly desirable.

The data is also stored using the same alphanumeric code form. Consistent use of the same code is required to allow later retrieval of the data, as well as for operations using data entered into the computer at different times, such as during merge operations.

It also matters that the programs within the computer know something about the particular data code that was used as input so that conversion of the characters that make up numbers into the numbers themselves can be done correctly, and also so that such operations as sorting can be done. It would not make a lot of sense to pick a code in which the letters of the alphabet are scrambled, for example. By choosing a code in which the value of the binary number representing a character corresponds to the placement of the character within the alphabet, we can provide programs that sort data without even knowing what the data is, just by numerically sorting the codes that correspond to each character.

Three alphanumeric codes are in common use. The three codes are known as **Unicode**, **ASCII** (which stands for American Standard Code for Information Interchange, pronounced "as-key" with a soft "s"), and **EBCDIC** (Extended Binary Coded Decimal Interchange Code, pronounced "ebb-see-dick"). EBCDIC was developed by IBM. Its use is restricted mostly to older IBM and IBM-compatible mainframe computers and terminals. The Web makes EBCDIC particularly unsuitable for current work. Nearly everyone today uses Unicode or ASCII. Still, it will be many years before EBCDIC totally disappears from the landscape.

The translation table for ASCII code is shown in Figure 4.3. The EBCDIC code is somewhat less standardized; the punctuation symbols have changed over the years. A recent EBCDIC code table is shown in Figure 4.4. The codes for each symbol are given in hexadecimal, with the most significant digit across the top and the least significant digit down the side. Both ASCII and EBCDIC codes can be stored in a byte. For example, the ASCII value for "G" is 47_{16}. The EBCDIC value for "G" is $C7_{16}$. When comparing the two tables, note that the standard ASCII code was originally defined as a 7-bit code, so there are only 128 entries in the ASCII table. EBCDIC is defined as an 8-bit code. The additional special characters in both tables are used as process and communication control characters.

The ASCII code was originally developed as a standard by the American National Standards Institute (**ANSI**). ANSI also has defined 8-bit extensions to the original ASCII codes that provide various symbols, line shapes, and accented foreign letters for the additional 128 entries not shown in the figure. Together, the 8-bit code is known as Latin-1. Latin-1 is an ISO (International Standards Organization) standard.

Both ASCII and EBCDIC have limitations that reflect their origins. The 256 code values that are available in an 8-bit word limit the number of possible characters severely.

FIGURE 4.3

ASCII Code Table

LSD↓ \ MSD→	0	1	2	3	4	5	6	7
0	NUL	DLE	space	0	@	P	`	p
1	SOH	DC1	!	1	A	Q	a	q
2	STX	DC2	"	2	B	R	b	r
3	ETX	DC3	#	3	C	S	c	s
4	EOT	DC4	$	4	D	T	d	t
5	ENQ	NAK	%	5	E	U	e	u
6	ACK	SYN	&	6	F	V	f	v
7	BEL	ETB	'	7	G	W	g	w
8	BS	CAN	(	8	H	X	h	x
9	HT	EM	)	9	I	Y	i	y
A	LF	SUB	*	:	J	Z	j	z
B	VT	ESC	+	;	K	[	k	{
C	FF	FS	,	<	L	\	l		
D	CR	GS	-	=	M	]	m	}
E	SO	RS	.	>	N	^	n	~
F	SI	US	/	?	O	_	o	DEL

Both codes provide only the Latin alphabet, Arabic numerals, and standard punctuation characters that are used in English; Latin-1 ASCII also includes a small set of accents and other special characters that extend the set to major western European cultures. Older forms of EBCDIC omit certain characters, in particular, the "[" and "]" characters that are used to represent subscripts in the C and Java programming languages, the "^" character, used as a mathematical operator in a number of languages, "{" and "}", used to enclose code blocks in many languages, and the "~" character, used for UNIX system commands and Internet and Internet URLs. These shortcomings led to the development of a new, mostly 16-bit, international standard, Unicode, which is quickly supplanting ASCII and EBCDIC for alphanumeric representation in most modern systems. Unicode supports approximately a million characters, using a combination of 8-bit, 16-bit and 32-bit words. The ASCII Latin-1 code set is a subset of Unicode, occupying the values 0–255 in the Unicode table, and therefore conversion from ASCII to Unicode is particularly simple: it is only necessary to extend the 8-bit code to 16 bits by setting the eight most significant bits to zero. Unicode to ASCII conversion is also simple, provided that the characters used are limited to the ASCII subset.

The most common form of Unicode, called UTF-16 can represent 65,536 characters directly, of which approximately forty-nine thousand are defined to represent the world's most used characters. An additional 6,400 16-bit codes are reserved permanently for private use. A more recent standard, Unicode 5.0, allows for multiple code pages; presently about one hundred thousand different characters have actually been defined. Unicode

FIGURE 4.4

An EBCDIC Code Table

	0	1	2	3	4	5	6	7
0	NUL	DLE	DS		space	&	-	
1	SOH	DC1	SOS		RSP		/	
2	STX	DC2	FS	SYN				
3	ETX	DC3	WU5	IR				
4	SEL	ENP	BYP/INP	PP				
5	HT	NL	LF	TRN				
6	RNL	BS	ETB	NBS				
7	DEL	POC	ESC	EOT				
8	GE	CAN	SA	SBS				
9	SPS	EM	SFE	IT				
A	RPT	UB5	SM/SW	RFF	¢	!	|	:
B	VT	CU1	CSP	CU3	.	$	,	#
C	FF	IFS	MFA	DC4	<	*	%	@
D	CR	IGS	ENQ	NAK	(	)	~	'
E	SO	IRS	ACK		+	;	>	=
F	SI	IUS	BEL	SUB	¦	¬	?	"

	8	9	A	B	C	D	E	F
0				∧	{	}	\	0
1	a	j	~		A	J	NSP	1
2	b	k	s		B	K	S	2
3	c	l	t		C	L	T	3
4	d	m	u		D	M	U	4
5	e	n	v		E	N	V	5
6	f	o	w		F	O	W	6
7	g	p	x		G	P	X	7
8	h	q	y		H	Q	Y	8
9	i	r	z		I	R	Z	9
A				[	5HY			
B				]				
C								
D								
E								
F								EO

FIGURE 4.5

Two-byte Unicode Assignment Table

**Code range
(in hexadecimal)**

```
0000 –⎫ 0000–00FF Latin-I (ASCII)
1000 –⎬
       │ General character alphabets: Latin, Cyrillic, Greek, Hebrew, Arabic, Thai, etc.
2000 –⎧
       │ Symbols and dingbats: punctuation, math, technical, geometric shapes, etc.
3000 –⎨ 3000–33FF Miscellaneous punctuations, symbols, and phonetics for Chinese, Japanese, and Korean
4000 –⎬ Unassigned
5000 –⎤
   •  │
   •  ⎬ 4E00–9FFF Chinese, Japanese, Korean ideographs
   •  │
A000 –⎦
       } Unassigned
B000 –⎤
C000 –⎬ AC00–D7AF Korean Hangui syllables
D000 –⎦
E000 –} Space for surrogates
F000 –⎫ E000–F8FF Private use
FC00 –} FC00–FFFF Various special characters
```

is multilingual in the most global sense. It defines codes for the characters of nearly every character-based alphabet of the world in modern use, as well as codes for a large set of ideographs for the Chinese, Japanese, and Korean languages, codes for a wide range of punctuation and symbols, codes for many obsolete and ancient languages, and various control characters. It supports composite characters and syllabic clusters. Composite characters are those made up of two or more different components, only one of which causes spacing to occur. For example, some vowels in Hebrew appear beneath a corresponding consonant. Syllabic clusters in certain languages are single characters, sometimes made up of composite components, that make up an entire syllable. The private space is intended for user-defined and software-specific characters, control characters, and symbols. Figure 4.5 shows the general code table layout for the common, 2-byte, form of Unicode.

Reflecting the pervasiveness of international communications, Unicode is gradually replacing ASCII as the alphanumeric code of choice for most systems and applications. Even IBM uses ASCII or Unicode on its smaller computers, and provides two-way Unicode-EBCDIC conversion tables for its mainframes. Unicode is the standard for use in current Windows and Linux operating systems. However, the vast amount of archival data in storage and use assures that ASCII and EBCDIC will continue to exist for some time to come.

Returning to the ASCII and EBCDIC tables, there are several interesting ideas to be gathered by looking at the tables together. First, note, not surprisingly, that the codes for particular alphanumeric characters are different in the two tables. This simply reemphasizes that, if we use an ASCII terminal for the input, the output will also be in ASCII form unless some translation took place within the computer. In other words, printing ASCII characters on an EBCDIC terminal would produce garbage.

More important, note that both ASCII and EBCDIC are designed so that the order of the letters is such that a simple numerical sort on the codes can be used within the computer to perform alphabetization, provided that the software converts mixed upper- and lowercase codes to one form or the other. The order of the codes in the representation table is known as its **collating sequence**. The collating sequence is of great importance in routine character processing, since much character processing centers on the sorting and selection of data.

Uppercase and lowercase letters, and letters and numbers, have different collating sequences in ASCII and EBCDIC. Therefore, a computer program designed to sort ASCII-generated characters will produce a different, and perhaps not desired, result when run with EBCDIC input. Particularly note that small letters *precede* capitals in EBCDIC, but the reverse is true in ASCII. The same situation arises for strings that are a mix of alphabetical characters and numbers. In ASCII the numbers collate first, in EBCDIC, last.

Both tables are divided into two classes of codes, specifically *printing* characters and *control* characters. Printing characters actually produce output on the screen or on a printer. Control characters are used to control the position of the output on the screen or paper, to cause some action to occur, such as ringing a bell or deleting a character, or to communicate status between the computer and an I/O device, such as the Control–"C" key combination, which is used on many computers to interrupt execution of a program. Except for position control characters, the control characters in the ASCII table are struck by holding down the Control key and striking a character. The code executed corresponds in table position to the position of the same alphabetic character. Thus, the code for SOH is generated by the Control-"A" key combination and SUB by the Control-"Z" key combination. Looking at the ASCII and EBCDIC tables can you determine what **control codes** are generated by the tab key? An explanation of each control character in the ASCII table is shown in Figure 4.6. Many of the names and descriptions of codes in this table reflect the use of these codes for data communications. There are also additional control codes in EBCDIC that are specific to IBM mainframes, but we won't define them here.

Unless the application program that is processing the text reformats or modifies the data in some way, textual data is normally stored as a string of characters, including alphanumeric characters, spaces, tabs, carriage returns, plus other control characters and escape sequences that are relevant to the text. Some application programs, particularly word processors, add their own special character sequences for formatting the text.

In Unicode, each UTF-16 alphanumeric character can be stored in two bytes, thus, half the number of bytes in a pure text file (one with no images) is a good approximation of the number of characters in the text. Similarly, the number of available bytes also defines the capacity of a device to store textual and numerical data. Only a small percentage of the storage space is needed to keep track of information about the various files; almost all the space is thus available for the text itself. Thus, a 1 GB flash drive will hold about sixty million characters (including spaces—note that spaces are also characters, of course!). If

FIGURE 4.6

Control Code Definitions [STAL96]

NUL	(Null) No character; used to fill space	**DLE**	(Data Link Escape) Similar to escape, but used to change meaning of data control characters; used to permit sending of data characters with any bit combination
SOH	(Start of Heading) Indicates start of a header used during transmission		
STX	(Start of Text) Indicates start of text during transmission	**DC1,DC2, DC3, DC4**	(Device Controls) Used for the control of devices or special terminal features
ETX	(End of Text) Similar to above	**NAK**	(Negative Acknowledgment) Opposite of ACK
EOT	(End of Transmission)		
ENQ	(Enquiry) A request for response from a remote station; the response is usually an identification	**SYN**	(Synchronous) Used to synchronize a synchronous transmission system
ACK	(Acknowledge) A character sent by a receiving device as an affirmative response to a query by a sender	**STB**	(End of Transmission Block) Indicates end of a block of transmitted data
		CAN	(Cancel) Cancel previous data
BEL	(Bell) Rings a bell	**EM**	(End of Medium) Indicates the physical end of a medium such as tape
BS	(Backspace)		
HT	(Horizontal Tab)	**SUB**	(Substitute) Substitute a character for one sent in error
LF	(Line Feed)		
VT	(Vertical Tab)	**ESC**	(Escape) Provides extensions to the code by changing the meaning of a specified number of contiguous following characters
FF	(Form Feed) Moves cursor to the starting position of the next page, form, or screen		
CR	(Carriage return)	**FS, GS, RS, US**	(File, group, record, and united separators) Used in optional way by systems to provide separations within a data set
SO	(Shift Out) Shift to an alternative character set until SI is encountered		
SI	(Shift In) see above	**DEL**	(Delete) Delete current character

you assume that a page has about fifty rows of sixty characters, then the flash drive can hold almost twenty thousand pages of text or numbers.

In reality, the flash drive will probably hold less because most modern word processors can combine text with graphics, page layout, font selection, and other features. And it probably has a YouTube video or two on there, as well. Graphics and video, in particular, consume a lot of disk space. Nonetheless, this book, graphics and all, fits comfortably on a single 1 GB flash drive.

Keyboard Input

Most alphanumeric data in the computer results from keyboard input, although alternative forms of data input can be used. Operation of a keyboard is quite simple and straightforward: when a key is struck on the keyboard, the circuitry in the keyboard generates a binary code, called a **scan code**. When the key is released, a different scan code is generated. There are two different scan codes for every key on the keyboard. The scan codes are converted to the appropriate Unicode, ASCII, or EBCDIC codes by software within the terminal or personal computer to which the keyboard is connected. The advantage of software conversion is

FIGURE 4.7

Keyboard Operation

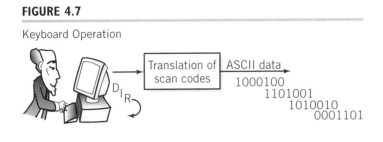

that the use of the keyboard can be easily changed to correspond to different languages or keyboard layouts. The use of separate scan codes for key press and release functions allows the system to detect and process multiple key combinations, such as those used by the shift and control keys.

The keyboard operation is shown in Figure 4.7. In the figure, the user has typed the three letters "D," "I," "R," followed by the carriage return character. The computer translates the four scan codes to ASCII binary codes 1000100, 1001001, 1010010, 0001101, or their Unicode equivalents. Nonprinting characters, such as Control characters, are treated identically to Printing characters. To the computer, keyboard input is treated simply as a **stream** of text and other characters, one character after another, in the sequence typed. Note that the carriage return character is part of the stream.

The software in most computer systems echoes printable keyboard input characters directly back to the display screen, to allow the user to verify that the input has been typed correctly. Since the display circuitry and software recognizes the same character code set as the input, the characters are correctly echoed on the screen. In theory, a system could accept Unicode input from a keyboard and produce EBCDIC output to a display screen, using software to convert from one code set to the other. In practice, this is almost never done.

Alternative Sources of Alphanumeric Input

OPTICAL CHARACTER RECOGNITION   Alphanumeric data may also be entered into a computer using other forms of input. One popular alternative is to scan a page of text with an image scanner and to convert the image into alphanumeric data form using **optical character recognition (OCR)** software. Early OCR software required the use of special typefaces for the scanned image and produced a lot of errors. The amount of proofreading required often nullified any advantage to using the scanner. As OCR software continues to improve, the use of scanners to read typed text directly from the page will undoubtedly increase as a source of alphanumeric data input.

A variation on OCR is also used to read specially encoded characters, such as those printed magnetically on checks. Another variation, handwriting recognition, is used to identify characters entered as input to a graphics tablet pad or the touch screen of a tablet PC, personal digital assistant, or cell phone. This technology continues to improve, but is still limited to small quantities of data, carefully printed. Attempts to extend character recognition to scanned documents and to characters written in cursory script have been largely unsuccessful to date.

BAR CODE READERS   Another alternative form of data input is the bar code reader. Bar code input is practical and efficient for many business applications that require fast, accurate, and repetitive input with minimum employee training. You are probably most familiar with its use at grocery checkout counters, but many organizations use bar codes, particularly for inventory control and order filling.

FIGURE 4.8

UPC Bar Code

Bar codes represent alphanumeric data. The UPC bar code in Figure 4.8, for example, translates to the alphanumeric value 780471 108801 90000. Bar codes are read optically using a device called a wand that converts a visual scan of the code into electrical binary signals that a bar code translation module can read. The module translates the binary input into a sequence of number codes, one code per digit, that can then be input into the computer. The process is essentially similar to those already discussed. The code is usually then translated to Unicode or ASCII.

MAGNETIC STRIPE READERS Magnetic stripe readers are used to read alphanumeric data from credit cards and other similar devices. The technology used is very similar to that used for magnetic tape.

RFID INPUT **RFID** (Radio Frequency IDentification) is an inexpensive technology that can be used to store and transmit data to computers. RFID technology can be embedded in RFID tags or "smart cards" or even implanted in humans or animals. One familiar type of RFID tag is shown in Figure 4.9. An RFID tag can store anywhere from a few kilobytes to many megabytes of data. Using radio waves, RFID tags can communicate with a nearby transmitter/receiver that captures and passes the data as input to a computer for processing. Most RFID data is alphanumeric, although it is also possible with some RFID systems to provide graphical images, photographs, and even video. RFID technology is used for a wide variety of applications, including store inventory, theft prevention, library book and grocery checkout, car key verification, passport identification, cargo tracking, automobile toll and public transportation fare collection, golf ball tracking (!), animal identification, implanted human medical record storage, and much more.

VOICE INPUT It is currently possible and practical to digitize audio for use as input data. As we discuss in Section 4.4, most digitized audio data is simply stored for later output or is processed in ways that modify the sound of the data. The technology necessary

FIGURE 4.9

An RFID tag used at WalMart

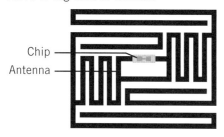

Chip
Antenna

to interpret audio data as voice input and to translate the data into alphanumeric form is still relatively primitive. The translation process requires the conversion of voice data into sound patterns known as **phonemes**. Each phoneme in a particular language represents one or more possible groupings of letters in that language. The groupings must then be matched and manipulated and combined to form words and sentences. Pronunciation rules, grammar rules, and a dictionary aid in the process. The understanding of sentence context is also necessary to correctly identify words such as to, too, or two. As you can see, the task is a daunting one! Progress is being made, however, and it is expected that voice input will be a major source of alphanumeric input in the foreseeable future.

4.3 IMAGE DATA

Although alphanumeric data was long the traditional medium of business, improved computer technology and the growth of the Web have elevated the importance of images in the business computing environment. Photographs can be stored within the computer to provide rapid identification of employees. Drawings can be generated rapidly and accurately using tools that range from simple drawing packages to sophisticated CAD/CAM systems. Charts and graphs provide easily understood representations of business data and trends. Presentations and reports contain images and video for impact. Multimedia of all kinds is central to the success of the Web.

Images come in many different shapes, sizes, textures, colors, and shadings. Different processing requirements require different forms for image data. All these differences make it difficult to define a single universal format that can be used for images in the way that the standard alphanumeric codes are used for text. Instead, the image will be formatted according to processing, display, application, storage, communication, and user requirements.

Images used within the computer fall into two distinct categories. Different computer representations, processing techniques, and tools are used for each category:

- Images such as photographs and paintings that are characterized by continuous variations in shading, color, shape, and texture. Images within this category may be entered into the computer using an image scanner, digital camera, or video camera frame grabber. They may also be produced within the computer using a paint program. To maintain and reproduce the detail of these images, it is necessary to represent and store each individual point within the image. We will refer to such images as **bitmap images**. Sometimes, they are called **raster images** because of the way the image is displayed. (See Figure 10.16, page 324). The GIF and JPEG formats commonly used on the Web are both examples of bitmap image formats.

- Images that are made up of graphical shapes such as lines and curves that can be defined geometrically. The shapes themselves may be quite complex. Many computer experts refer to these shapes as **graphical objects**. For these images, it is sufficient to store geometrical information about each object and the relative position of each object in the image. We will refer to these images as **object images**. They are also known, somewhat incorrectly, as **vector images**, because the image is often (but not always) made up of straight-line segments called vectors. Object images are normally produced within the computer using some sort of drawing or design package. They may also result from other types of processing, for example, as data plots or graphs representing the data in a spreadsheet. More rarely, they may occur as the result of the translation by special software of scanned bitmap images that are simple enough to reduce to object form.

  Most object image formats are proprietary. However, W3C, the international consortium that oversees the Web, has defined a standard, SVG (scalable vector graphics), based on XML Web description language tags. Macromedia Flash is also in popular use.

With only rare exceptions[1], the nature of display technology make it much more convenient and cost effective to display and print all images as bitmaps. Object images are converted to bitmap for display. Looking at an image, it can sometimes be difficult to determine whether the original form is bitmap or object. It is possible, for example, to describe subtle gradations of color within an image geometrically. The processing required to create movement in computer-animated images may dictate the use of object images, even if the objects themselves are very complex. The type of image representation is often chosen on the basis of the computer processing to be performed on the image. The movies *Shrek* and *Toy Story* are amazing examples of the possibilities of object images. (See Figure 4.14, for example.)

Sometimes, both types of image data occur within the same image. It is always possible to store graphical objects in a bitmap format, but it is often desirable in such cases to maintain each type of image separately. Most object image representations provide for the inclusion of bitmap images within the representation.

Bitmap Images

Most images—photographs, graphical images and the like—are described most easily using a bitmap image format. The basic principle for representing an image as a digital bitmap is simple. A rectangular image is divided into rows and columns, as shown in Figure 4.10. The junction of each row and column is a point (actually a small area) in the image known as a **pixel**, for pi[x]cture *el*ement. Corresponding to each pixel is a set of one or more binary numerical values that define the visual characteristics of that point.

FIGURE 4.10

A 16 × 8 Bitmap Image Format

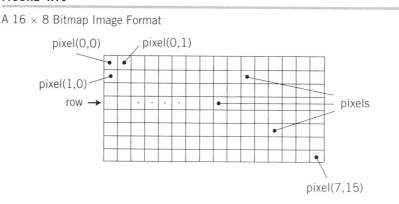

pixels stored in order p(0,0), p(0,1),... p(0,15), p(1,0),... p(1,15),... p(7,15)

---

[1]The exceptions are the circular scan screens used for radar display and ink plotters used for architectural and engineering drawings.

FIGURE 4.11

Image Pixel Data

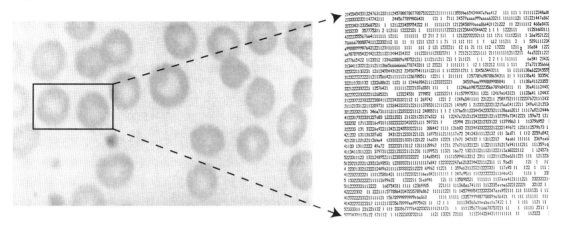

Most commonly, color and color intensity are the primary characteristics of interest, but secondary characteristics such as transparency may also be present. The meaning and scales for these values are defined within the image metadata that is included with the image, along with the number of rows and columns, identification of the bitmap format in use, and other relevant information about the image.

A pixel aspect ratio may also be included so that display of the image may be adjusted if the pixel is rectangular rather than square. The specific metadata included with an image is part of the definition for a particular bitmap format.

Pixel data is normally stored from top to bottom, one row at a time, starting from pixel(0, 0), the top, leftmost pixel, to pixel($n_{row}-1$, $n_{col}-1$), representing the pixel at the bottom right corner of the image. (For quirky reasons, this image would be known as a n_{col} × n_{row} image, instead of the other way around.) Because the representation is so similar to the way in which television images are created, this layout is called a raster, and the presentation of pixels as input or output, one pixel at a time, in order, is called a raster scan. The actual pixel coordinates, pixel(row,column), do not need to be stored with their values, because the pixels are stored in order, and the number of rows and columns is known.

The actual data value representing a pixel could be as simple as one bit, for an image that is black and white (0 for black, 1 for white, for example) or quite complex. Each pixel in a high-quality color image, for example, might consist of many bytes of data: a byte for red, a byte for green, and a byte for blue, with additional bytes for other characteristics such as transparency and color correction.

As a simple example, look at the image shown in Figure 4.11. Each point in the photograph on the left is represented by a 4-bit code corresponding to one of sixteen gray levels. For this image, hexadecimal F represents black, and hexadecimal 0 represents white. The representation of the image shown on the right indicates the corresponding values for each pixel.

The storage and processing of bitmap images frequently requires a large amount of memory, and the processing of large arrays of data. A single color picture containing 768 rows of 1024 pixels each, (i.e., a 1024 × 768 image) with a separate byte to store each of three colors for each pixel, would require nearly 2.4 megabytes of storage. An alternative representation method that is useful for display purposes when the number of different colors is small reduces memory requirements by storing a code for each pixel, rather than the actual color values. The code for each pixel is translated into actual color values using a color translation table known as a **palette** that is stored as part of the image metadata. This method is discussed in Chapter 10. Data compression may also be used to reduce storage and data transmission requirements.

The image represented within the computer is really only an approximation to the original image, since the original image presents a continual range of intensity, and perhaps also of color. The faithfulness of the computer representation depends on the size of the pixels and the number of levels representing each pixel. Reducing the size of each pixel improves the **resolution**, or detail level, of the representation by increasing the number of pixels per inch used to represent a given area of the image. It also reduces the "stepping" effects seen on diagonal lines. Increasing the range of values available to describe each pixel increases the number of different gray levels or colors available, which improves the overall accuracy of the colors or gray tones in the image. The trade-off, of course, is in storage requirements and processing and transmission time.

Bitmap representations are particularly useful when there is a great amount of detail within an image, and for which the processing requirements are fairly simple. Typical processing on bitmap images includes storage and display, cutting and pasting of pieces of the image, and simple transformations of the image such as brightness and contrast changes, changing a dimension, or color alterations. Most bitmap image processing involves little or no direct processing of the objects illustrated within the image.

EXAMPLE

As an example of a bitmap image storage format, consider the popular **Graphics Interchange Format (GIF)**, method of storing images. GIF was first developed by CompuServe in 1987 as a proprietary format that would allow users of the online service to store and exchange bitmap images on a variety of different computing platforms. A second, more flexible, form of GIF was released in 1989. The later version, GIF89a, also allows a series of GIF images to be displayed sequentially at fixed time intervals to created "animated GIF images." The GIF format is used extensively on the Web.

GIF assumes the existence of a rectangular "screen" upon which is located one or more rectangular images of possibly different sizes. Areas not covered with images are painted with a background color. Figure 4.12 illustrates the layout of the screen and its images. The format divides the picture information and data into a number of blocks, each of which describes different aspects of the image. The first block, called the header block, identifies the file as a GIF file and specifies the version of GIF that is being used.

Following the header block is a logical screen-descriptor block, which identifies the width and height of the screen, describes an optional color table for the images on the screen (the palette), indicates the number of bits per color available, identifies the background screen color, and specifies the pixel aspect ratio.

Each image within the screen is then stored in its own block, headed by an image-descriptor block. The image-descriptor block identifies the size and position of the image on the screen, and also allows for a palette specific to the particular image, if desired. The block also contains information that makes it possible to display individual

FIGURE 4.12

GIF Screen Layout

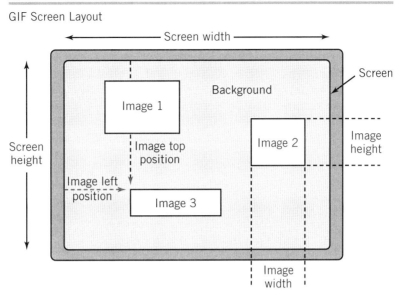

FIGURE 4.13

GIF File Format Layout

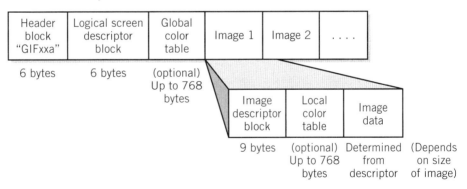

images at different resolutions. The actual pixel data for the image follows. The pixel data is compressed, using an algorithm called LZW. The basic GIF file format layout is shown in Figure 4.13.

Even though we have simplified the description, you can see that a graphical data format can be quite complex. The complexity is required to provide all the information that will allow the use of the image on a variety of different equipment.

There are a number of alternatives to the GIF format. In particular, the GIF format is limited to 256 colors, which is sometimes insufficient to display the details of a painting or photograph, for example. A popular alternative, **JPEG format** (Joint Photographers Expert Group), addresses this concern by allowing more than sixteen million colors to be represented and displayed. JPEG employs a lossy compression algorithm to reduce the amount of data stored and transmitted, but the algorithm used reduces image resolution under certain circumstances, particularly for sharp edges and lines. This makes JPEG more suitable for the representation of highly detailed photographs and paintings, but GIF is preferable for line drawings and simple images. Other formats include TIFF, which is popular on Macintosh platforms, BMP, a Windows format, and PCX, a format originally designed for use with PC Paintbrush software. PNG is a recent format that eliminates many GIF and JPEG shortcomings. It is intended to replace GIF and JPEG for many Internet applications.

Object Images

When an image is made up of geometrically definable shapes, it can be manipulated efficiently, with great flexibility, and stored in a compact form. Although it might seem that such images are rare, this turns out not to be the case.

Object images are made up of simple elements like straight lines, curved lines (known as Bezier curves), circles and arcs of circles, ovals, and the like. Each of these elements can be defined mathematically by a small number of parameters. For example, a circle requires only three parameters, specifically, the X and Y coordinates locating the circle in the image, plus the radius of the circle. A straight line needs the X and Y coordinates of its end points, or alternatively, by its starting point, length, and direction. And so on.

Because objects are defined mathematically, they can be easily moved around, scaled, and rotated without losing their shape and identity. For example, an oval can be built from a circle simply by scaling the horizontal and vertical dimensions differently. Closed objects can be shaded and filled with patterns of color, also described mathematically. Object elements can be combined or connected together to form more complex elements, and then those elements can also be manipulated and combined. You might be surprised to learn that Shrek, the image in Figure 4.14, is an example of an object image.

Object images have many advantages over bitmap images. They require far less storage space. They can be manipulated easily, without losing their identity. Note, in contrast, that if a bitmap image is reduced in size and reenlarged, the detail of the image is permanently lost. When such a process is applied to a bitmapped straight line,

FIGURE 4.14

An Object Image

Dreamworks LLC/Photofest.

the result is "jaggies." Conversely, images such as photographs and paintings cannot be represented as object images at all and must be represented as bitmaps.

Because regular printers and display screens produce their images line by line, from the top to the bottom of the screen or paper, object images also cannot be displayed or printed directly, except on plotters. Instead, they must be converted to bitmap images for display and printing. This conversion can be performed within the computer, or may be passed on to an output device that has the capability to perform the conversion. A PostScript printer is an example of such a device. To display a line on a screen, for example, the program would calculate each of the pixels on the screen that the line passes through, and mark them for display. This is a simple calculation for a computer to perform. If the line is moved or resized, it is only necessary to perform the calculation again to display the new image.

EXAMPLE

The **PostScript page description language** is an example of a format that can be used to store, transmit, display, and print object images. A page description is a list of procedures and statements that describe each of the objects on a page. PostScript embeds page descriptions within a programming language. Thus, an image consists of a program written in the PostScript language.

The programming language is stored in ASCII or Unicode text form. Thus, PostScript files can be stored and transmitted as any other text file. An interpreter program in the computer or output device reads the PostScript language statements and uses them to create pages that can then be printed or displayed. The interpreter produces an image that is the same, regardless of the device it is displayed or printed on. Compensation for differences in device resolution and pixel shape is built into the interpreter.

PostScript provides a large library of functions that facilitate every aspect of an object-based image. There are functions that draw straight lines, Bezier curves, and arcs of a circle, functions that join simple objects into more complex ones, translate an object to a different location on the page, scale or distort an object, rotate an object, and create the mirror image of an object, and functions that fill an object with a pattern, or adjust the width and color of a line. There are methods for building and calling procedures, and IF-THEN-ELSE and loop programming structures. The list goes on and on.

A simple program that draws a pair of shaded and concentric circles within a rectangle in the middle of an $8\,1/2 \times 11$-inch page is shown in Figure 4.15. This example shows a number of features of the language. The page is laid out as an X, Y grid, with the origin at the lower left corner. Each unit in the grid is 1/72 of an inch, which corresponds to 1 point in publishing. Each line contains a function, with a number of parameters that provide the specific details for the function. The parameters precede the function call. Text following the % symbols are comments.

The first line contains a *translate* function that moves the X, Y origin to the center of the page. The parameters for this function, 288 and 396, represent the X and Y distances moved in points. (Note that $288/72 = 4$ inches in X and $396/72 = 5$ inches in Y.) Each circle is created with an *arc* function. The parameters for the arc function are X origin and Y origin for the arc, radius, and starting and finishing angle in degrees. (0 to 360 produces a full circle.) You should be able to follow the remainder of the program on your own. Note that the statements are interpreted in sequence: the second, gray circle is layered on top of the first.

FIGURE 4.15

A PostScript Program

```
288 396 translate    % move origin to center of page
0 0 144 0 360 arc    % define 2" radius black circle
fill

0.5 setgray          % define 1" radius gray circle
0 0 72 0 360 arc
fill

0 setgray            % reset color to black
-216 -180 moveto     % start at lower left corner
0 360 rmoveto        % and define rectangle
432 0 rmoveto        % ...one line at a time
0 -360 rmoveto
closepath            % completes rectangle
stroke               % draw outline instead of fill

showpage             % produce the image
```

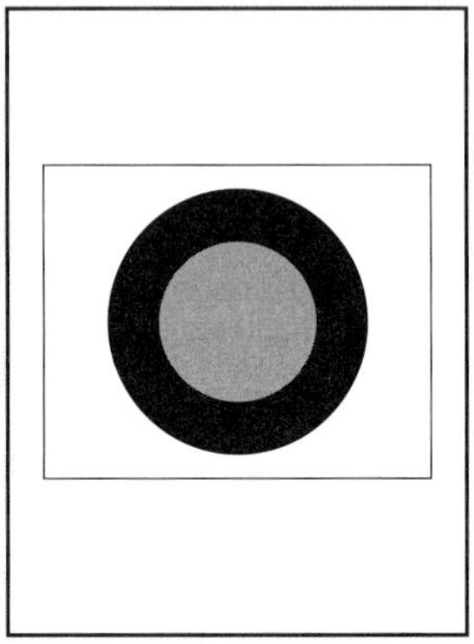

FIGURE 4.16

Another PostScript Program

```
% procedure to draw pie slice
%arguments graylevel, start angle, finish angle
/wedge {
     0 0 moveto
     setgray
     /angle1 exch def
     /angle2 exch def
     0 0 144 angle1 angle2 arc
     0 0 lineto
     closepath } def

%set up text font for printing
/Helvetica-Bold findfont
     16 scalefont
      setfont

.4 72 108 wedge fill % 108-72 = 36 = .1 circle
.8 108 360 wedge fill % 70%
% print wedge in three parts
32 12 translate
0 0 72 wedge fill
gsave
-8 8 translate
1 0 72 wedge fill
0 setgray stroke
grestore
```

```
% add text to drawing
0 setgray
144 144 moveto
(baseball cards) show
-30 200 (cash) show
-216 108 (stocks) show
32 scalefont
(Personal Assets) show

showpage
```

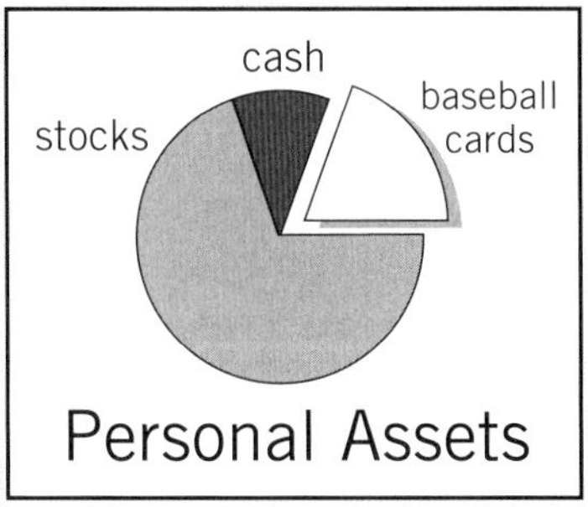

Arguably, the most important feature in PostScript is the inclusion of scalable **font** support for the display of text. Font outline objects are specified in the same way as other objects. Each font contains an object for each printable character in the extended ASCII character set. PostScript includes objects for thirty-five standard fonts representing eight font families, plus two symbol fonts, and others can be added. Unicode fonts are also available. Fonts can be manipulated like other objects. Text and graphics can be intermixed in an image. The graphic display of text is considered further in the next subsection.

Figure 4.16 shows another, more complicated, example of a PostScript program. This one presents a pie chart with an expanded slice, and labels. The expanded slice includes a shadow to improve its appearance. Each slice of the pie is drawn using a procedure called *wedge*. The shadow is drawn by drawing the wedge three times, once in black, then moved a bit and drawn in white and as an outline.

PostScript is a format for storing images in object form. Nonetheless, there are occasions when it is necessary to embed a bitmap image into what is primarily an object-based image. PostScript provides this capability. It even provides the ability to crop, enlarge, shrink, translate, and rotate the embedded bitmap images, within the limits of the bitmap format, of course.

Representing Characters as Images

The representation of character-based data in a typical modern, graphically based systems presents an additional challenge. In graphically based systems it is necessary to distinguish between characters and the object image-based representations of characters, known as **glyphs**. Individual glyphs are based on a particular character in a particular font. In some cases, a glyph may also depend on neighboring characters. Should the data be represented and stored as characters or as glyphs? The answer depends on what the text is to be used for. Most text is processed and stored primarily for its content. A typical word processor, for example, stores text as character data, in Unicode format; fonts are embedded into the text file using special sequences of characters stored with the data, often in a proprietary file format supported by the particular application software. Conversion of the character data to glyphs for presentation is known as **rendering** and is performed by a **rendering engine** program. The glyphs are then converted to bitmap graphics for presentation according to the characteristics of the display device or printer. For the rare occasion where the text is actually embedded within an image, the glyphs that represent the characters may be combined, stored, and manipulated as an object image.

Video Images

Although GIF images are adequate for simple animation loops, there are a number of additional considerations for the storage, transmission, and display of true video. The most important consideration is the massive amount of data created by a video application. A video camera producing full screen 1024×768 pixel true-color images at a frame rate of thirty frames per second, for example, will generate 1024 pixels $\times$ 768 pixels $\times$ 3 bytes of color/image $\times$ 30 frames per second = 70.8 megabytes of data per second! A one-minute film clip would consume 4.25 gigabytes of storage.

There are a number of possible solutions: reduce the size of the image, limit the number of colors, or reduce the frame rate. It is also possible, or, more likely, necessary to compress the video data. Each of these options has obvious drawbacks. The solution chosen also depends on the nature of the method used to make the video available to the user. One option is to present the video as a file on the system. The video file is either accessed from a removable medium, such as a DVD-ROM, or downloaded and stored on the system.

Alternatively, the video may be made available to the system in real time. The latter technique is called **streaming video**. Streaming video is normally downloaded continuously from a Web server or network server. Video conferencing is an example of a streaming video application. The requirements for streaming video are much more stringent than for locally stored video, because the amount of data that can be downloaded per unit time is limited by the capability of the network connection. Furthermore, the processor must be able to uncompress and decode the data fast enough to keep up with the incoming data stream. Generally speaking, streaming video is of lower display quality than video that is available locally.

Various mixes of these solutions are used. There are a number of proprietary formats in use, including RealPlayer from Real.com, Windows Media Format from Microsoft, and Flash Video from Macromedia. The output, although less than ideal, is adequate for many applications.

When the video data is local to the system, it is possible to generate and display high-quality video using sophisticated data compression techniques, but the processing required for generation of the compressed data is beyond the capabilities of most computer systems and users at the present time. The **MPEG-2** and **MPEG-4** formats store real-time video that produces movie quality images, with the video data compressed to 30–60 megabytes or less of data per minute, even for high definition images. Even the re-creation of the original images for display requires substantial computing power. Although high-end modern personal computer systems have adequate processing power to decode high-quality video data, many computer systems provide additional hardware support for the reading, decoding, and displaying of real-time video data from DVDs. Direct transmission of high-quality digital video data is still confined to very high-speed networks and satellite systems.

Image and Video Input

Of course the obvious input source for images and video these days is the Web. Still, those images and videos had to originate somewhere, so we'll take a brief look at the various means used to input them and convert them to the digital formats that we use. Three classes of devices provide most of the imaging capability that we use.

IMAGE SCANNING   One common way to input image data is with an image scanner. Data from an image scanner takes the form of a bitmap that represents some sort of image—a graphic drawing, a photograph, magnetically inked numbers on a check, perhaps even a document of printed text. The scanner electronically moves over the image, converting the image row by row into a stream of binary numbers, each representing a pixel. Software in the computer then converts this raw data into one of the standard bitmap data formats in use, adding appropriate metadata, applying data compression when desired, reconfiguring the data as necessary, and storing the data as a file that is then available for use.

DIGITAL CAMERAS AND VIDEO CAPTURE DEVICES Digital cameras and video cameras can be used to capture bitmap images and video. An electronic raster scan mechanism is used to collect light and digitize the data from the lens. Most modern cameras collect the data in a simple, vendor-specific so-called raw format. Because the amount of data generated for a single image in a modern camera is large (a common value is 8.1 megapixels $\times$ 3 or more bytes per pixel for example), the camera usually contains software to convert the raw data to a compressed JPEG or MPEG image for storage and transfer to a computer. Some cameras allow the direct transfer of raw images to a computer for more precise processing control.

GRAPHICAL INPUT USING POINTING DEVICES Mice, pens, and other pointing devices can be used in conjunction with drawing or painting programs to input graphical data. The input from most of these devices is a pair of binary numbers representing either X and Y coordinates on the screen or relative movements in X and Y directions. Some drawing tablets also provide a measure of the pressure applied to the drawing pen. The pointing device is an input device. The appearance of a cursor on the output screen results from a calculation within the program that detects the current set of coordinates. The program then outputs a cursor as part of the screen image bitmap at the appropriate location on the screen. Internally, the image drawn will depend on the application program being used. Paint packages provide tools that use the pointing device to create "paintings" in a bitmap image form. Drawing packages provide tools that create and manipulate objects. In this case, the result is an object image.

4.4 AUDIO DATA

Sound has become an important component in modern computer applications. Sound is used as an instructional tool, as an element of multimedia presentations, to signal events within the computer, and to enhance the enjoyment of games. Sound can be stored in digital form on CD-ROMs and other media and made available to accompany a film clip, illustrate the nuances of a symphony, or reproduce the roar of a lion. Sound can be manipulated in the computer to compose music and to create the sounds of different musical instruments, even an entire orchestra.

Sound is normally digitized from an audio source, such as a microphone or amplifier, although it is possible to purchase instrumentation that connects the computer directly to a musical keyboard and synthesizer. For most users, the sound was previously digitized and provided on a CD-ROM or downloaded from a Web site.

Since the original sound wave is analog in nature, it is necessary to convert it to digital form for use in the computer. The technique used is the same as that used for music CDs and many other types of analog waveforms. The analog waveform is sampled electronically at regular time intervals. Each time a sample is taken, the amplitude of the sample is measured by an electronic circuit that converts the analog value to a binary equivalent. The circuit that performs this function is known as an **A-to-D converter**. The largest possible sample, which represents the positive peak of the loudest possible sound, is set to the maximum positive binary number being used, and the most negative peak is set to the largest negative number. Binary 0 falls in the middle. The amplitude scale is divided uniformly between the two limits. The sampling rate is chosen to be high enough to capture every nuance in the signal being converted. For audio signals, the sampling rate is normally around 50 kilohertz, or fifty thousand times a second. The basic technique is illustrated in Figure 4.17. A typical audio signal is shown in the upper diagram. A portion of the signal is shown in expanded form below. In this diagram, the signal is allowed to fall between −64 and 64. Although we haven't discussed the representation of negative numbers yet, the consecutive values for the signal in this diagram will be the binary equivalents to −22, −7, +26, 52, 49, and 2. The A-to-D conversion method is discussed more thoroughly in Chapter 14.

Within the computer, most programs would probably treat this data as a one-dimensional array of integers. Like graphics images, however, it is necessary to maintain, store, and transmit metadata *about* the waveform, in addition to the waveform itself. To process and reproduce the waveform, a program would have to know the maximum possible amplitude, the sampling rate, and the total number of samples, at the very least. If several waveforms are stored together, the system would have to identify each individual waveform somehow and establish the relationships between the different waveforms. Are the waveforms played together, for example, or one right after another?

As you might expect, there are a number of different file formats for storing audio waveforms, each with its own features, advantages, and disadvantages. The .*MOD* format, for example, is used primarily to store samples of sound that will be manipulated and combined to produce a new sound. A .MOD file might store a sample of a piano tone.

FIGURE 4.17

Digitizing an Audio Waveform

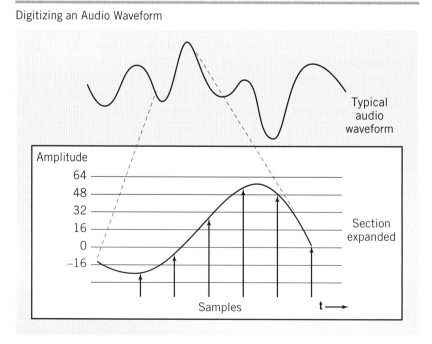

Software could then manipulate the sample to reproduce all the different keys on the keyboard, it could alter the loudness of each tone, and it could combine them to synthesize the piano lines in a piece of music. Other instruments could be synthesized similarly. The *MIDI* format is used to coordinate the sounds and signals between a computer and connected musical instruments, particularly keyboards. MIDI software can "read" the keyboard and can also reproduce the sounds. The *.VOC* format is a general sound format that includes special features such as markers within the file that can be used to repeat (loop) a block or synchronize the different components of a multimedia presentation. Block looping can extend a sound by repeating it over and over again. The *.WAV* format is a general-purpose format used primarily to store and reproduce snippets of sound. *MP3* is a derivative of the MPEG-2 specification for the transmission and storage of music. It has gained popularity because of the large numbers of MP3-coded recordings posted on the Web and because of the availability of low-cost portable devices that can download, store, decode, and reproduce MP3 data.

Like video, audio data can also be generated and stored locally or streamed from a network or website. The data transmission and processing requirements for audio are much less stringent than those for video, however. Audio is routinely streamed from the Web. There are numerous websites broadcasting audio from radio stations and other sources, and streaming audio is also used for Internet telephony.

EXAMPLE

The .WAV format was designed by Microsoft as part of its multimedia specification. The format supports 8- or 16-bit sound samples, sampled at 11.025 KHz, 22.05 KHz, or 44.1 KHz in mono or stereo. The .WAV format is very simple and does not provide support for a lot of features, such as the looping of sound blocks .WAV data is not compressed.

The format consists of a general header that identifies a "chunk" of data and specifies the length of a data block within the chunk. The header is followed by the data block. The general header is used for a number of different multimedia data types.

The layout of a .WAV file is shown in Figure 4.18. The data block is itself broken into three parts. First, a 4-byte header identifies a sound file with the ASCII word "WAVE." A format chunk follows. This chunk contains such information as the method used to digitize the sound, the sampling rate in samples per second, the data transfer rate in average number of bytes per second, the number of bits per sample, and whether the sound is recorded in mono or stereo. The actual data follows.

FIGURE 4.18

.WAV Sound Format

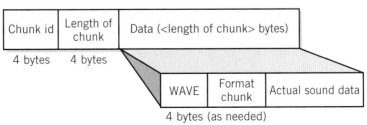

If you have a personal computer that runs Windows and supports sound, you will probably find .WAV files in one of your Windows directories. Look for the file *tada.wav*, which holds the brief trumpet fanfare that sounds when Windows is started.

EXAMPLE

MP3 is the predominant digital audio data format for the storage and transmission of music. It is characterized by reasonable audio quality and small file size. MP3 uses a number of different tactics and options to achieve its small file sizes. These include options for different audio sampling rates, fixed or variable bit rates, and a wide range of bit rates that represent different levels of compression. The bit rate, measured in Kbits/second is, of course, directly related to the size of the file, however lower bit rates result in lower audio quality. The options chosen are made by the creator of the file during the encoding process, based on the trade-off between tolerable audio quality versus transmission rate or file size. An MP3 player must be capable of correctly decoding and playing any of the format variations specified in the MP3 standard.

The primary contributor to the small MP3 file size is the use of psychoacoustic lossy compression. The size of an MP3 file is typically about 1/10th the size of an equivalent uncompressed .WAV file. Psychoacoustic compression is based on the assumption that there are sounds that a listener cannot hear or will not notice, which can then be eliminated. As an example, a soft sound in the background is not usually noticeable against a loud foreground sound. The level of compression depends on the tolerable level of sound quality, but also on the nature of the audio being compressed. A typical MP3 file samples the audio data 44,100 times per second, which is the same as the data rate used on audio CDs, and presents the data to the listener at a rate of either 128 or 192 Kb/second.

Figure 4.19 shows the structure of an MP3 file. The file consists of an optional ID field that contains such information as song title and artist, followed by multiple data frames. Each frame has a 32-byte header that describes the frame data, followed by an optional

FIGURE 4.19

MP3 Audio Data Format

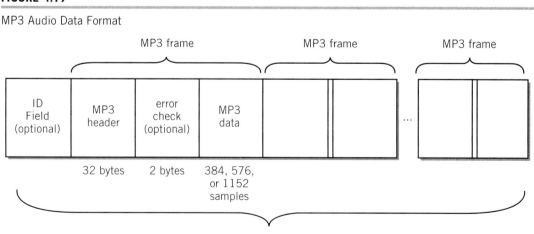

MP3 file

2-byte error-checking code, followed by the data itself. The header contains 2 bytes of synchronization and MP3 version data followed by the bit rate, the audio sample rate, the type of data (for example, stereo or monaural audio), copy protection, and other information. The MP3 standard requires that each frame contains 384, 576, or 1152 audio samples of data. Note that this format allows the bit rate to vary for each frame, allowing for more efficient compression, but more difficult encoding procedures.

4.5 DATA COMPRESSION

The volume of multimedia data, particularly video, but also sound and even high resolution still images, often makes it impossible or impractical to store, transmit, and manipulate the data in its normal form. Instead it is desirable or, in some cases, necessary to compress the data. This is particularly true for video clips, real-time streaming video with sound, lengthy sound clips, and images that are to be transmitted across the Internet through modem connections. (It is also true of large data and program files of any type.)

There are many different data compression algorithms, but all fall into one of two categories, **lossless** or **lossy**. A lossless algorithm compresses the data in such a way that the application of a matching inverse algorithm restores the compressed data exactly to its original form. Lossy data compression algorithms operate on the assumption that the user can accept a certain amount of data degradation as a trade-off for the savings in a critical resource such as storage requirements or data transmission time. Of course, only lossless data compression is acceptable for files where the original data must be retained, including text files, program files and numerical data files, but lossy data compression is frequently acceptable in multimedia applications. In most applications, lossy data compression ratios far exceed those possible with lossless compression.

Lossless data algorithms work by attempting to eliminate redundancies in the data. For example, suppose that you have the following string of data:

> 0 5 5 7 3 2 0 0 0 0 1 4 7 3 2 9 1 0 0 0 0 0 6 6 8 2 7 3 2 7 3 2 ...

There are two simple steps you could take to reduce this string. First, you could reduce the amount of data by counting the strings of consecutive 0s, and maintaining the count instead of the string. The character is reproduced once, followed by its count:

> 0 1 5 5 7 3 2 0 4 1 4 7 3 2 9 1 0 5 6 6 8 2 7 3 2 7 3 2 ...

Notice that we actually had to add a character when the 0 appeared singly in the string. Otherwise, the inverse algorithm would have assumed that the first 0 appeared five times rather than recognizing the data to be a single 0 followed by a 5.

As a second step, the algorithm attempts to identify larger sequences within the string. These can be replaced with a single, identifiable value. In the example string, the sequence "7 3 2" occurs repeatedly. Let us replace each instance of the sequence with the special character "Z":

> 0 1 5 5 Z 0 3 1 4 Z 9 1 0 5 6 6 8 2 Z Z ...

Application of these two steps has reduced the sample string by more than 35 percent. A separate attachment to the data would identify the replacements that were made, so that the original data can be restored losslessly. For the example, the attachment would indicate that 0s were replaced by a single 0 followed by their count and the sequences "7 3 2" were replaced by "Z." You might wish to restore the original string in this example for practice.

There are many variations on the methods shown in the example. You should also notice that the second step requires advance access to the entire sequence of data to identify the repetitive sequences. Thus, it is not useful with streaming data. There are other variations that are based on the known properties of the data stream that can be used, however. For example, MPEG-2 uses the knowledge that the image is repeated at a frame rate of, say, thirty times per second, and that in most instances, very little movement occurs within small parts of the image between consecutive frames. GIF images and ZIP files are compressed losslessly.

Lossy algorithms operate on the assumption that some data can be sacrificed without significant effect, based on the application and on known properties of human perception. For example, it is known that subtle color changes will not be noticeable in the area of an image where the texture is particularly vivid. Therefore, it is acceptable to simplify the color data in this circumstance. There is no attempt to recover the lost data. The amount of data reduction possible in a particular circumstance is determined experimentally. Lossy algorithms can often reduce the amount of data by a factor of 10:1 or more. JPEG and MP3 are examples of lossy algorithms.

MPEG-2 uses both variations on both forms of compression simultaneously to achieve compression ratios of 100:1 or more with very little noticeable degradation in image quality; however, the compression process itself requires tremendous amounts of computing power.

Ongoing advances in data compression technology have resulted in improved performance with existing compression techniques, as well as a number of new video formats, including new versions of Microsoft's Windows Media Video format and new formats based on the MPEG-4 standard, as well as a new JPEG bitmap format, JP-2. As of this writing, these formats have not yet achieved general acceptance, but there is much promise for greatly improved video performance.

In general, the use of data compression is a trade-off between the use of processing power and the need to reduce the amount of data for transmission and storage. In most cases, the higher the compression ratio, the greater the demand upon the computer processing resources. At some point, the incremental improvement in compression to be achieved will no longer justify the additional cost in processing or the degradation of the result.

4.6 PAGE DESCRIPTION LANGUAGES

A **page description language** is a language that describes the layout of objects on a displayed or printed page. (In this context we are using the word "object" in the more general object-oriented programming language sense, rather than as a specific reference to object images.) Page description languages incorporate various types of objects in various data formats, including, usually, text, object images, and bitmap images. The page description language provides a means to position the various items on the page. Most page description languages also provide the capability to extend the language to include new data formats and new objects using language stubs called **plug-ins**. Most audio and video extensions fall into this category.

Some page description languages are extremely simple, with limited innate functionality. **HTML** (HyperText Markup Language), for example, provides little more than a shell. Except for text, most objects are stored in separate files, the details of layout are left mostly to the Web browser that is recreating the page, and programming language capability and other features are provided as extensions. We have already shown you many of the data formats that are used with HTML. Others, such as **PDF** (Portable Document Format) and PostScript offer the ability to recreate sophisticated pages with surprising faithfulness to the intentions of the original page designer.

PDF, for example, incorporates its own bitmap formats, object image format, and text format, all optimized for rapid page creation and presentation. It is often difficult to extract data in their original data formats from a PDF file. Interestingly, PDF does not provide programming language features. Instead, PDF is treated as a file format. The file contains objects, along with page positioning information for each object, and that's about it. It is presumed that any program execution required to preprocess the objects in the file for presentation was done prior to the creation of the file.

PostScript, on the other hand, contains a full-featured programming language that can be processed at display time. In that sense, PDF is something of a subset of PostScript, though with somewhat different goals and strengths. Many of the features of PDF are derived from postprocessed PostScript. In particular, the object image descriptions in PDF are based on the PostScript formats shown as examples earlier in this chapter.

4.7 INTERNAL COMPUTER DATA FORMAT

So now you have an idea of the various forms that data takes when it reaches the computer. Once inside the computer, however, *all* data is simply stored as binary numbers of various sizes, ranging from 1 to 8 bits, or even larger. The interpretation of these binary numbers depends upon two factors:

- The actual operations that the computer processor is capable of performing
- The data types that are supported by the programming language used to create the application program

As you will see in later chapters, computer processors provide instructions to manipulate data, for searching and sorting, for example, and to manipulate and perform basic mathematical operations on signed and unsigned integers. They also provide a means to point to data, using a stored binary value as a pointer or locator to another stored binary number. Since these pointer values are themselves stored as numbers, they can also be manipulated and used in calculations. A pointer value might represent the index in an array, for example. Most recent computers also provide instructions for the direct manipulation of floating point, or real, numbers. In other computers, floating point numbers are manipulated using software procedures.

The processor instruction set also establishes formats for each data type that it supports. If a number in the computer is supposed to be a floating point number, for example, the instructions are designed to assume that the number is laid out in a particular format. Specific formats that are used for integer and real numbers are discussed in Chapter 5.

Thus, the raw binary numbers stored in a computer can easily be interpreted to represent data of a variety of different types and formats. C, Java, Visual Basic, and other languages all provide a programmer with the capability to identify binary data with a particular data type. Typically, there are five different simple data types:

- *Boolean*: two-valued variables or constants with values of true or false.
- *char*: the character data type. Each variable or constant holds a single alpha-numeric character code representing, for example, the single strike of a key. It is also common to process groups of characters together as strings. Strings are simply arrays of individual characters. The ASC function in Visual Basic shows the actual binary number code representing a particular character. Thus, ASC("A") would show a different value on an ASCII-based system from that shown on an EBCDIC system.
- *enumerated* data types: user-defined simple data types, in which each possible value is listed in the definition, for example,

    ```
    type DayOfWeek = Mon, Tues, Wed, Thurs, Fri, Sat
    ```

- *integer*: positive or negative whole numbers. The string of characters representing a number is converted internally by a conversion routine built into the program by the compiler and stored and manipulated as a numerical value.
- *real* or *float*: numbers with a decimal portion, or numbers whose magnitude, either small or large, exceeds the capability of the computer to process and store as an integer. Again, the routine to convert a string of characters into a real number is built into the program.

In addition to the simple data types, many programming languages, including C, but not Java, support an explicit pointer variable data type. The value stored in a *pointer variable* is a memory address within the computer. Other, more complex, data types, structures, arrays, records, and other objects, for example, are made up of combinations of the simple data types.

The data types just listed correlate rather well with the instruction set capability of the processor. The integer and real types can be processed directly. The character type is translated into instructions that manipulate the data for basic character operations that are familiar to you from your programming classes. Boolean and enumerated data types are treated within the computer in a manner similar to integers. Most programming languages do not accept Boolean and enumerated data as input, but the conversion would be relatively straightforward. It would only be necessary to test the input character string against the various possibilities, and then set the value to the correct choice (see Exercise 4.10).

Other languages may support a completely different set of data types. There are even some languages that don't recognize any data types explicitly at all, but simply treat data in a way appropriate to the operation being performed.

Numerical Character to Integer Conversion

EXAMPLE

As you've already seen, the typical high-level language numerical input statement

$$READ(value)$$

where *value* is the name of an integer variable, requires a software conversion from the actual input, which is alphanumeric, to the numerical form specified for value. This conversion is normally provided by program code contributed by the language compiler that becomes part of your program. Some programmers choose instead to accept the input data in character form and include their own code to convert the data to numerical form. This allows more programmer control over the process; for example, the programmer might choose to provide more extensive error checking and recovery than that of the internal conversion program. (Many internal conversion programs simply crash if the user inputs an illegal character, say, a letter when a numeral is expected.)

Whether internal or programmer supplied, the conversion process is similar. Just to deepen your understanding of the conversion process, Figure 4.20 contains a simple

FIGURE 4.20

A Pseudocode Procedure that Performs String Conversion

```
//variables used
char key;
int number = 0;
boolean error, stop;
{
    stop = false;
    error = false;
    ReadAKey;
    while (NOT stop && NOT error) {
        number = 10 * number + (ASCIIVALUE(key) - 48);
        ReadAKey;
    } //end while
    if (error == true) {
        printout('Illegal Character in Input');
    else printout('input number is ' number);
    } //end if
} //end procedure

function ReadAKey(); {
    read(key);
    if (ASCIIVALUE(key) == 13 or ASCIIVALUE(key) == 32 or ASCIIVALUE(key) == 44)
        stop = true;
    else if ((key < '0' ) or (key > '9' )) error = true;
} //end function ReadAKey
```

pseudocode procedure that converts the string representing an unsigned integer into numerical form. This code contains simple error checking and assumes that the number ends with a space (ASCII 32), a comma (ASCII 44), or a carriage return (ASCII 13).

Conversion procedures for other data types are similar.

SUMMARY AND REVIEW

Alphanumeric data inputs and outputs are represented as codes, one code for each data value. Three commonly used code systems for interactive input and output are Unicode, ASCII, and EBCDIC. Within these codes, each character is represented by a binary number, usually stored 1 or 2 bytes per character.

The design and choice of a code is arbitrary; however, it is useful to have a code in which the collating sequence is consistent with search and sort operations in the language represented. Within the computer, programs must be aware of the code used to assure that data sorts, number conversions, and other types of character manipulation are handled correctly. There must also be agreement between input and output devices, so that the data is displayed correctly. If necessary, translation programs can be used to translate from one representation to another. When necessary, conversion programs within the computer convert the alphanumeric character strings into other numeric forms. Numeric data must be converted back to Unicode, ASCII, or EBCDIC form for output display, however. The most common source of alphanumeric data is the keyboard.

Data from a keyboard enters the computer in the form of a character stream, which includes nonprinting characters as well as printing characters. Image scanning with optical character recognition, voice input, and various special devices, such as bar code readers, can also be used to create alphanumeric data.

There are two different methods used for representing images in the computer. Bitmap images consist of an array of pixel values. Each pixel represents the sampling of a small area in the picture. Object images are made up of simple geometrical elements. Each element is specified by its geometric parameters, its location in the picture, and other details.

Within the constraint that object images must be constructed geometrically, they are more efficient in storage and more flexible for processing. They may be scaled, rotated, and otherwise manipulated without loss of shape or detail. Images with texture and shading, such as photographs and painting, must be stored in bitmap image form. Generally, images must be printed and displayed as bitmaps, so object images are converted to bitmap form by a page description language interpreter before printing or display. There are many different formats used for storing graphical images.

Video images are difficult to manage because of the massive amounts of data involved. Video may be stored local to the system, or may be streamed from a network or website. The quality of streamed video is limited by the capability of the network connection. Higher quality is possible with locally stored video data, but the processing requirements are demanding. Some systems provide auxiliary hardware to process video.

Audio signals are represented in the computer by a sequence of values created by digitizing the signal. The signal is sampled at regular time intervals. Each sample is then converted to an equivalent binary value that is proportional to the amplitude of the sample. Again, different formats are available for storing audio data, depending on the application.

Audio signals may be streamed or stored locally. The requirements for audio transmission and processing are far less stringent than for those of video.

For images, both still and video, as well as audio, data compression is often appropriate. Lossless data compression allows complete recovery of the original noncompressed data. Lossy data compression does not allow recovery of the original data, but is designed to be perceived as sufficient by the user.

Page description languages combine the characteristics of various specific data formats together with data indicating the position on the page to create data formats that can be used for display and printing layouts.

Internally, all data, regardless of use, are stored as binary numbers. Instructions in the computer support interpretation of these numbers as characters, integers, pointers, and in many cases, floating point numbers.

FOR FURTHER READING

The general concepts of data formats are fairly straightforward, but additional character-based exercises and practice can be found in the Schaum outline [LIPS82]. Individual codes can be found in many references. The actual characters mapped to the keyboard are directly observable using the *Character Map* accessory in Windows or the *Key Caps* desk accessory on the Macintosh. Extensive information about Unicode is available from the Unicode website at www.unicode.org.

For graphics formats, there are a number of good general books on graphics. Most of these books describe the difference between bitmap and object graphics clearly, and most also discuss some of the different graphics file formats, and the trade-offs between them. Additionally, there are more specialized books that are often useful in this area. Murray and Van Ryper [MURR96] provide a detailed catalog of graphics formats. Rimmer [RIMM93] discusses bitmapped graphics at length.

Smith [SMIT90] presents an easy approach to the PostScript language. The three Adobe books—[ADOB93], [ADOB99], and [ADOB85], often called the "green book", the "red book", and the "blue book", respectively—are detailed but clear explanations of PostScript. Adobe also offers the PDF Reference [ADOB06]. A simple introduction to PDF is the PDF Primer White Paper [PDFP05].

There are many books on various aspects of digital sound, but most are hard to read; the Web is a better resource. Similarly, new data formats of all types occur as the need arises. Because the need seems to arise continuously nowadays, your best source of current information is undoubtedly the Web.

KEY CONCEPTS AND TERMS

A-to-D converter	JPEG format	phoneme
alphanumeric data	lossless data compression	pixel
ANSI	lossy data compression	PostScript language
ASCII	metadata	plug-ins
bitmap or raster image	MP3	proprietary format
collating sequence	MPEG-2, MPEG-4	resolution
control code	numeric character versus	RFID (radio frequency
EBCDIC	number	identification)
font	object or vector image	scan code
glyph	optical character	stream, character
Graphics Interchange	recognition (OCR)	streaming (video)
Format (GIF)	page description language	Unicode
graphical objects	palette	

READING REVIEW QUESTIONS

4.1 When data is input to a computer, it is nearly always manipulated and stored in some standard data format. Why is the use of data standards considered important, or indeed, crucial in this case?

4.2 Name the three standards in common use for alphanumeric characters. Which standard is designed to support all of the world's written languages? Which language is used primarily with legacy programs that execute on mainframe computers?

4.3 What is a collating sequence?

4.4 What is the relationship between the ASCII Latin-1 character set and its Unicode equivalent that makes conversion between the two simple?

4.5 Name at least four alternative devices that can be used as sources of alphanumeric character input data.

4.6 What is image *metadata*? Give an at least three examples of metadata that would be required for a bitmap image.

4.7 What are the major characteristics of a *bitmap* image? What are the major characteristics of an *object* or *vector* image? Which is used for displays? What types of images <u>must</u> be stored and manipulated as bitmap images? Why?

4.8 Name two advantages to the use of object images.

4.9 Describe briefly the most important characteristics and features of an MP3 audio file.

4.10 Explain briefly how an A-to-D converter converts audio data into binary data.

4.11 Explain the difference between lossless and lossy data compression. Which type normally provides a smaller file? What is "lost" in lossy audio data compression? Under what circumstances is it impossible to use lossy data compression?

4.12   What is a *page description language*? Give an example of a page description language.

4.13   Explain the difference between numeric characters and numbers. Under what conditions would you expect the computer to use numeric characters? When would you expect the computer to use numbers? When numeric data is entered at the keyboard, which form is used? Which form is used for calculations? Which form is used for display?

4.14   Name five simple data types that are provided in most high-level programming languages.

EXERCISES

4.1   **a.**   What is the ASCII representation for the numeral −3.1415 in binary? in octal? in hexadecimal? in decimal?

     b.   What is the EBCDIC representation for the numeral +1,250.1? (Include the comma.)

4.2   What character string does the binary ASCII code

```
1010100 1101000 1101001 1110011 0100000 1101001 1110011
0100000 1000101 1000001 1010011 1011001 0100001
```

represent?

4.3   **a.**   Create a table that shows the ASCII and EBCDIC representations side-by-side for each of the uppercase letters, lowercase letters, and numerals.

     b.   Does the hexadecimal representation show you a simple method for converting individual numeric characters into their corresponding numerical values?

     c.   Does the hexadecimal representation suggest a simple method for changing lowercase letters into their corresponding capital letters?

     d.   Can you use the same methods for EBCDIC as you do for ASCII? If so, what changes would you need to make in a program to make (b) and (c) work?

4.4   Unicode is downward compatible with the Latin-1 version of 8-bit ASCII in the sense that a Unicode text file that is limited to the Latin-1 character set will be read correctly on a system that does not support Unicode, provided that an end delimiter is used, rather than a character count as the measure of the length of the message. Why is this so? (Hint: Consider the role of the ASCII NUL character.)

4.5   As an alternative alphanumeric code, consider a code where punched holes in the columns of a card represent alphanumeric codes. The punched hole represents a "1"; all other bits are "0". The Hollerith code shown in Figure E4.1 is an example of such a code. This code has been used to represent a message on the card in Figure E4.2. Each row represents a code level from 0 to 12. Levels 12 and 11, which are not labeled on the card, are the top row and next-to-top rows, respectively. Each column represents a single character, so the card can hold one eighty-column line of text. (This card, prevalent in the 1960s and 1970s as a means of data input, is the reason that text-based displays are still limited to eighty characters per line.) Translate the card in Figure E4.2.

FIGURE E4.1

Character	Punched code	Character	Punched code	Character	Punched code	Character	Punched code	Character	Punched code
A	12,1	L	11,3	W	0,6	7	7	<	12,8,4
B	12,2	M	11,4	X	0,7	8	8	(	12,8,5
C	12,3	N	11,5	Y	0,8	9	9	+	12,8,6
D	12,4	O	11,6	Z	0,9	0	0	$	11,8,3
E	12,5	P	11,7	0	0	&	12	*	11,8,4
F	12,6	Q	11,8	1	1	-	11	)	11,8,5
G	12,7	R	11,9	2	2	/	0,1	,	0,8,3
H	12,8	S	0,2	3	3	#	8,3	%	0,8,4
I	12,9	T	0,3	4	4	@	8,4	blank	none
J	11,1	U	0,4	5	5	'	8,5		
K	11,2	V	0,5	6	6	=	8,6		
						.	12,8,3		

FIGURE E4.2

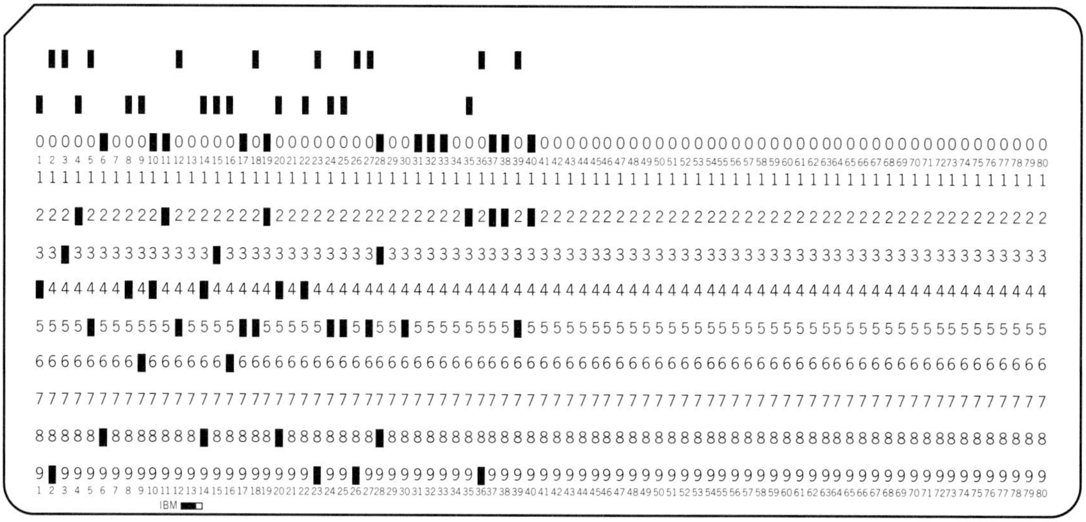

4.6   ASCII, Unicode, and EBCDIC are, of course, not the only possible codes. The Sophomites from the planet Collegium use the rather strange code shown in Figure E4.3. There are only thirteen characters in the Sophomite alphabet, and each character uses a 5-bit code. In addition, there are four numeric digits, since the Sophomites use base 4 for their arithmetic.

    a.   Given the following binary code, what is the message being sent by the Sophomites?

1100111010000011111100000010011011111111101111100000000100100

FIGURE E4.3

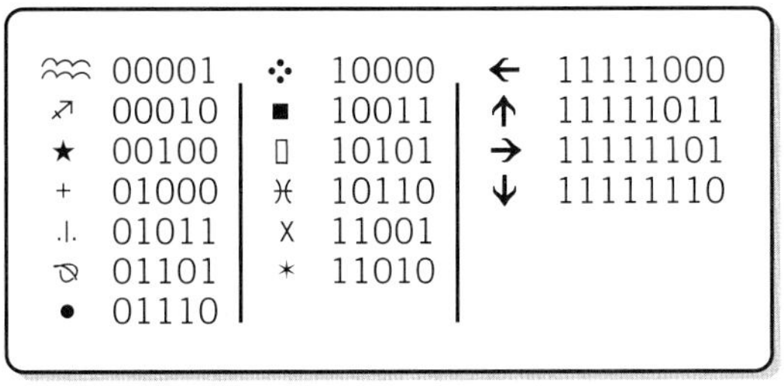

≈≈	00001	∴	10000	←	11111000
↗	00010	■	10011	↑	11111011
★	00100	▯	10101	→	11111101
+	01000	✳	10110	↓	11111110
⌁	01011	X	11001		
↻	01101	✶	11010		
●	01110				

    b. You noticed in part (a) that this code does not delimit between characters. How does one delimit this code? Suppose a bit was dropped during transmission. What happens? Suppose a single bit was altered (0 to 1 or 1 to 0). What happens?

4.7 Approximately how many pages of pure 16-bit Unicode text can a 650 MB CD-ROM hold?

4.8 Suppose you have a program that reads an integer, followed by a character, using the following prompt and READ statement:

```
WRITE ('Enter an integer and a character:')
READ (intval, charval);
```

When you run the program, you type in the following, in response to the prompt

```
Enter an integer and a character:
1257
z
```

When you check the value of charval, you discover that it does *not* contain "z." Why not? What would you expect to find there?

4.9 Without writing a program, predict the ORD value for your computer system for the letter "A," for the letter "B," for the letter "C." How did you know? Might the value be different on a different system? Why or why not?

4.10 If you have access to a debug program, load a text file into computer memory from your disk, and read the text from computer memory by translating the ASCII codes.

4.11 Write a program in your favorite language that will convert all ASCII uppercase and lowercase letters to EBCDIC code. For an additional challenge, also convert the punctuation symbols, indicating with a failure-to-convert message, those symbols that are not represented in the EBCDIC system.

4.12 Write a program that accepts one of the seven values "MON," "TUE," "WED," "THU," "FRI," "SAT," and "SUN" as input and sets a variable named TODAY to the correct value of type DayOfWeek, and then outputs the ORD value of TODAY to the screen. (Does the ORD value give you a hint as to the internal representation of the enumerated data type?)

4.13 Write a procedure similar to procedure Convert that converts a signed integer to a character string for output.

4.14 Using the Web as a resource, create a table that compares the features and capabilities of .PNG, .GIF, and .JPEG.

4.15 Find a book or article that describes the various bitmapped graphics formats, and compare .GIF, .PNG, and .BMP.

4.16 Find a book or article that describes the various bitmapped graphics formats, and compare .GIF and .RLE.

For Exercises 4.15 and 4.16, there are several books that describe graphics formats in detail. One of these is Murray [MURR96].

4.17 If you have studied COBOL, discuss the difference between numeric characters and numbers in the context of a COBOL program. Does COBOL distinguish clearly between the two? If so, in what ways?

4.18 Investigate several audio formats, and discuss the different features that each provides. Also discuss how the choice of features provided in different formats affects the type of processing that the format would be useful for.

4.19 The MP3 audio format is described as "almost CD quality." What characteristic of MP3 makes this description accurate?

4.20 Use the Web as a resource to investigate MPEG-2 [or MPEG-4]. Explain the data compression algorithm used by MPEG-2 [or MPEG-4].

4.21 Provide a line-by-line explanation for the PostScript code in Figure 4.14.

4.22 Use the Web as a resource to study the PDF format.

a. Describe how PDF provides output that is consistent across different types of devices, including printers and monitors of various resolutions.

b. Describe the format for storing, laying out, and managing the objects on a page. Explain the advantages to the use of this format over other formats, such as that used by HTML.

c. Explain how PDF manages the many different type fonts that might be found in a document.

d. How does PDF manage bitmap images? Object images?

e. Explain how PDF differs from PostScript.

f. Describe at least three major limitations that PDF places on the end-user of a PDF document.

CHAPTER 5

REPRESENTING NUMERICAL DATA

"It's OK, Mrs. Grumpworthy,
my brother's teaching me arithmetic
on our computer at home."

Thomas Sperling, adapted by Benjamin Reece

5.0 INTRODUCTION

As we have noted previously, the computer stores all data and program instructions in binary form, using only groups of zeros and ones. No special provision is made for the storage of the algebraic sign or decimal point that might be associated with a number; all responsibility for interpretation of those zeros and ones is left to the programmers whose programs store and manipulate those binary numbers. Thus the binary numbers in a computer might represent characters, numbers, graphics images, video, audio, program instructions, or something else.

The ability of a computer to manipulate numbers of various kinds is, of course, of particular importance to users. In Chapter 4, we observed that nearly every high-level computing language provides a method for storage, manipulation, and calculation of signed integer and real numbers. This chapter discusses methods of representing and manipulating these numbers within the zeros-and-ones constraint of the computer.

We saw in Chapter 3 that unsigned **integer numbers** can be represented directly in binary form, and this provides a clue as to how we might represent the integer data type in the computer. There is a significant limitation, however: we have yet to show you a sign-free way of handling negative numbers that is compatible with the capabilities of the computer. In this chapter, we explore several different methods of storing and manipulating integers that may encompass both positive and negative numbers.

Also, as you know, it is not always possible to express numbers in integer form. **Real**, or floating point, **numbers** are used in the computer when the number to be expressed is outside of the integer range of the computer (too large or too small) or when the number contains a decimal fraction.

Floating point numbers allow the computer to maintain a limited, fixed number of digits of precision together with a power that shifts the point left or right within the number to make the number larger or smaller, as necessary. The range of numbers that the computer can handle in this way is huge. In a personal computer, for example, the range of numbers that may be expressed this way may be $\pm[10^{-38} < \text{number} < 10^{+38}]$ or more.

Performing calculations with floating point numbers provide an additional challenge. There are trade-offs made for the convenience of using floating point numbers: a potential loss of precision, as measured in terms of significant digits, larger storage requirements, and slower calculations. In this chapter we will also explore the properties of floating point numbers, show how they are represented in the computer, consider how calculations are performed, and learn how to convert between integer and floating point representations. We also investigate the importance of the trade-offs required for the use of floating point numbers and attempt to come up with some reasonable ground rules for deciding what number format to specify in various programming situations.

We remind you that numbers are usually input as characters and must be converted to a numerical format before they may be used in calculations. Numbers that will not be used in calculations, such as zip codes or credit card numbers, are simply manipulated as characters.

5.1 UNSIGNED BINARY AND BINARY-CODED DECIMAL REPRESENTATIONS

In conventional notation, numbers can be represented as a combination of a value, or magnitude, a sign, plus or minus, and, if necessary, a decimal point. As a first step in our discussion, let's consider two different approaches to storing just the value of the number in the computer.

The most obvious approach is simply to recognize that there is a direct binary equivalent for any decimal integer. We can simply store any positive or unsigned whole number as its binary representation. This is the approach that we already discussed in Chapter 3. The range of integers that we can store this way is determined by the number of bits available. Thus, an 8-bit storage location can store any **unsigned integer** of value between 0 and 255, a 16-bit storage location, 0–65535. If we must expand the range of integers to be handled, we can provide more bits. A common way to do this is to use multiple storage locations. In Figure 5.1, for example, four consecutive 1-byte storage locations are used to provide 32 bits of range. Used together, these four locations can accept 2^{32}, or 4,294,967,296 different values.

The use of multiple storage locations to store a single binary number may increase the difficulty of calculation and manipulation of these numbers because the calculation may have to be done one part at a time, possibly with carries or borrows between the parts, but the additional difficulty is not unreasonable. Most modern computers provide built-in

FIGURE 5.1

Storage of a 32-bit Data Word

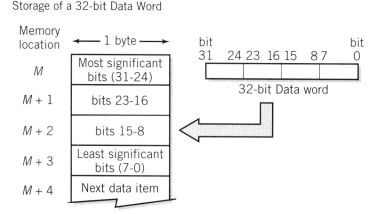

FIGURE 5.2

Value Range for Binary Versus Binary-coded Decimal

No. of Bits	BCD range		Binary range	
4	0–9	1 digit	0–15	1+ digit
8	0–99	2 digits	0–255	2+ digits
12	0–999	3 digits	0–4,095	3+ digits
16	0–9,999	4 digits	0–65,535	4+ digits
20	0–99,999	5 digits	0–1 Million	6 digits
24	0–999,999	6 digits	0–16 Million	7+ digits
32	0–99,999,999	8 digits	0–4 Billion	9+ digits
64	$0-(10^{16}-1)$	16 digits	0–16 Quintillion	19+ digits

instructions that perform data calculations 32 bits or 64 bits at a time, storing the data automatically in consecutive bytes. For other number ranges, and for computers without this capability, these calculations can be performed using software procedures within the computer.

An alternative approach known as **binary-coded decimal (BCD)**, may be used in some applications. In this approach, the number is stored as a digit-by-digit binary representation of the original decimal integer. Each decimal digit is individually converted to binary. This requires 4 bits per digit. Thus, an 8-bit storage location could hold two binary-coded decimal digits—in other words, one of one hundred different values from 00 to 99. For example, the decimal value 68 would be represented in BCD as 01101000. (Of course you remember that $0110_2 = 6_{10}$ and $1000_2 = 8_{10}$.) Four bits can hold sixteen different values, numbered 0 to F in hexadecimal notation, but with BCD the values A to F are simply not used. The hexadecimal and decimal values for 0 through 9 are equivalent.

The table in Figure 5.2 compares the decimal range of values that can be stored in binary and BCD forms. Notice that for a given number of bits the range of values that can be held using the binary-coded decimal method is substantially less than the range using conventional binary representation. You would expect this because the values A–F are being thrown away for each group of 4 bits. The larger the total number of bits, the more pronounced the difference. With 20 bits, the range for binary is an entire additional decimal digit over the BCD range.

Calculations in BCD are also more difficult, since the computer must break the number into the 4-bit binary groupings corresponding to individual decimal digits and use base 10 arithmetic translated into base 2 to perform calculations. In other words, the calculation for each 4-bit grouping must be treated individually, with arithmetic carries moving from grouping to grouping. Any product or sum of any two BCD integers that exceeds 9 must be reconverted to BCD each time to perform the carries from digit to digit.

EXAMPLE

One method of performing a "simple" one- by two-digit multiplication is shown as an example in Figure 5.3. In the first step, each digit in the multiplicand is multiplied by the single-digit multiplier. This yields the result $7 \times 6 = 42$ in the units place and the result $7 \times 7 = 49$ in the 10's place. Numerically, this corresponds to the result achieved performing the multiplication in decimal, as is shown at the left of the diagram.

FIGURE 5.3

A Simple BCD Multiplication

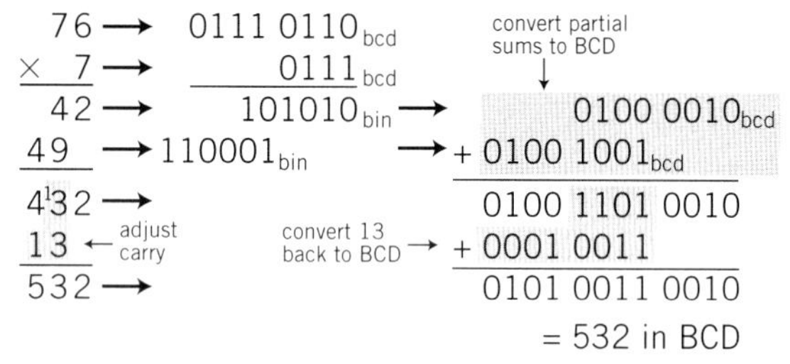

To continue, the binary values for 42 and 49 must be converted back to BCD. This is done in the second step. Now the BCD addition takes place. As in the decimal version, the sum of 9 and 4 results in a carry. The binary value 13 must be converted to BCD 3, and the 1 added to the value 4 in the hundreds place. The final result is BCD value 532.

If the number contains a decimal point, the same approach can be used, but the application program must keep track of the decimal point's location. For example, many business applications have to maintain full accuracy for real numbers. In many cases, the real numbers being used represent dollars and cents figures. You are aware from Chapter 3 that rational decimal real numbers do not necessarily remain so when converted into binary form. Thus, it is possible that a number converted from decimal to binary and back again may not be exactly the same as the original number. You would not want to add two financial numbers and have the result off by a few cents. (In fact, this was a problem with early versions of spreadsheet programs!)

For this reason, business-oriented high-level languages such as COBOL provide formats that allow the user to specify the number of desired decimal places exactly. Large computers support these operations by providing additional instructions for converting, manipulating, and performing arithmetic operations on numbers that are stored in a BCD format.

EXAMPLE

IBM zSeries computers support numbers stored in a BCD format called packed decimal format, shown in Figure 5.4. Each decimal digit is stored in BCD form, two digits to a byte. The most significant digit is stored first, in the high-order bits of the first byte. The sign is stored in the low-order bits of the last byte. Up to thirty-one digits may be stored. The binary values 1100 and 1101 are used for the sign, representing "+" and "−" respectively. The value 1111 can be used to indicate that the number is unsigned. Since these values do not represent any valid decimal number, it is easy to detect an error, as well as to determine the end of the number. As we noted earlier, the location of the decimal point is not stored and must be maintained by the application program. Intel CPUs provide a more limited packed format that holds two digits (00–99) in a single byte. As an example, the decimal number -324.6 would be stored in packed decimal form as

0000 0011   0010 0100   0110 1101

FIGURE 5.4

Packed Decimal Format

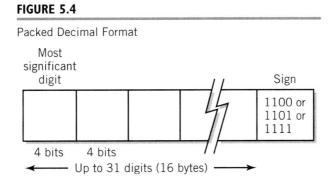

The leading 0s are required to make the number fit exactly into 3 bytes. IBM provides additional formats that store data one digit to a byte, but provides no instructions for performing calculations in this format. This format is used primarily as a convenience for conversion between text and packed decimal format. IBM also provides a compressed version of its packed decimal format to save storage space.

Even with computer instructions that perform BCD arithmetic, BCD arithmetic is nearly always much slower. As an alternative, some computers convert each BCD number to binary form, perform the calculation, and then convert the result back to BCD.

Despite its drawbacks, binary-coded decimal representation is sometimes useful, especially in business applications, where it is often desirable to have an exact digit-for-digit decimal equivalent in order to mimic decimal arithmetic, as well as to maintain decimal rounding and decimal precision. Translation between BCD and character form is also easier, since the last 4 bits of ASCII, EBCDIC, and Unicode numeric character forms correspond exactly to the BCD representation of that digit. Thus, to convert from alphanumeric form to BCD you simply chop off everything but the rightmost 4 bits of the character to get its BCD value. This makes BCD an attractive option when the application involves a lot of input and output, but limited calculation. Many business applications fit this description. In most cases, though, binary representation is preferred and used.

5.2 REPRESENTATIONS FOR SIGNED INTEGERS

With the shortcomings of BCD, it shouldn't surprise you that integers are nearly always stored as binary numbers. As you have already seen, unsigned integers can be converted directly to binary numbers and processed without any special care. The addition of a sign, however, complicates the problem, because there is no obvious direct way to represent the sign in binary notation. In fact, there are several different ways used to represent negative numbers in binary form, depending on the processing that is to take place. The most common of these is known as **2's complement representation**. Before we discuss 2's complement representation, we will take a look at two other, simpler methods: **sign-and-magnitude representation** and **1's complement representation**. Each of these latter methods has some serious limitations for computer use, but understanding these methods and their limitations will clarify the reasoning behind the use of 2's complementation.

Sign-and-magnitude Representation

FIGURE 5.5

Examples of Sign-and-Magnitude
Representation

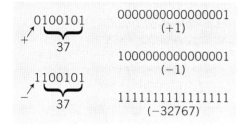

0000000000000001
(+1)

1000000000000001
(−1)

1111111111111111
(−32767)

In daily usage, we represent **signed integers** by a plus or minus sign and a value. This representation is known, not surprisingly, as *sign-and-magnitude* representation.

In the computer we cannot use a sign, but must restrict ourselves to 0's and 1's. We could select a particular bit, however, and assign to it values that we agree will represent the plus and minus signs. For example, we could select the leftmost bit and decide that a 0 in this place represents a plus sign and a 1 represents a minus. This selection is entirely arbitrary, but if used consistently, it is as reasonable as any other selection. In fact, this is the representation usually selected. Figure 5.5 shows examples of this representation.

Note that since the leftmost digit is being used as a sign, it cannot represent any value. This means that the positive range of the signed integer using this technique is one-half as large as the corresponding unsigned integer of the same number of bits. On the other hand, the signed integer also has a negative range of equal size to its positive range, so we really haven't lost any capability, but have simply shifted it to the negative region. The total range remains the same, but is redistributed to represent numbers both positive and negative, though in magnitude only half as large.

Suppose 32 bits are available for storage and manipulation of the number. In this case, we will use 1 bit for the sign and 31 bits for the magnitude of the number. By convention, the leftmost, or most significant, bit is usually used as a sign, with 0 corresponding to a plus sign and 1 to a minus sign. The binary range for 32 bits is 0 to 4,294,967,295; we can represent the numbers $-2,147,483,647$ to $+2,147,483,647$ this way.

There are several inherent difficulties in performing calculations when using sign-and-magnitude representation. Many of these difficulties arise because the value of the result of an addition depends upon the signs and relative magnitudes of the inputs. This can be easily seen from the following base 10 examples. Since the numbers are exactly equivalent, the same problem of course occurs with binary addition.

EXAMPLE

Consider the base 10 sum of 4 and 2:

$$\begin{array}{r} 4 \\ +\,2 \\ \hline 6 \end{array}$$

The sum of 4 and −2, however, has a different numerical result:

$$\begin{array}{r} 4 \\ -\,2 \\ \hline 2 \end{array}$$

Notice that the addition method used depends on the signs of the operands. One method is used if both signs agree; a different method is used if the signs differ. Even worse, the presence of a second digit that can result in a carry or borrow changes the result yet again:

$$\begin{array}{r} 2 \\ -\ 4 \\ \hline -\ 2 \end{array}$$

But

$$\begin{array}{r} 12 \\ -4 \\ \hline 8 \end{array}$$

Interestingly enough, we have been so well trained that we alter our own mental algorithm to fit the particular case without even thinking about it, so this situation might not even have crossed your mind. The computer requires absolute definition of every possible condition, however, so the algorithm must include every possibility; unfortunately, sign-and-magnitude calculation algorithms are complex and difficult to implement in hardware.

In addition to the foregoing difficulty, there are two different binary values for 0,

$$00000000 \text{ and } 10000000$$

representing $+0$ and -0, respectively. This seems like a minor annoyance, but the system must test at the end of every calculation to assure that there is only a single value for 0. This is necessary to allow program code that compares values or tests a value for 0 to work correctly. Positive 0 is preferred because presenting -0 as an output result would also be confusing to the typical user.

The one occurrence where sign-and-magnitude is a useful representation is when binary-coded decimal is being used. Even though the calculation algorithms are necessarily complex, other algorithms for representing signed integers that you will be introduced to in this chapter are even more impractical when using BCD. Furthermore, as we have already discussed, BCD calculation is complex in any case, so the additional complexity that results from handling sign-and-magnitude representations is just more of the same.

With BCD, the leftmost bit can be used as a sign, just as in the case of binary. With binary, however, using a sign bit cuts the range in half; the effect on range is much less pronounced with BCD. (Remember, though, that BCD already has a much smaller range than binary for the same number of bits.) The leftmost bit in an unsigned BCD integer only represents the values 8 or 9; therefore, using this bit as a sign bit still allows the computer 3 bits to represent the leftmost digit as a number within the range 0–7.

As an example, the range for a signed 16-bit BCD integer would be

$$-7999 \le \text{value} \le +7999.$$

Nine's Decimal and 1's Binary Complementary Representations

For most purposes, computers use a different method of representing signed integers known as complementary representation. With this method, the sign of the number is a natural result of the method and does not need to be handled separately. Also, calculations using complementary representation are consistent for all different signed combinations of input numbers. There are two forms of complementary representation in common use. One, known as the radix complement, is discussed in the next section. In this section, we will introduce a representation known as *diminished radix* complementary representation, so called because the value used as a basis for the complementary operation is *diminished* by one from the radix, or base. Thus, base 10 diminished radix complementary representation uses the value 9 as its basis, and binary uses 1. Although the computer obviously uses the 1's representation, we will introduce the 9's representation first, since we have found that it is easier for most students to understand these concepts in the more familiar decimal system.

NINE'S DECIMAL REPRESENTATION Let us begin by considering a different means of representing negative and positive integers in the decimal number system. Suppose that we manipulate the range of a three-digit decimal number system by splitting the three-digit decimal range down the middle at 500. Arbitrarily, we will allow any number between 0 and 499 to be considered positive. Positive numbers will simply represent themselves. This will allow the value of positive numbers to be immediately identified. Numbers that begin with 5, 6, 7, 8, or 9 in the most significant digit will be treated as representations of negative numbers. Figure 5.6 shows the shift in range.

One convenient way to assign a value to the negative numbers is to allow each digit to be subtracted from the largest numeral in the radix. Thus, there is no carry, and each digit can be converted independently of all others. Subtracting a value from some standard basis value is known as taking the **complement** of the number. Taking the complement of a number is almost like using the basis value as a mirror. In the case of base 10 radix, the largest numeral is 9; thus, this method is called 9's complementary representation.

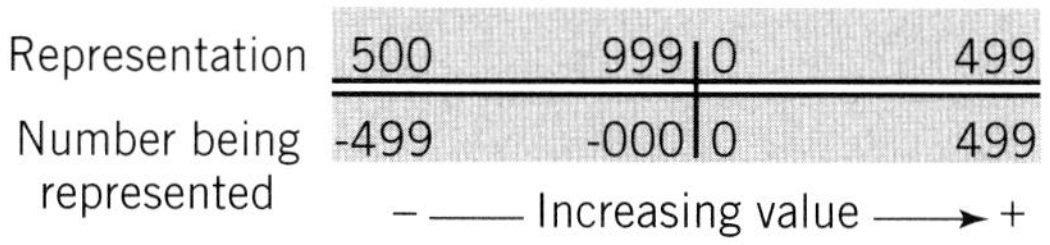

The facing page shows several examples of this technique.

If we now use the 9's complement technique to assign the negative values to the chart in Figure 5.6, you see that 998 corresponds to a value of -1 and 500 to the value -499. This results in the relationship shown in Figure 5.7.

An important consideration in the choice of a representation is that it is consistent with the normal rules of arithmetic. For the representation to be valid, it is necessary that, for any value within the range,

$$-(-\text{value}) = \text{value}$$

Simply stated, this says that if we complement the value twice, it should return to its original value. Since the complement is just

$$\text{comp} = \text{basis} - \text{value}$$

then complementing twice,

$$\text{basis} - (\text{basis} - \text{value}) = \text{value}$$

which confirms that this requirement is met.

FIGURE 5.6

Range Shifting Decimal Integers

Representation	500	999	0	499
Number being represented	-499	-000	0	499

$-$ ——— Increasing value ——→ +

FIGURE 5.7

Addition as a Counting Process

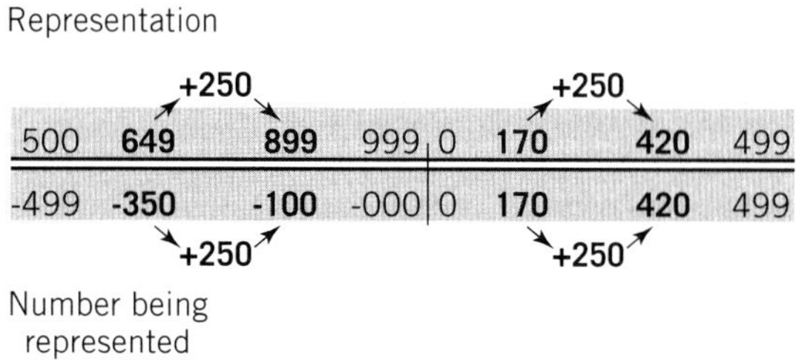

Representation

	+250				+250	
500	649	899	999, 0	170	420	499
-499	-350	-100	-000 0	170	420	499
	+250				+250	

Number being represented

EXAMPLES

Find the 9's complementary representation for the three-digit number −467.

$$\begin{array}{r} 999 \\ -467 \\ \hline 532 \end{array}$$

532 represents the value for −467. Notice that the three-digit value range is limited to 0–499, since any larger number would start with a digit of 5 or greater, which is the indicator for a negative number.

■ ■ ■

Find the 9's complementary representation for the four-digit number −467.

$$\begin{array}{r} 9999 \\ -467 \\ \hline 9532 \end{array}$$

Notice that in this system, it is necessary to specify the number of digits, or *word size*, being used. In a four-digit representation, the number (0)532 represents a positive integer, since it is less than 4999 in value. Care is required in maintaining the correct number of digits.

■ ■ ■

What is the sign-and-magnitude value of the four-digit number represented in 9's complement by 3789?

In this case, the leftmost digit is in the range 0–4. Therefore, the number is positive, and is already in correct form. The answer is +3789.

This example emphasizes the difference between the representation of a number in complementary form and the operation of taking the complement of a number. The representation just tells us what the number looks like in complementary form. The operation of finding the complement of a number consists of performing the steps that are necessary to change the number from one sign to the other. Note that if the value represents a negative number, it is necessary to perform the operation if we wish to convert the number into sign-and-magnitude form.

■ ■ ■

What is the sign-and-magnitude value of the four-digit number represented by 9990?

This value is negative. To get the sign-and-magnitude representation for this number, we take the 9's complement:

$$\begin{array}{r} 9999 \\ -9990 \\ \hline 9 \end{array}$$

Therefore, 9990 represents the value −9.

Next, let's consider the operation of addition when the numbers being added are in 9's complementary form. When you studied programming language, you learned that modular arithmetic could be used to find the remainder of an integer division. You recall that in modular arithmetic, the count repeats from 0 when a limit, called the *modulus*, is exceeded. Thus, as an example, 4 mod 4 has the value 0 and 5 mod 4 has the value 1.

The 9's complement scale shown in Figure 5.6 shares the most important characteristic of modular arithmetic; namely, in counting upward (from left to right on the scale), when 999 is reached, the next count results in a modular rotation to a value of 0. (Notice that when you reach the right end of the scale, it continues by flowing around to the left end.)

Counting corresponds to addition; thus, to add a number to another is simply to count upward from one number by the other. This idea is illustrated in Figure 5.7. As you can see from the examples in this diagram, simple additions are straightforward and work correctly. To understand how this process works in a "wraparound" situation, consider the example shown in Figure 5.8. As you can see in this case, adding 699 to the value 200 leads to the position 899 by wrapping around the right end. Since 699 is equivalent to −300 and 899 is equivalent to −100, 699 + 200 is equivalent to (−300) + 200, and the result of the addition is correct.

The reason this technique works can also be seen in the diagram. The **wraparound** is equivalent to extending the range to include the addition on the scale.

The same final point should also be reached by moving to the left 300 units, which is equivalent to subtracting 300. In fact, the result is off by 1. This occurs because we have again picked a scale with two values for 0, namely, 0 for +0 and 999 for −0. This means that any count that crosses the modulus will be short one count, since 0 will be counted twice. In this particular example, the count to the right, which is the a addition 200 + 699, yielded the correct result, since the modulus was not crossed. The count to the left, the subtraction 200 − 300, is off by one because of the double zero. We could correct for this situation on the chart by moving left an additional count any time the subtraction requires "borrowing" from the modulus. For example, subtracting 200 − 300 requires treating the value 200 as though it were 1200 to stay within the 0–999 range. The borrow can be used to indicate that an additional unit should be subtracted.

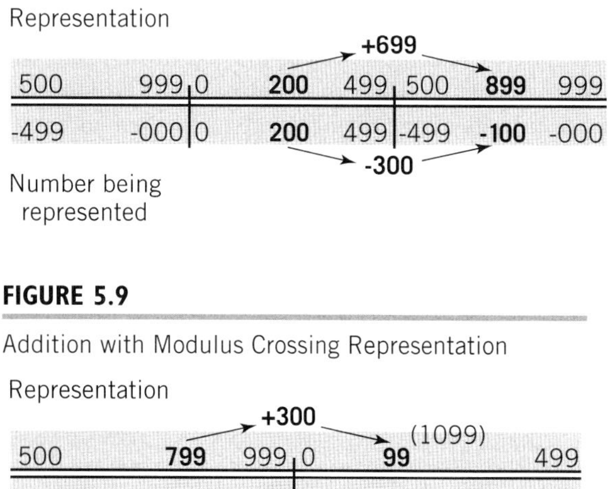

Next, consider the situation shown in Figure 5.9. In this case, counting to the right, or adding, also results in crossing the modulus, so an additional count must be added to obtain the correct result. This is an easier situation, however. Since the result of any sum that crosses the modulus must initially contain a carry digit (the 1 in 1099 in the diagram), which is then dropped in the modular addition, it is easy to tell when the modulus has been crossed to the right. We can then simply add the extra count in such cases.

FIGURE 5.8

Addition with Wraparound

Number being represented

FIGURE 5.9

Addition with Modulus Crossing Representation

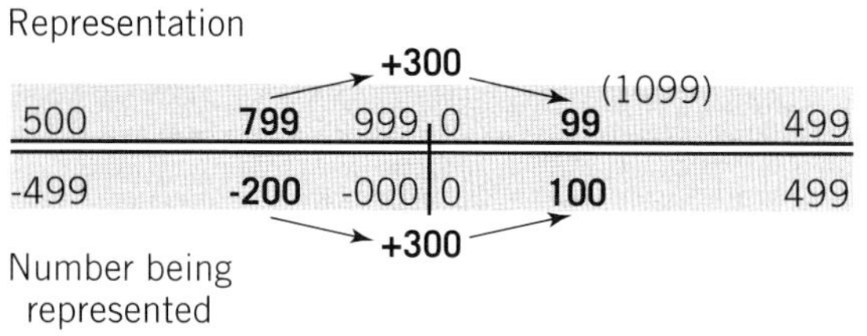

Number being represented

FIGURE 5.10

End-around Carry Procedure

```
                              799
      799                     300
      100                    1099
      899                     └─→1
                              100
No end-around carry
                         End-around carry
```

This leads to a simple procedure for adding two numbers in 9's complementary arithmetic: Add the two numbers. If the result flows into the digit beyond the specified number of digits, add the carry into the result. This is known as **end-around carry**. Figure 5.10 illustrates the procedure. Notice that the result is now correct for both examples.

Although we could design a similar algorithm for subtraction, there is no practical reason to do so. Instead, subtraction is performed by taking the complement of the subtrahend (the item being subtracted) and adding to the minuend (the item being subtracted from). In this way, the computer can use a single addition algorithm for all cases.

There is one further consideration. A fixed word size results in a range of some particular fixed size; it is always possible to have a combination of numbers that adds to a result outside the range. This condition is known as **overflow**. If we have a three-digit plus sign word size in a sign-and-magnitude system, and add 500 to 500, the result overflows, since 1000 is outside the range. The fourth digit would be evidence of overflow.

It is just as easy to detect overflow in a 9's complement system, even though the use of modular arithmetic assures that an extra digit will never occur. In complementary arithmetic, numbers that are out of range represent the opposite sign. Thus, if we add

$$300 + 300 = 600 \, (\text{i.e.,} -399)$$

both inputs represent positive numbers, but the result is negative. Then the test for overflow is this: *If both inputs to an addition have the same sign, and the output sign is different, overflow has occurred*.

ONE'S COMPLEMENT   The computer can use the binary version of the same method of representation that we have just discussed. In base 2, the largest digit is 1. Splitting the range down the middle, as we did before, numbers that begin with 0 are defined to be positive; numbers that begin with 1 are negative. Since

$$
\begin{array}{c}
1 \\
-0 \\
\hline
1
\end{array}
\quad \text{and} \quad
\begin{array}{c}
1 \\
-1 \\
\hline
0
\end{array}
$$

the 1's complement of a number is performed simply by changing every 0 to a 1 and every 1 to a 0. How elegantly simple! This exchange of 0s and 1s is also known as **inversion**. (Of course, this means that both 000 . . . and 111 . . . represent 0, specifically, +0 and −0, respectively.) The 1's complement scale for 8-bit binary numbers is shown in Figure 5.11.

Addition also works in the same way. To add two numbers, regardless of the implied sign of either input, the computer simply adds the numbers as though they were unsigned integers. If there is a carryover into the next bit beyond the leftmost specified bit, 1 is added to the result, following the usual end-around carry rule. Subtraction is done by inverting the subtrahend (i.e., changing every 0 to 1 and every 1 to 0) and adding. Overflows are

FIGURE 5.11

One's Complement Representation

10000000	11111111	00000000	01111111
-127_{10}	-0_{10}	0_{10}	127_{10}

detected in the same way as previously discussed: if both inputs are of the same sign, and the sign of the result is different, overflow has occurred; the result is outside the range. Notice that this test can be performed simply by looking at the leftmost bit of the two inputs and the result.

An important comment about conversion between signed binary and decimal integers in their complementary form: although the technique used is identical between 9's complement decimal and 1's complement binary, the modulus used in the two systems is obviously *not the same!* For example, the modulus in three-digit decimal is 999, with a positive range of 499. The modulus in 8-bit binary is 11111111, or 255_{10}, with a positive range of 01111111, or 127_{10}.

This means that you *cannot* convert directly between 9's complement decimal and 1's complement binary. Instead, you must change the number to sign-and-magnitude representation, convert, and then change the result to the new complementary form. Of course, if the number is positive, this process is trivial, since the complementary form is the same as the sign-and-magnitude form. But you must remember to follow this procedure if the sign is negative. Remember, too, that you must check for overflow to make sure that your number is still in range in the new base.

Here are several examples of 1's complement addition and subtraction, together with the equivalent decimal results:

EXAMPLES

Add

$$
\begin{array}{r}
00101101 = 45 \\
00111010 = 58 \\
\hline
01100111 = 103
\end{array}
$$

■ ■ ■

Add the 16- bit numbers

$$
\begin{array}{r}
0000000000101101 = 45 \\
1111111111000101 = -58 \\
\hline
1111111111110010 = -13
\end{array}
$$

Note that the addend 1111111111000101 is the inversion of the value in the previous example with eight additional 0s required to fill up 16 bits. The decimal result, -13, is found by inverting 1111111111110010 to 0000000000001101 to get a positive magnitude and adding up the bits.

EXAMPLES

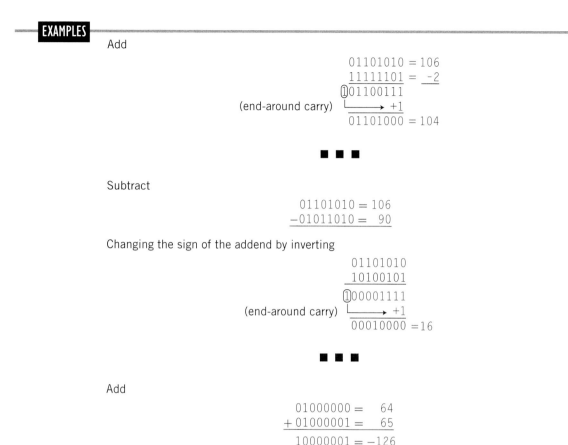

Add

$$01101010 = 106$$
$$11111101 = -2$$
$$\boxed{1}01100111$$
(end-around carry) $\longrightarrow +1$
$$01101000 = 104$$

■ ■ ■

Subtract

$$01101010 = 106$$
$$-01011010 = 90$$

Changing the sign of the addend by inverting

$$01101010$$
$$10100101$$
$$\boxed{1}00001111$$
(end-around carry) $\longrightarrow +1$
$$00010000 = 16$$

■ ■ ■

Add

$$01000000 = 64$$
$$+\,01000001 = 65$$
$$10000001 = -126$$

This is an obvious example of overflow. The correct positive result, 129, exceeds the range for 8 bits. Eight bits can store 256 numbers; splitting the range only allows positive values 0–127.

The overflow situation shown in the last example occurs commonly in the computer, and some high-level languages do not check adequately. In some versions of BASIC, for example, the sum

$$16384 + 16386$$

will show an incorrect result of −32765 or −32766. (The latter result comes from use of a different complementary representation, discussed in the next section.) What has happened is that overflow has occurred in a system that uses 16 bits for integer calculations. The positive range limit for 16 bits is +32767 (a 0 for the sign plus fifteen 1s). Since the sum of 16384 and 16386 is 32770, the calculation overflows. Unfortunately, the user may never notice, especially if the overflowing calculation is buried in a long series of calculations. A good programmer takes such possibilities into account when the program is written. (This type of error caused some embarrassment when it showed up in a recent version of Microsoft Excel.)

Ten's Complement and 2's Complement

FIGURE 5.12

Ten's Complement Scale

Representation	500	999|0	499
Number being represented	-500	-001|0	499
		−	+

TEN'S COMPLEMENT You have seen that complementary representation can be effective for the representation and calculation of signed integer numbers. As you are also aware, the system that we have described, which uses the largest number in the base as its complementary reflection point, suffers from some disadvantages that result from the dual zero on its scale.

By shifting the negative scale to the right by one, we can create a complementary system that has only a single zero. This is done by using the radix as a basis for the complementary operation. In decimal base, this is known as the 10's complement representation. The use of this representation will simplify calculations. The trade-off in using 10's complement representation is that it is slightly more difficult to find the complement of a number. A three-digit decimal scale is shown in Figure 5.12. Be sure to notice the differences between this diagram and Figure 5.6.

The theory and fundamental technique for 10's complement is the same as that for 9's complement. The 10's complement representation uses the modulus as its reflection point. The modulus for a three-digit decimal representation is 1000, which is one larger than the largest number in the system, 999.

Complements are found by subtracting the value from the modulus, in this case, 1000. This method assures a single zero, since $(1000 - 0)$ mod 1000 is zero. Again, as with the previously discussed complementary methods, notice that the complement of the complement results in the original value. See the examples on the facing page.

There is an alternative method for complementing a 10's complement number. First, observe that

$$1000 = 999 + 1$$

You recall that the 9's complement was found by subtracting each digit from 9:

$$9's \text{ comp} = 999 - \text{value}$$

From the previous equation, the 10's complement can be rewritten as

$$10's \text{ comp} = 1000 - \text{value} = 999 + 1 - \text{value} = 999 - \text{value} + 1$$

or, finally,

$$10's \text{ comp} = 9's \text{comp} + 1$$

This gives a simple alternative method for computing the 10's complement value: find the 9's complement, which is easy, and add 1 to the result. Either method gives the same result. You can use whichever method you find more convenient. This alternative method is usually easier computationally, especially when working with binary numbers, as you will see.

Addition in 10's complement is particularly simple. Since there is only a single zero in 10's complement, sums that cross the modulus are unaffected. Thus, the carry that results

EXAMPLES

Find the 10's complement of 247.

As a reminder, note that the question asks for the 10's *complement* of 247, not the 10's *complement representation*. Since 247 represents a positive number, its 10's complement representation is, of course, 247.

The 10's complement of 247 is

$$1000 - 247 = 753$$

Since 247 is a positive representation, 753 represents the value -247.

■ ■ ■

Find the 10's complement of 17.

As in the 9's complement work, we always have to be conscious of the number of specified digits. Since all the work so far has assumed that the numbers contain three digits, let's solve this problem from that assumption:

$$1000 - 017 = 983$$

■ ■ ■

Find the sign and magnitude of the three-digit number with 10's complement representation: 777

Since the number begins with a 7, it must be negative. Therefore,

$$1000 - 777 = 223$$

The sign-magnitude value is -223.

when the addition crosses the zero point is simply ignored. To add two numbers in 10's complement, one simply adds the digits; any carry beyond the specified number of digits is thrown away. (Actually, in the computer, the carry is saved in a special "carry bit," just in case it is to be used to extend the addition to another group of bits for multiple-word additions.) Subtraction is again performed by inverting the subtrahend and adding.

The range of numbers in 10's complement for three digits can be seen in Figure 5.12. Of particular interest is the fact that the positive and negative regions are of different size: there is one negative number, 500, that cannot be represented in the positive region. (The 10's complement of 500 is itself.) This peculiarity is a consequence of the fact that the total range of numbers is even for any even-numbered base, regardless of word size (in this case, 10^W). Since one value is reserved for zero, the number of remaining values to be split between positive and negative is odd and, thus, could not possibly be equal.

TWO'S COMPLEMENT.   Two's complement representation for binary is, of course, similar to 10's complement representation for decimal. In binary form, the modulus consists of a base 2 "1" followed by the specified number of 0s. For 16 bits, for example, the modulus is

10000000000000000

FIGURE 5.13

Two's Complement Representation

10000000	11111111	00000000	01111111
-128_{10}	-1_{10}	0_{10}	127_{10}

As was true for the 10's complement, the 2's complement of a number can be found in one of two ways: either subtract the value from the modulus or find the 1's complement by inverting every 1 and 0 and adding 1 to the result.

The second method is particularly well suited to implementation in the computer, but you can use whichever method you find more convenient.

Figure 5.13 shows an 8-bit scale for 2's complement representation.

Two's complement addition, like 10's complement addition in decimal, consists of adding the two numbers *mod* <the modulus>. This is particularly simple for the computer, since it simply means eliminating any 1s that don't fit into the number of bits in the word. Subtraction and overflow are handled as we have already discussed.

As in 10's complement, the range is unevenly divided between positive and negative. The range for 16 bits, for example, is $-32768 \leq$ value ≤ 32767.

There are many 2's complement problems at the end of the chapter for you to practice on.

The use of 2's complement is more common in computers than is 1's complement, but both methods are in use. The trade-off is made by the designers of a particular computer: 1's complement makes it easier to change the sign of a number, but addition requires an extra end-around carry step. One's complement has the additional drawback that the algorithm must test for and convert -0 to 0 at the end of each operation. Two's complement simplifies the addition operation at the expense of an additional add operation any time the sign change operation is required.

As a final note, before we conclude our discussion of binary complements, it is useful to be able to predict approximate sizes of integers that are represented in complementary form without going through the conversion. A few hints will help:

1. Positive numbers are always represented by themselves. Since they always start with 0, they are easily identified.

2. Small negative numbers, that is, negative numbers close to 0, have representations that start with large numbers of 1s. The number -2 in 8-bit 2's complement, for example, is represented by

    11111110

    whereas -128, the largest negative 2's complement number, is represented by

    10000000

    This is evident from the scale in Figure 5.13.

3. Since there is only a difference in value of 1 between 1's and 2's complement representations of negative numbers (positive numbers are, of course, identical

in both representations), you can get a quick idea of the value in either representation simply by inverting all the 1s and 0s and approximating the value from the result.

Overflow and Carry Conditions

We noted earlier in this discussion that overflows occur when the result of a calculation does not fit into the fixed number of bits available for the result. In 2's complement, an addition or subtraction overflow occurs when the result overflows into the sign bit. Thus, overflows can occur only when both operands have the same sign and can be detected by the fact that the sign of the result is opposite that of the operands.

Computers provide a flag that allows a programmer to test for an overflow condition. The overflow flag is set or reset each time a calculation is performed by the computer. In addition, the computer provides a **carry flag** that is used to correct for carries and borrows that occur when large numbers must be separated into parts to perform additions and subtractions. For example, if the computer has instructions that are capable of adding two 32-bit numbers, it would be necessary to separate a 64-bit number into two parts, add the least significant part of each, then add the most significant parts, together with any carry that was generated by the previous addition. For normal, single precision 2's complement addition and subtraction the carry bit is ignored.

Although overflow and carry procedures operate similarly, they are not quite the same, and can occur independently of each other. The carry flag is set when the result of an addition or subtraction exceeds the fixed number of bits allocated, without regard to sign. It is perhaps easiest to see the difference between overflow and carry conditions with an example. This example shows each of the four possible outcomes that can result from the addition of two 4-bit 2's complement numbers.

EXAMPLE

```
(+4) + (+2)                                    (+4) + (+6)
0100          no overflow,                     0100          overflow,
0010          no carry                         0110          no carry
0110 = (+6)   the result is correct  1010 = (−6)   the result is incorrect


(−4) + (−2)                                    (−4) + (−6)
1100          no overflow,                     1100          overflow,
1110          carry                            1010          Carry
110106 = (−6) ignoring carry,        10110 = (+6)  ignoring the carry,
              the result is correct                  the result is incorrect
```

If an overflow occurs on any but the most significant part of a multiple part addition, it is ignored (see exercise 5.13).

Other Bases

Any even-numbered base can be split the same way to represent signed integers in that base. Either the modulus or the largest-digit value can be used as a mirror for the complementary representation. Odd bases are more difficult: either the range must be split unevenly to use the leftmost digit as an indicator, or the second left digit must be used together with the first to indicate whether the represented number is positive or negative. We will not consider odd bases any further.

Of particular interest are the corresponding 7's and 8's complements in octal and 15's and 16's complements in hexadecimal. These correspond exactly to 1's and 2's complement in binary, so you can use calculation in octal or hexadecimal as a shorthand for binary.

As an example, consider four-digit hexadecimal as a substitute for 16-bit binary. The range will be split down the middle, so that numbers starting with $0-7_{16}$ are positive and those starting with 8–F are negative. But note that hex numbers starting with 8–F all have a binary equivalent with 1 in the leftmost place, whereas 0–7 all start with 0. Therefore, they conform exactly to the split in 16-bit binary.

You can carry the rest of the discussion by yourself, determining how to take the complement, and how to add, from the foregoing discussions. There are practice examples at the end of the chapter.

Finally, note that since binary-coded decimal is essentially a base 10 form, the use of complementary representation for BCD would require algorithms that analyze the first digit to determine the sign and then perform 9's or 10's complement procedures. Since the purpose of BCD representation is usually to simplify the conversion process, it is generally not practical to use complementary representation for signed integers in BCD.

Summary of Rules for Complementary Numbers

The following points summarize the rules for the representation and manipulation of complementary numbers, both radix and diminished radix, in any even number base. For most purposes you will be interested only in 2's complement and 16's complement:

1. Remember that the word "complement" is used in two different ways. To complement a number, or take the complement of a number, means to change its sign. To find the complementary representation of a number means to translate or identify the representation of the number just as it is given.

2. Positive numbers are represented the same in complementary form as they would be in sign and magnitude form. These numbers will start with 0, 1, . . . N/2−1. For binary numbers, positive numbers start with 0, negative with 1.

3. To go from negative sign-and-magnitude to complementary form, or to change the sign of a number, simply subtract each number from the largest number in the base (diminished radix) or from the value 100 . . . , where each zero corresponds to a number position (radix). Remember that implied zeros must be included in the procedure. Alternatively, the radix form may be calculated by adding 1 to the diminished radix form. For 2's complement, it is usually easiest to invert every digit and add 1 to the result.

4. To get the sign-and-magnitude representation for negative numbers, use the procedure in (2) to get the magnitude. The sign will, of course, be negative. Remember that the word size is fixed; there may be one or more implied 0s at the beginning of a number that mean the number is really positive.

5. To add two numbers, regardless of sign, simply add in the usual way. Carries beyond the leftmost digit are ignored in radix form, added to the result in diminished radix form. To subtract, take the complement of the subtrahend and add.

6. If we add two complementary numbers of the same sign and the result is of opposite sign, the result is incorrect. Overflow has occurred.

5.3 REAL NUMBERS

A Review of Exponential Notation

Real numbers add an additional layer of complexity. Because the number contains a radix point (decimal in base 10, binary in base 2), the use of complementary arithmetic must be modified to account for the fractional part of the number. The representation of real numbers in exponential notation simplifies the problem by separating the number into an integer, with a separate **exponent** that places the **radix point** correctly. As before, we first present the techniques in base 10, since working with decimal numbers is more familiar to you. Once you have seen the methods used for the storage and manipulation of floating point numbers, we will then extend our discussion to the binary number system. This discussion will include the conversion of floating point numbers between the decimal and binary bases (which requires some care) and the consideration of floating point formats used in actual computer systems.

Consider the whole number

$$12345$$

If we allow the use of exponents, there are many different ways in which we can represent this number. Without changing anything, this number can be represented as

$$12345 \times 10^0$$

If we introduce decimals, we can easily create other possible representations. Each of these alternative representations is created by shifting the decimal point from its original location. Since each single-place shift represents a multiplication or division of the value by the base, we can decrease or increase the exponent to compensate for the shift. For example, let us write the number as a decimal fraction with the decimal point at the beginning:

$$0.12345 \times 10^5$$

or, as another alternative,

$$123450000 \times 10^{-4}$$

or even,

$$0.0012345 \times 10^7$$

Of course, this last representation will be a poor choice if we are limited to five digits of magnitude,

$$0.00123 \times 10^7$$

since we will have sacrificed two digits of precision in exchange for the two zeros at the beginning of the number which do not contribute anything to the precision of the number. (You may recall from previous math courses that they are known as insignificant digits.) The other representations do retain full precision, and any one of these representations would be theoretically as good as any other. Thus, our choice of representation is somewhat arbitrary and will be based on more practical considerations.

The way of representing numbers described here is known as **exponential notation** or, alternatively, as scientific notation. Using the exponential notation for numbers requires the specification of four separate components to define the number. These are

1. The sign of the number ("+", for our original example)
2. The magnitude of the number, known as the **mantissa** (12345)
3. The sign of the exponent ("+")
4. The magnitude of the exponent (3, see below)

Two additional pieces of information are required to complete the picture:

5. The base of the exponent (in this case, 10)
6. The location of the decimal (or other base) radix point

Both these latter factors are frequently unstated, yet extremely important. In the computer, for example, the base of the exponent is usually, but not always, specified to be 2. In some computers, 16 or 10 may be used instead, and it is obviously important to know which is being used if you ever have to read the numbers in their binary form. The location of the decimal point (or *binary* point, if we're working in base 2) is also an essential piece of information. In the computer, the binary point is set at a particular location in the number, most commonly the beginning or the end of the number. Since its location never changes, it is not necessary to actually store the point. Instead, the location of the binary point is implied.

Knowing the location of the point is, of course, essential. In the example that accompanies the rules just given, the location of the decimal point was not specified. Reading the data suggests that the number might be

$$+12345 \times 10^{+3}$$

which, of course, is not correct if we're still using the number from our original example. The actual placement of the decimal point should be

$$12.345 \times 10^3$$

Let us summarize these rules by showing another example, with each component specifically marked. Assume that the number to be represented is

$$-0.0000003579$$

One possible representation of this number is

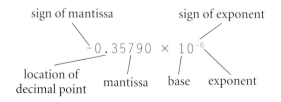

Floating Point Format

As was the case with integers, floating point numbers will be stored and manipulated in the computer using a "standard", predefined format. For practical reasons, a multiple of 8 bits is usually selected as the word size. This will simplify the manipulation and arithmetic that is performed with these numbers.

In the case of integers, the entire word is allocated to the magnitude of the integer and its sign. For floating point numbers, the word must be divided: part of the space is reserved for the exponent and its sign; the remainder is allocated to the mantissa and its sign. The base of the exponent and the implied location of the binary point are standardized as part of the format and, therefore, do not have to be stored at all.

You can understand that the format chosen is somewhat arbitrary, since you have already seen that there are many different ways to represent a floating point number. Among the decisions made by the designer of the format are the number of digits to use, the implied location of the binary or decimal point, the base of the exponent, and the method of handling the signs for the mantissa and the exponent.

For example, suppose that the standard word consists of space for seven decimal digits and a sign:

SMMMMMMM

This format would allow the storage of any integer in the range

$$-9,999,999 < I < +99,999,999$$

with full, seven-digit precision. Numbers of magnitude larger than 9,999,999 result in overflow. Numbers of magnitude less than 1 cannot be represented at all, except as 0.

For floating point numbers, we might assign the digits as follows:

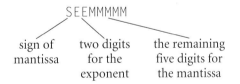

In addition we have to specify the implied location for the decimal point.

In this example we have "traded" two digits of exponent in exchange for the loss of two digits of precision. We emphasize that we have not increased the number of values that can be represented by seven digits. Seven digits can represent exactly 10,000,000 different values, no matter how they are used. We have simply chosen to use those digits differently—to increase the expressible range of values by giving up precision throughout the range. If we wish to increase the precision, one option is to increase the number of digits.

There are other possible trades. We could, for example, increase precision by another digit by limiting the exponent to a single digit. This might not be as limiting as it first appears. Since each increment or decrement of the exponent changes the number by a factor equivalent to the base (in this case, 10), a fairly substantial range of numbers can be accommodated with even a single digit, in this case 10^9 to 10^0, or 1 billion to 1.

The sign digit will be used to store the sign of the mantissa. Any of the methods shown earlier in this chapter for storing the sign and magnitude of integers could be used for

FIGURE 5.14

Excess-50 Representation

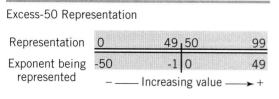

the mantissa. Most commonly, the mantissa is stored using sign-magnitude format. A few computers use complementary notation.

Notice that we have made no specific provision for the sign of the exponent within the proposed format. We must therefore use some method that includes the sign of the exponent within the digits of the exponent itself. One method that you have already seen for doing this is the complementary representation. (Since the exponent and mantissa are independent of each other, and are used differently in calculations, there is no reason to assume that the same representation would be used for both.)

The manipulations used in performing exponential arithmetic allow us to use a simple method for solving this problem. If we pick a value somewhere in the middle of the possible values for the exponent, for example, 50 when the exponent can take on values 0 to 99, and declare that value to correspond to the exponent 0, then every value lower than that will be negative and those above will be positive. Figure 5.14 shows the scale for this offset technique.

What we have done is *offset*, or bias, the value of the exponent by our chosen amount. Thus, to convert from exponential form to the format used in our example, we add the offset to the exponent, and store it in that form. Similarly, the stored form can be returned to our usual exponential notation by subtracting the offset.

This method of storing the exponent is known as **excess-N notation**, where N is the chosen midvalue. It is simpler to use for exponents than the complementary form, and appropriate to the calculations required on exponents. In our example we have used excess-50 notation. This allows us to store an exponential range of -50 to $+49$, corresponding to the stored values 00 to 99. We could, if we wished, pick a different offset value, which would expand our ability to handle larger numbers at the expense of smaller numbers, or vice versa.

If we assume that the implied decimal point is located at the beginning of the five-digit mantissa, excess-50 notation allows us a magnitude range of

$$0.00001 \times 10^{-50} < \text{number} < 0.99999 \times 10^{+49}$$

This is an obviously much larger range than that possible using integers, and at the same time gives us the ability to express decimal fractions. In practice, the range may be slightly more restricted, since many format designs require that the most significant digit not be 0, even for very small numbers. In this case, the smallest expressible number becomes 0.10000×10^{-50}, not a great limitation. The word consisting of all 0s is frequently reserved to represent the special value 0.0.

If we were to pick a larger (or smaller) value for the offset, we could skew the range to store smaller (or larger) numbers. Generally, values somewhere in the midrange seem to satisfy the majority of users, and there seems little reason to choose any other offset value.

Notice that, like the integer, it is still possible, although very difficult, to create an overflow by using a number of magnitude too large to be stored. With floating point numbers it is also possible to have **underflow**, where the number is a decimal fraction of magnitude too small to be stored. The diagram in Figure 5.15 shows the regions of underflow and overflow for our example. Note that in the diagram 0.00001×10^{-50} is expressed equivalently as 10^{-55}.

FIGURE 5.15

Regions of Overflow and Underflow

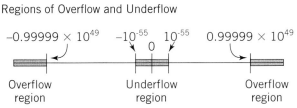

There is one more consideration. As you are already aware, the computer is actually capable of storing only numbers, no signs or decimal points. We have already handled the decimal point by establishing a fixed, implied point. We must also represent the sign of the number in a way that takes this limitation into account.

Here are some examples of floating point decimal representations. The format used is that shown on page 157: a sign, two digits of exponent stored excess-50, and five digits of mantissa. The value 0 is used to represent a "+" sign; 5 has been arbitrarily chosen to represent a "−" sign, just as 1 is usually chosen within the computer for the same purpose. The base is, of course, 10; the implied decimal point is at the beginning of the mantissa. You should look at these examples carefully to make sure that you understand all the details of the **floating point format**.

EXAMPLES

$$05324657 = 0.24657 \times 10^3 = 246.57$$
$$54810000 = -0.10000 \times 10^{-2} = -0.0010000$$

(Note that five significant digits are maintained.)

$$55555555 = -0.55555 \times 10^5 = -55555$$
$$04925000 = 0.25000 \times 10^{-1} = 0.025000$$

Normalization and Formatting of Floating Point Numbers

The number of digits used will be determined by the desired precision of the numbers. To maximize the precision for a given number of digits, numbers will be stored whenever possible with no leading zeros. This means that, when necessary, numbers are shifted left by increasing the exponent until leading zeros are eliminated. This process is called **normalization**.

Our standard format, then, will consist of a mantissa of fixed, predetermined size with a decimal point placed at a fixed, predetermined location. The exponent will be adjusted so that numbers will be stored in this format with no leading zeros.

As an example, let us set up a standard format that reflects the storage capabilities suggested in the previous section. Our format will consist of a sign and five digits, with the decimal point located at the beginning of the number:

$$.MMMMM \times 10^{EE}$$

There are four steps required to convert any decimal number into this standard format:

1. Provide an exponent of 0 for the number, if an exponent was not already specified as part of the number.
2. Shift the decimal point left or right by increasing or decreasing the exponent, respectively, until the decimal point is in the proper position.

3. Shift the decimal point right, if necessary, by decreasing the exponent, until there are no leading zeros in the mantissa.

4. Correct the precision by adding or discarding digits as necessary to meet the specification. We discard or round any digits in excess of the specified precision by eliminating the least significant digits. If the number has fewer than the specified number of digits, we supply zeros at the end.

Once we have normalized the number and put it into a standard exponential form, we can perform a fifth step to convert the result into the desired word format. To do this, we change the exponent into excess-50 notation and place the digits into their correct locations in the word.

Conversions between integer and floating point format are similar. The integer is treated as a number with an implied radix point at the end of the number. In the computer, an additional step may be required to convert the integer between complementary and sign-magnitude format to make it compatible with floating point format.

Here are some examples of a decimal to floating point format conversion:

EXAMPLES

Convert the number

$$246.8035$$

into our standard format.

1. Adding an exponent makes the number

$$246.8035 \times 10^0$$

2. We shift the decimal to the left three places, thereby increasing the exponent by 3:

$$0.2468035 \times 10^3$$

3. Since the number is already normalized (no leading zeros), there is no adjustment required.

4. There are seven digits, so we drop the two least significant digits, and the final exponential representation is

$$0.24680 \times 10^3$$

5. The exponent is 3, which in excess-50 notation is represented as 53. If we represent a "+" sign with the digit 0, and a "−" sign with the digit 5 (this choice is totally arbitrary, but we needed to select some digits since the sign itself cannot be stored), the final stored result becomes

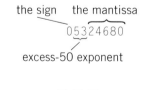

the sign   the mantissa
05324680
excess-50 exponent

■ ■ ■

Assume that the number to be converted is

$$1255 \times 10^{-3}$$

1. The number is already in exponential form.
2. We must shift the decimal to the left four places, so the number becomes

$$0.1255 \times 10^{+1}$$

   The positive exponent results from adding 4 to the original −3 exponent.
3. The number is normalized, so no additional adjustment is required.
4. A zero is added to provide five digits of precision. The final result in exponential form is

$$0.12550 \times 10^1$$

5. The exponent in excess-50 notation becomes 51, and the result in word format is

$$05112550$$

■ ■ ■

Assume that the number to be converted is

$$-0.00000075$$

1. Converting to exponential notation, we have

$$-0.00000075 \times 10^0$$

2. The decimal point is already in its correct position, so no modification is necessary.
3. Normalizing, the number becomes

$$-0.75 \times 10^{-6}$$

4. And the final exponential result,

$$-0.75000 \times 10^{-6}$$

5. In our word format, this becomes

$$54475000$$

Although the technique is simple and straightforward, it will still require some practice for you to feel comfortable with it. We suggest that you practice with a friend, inventing numbers for each other to put into a standard format.

Some students have a bit of difficulty remembering whether to increase or decrease the exponent when shifting the number left or right. There is a simple method that may help you to remember which way to go: when you shift the decimal to the right, it makes the resulting number larger. (For example, 1.5 becomes 15.) Thus, the exponent must become smaller to keep the number the same as it was originally.

A Programming Example

Perhaps representing the steps as a pseudocode procedure will clarify these concepts even further. The procedure in Figure 5.16 converts numbers in normal decimal format to the floating point format

SEEMMMMM

The implied decimal point is at the beginning of the mantissa, and the sign is stored as 0 for positive, 5 for negative. The mantissa is stored in sign-magnitude format. The exponent is stored in excess-50 format. The number 0.0 is treated as a special case, with an all-zero format.

We suggest that you trace through the procedure carefully, until you understand each step.

FIGURE 5.16

A Procedure to Convert Decimal Numbers to Floating Point Format

```
function ConvertToFloat();
//variables used:
real decimalin; //decimal number to be converted
//components of the output
integer sign, exponent, integermantissa;
float mantissa; //used for normalization
integer floatout; //final form of output
{
    if (decimalin == 0.0) floatout = 0;
    else {
        if (decimalin > 0.0) sign = 0;
        else sign = 50000000;
        exponent = 50;
        StandardizeNumber;
        floatout = sign + exponent * 100000 + integermantissa;
        } //end else

function StandardizeNumber(); {
    mantissa = abs (mantissa);
    //adjust the decimal to fall between 0.1 and 1.0.
        while (mantissa >= 1.00) {
            mantissa = mantissa / 10.0;
            exponent = exponent + 1;
        } //end while
        while (mantissa < 0.1) {
            mantissa = mantissa * 10.0;
            exponent = exponent - 1;
        } //end while
        integermantissa = round (10000.0 * mantissa)
    } //end function StandardizeNumber
} //end ConvertToFloat
```

Floating Point Calculations

Floating point arithmetic is obviously more complex than integer arithmetic. First, the exponent and the mantissa have to be treated separately. Therefore, each has to be extracted from each number being manipulated.

ADDITION AND SUBTRACTION   You recall that in order to add or subtract numbers that contain decimal fractions, it is necessary that the decimal points line up. When using exponential notation, it is thus a requirement that the implied decimal point in both numbers be in the same position; the exponents of both numbers must agree.

The easiest way to align the two numbers is to shift the number with the smaller exponent to the right a sufficient number of spaces to increase the exponent to match the larger exponent. This process inserts insignificant zeros at the beginning of the number. Note that this process protects the precision of the result by maintaining all the digits of the larger number. It is the least significant digits of the smaller number that will disappear.

Once alignment is complete, addition or subtraction of the mantissas can take place. It is possible that the addition or subtraction may result in an overflow of the most significant digit. In this case, the number must be shifted right and the exponent incremented to accommodate the overflow. Otherwise, the exponent remains unchanged.

It is useful to notice that the exponent can be manipulated directly in its excess form, since it is the difference in the two exponents that is of interest rather than the value of the exponent itself. It is thus not necessary to change the exponents to their actual values in order to perform addition or subtraction.

EXAMPLE

Add the two floating point numbers

```
05199520
04967850
```

Assume that these numbers are formatted using sign-and-magnitude notation for the mantissa and excess-50 notation for the exponent. The implied decimal point is at the beginning of the mantissa, and base 10 is used for the exponent.

Shifting the lower mantissa right two places to align the exponent, the two numbers become

```
05199520
0510067850
```

Adding the mantissas, the new mantissa becomes

```
(1)0019850
```

We have put the 1 in parentheses to emphasize the fact that it is a carry beyond the original left position of the mantissa. Therefore, we must again shift the mantissa right one place and increment the exponent to accommodate this digit:

```
05210019(850)
```

Rounding the result to five places of precision, we finally get

```
05210020
```

Checking the result,

$$05199520 = 0.99520 \times 10^1 \;=\; 9.9520$$
$$04967850 = 0.67850 \times 10^{-1} = \underline{0.06785}$$
$$10.01985 = 0.1001985 \times 10^2$$

which converts to the result that we previously obtained.

MULTIPLICATION AND DIVISION Alignment is not necessary in order to perform multiplication or division. Exponential numbers are multiplied (or divided) by multiplying (dividing) the two mantissas and adding (subtracting) the two exponents. The sign is dealt with separately in the usual way. This procedure is relatively straightforward. There are two special considerations that must be handled, however:

1. Multiplication or division frequently results in a shifting of the decimal point (e.g., $0.2 \times 0.2 = 0.04$) and normalization must be performed to restore the location of the decimal point and to maintain the precision of the result.

2. We must adjust the excess value of the resulting exponent. Adding two exponents, each of which contains an excess value, results in adding the excess value to itself, so the final exponent must be adjusted by subtracting the excess value from the result. Similarly, when we subtract the exponents, we subtract the excess value from itself, and we must restore the excess value by adding it to the result.

This is seen easily with an example. Assume we have two numbers with exponent 3. Each is represented in excess-50 notation as 53. Adding the two exponents,

$$
\begin{array}{r}
53 \\
\underline{53} \\
106
\end{array}
$$

We have added the value 50 twice, and so we must subtract it out to get the correct excess-50 result:

$$
\begin{array}{r}
106 \\
\underline{-50} \\
56
\end{array}
$$

3. The multiplication of two five-digit normalized mantissas yields a ten-digit result. Only five digits of this result are significant, however. To maintain full, five-digit precision, we must first normalize and then round the normalized result back to five digits.

EXAMPLE

Multiply the two numbers

$$
\begin{array}{r}
05220000 \\
\times 04712500
\end{array}
$$

Adding the exponents and subtracting the offset results in a new, excess-50 exponent of

$$52 + 47 - 50 = 49$$

Multiplying the two mantissas,

$$0.20000 \times 0.12500 = 0.025000000$$

Normalizing the result by shifting the point one space to the right decreases the exponent by one, giving a final result

$$04825000$$

Checking our work,

$$05220000 \text{ is equivalent to } 0.20000 \times 10^2,$$
$$04712500 \text{ is equivalent to } 0.12500 \times 10^{-3}$$

which multiplies out to

$$0.0250000000 \times 10^{-1}$$

Normalizing and rounding,

$$0.0250000000 \times 10^{-1} = 0.25000 \times 10^{-2}$$

which corresponds to our previous result.

Floating Point in the Computer

The techniques discussed in the previous section can be applied directly to the storage of floating point numbers in the computer simply by replacing the digits with bits. Typically, 4, 8, or 16 bytes are used to represent a floating point number. In fact, the few differences that do exist result from "tricks" that can be played when "0" and "1" are the only options.

A typical floating point format might look like the diagram in Figure 5.17. In this example, 32 bits (4 bytes) are used to provide a range of approximately 10^{-38} to 10^{+38}. With 8 bits, we can provide 256 levels of exponent, so it makes sense to store the exponent in excess-128 notation.

EXAMPLE

Here are some examples of binary floating point format using this notation. Again we have assumed that the binary point is at the start of the mantissa. The base of the exponent is 2.

$$0\ 10000001 \quad 11001100000000000000000 =$$
$$+1.1001100000000000000000$$
$$1\ 10000100 \quad 10000111100000000000000 =$$
$$-1000.0111100000000000000$$
$$1\ 01111110 \quad 10101010101010101010101 =$$
$$-0.0010101010101010101010101$$

FIGURE 5.17

Typical Floating Point Format

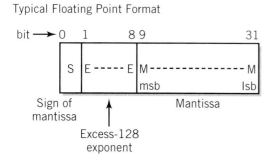

Thanks to the nature of the binary system, the 23 bits of mantissa can be stretched to provide 24 bits of precision, which corresponds to approximately seven decimal digits of precision. Since the leading bit of the mantissa must be "1" if the number is normalized, there is no need to store the most significant bit explicitly. Instead, the leading bit can be treated implicitly, similar to the binary point.

There are three potential disadvantages to using this trick. First, the assumption that the leading bit is always a "1" means that we cannot store numbers too small to be normalized, which slightly limits the small end of the range. Second, any format that may require a "0" in the most significant bit for any reason cannot use this method. Finally, this method requires that we provide a separate way to store the number 0.0, since the requirement that the leading bit be a "1" makes a mantissa of 0.0 an impossibility!

Since the additional bit doubles the available precision of the mantissa in all numbers, the slightly narrowed range is usually considered an acceptable trade-off. The number 0.0 is handled by selecting a particular 32-bit word and assigning it the value 0.0. Twenty-four bits of mantissa corresponds to approximately seven decimal digits of precision.

Don't forget that the base and implied binary point must also be specified.

There are many variations, providing different degrees of precision and exponential range, but the basic techniques for handling floating point numbers in the computer are identical to those that we have already discussed in the previous sections of this chapter.

IEEE 754 STANDARD   Most current computers conform to IEEE 754 standard formats. The IEEE Computer Society is a society of computer professionals. Among its tasks, the IEEE Computer Society develops technical standards for use by the industry. The IEEE 754 standard defines formats for 32-bit and 64-bit floating point arithmetic. Instructions built into modern computers utilize the standard to perform floating point arithmetic, normalization, and conversion between integer and floating point representations internally under program command. The standard also facilitates the portability of programs between different computers that support the standard.

In addition to the IEEE 754 format, there are a number of older, machine-specific formats still in use for legacy data. The Macintosh also provides an additional 80-bit format. Sun UltraSparc and IBM mainframes systems include additional 128-bit formats. The Intel IA-64 architecture conforms to the IEEE 754 format, but also provides 64-bit significand/17-bit exponent range capability; the programmer can set individual precision control and widest-range exponent values in the floating point status register for additional flexibility.

The standard defines a **single-precision floating point format** consisting of 32 bits, divided into a sign, 8 bits of exponent, and 23 bits of mantissa. Since normalized numbers must always start with a 1, the leading bit is not stored, but is instead implied; this bit is located to the left of the implied binary point. Thus, numbers are normalized to the form

$$1.MMMMMMM\dots$$

FIGURE 5.18

IEEE Standard 32-bit Floating Point Value
Definition

Exponent	Mantissa	Value
0	± 0	0
0	not 0	± 2^{-126} × 0.M
1-254	any	± 2^{E-127} × 1.M
255	± 0	± ∞
255	not 0	NaN (Not a Number)

The exponent is formatted using excess-127 notation, with an implied base of 2. This would theoretically allow an exponent range of 2^{-127} to 2^{128}. In actuality, the stored exponent values 0 and 255 are used to indicate special values, and the exponential range of this format is thus restricted to

$$2^{-126} \text{ to } 2^{127}$$

The number 0.0 is defined by a mantissa of 0 together with the special exponential value 0. The IEEE standard also allows the values ±∞, very small denormalized numbers, and various other special conditions. Overall, the standard allows approximately seven significant decimal digits and an approximate value range of 10^{-45} to 10^{38}.

The double-precision floating point format standard works similarly. Sixty-four bits (8 bytes) are divided into a sign, 11 bits of exponent, and 52 bits of mantissa. The same format is used, with excess-1023 notation for the exponent, an implied base of 2, and an implied most significant bit to the left of the implied binary point. The double-precision standard supports approximately fifteen significant decimal digits and a range of more than 10^{-300} to 10^{300}!

The values defined for all possible 32-bit words are shown in Figure 5.18. The 64-bit table is similar, except for the limiting exponent of 2047, which results in an excess 1023 offset.

Conversion between Base 10 and Base 2

On occasion, you may find it useful to be able to convert real numbers between decimal and binary representation. This task must be done carefully. There are two major areas that sometimes cause students (and others!) difficulty:

1. The whole and fractional parts of numbers with an embedded decimal or binary point must be converted separately.
2. Numbers in exponential form must be reduced to a pure decimal or binary mixed number or fraction before the conversion can be performed.

We dealt with the first issue in Section 3.8. Recall from that section that in converting from one base to another that one must deal with the different multipliers associated with each successive digit. To the left of the radix point, the multipliers are integer, and there is a direct relationship between the different bases. To the right of the point, the multipliers are fractional, and there may or may not be a rational relationship between the multipliers in the different bases.

The solution is to convert each side of the radix point separately using the techniques discussed in Chapter 3. As an alternative, you can multiply the entire number in one base by whatever number is required to make the entire number an integer, and then convert the number in integer form. When this is complete, however, you must divide the converted result by *that same multiplier* in the new base. It is not correct to simply shift the radix point back, since each shift has a different value in the new base! Thus, if you shift a binary point right by seven places, you have effectively multiplied the number by 128, and you must divide the converted number by 128 in the new base. This latter method is best illustrated with an example.

EXAMPLE

Convert the decimal number 253.75 to binary floating point form.

Begin by multiplying the number by 100 to form the integer value 25375. This is converted to its binary equivalent 110001100011111, or $1.10001100011111 \times 2^{14}$. The IEEE 754 floating point equivalent representation for this integer would be

$$0 \mid 10001101 \mid 10001100011111$$

Sign   Excess-127   Mantissa (initial 1 is dropped)

Exponent = 127 + 14

One more step is required to complete the conversion. The result must be divided by the binary floating point equivalent of 100_{10} to restore the original decimal value. 100_{10} converts to binary 1100100_2, or 010000101100100 in IEEE 754 form. The last step is to divide the original result by this value, using floating point division. We will omit this step, as it is both difficult and irrelevant to this discussion. Although this method looks more difficult than converting the number directly as a mixed fraction, it is sometimes easier to implement within the computer.

The problem with converting floating point numbers expressed in exponential notation is essentially the same problem; however, the difficulty is more serious because it looks as though it should be possible to convert a number, keeping the same exponent, and this is of course not true.

If you always remember that the exponent actually represents a multiplier of value B^e, where B is the base and e is the actual exponent, then you will be less tempted to make this mistake. Obviously it is incorrect to assume that this multiplier would have the same value for a different B.

Instead, it is necessary to follow one of the two solutions just outlined: either reduce the exponential notation to a standard mixed fraction and convert each side separately, or use the value B^e as a multiplier to be divided in the new base at the end of the conversion.

5.4 PROGRAMMING CONSIDERATIONS

In this chapter you have been exposed to a number of different ways of storing and manipulating numeric values. It should be of interest to you to consider how a programmer might make an intelligent choice between the many different options available.

The trade-offs between integer and floating point are clear. Integer calculations are easier for the computer to perform, have the potential to provide higher precision, and are obviously much faster to execute. Integer values usually take up fewer storage locations. As you will see later, it takes a certain amount of time to access each storage location; thus, the use of fewer storage locations saves time, as well as space.

Clearly, the use of integer arithmetic is preferred whenever possible. Most modern high-level languages provide two or more different integer word sizes, usually at least a "short" integer of 16 bits and a "long" integer of 64 bits. Now that you understand the range limitations of integer arithmetic, you are in a position to determine whether a particular variable or constant can use the integer format, and whether special error checking may be required in your program.

The longer integer formats may require multiple-word calculation algorithms, and as such are slower to execute than short formats. The short format is preferable when it is sufficient for the values that you expect. It may also be necessary to consider the limitations of other systems that the same program may have to operate on.

The use of real numbers is indicated whenever the variable or constant has a fractional part, whenever the number can take on very large or very small values that are outside of integer range, or whenever the required precision exceeds the number of different values that are possible in the longest integer format available to you. (As you've seen, most systems provide a floating point format of very high precision.) Of course, it is sometimes possible to multiply a mixed number by some multiplier to make it integer, perform the calculations in integer form, and then divide back. If the number of calculations is large, and the numbers can be adjusted to operate as integers, this can be a worthwhile option to consider, especially for the gain in execution speed.

As with integers, it is desirable to use the real number with the least precision that is sufficient for the task. Higher-precision formats require more storage and usually must use multiple-word floating point or packed decimal calculation algorithms that are much slower than the lower-precision formats.

Recall that decimal fractions may convert into irrational binary fractions. For those languages that provide the capability, the use of packed decimals represents an attractive alternative to floating point for those business applications where exact calculations involving mixed decimal numbers are required.

SUMMARY AND REVIEW

Computers store all data as binary numbers. There are a number of different ways to format these binary numbers to represent the various types of numbers required for computer processing. Conceptually, the simplest formats are sign-and-magnitude and binary-coded decimal. Although BCD is sometimes used for business programming, both of these formatting methods have shortcomings in terms of number manipulation and calculation.

Unsigned integers can of course be directly represented by their binary equivalents. Complementary arithmetic is usually the method of choice for signed integers. Nine's decimal complement, and its binary equivalent 1's complement, split the number range in two, using the upper half of the range to represent negative numbers. Positive numbers represent themselves. These representations are convenient and especially simple to use, since the complement is found by subtracting the number from a row of the largest digits in the base. Binary complements may be found by simply inverting the 0s and 1s in the number. Calculations are a bit more difficult due to the existence of both positive and negative values for zero, but end-around carry addition may be used for this purpose.

Ten's complement and 2's complement split the range similarly, but use a single value 0 for zero. This requires the use of a complement based on a value one larger than the largest number in the base for the given number of digits. This "base value" will always consist of a 1 followed by N zeros, where N is the number of digits being used. Complementation may be taken by inverting the number as before, and adding 1 to the result, or by subtracting the number from the base value. Calculation is straightforward, using modulo arithmetic. Most computer arithmetic instructions are based on 2's complement arithmetic.

Both 1's and 2's complement representations have the additional convenience that the sign of a number may be readily identified, since a negative number always begins with a "1." Small negative numbers have large values, and vice versa. Complementary representations for other even-numbered bases can be built similarly.

Numbers with a fractional part and numbers that are too large to fit within the constraints of the integer data capacity are stored and manipulated in the computer as real, or floating point, numbers. In effect, there is a trade-off between accuracy and range of acceptable numbers.

The usual floating point number format consists of a sign bit, an exponent, and a mantissa. The sign and value of the exponent are usually represented in an excess-N format. The base of the exponent is 2 for most systems, but some systems use a different base for the exponent. The radix point is implied. When possible, the mantissa is normalized.

In some systems the leading bit is also implied, since normalization requires that the leading bit of the mantissa be a 1.

Floating point numbers are subject to overflow or underflow, where the exponent of the number is too large or too small to represent, respectively. Zero is treated as a special case. Sometimes there is also a special representation for ∞.

Addition and subtraction require that the exponents in each number be equal. This is equivalent to lining up the decimal point in conventional decimal arithmetic. In multiplication and division, the exponents are added or subtracted, respectively. Special care must be taken with exponents that are expressed in excess-N notation.

Most computers conform to the format defined in IEEE Standard 754. Other formats in use include extra-precision formats and legacy formats.

FOR FURTHER READING

The representation and manipulation of integers and real numbers within the computer is discussed in most computer architecture texts. A particularly effective discussion is found in Stallings [STAL05]. This discussion presents detailed algorithms and hardware implementations for the various integer operations. A simpler discussion, with many examples, is found in Lipschutz [LIPS82]. More comprehensive treatments of computer arithmetic can be found in the two-volume collection of papers edited by Swartzlander [SWAR90] and in various textbooks on the subject, including those by Kulisch and Maranker [KUL81] and Spaniol [SPAN81]. A classical reference on computer algorithms, which includes a substantial discussion on computer arithmetic, is the book by Knuth [KNUT97]. One additional article of interest is the article titled "What Every Computer Scientist Should Know About Floating-Point Arithmetic" [GOLD91].

KEY CONCEPTS AND TERMS

binary-coded decimal (BCD)	integer numbers	sign-and-magnitude representation
carry flag	integer representation	signed integers
complement	inversion	single-precision floating point format
end-around carry	mantissa	2's complement representation
excess-*N* notation	normalization	underflow
exponent	1's complement representation	unsigned integer
exponential notation	overflow	wraparound
floating point format	radix point	
floating point numbers	real numbers	

READING REVIEW QUESTIONS

5.1 What is the largest unsigned integer that can be stored as a 16-bit number?

5.2 What does *BCD* stand for? Explain at least two important disadvantages of storing numbers in BCD format. Offer one advantage for using a BCD format for storing numbers.

5.3 Give an example that shows the disadvantage of using a sign-and-magnitude format for manipulating signed integers.

5.4 What is a quick way to identify negative numbers when using 1's complement arithmetic?

5.5 What is the relationship between complementary representation and sign-and-magnitude representation for positive numbers?

5.6 How do you change the sign of an integer stored in 1's complement form? As an example, the 8-bit representation for the value 19 is 00010011_2. What is the 1's complement representation for -19?

5.7 Explain the procedure for adding two numbers in 1's complement form. As an example, convert $+38$ and -24 to 8-bit 1's complement form and add them. Convert your result back to decimal and confirm that your answer is correct.

5.8 How do you identify an *overflow* condition when you add two numbers in 1's complement form?

5.9 How do you change the sign of an integer stored in 2's complement form? As an example, the 8-bit representation for the value 19 is 00010011_2. What is the 2's complement representation for -19?

5.10 If you see a 2's complement number whose value is 11111110_2, what rough estimate can you make about the number?

5.11 Explain the procedure for adding two numbers in 2's complement form. As an example, convert $+38$ and -24 to 8-bit 2's complement form and add them. Convert your result back to decimal and confirm that your answer is correct.

5.12 How do you detect overflow when adding two numbers in 2's complement form?

5.13   Real numbers in a computer (or *float*, if you prefer), are most often represented in exponential notation. Four separate components are needed to represent numbers in this form. Identify each component in the number 1.2345×10^{-5}. What is the advantage of this type of representation, rather than storing the number as 0.000012345?

5.14   To represent a number in exponential form in the computer, two additional assumptions must be made about the number. What are those assumptions?

5.15   Exponents are normally stored in *excess-N* notation. Explain excess-N notation. If a number is stored in excess-31 notation and the actual exponent is 2^{+12}, what value is stored in the computer for the exponent?

5.16   When adding two floating point numbers, what must be true for the exponents of the two numbers?

5.17   The IEEE provides a standard 32-bit format for floating point numbers. The format for a number is specified as $\pm 1.M \times 2^{E-127}$. Explain each part of this format.

EXERCISES

5.1   The following decimal numbers are already in six-digit 10's complementary form. Add the numbers. Convert each number and your result to sign and magnitude, and confirm your results.

a.
$$\begin{array}{r} 1250 \\ \underline{772950} \end{array}$$

b.
$$\begin{array}{r} 899211 \\ \underline{999998} \end{array}$$

c.
$$\begin{array}{r} 970000 \\ \underline{30000} \end{array}$$

5.2   Add the following decimal numbers by converting each to five-digit 10's complementary form, adding, and converting back to sign and magnitude.

a.
$$\begin{array}{r} 24379 \\ \underline{5098} \end{array}$$

b.
$$\begin{array}{r} 24379 \\ \underline{-5098} \end{array}$$

c.
$$\begin{array}{r} -24379 \\ \underline{5098} \end{array}$$

5.3   Subtract the second number from the first by taking the six-digit 10's complement of the second number and adding. Convert the result back to sign and magnitude if necessary.

a.

$$
\begin{array}{r}
37968 \\
(-)\ 24109 \\ \hline
\end{array}
$$

b.

$$
\begin{array}{r}
37968 \\
(-) - 70925 \\ \hline
\end{array}
$$

c.

$$
\begin{array}{r}
-10255 \\
(-) - 7586 \\ \hline
\end{array}
$$

5.4   Given the positive number 2468, what is the largest positive digit that you can add that will not cause overflow in a four-digit decimal, 10's complement number system?

5.5   Data is stored in the R4-D4 computer using eight-digit base 4 notation. Negative numbers are stored using 4's complement.

   a.   What is the sign-and-magnitude value of the following 4's complement number?

$$33333210_4$$

   Leave your answer in base 4.

   b.   Add the following eight-digit 4's complement numbers. Then, show the sign-and-magnitude values (in base 4) for each of the input numbers and for your result.

$$
\begin{array}{r}
13220231 \\
120000 \\ \hline
\end{array}
$$

5.6   Data was stored in the Digital PDP-9 computer using six-digit octal notation. Negative numbers were stored in 8's complement form.

   a.   How many bits does six-digit octal represent? Show that 8's complement octal and 2's complement binary are exactly equivalent.

   b.   What is the largest positive octal number that can be stored in this machine?

   c.   What does the number in (b) correspond to in decimal?

   d.   What is the largest possible negative number? Give your answer in both octal and decimal form.

5.7   **a.**   Find the 16-bit 2's complementary binary representation for the decimal number 1987.

   b.   Find the 16-bit 2's complementary binary representation for the decimal number -1987.

   c.   From your answer in (b) find the six-digit 16's complement hexadecimal representation for the decimal number -1987.

5.8   Convert the decimal number -19575 to a 15-bit 2's complement binary number. What happens when you perform this conversion? After the conversion is complete, what values (base 2 and base 10) does the computer think it has?

5.9   What are the 16-bit 1's and 2's complements of the following binary numbers?

    a.   10000

    b.   100111100001001

    c.   0100111000100100

5.10   Add the following two 12-bit binary 2's complement numbers. Then convert each number to decimal and check the results.

    a.

$$11001101101$$
$$\underline{111010111011}$$

    b.

$$101011001100$$
$$\underline{111111111100}$$

5.11   Add the following 16's complement hexadecimal numbers

$$4F09$$
$$\underline{D3A5}$$

   Is your result positive or negative? How do you know? Convert each number to binary and add the binary numbers. Convert the result back to hexadecimal. Is the result the same?

5.12   Consider a machine that performs calculations 4 bits at a time. Eight-bit 2's complement numbers can be added by adding the four least significant bits, followed by the four most significant bits. The leftmost bit is used for the sign, as usual. With 8 bits for each number, add -4 and -6, using 4-bit binary 2's complement arithmetic. Did overflow occur? Did carry occur? Verify your numerical result.

5.13   In 12's complement base 12, how would you know if a number is positive or negative?

5.14   Most computers provide separate instructions for performing unsigned additions and complementary additions. Show that for unsigned additions, carry and overflow are the same. (Hint: Consider the definition of overflow.)

5.15   **a.**   Convert the decimal number 19557 to floating point. Use the format SEEM M M M. All digits are decimal. The exponent is stored excess-40 (not excess-50). The implied decimal point is at the *beginning* of the mantissa. The sign is 1 for a positive number, 7 for a negative number. Hint: Note carefully the number of digits in the mantissa!

    b.   What is the range of numbers that can be stored in this format?

    c.   What is the floating point representation for -19557?

    d.   What is the six-digit 10's complement representation for -19557?

    e.   What is the floating point representation for 0.0000019557?

5.16   **a.**   Convert the number 123.57×10^{15} to the format SEEM M M M, with the exponent stored excess-49. The implied decimal point is to the right of the first mantissa digit.

    b.   What is the smallest number you can use with this format before underflow occurs?

5.17   Real numbers in the R4-D4 computer are stored in the format

$$SEEMMMMM_4$$

where all the digits, including the exponent, are in base 4. The mantissa is stored as sign and magnitude, where the sign is 0 for a positive number and 3 for a negative number. The implied quadrinary (base 4!) point is at the beginning of the mantissa:

$$.MMMMM$$

a.   If you know that the exponent is stored in an excess-something format, what would be a good choice of value for "something?"

b.   Convert the real, decimal number 16.5 to base 4, and show its representation in the format of the R4-D4 computer. Use the excess value that you determined in part (a).

5.18   In the Pink-Lemon-8 computer, real numbers are stored in the format

$$SEEMMMM_8$$

where all the digits, including the exponent, are in octal. The exponent is stored excess-40_8. The mantissa is stored as sign and magnitude, where the sign is 0 for a positive number and 4 for a negative number. The implied octal point is at the end of the mantissa: $MMMM$.
Consider the real number stored in this format as

$$4366621$$

a.   What real number is being represented? Leave your answer in octal.

b.   Convert your answer in part (a) to decimal. You may leave your answer in fractional form if you wish.

c.   What does changing the original exponent from 36 to 37 do to the magnitude of the number? (Stating that it moves the octal point one place to the right or left is not a sufficient answer.) What would be the new magnitude in decimal?

5.19   Convert the following binary and hexadecimal numbers to floating point format. Assume a binary format consisting of a sign bit (negative = 1), a base 2, 8-bit, excess-128 exponent, and 23 bits of mantissa, with the implied binary point to the right of the first bit of the mantissa.

a. 110110.011011_2

b. -1.1111001_2

c. $-4F7F_{16}$

d. 0.00000000111111_2

e. 0.1100×2^{36}

f. 0.1100×2^{-36}

5.20   For the format used in Exercise 5.19, what decimal number is represented by each of the following numbers in floating point format?

a. $C2F00000_{16}$

b. $3C540000_{16}$

5.21   The following decimal numbers are stored in excess-50 floating point format, with the decimal point to the left of the first mantissa digit. Add them. A 9 is used as a negative sign. Present your result in standard decimal sign-and-magnitude notation.

a.

```
05225731
04833300
```

b.

```
05012500
95325750
```

5.22   Using the same notation as in Exercise 5.9, multiply the following numbers. Present your answer in standard decimal notation.

a.

```
05452500
04822200
```

b.

```
94650000
94450000
```

5.23   Using the same format found in Exercise 5.19, add and multiply the following floating point numbers. Present your answers in both floating point and sign-and-magnitude formats.

$$3DEC0000_{16}$$
$$C24C0000_{16}$$

5.24   Represent the decimal number 171.625 in IEEE 754 format.

5.25   Write a program in your favorite language that converts numbers represented in the decimal floating point format

SEEMMMMM

into 10's complementary integer form. Round any fractional decimal value.

5.26   Show the packed decimal format for the decimal number −129975.

5.27   What base is the student in the chapter cartoon using to perform his addition?

PART THREE

The basic operation of a computer is defined by its hardware architecture. The hardware architecture establishes the CPU instruction set and the type of operations that are permitted. It defines the passage of data from one part of the computer to another. It establishes the ground rules for input and output operation.

The next six chapters introduce the fundamental architectural concepts that define computer operations and hardware organization. We will attempt to convey the basic simplicity and elegance of computer instruction sets. We will expose the inner workings of computer peripherals and show how the various pieces fit together to create a system.

For the past sixty plus years, and for the foreseeable future, basic computer architecture conforms to the general principles established by von Neumann that were introduced in Chapter 1. Chapter 6 introduces the principles of von Neumann architecture using a classic model of the computer called the Little Man Computer as an example. The Little Man Computer introduces the stored program concept, demonstrates the role of memory, describes the essential instructions that make up a computer instruction set, and explains the simple set of operations that implement an instruction set. We also show how the basic instructions of a computer work together to make up a program.

In Chapter 7 we extend the ideas introduced in Chapter 6 to the operation of a real computer. We consider the basic components of a CPU, explain the concept of a bus, discuss the operation of memory, and show how each of these architectural elements fit together to create a computer system. We also show the individual operations that make up the execution of instructions, the so-called fetch-execute cycle. We also discuss the formats for instruction words and present a general classification of the instruction set.

In Chapter 8, we consider the variations that distinguish one CPU architecture from another. The major topics in Chapter 8 deal with CPU design and organization. We present different CPU models, and compare them. We investigate alternatives to the traditional CPU organization and explain the benefits to be gained. We look at improvements to memory and, especially, the use of cache memory.

COMPUTER ARCHITECTURE
AND HARDWARE OPERATION

In Chapter 9 we shift our focus to I/O. Chapter 9 introduces the various methods that are used to move data between computer peripherals and memory, including the use of interrupts and direct access paths between peripherals and memory as efficient ways to perform I/O with minimal impact on the processing unit. We also introduce the concept of I/O modules as an interface between the various I/O devices and the CPU and memory components.

Chapter 10 provides explanations of the requirements and operation of various I/O peripheral components, including flash memory, disks, displays, tapes, printers, and other components. This chapter also presents a hierarchical model of storage.

Chapter 11 integrates the major ideas of the previous five chapters and then explores additional features and innovative techniques at the system level that have expanded the performance and capability of computers. While these techniques are substantial exten- sions to the basic design, they do not change the fundamental concepts and operating methods that are discussed in the earlier chapters. Beyond the discussion of basic com- puter system hardware architecture, the most important topics in this chapter are the modern buses and I/O channels that are used to expand I/O capability, and the inter- connection of computer systems into clusters to increase computing power and improver reliability.

There are four additional supplementary chapters on the Web at www.wiley.com/ college/Englander. Three of these provide additional insight into material presented in Part 3. Supplementary Chapter 1 offers an overview of Boolean algebra and the digital logic circuits that are used to implement CPU hardware circuits. Supplementary Chapter 2 illustrates many of the previous concepts with case studies of three important current systems, representing three different approaches to computer design. Supplementary Chapter 3 expands on the discussion of CPU addressing techniques that is touched only briefly in Chapter 8.

CHAPTER 6

THE LITTLE MAN COMPUTER

6.0 INTRODUCTION

The power of a computer does not arise from complexity. Instead, the computer has the ability to perform simple operations at an extremely high rate of speed. These operations can be combined to provide the computer capabilities that you are familiar with.

Consistent with this idea, the actual design of the computer is also simple, as you will see.

(The beauty of the design is that these simple operations can be used to solve extremely complex problems. The programmer's challenge, of course, is to produce the exact sequence of operations to perform a particular task correctly under all possible circumstances, since any error in selection or sequence of operations will result in a "buggy" program. With the large number of instructions required by modern programs, it is not surprising that few of today's programs are truly bug-free.)

In this chapter, we will begin to explore the operations that the computer is capable of performing and look at how those operations work together to provide the computer with its power. To simplify our exploration, we will begin by introducing a model of the computer; a model that operates in a very similar way to the real computer but that is easier to understand instinctively.

The model that we will use is called the **Little Man Computer** (**LMC**). The original LMC was created by Dr. Stuart Madnick at MIT in 1965. In 1979, Dr. Madnick produced a new version of the LMC, with a slightly modified instruction set; the later version is used in this book. It is a strength of the original model that it operates so similarly to a real computer that it is still an accurate representation of the way that computers work thirty-five years after its introduction.

Using this model we will introduce a simplified, but typical, set of instructions that a computer can perform. We will show you exactly how these instructions are executed in the Little Man Computer. Then we will demonstrate how these instructions are combined to form programs.

6.1 LAYOUT OF THE LITTLE MAN COMPUTER

We begin by describing the physical layout of the Little Man Computer. A diagram for the Little Man Computer appears in Figure 6.1.

The LMC consists of a walled mailroom, represented by the dark line surrounding the model in the diagram. Inside the mailroom are several objects:

First, there is a series of one hundred *mailboxes*, each numbered with an address ranging from 00 to 99. This numbering system is chosen because each mailbox address can be represented by two digits, and this is the maximum number of mailboxes that can be represented by two decimal digits.

Each mailbox is designed to hold a single slip of paper, upon which is written a three-digit decimal number. Note carefully that the *contents* of a mailbox are not the same as the *address* of a mailbox. This idea is consistent with what you already know about your post office box: your post office box number identifies where you go

FIGURE 6.1

The Little Man Computer

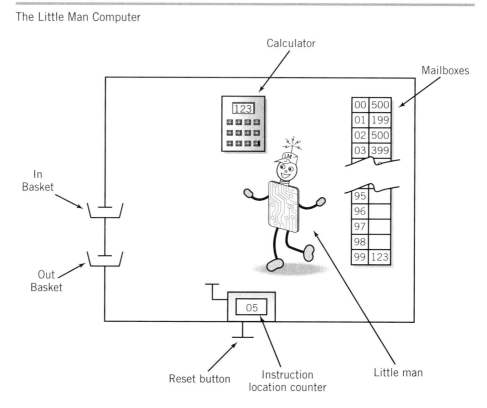

to pick up your mail, but this has no relationship to the actual contents of the letters that you find in that mailbox.

Next, there is a *calculator* . . . basically a simple pocket calculator. The calculator can be used to enter and temporarily hold numbers, and also to add and subtract. The display on the calculator is three digits wide. At least for the purposes of this discussion, there is no provision made for negative numbers, or for numbers larger than three digits. As you are already aware, 10's complement arithmetic could be used for this purpose, but that is not of interest here.

Third, there is a two-digit *hand counter*, the type that you click to increment the count. The reset button for the hand counter is located outside the mailroom. We will call this counter an *instruction location counter*.

Finally, there is the Little Man. It will be his role to perform certain tasks that will be defined shortly.

Other than the reset switch on the hand counter, the only interaction between the Little Man Computer and the outside environment are an *in basket* and an *out basket*.

A user outside of the mailroom can communicate with the Little Man in the mailroom by putting a slip of paper with a three-digit number on it into the in basket, to be read by the Little Man at the appropriate time. Similarly, the Little Man can write a three-digit number on a slip of paper and leave it in the out basket, where it can be retrieved by the user.

Note that *all communication* between the Little Man Computer and the outside world takes place using three-digit numbers. Except for the reset button on the instruction location counter, no other form of communication is possible. The same is true within the mailroom: all instructions to the Little Man must be conveyed as three-digit numbers.

6.2 OPERATION OF THE LMC

We would like the Little Man to do some useful work. For this purpose we have invented a small group of instructions that he can perform. Each instruction will consist of a single digit. We will use the first digit of a three-digit number to tell the Little Man which operation to perform.

In some cases, the operation will require the Little Man to use a particular mailbox to store or retrieve data (in the form of three-digit numbers, of course!). Since the instruction only requires one digit, we can use the other two digits in a three-digit number to indicate the appropriate mailbox address to be used as a part of the instruction. Thus, using the three digits on a slip of paper we can describe an instruction to the Little Man according to the following diagram:

The instruction part of the three-digit code is also known as an "operation code," or **op code** for short. The op code number assigned to a particular instruction is arbitrary, selected by the computer designer based on various architectural and implementation factors. The op codes used by the author conform to the 1979 version of the Little Man Computer model.

Now let's define some instructions for the Little Man to perform:

LOAD instruction—op code 5

The Little Man walks over to the mailbox address specified in the instruction. He reads the three-digit number located in that mailbox, and then walks over to the calculator and punches that number into the calculator. The three-digit number in the mailbox is left unchanged, but of course the original number in the calculator is replaced by the new number.

STORE instruction—op code 3

This instruction is the reverse of the LOAD instruction. The Little Man walks over to the calculator and reads the number there. He writes that number on a slip of paper and puts it in the mailbox whose address was specified as the address part of the instruction. The number in the calculator is unchanged; the original number in the mailbox is replaced with the new value.

ADD instruction—op code 1

This instruction is very similar to the LOAD instruction. The Little Man walks over to the mailbox address specified in the instruction. He reads the three-digit number located in the mailbox and then walks over to the calculator and *adds it to the number already in the calculator*. The number in the mailbox is unchanged.

SUBTRACT instruction—op code 2

This instruction is the same as the ADD instruction, except that the Little Man subtracts the mailbox value from the value in the calculator. The result of a subtraction can leave a negative value in the calculator. Chapter 5 discussed the use of complements to implement negative values, but for simplicity, the LMC model ignores this solution. For the purposes of our LMC model, we will simply assume that the calculator holds and handles negative values correctly, and provides a minus sign as a flag to indicate that the value is negative. The Little Man cannot handle negative numbers outside of the calculator, however, because there is no provision in the model for storing the negative sign within the constraint of the three-digit number system used.

INPUT instruction (or read, if you prefer)—op code 9, "address" 01

The Little Man walks over to the in basket and picks up the slip of paper in the basket. He then walks over to the calculator and punches it into the calculator. The number is no longer in the in basket, and the original calculator value has been replaced by the new number. If there are multiple slips of paper in the basket, the Little Man picks them up in the order in which they were submitted, but each INPUT instruction handles only a single slip of paper; other input values must await the execution of subsequent INPUT instructions. Some authors use the concept of a conveyor belt in place of the in basket, to emphasize this point.

OUTPUT instruction (or print)—op code 9, "address" 02

The Little Man walks over to the calculator and writes down the number that he sees there on a slip of paper. He then walks over to the out basket and places the slip of paper there for the user outside the mailroom to retrieve. The original number in the calculator is unchanged. Each OUTPUT instruction places a single slip of paper in the out basket. Multiple outputs will require the use of multiple OUTPUT instructions.

Note that the INPUT and OUTPUT instructions do not use any mailboxes during execution, since the procedure for each only involves the transfer of data between an in or out basket and the calculator. Because this is true, the address part of the instruction can be used to extend the capability of the instruction set, by using the same op code with different "address" values to create a number of different instructions. In the LMC, 901 is the code for an INPUT instruction, while 902 is used for an OUTPUT instruction. In a real computer, for example, the instruction address might be used to specify the particular I/O device to be used for input or output.

COFFEE BREAK (or HALT) instruction—op code 0

The Little Man takes a rest. The Little Man will ignore the address portion of the instruction.

The instructions that we have defined so far fall into four categories:

- instructions that move data from one part of the LMC to another (LOAD, STORE)
- instructions that perform simple arithmetic (ADD, SUBTRACT)

- ■ instructions that perform input and output (INPUT, OUTPUT)
- ■ instructions that control the machine (COFFEE BREAK)

This is enough for now. We will discuss instructions 6, 7, and 8 later in this chapter.

6.3 A SIMPLE PROGRAM

Now let's see how we can combine these instructions into a program to have the Little Man do some useful work.

Before we do this, we need to store the instructions somewhere, and we need a method to tell the Little Man where to find the particular instruction that he is supposed to perform at a given time.

Without discussing how they got there, for now we will assume that the instructions are stored in the mailboxes, starting at mailbox number 00. The Little Man will perform instructions by looking at the value in the instruction location counter and executing the instruction found in the mailbox whose address has that value. Each time the Little Man completes an instruction, he will walk over to the instruction location counter and increment it. Again he will perform the instruction specified by the counter. Thus, the Little Man will execute the instructions in the mailboxes sequentially, starting from mailbox 00. Since the instruction location counter is reset from outside the mailroom, the user can restart the program simply by resetting the counter to 00.

Now that we have a method for guiding the Little Man through a program of instruction steps, let's consider a simple program that will allow the user outside the mailroom to use the Little Man Computer to add two numbers together. The user will place two numbers in the in basket. The sum of the two will appear as a result in the out basket. The question is what instructions we will need to provide to have the Little Man perform this operation.

INPUT   **901**

Since the Little Man must have access to the data, the first step, clearly, is to have the Little Man read the first number from the in basket to the calculator. This instruction leaves the first number to be added in the calculator.

STORE 99   **399**

Note that it is not possible for the Little Man to simply read another number into the calculator. To do so would destroy the first number. Instead, we must first save the first number somewhere.

Mailbox 99 was chosen simply because it is clearly out of the way of the program. Any other location that is beyond the end of the program is equally acceptable.

Storing the number at a location that is within the program would destroy the instruction at that location. This would mean that when the Little Man went to perform that instruction, it wouldn't be there.

More seriously, there is no way for the Little Man to distinguish between an instruction and a piece of data—both are made up of three-digit numbers. Thus, if we were to store data in a location that the Little Man is going to use as an instruction, the Little Man would simply attempt to perform the data as though it were an instruction. Since there is no way to predict what the data might contain, there is no way to predict what the program might do.

The concept that there is no way to distinguish between instructions and data except in the context of their use is a very important one in computing. For example, it allows a programmer to treat an instruction as data, to modify it, and then to execute the modified instruction.

INPUT   **901**

With the first number stored away, we are ready to have the Little Man read the second number into the calculator.

ADD 99   **199**

Note that there is no specific reason to save the second number. If we were going to perform some operation that required the reuse of the second number, it could be stored somewhere.

In this program, however, we have both numbers in place to perform the addition. The result is, of course, left in the calculator.

OUTPUT   **902**

All that remains is for us to have the Little Man output the result to the out basket.

COFFEE BREAK   **000**

The program is complete, so we allow the Little Man to take a rest.

These instructions are stored sequentially starting from mailbox 00, where the Little Man will retrieve and execute them one at a time, in order. The program is reshown in Figure 6.2.

Since we were careful to locate the data outside the program, this program can be rerun simply by telling the Little Man to begin again.

6.4 AN EXTENDED INSTRUCTION SET

The instructions that we have defined must always be executed in the exact sequence specified. Although this is sufficient for simple program segments that perform a sequence of operations, it does not provide any means for branching or looping, both constructs that you know are very important in programming. Let us extend the instruction set by adding three more instructions for this purpose:

BRANCH UNCONDITIONALLY instruction (sometimes known as JUMP)—op code 6

This instruction tells the Little Man to walk over to the instruction location counter and actually *change* the counter to the location shown in the two address digits of the instruction. (Assume that the hand counter has thumbwheels for this purpose.) This means that the next instruction that the Little Man will execute is located at that mailbox address.

This instruction is very similar, conceptually, to the GOTO instruction in BASIC. Its execution will always result in a break in the sequence to another part of the program.

FIGURE 6.2

Program to Add Two Numbers

Mailbox code		Instruction description
00	901	INPUT
01	399	STORE DATA
02	901	INPUT 2ND #
03	199	ADD 1ST # TO IT
04	902	OUTPUT RESULT
05	000	STOP
99		DATA

Note that this instruction also uses the address digits in an unusual way, since the Little Man does not use the data at the address specified. Indeed, the Little Man expects to find an instruction at that address, the next to be performed.

BRANCH ON ZERO instruction—op code 7

The Little Man will walk over to the calculator and will observe the number stored there. If its current value is zero, he will walk over to the instruction location counter and modify its value to correspond to the address specified within the instruction. The next instruction executed by the Little Man will be located at that address.

If the value in the calculator is not zero, he will simply proceed to the next instruction in sequence.

BRANCH ON POSITIVE instruction—op code 8

The Little Man will walk over to the calculator and will observe the number stored there. If its current value is positive, he will walk over to the instruction location counter and modify its value, to correspond to the address specified within the instruction. The next instruction executed by the Little Man will be located at that address.

If the value in the calculator is negative, he will simply proceed to the next instruction in sequence. Zero is considered to be a positive value.

Note that is it not necessary to provide BRANCH ON NEGATIVE or BRANCH ON NONZERO instructions. The instructions supplied can be used together to achieve equivalent results.

These three instructions make it possible to break from the normal sequential processing of instructions. Instructions of this type are used to perform branches and loops. As an example, consider the following WHILE-DO loop, common to many programming languages:

```
WHILE Value = 0 DO
        Task;
    NextStatement
```

This loop could be implemented using the Little Man BRANCH instruction as follows. Assume that these instructions are located starting at mailbox number 45 (comments are provided to the right of each line):

```
45   LDA 90     590   90 is assumed to contain value
46   BRZ 48     748   Branch if the value is zero
47   BR 60      660   Exit loop; Jump to NextStatement
48     :              This is where the task is located
       :
59   BR 45      645   End to Task; loop to test again
60                    Next statement
```

EXAMPLE

Here is an example of a Little Man program that uses the BRANCH instructions to alter the flow of the program. This program finds the positive difference between two numbers (sometimes known as the absolute magnitude of the difference). For convenience, we are introducing a set of abbreviations for each instruction. These abbreviations are known as **mnemonics**

FIGURE 6.3

Little Man Mnemonic Instruction Codes with
Their Corresponding OP Codes

LDA	5xx	Load
STO	3xx	Store
ADD	1xx	Add
SUB	2xx	Subtract
IN	901	Input
OUT	902	Output
COB or HLT	000	Coffee break (or Halt)
BRZ	7xx	Branch if zero
BRP	8xx	Branch if positive or zero
BR	6xx	Branch unconditional
DAT		Data storage location

(the first "m" is silent). Once you learn to read these mnemonics, you'll find that programs written with mnemonics are generally easy to read. It is more common to write programs this way. For a while, we will continue to print both the mnemonic and the code, but eventually, we will stop printing the code. Most programs are also written with *comments*, which help to clarify the code. The mnemonic instructions that we will use are shown in Figure 6.3. The DAT abbreviation is used to indicate that a particular mailbox will be used to store data. The data may be specified in advance, for example, to use as a constant, or it may be zero if the particular location is to be used to store the data later, during execution of the program.

The program, shown in Figure 6.4, works as follows: the first four instructions simply input and store the two numbers. The fifth instruction, in mailbox 04, subtracts the first

FIGURE 6.4

LMC Program to Find Positive Difference of Two
Numbers

00	IN		901	
01	STO	10	310	
02	IN		901	
03	STO	11	311	
04	SUB	10	210	
05	BRP	08	808	test
06	LDA	10	510	negative; reverse order
07	SUB	11	211	
08	OUT		902	print result and
09	COB		000	stop.
10	DAT	00	000	used for data
11	DAT	00	000	"

number from the second. Instruction 05 tests the result. If the result is positive, all that's left to do is print out the answer. So, the instruction can be used to branch to the printout instruction. If the answer is negative, the subtraction is performed in the other order. Then the result is output, and the Little Man takes his break. Note that if the COB instruction is omitted (as in forgotten—this is a very common error!), the Little Man will attempt to execute the data stored in locations 10 and 11. Please study the example until you understand how it works in every detail.

The nine instructions that make up the instruction set that we have presented are sufficient to perform the steps of any computer program, although not necessarily in the most efficient way. It is important for you to realize that, although simplified, the Little Man instruction set is very similar to the instruction sets that appear in most real computers. In real computers, as in the Little Man Computer, most instruction steps are involved with the movement of data between the equivalent of mailbox locations and calculators, with very simple calculations, and with program branching.

The real computer differs mostly in the variations to these instructions that are provided, and with the addition of a few instructions that provide programming convenience, particularly multiplication and division instructions, and also instructions that shift the data in a word left or right. (Note that the traditional method of performing multiplication can be done in the computer using SHIFT and ADD instructions.)

We will discuss many of these variations when we look at the instruction sets in some real computers, in Chapters 7, 8, 11, and Supplementary Chapters 2 and 3.

6.5 THE INSTRUCTION CYCLE

We will refer to the steps that the Little Man takes to perform an instruction as the **instruction cycle**. This cycle, which is similar for all the instructions, can be broken into two parts:

1. The *fetch* portion of the cycle, in which the Little Man finds out what instruction he is to execute, and

2. The *execute* portion of the cycle, in which he actually performs the work specified in the instruction.

The fetch portion of the cycle is identical for every instruction. The Little Man walks to the location counter and reads its value. He then goes to the mailbox with the address that corresponds to that value and reads the three-digit number stored there. That three-digit number is the instruction to be performed. This is depicted in the drawings of Figure 6.5a.

The fetch portion of the cycle has to occur first: until the Little Man has performed the fetch operation, he does not even know what instruction he will be executing!

The execute portion of each instruction is, of course, different for each instruction. But even here, there are many similarities. The first six instructions all require the Little Man to move data from one place in the mailroom to another. The first four instructions all involve the use of a second mailbox location for the data.

The LOAD instruction is typical. First, the Little Man fetches the instruction. To perform the execute phase of the LOAD instruction, the Little Man first looks at the mailbox with the address that is contained in the instruction. He reads the three-digit number on the slip

FIGURE 6.5(a)

The Fetch Portion of the Instruction Cycle

(1) The Little Man reads the address from the location counter

(2) . . . walks over to the mailbox that corresponds to the location counter

(3) . . . and reads the number on the slip of paper. (He then puts the slip of paper back, in case he should need to read it again later.)

of paper in that mailbox and returns the slip of paper to its place. Then he walks over to the calculator and punches the number into the calculator. Finally, he walks over to the location counter and increments it. He has completed one instruction cycle and is ready to begin the next. These steps are shown in Figure 6.5b.

With the exception of the step in which the Little Man increments the location counter, the steps must be performed in the exact sequence shown. (The location counter can be incremented anytime after the fetch has occurred.) The fetch steps must occur before the

FIGURE 6.5(b)

The Execute Portion of the Instruction Cycle (LOAD Instruction)

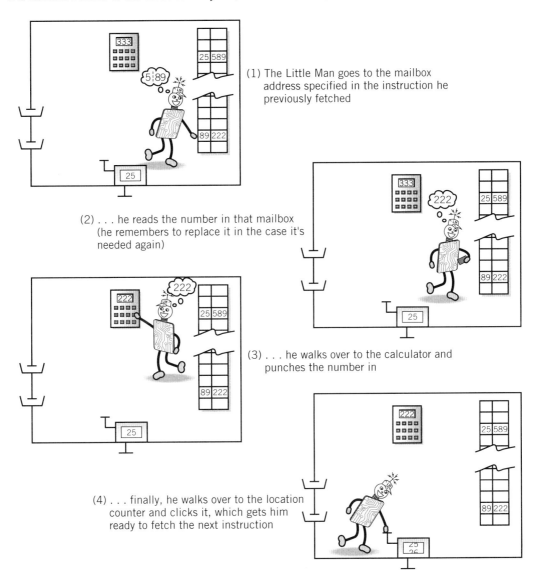

(1) The Little Man goes to the mailbox address specified in the instruction he previously fetched

(2) . . . he reads the number in that mailbox (he remembers to replace it in the case it's needed again)

(3) . . . he walks over to the calculator and punches the number in

(4) . . . finally, he walks over to the location counter and clicks it, which gets him ready to fetch the next instruction

execution steps; within the fetch, the Little Man must look at the location counter before he can pull the instruction from its mailbox.

Just as the sequence of instructions in a program is important—and you know that this is true for any language, Pascal, Little Man, or any other—so it is also true that the steps within each instruction must be performed in a particular order.

Notice that the ADD and SUBTRACT instructions are almost identical to the LOAD instruction. The only difference occurs during the execute step, when the Little Man enters the number into the calculator. In the case of the arithmetic instructions, the Little Man adds or subtracts the number that he is carrying into the calculator, rather than simply entering it.

The other instructions are slightly different, although not any more difficult to trace through and understand. To improve your understanding, you should trace the steps of the Little Man through the remaining six instructions.

6.6 A NOTE REGARDING COMPUTER ARCHITECTURES

As we noted in Chapter 1, John von Neumann is usually considered to be the developer of the computer as we know it today. Between 1945 and 1951 von Neumann set down a series of guidelines that came to be known as the **von Neumann architecture** for computers. Although other experimental computer architectures have been developed and built, the von Neumann architecture continues to be the standard architecture for computers; no other architecture has had any commercial success to date. It is significant that, in a field where technological change occurs almost overnight, the architecture of computers is virtually unchanged since 1951.

The major guidelines that define a von Neumann architecture include:

- Memory holds both programs and data; this is known as the **stored program concept**. The stored program concept allows programs to be changed easily.
- Memory is addressed **linearly**; that is, there is a single sequential numeric address for each and every memory location.
- Memory is addressed by the location number without regard to the data contained within.

Instructions are executed sequentially unless an instruction or an outside event (such as the user resetting the location counter) causes a branch to occur.

In addition, von Neumann defined the functional organization of the computer to be made up of a control unit that executes instructions, an arithmetic/logic unit that performs arithmetic and logical calculations, and memory. The control unit and arithmetic/logic unit together make up the CPU, or central processing unit.

If you check over the guidelines just given, you will observe that the Little Man Computer is an example of a von Neumann architecture. In fact, we took care to point out features of the von Neumann architecture during our discussion of the Little Man Computer.

SUMMARY AND REVIEW

The workings of the computer can be simulated by a simple model. The Little Man Computer model consists of a Little Man in a mailroom with mailboxes, a calculator, and a counter. Input and output baskets provide communication to the outside world. The Little Man Computer meets all the qualifications of a von Neumann computer architecture.

The Little Man performs work by following simple instructions, which are described by three-digit numbers. The first digit specifies an operation. The last two digits are used for various purposes, but most commonly to point to an address. The instructions provide operations that can move data between the mail slots and the calculator, move data between the calculator and the input and output baskets, perform addition and subtraction, and allow the Little Man to stop working. There are also instructions that cause the Little Man to change the order in which instructions are executed, either unconditionally or based on the value in the calculator.

Both data and instructions are stored in individual mail slots. There is no differentiation between the two except in the context of the particular operation taking place. The Little Man normally executes instructions sequentially from the mail slots except when he encounters a branching instruction. In that case he notes the value in the calculator, if required, and resumes executing instructions from the appropriate location.

The exact steps performed by the Little Man are important because they reflect closely the steps performed in a real CPU in executing an instruction.

KEY CONCEPTS AND TERMS

instruction cycle	mnemonics
linear memory addressing	op code
Little Man Computer	stored program concept
(LMC)	von Neumann architecture

READING REVIEW QUESTIONS

6.1   Without looking at the book, draw a Little Man Computer. Label each of the components in your drawing.

6.2   Instructions in the Little Man Computer are three digits, divided into two parts. Show the format of an LMC instruction.

6.3   Describe, step by step, what the Little Man does to execute an INPUT instruction.

6.4   Describe, step by step, what the Little Man does to execute a STORE instruction.

6.5   If a user wants to enter two numbers, what must the Little Man program do before she enters the second number? Why?

6.6   Write a Little Man program that accepts two numbers as input and outputs the numbers in reverse order.

6.7   Write a Little Man program that accepts two numbers as input, subtracts the first from the second and outputs the result.

6.8   Extend the simple program shown in Section 6.3 to accept *three* inputs from a user, add them, and output the result.

6.9   Explain carefully what the Little Man will do when he executes a JUMP instruction.

6.10   Explain carefully, step by step, what the Little Man will do when he executes a BRANCH ON ZERO instruction.

6.11   Even if he runs out of instructions to execute, the Little Man only stops trying to execute instructions under one condition. What is that condition? What happens if the Little Man runs out of instructions and that condition is not met?

6.12 What does the Little Man do during the second phase of a COFFEE BREAK or HALT instruction?

6.13 Why is the instruction cycle called a *cycle*?

6.14 The instruction cycle is divided into two phases. Name each phase. The first phase is the same for every instruction. What is the purpose of the first phase that makes this true? Explain what the Little Man does during the first phase.

EXERCISES

6.1 Write a Little Man program that accepts three values as input and produces the largest of the three as output.

6.2 Consider the example in this chapter in which we enter and add two numbers. Suppose we had stored the first input entry in mailbox location 00. Would the program have produced the same result? What would have happened if the program were executed a second time? What characteristic of the computer makes this true?

6.3 Write a Little Man program that accepts three values as input and outputs them in order of size, largest to smallest. (This is a more challenging variation on Exercise 6.6.)

6.4 Write a Little Man program that prints out the odd numbers from 1 to 99. No input is required.

6.5 Write a Little Man program that prints out the sums of the odd values from 1 to 39. The output will consist of $1, 1+3, 1+3+5, 1+3+5+7 \ldots$. No input is required.

As an aside, do you notice anything interesting about the output results that are produced by this series? (Hint: This series is sometimes used as part of an algorithm for finding square roots of numbers.)

6.6 Write a Little Man program to accept an indefinite number of input values. The output value will be the largest of the input values. You should use the value 0 as a flag to indicate the end of input.

6.7 Write a Little Man program that adds a column of input values and produces the sum as output. The first input value will contain the number of values that follow as input to be added.

6.8 The following Little Man program is supposed to add two input numbers, subtract a third input number from the sum, and output the result, i.e.,

$$OUT = IN1 + IN2 -- IN3$$

mailbox	mnemonic code	numeric code
00	IN	901
01	STO 99	399
02	IN	901
03	ADD 99	199
04	STO 99	399
05	IN	901
06	SUB 99	299
07	OUT	902
08	COB	000

What is wrong with this program? Modify the program so that it produces the correct result.

6.9 The steps that the Little Man performs are closely related to the way in which the CPU actually executes instructions. Draw a flow chart that carefully describes the steps that the Little Man follows to execute a branch instruction.

6.10 Repeat Exercise 6.9 for a subtract instruction.

6.11 Repeat Exercise 6.9 for a branch on positive instruction.

6.12 Show carefully how you would implement an IF-ELSE statement using Little Man instructions.

6.13 Show how you would implement a DO-WHILE statement using Little Man instructions.

6.14 When we discussed conditional branching we claimed that a BRANCH NEGATIVE instruction is not necessary. Show a sequence of BRANCH instructions that will cause a program to branch to location 50 if the value in the calculator is negative.

6.15 The programs that we have discussed in this chapter seem to have appeared in the mailboxes by magic. Consider a more realistic alternative:

Suppose a small program is permanently stored in the last few mailbox locations. A BRANCH instruction at location 0, also permanent, will start this program. This program will accept input values and will store them at consecutive mailbox locations, starting with mailbox 001. You may assume that these values represent the instructions and data of a user's program to be executed. When a 999 is received as input data, the program jumps to location 001 where it will proceed to execute the values just entered.

The small program described here is known as a *program loader*, or, under certain circumstances as a *bootstrap*. Write a Little Man program loader. (Hint: It may be useful to remember that instructions and data are indistinguishable. Thus, instructions could be treated as if they were data, if necessary.)

6.16 Suppose we have a need to handle both negative and positive data beyond the simple test in the various conditional branch instructions. One way to do this would be to replace the subtract instruction with a 10's complement instruction. The COMP instruction complements the value in the calculator and leaves the value in the calculator.

a. How would subtraction be performed in this case?

b. Carefully trace the steps that the Little Man would perform to execute the new COMP instruction.

c. What is the new range of values possible with this modification, and how are these values represented in the Little Man Computer?

d. What would the Little Man do to execute a BRANCH ON POSITIVE instruction?

6.17 The original version of the Little Man Computer used op code 7 (i.e., instruction 700) for a COFFEE BREAK instruction instead of op code 0. What is the advantage of using 000 for the COB instruction instead of 700? (Hint: Consider what happens if the programmer forgets to put a COB instruction at the end of a program.)

6.18 The input data values in our problems have always been entered in the order that they were to be used. This is not always possible or convenient. Can you think of a simple way to accept input data in the wrong order and still use it correctly?

6.19   Show a sequence of instructions that will cause a program to branch to location 75 if the value in the calculator is *greater than* zero.

6.20   Suppose the Little Man Computer had been implemented as a 16-bit binary machine. Assume that the binary LMC provides the same instruction set, with the same op codes (in binary, of course), and the same instruction format (op code followed by address). How many bits would be required for the op code portion of the instruction? How many mailboxes could the binary machine accommodate? What is the range of 2's complement data that this machine could handle?

6.21   What are the criteria that define a von Neumann architecture? How does the example in this chapter in which we enter and add two numbers illustrate each of the criteria?

CHAPTER 7

THE CPU AND MEMORY

7.0 INTRODUCTION

The previous chapter provided a detailed introduction to the Little Man model of a computer. In that chapter we introduced a format, using a three-digit number divided into op code and address fields, for the instructions that a computer can perform. We introduced an instruction set that we indicated was representative of those found in a real computer. We also showed the steps that are performed by the Little Man in order to execute one of these instructions.

In this chapter and the next we will extend these concepts to the real computer. Our primary emphasis in this chapter is on the central processing unit (CPU), together with memory. In the real computer, memory is actually separated both physically and functionally from the CPU. Memory and the CPU are intimately related in the operation of the computer, however, and so we will treat memory together with the CPU for the convenience of our discussion. Since every instruction requires memory access,[1] it makes sense to discuss the two together.

We will use the Little Man model and its instruction set as a guideline for our discussion. The Little Man instruction set is fundamentally similar to the instruction sets of many different computers. Of course, the Little Man instruction set is based on a decimal number system, and the real CPU is binary, but this is a detail that won't concern us for most of this discussion. The CPU architectural model that we shall discuss is not based on a particular make and model, but is typical of most computers. Chapter 8 will discuss the implementation of this model in modern technology. In Supplementary Chapter 2, we shall look specifically at several popular computer models.

In this chapter you will see that the execution of instructions in the CPU together with memory is nearly identical functionally to the Little Man Computer. There is a one-to-one relationship between the various contents of the mailroom and the functional components of the CPU plus memory. The major differences occur in the facts that the CPU instruction set is created using binary numbers rather than decimal and that the instructions are performed in a simple electronic way using logic based upon Boolean algebra instead of having a Little Man running around a mailroom.

Sections 7.1 through 7.3 present a systematic introduction to the components of the CPU and memory, offering a direct comparison with the components of the Little Man Computer, and focusing on the concept of the register as a fundamental element of CPU operation. In Section 7.4, we show how simple CPU and memory register operations serve as the basic mechanism to implement the real computer's instruction set.

In Section 7.5, we turn our attention to the third major computer system component, the bus component. Buses provide the interconnection between various internal parts of the CPU, and between the CPU and memory, as well as providing

---

[1] Recall that in the LMC every instruction must be fetched from a mailbox to be executed. The same is true in the real computer.

connections between input and output devices, the CPU, and memory. There are many different types of buses in a computer system, each optimized for a different type of task. Buses can connect two components in a point-to-point configuration or may interconnect several modules in a multipoint configuration. In general, the lines on buses carry signals that represent data, addresses, and control functions. We consider the general requirements for a bus, the features, advantages and disadvantages of different types of buses. In Chapter 11, we will focus on the specific buses that interconnect the various components of a computer system, and show you the ways in which the buses connect different parts of an entire computer system together.

In Sections 7.6, 7.7, and 7.8, we return our attention to the CPU to discuss the characteristics and features of the instruction sets provided in real computers: the different types of instructions, the formats of instruction words, and the general requirements and restraints that are required for instruction words.

You already understand from Chapter 6 how simple instructions can be combined to form the programs that you write. When you complete this chapter, you will have a good understanding of how those instructions are executed in a computer.

7.1 THE COMPONENTS OF THE CPU

A simplified conceptual block diagram of a CPU with memory is shown in Figure 7.1.[2] For comparison purposes, the block diagram for the Little Man Computer is repeated in Figure 7.2, with labels corresponding to the components in Figure 7.1.

Note the similarities between the two figures. As noted in Chapter 1, the computer unit is made up conceptually of three major components, the **arithmetic/logic unit (ALU)**, the **control unit (CU)**, and **memory**. The ALU and CU together are known as the **central processing unit (CPU)**. An input/output (I/O) interface is also included in the diagram. The I/O interface corresponds in function roughly to the input and output baskets, although its implementation and operation differ from that of the Little Man Computer in many respects.

The arithmetic/logic unit is the component of the CPU where data is held temporarily and where calculations take place. It corresponds directly to the calculator in the Little Man Computer.

The control unit controls and interprets the execution of instructions. It does so by following a sequence of actions that correspond to the fetch-execute instruction cycle that was described in the previous chapter. Most of these actions are retrievals of instructions from memory followed by movements of data or addresses from one part of the CPU to another.

The control unit determines the particular instruction to be executed by reading the contents of a **program**

FIGURE 7.1

System Block Diagram

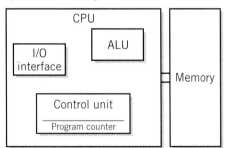

---

[2]This diagram is first attributed to John von Neumann in 1945. As discussed in Chapter 8, current technology results in a different physical layout for the components in the model; nevertheless, the basic execution of instructions is still consistent with the original model.

FIGURE 7.2

The Little Man Computer

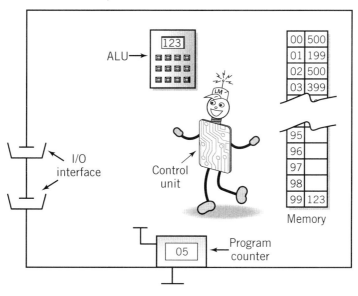

counter **(PC)**, sometimes called an **instruction pointer**, which is a part of the control unit. Like the Little Man's location counter, the program counter contains the address of the current instruction or the next instruction to be executed. Normally, instructions are executed sequentially. The sequence of instructions is modified by executing instructions that change the contents of the program counter. The Little Man branch instructions are examples of such instructions. A **memory management unit** within the control unit supervises the fetching of instructions and data from memory. The I/O interface is also part of the control unit. In some CPUs, these two functions are combined into a single **bus interface unit**. The program counter in the CPU obviously corresponds to the location counter in the Little Man Computer, and the control unit itself corresponds to the Little Man.

Memory, of course, corresponds directly to the mailboxes in the LMC.

7.2 THE CONCEPT OF REGISTERS

Before we discuss the way in which the CPU executes instructions, it is necessary to understand the concept of a register. A **register** is a single, permanent storage location within the CPU used for a particular, defined purpose. A register is used to hold a binary value temporarily for storage, for manipulation, and/or for simple calculations. Note that each register is wired within the CPU to perform its specific role. That is, unlike memory, where every address is just like every other address, each register serves a particular purpose. The register's size, the way it is wired, and even the operations that take place in the register reflect the specific function that the register performs in the computer.

Registers also differ from memory in that they are not addressed as a memory location would be, but instead are manipulated directly by the control unit during the execution of instructions. Registers may be as small as a single bit or as wide as several bytes, ranging usually from 1 to 128 bits.

Registers are used in many different ways in a computer. Depending on the particular use of a register, a register may hold data being processed, an instruction being executed, a memory or I/O address to be accessed, or even special binary codes used for some other purpose, such as codes that keep track of the status of the computer or the conditions of calculations that may be used for conditional branch instructions. Some registers serve many different purposes, while others are designed to perform a single, specialized task. There are even registers specifically designed to hold a number in floating point format, or a set of related values representing a list or vector, such as multiple pixels in an image.

Registers are basic working components of the CPU. You have already seen, in Chapter 6, that the computer is unable to distinguish between a value that is used as a number in a program and a value that is actually an instruction or address, except in the context of current use. When we refer to the "data" in a register, we might be talking about any of these possibilities.

You have already become acquainted with two "registers" in the Little Man Computer, namely, the calculator and the location counter.

In the CPU, the equivalent to the calculator is known as an **accumulator**. Even the short example to add two numbers in Chapter 6 showed that it is often necessary to move data to and from the accumulator to make room for other data. As a result, modern CPUs provide several accumulators; these are often known as **general-purpose registers**. Some vendors also refer to general-purpose registers as **user-visible** or **program-visible registers** to indicate that they may be accessed by the instructions in user programs. Groups of similar registers are also sometimes referred to collectively as a **register file**. General-purpose registers or accumulators are usually considered to be a part of the arithmetic/logic unit, although some computer manufacturers prefer to consider them as a separate register unit. As in the Little Man Computer, accumulator or general-purpose registers hold the data that are used for arithmetic operations as well as the results. In most computers, these registers are also used to transfer data between different memory locations, and between I/O and memory, again similar to the LMC. As you will see in Chapter 8, they can also be used for some other similar purposes.

The control unit contains several important registers.

- As already noted, the **program counter register** holds the address of the current instruction being executed.
- The **instruction register (IR)** holds the actual instruction being executed currently by the computer. In the Little Man Computer this register was not used; the Little Man himself remembered the instruction he was executing. In a sense, his brain served the function of the instruction register.
- The **memory address register (MAR)** holds the address of a memory location.
- The **memory data register (MDR)**, sometimes known as the *memory buffer register*, will hold a data value that is being stored to or retrieved from the memory location currently addressed by the memory address register.

The last two registers will be discussed in more detail in the next section, when we explain the workings of memory. Although the memory address register and memory data register are part of the CPU, operationally these two registers are more closely associated with memory itself.

The control unit will also contain several 1-bit registers, sometimes known as **flags**, that are used to allow the computer to keep track of special conditions such as arithmetic carry and overflow, power failure, and internal computer error. Usually, several flags are grouped into one or more **status registers**.

In addition, our typical CPU will contain an I/O interface that will handle input and output data as it passes between the CPU and various input and output devices, much like the LMC *in* and *out* baskets. For simplification, we will view the I/O interface as a pair of I/O registers, one to hold an I/O address that addresses a particular I/O device, the other to hold the I/O data. These registers operate similarly to the memory address and data registers. Later, in Chapter 9, we will discuss a more common way of handling I/O that uses memory as an intermediate storage location for I/O data.

Most instructions are executed by the sequenced movement of data between the different registers in the ALU and the CU. Each instruction has its own sequence.

Most registers support four primary types of operations:

1. Registers can be loaded with values from other locations, in particular from other registers or from memory locations. This operation destroys the previous value stored in the destination register, but the source register or memory location remains unchanged.

2. Data from another location can be added to or subtracted from the value previously stored in a register, leaving the sum or difference in the register.

3. Data in a register can be shifted or rotated right or left by one or more bits. This operation is important in the implementation of multiplication and division. The details of the shift operation are discussed in Section 7.6.

4. The value of data in a register can be tested for certain conditions, such as zero, positive, negative, or too large to fit in the register.

In addition, special provision is frequently made to load the value zero into a register, which is known as clearing a register, and also to invert the 0s and 1s (i.e., take the 1's complement of the value) in a register, an operation that is important when working with complementary arithmetic. It is also common to provide for the addition of the value 1 to the value in a register. This capability, which is known as incrementing the register, has many benefits, including the ability to step the program counter, to count in for loops, and to index through arrays in programs. Sometimes decrementing, or subtraction of 1, is also provided. The bit inversion and incrementing operations are combined to form the 2's complement of the value in a register. Most computers provide a specific instruction for this purpose, and also provide instructions for clearing, inverting, incrementing, and decrementing the general-purpose registers.

The control unit sets ("1") or resets ("0") status flags as a result of conditions that arise during the execution of instructions.

As an example, Figure 7.3 identifies the programmer-accessible registers in the IBM System z computers, which includes a variety of IBM mainframe models. Internal registers, such as the instruction, memory address, and memory buffer registers are not specifically

FIGURE 7.3

Programmer-Accessible Registers in IBM zSeries Computers

Register type	Number	Size of each in bits	Notes
General	16	64	For arithmetic, logical, and addressing operations; adjoining registers may be joined to form up to eight 128-bit registers
Floating point	16	64	Floating point arithmetic; registers may be joined to form 128-bit registers
PSW	1	128	Combination program counter and status-flag register, called the **Program Status Word (PSW)**
Control (+1 32-bit floating point control)	16	64	Various internal functions and parameters connected with the operating system; accessible only to systems programmers

identified in the table, since they are dependent on the implementation of the particular model in the series.

7.3 THE MEMORY UNIT

The Operation of Memory

To understand the details of instruction execution for the real CPU, you need first to see how instructions and data can be retrieved from memory. Real memory, like the mailboxes in the Little Man Computer, consists of cells, each of which can hold a single value, and each of which has a single address.

Two registers, the memory address register and the memory data register, act as an interface between the CPU and memory. The memory data register is called the memory buffer register by some computer manufacturers.

Figure 7.4 is a simplified representation of the relationship between the MAR, the MDR, and memory. Each cell in the memory unit holds 1 bit of data. The cells in Figure 7.4 are organized in rows. Each row consists of a group of one or more bytes. Each group represents the data cells for one or more consecutive memory addresses, shown in the figure as addresses $000, 001, \ldots, 2^n - 1$.

In modern computers, it is common to address 8 bytes at a time to speed up memory access between the CPU and memory. The CPU can still isolate individual bytes from the group of eight for its use, however.

The memory address register holds the address in the memory that is to be "opened" for data. The MAR is connected to a decoder that interprets the address and activates a single address line into the memory. There is a separate address line for each group of cells in the memory; thus, if there are n bits of addressing, there will be 2^n address lines. (In actuality, the decoding process is somewhat more complex, involving several levels of address decoding, since there may be several millions or billions of addresses involved, but the concept described here is correct.)

FIGURE 7.4

The Relationship Between the MDR, the MAR, and Memory

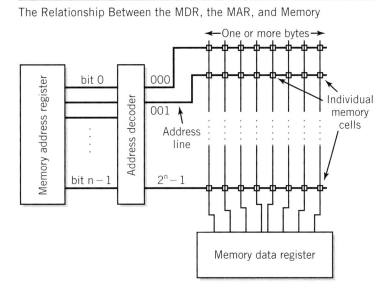

The memory data register is designed such that it is effectively connected to every cell in the memory unit. Each bit of the MDR is connected in a column to the corresponding bit of every location in memory. However, the addressing method assures that only a single row of cells is activated at any given time. Thus, only one memory location is addressed at any one time. A specific example of this is shown in Figure 7.5. (Note that in the drawing *msb* stands for most significant bit and *lsb* for least significant bit.)

FIGURE 7.5

MAR-MDR Example

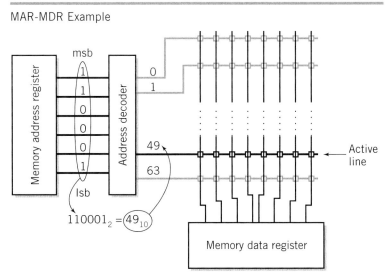

As a simple analogy to the operation we've just described, consider the memory as being stored in a glass box, as shown in Figure 7.6. The memory data register has a window into the box. The viewer, who represents each cell in the memory data register, can see the cells in corresponding bit position for every location in memory through the window. The cells themselves are light bulbs that can be turned on (1) or off (0). The output from the memory address register is passed to an address decoder. The output from the address decoder in our analogy consists of a series of lines, each of which can light up the bulbs in a single row of cells. Only one line at a time can be activated—specifically, the one corresponding to the decoded address. The active line will light the bulbs that correspond to "1s," leaving the "0s" dark. The viewer therefore will see only the single group of cells that is currently addressed by the memory address register. We can extend the analogy to include a "master switch" that controls all the lights, so that the data can be read only at the appropriate instant.

A more detailed picture of an individual memory cell is shown in Figure 7.7. Although this diagram is a bit complicated, it may help to clarify how data is transferred between the MDR and memory. There are three lines that control the memory cell: an address line, a read/write line, and an activation line. The address line to a particular cell is turned on only if the computer is addressing the data within that cell. The read/write line determines whether the data will be transferred from the cell to the MDR (read) or from the MDR to the cell (write). This line works by turning on one of two switches in conjunction with the address line and the activation line. The read switch, R, in the diagram turns on when the

FIGURE 7.6

A Visual Analogy for Memory

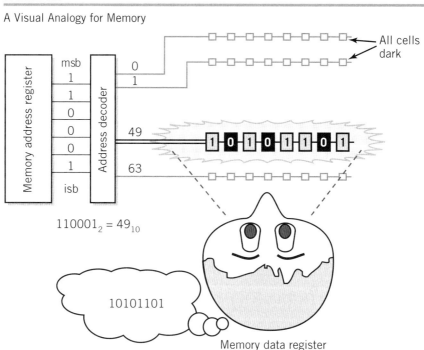

FIGURE 7.7

An Individual Memory Cell

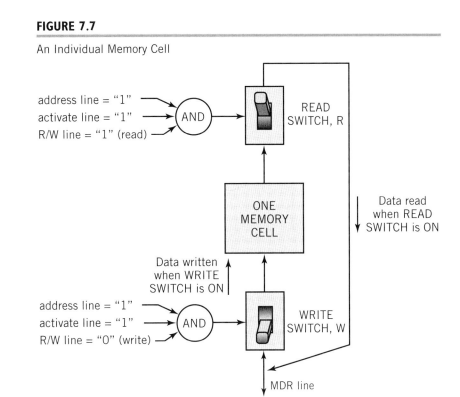

The interaction between the CPU and the memory registers takes place as follows: to address line and the activation line are both on (on is usually represented by 1, off by 0), and the read/write line is set to read; the switch then connects the output of the cell to the MDR line. The write switch, W, works similarly; switch W turns on when the address line and activation line are both on and the read/write switch is set to write. Switch W connects the MDR line to the input of the cell, which transfers the data bit on the MDR line to the cell for storage. Note that only one switch, at most, can be on at a given time.

The interaction between the CPU and the memory registers takes place as follows: to retrieve or store data at a particular memory location, the CPU copies an address from some register in the CPU to the memory address register. *Note that addresses are always moved to the MAR; there would never be a reason for an address transfer from the MAR to another register within the CPU*, since the CPU controls memory transfers and is obviously aware of the memory address being used. At the same time that the MAR is loaded, the CPU sends a message to the memory unit indicating whether the memory transfer is a retrieval from memory or a store to memory. This message is sent by setting the read/write line appropriately.

At the appropriate instant, the CPU momentarily turns on the switch that connects the MDR with the register by using the activation line, and the transfer takes place between memory and the MDR. The MDR is a two-way register. When the instruction being executed is to store data, the data will be transferred from another register in the CPU to the MDR, and from there it will be transferred into memory. The original data at that location will be destroyed, replaced by the new data from the MDR. Conversely, when the instruction is to load data from memory, the data is transferred from memory to the MDR, and it will subsequently be transferred to the appropriate register in the CPU. In this case, the memory data are left intact, but the previous data value in the MDR is replaced by the new data from memory.

Memory Capacity

The number of possible memory locations in the Little Man Computer, one hundred locations, was established by the two-digit address space in each instruction. The location counter also addresses one hundred locations. There is no memory address register per se, but the Little Man is certainly aware that each memory location requires two digits. In theory, a larger location counter, say, three digits, would allow the Little Man to fetch more *instructions*, but notice that his *data* fetches and stores are still limited to the one hundred locations that the two digits of the address field in the instruction word can address.

Similarly, there are two factors that determine the capacity of memory in a real computer. The number of bits in the memory address register determines how many different address locations can be decoded, just as the two-digit addresses in the Little Man Computer resulted in a maximum of one hundred mailboxes. For a memory address register of width k bits, the number of possible memory addresses is

$$M = 2^k$$

The other factor in establishing memory capacity is of course the number of bits in the address field of the instruction set, which establishes how many memory locations can be directly addressed from the instruction.

In the Little Man Computer, we have assumed that these two size factors are the same, but in a real computer, that is not necessarily the case. Even if the size of the instruction address field is sufficient to support a larger amount of memory, the number of physical memory locations is, in fact, determined by the size of the memory address register. There are also other ways of extending the addresses specified within instructions so that we can reach more addresses than the size of the instruction address field would allow. Just to give you one common method, consider a computer that can use one of the general-purpose registers to hold an address. To find a memory location, the computer would use the value in that register as a pointer to the address. Instead of an address field, the instruction needs only to indicate which register contains the address. Using this technique, the addressing capability of the computer is determined by the size of the register. For example, a computer with 64-bit registers could address 2^{64} addresses if the MAR were wide enough. Such an extension would suggest that the MAR, and thus the actual memory capacity, is normally at least as large as the instruction address field, but it may be much larger. There is a brief discussion of simple addressing methods in Chapter 8. Additional, more sophisticated addressing methods are presented in Supplementary Chapter 3.

Ultimately, the width of the MAR determines the maximum amount of addressable memory in the computer. Today, a typical memory address register will be at least 32 bits wide, and probably much wider. Many modern CPUs support 64-bit memory addresses. A 32-bit memory address allows a memory capacity of 4 gigabytes (GB) (4×10^9 byte-size spaces), whereas 64 bits allows a memory capacity of 16×10^{18} bytes (16 exabytes or

16 billion gigabytes). In modern computers, the ultimate size of memory is more likely limited by physical space for the memory chips or by the time required to decode and access addresses in a large memory, rather than by the capability of the CPU to address such a large memory.

Of course the size of memory also affects the speed of access. The time needed for the address decoder to identify a single line out of four billion is necessarily larger than that required for a memory that is much smaller.

As an aside, it is worth noting that early models of IBM's largest mainframe computer systems had a total memory capacity of only 512 KB, (1/4000th the memory of a typical modern PC with 2 GB of memory!) and that the original IBM PC came supplied with 64 KB of memory, with a maximum capacity of 640 KB. In fact, Bill Gates, of Microsoft, was quoted at the time as saying that he could see no need for more than 640 KB of memory, ever!

The size of the data word to be retrieved or stored in a single operation is determined by the size of the memory data register and by the width of the connection between memory and the CPU. In most modern computers, data and instructions found in memory are addressed in multiples of 8-bit bytes. This establishes the minimum instruction size as 8 bits. Most instructions cannot fit practically into 8 bits. If one were to allow 3 bits for the op code (eight instruction types), only 5 bits remain for addressing. Five bits allows $2^5 = 32$ different addresses, which is clearly insufficient address space. As a result, longer instructions of 16, 24, 32, or even more bits will be stored in successive memory locations. In the interest of speed, it is generally desirable to retrieve an entire instruction with a single fetch, if possible. Additionally, data to be used in arithmetic calculations frequently requires the precision of several bytes. Therefore, most modern computer memories are designed to allow the retrieval or storage of at least 4 and, more commonly, 8 or even 16, successive bytes in a single operation. Thus, the memory data register is usually designed to retrieve the data or instruction(s) from a sequence of several successive addresses all at once, and the MDR will be several bytes wide.

Primary Memory Characteristics and Implementation

Through the history of computing there have been several different types of primary memory used, reflecting the technology and the system requirements and capabilities of the times. In the 1960s and 1970s, the dominant technology was magnetic core memory, which used a tiny core of magnetic material to hold a bit of data, and the largest machines might have had 512 KB of memory. Today, the primary memory in most computer systems is dynamic **RAM**, and most machines have 1 GB of memory, or more. RAM is an acronym that stands for *random access memory*, which is a slight misnomer, since other types of semiconductor memory can also be accessed randomly (i.e., their addresses can be accessed in any order). A more appropriate name would be *read-write memory*.

Memory today is characterized by two predominant operational factors and by a number of technical considerations. Operationally, the most important memory characteristic is whether the memory is read-write capable or read-only. Almost as important is whether the memory is **volatile** or **nonvolatile**. Nonvolatile memory retains its values when power is removed. Volatile memory loses its contents when power is removed. Magnetic core memory was nonvolatile. RAM is volatile.

Important technical considerations include the speed of memory access, the total amount of memory that can be addressed, the data width, the power consumption and heat generation, and the bit density (specified as the number of bits per square centimeter). Cost is an additional factor.

Most current computers use a mix of static and dynamic RAM for memory. The difference between static and dynamic RAM is in the technical design and is not of importance here. However, **dynamic RAM** is less expensive, requires less electrical power, generates less heat, and can be made smaller, with more bits of storage in a single integrated circuit. Dynamic RAM also requires extra electronic circuitry that "refreshes" memory periodically; otherwise the data fades away after a while and is lost. Static RAM does not require refreshing. **Static RAM** is also faster to access than dynamic RAM and is therefore useful in very-high-speed computers and for small amounts of high-speed memory, but static RAM is lower in bit density and more expensive. Both dynamic and static RAM are volatile: their contents are lost when power is turned off.

At the time of this writing, dynamic RAM is standard for most applications. The amount of data that can be stored in a single dynamic RAM chip has increased rapidly in the past few years, going from 64 Kilobits(Kb) to 512 Megabits (Mb) in fewer than fifteen years. Currently, most systems are built with chips that can hold 256 or 512 Mb of data. These chips are also designed to be packaged together in convenient plug-in packages that can supply 1–2 gigabytes of memory, or more, in a single unit. 1 gigabit (Gb) and 2 Gb RAM chips are also in production, but have not yet replaced 512 Mb chips for most system applications, with the exception of mainframe systems. Most modern systems also provide a small amount of static RAM memory that is used for high-speed access. This memory is known as *cache memory*. The use of cache memory is discussed in Chapter 8.

Although current RAM technology is fast, inexpensive, and efficient, its volatility makes some applications difficult or impossible. For example, nonvolatile RAM would make it possible to shut off a computer without losing the programs and data in memory. This would make it possible to restart the computer into its previous state without rebooting, would eliminate the undesirable effects of power failures and laptop battery discharge, and would simplify the use of computers in situations where power conservation is critical, such as in long distance space missions. The desire for nonvolatile RAM has led to considerable research on alternative technologies for creating and producing nonvolatile RAM.

There are a small number of memory technologies in current use that are capable of nonvolatile random access, but none in current large-scale production is capable of replacing standard SRAM and DRAM for use in primary memory. Foremost among these technologies is **flash memory**. Flash memory uses a concept called *hot carrier injection* to store bits of data. Flash memory allows rewriting of cells by erasing groups of memory cells selectively, and then writing the new pattern into the cells. Flash memory serves as an inexpensive form of nonvolatile storage for portable computer storage, digital cameras. MP3 players, and other electronic devices; however it is unsuitable for primary memory because the rewrite time is extremely slow compared to standard RAM and the number of rewrites over the lifetime of the ROM is somewhat limited. Flash memory is viewed primarily as a potential replacement for slow long-term storage devices such as magnetic disks and CD or DVD devices, although the significantly higher cost of flash memory is still a factor at this point in time.

A number of nonvolatile memory technologies that might be capable of replacing traditional RAM appear to be nearing production. These include magnetorestrictive RAM (MRAM), ferroelectric RAM (FeRAM), phase-change RAM (PRAM), and carbon nano[tube] RAM (NRAM). You will probably be reading about one or more of these in the future.

ROM, or *read-only memory*, is used for situations where the software is built semi-permanently into the computer, is required as part of the computer's software, and is not expected to change over the life of the computer, except perhaps very infrequently. Bootstrap programs and basic I/O system drivers fall into this category. Early ROM memory was made up of integrated circuits with fuses in them that could be blown. These fuses were similar to, but much smaller than, the fuses that you might have in your home. A blown fuse might represent a "0," an intact fuse a "1." Modern ROM memories use a different technology, such as **EEPROM** or flash memory. EEPROM (Erasable Electrically Programmable ROM) uses a concept called Fowler-Nordheim tunneling to achieve rewritability. Because of its cost, need for special circuitry, and speed, EEPROM has mostly been replaced by flash memory. Regardless of technology, ROM is nonvolatile. Thus, although electrical power is required to access the data, the data remains consistent with or without power.

7.4 THE FETCH-EXECUTE INSTRUCTION CYCLE

The fetch-execution instruction cycle is *the* basis for every capability of the computer. This seems like a strong statement, but think about it: the purpose of the computer is to execute instructions similar to those that we have already introduced. And, as you've already seen from the Little Man Computer, the operation of every instruction is defined by its fetch-execute instruction cycle. Ultimately, the operation of a computer as a whole is defined by the primary operations that can be performed with registers, as explained in Section 7.2: to move data between registers, to add or subtract data to a register, to shift data within a register, and to test the value in a register for certain conditions, such as negative, positive, or zero.

With the importance of the instruction cycle in mind, we can consider how these few operations can be combined to implement each of the instructions in a computer. The registers that will be of the most importance to us for this discussion will be the general-purpose registers or accumulators used to hold data values between instructions (A or GR), the program counter (PC), which holds the address of the current instruction, the instruction register (IR), which will hold the current instruction while it is being executed, and the memory address and data registers (MAR and MDR), used for accessing memory.

To begin, review carefully the steps that the Little Man took to execute an instruction. (You may want to read Section 6.6 again to refresh your memory.) You will recall that there were two phases in the process. First, the Little Man fetched the instruction from memory and read it. This phase was identical for every instruction. Then, he interpreted the instruction and performed the actions required for that particular instruction.

He repeated this cycle endlessly, until he was given the instruction to stop.

The **fetch-execute instruction cycle** in a CPU works similarly. As noted, much of the procedure consists of copying data from one register to another. You should always be aware that data copying does not affect the "from" register, but it obviously replaces the previous data in the "to" register with the new data being copied.

Remember that every instruction must be fetched from memory before it can be executed. Therefore, the first step in the instruction cycle always requires that the instruction must be fetched from memory. (Otherwise, how would the computer know what instruction to perform?) Since the address of the current instruction to be executed is identified by the value in the program counter register, the first step will be to transfer that value into the memory address register, so that the computer can retrieve the instruction located at that address.

We will use the following notation to indicate the transfer of a data value from one register to another:

$$REG_a \rightarrow REG_b$$

Then, in this notation, the first step in the execution of every instruction will be

(step 1) $PC \rightarrow MAR$

As explained in the description of memory, this will result in the instruction being transferred from the specified memory location to the memory data register. The next step is to transfer that instruction to the instruction register:

(step 2) $MDR \rightarrow IR$

The instruction register will hold the instruction through the rest of the instruction cycle. It is the particular instruction in the IR that will control the particular steps that make up the remainder of the cycle. These two steps comprise the fetch phase of the instruction cycle.

The remaining steps are, of course, instruction dependent. Let us consider the steps required to complete a LOAD instruction.

The next thing that the Little Man did was to read the address part of the LOAD instruction. He then walked over to the mailbox specified by that address, read the data, and copied it into the calculator. The real CPU will operate similarly, substituting register transfers for the Little Man, of course. Thus,

(step 3) $IR[address] \rightarrow MAR$

The notation IR [address] is used to indicate that only the address part of the contents of the instruction register is to be transferred. This step prepares the memory module to read the actual data that will be copied into the "calculator," which in this case will be the accumulator:

(step 4) $MDR \rightarrow A$

The CPU increments the program counter, and the cycle is complete and ready to begin the next instruction (actually this step can be performed any time after the previous instruction is retrieved, and is usually performed early in the cycle in parallel with other steps).

(step 5) $PC + 1 \rightarrow PC$

Notice the elegant simplicity of this process! The LOAD instruction requires only five steps. Four of the steps simply involve the movement of data from one register to another.

The fifth step is nearly as simple. It requires the addition of the value 1 to the contents of a register, and the new value is returned to the same register. This type of addition is common in computers. In most cases, the result of an addition or subtraction is returned to one of the original registers.

The remaining instructions operate similarly. Compare, for example, the steps required to perform the STORE and the ADD instructions with those of the LOAD instruction, discussed earlier.

The STORE instruction

```
PC → MAR
MDR → IR
IR[address] → MAR
A → MDR
PC + 1 → PC
```

The ADD instruction

```
PC → MAR
MDR → IR
IR[address] → MAR
A + MDR → A
PC + 1 → PC
```

Study these examples carefully. For practice, relate them to the steps the Little Man performs to execute the corresponding instruction. Notice that the only step that changes in these three instructions is the fourth step.

The fetch-execute cycles for the remaining instructions are left as an exercise (see Exercise 7.5 at the end of this chapter).

The following example, with comments, recaps the above discussion in the context of a three-instruction program segment that loads a number from memory, adds a second number to it, and stores the result back to the first memory location. Note that each instruction is made up of its corresponding fetch-execute cycle. The program segment is executed by processing each step of each fetch-execute cycle in sequence.

Assume that the following values are present just prior to execution of this segment:

```
Program Counter: 65
Value in Mem Location 65: 590 (LOAD 90)
Value in Mem Location 66: 192 (ADD 92)
Value in Mem Location 67: 390 (STORE 90)
Value in Mem Location 90: 111
Value in Mem Location 92: 222
```

EXAMPLE

1st instruction LOAD 90:	PC → MAR	MAR now has 65
	MDR → IR	IR contains the instruction: 590
	- - - - - - - - - - - - ← end of fetch	
	IR[address] → MAR	MAR now has 90, the location of the data
	MDR → A	Move 111 from MDR to A
	PC + 1 → PC	PC now points to 66.

end of execution, end of first instruction

2nd instruction ADD 92: PC → MAR MAR now contains 66

MDR → IR IR contains the instructions: 192

- - - - - - - - - - - - ← end of fetch

IR [address] → MAR MAR now has 92

A + MDR → A 111+222=333 in A

PC + 1 → PC PC now points to 67

——————————————————————— end of execution, end of second instruction

3rd instruction STORE 90: PC → MAR MAR now contains 67

MDR → IR IR contains 390

- - - - - - - - - - - - ← end of fetch

IR [address] → MAR MAR now holds 90

A → MDR The value in A, 333, moves to mem location 90

PC + 1 → PC PC now points to 68

——————————————————————— end of execution, end of third instruction

← ready for next instruction

7.5 BUSES

Bus Characteristics

You have already seen that instructions are executed within the CPU by moving "data" in many different forms from register to register and between registers and memory. The different forms that the "data" can take include instructions and addresses, in addition to actual numerical data. "Data" moves between the various I/O modules, memory, and the CPU in similar fashion. The physical connection that makes it possible to transfer data from one location in the computer system to another is called a **bus**. From our previous discussion of the way that the CPU and memory work together, it is probably already obvious to you that there must be a bus of some kind linking the CPU and memory; similarly, buses internal to the CPU can be used to link registers together at the proper times to implement the fetch-execute cycles introduced in Section 7.4.

Specifically, a bus may be defined as a group of electrical, or, less commonly, optical, conductors suitable for carrying computer signals from one location to another. The electrical conductors may be wires, or they may be conductors on a printed circuit. Optical conductors work similarly, using light that is directed from point to point in special thin clear glass fibers. Optical conductors can carry data much faster than electrical conductors, but their cost is high, which has limited their use to date. Nonetheless, there is considerable lab research into ways to integrate more optical circuits into computers.

Buses are used most commonly for transferring data between computer peripherals and the CPU, for transferring data between the CPU and memory, and for transferring data between different points within the CPU. A bus might be a tiny fraction of an inch long, carrying data between various parts of the CPU within an integrated circuit chip; it might be a few inches long, carrying data between the CPU chip and memory; it might even be hundreds of feet long, carrying data between different computers connected together in a network.

The characteristics of buses are dependent on their particular use within the computer environment. A bus can be characterized by the number of separate wires or optical conductors in the bus; by its *throughput*, that is, the data transfer rate measured in bits per second; by the data width (in bits) of the data being carried; by the number and type of attachments that the bus can support; by the distance between the two end points; by the type of control required; by the defined purpose of the bus; by the addressing capacity; by whether the lines on the bus are uniquely defined for a single type of signal or shared; and by the various features and capabilities that the bus provides. The bus must also be specified electrically and mechanically; by the voltages used; by the timing and control signals that the bus provides, by the protocol used to operate and control the bus, by the number of pins on the connectors, if any; even by the size of the cards that plug into the connector. A bus would not be very useful if the cards that it was to interconnect did not fit into the space allotted! Unfortunately for the concept of standardization, there are dozens of different buses in use, although a few are far more common than others.

The need to characterize buses comes from the necessity of interfacing the bus to other components that are part of the computer system. Buses that are internal to the CPU are usually not characterized formally at all, since they serve special purposes and do not interface to the outside world. Buses that are used in this way are sometimes known as *dedicated* buses. Buses that are intended for more general use must have a well-defined standard; standard buses generally have a name. PCI Express, USB, IDE, and SATA are all examples of named buses.

Each conductor in the bus is commonly known as a **line**. Lines on a bus are often assigned names, to make individual lines easier to identify. In the simplest case, each line carries a single electrical signal. The signal might represent one bit of a memory address, or a sequence of data bits, or a timing control that turns a device on and off at the proper time. Sometimes, a conductor in a bus might also be used to carry power to a module. In other cases, a single line might represent some combination of functions.

The lines on a bus can be grouped into as many as four general categories: data, addressing, control, and power. Data lines carry the "data" that is being moved from one location to another. Address lines specify the recipient of data on the bus. Control lines provide control and timing signals for the proper synchronization and operation of the bus and of the modules and other components that are connected to the bus. A bus connecting only two specific 32-bit registers within a CPU, for example, may require just thirty-two data lines plus one control line to turn the bus on at the correct time. A backplane that interconnects a 64-bit data width CPU, a large memory, and many different types of peripherals might require many more than a hundred lines to perform its function.

The bus that connects the CPU and memory, for example, needs address lines to pass the address stored in the MAR to the address decoder in memory and data lines to transfer data between the CPU and the memory MDR. The control lines provide timing signals for the data transfer, define the transfer as a read or write, specify the number of bytes to transfer, and perform many other functions.

In reality, all of the lines except for the power lines in a bus can be used in different ways. Each line in a bus may serve a single, dedicated purpose, such as a bus line that carries the twelfth bit of an address, for example. Alternatively, a line may be configured to serve different purposes at different times. A single line might be used to carry each of the bits of an address in sequence, followed by the bits of data, for example. At their two extremes, buses are characterized as **parallel** or **serial**. By definition, a parallel bus is simply a bus in which there is an individual line for each bit of data, address, and control being used. This means that all the bits being transferred on the bus can be transferred simultaneously. A serial bus is a bus in which data is transferred sequentially, one bit at a time, using a single data line pair. (A data return line is required to complete the circuit, just as there are two wires in a standard 110-volt power circuit. Multiple data lines can share the same data return line, commonly known as a *ground* line, but in some cases it is possible to reduce noise and other interference by using a separate return line for each data line.)

A bus line may pass data in one direction only, or may be used to pass data in both directions. A unidirectional line is called a **simplex line**. A bidirectional line may carry data one direction at a time, in which case it is called a **half-duplex line**, or in both directions simultaneously, known as a **full-duplex line**. The same nomenclature is also used to describe data communication channels, because, ultimately, the basic concepts of bus lines and communication channels are essentially similar.

Buses are also characterized by the way that they interconnect the various components to which they are attached. A bus that carries signals from a single specific source to a single specific destination is identified as a **point-to-point bus**. Point-to-point buses that connect an external device to a connector are often referred to as **cables**, as in a printer cable or a network cable. Thus, the cable that connects the USB port in a personal computer from the computer to a printer is an example of a point-to-point bus. The internal connectors into which external cables can be plugged are often called **ports**. Typical ports on a personal computer might include parallel printer ports, network ports, USB ports, and firewire ports.

Alternatively, a bus may be used to connect several points together. Such a bus is known as a **multipoint bus**, or sometimes as a *multidrop bus*. It is also referred to as a **broadcast bus**, because the signals produced by a source on the bus are "broadcast" to every other point on the bus in the same way as a radio station broadcasts to anyone who tunes in. The bus in a traditional Ethernet network is an example of a broadcast bus: the signal being sent by a particular computer on the network is received by every other computer connected to the network. (The operation of Ethernet is discussed in Chapter 13.) In most cases, a multipoint bus requires addressing signals on the bus to identify the desired destination that is being addressed by the source at a particular time. Addressing is not required with a point-to-point bus, since the destination is already known, but an address may be required if the message is being passed *through* the destination point to another location. Addressing is also not required for a multipoint bus where the signal is actually intended to reach all the other locations at once; this is sometimes the case for buses that are internal to the CPU. Addressing may be integral to the lines of the bus itself, or may be part of the protocol that defines the meaning of the data signals being transported by the bus.

Typical point-to-point and multipoint bus configurations are illustrated in Figure 7.8

A parallel bus that carries, say, 64 bits of data and 32 bits of address on separate data and address lines would require a bus width of 96 lines, even before control lines are considered. The parallel bus is characterized by high throughput capability because all the bits of a data word are transferred at once. Virtually every bus internal to the CPU is a parallel bus, since the high speed is essential to CPU operation. Also most internal

FIGURE 7.8

Point-to-Point and Multipoint Buses

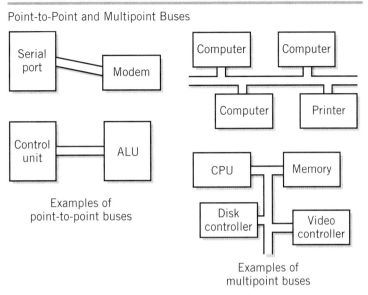

Examples of
point-to-point buses

Examples of
multipoint buses

operations and registers are inherently parallel, and the use of serial buses would require additional circuitry to convert the parallel data to serial and back again. Until recently, the buses that connected the CPU with memory and various high speed I/O modules such as disk and display controllers were also parallel, for similar reasons.

The parallel bus does have a number of disadvantages, though. Parallel buses are expensive and consume a considerable amount of space. Connectors used with parallel buses are also expensive because of the large number of pins involved. External parallel buses, such as printer cables are also expensive because of the large number of lines required. More seriously, parallel buses are subject to radio-generated electrical interference between the different lines at high data transfer rates. The higher the data rate, the worse the interference, which ultimately limits the speed at which the parallel bus can operate. Additionally, there is a slight difference in time delay on different lines, known as *skew*, as signals traverse the bus. The transfer rate, and thus the clock speed of the bus, is also limited by the requirement that the data must not change faster than the maximum skew time. Both of these problems can cause data corruption. Finally, the cost of fiber optic technology makes a parallel optical cable impractical.

Data on a serial bus is transferred sequentially, one bit at a time. Although you might think that the throughput of a serial bus would be lower than that of a parallel bus theoretically capable of the same per line transfer rate, the limitations noted above make serial bus transmission attractive in many circumstances. Indeed, with advances in serial bus technology, serial buses are now preferred for many, if not most, applications requiring high data transfer rates.

Generally, a serial bus has a single data line pair and perhaps a few control lines. (For simultaneous two-way communication, a second data line pair can be added.) There are

FIGURE 7.9

Alternative Bus Notations

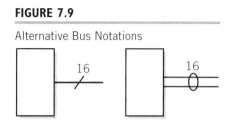

no separate address lines in a serial bus. Serial buses are often set up for point-to-point connection; no addressing is required in this case. If addressing is required in a serial bus application, the address may be **multiplexed** with the data. What this means is that the same line is used for both address and data at different times; if an address is required, for example, the address might be sent first, one bit at a time, followed by the data. At its simplest, the serial bus can be reduced to a single data line pair, used for data, control, and addressing. Using modern materials such as fiber optics, very high transfer rates may be achieved. In general, control is handled using a bus protocol that establishes agreement as to the meaning and timing of each signal on the line among the components connected to the line.

It is also possible to design a parallel bus that multiplexes addresses and data on the same lines, as the PCI bus does, or multiplexes 32-bit data on sixteen data lines, for example. For example, the Pentium 4 multiplexes 128-bit data words to fit a 64-bit data path on the Pentium system bus.

To use a bus, the circuits that are connected to the bus must agree on a **bus protocol**. Recall from Chapter 1 that a protocol is an agreement between two or more entities that establishes a clear, common path of communication and understanding between them. A bus protocol is simply a specification that spells out the meaning of each line and each signal on each line for this purpose. Thus, a particular control line on a bus might be defined as a line that determines if the bus is to be used for memory read or memory write. Both the CPU and memory would have to agree, for example, that a "0" on that particular line means "memory read" and a "1" on the line means "memory write". The line might have a name like MREAD/$\overline{\text{MWRITE}}$, where the bar over MWRITE means that a "0" is the active state. The bar itself stands for "NOT".[3]

Buses are frequently notated on diagrams using widened lines to indicate buses. Sometimes a number is also present on the diagram. The number indicates the number of separate lines in the bus. Two alternative ways of notating buses in diagrams are shown in Figure 7.9.

7.6 CLASSIFICATION OF INSTRUCTIONS

Nearly every instruction in a computer performs some sort of operation on one or more source data values, which results in one or more destination data values. The operation may be a move or load, it may be an addition or subtraction, it may be an input or output, or it may be one of many other operations that we have already discussed.

---

[3]A pound sign (#) following the name is sometimes used to stand for "NOT" instead.

Actually, if you think about the classes of instructions that we have discussed, you will realize that there are only a very few instructions that do *not* operate on data. Some of these are concerned with the flow of the program itself, such as unconditional JUMP instructions. There are also instructions that control the administration of the computer itself; the only example in the Little Man Computer instruction set is the COFFEE BREAK or HALT that causes the computer to cease executing instructions. Another example on many computers is the NO OPERATION instruction that does nothing but waste time (which can be useful when a programmer wants to create a time delay for some reason).

Most modern computers also provide instructions that aid the operating system software in its work, by providing security, controlling memory access, and performing other functions. Because the operating system will frequently be controlling many tasks and users, these instructions must not be available to the users' application programs. Only the operating system can execute these instructions. These instructions are known as **privileged instructions**. The HALT instruction is usually a privileged instruction, because you would not want an individual user to stop the computer while other users are still in the middle of their tasks.

Computer manufacturers usually group the instruction set into various categories of instructions, such as data movement instructions, arithmetic instructions, shift and rotate instructions, input/output instructions, conditional branch instructions, jump instructions, and special-purpose instructions.

Within each category, the instructions usually have a similar instruction word format, support similar addressing modes, and execute in a similar way. A typical instruction set, divided into eight categories, appears in Figure 7.10. This figure represents nearly all the user-accessible instructions in the Motorola 68000 series of microprocessors used in early Apple Macintosh computers.[4] The privileged instructions are not listed in the diagram, nor are exception-handling instructions that are used primarily by system programmers. These constitute an additional two categories for the 68000 series CPUs. Incidentally, notice that this CPU does not have any I/O instructions. That is because the CPU is designed in such a way that the move instructions can also be used for I/O. Notice particularly that, except for the lack of I/O instructions, the categories conform fairly well to the Little Man Computer instruction set. The additional instructions in this CPU are mostly variations on instructions that are familiar to you plus special control instructions. The 68000 series CPUs also support a math coprocessor, which adds a category of floating point arithmetic instructions. The floating point math instructions are built directly into 68000 series processors starting with the 68040 CPU.

Data Movement Instructions (LOAD, STORE, and Other Moves)

Because the move instructions are the most frequently used, and therefore the most basic to the computer, computer designers try to provide a lot of flexibility in these instructions. The MOVE category commonly includes instructions to move data from memory to general registers, from general registers to memory, between different general registers, and, in

---

[4] Although the 68000 CPU series is old, it is still used in embedded computer systems. It was selected for this illustration because of its clean design, with few extraneous bells and whistles.

FIGURE 7.10

68000 Instruction Set

Mnemonic	Operation	Mnemonic	Operation
Data Movement Instructions		**Shift and Rotate Instructions**	
CAS*	Compare and swap with operand	ASL	Arithmetic shift register left
CAS2*	Compare upper/lower and swapASR	ASR	Arithmetic shift right
EXG	Exchange registers	LSL	Logical shift left
LEA	Load effective address	LSR	Logical shift right
LINK	Link and allocate stack	ROL	Rotate left
MOVE	Move src to dst	ROR	Rotate right
MOVE16	Move src to dst (68030-68060 only)	ROXL	Rotate left with extend bit
MOVEA	Move src to address register	ROXR	Rotate right with extend bit
MOVEM	Move multiple registers at once	SWAP	Swap words of a long word
MOVEP	Move to peripheral		
MOVEQ	Move short data to dst	**Bit Manipulation Instructions**	
PEA	Push effective address to stack	BCHG	Change bit
UNLK	Unlink stack	BCLR	Clear bit
		BTEST	Set bit
Integer Arithmetic Instructions		BTST	Test bit
ADD	Add src to dst		
ADDA	Add src to address register	**Bit Field Instructions**	
ADDI	Add immediate data to dst	BFCHG*	Change bit field
ADDQ	Add short data to dst	BFCLR*	Clear bit field
ADDX	Add with extend bit to dst	BFEXTS*	Extract and sign extend bit field
SUB, SUBA,	Subtracts act similarly to adds	BFEXTU*	Extract and zero extend bit field
SUBI, SUBQ,		BFFFO*	Find first set bit in bit field
SUBX		BFINS*	Insert bit field
MULS	Signed multiply	BFSET*	Set bit field
MULU	Unsigned multiply	BFTST*	Test bit field
DIVS	Signed divide		
DIVU	Unsigned divide	**Binary Coded Decimal Instructions**	
DIVSL*	Long signed divide	ABCD	Add src to dst
DIVUL*	Unsigned long divide	NBCD	Negate destination
CLR	Clear value in register	PACK*	Pack src to dst
CMP	Compare src to dst	SBCD*	Subtract src from dst
CMPA	Compare src to address register	UNPK*	Unpack src to dst
CMPI	Compare immediate data to dst		
CMPM	Compare memory	**Program Flow Instructions**	
CMP2*	Compare register to upper/lower bounds	Bcc	Branch on condition code cc
EXT	Sign extend	BRA	Branch unconditionally
EXTB	Sign extend byte	BSR	Branch to subroutine
NEG	Negate register	CALLM*	Call module
NEGX	Negate with extend	DBcc	Test, decrement, and branch on condition
		JMP	Jump to address
Boolean Logic Instructions		JSR	Jump to subroutine
AND	AND src to dst	NOP	No operation
ANDI	AND immediate data to dst	RTD*	Return and deallocate stack (also 68010)
EOR	Exclusive OR src to dst	RTE	Return from exception (privileged)
EORI	Exclusive OR immediate data to dst	RTM*	Return from module
NOT	NOT destination	RTR	Return and restore condition codes
OR	OR src to dst	RTS	Return from subroutine
ORI	OR immediate data to dst	TRAP	Trap to system
Scc	Test condition codes and set operand		
TAS	Test and set operand	*(68020–68060 only)	
TST	Test operand and set condition codes	(src = source; dst = destination; cc = condition code	
TRAPcc*	Trap on condition	indicator, e.g. BGT branch of greater than)	

some computers, directly between different memory locations without affecting any general register. There may be many different addressing modes available within a single computer.

Additionally, variations on these instructions are frequently used to handle different data sizes. Thus, there may be a LOAD BYTE instruction, a LOAD HALF-WORD (2 bytes), a LOAD WORD (4 bytes), and a LOAD DOUBLE WORD (8 bytes) within the same instruction set. (Incidentally, the concept of a "word" is not consistent between manufacturers. To some manufacturers the size of a word is 16 bits; to others, it is 32 or even 64 bits).

The Little Man LOAD and STORE instructions are simple, though adequate, examples of MOVE instructions. Other than expanding the addressing mode capabilities and adding multiple word size capabilities, which we have already discussed, the major limitation of the Little Man LOAD and STORE instructions is the fact that they are designed to operate with a single accumulator.

When we expand the number of accumulators or general-purpose registers, we must expand the instruction to determine which register we wish to use. Thus, the instruction must provide a field for the particular register. Fortunately, it takes very few bits to describe a register. Even sixteen registers require only 4 bits. On the other hand, if the computer uses the registers to hold pointers to the actual memory addresses as its standard addressing mode, the required instruction size may actually decrease, since fewer bits are required for the address field in this case.

Additionally, it is desirable to have the capability to move data directly between registers, since such moves do not require memory access and are therefore faster to execute. In fact, some modern CPUs, including the Sun SPARC and IBM PowerPC architectures, provide only one pair of LOAD/STORE or MOVE instructions for moving data between the CPU and memory. All other instructions in these CPUs move and manipulate data only between registers. This allows the instruction set to be executed much more rapidly. There is a detailed examination of the Power PC computer and its variants in Supplementary Chapter 2.

Arithmetic Instructions

Every CPU instruction set includes integer addition and subtraction. Except for a few special-purpose CPUs, every CPU today also provides instructions for integer multiplication and division. Many instruction sets provide integer arithmetic for several different word sizes. As with the MOVE instructions, there may be several different integer arithmetic instruction formats providing various combinations of register and memory access in different addressing modes.

In addition, most current CPUs also provide floating point arithmetic capabilities. On older PCs with 80386 or earlier processors, a floating point math coprocessor unit had to be purchased separately and installed in a socket provided for that purpose on the motherboard of the computer. Because of the expense, most users would not exercise this option. Extensive floating point calculations are required for many graphics applications, such as CAD/CAM programs, animation, and computer games; the presence of floating point instructions reduces the processing time significantly. Floating point instructions usually operate on a separate set of floating point data registers with 64-, 80-, or 128-bit word sizes. The modern instruction set usually also contains instructions that convert data between integer and floating point formats.

As noted in Chapter 5, most modern CPUs also provide at least a minimal set of arithmetic instructions for BCD or packed decimal format, which simplifies the programming of business data processing applications.

Of course, it is not absolutely necessary to provide all these different instruction options. Multiplication and division can be performed with repeated addition and subtraction, respectively. In computers there is an even easier technique. In elementary school you probably learned the "long" multiplication and division methods which multiply or divide numbers one digit at a time and shift the results until the entire operation is complete. Because of the simplicity of binary multiplication ($1 \times 1 = 1$, all other results are 0), the computer can implement the same method using only adds or subtracts together with shift instructions. Internally, the multiplication and division instructions simply implement in hardware this same method. Since the fetch-execute cycle requires a single-bit shift and register add step for each bit in the multiplier, multiply and divide instructions execute slowly compared to other instructions.

Even the subtract instruction is theoretically not necessary, since we showed in Chapter 4 that integer subtraction is performed internally by the process of complementing and adding.

As we already noted, the same is true of BCD and floating point instructions. On the now rare computers that do not provide floating point instructions, there is usually a library of software procedures that are used to simulate floating point instructions.

Boolean Logic Instructions

Most modern instruction sets provide instructions for performing Boolean algebra. Commonly included are a NOT instruction, which inverts the bits on a single operand, as well as AND, (inclusive) OR, and EXCLUSIVE-OR instructions, which require two source arguments and a destination.

Single Operand Manipulation Instructions

In addition to the NOT instruction described in the previous paragraph, most computers provide other convenient single operand instructions. Most of these instructions operate on the value in a register, but some instruction sets provide similar operations on memory values as well. Most commonly, the instruction set will contain instructions for NEGATing a value, for INCREMENTing a value, for DECREMENTing a value, and for setting a register to zero. There are sometimes others. On some computers, the increment or decrement instruction causes a branch to occur automatically when zero is reached; this simplifies the design of loops by allowing the programmer to combine the test and branch into a single instruction.

Bit Manipulation Instructions

Most instruction sets provide instructions for setting and resetting individual bits in a data word. Some instruction sets also provide instructions for operating on multiple bits at once. Bits can also be tested, and used to control program flow. These instructions allow programmers to design their own "flags" in addition to commonly provided negative/positive, zero/nonzero, carry/borrow, and overflow arithmetic flags.

Shift and Rotate Instructions

Shift and **rotate operations** have been mentioned previously as a means to implement multiplication and division. Shifts and rotate operations have other programming applications, and CPU instruction sets commonly provide a variety of different shift and rotate instructions for the programmer to use. As shown in Figure 7.11, shift instructions move the data bits left or right one or more bits. Rotate instructions also shift the data bits left or right, but the bit that is shifted out of the end is placed into the vacated space at the other end. Depending on the design of the particular instruction set, bits shifted out the end of the word may be shifted into a different register or into the carry or overflow flag bit, or they may simply "fall off the end" and be lost.

Two different kinds of shifts are usually provided. The data word being shifted might be logical or it might be numeric. **Logical shift** instructions simply shift the data as you would expect, and zeros are shifted in to replace the bit spaces that have been vacated. **Arithmetic shift** instructions are commonly used to multiply or divide the original value by a power of 2. Therefore, the instruction does not shift the leftmost bit, since that bit usually represents the algebraic sign of the numeric value—obviously the sign of a number must be maintained. Left arithmetic shifts do not shift the left bit, but zeros replace the bits from the right as bits are moved to the left. This will effectively double the numeric value for each shift of one bit. On the other hand, right arithmetic shifts fill the space of moved bits with the sign bit rather than with zero. This has the effect of halving the value

FIGURE 7.11

Typical Register Shifts and Rotates

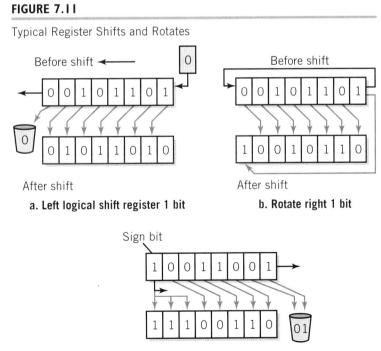

a. Left logical shift register 1 bit

b. Rotate right 1 bit

c. Right arithmetic shift 2 bits

for each bit shifted, while maintaining the sign of the value. It may not seem obvious to you that this works correctly, but it becomes more apparent if you recall that negative numbers in complementary arithmetic count backward starting from the value −1, which is represented in 2's complement by all ones.

Rotate instructions take the bits as they exit and rotate them back into the other end of the register. Some instructions sets include the carry or overflow bit as part of the rotation. Some CPUs also allow the rotation to take place between two registers. Rotate instructions can be used to exchange the 2 bytes of data in a 16-bit word, for example, by rotating the word by 8 bits.

Program Control Instructions

Program control instructions control the flow of a program. Program control instructions include jumps and branches, both unconditional and conditional, and also **subroutine** CALL **and** RETURN instructions. Various conditional tests are provided, including those with which you are already familiar: branch on zero, branch on nonzero, branch on positive, branch on negative, branch on carry, and so on.

CALL instructions, sometimes known as JUMP SUBROUTINE instructions, are used to implement subroutine, procedure and function calls. Thus, CALL instructions are important as a means to enable program modularization.

From your programming experience, recall what happens when your program calls a subroutine or procedure. The program jumps to the starting location of the subroutine and executes the code in the subroutine. When the subroutine is completed, program execution returns to the calling program and continues with the instruction following the call. The machine language CALL instruction works the same way. A jump to the starting location of the subroutine occurs, and execution continues from that point. The only difference between a CALL instruction and a normal JUMP instruction is that the CALL instruction must also save somewhere the program counter address from which the jump occurred, so that the program may return to the instruction in the calling program following the call after the subroutine is completed. The RETURN instruction restores the original value to the program counter, and the calling program proceeds from where it left off. Operation of the CALL and RETURN instructions are illustrated in Figure 7.12.

FIGURE 7.12

Operation of CALL and RETURN Instructions

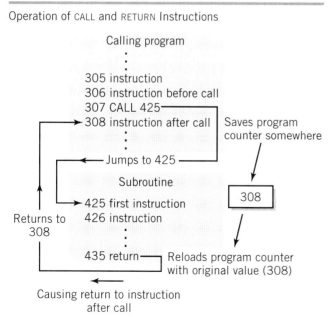

Different computers use different methods to save the return address. One common method is to store the return address on a memory stack; the RETURN instruction operates by removing the address from the stack and moving it to the program counter. The use of stacks is discussed briefly in the next section. Another method for performing CALLs and RETURNS is explored in Exercise S3.14.

Stack Instructions

One of the most important data storage structures in programming is the **stack**. A stack is used to store data when the most recently used data will also be the first needed. For that reason, stacks are also known as *LIFO*, for *last-in, first-out*, structures. As an analogy, stacks are frequently described by the way plates are stored and used in a cafeteria. New plates are added to the top of the stack, or *pushed*, and plates already on the stack move down to make room for them. Plates are removed from the top of the stack, or *popped*, so that the last plates placed on the stack are the first removed. Similarly, the last number entered onto a computer memory stack will be the first number available when the stack is next accessed. Any data that must be retrieved in reverse order from the way it was entered is a candidate for the use of stacks. Figure 7.13 shows the process of adding to and removing numbers from the stack.

Stacks are an efficient way of storing intermediate data values during complex calculations. In fact, storage in Hewlett-Packard calculators is organized around a stack of memory. As we already noted, stacks are also an excellent method for storing the return addresses and arguments from subroutine calls. Program routines that are recursive must "call themselves." Suppose the return address were stored in a fixed location, as shown in Figure 7.14a. If the routine is called a second time, from within itself, Figure 7.14b, the original returning address (56) is lost and replaced by the new return address (76). The program is stuck in an infinite loop between 76 and 85. In Figure 7.15, the return address is stored on a stack. This time when the routine is again called, the original address is simply

FIGURE 7.13

Using a Stack

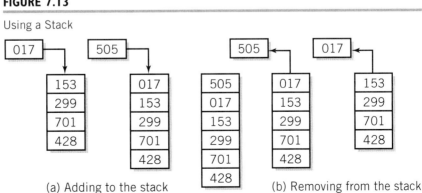

(a) Adding to the stack   (b) Removing from the stack

FIGURE 7.14

Fixed Location Subroutine Return Address Storage

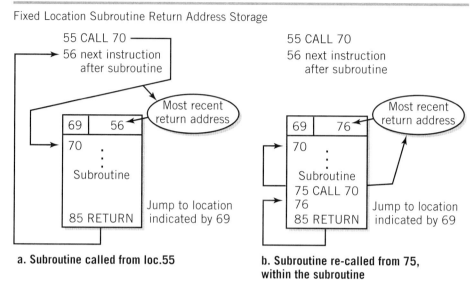

a. Subroutine called from loc.55

b. Subroutine re-called from 75, within the subroutine

pushed down the stack, below the most recent address. Notice that the program "winds its way back out" in the reverse order from which the routines were entered. This is exactly what we want: we always return from the last called subroutine to the one just previous. J. Linderman of Bentley University notes that the same technique would be used to back out of a maze for which the explorer has written down each turn that she made after entering.

There are many other interesting applications for stacks in computers, but further discussion is beyond the scope of this book. The curious reader is referred to *For Further Reading* for references.

Computers do not generally provide special memory for stack use, although many machines provide special STACK instructions to simplify the bookkeeping task. Instead, the programmer sets aside one or more blocks of regular memory for this purpose. The "bottom" of the stack is a fixed memory location, and a **stack pointer** points to the "top" of the stack, that is, the most recent entry. This is shown in Figure 7.16. A new entry is added to the stack, or pushed, by incrementing the stack pointer, and then storing the data at that location. An entry is removed from the stack, or popped, by copying the value pointed to and then decrementing the stack pointer. If a register is provided for the stack pointer, register-deferred addressing can be used for this purpose. (You should note that memory is drawn upside-down in Figure 7.16 so that incrementing the stack pointer moves it *upward*.)

Many instruction sets provide PUSH and POP instructions as direct support for stacks, but stacks can be implemented easily without special instructions. (Exercise S3.15 illustrates one solution.) Some computers also specify the use of a particular general-purpose register as a stack pointer register.

FIGURE 7.15

Stack Subroutine Return Address Storage

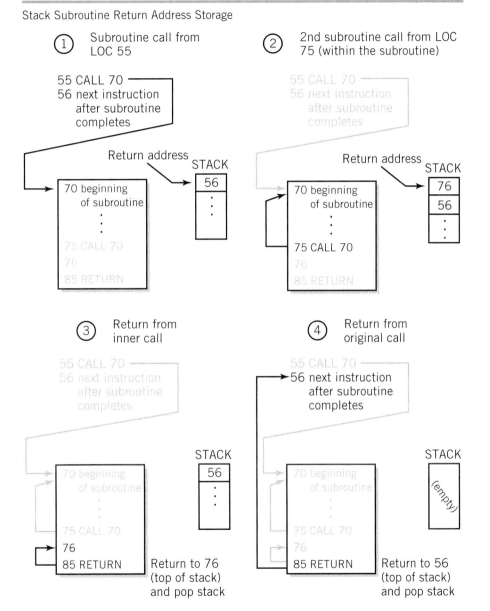

FIGURE 7.16

Using a Block of Memory as a Stack

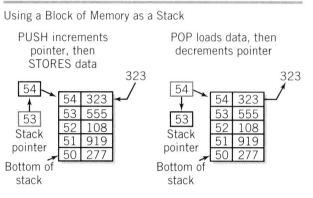

Multiple Data Instructions

Multimedia applications rank high in computational demands on the CPU in modern PCs and workstations. In response to the demand, CPU designers have created specialized instructions that speed up and simplify multimedia processing operations.

Multimedia operations are commonly characterized by a number of simple operations applied identically to every piece of data in the set. As a simple example, the brightness of an image might be modified by multiplying the value of every pixel in the image by a common scale factor. Or, a measure of similarity between two images could be established by subtracting all the pixel values in one image from the corresponding pixel values in a second image and averaging the results.

Multiple data instructions perform a single operation on multiple pieces of data simultaneously. For this reason they are also known as **SIMD** instructions. SIMD stands for **S**ingle **I**nstruction, **M**ultiple **D**ata. The SIMD instructions provided on Intel Pentium processors are typical. The processor provides eight 128-bit registers specifically for SIMD instruction use and also allows the use of the standard 64-bit floating point registers for this purpose. The Pentium CPU SIMD instructions can process from two 64-bit integers up to sixteen 8-bit integer arithmetic operations or up to two 64-bit floating point number operations simultaneously as well as providing instructions for packing and unpacking the values and moving them between registers and memory, and a variety of other related instructions. Other vendors, including AMD, IBM, Sun, Transmeta, and VIA provide compatible or similar SIMD instructions. The IBM Cell processor, which serves as the CPU in the Sony Playstation 3, provides a particularly powerful SIMD capability that accounts for much of the Playstation's graphics strength. Figure 7.17 shows the operation of a SIMD ADD instruction.

Although multimedia operations are a primary application for these instructions, these instructions can be applied to any vector or array processing application, and are useful for a number of purposes in addition to multimedia processing, including voice-to-text processing, the solutions to large-scale economics problems, weather prediction, and data encryption and decryption.

FIGURE 7.17

Operation of a 4-Wide SIMD ADD Instruction

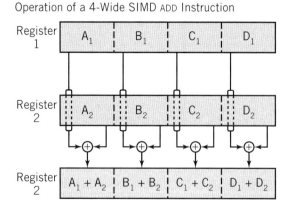

Other Instructions

The remainder of the instructions includes input/output instructions and machine control instructions. In most systems both groups are privileged instructions. Input/output instructions are generally privileged instructions because we do not want input and output requests from different users and programs interfering with each other. Consider, for example, two users requesting printer output on a shared printer at the same time, so that each page of output is divided back and forth between the two users. Obviously, such output would not be acceptable. Instead, these requests would be made to the operating system that controls the printer, which would set priorities, maintain queues, and service the requests. We will deal with the subject of input/output in Chapters 9 and 10, and with operating systems in Chapters 15 through 18.

7.7 INSTRUCTION WORD FORMATS

Instructions in the Little Man Computer were made up entirely of three-digit decimal numbers, with a single-digit op code, and a two-digit **address field**. The address field was used in various ways: for most instructions, the address field contained the two-digit address where data for the instruction could be found (e.g., LOAD) or was to be placed (STORE). In a few instructions, the address field was unused (e.g., HALT). For the branch instructions, the address field space was used instead to hold the address of the next instruction to be executed. For the I/O instructions, the address field became a sort of extension of the op code. In reality, the I/O address field contained the ''address'' of an I/O device, in our case 01 for the in basket and 02 for the out basket.

The instruction set in a typical real CPU is similar. Again, the instruction word can be divided into an op code and zero or more address fields. A simple 32-bit instruction format with one address field might look like that shown in Figure 7.18. In this example, the 32 bits are divided into an 8-bit op code and 24 bits of address field.

In the Little Man Computer, reference to an *address* specifically referred to a *memory* address. However, we have already noted that the computer might have several general-purpose registers and that it would be necessary for the programmer to select a particular register to use as a part of the instruction. To be more general, we will use the word ''address'' to refer to any data location, whether it is a user-accessible register or a memory location. We will use the more specific expression *memory address* when we want to specify that the address is actually a memory location.

In general, computer instructions that manipulate data require the specification of at least two locations for the data: one or more *source* locations and one *destination* location. These locations may be expressed *explicitly*, as address fields in the instruction word, or *implicitly*, as part of the definition of the instruction itself. The instruction format of the Little Man LOAD instruction, for example, takes the data from the single address field as the

FIGURE 7.18

A Simple 32-bit Instruction Format

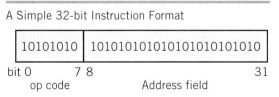

bit 0   7 8   31
   op code   Address field

FIGURE 7.19

Typical Two Operation Register Move Format

op code	source register	destination register
MOVE	5	10

explicit source address. Explicit addresses in the Little Man Computer are always memory addresses. The destination address in this case is **implicit**: this instruction always uses the accumulator register as a destination. The Little Man ADD and SUBTRACT instructions require *two* sources and a destination. Source data addressed by the instruction's single explicit address field is added to the value in the implicitly stated accumulator, with the result placed implicitly in the accumulator.

For a particular instruction, the source(s) and destination may be the same or may be different. For example, an instruction that complements a value to change its sign would usually be done "in place"; that is, the source and destination register or memory location is usually the same. The Little Man ADD instruction uses the accumulator register both as a source for one of the numbers to be added and as the destination for the result. On the other hand, when we move data, using a LOAD or STORE or some other type of MOVE operation, two operands are required. The source and destination are obviously different, or the move would not be useful! A register-to-register MOVE, for example, might use an instruction format such as that shown in Figure 7.19. In the figure, the instruction word consists of an opcode and two fields that point to registers. As shown, this instruction would move data from register 5 to register 10. Unless the operation is done in place, the sources are normally left unchanged by the instruction, whereas the destination is almost always changed.

The source and destination addresses may be registers or memory locations. Since most modern computers have multiple registers available to the user it is usually necessary to provide at least two explicit address fields, even for an address-register move, since the number of the particular register must be specified in the instruction.

The sources and destinations of data for an instruction, whether implicit or explicit, are also known as **operands**. Thus, instructions that move data from one place to another have two operands: one source operand and one destination operand. Arithmetic operations such as ADD and SUBTRACT require three operands. Explicit address fields are also known as *operand fields*.

Most commonly, instructions that manipulate data will have one address field for operations that happen in place, and two or three address fields for move and arithmetic operations. On some computers one or more of the addresses may be implicit, and no address field is required for the implicit address. However, in modern computers most address references are explicit, even for register addresses, because this increases the generality and flexibility of the instruction. Thus, most computer instructions will consist of an op code and one, two, or three explicit address fields. Some textbooks refer to instructions with one, two, or three explicit address fields as *unary*, *binary*, or *ternary* instructions, respectively.

7.8 INSTRUCTION WORD REQUIREMENTS AND CONSTRAINTS

The size of the instruction word, in bits, is dependent on the particular CPU architecture, particularly by the design of its instruction set. The size of the instruction word may be fixed at, say, 32 bits, or it may vary depending on the usage of the address fields. The Sun Sparc CPU, for example, takes the former approach: every instruction word is exactly 32 bits wide. Conversely, some of the basic instruction words for the x86 microprocessor line used in the common PC, for example, are as small as 1 or 2 bytes long, but there are some instructions in the Pentium microprocessor that are as many as 15 bytes long. The IBM Series z architecture is an evolutionary extension of upward compatible CPU architectures dating back to the 1960s. The legacy instructions in the IBM Series z CPU are mostly 4 bytes, or 32 bits long, with a few 2-byte or 6-byte long instructions. To expand the architecture to 64-bit addressing and data, IBM added a number of new instructions. These are all 6 bytes in length.

The challenge in establishing an instruction word size is the need to provide both enough op code bits to support a reasonable set of different instructions as well as enough address field bits to meet the ever growing demand for increasing amounts of addressable memory. Consider again, for example, the extremely straightforward instruction format shown in Figure 7.18. This format assumes a single address field with a 32-bit fixed length instruction. With the division shown, we have access to $2^8 = 256$ different instructions and $2^{24} =$ approximately 16 million memory addresses.

Even if the designer creates a smaller instruction set, with fewer op codes, the amount of memory that may be specified in a 32-bit instruction word is severely limited by modern standards. Most of today's computers support an address size of at least 32 bits. Many newer machines support 64-bit addresses.

Further, with additional registers, the simple instruction format shown in Figure 7.18 must be expanded to handle explicit addressing of multiple registers, including moves between registers, as well as identifying the proper register in operations between registers and memory. In short, the simple instruction format used in the Little Man Computer is inadequate for the instruction sets in modern computers.

The use of instructions of different lengths is one of several techniques developed by instruction set designers to allow more flexibility in the design of the instruction set. Simple instructions can be expressed in a small word, perhaps even a single byte, whereas more complicated instructions will require instruction words many bytes long. Longer instructions are stored in successive bytes of memory. Thus, a Little Man HALT, IN, or OUT instruction would be stored in a single location. A LOAD might require two successive locations to store memory addresses of five digits or three locations for an eight-digit address. The use of variable length instructions is efficient in memory usage, since each instruction is only as long as it needs to be.

There are a number of important disadvantages to variable length instructions, however. Most modern computers increase CPU processing speed by "pipelining" instructions, that is, by fetching a new instruction while the previous one is still completing execution, similar to the processing on an automobile assembly line. Variable length instructions complicate pipelining, because the starting point of the new instruction is not known until the length of the previous instruction has been determined. If you extend this idea to multiple instructions, you can see the difficulty of maintaining a smooth assembly line. This issue is discussed in more detail in Chapter 8. Because pipelining has become so important to processing speed in modern computers, the use of variable length instructions has fallen out of favor for new CPU designs. Nearly all new CPU designs use fixed length instructions exclusively.

As we mentioned previously in our discussion of memory size, an effective alternative to large instructions or variable instruction words is to store the address that would otherwise be located in an instruction word address field at some special location that can hold a large address, such as a general purpose register, and use a small address field within the instruction to point to the register location. There are a number of variations on this theme. This technique is used, even on systems that provide variable length instructions. A single CPU might provide a number of different variations to increase the flexibility of the instruction set. This flexibility also includes the ability to code programs that process lists of data more efficiently. The various ways of addressing registers and memory are known as addressing modes. The Little Man Computer provides only a single mode, known as direct addressing. The alternative just described is called register deferred addressing. An example of a deferred LOAD instruction is shown in Figure 7.20. This instruction would load the data value stored at memory address 3BD421 into general purpose register 7. There are a number of addressing modes discussed in detail in Supplementary Chapter 3. The use of different addressing modes is the most important method for minimizing the size of instruction words and for writing efficient programs.

Examples of instruction formats from two different CPUs are shown in Figure 7.21. There may be several different formats within a single CPU. We have shown only a partial set for each machine, although the SPARC set is complete except for small variations. (There are twenty-three different IBM formats in all.) It is not necessary that you understand every detail in Figure 7.21, but it is useful to note the basic similarities between the instruction set formats in different computers.

FIGURE 7.20

Deferred Register Addressing

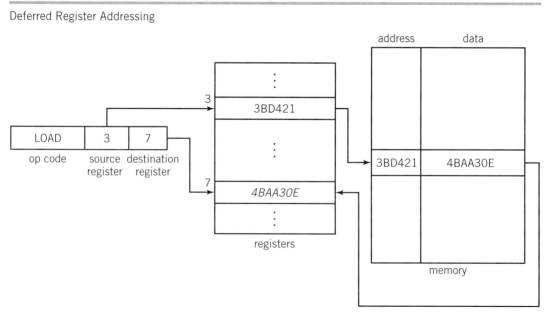

FIGURE 7.21

Examples of Instruction Formats

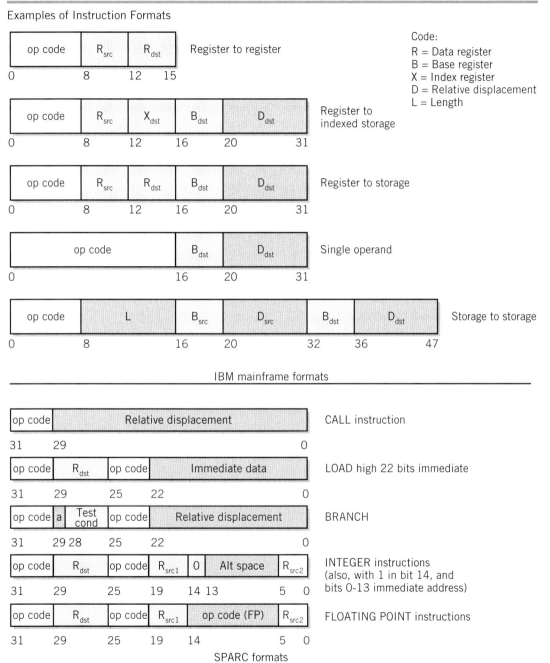

Code:
R = Data register
B = Base register
X = Index register
D = Relative displacement
L = Length

IBM mainframe formats

SPARC formats

SUMMARY AND REVIEW

Functionally, the operation of the CPU, together with memory, is essentially identical to that of the Little Man Computer. For each component of the Little Man Computer, there is a corresponding component in the computer unit.

Within the CPU, the most important components are registers. Data may be moved between registers, may be added or subtracted from the current contents of a register, and can be shifted or rotated within a register or between registers. Each instruction in the instruction set is executed by performing these simple operations, using the appropriate choice of registers and operations in the correct sequence for the particular instruction. The sequence of operations for a particular instruction is known as its fetch-execute cycle. A fetch-execute cycle exists for every instruction in the instruction set. Fetch-execute instruction cycles constitute the basis for all program execution in the computer. The sequence for each instruction corresponds closely to the actions taken by the Little Man in performing a similar instruction.

The operation of memory is intimately related to two registers in particular, the memory address register and the memory data register. Addresses placed into the MAR are decoded in memory, resulting in the activation of a single memory address line. At the proper instant, data can then be transferred in either direction between that memory location and the MDR. The direction is specified by a read/write control line. The number of available memory locations is established by the size of the MAR; the data word size is established by the size of the MDR.

Interconnections between various parts of a computer are provided by buses. There are many different types of buses. Buses connect different modules within the CPU. They also connect the CPU to memory and to the I/O peripherals. Buses can connect two components in a point-to-point configuration or may interconnect several modules in a multipoint configuration. Buses may be parallel or serial. In general, the lines on buses carry signals that represent data, address, and control functions.

Instructions fall naturally into a small number of categories: moves, integer arithmetic, floating point arithmetic, data flow control, and so forth. There are also privileged instructions, which control functions internal to the CPU and are accessible only to the operating system.

Instructions in a real CPU are made up of an op code and up to three address field operands. The size of the instruction word is CPU dependent. Some computers use variable length instruction words. Other computers use a fixed length instruction, most commonly, 32 bits in length.

FOR FURTHER READING

There are many excellent textbooks that describe the implementation and operation of the components of the computer system. A brief, but very clear, explanation of the fetch-execute cycle can be found in Davis and Rajkumar [DAV02]. Three classic engineering textbooks that discuss the topics of this chapter in great detail are those authored by Stallings [STAL05], Patterson and Hennessy [PATT07], and Tanenbaum [TAN05]. Wikipedia offers a brief, but clear, introduction to the principal concepts of von Neumann architecture. There are many books and papers describing various components and techniques associated with the implementation and operation of the CPU and memory. Also see the For Further Reading section in Chapter 8 for more suggestions.

KEY CONCEPTS AND TERMS

accumulator
address field
arithmetic/logic unit (ALU)
arithmetic shift
broadcast bus
bus
bus interface bridge
bus protocol
cable
central processing unit (CPU)
control unit (CU)
dynamic RAM
EEPROM (electronically erasable programmable ROM)
explicit source address
fetch-execute instruction cycle
flag
flash memory

full-duplex line
general-purpose register
half-duplex line
implicit source address
instruction pointer
instruction register (IR)
line (bus)
logical shift
memory
memory address register (MAR)
memory data register (MDR)
memory management unit
multiplex
multipoint bus
nonvolatile memory
operands
parallel bus
point-to-point bus
port

program counter (PC)
program counter register
Program Status Word (PSW)
privileged instruction
RAM
register
register file
ROM
rotate operation
serial bus
shift operation
SIMD
simplex line
stack
stack pointer
static RAM
status register
subroutine call and return
user-visible register
volatile memory

READING REVIEW QUESTIONS

7.1   What does *ALU* stand for? What is its corresponding component in the Little Man Computer? What does *CU* stand for? What is its corresponding LMC component?

7.2   What is a *register*? Be precise. Name at least two components in the LMC that meet the qualifications for a register. Name several different kinds of values that a register might hold.

7.3   There are four primary operations that are normally performed on a register. Describe each operation.

7.4   What is the purpose of the *instruction register*? What takes the place of the instruction register in the LMC?

7.5   When a value is copied from one register to another, what happens to the value in the source register? What happens to the value in the destination register?

7.6   Registers perform a very important role in the fetch-execute cycle. What is the function of registers in the fetch-execute instruction cycle?

7.7   Explain the relationship between the memory address register, the memory data register, and memory itself.

7.8   If the memory register for a particular computer is 32 bits wide, how much memory can this computer support?

7.9   What is the difference between volatile and nonvolatile memory? Is RAM volatile or nonvolatile? Is ROM volatile or nonvolatile?

7.10   Explain each step of the fetch part of the fetch-execute cycle. At the end of the fetch operation, what is the status of the instruction? Specifically, what has the fetch operation achieved that prepares the instruction for execution? Explain the similarity between this operation and the corresponding operation performed steps performed by the Little Man.

7.11   Assume the following values in various registers and memory locations at a given point in time:
PC: 20   A: 150   Memory location 20: 160 [ADD 60]   Memory location 60: 30.
Show the values that are stored in each of the following registers at the completion of the instruction: PC, MAR, MDR, IR, and A.

7.12   Once the fetch operation is complete, what is the first step of the execution phase for any instruction that accesses a memory address for data (e.g., LOAD, STORE)?

7.13   Using the ADD instruction as a model, show the fetch-execute cycle for a SUBTRACT instruction.

7.14   Define a *bus*. What are buses used for?

7.15   What is the difference between a *multipoint* bus and a *point-to-point* bus? Draw diagrams that illustrate the difference.

7.16   What three types of "data" might a bus carry?

7.17   Explain how data travels on a bus when the bus is *simplex. Half-duplex. Full-duplex.*

7.18   Briefly describe each of the major disadvantages of parallel buses.

7.19   Which Little Man Computer instructions would be classified as *data movement* instructions?

7.20   What operations would you expect the arithmetic class of instructions to perform?

7.21   What do *program control instructions* do? Which LMC instructions would be classified as program control instructions?

7.22   What is a stack? Explain how a stack works. Create a diagram that shows how PUSH and POP instructions are used to implement a stack.

7.23   Explain the difference between SHIFT and ROTATE instructions.

7.24   What is a *privileged instruction*? Which LMC instructions would normally be privileged?

7.25   Show an instruction format that could be used to move data or perform arithmetic between two registers. Assume that the instruction is 32 bits wide and that the computer has sixteen general-purpose data registers. If the op code uses 8 bits, how many bits are spares, available for other purposes, such as special addressing techniques?

7.26   Show a 32-bit instruction format that allows 32 different op codes. How many bits are available for addressing in your format?

EXERCISES

7.1   Suppose that the following instructions are found at the given locations in memory:

```
20 LDA 50
21 ADD 51
50 724
51 006
```

    a.   Show the contents of the IR, the PC, the MAR, the MDR, and A at the conclusion of instruction 20.

    b.   Show the contents of each register as each step of the fetch-execute cycle is performed for instruction 21.

7.2   Draw side-by-side flow diagrams that show how the Little Man executes a store instruction and the corresponding CPU fetch-execute cycle.

7.3   Show the steps of the CPU fetch-execute cycle for the remaining instructions in the Little Man instruction set.

7.4   Using the register operations indicated in this chapter, show the fetch-execute cycle for an instruction that produces the 2's complement of the number in A. Show the fetch-execute cycle for an instruction that clears A (i.e., sets A to 0).

7.5   Many older computers used an alternative to the BRANCH ON CONDITION instruction called SKIP ON CONDITION that worked as follows: if the condition were true, the computer would skip the following instruction and go on to the one after; otherwise, the next instruction in line would be executed. Programmers usually place a jump instruction in the "in-between" location to branch on a FALSE condition. Normally, the skip instruction was designed to skip one memory location. If the instruction set uses variable length instructions, however, the task is more difficult, since the skip must still skip around the entire instruction. Assume a Little Man mutant that uses a variable length instruction. The op code is in the first word, and there may be as many as three words following. To make life easy, assume that the third digit of the op code word is a number from 1 to 4, representing the number of words in the instruction. Create a fetch-execute cycle for this machine.

7.6   The Little Prince Computer (LPC) is a mutant variation on the LMC. (The LPC is so named because the differences are a royal pain.) The LPC has one additional instruction. The extra instruction requires two consecutive words:

```
0XX
0YY
```

This instruction, known as move, moves data directly from location XX to location YY without affecting the value in the accumulator. To execute this instruction, the Little Prince would need to store the XX data temporarily. He can do this by writing the value on a piece of paper and holding it until he retrieves the second address. The equivalent in a real CPU might be called the intermediate address register, or IAR. Write the fetch-execute cycle for the LPC MOVE instruction.

7.7   Generally, the distance that a programmer wants to move from the current instruction location on a BRANCH ON CONDITION is fairly small. This suggests that it might be appropriate to design the BRANCH instruction in such a way that the new location is calculated relative to the current instruction location. For example, we could design a different LMC instruction 8CX. The C digit would specify the condition on which to branch, and X would be a single-digit relative address. Using 10's complement, this would allow a branch of −5 to +4 locations from the current address. If we were currently executing this instruction at location 24, 803 would cause a branch on negative to location 27. Write a fetch-execute cycle for this BRANCH ON NEGATIVE RELATIVE instruction. You may ignore the condition code for this exercise, and you may also assume that the complementary addition is handled correctly. The single-digit address, X, is still found in IR [address].

7.8   Suppose that the instruction format for a modified Little Man Computer requires two consecutive locations for each instruction. The high-order digits of the instruction are located in the first mail slot, followed by the low-order digits. The IR is large enough to hold the entire instruction and can be addressed as IR [high] and IR [low] to load it. You may assume that the op code part of the instruction uses IR [high] and that the address is found in IR [low]. Write the fetch-execute cycle for an ADD instruction on this machine.

7.9   Create the fetch-execute cycle for an instruction that moves a value from general purpose register-1 to general purpose register-2. Compare this cycle to the cycle for a LOAD instruction. What is the major advantage of the MOVE over the LOAD?

7.10   Most modern computers provide a large number of general-purpose registers and very few memory access instructions. Most instructions use these registers to hold data instead of memory. What are the advantages to such an architecture?

7.11   Why are there two different registers (MAR and MDR) associated with memory? What are the equivalents in the Little Man Computer?

7.12   One large modern computer has a 48-bit memory address register. How much memory can this computer address?

7.13   Most of the registers in the machine have two-way copy capability; that is, you can copy to them from another register, and you can copy from them to another register. The MAR, on the other hand, is always used as a destination register; you only copy to the MAR. Explain clearly why this is so.

7.14   If you were building a computer to be used in outer space, would you be likely to use some form of flash memory or RAM as main memory? Why?

7.15
   a.   What is the effect of shifting an unsigned number in a register two bits to the left? One bit to the right? Assume that 0s are inserted to replace bit locations at the end of the register that have become empty due to the shift.

   b.   Suppose the number is signed, that is, stored using 2's complement. Now what is the effect of shifting the number?

   c.   Suppose that the shift excludes the sign bit, so that the sign bit always remains the same. Furthermore, suppose that during a right shift, the sign bit is always used as the insertion bit at the left end of the number (instead of 0). Now what is the effect of these shifts?

7.16   As computer words get larger and larger, there is a law of diminishing returns: the speed of execution of real application programs does not increase and may, in fact, decrease. Why do you suppose that this is so?

7.17   Until recently, most personal computers used a parallel PCI bus as a backplane to interconnect the various components within the computer, but the PCI bus was rarely, if ever, used to connect external devices to the computer. Modern computers often use a serial adaptation of the PCI bus called PCI Express, which is sometimes made available as a port to connect external devices. Identify at least three shortcomings of the original PCI bus that made external use of the bus impractical. Explain how the PCI Express bus overcomes each of these limitations.

7.18   What are the trade-offs in using a serial bus versus a parallel bus to move data from one place to another?

7.19   Point-to-point buses generally omit lines for addressing. Why is this possible? Suppose a point-to-point bus is used to connect two components together where one of the components actually represents multiple addresses. How could a bus with no address lines be used to satisfy the requirement for different addresses in this case?

7.20   Explain why skew is not a factor in a serial bus.

CHAPTER 8

CPU AND MEMORY: DESIGN, ENHANCEMENT, AND IMPLEMENTATION

Adapted by Benjamin Reece

8.0 INTRODUCTION

The Little Man Computer design, implemented in binary form, may be sufficient to implement any program, but it is not necessarily a convenient way to do so. It is like traveling overseas by freight steamer instead of by fast plane: it might be fun, but it sure ain't the easiest way to get the job done! Computers today are more sophisticated and flexible, providing a greater variety of instructions, improved methods of addressing memory and manipulating data, and implementation techniques that allow instructions to be executed quickly and efficiently.

In Chapter 7, we discussed the principal features of a CPU: the basic architecture of the CPU, register concept, instruction set, instruction formats, means of addressing memory, and the fetch-execute cycle. In this chapter we will investigate some of the additional design features and implementation techniques that help to give the modern CPU its power.

It probably won't surprise you to know that there are a large number of different ways of performing these tasks. At the same time, it is important to recognize, right from the outset, that additional features and a particular choice of organization do not change the fundamental operation of the computer as we have already described it. Rather, they represent variations on the ideas and techniques that we have already described. These variations can simplify the programmer's task and possibly speed up program execution by creating shortcuts for common operations. However, nothing introduced in this chapter changes the most important idea: that the computer is nothing more than a machine capable of performing simple operations at very high speeds.

The first section investigates different CPU architectures, with particular focus on the modern manifestation and organization of traditional architectures The section also briefly considers two interesting recent architectures, the Transmeta VLIW and Intel EPIC architectures.

In the second section we consider various CPU features and enhancements, with an emphasis on alternatives to the traditional control unit/ALU CPU organization. We explain how these alternative organizations address major bottlenecks that limit CPU execution speed, with a number of innovative techniques for improving CPU performance.

Section 8.3 looks at memory enhancements. The most significant improvement in memory access speed is cache memory. Cache memory is discussed in considerable depth.

In Section 8.4, we present a general model that includes the features, enhancements, and techniques described in Section 8.2. This model represents the organization of most current CPUs.

Section 8.5 considers the concept of multiprocessing: a computer organization consisting of multiple CPUs directly connected together, sharing memory, major buses, and I/O. This organization adds both performance enhancement and additional design challenges. We also briefly introduce a complementary feature, simultaneous multithreading. Two types of multiprocessors are presented: the symmetrical multiprocessor is more common. It is well-suited for general purpose computing. An alternative, the master-slave multiprocessor is useful for computer applications characterized by computationally intense, repetitive operations, such as graphics processing.

Finally, in Section 8.6, we present a brief commentary on the implementation of the CPU organization that we have discussed in previous sections.

It is not our intention to overwhelm you in this chapter with myriad details to memorize, nor to help you create a new career as an assembly language programmer or computer hardware engineer, but this chapter will at least introduce you to the major concepts, methods, and terminology used in modern computers. When reading this chapter, remember to keep your focus on the larger picture: the details are just variations on a theme.

8.1 CPU ARCHITECTURES

Overview

A CPU architecture is defined by the basic characteristics and major features of the CPU. (CPU architecture is sometimes called **instruction set architecture (ISA)**.) These characteristics include such things as the number and types of registers, methods of addressing memory, and basic design and layout of the instruction set. It does *not* include consideration of the implementation, instruction execution speed, details of the interface between the CPU and associated computer circuitry, and various optional features. These details are usually referred to as the computer's **organization**. The architecture may or may not include the absence or presence of particular instructions, the amount of addressable memory, or the data widths that are routinely processed by the CPU. Some architectures are more tightly defined than others.

These ideas about computer architecture should not surprise you. Consider house architecture. A split-level ranch house, for example, is easily recognized by its general characteristics, even though there may be wide differences in features, internal organization, and design from one split-level ranch to the next. Conversely, an A-frame house or a Georgian house is recognized by specific, well-defined features that must be present in the design to be recognized as A-frame or Georgian.

There have been many CPU architectures over the years, but only a few with longevity. In most cases, that longevity has resulted from evolution and expansion of the architecture to include new features, always with protection of the integrity of the original architecture, as well as with improved design, technology, and implementation of the architecture.

At present, important CPU architectural families include the IBM mainframe series, the Intel x86 family, the IBM POWER/PowerPC architecture, and the Sun SPARC family. Each of these is characterized by a lifetime exceeding twenty years. The original IBM mainframe architecture is more than forty-five years old. Architectural longevity protects the investment of users by allowing continued use of program applications through system upgrades and replacements.

Most CPU architectures today are variations on the traditional design described in Chapter 7.[1] There have also been a few interesting attempts to create other types, including a stack-based CPU with no general-purpose registers, and two recent architectures called **very long instruction word (VLIW)** from Transmeta and **explicitly parallel instruction computers (EPIC)** from Intel. VLIW and EPIC architectures are too new to assess their long-term value.

It should be noted that each of these architectures is consistent with the broad characteristics that define a von Neumann computer.

Traditional Modern Architectures

Early CPU architectures were characterized by comparatively few general-purpose registers, a wide variety of memory addressing techniques, a large number of specialized instructions, and instruction words of varying sizes. Researchers in the late 1970s and early 1980s concluded that these characteristics inhibited the efficient organization of the CPU. In particular, their studies revealed that

- Specialized instructions were used rarely, but added hardware complexity to the instruction decoder that slowed down execution of the other instructions that are used frequently.

- The number of data memory accesses and total MOVE instructions could be reduced by increasing the number of general-purpose registers and using those registers to manipulate data and perform calculations. The time to locate and access data in memory is much longer than that required to process data in a register and requires more steps in the fetch-execute cycle of instructions that access memory than those that don't.

- Permitting the use of general purpose registers to hold memory addresses, also, would allow the addressing of large amounts of memory while reducing instruction word size, addressing complexity, and instruction execution time, as well as simplifying the design of programs that require indexing. Reducing the number of available addressing methods simplifies CPU design significantly.

- The use of fixed-length, fixed-format instruction words with the op code and address fields in the same position for every instruction would allow instructions to be fetched and decoded independently and in parallel. With variable-length instructions it is necessary to wait until the previous instruction is decoded in order to establish its length and instruction format.

The Intel x86 is characteristic of older architectures; it has comparatively few general purpose registers, numerous addressing methods, dozens of specialized instructions, and instruction word formats that vary from 1 to 15 bytes in length. In contrast, every instruction

---

[1] Historically, traditional architecture was loosely categorized into one of two types, CISC (complex instruction set computers) or RISC (reduced instruction set computers). In modern times, the dividing line between CISC and RISC architectures has become increasingly blurred as many of the features of each have migrated across the dividing line. Because modern architectures contain the major features of both, it is no longer useful to distinguish one from the other.

in the newer Sun SPARC architecture is the same 32-bit length; there are only five primary instruction word formats, shown earlier in Figure 7.21; and only a single, register-based, LOAD/STORE memory addressing mode.

VLIW and EPIC Architectures

VLIW (very long instruction word) and EPIC (explicitly parallel instruction computer) architectures represent recent approaches to architectural design. VLIW architecture is represented by the Transmeta Crusoe and Efficeon families of CPU processors. The Intel Itanium IA-64 series is based on EPIC architecture. The basic goal of each of these architectures is to increase execution speed by processing instruction operations in parallel. The primary difficulty in doing so results from the inherently sequential order of the instructions in a program. In particular, the data used in an instruction may depend on the result from a previous instruction. This situation is known as a **data dependency**. Also, branches and loops may alter the sequence, resulting in **control dependency**. Data and control dependencies are discussed in more depth in Section 8.2.

The Transmeta Crusoe architecture is based on a 128-bit instruction word called a molecule. The molecule is divided into four 32-bit *atoms*. Each atom represents an operation similar to those of a normal 32-bit instruction word, however, the atoms are designed in such a way that all four operations may be executed simultaneously in separate execution units. Figure 8.1 shows an example of a typical molecule.

The Crusoe CPU provides 64 general-purpose registers to assure adequate register space for rapid register-to-register processing.

Although a programmer could write programs directly for a Crusoe CPU with the 128-bit word instruction set, that is not the primary goal of the Crusoe architecture. Indeed, the fine details of the instruction set have not been publicly released to date. Instead, the Crusoe CPU is intended for use with a specific software program that translates instruction sets on the fly from other types of CPUs to the Crusoe instruction set for execution on

FIGURE 8.1

VLIW Format

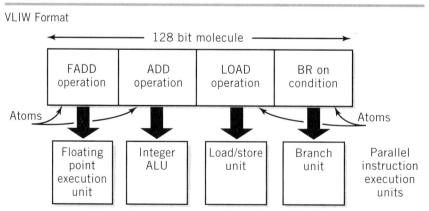

the Crusoe CPU. This translator is called a **code-morphing layer**.[2] It is a fundamental component within the Crusoe architecture. It is permanently resident in memory and processes every instruction prior to execution. In addition to instruction translation, the code-morphing layer also reorders the instructions as necessary to eliminate data dependencies and other bottlenecks. Although this sounds like an inefficient way to process instructions, Transmeta has demonstrated that the simplicity of its VLIW design and the sophistication of its code-morphing software allow execution of the Pentium instruction set at speeds comparable to the native execution speeds of a Pentium processor. Transmeta claims, with apparent justification, that this simplicity allows a much simpler CPU design, with fewer transistors and a much lower power consumption, resulting from the elimination of complicated hardware implementation features commonly used to achieve high execution speeds in a conventional CPU design. The Efficeon CPU extends the Crusoe architecture to 256 bits, representing eight 32-bit atoms to be executed simultaneously.

At present, Transmeta has provided a code-morphing layer only for the Pentium CPU family. However, if there were reason to do so, Transmeta could easily create code-morphing layers for other CPUs.

The EPIC architecture, designed by Intel for its IA-64 processor family, attempts to achieve similar goals by slightly different means. The basic instruction set architecture is new, although Intel has built x86 capability into the CPU to support compatibility with its earlier architecture. The IA-64 offers 128 64-bit general-purpose registers and 128 82-bit floating point registers. All instructions are 41 bits wide.

Like the VLIW architecture, the EPIC architecture also organizes instructions into bundles prior to CPU execution, however the methodology and goal are somewhat different. In this case, the instructions *do* represent the native instruction set of the architecture. Instructions are presented to the CPU for execution in 128-bit bundles that include a group of three instructions plus 5 bits that identify the type of each instruction in the bundle.

An assembly language programmer is expected to follow a set of published guidelines that identify dependencies and allow the parallel execution of each bundle. Additionally, bits within each instruction word provide information to the execution unit that identify potential dependencies and other bottlenecks and help the programmer to optimize the code for fast execution. High-level language EPIC compilers must also create code that satisfies the guidelines.

A fundamental difference between the Transmeta VLIW and the Intel EPIC architectures is the placement of responsibility for correct instruction sequencing. The VLIW architecture allows any sequence of instructions to enter the CPU for processing. The code-morphing software, integral to the architecture, handles proper sequencing. The EPIC architecture places the burden on the assembly language programmer or on the program compiler software.

This does not suggest that one architecture is superior to the other. It simply indicates a different approach to the solution of dependencies. Note that the Transmeta VLIW does

---

[2]On a lesser scale, code morphing can also be used to translate complex variable-width instruction words to simpler fixed-width equivalents for faster execution. This technique allows the retention of legacy architectures while permitting the use of modern processing methods. Modern x86 implementations use this approach.

not allow direct assembly language access to the CPU. *All* program code must be processed through code-morphing software. Each architecture offers an interesting new approach to program execution with potential benefits.

8.2 CPU FEATURES AND ENHANCEMENTS

Introduction

We have already introduced you to the fundamental model of a traditional CPU, represented by an instruction set, registers, and a fetch-execute instruction cycle. Additionally, we have presented some of the bells and whistles that have enhanced CPU capability and performance. Some of the enhancements that were introduced in Chapter 7 include direct support for floating point arithmetic, BCD arithmetic, and multimedia processing, as well as the inclusion of additional addressing modes, which simplify data access, increase potential memory size capability while maintaining reasonable instruction word sizes, and improve list and array processing. In this chapter we have already presented a number of architectural enhancements that can improve performance including features that allow parallel execution of instructions to improve processing speed, register-oriented instructions, the use of fixed-width instructions, and integral code-morphing software.

Since the purpose of a computer is to execute programs, the ability of the CPU to execute instructions quickly is an important contributor to performance. Once a particular architecture is established, there remain a number of different ways to increase the instruction execution performance of a computer. One method is to provide a number of CPUs in the computer rather than just one. Since a single CPU can process only one instruction at a time, each additional CPU would, in theory, multiply the performance of the computer by the number of CPUs included. We will return to a discussion of this technique later, in Section 8.5.

Of more interest at the moment are approaches that can be used to improve the performance of an individual CPU. In our introduction to CPU architectures, we suggested a number of possibilities. Some of these require new design, such as the large number of registers and register-to-register instructions that are characteristic of newer architectures. As we already noted, even with older instruction sets, it is often possible to use code morphing to create an intermediate instruction set that is used within the CPU as a substitute for the more complex, original instruction set.

Another difficulty to be overcome when attempting system optimization is that some computer instructions inherently require a large number of fetch-execute steps. Integer division and floating point arithmetic instructions are in this category. Obviously, CPU architects cannot create modern instruction sets that omit these instructions.

In this section, we consider a number of different, but interrelated, approaches to CPU optimization that are applicable to nearly any CPU design. Interestingly enough, you will see that similar approaches can be found in such diverse operations as automobile assembly plants and restaurants.

In Chapter 7, you learned that the fetch-execute cycle is the basic operation by which instructions get executed. You also observed that the steps in a fetch-execute cycle generally must be performed in a particular sequence: an instruction must be fetched and identified before it can be executed, for example. Otherwise the machine would have no way of knowing what to execute. And so on, step by step, through the entire instruction cycle. *(The first step in cooking spaghetti is to add water to the pot.)* CPU performance can be improved by any method that can perform the fetch-execute cycle steps more quickly or more efficiently.

Then, a program is executed by performing the fetch-execute cycle in a specified sequence, where the sequence is sometimes determined by the program itself during execution. To be provably correct during program execution, the sequence must be maintained and data dependencies resolved in proper order. *(The "cook spaghetti," "drain spaghetti," and "prepare sauce" instructions must be completed before the sauce is mixed into the spaghetti.)*

Observe that the limitation to performance results from the serial nature of CPU processing: each instruction requires a sequence of fetch-execute cycle steps, and the program requires the execution of a sequence of these instructions. Thus, the keys to increased performance must rely on methods that either reduce the number of steps in the fetch-execute cycle or reduce the time required for each step in the cycle and, ultimately, reduce the time for each instruction in the program.

Fetch-Execute Cycle Timing Issues

As a first step, consider the problem of controlling the timing of each step in the fetch-execute cycle to guarantee perfect CPU operation, to assure that each step follows the previous step, in perfect order, as quickly as possible. There must be enough time between steps to assure that each operation is complete and that data is where it is supposed to be before the next step takes place. As you saw in Chapter 7, most steps in the fetch-execute cycle work by copying, combining, or moving data between various registers. When data is copied, combined, or moved between registers, it takes a short, but finite, amount of time for the data to "settle down" in the new register, that is, for the results of the operation to be correct. This occurs in part because the electronic switches that connect the registers operate at slightly different speeds. (We're actually talking billionths of a second here!) Also, design allowances must be made for the fact that some operations take longer than others; for example, addition takes more time than a simple data movement. Even more significant is the amount of time that it takes for the address stored in the MAR to activate the correct address in memory. The latter time factor is due to the complex electronic circuitry that is required to identify one group of memory cells out of several million or billion possibilities. This means that reducing the number of memory access steps by using registers for most data operations will inherently improve performance. (We discuss methods to reduce the memory access time, itself, in Section 8.3.) To assure adequate time for each step, the times at which different events take place are synchronized to the pulses of an electronic clock. The **clock** provides a master control as to when each step in the instruction cycle takes place. The pulses of the clock are separated sufficiently to assure that each step has time to complete, with the data settled down, before the results of that step are required by the next step. Thus, use of a faster clock alone does not work if the circuitry cannot keep up.

A timing cycle for a Little Man ADD instruction is shown in Figure 8.2. Each block in the diagram represents one step of the fetch-execute cycle. Certain steps that do not have to access memory and which are not dependent on previous steps can actually be performed at the same time. This can reduce the overall number of cycles required for the

FIGURE 8.2

Fetch-Execute Timing Diagram

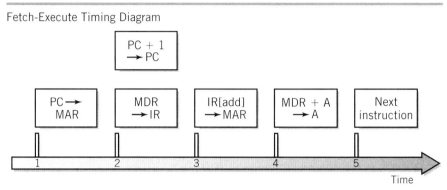

instruction, which speeds up the computer. In this diagram, the data from the program counter has been copied into the memory address register in the first step and is no longer needed. Therefore, the program counter can be incremented at any time after the first step. In Figure 8.2 the PC is incremented in parallel with the MDR → IR step. As shown in the figure, the ADD instruction is completed in four clock cycles.

Figure 8.3 shows the improvement possible by using multiple data registers to implement an ADD instruction. Since the register-to-register add can be done directly, the number of steps in the cycle is reduced from four to three, with only a single execute step, and the extra time required for the memory access is eliminated.

The built-in clock runs continuously whenever the power to the computer is on. The frequency of its pulses is controlled by a quartz crystal, similar to that which might control your wristwatch. The frequency of the clock and the number of steps required by each instruction determine the speed with which the computer performs useful work.

The pulses of the clock are combined with the data in the instruction register to control electronic switches that open and close in the right sequence to move data from

FIGURE 8.3

Fetch-Execute Cycle for Register-to-Register ADD Instruction

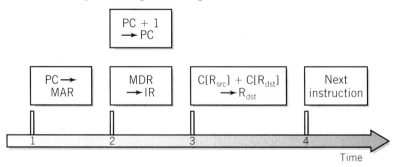

Note: $C[R_{dst}]$ = contents of destination register

register to register in accordance with the instruction cycle for the particular instruction. The memory activation line described in Section 7.3 is an example of a timing line. The activation line is set up so that it will not turn on until the correct address decode line in the MAR has had time to settle down. If this were not the case, several address lines might be partially turned on, and the data transferred between the memory and MDR might be incorrect. Such errors can obviously not be tolerated, so it is important to control timing accurately.

Conceptually, each pulse of the clock is used to control one step in the sequence, although it is sometimes possible to perform multiple operations within a single step. The clock in the original IBM PC, for example, ran at 4.77 MHz (MHz is pronounced megahertz), which meant that the machine could perform 4.77 million steps every second. If a typical instruction in the IBM PC requires about ten steps, then the original IBM PC could execute about (4.77/10) or about 0.5 million PC instructions per second. A PC running at 8 MHz, with everything else equal, would perform approximately twice as fast.

There are several factors that determine the number of instructions that a computer can perform in a second. Obviously the clock speed is one major factor. Some current PC computers run their clocks at 3 GHz (pronounced gigahertz) or even more to achieve higher instruction cycle rates.

A Model for Improved CPU Performance

The current organizational model of a CPU uses three primary, interrelated techniques to address the limitations of the conventional CU/ALU model and to improve performance.

- Implementation of the fetch-execute cycle is divided into two separate units: a fetch unit to retrieve and decode instructions and an execution unit to perform the actual instruction operation. This allows independent, concurrent operation of the two parts of the fetch-execute cycle.

- The model uses an assembly line technique called *pipelining* to allow overlapping between the fetch-execute cycles of sequences of instructions. This reduces the average time needed to complete an instruction.

- The model provides separate execution units for different types of instructions. This makes it possible to separate instructions with different numbers of execution steps for more efficient processing. It also allows the parallel execution of unrelated instructions by directing each instruction to its own execution unit. You have already seen this method applied to the Transmeta and Itanium architectures in Section 8.1.

We next consider each of these techniques in turn.

SEPARATE FETCH UNIT/EXECUTE UNIT   Picture a modified Little Man Computer in which the Little Man has been given an assistant. The assistant will fetch and decode the instructions from the mailboxes at a pace that allows the Little Man to spend his time executing instructions, one after another. Note that a similar division of labor is used in a restaurant: waiters and waitresses gather the food orders from the customers and pass them to the cooks for processing.

The current preferred CPU implementation model divides the CPU similarly into two units, which correspond roughly to the fetch and execute parts of the instruction cycle. To achieve maximum performance, these two parts operate as independently from each other as possible, recognizing, of course, that an instruction must be fetched before it can be decoded and executed. Figure 8.4 illustrates this alternative CPU organization.

The **fetch unit** portion of the CPU consists of an instruction fetch unit and an instruction decode unit. Instructions are fetched from memory by the fetch unit, based on the current address stored in an instruction pointer (IP) register. The fetch unit is designed to fetch several instructions at a time in parallel. The IP register effectively acts as a program counter, but is given a different name to emphasize that there are a number of instructions in the pipeline simultaneously. There is a bus interface unit that provides the logic and memory registers necessary to address memory over the bus. Once an instruction is fetched, it is held in a buffer until it can be decoded and executed. The number of instructions held will depend upon the size of each instruction, the width of the memory bus and memory

FIGURE 8.4

Alternative CPU Organization

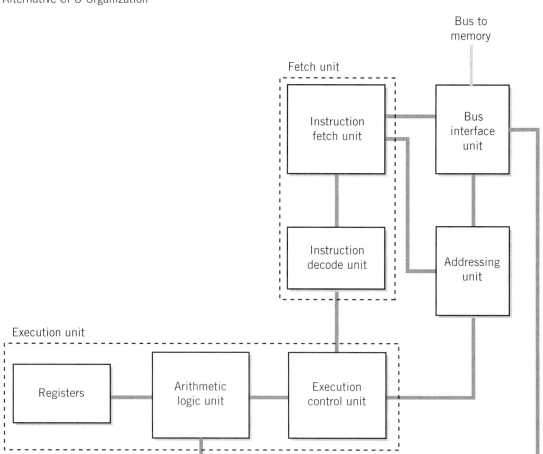

data register[3], and the size of the buffer. As instructions are executed, the fetch unit takes advantage of time when the bus is not otherwise being used and attempts to keep the buffer filled with instructions. In general, modern memory buses are wide enough and fast enough that they do not limit instruction retrieval.

Recall that in Figure 8.3 we showed that register-to-register operations could be implemented with only a single memory access, in the fetch portion of the fetch-execute cycle. Fetching the instructions in advance allows the execution of these instructions to take place quickly, without the delay required to access memory.

Instructions in the fetch unit buffer are sent to the instruction decoder unit. The decoder unit identifies the op code. From the op code it determines the type of the instruction. If the instruction set is made up of variable length instructions, it also determines the length of the particular instruction. The decoder then assembles the complete instruction with its operands, ready for execution.

The **execution unit** contains the arithmetic/logic unit and the portion of the control unit that identifies and controls the steps that comprise the execution part for each different instruction. The remainder of what we previously called the control unit is distributed throughout the model, controlling the fetching and decoding of instructions at the correct times, and in the correct order, address generation for instructions and operands, and so forth. The ALU provides the usual computational abilities for the general registers and condition flags.

When the execution unit is ready for an instruction, the instruction decoder unit passes the next instruction to the control unit for execution. Instruction operands requiring memory references are sent to the addressing unit. The addressing unit determines the memory address required, and the appropriate data read or write request is then processed by the bus interface unit.

The bus interface and addressing units operate independently of the instruction pipeline and provide services to the fetch, decode, and execution units as requested by each unit.

PIPELINING   Look at Figure 8.2 again. In the figure, there are two stages to the execution phase of the instruction cycle. If each stage is implemented separately, so that the instruction simply passes from one stage to the next as it is executed, only one stage is in use at any given time. If there are more steps in the cycle, the same is still true. Thus, to speed up processing even more, modern computers overlap instructions, so that more than one instruction is being worked on at a time. This method is known as **pipelining**. The pipelining concept is one of the major advances in modern computing design. It has been responsible for large increases in program execution speed.

In its simplest form, the idea of pipelining is that as each instruction completes a step, the following instruction moves into the stage just vacated. Thus, when the first instruction is completed, the next one is already one stage short of completion. If there are many steps in the fetch-execute cycle, we can have several instructions at various points in the cycle. The method is similar to an automobile assembly line, where several cars are in different degrees of production at the same time. It still takes the same amount of time to complete

---

[3]Recall that in Chapter 7 we noted that it is common modern practice to retrieve several bytes from memory with each memory access.

one instruction cycle (or one car), but the pipelining technique results in a large overall increase in the average number of instructions performed in a given time.

Of course, a branch instruction may invalidate all the instructions in the pipeline at that instant if the branch is taken, and the computer still must have the data from the previous instruction if the next instruction requires it in order to proceed. Modern computers use a variety of techniques to compensate for the branching problem. One common approach is to maintain two or more separate pipelines so that instructions from both possible outcomes can be processed until the direction of the branch is clear. Another approach attempts to predict the probable branch path based on the history of previous execution of the same instruction. The problem of waiting for data results from previous instructions can be alleviated by separating the instructions so that they are not executed one right after the other. Many modern computer designs contain logic that can reorder instructions as they are executed to keep the pipelines full and to minimize situations where a delay is necessary. **Instruction reordering** also makes it possible to provide parallel pipelines, with duplicate CPU logic, so that multiple instructions can actually be executed simultaneously. This technique is equivalent to providing multiple car assembly lines. It is known as superscalar processing. We will look at superscalar processing again in the next section.

Pipelining and instruction reordering complicate the electronic circuitry required for the computer and also require careful design to eliminate the possibility of errors occurring under unusual sequences of instructions. (Remember that the programmer must always be able to assume that instructions are executed in the specified order.) Despite the added complexity, these methods are now generally accepted as a means for meeting the demand for more and more computer power. The additional task of analyzing, managing, and steering instructions to the proper execution unit at the proper time is usually combined with instruction fetching and decoding to form a single **instruction unit** that handles all preparation of instructions for execution.

A diagram illustrating pipelining is shown in Figure 8.5. For simplicity, instruction reordering has not been included. The figure shows three instructions, one for each row in the diagram. The "steps" in the diagram represent the sequence of steps in the fetch-execute

FIGURE 8.5

Pipelining

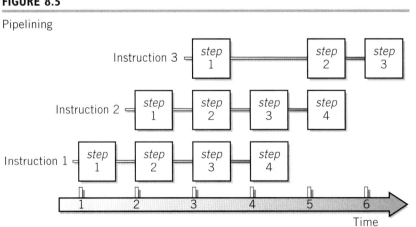

cycle for each instruction. Timing marks are indicated along the horizontal axis. The F-E cycle for instruction 3 shows a delay between step 1 and step 2; such a delay might result because the second step of the instruction needs a result from step 3 of the previous instruction, for example, the data in a particular register.

MULTIPLE, PARALLEL EXECUTION UNITS   It is not useful to pipe different types of instructions through a single pipeline. Different instructions have different numbers of steps in their cycles and, also, there are differences in each step. Instead, the instruction decode unit steers instructions into specific execution units. Each execution unit provides a pipeline that is optimized for one general type of instruction. Typically, a modern CPU will have a LOAD/STORE unit, an integer arithmetic unit, a floating point arithmetic unit, and a branch unit. More powerful CPUs may have multiple execution units for the more commonly used instruction types and, perhaps, may provide other types of execution units as well. Again, an analogy may aid in understanding the concept of multiple, parallel execution units. A simple automobile plant analogy would note that most automobile plants have separate assembly lines for different car models. The most popular models might have multiple assembly lines operating in parallel.

The use of multiple execution units operating in parallel makes it possible to perform the actual execution of several instructions simultaneously.

Scalar and Superscalar Processor Organization

The previous discussion has shown you that modern CPUs achieve high performance by separating the two major phases of the fetch-execute cycle into separate components, then further separating the execution phase into a number of independent execution units, each with pipeline capability. Once a pipeline is filled, an execution unit can complete an instruction with each clock tick. With a single execution unit pipeline, ignoring holes in the pipeline resulting from different instruction types and branch conditions, the CPU can average instruction execution approximately equal to the clock speed of the machine. A processor fulfilling this condition is called a **scalar processor**. With multiple execution units it is possible to process instructions in parallel, with an average rate of more than one instruction per clock cycle. The ability to process more than one instruction per clock cycle is known as **superscalar processing**. Superscalar processing is a standard feature in modern CPUs. Superscalar processing can increase the throughput by double or more. Commonly, current CPU designs produce speed increases of between two and five times.

It is important to remember that pipelining and superscalar processing techniques do not affect the cycle time of any individual instruction. An instruction fetch-execute cycle that requires six clock cycles from start to finish will require six clock cycles whether instructions are performed one at a time or pipelined in parallel with a dozen other instructions. It is the average instruction cycle time that is improved by performing some form of parallel execution. If an individual instruction must be completed for any reason before another can be executed, the CPU must stall for the full cycle time of the first instruction.

Figure 8.6 illustrates the difference between scalar and superscalar processing with pipelining in the execution unit. In the illustration the execution phase of the fetch-execute

FIGURE 8.6

Scalar versus Superscalar Processing

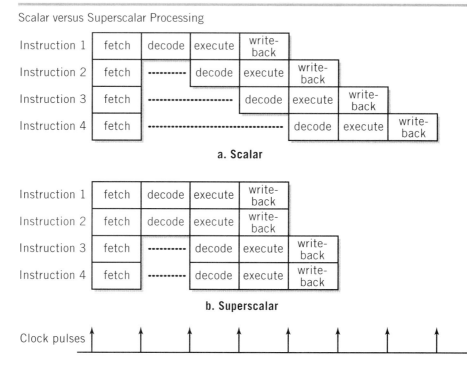

a. Scalar

b. Superscalar

Clock pulses

cycle is divided into three parts that can be executed separately. Thus, the diagram is divided into steps that fetch, decode, execute, and write back the results of the execute operation. Presumably, each step is carried out by a separate component within the execution unit. To simplify the illustration, we have also assumed that in each case the pipeline is full. Generally, a single fetch unit pipeline is sufficient to fetch multiple instructions, even when multiple execution units are present.

In the scalar processor, Figure 8.6a, each step is assumed to take one clock cycle. If the instructions are all of the same length, they will finish consecutively, as shown in the diagram. More complexity in the instruction set will create bubbles in the pipeline, but does not alter the basic idea that we are illustrating. Panel b of the figure assumes the presence of two execution units. It also assumes that the instructions executing in parallel are independent of each other; that is, the execution of one does not depend upon results from the other. Therefore, two instructions can be executed at a time in parallel, resulting in a substantial improvement in overall instruction completion performance.

Superscalar processing complicates the design of a CPU considerably. There are a number of difficult technical issues that must be resolved to make it possible to execute multiple instructions simultaneously. The most important of these are

- Problems that arise from instructions completing in the wrong order
- Changes in program flow due to branch instructions
- Conflicts for internal CPU resources, particularly general-purpose registers

OUT-OF-ORDER PROCESSING   Out-of-order instruction execution can cause problems because a later instruction may depend on the results from an earlier instruction. This situation is known as a **hazard** or a *dependency*. If the later instruction completes ahead of the earlier one, the effect of the earlier instruction upon the later cannot be satisfied. The most common type of a dependency is a **data dependency**. This is a situation in which the later instruction is supposed to use the results from the earlier instruction in its calculation. There are other types of dependencies also.

With multiple execution units, it is possible for instructions to complete in the wrong order. There are a number of ways in which this can occur. In the simplest case, an instruction with many steps in its cycle may finish after an instruction with just a few steps, even if it started earlier. As a simple example, a MULTIPLY instruction takes longer to execute than a MOVE or ADD instruction. If a MULTIPLY instruction is followed in the program by an ADD instruction that adds a constant to the results of the multiplication, the result will be incorrect if the ADD instruction is allowed to complete ahead of the MULTIPLY instruction. This is an example of data dependency. Data dependency can take several different forms.

Many data dependencies are sufficiently obvious that they can be detected by the CPU. In this case, execution of the dependent instruction is suspended until the results of the earlier instruction are available. This suspension may, itself, cause out-of-order execution, since it may allow another, still later, instruction to complete ahead of the suspended instruction. Some CPUs provide reservation stations within each execution unit or a general instruction pool to hold suspended instructions so that the execution unit may continue processing other instructions.

Finally, some systems intentionally allow out-of-order instruction execution. These CPUs can actually search ahead for instructions without apparent dependencies, to keep the execution units busy. Current Intel x86 CPUs, for example, can search twenty to thirty instructions ahead, if necessary, to find instructions available for execution.

BRANCH INSTRUCTION PROCESSING   Branch instructions must always be processed ahead of subsequent instructions, since the addresses of the proper subsequent instructions to fetch are determined from the branch instruction. For unconditional branch instructions, this is simple. Branch instructions are identified immediately as they enter the instruction fetch pipeline. The address in the instruction is decoded and used to fill the instruction fetch pipeline with instructions from the new location. Normally, no delay is incurred.

Unfortunately, conditional branch instructions are more difficult, because the condition decision may depend on the results from instructions that have not yet been executed. These situations are known as *flow* or *branch dependencies*. If the wrong branch is in the pipeline, the pipeline must be flushed and refilled, wasting time. Worse yet, an instruction from the wrong branch, that is, one that should not have been executed, can alter a previous result that is still needed.

The solution to the conditional branching problem may be broken into two parts: methods to optimize correct branch selection and methods to prevent errors as a result of conditional branch instructions. Selection of the wrong branch is time wasting, but not fatal. By contrast, incorrect results *must* be prevented.

Errors are prevented by setting the following guideline: although instructions may be executed out of order, they must be completed in the correct order. Since branches and subtle data dependencies can occur, the execution of an instruction out of order may or may not be valid, so the instruction is executed *speculatively*, that is, on the assumption that its execution will be useful. For this purpose, a separate bank of registers is used to hold results from these instructions until previous instructions are complete. The results are then transferred to their actual register and memory locations, in correct program instruction order. This technique of processing is known as **speculative execution**. On occasion, the results from some speculatively executed instructions must be thrown away, but on the whole, speculative execution results in a performance boost sufficient to justify the extra complexity required.

A few systems place the burden for error prevention on the assembly language programmer or program language compiler by requiring that a certain number of instructions following a conditional branch instruction be independent of the branch. In these systems, one or more instructions sequentially following the branch are *always* executed, regardless of the outcome of the branch.

There are various creative methods that are used in CPUs to optimize conditional branch processing. One possible solution to this problem is to maintain two separate instruction fetch pipelines, one for each possible branch outcome. Instructions may be executed speculatively from *both* branches until the correct pipeline is known. Another solution is to have the CPU attempt to predict the correct path based on program usage or past performance. A loop, for example, may be expected to execute many times before exiting. Therefore, the CPU might assume that a branch to a previous point in the program is usually taken. Some systems provide a **branch history table**, a small amount of dedicated memory built into the CPU that maintains a record of previous choices for each of several branch instructions that have been used in the program being executed to aid in prediction. A few systems even include a "hint" bit in the branch instruction word that can be set by the programmer to tell the CPU the more probable outcome of the branch. Of course, when a branch prediction is incorrect, there is a time delay to purge and refill the fetch pipeline and speculative instructions, but, overall, branch prediction is effective.

CONFLICT OF RESOURCES   Conflicts between instructions that use the same registers can be prevented by using the same bank of registers that is used to hold the results of speculative instructions until instruction completion. This register bank is given different names by different vendors. They are called variously **rename registers** or **logical registers** or **register alias tables**. The registers in the bank can be renamed to correspond logically to any physical register and assigned to any execution unit. This would allow two instructions using the "same" register to execute simultaneously without holding up each other's work At completion of an instruction, the CPU then selects the corresponding physical register and copies the result into it. This must occur in the specified program instruction order.

8.3 MEMORY ENHANCEMENTS

Within the instruction fetch-execute cycle, the slowest steps are those that require memory access. Therefore, any improvement in memory access can have a major impact on program processing speed.

The memory in modern computers is usually made up of dynamic random access memory circuit chips. DRAM is inexpensive. Each DRAM chip is capable of storing millions of bits of data. Dynamic RAM has one major drawback, however. With today's fast CPUs, the access time of DRAM is too slow to keep up with the CPU, and delays must be inserted into the LOAD/STORE execution pipeline to allow memory to keep up. Thus, the use of DRAM is a potential bottleneck in processing. Instructions must be fetched from memory and data must be moved from memory into registers for processing.

The fetch-execute CPU implementation introduced in Section 8.2 reduces instruction fetch delay to a minimum with modern instruction prefetch and branch control technologies, and the increased adoption of register-to-register instructions also reduces delays. Nonetheless, memory accesses are always required ultimately to move the data from memory to register and back, and improvements in memory access still have an impact on processing speed.

As mentioned in Chapter 7, static RAM, or SRAM, is an alternative type of random access memory that is two to three times as fast as DRAM. The inherent memory capacity of SRAM is severely limited, however. SRAM design requires a lot of chip real estate compared to DRAM, due to the fact that SRAM circuitry is more complex and generates a lot of heat that must be dissipated. One or two MB of SRAM requires more space than 64 MB of DRAM, and will cost considerably more.

With today's memory requirements, SRAM is not a practical solution for large amounts of memory except in very expensive computers; therefore, designers have created alternative approaches to fulfill the need for faster memory access. Three different approaches are commonly used to enhance the performance of memory:

- Wide path memory access
- Memory interleaving
- Cache memory

These three methods are complementary. Each has slightly different applicability, and they may be used together in any combination to achieve a particular goal. Of these techniques, the use of cache memory has the most profound effect on system performance.

Wide Path Memory Access

As mentioned in Chapter 7, Section 7.3, the simplest means to increase memory access is to widen the data path so as to read or write several bytes or words between the CPU and memory with each access; this technique is known as **wide path memory access**. Instead of reading 1 byte at a time, for example, the system can retrieve 2, 4, 8, or even 16 bytes, simultaneously. Most instructions are several bytes long, in any case, and most data is at least 2 bytes, and frequently more. This solution can be implemented easily by widening the bus data path and using a larger memory data register. The system bus on most modern CPUs, for example, has a 64-bit data path and is commonly used to read or write 8 bytes of data with a single memory access.

Within the CPU, these bytes can be separated as required and processed in the usual way. With modern CPU implementation, instruction groups can be passed directly to the instruction unit for parallel execution. As the number of bytes simultaneously accessed is increased, there is a diminishing rate of return, since the circuitry required to separate and direct the bytes to their correct locations increases in complexity, fast memory access becomes more difficult, and yet it becomes less likely that the extra bytes will actually be used. Even a 64-bit data path is adequate to assure that a pipeline will remain filled and bursts of consecutive 64-bit reads or writes can handle situations that require high-speed access to large blocks of data. Very few systems read and write more than 8 bytes at a time. Most systems read and write a fixed number of bytes at a time, but there are a few systems that can actually read and write a variable number of bytes.

Modern computers are commonly built with standard, off-the-shelf memory circuits and chips that include wide path memory access as a standard feature.

Memory Interleaving

Another method for increasing the effective rate of memory access is to divide memory into parts, called **memory interleaving**, so that it is possible to access more than one location at a time. Then, each part would have its own address register and data register, and each part is independently accessible. Memory can then accept one read/write request from each part simultaneously. Although it might seem to you that the obvious way to divide up memory would be in blocks, for example, by separating the high addresses into one block and the low addresses into the other, it turns out that as a practical matter it is usually more useful to divide the memory so that successive access points, say, groups of 8 bytes (see above), are in different blocks. Breaking memory up this way is known as ***n*-way interleaving**, where a value of 2 or 4 or some other value is substituted for *n*, depending on the number of separate blocks. For example, two-way interleaving would be designed so that it would be possible to access an odd memory address and an even memory address concurrently. If 8-byte wide access is provided, this would allow the concurrent access to 16 successive bytes at a time. A memory with eight-way interleaving would allow access to eight different locations simultaneously, but the system could not access locations 0, 8, 16, or 24 at the same time, for instance, nor 1, 9, 17, or 25. It *could* access locations 16 and 25 or 30 and 31 concurrently, however. Since memory accesses tend to be successive, memory interleaving can be effective. A diagram of four-way interleaving is shown in Figure 8.7.

FIGURE 8.7

Four-Way Memory Interleaving

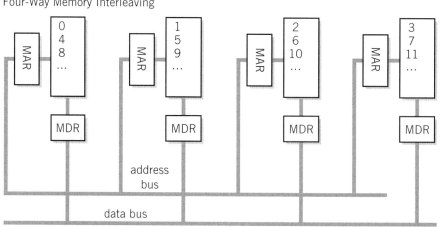

This method is particularly applicable when multiple devices require access to the same memory. The IBM mainframe architecture, for example, is designed to allow multiple CPUs to access a common memory area; the I/O channel subsystem also has access to the storage area. Thus, several different components may make memory requests at the same time. The IBM S/3033 computer, for example, partitioned memory into eight **logical storage elements**. Each element can independently accept a memory request. Thus, eight memory requests can be processed concurrently.

The personal computer memory that holds images while they are being displayed, known as video RAM, is another example. Changes to part of the video RAM can be made at the same time that another part of the video RAM is being used to produce the actual display on the monitor.

Cache Memory

A different strategy is to position a small amount of high-speed memory, for example, SRAM, between the CPU and main storage. This high-speed memory is invisible to the programmer and cannot be directly addressed in the usual way by the CPU. Because it represents a "secret" storage area, it is called **cache memory**. This concept is illustrated in Figure 8.8.

Cache memory is organized differently than regular memory. Cache memory is organized into blocks. Each block provides a small amount of storage, perhaps between 8 and 64 bytes, also known as a **cache line**. The block will be used to hold an exact reproduction of a corresponding amount of storage from somewhere in main memory. Each block also holds a **tag**. The tag identifies the location in main memory that corresponds to the data being held in that block. In other words, taken together, the tags act as a directory that can be used to determine exactly which storage locations from main memory are also available in the cache memory. A typical 64 KB cache memory might consist of 8000 (actually 8192) 8-byte blocks, each with tag.

A simplified, step-by-step illustration of the use of cache memory is shown in Figure 8.9. Every CPU request to main memory, whether data or instruction, is seen first by cache memory. A hardware **cache controller** checks the tags to determine if the memory location of the request is presently stored within the cache. If it is, the cache memory is used as if it were main memory. If the request is a read, the corresponding word from cache memory is simply passed to the CPU. Similarly, if the request is a write, the data from the CPU is stored in the appropriate cache memory location. Satisfying a request in this way is known as a **hit**.

If the required memory data is not already present in cache memory, an extra step is required. In this case, a cache line that includes the required location is copied from memory to the cache. Once this is done, the transfer is made to or from cache memory, as before. The situation in which the request is not already present in cache memory is known as a **miss**. The ratio of hits to the total number of requests is known as the **hit ratio**.

When cache memory is full, some block in cache memory must be selected for replacement. Various algorithms

FIGURE 8.8

Cache Memory

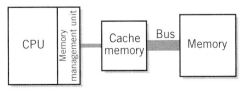

FIGURE 8.9

Step-by-Step Use of Cache

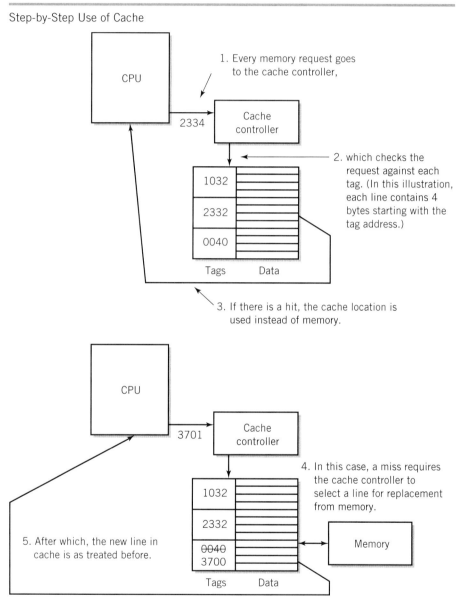

1. Every memory request goes to the cache controller,

2. which checks the request against each tag. (In this illustration, each line contains 4 bytes starting with the tag address.)

3. If there is a hit, the cache location is used instead of memory.

4. In this case, a miss requires the cache controller to select a line for replacement from memory.

5. After which, the new line in cache is as treated before.

have been implemented by different computer designers to make this selection, but most commonly, some variation on a *least recently used*, or *LRU*, algorithm is used. An LRU algorithm, as the name implies, keeps track of the usage of each block and replaces the block that was last used the longest time ago.

Cache blocks that have been read, but not altered, can simply be read over during replacement. Memory write requests impose an additional burden on cache memory operations, since written data must also be written to the main memory to protect the integrity of the program and its data. Two different methods of handling the process of returning changed data from cache to main storage are in common use. The first method, **write through**, writes data back to the main memory immediately upon change in the cache. This method has the advantage that the two copies, cache and main memory, are always kept identical. Some designers use an alternative technique known variously as *store in, write back*, or *copy back*. With this technique, the changed data is simply held in cache until the cache line is to be replaced. The **write back** method is faster, since writes to memory are made only when a cache line is actually replaced, but more care is required in the design to ensure that there are no circumstances under which data loss could occur. If two different programs were using the same data in separate cache blocks, for example, and one program changed the data, the design must assure that the other program has access to the updated data.

The entire cache operation is managed by the cache controller. This includes tag searching and matching, write through or write back, and implementation of the algorithm that is used for cache block replacement. The CPU and software are unaware of the presence of cache memory and the activities of the cache controller. We note in passing that to be effective, these operations must be controlled completely by hardware. It is possible to envision using a program to implement the cache block replacement algorithm, for example, but this is not feasible. Since memory accesses would be required to execute the program, this would defeat the entire purpose of cache memory, which is to provide access quickly to a single memory location.

Cache memory works due to a principle known as **locality of reference**. The locality of reference principle states that at any given time, most memory references will be confined to one or a few small regions of memory. If you consider the way that you were taught to write programs, this principle makes sense. Instructions are normally executed sequentially; therefore, adjoining words are likely to be accessed. In a well-written program, most of the instructions being executed at a particular time are part of a small loop or a small procedure or function. Likewise, the data for the program is likely taken from an array. Variables for the program are all stored together. Studies have verified the validity of the locality principle. Cache memory hit ratios of 90 percent and above are common with just a small amount of cache. Since requests that can be fulfilled by the cache memory are fulfilled much faster, the cache memory technique can have a significant impact on the overall performance of the system. Program execution speed improvements of 50 percent and more are common.

The hit ratio is an important measure of system performance. Cache hits can access memory data at or near the speed that instructions are executed, even with sophisticated instruction steering and multiple execution units. When a miss occurs, however, there is a time delay while new data is moved to the cache. The time to move data to the cache is called **stall time**. The stall time is typically long compared to instruction execution time. This can result in a condition in which there are no instructions available to feed to the execution units; the pipelines empty and instruction execution is stalled until the needed cache line is available, reducing performance.

Some modern architectures even provide program instructions to request cache preloading for data or instructions that will be needed soon. This improves execution speed even more. Also, some system designers interleave the cache or implement separate caches for instructions and data. This allows even more rapid access, since the instruction and its operands can be accessed simultaneously much of the time. Furthermore, design of a separate instruction cache can be simplified, since there is no need to write the instruction cache back to main memory if the architecture imposes a pure coding requirement on the programmer. The trade-off is that accommodating separate instruction and data caches requires additional circuit complexity, and many system designers opt instead for a combined, or *unified*, cache that holds both data and instructions.

It is also possible to provide more than one level of cache memory. Consider the two level cache memory shown in Figure 8.10. This memory will work as follows. The operation begins when the CPU requests an instruction (or piece of data) be read (or written) from memory. If the cache controller for the level closest to the CPU, which we'll call level 1 (normally abbreviated as L1), determines that the requested memory location is presently in the level 1 cache, the instruction is immediately read into the CPU.

Suppose, however, that the instruction is *not* presently in level 1 cache. In this case, the request is passed on to the controller for level 2 cache. Level 2 cache works in exactly the same way as level 1 cache. If the instruction is presently in the level 2 cache, a cache line containing the instruction is moved to the level 1 cache and then to the CPU. If not, then the level 2 cache controller requests a level 2 cache line from memory, the level 1 cache receives a cache line from the level 2 cache, and the instruction is transferred to the CPU. This technique can be extended to more levels, but there is usually little advantage in expanding beyond level 3.

What does the second level buy us? Most system designers believe that more cache would improve performance enough to be worthwhile. In this case, the system designers provide a second level of cache, external to the chip. A personal computer secondary cache commonly provides an additional 512 KB–2 MB of cache. A typical AMD Athlon 64 processor provides 64 KB of L1 data cache, 64 KB of L1 instruction cache, and 512 KB or 1 MB of level 2 cache within the same package as the CPU. The use of a dedicated on-chip bus between level 1 cache and level 2 cache provides faster response than connecting the level 1 cache to memory or to a level 2 cache on the regular memory bus.

To be useful, the second level of cache must have significantly more memory than the first level; otherwise, the two cache levels would contain the same data, and the secondary cache would serve no purpose. It is also normal to provide a larger cache line in the secondary cache. This increases the likelihood that requests to the secondary cache can be met without going out to main memory every time.

FIGURE 8.10

Two-Level Cache

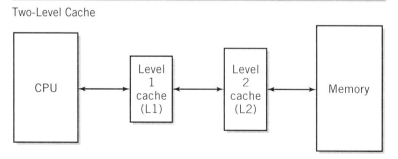

Before leaving the subject of memory caching, a side note: the concept of caching also shows up in other, unrelated but useful, areas of computer system design. For example, caching is used to reduce the time necessary to access data from a disk. In this case, part of main memory can be allocated for use as a **disk cache**. When a disk read or write request is made, the system checks the disk cache first. If the required data is present, no disk access is necessary; otherwise, a disk cache line made up of several adjoining disk blocks is moved from the disk into the disk cache area of memory. Most disk manufacturers now provide separate buffer memory for this purpose. This feature is implemented within the hardware of a disk controller. Another example is the cache of previous Web pages provided by Web browser application software.

All of these examples of caching share the common attribute that they increase performance by providing faster access to data, anticipating its potential need in advance, then storing that data temporarily where it is rapidly available.

8.4 THE COMPLEAT MODERN SUPERSCALAR CPU

Figure 8.11 is a model of a CPU block diagram that includes all the ideas just discussed. The design shown in this diagram is very similar to the one used in Sun SPARC and IBM Power and PowerPC processors and, with minor variations, to that used in various generations of the Intel Pentium and Itanium families, as well as various IBM mainframe processors. As you would expect, the CPU is organized into modules that reflect the superscalar, pipelined nature of the architecture. Although it is difficult to identify the familiar components that we introduced in Chapter 7, the control unit, arithmetic/logic unit, program counter, and the like, they are indeed embedded into the design, as you saw in Figure 8.4. The control unit operation is distributed through much of the diagram, controlling each step of the usual fetch-execute cycle as instructions flow through different blocks in the CPU. The functions of the arithmetic/logic unit are found within the integer unit. The program counter is part of the instruction unit.

In operation, instructions are fetched from memory by the memory management unit as they are needed for execution, and placed into a pipeline within the instruction unit. The instructions are also partially decoded within the instruction unit, to determine the type of instruction that is being executed. This allows branch instructions to be passed quickly to the branch processing unit for analysis of future instruction flow.

Instructions are actually executed in one of several types of execution units. Each execution unit has a pipeline designed to optimize the steps of the execute cycle for a particular type of instruction.

As you can see from the block diagram, there are separate execution units for branch instructions, for integer instructions, for floating point instructions, and for load and store instructions. Some processors provide multiple integer execution units to increase the processing capacity of the CPU still further. Some models also have a separate system register unit for executing system-level instructions. Some CPUs combine the load/store instructions into the integer unit. The PowerPC provides reservation stations in each execution unit. The Intel Pentium processors provide a general instruction pool where decoded instructions from the instruction unit are held as they await operand data from memory and from unresolved data dependencies. The Pentium instruction pool also holds

FIGURE 8.11

Modern CPU Block Diagram

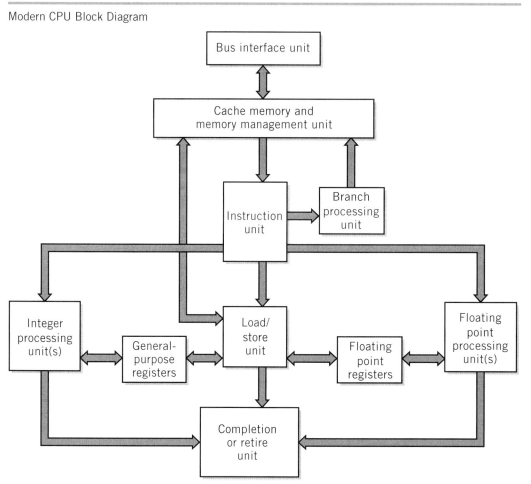

completed instructions after execution until they can be retired in order. The Pentium also separates the LOAD and STORE execution units.

The instruction unit is responsible for maintaining the fetch pipeline and for dispatching instructions. Because branch instructions affect the addresses of the following instructions in the pipeline, they are processed immediately. Other instructions are processed as space becomes available in the appropriate execution unit(s). Branch prediction is usually built into the branch unit. When conditional branches occur, execution of instructions continues speculatively along the predicted branch until the condition is resolved. Also, the use of multiple execution units makes it possible that instructions will execute in the wrong order, since some instructions may have to wait for operands resulting from other instructions and since the pipelines in each execution unit are of different lengths. As we noted earlier, some current superscalar processors can look ahead several instructions to find instructions that can be processed independently of the program order to prevent delays or errors arising from data dependency. The ability to process instructions out of order is an important factor in the effectiveness of these processors. The completion or "retire" unit accepts or rejects speculative instructions, stores results in the appropriate physical registers and cache memory locations, and retires instructions in the correct program order, assuring correct program flow. The Crusoe and Itanium architectures prevent out-of-order retirement by reordering the instructions prior to execution. This simplifies the CPU design.

From this discussion, you can see that the modern CPU includes many sophisticated features designed to streamline the basically simple fetch-execute cycle for high-performance processing. The modern CPU features different types of execution units, tailored to the needs of different types of instructions, and a complex steering system that can steer instructions through the instruction unit to available execution units, manage operands, and retire instructions in correct program order. The goal of each of these techniques is to increase the parallelism of instruction execution, while maintaining the basic sequential characteristic of a von Neumann computer architecture.

As a brief diversion, consider the similarities between the operation of the modern CPU and the operation of a moderately large restaurant. Each of the waiters and waitresses taking orders represent the fetch unit fetching instructions. Customers' orders are fed to the kitchen, where they are sorted into categories: soup orders to the soup chef, salads to the salad chef, entrées to the entrée chef, and so on. Typically, the entrée chef will have the most complex orders to fill, equivalent to the longest pipeline in the CPU. If the kitchen is large, the entrée area will be further subdivided into multiple execution areas: frying, baking, and so on, and there may be multiple cooks working in the busiest areas. As with the programs being executed in a computer, there are dependencies between the various cooks. For example, green beans must be blanched before they may be placed in the salad. Finally, we observe that, like computer program instructions, the restaurant must provide food from the kitchen to the customers in the proper sequence, and with appropriate timing, to satisfy the customers' requirements.

In this section we have introduced the basic ideas of superscalar processing, briefly indicated the difficulties, and explained the reasoning for its use. There are many excellent references listed in the For Further Reading if you are interested in more of the details of superscalar processing and modern CPU design.

8.5 MULTIPROCESSING

One obvious way to increase performance in a computer system is to increase the number of CPUs. Computers that have multiple CPUs within a single computer, sharing some or all of the system's memory and I/O facilities, are called **multiprocessor systems**, or sometimes **tightly coupled systems**. When multiple CPU processors are supplied within a single integrated circuit, they are more commonly called **multicore processors**. Figure 8.12 shows a typical multiprocessor configuration. All the processors in a multiprocessor configuration have access to the same programs and data in shared memory and to the same I/O devices, so it is possible to divide program execution between different CPUs. Furthermore, programs or pieces of programs may be run in any CPU that is available, so that each additional processor extends the power available for multitasking in a multiprocessing system, at least within the capability of the shared components, the memory, buses, and I/O controllers.

FIGURE 8.12

Typical Multiprocessing System Configuration

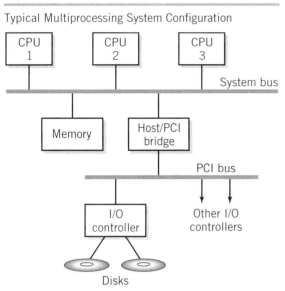

Under ideal conditions, each CPU processes its own assigned sequence of program instructions independently. Thus, a dual-core processor effectively doubles the number of instructions executed in a given time, a quad-core processor would quadruple the rate, and so forth. Of course this assumes that there are multiple independent tasks available to be executed simultaneously. Since modern computer systems are normally executing many programs and segments of programs concurrently this is nearly always the case.

In practice, increasing the number of CPUs is, in fact, usually effective, although, as the number of CPUs increases, the value of the additional CPUs diminishes because of the overhead required to distribute the instructions in a useful way among the different CPUs and the conflicts among the CPUs for shared resources, such as memory, I/O, and access to the shared buses. With the exception of certain, specialized systems, there are rarely more than sixteen CPUs sharing the workload in a multiprocessing computer; more commonly today, a multiprocessor might consist of two, four, or eight core CPUs within a single chip. Still, each core in the chip is a full-blown superscalar CPU, of the type discussed in the previous sections of this chapter.

Although increased computing power is a significant motivation for multiprocessing, there are other considerations that make multiprocessing attractive:

- Since the execution speed of a CPU is directly related to the clock speed of the CPU, equivalent processing power can be achieved at much lower clock speeds, reducing power consumption, heat, and stress within the various computer components.

- Programs can be divided into independent pieces, and the different parts executed simultaneously on multiple CPUs.

- With multiprocessing, increasing computational power may be achieved by adding more CPUs, which is relatively inexpensive.

- Data dependencies and cache memory misses can stall the pipelines in a single CPU. Multiprocessing allows the computer to continue instruction execution in the other CPUs, increasing overall throughput.

Assignment of work to the various processors is the responsibility of the operating system. Work is assigned from among the programs available to be executed, or, more commonly, from independent segments of those programs called **threads**. Since each of the CPUs has access to the same memory and I/O, any CPU can theoretically execute any thread or program currently in memory, including the operating system. This raises the question of control of the system. There are two basic ways of configuring a multiprocessing system:

- **Master-slave multiprocessing**, in which one CPU, the *master*, manages the system, and controls all resources and scheduling. Only the master may execute the operating system. Other CPUs are *slaves*, performing work assigned to them by the master.
- **Symmetrical multiprocessing (SMP)**, in which each CPU has identical access to the operating system, and to all system resources, including memory. Each CPU schedules it own work, within parameters, constraints, and priorities set by the operating system. In a normal SMP configuration, each of the CPUs is identical.

A number of CPUs also implement a simplified, limited form of multiprocessing using parallel execution units within a single CPU to process two or more threads simultaneously. This technique is called **simultaneous thread multiprocessing (STM)**. STM is also known as *hyperthreading*. STM is particularly useful in dealing with cache stalls, because the CPU can be kept busy working on the alternative thread or threads. The operating system manages STM in a manner similar to SMP. Since STM operates within a single CPU and SMP operates between CPUs, STM and SMP can be used together.

For general purpose computing, the symmetrical configuration has many advantages. Because every CPU is equal, every CPU has equal access to the operating system. Any CPU can execute any task and can process any interrupt.[4] Processors are all kept equally busy, since each processor can dispatch its own work as it needs it. Thus, the workload is well balanced. It is easy to implement fault-tolerant computing with a symmetrical configuration—critical operations are simply dispatched to all CPUs simultaneously. Furthermore, a failure in a single CPU may reduce overall system performance, but it will not cause system failure. As an interesting aside, note that a program may execute on a different CPU each time it is dispatched, although most SMP systems provide a means to *lock* a program onto a particular CPU, if desired. Thus, the symmetrical configuration offers important capabilities for multiprocessing: maximum utilization of each CPU, flexibility, high reliability, and optional support for fault-tolerant computing. Most modern general purpose multiprocessing systems are SMP systems.

Because of the somewhat limited flexibility in distributing the workload, the master-slave configuration is usually considered less suitable for general purpose computing. In a master-slave configuration the master is likely to be the busiest CPU in the system. If a slave requires a work assignment while the master is busy, the slave will have to wait until the master is free. Furthermore, since the master handles all I/O requests and interrupts, a heavily loaded system will cause a backload in the master. If slaves are dependent on the results of these requests, the system is effectively stalled.

Conversely, there are a number of specialized computing applications for which the master-slave configuration is particularly well suited. These applications are characterized by a need for a master control program, supported by repetitive or continuous, computation- and data-intensive, time-critical tasks. For example, the processor in a game controller

---

[4]Interrupts are a special feature of the CPU in which outside events such as mouse movements and power interruptions can affect the sequence of instructions processed by the CPU. Interrupts are discussed in detail in Chapter 9.

must execute the code that plays the game. At the same time, it requires support that can rapidly calculate and display new images based on movements of the objects in the image, compute shadings and light reflections resulting from the movements; often, the processor must create new pixel values for every pixel in the image. It must also be able to create the appropriate reactions and display in response to events that occur, such as explosions or fires or objects bouncing off a wall, and more.

Many important applications in economics, biology, physics, and finance, particularly those based on simulation and modeling, have similar requirements.

EXAMPLE

The recently developed Cell Broadband Engine processor is organized in a master-slave configuration. It was developed jointly by IBM, Sony, and Toshiba as the first of a new generation of processors intended for use in high-performance intensive computing applications. It is the main processor used in the Sony PlayStation 3.

A block diagram of the Cell processor is shown in Figure 8.13. The master processor is similar to a 64-bit PowerPC CPU. There are eight slave processors. A high-speed bus interconnects the master processor and each of the slave processors. For those interested, a more detailed description of the PowerPC Cell processor can be found in Gschwind, et. al. [GSCH06].

FIGURE 8.13

Cell Processor Block Diagram

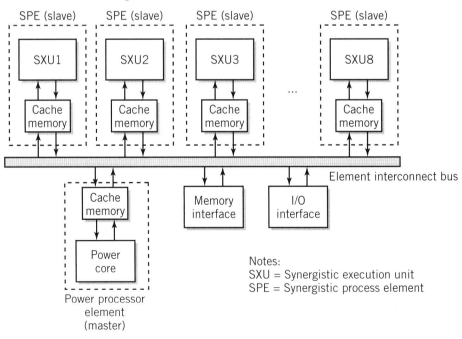

Notes:
SXU = Synergistic execution unit
SPE = Synergistic process element

8.6 A FEW COMMENTS ON IMPLEMENTATION

It is not the intention of this book to discuss the electronic implementation of the computer in any detail. A brief introduction is provided in Supplementary Chapter 1, but the details of such a discussion are better left to an engineering textbook. There are several good computer engineering textbooks listed in the *For Further Reading* for the supplementary chapter if you are interested in learning more about how the computer works.

Although the increased capacity of current integrated circuit technology has allowed computer designers the option of creating very complex circuits, much of that capacity is currently used to provide increased capability in the form of multiple execution units, increased amounts of cache memory, and multicore processing; the basic design and implementation of a processor is simpler than you might imagine.

If you look again at the instruction classes that constitute the operations of a CPU together with the fetch-execute cycles that make up each of the instructions, you can see that the great majority of operations within the CPU consist of moving data from one register to another. The steps

```
PC  →  MAR and
MDR  →  IR
```

are examples of this type of operation.

In addition, we must include the capability to add data to a register with data from another register or from a constant (usually the constant 1 or −1), the capability to perform simple Boolean functions (AND, OR, NOT) on data in registers, and the capability to shift the data in a register to the left or right. Finally, the CPU must include the capability to make simple decisions based on the values stored in flags and registers (conditional branches). All of these operations are under the timed control of a clock. Control unit logic opens and closes switches at the right times to control the individual operations and the movement of data from one component within the CPU to another.

And for all practical purposes, that's about it. The small number of different operations used in a CPU suggest that the CPU can be directly implemented in electronic hardware, and indeed that is the case. In Supplementary Chapter 1, we demonstrate for the curious reader, in somewhat simplified fashion, that all of the preceding functions can be implemented using logic gates that perform Boolean algebra. The registers, flags, and counters that control timing are made up of electronic devices called flip-flops, which are, themselves, made up of logic gates.

So, as you can see, the basic hardware implementation of the CPU is relatively straightforward and simple. Although the addition of pipelining, superscaling, and other features complicates the design, it is possible, with careful design, to implement and produce an extremely fast and efficient CPU at low cost and in large quantities.

SUMMARY AND REVIEW ────────────────────────────────────

In this chapter we presented a number of different techniques that are used to enhance the power and flexibility of a CPU. We began with a discussion of three different approaches to CPU architecture, with particular emphasis on traditional computer architecture. We presented the advantages, disadvantages, and trade-offs for each architecture.

Next, we looked at the various aspects of instruction execution in a CPU, with the purpose of improving performance. This discussion culminated in the presentation of a model for an alternative organization that preserves the basic rules of execution, but allows much faster instruction execution. The important features of this model include separating the fetch-execute cycle into two separate fetch and execute units that can operate in parallel, pipelining to allow instructions to execute in an assembly line, and multiple execution units to allow parallel execution of unrelated instructions. A variety of innovative techniques, including rename registers, speculative execution, out-of-order execution, and branch prediction help to reduce bottlenecks and contribute to the performance. We noted that the resulting model is capable of superscalar processing, with instructions processed at average rates far exceeding the cycle rate of the clock.

We then turned our attention to memory enhancements, particularly the techniques and benefits of cache memory, a fast, intermediate memory between then CPU and regular memory. Following this, we put together a model of the compleat susperscalar CPU that contained all of the features that we had presented up to this point.

To increase performance even further, it is possible to combine CPUs into multiple units that share memory, buses, I/O, and other resources, a concept called multiprocessing. We presented two different configurations of multiprocesors.

We concluded the chapter with a brief introduction to the technology used to implement the modern processor.

With all of the advances and variations in technology, architecture, and organization that we have introduced in this chapter, and despite all of the different types of computers, applications, and uses for computers that are available today, it is important to remember that, regardless of the specifics, every current CPU conforms to the basic model created by Von Neumann more than a half century ago. There is little evidence that the basic concepts that govern CPU operation are likely to change in the near future.

FOR FURTHER READING

The many references used to write this chapter are all listed in the bibliography section at the end of the book. The following books and articles are particularly useful for their clear descriptions and explanations of these topics. Stallings [STAL05] and Tanenbaum [TANE05] describe the different types of architectures, focusing on the differences between CISC and RISC architectures in great depth. Information about the VLIW and EPIC architectures may be found at the Transmeta and Intel websites, respectively. The IBM website contains a wealth of information about zSeries, POWER, and Cell architectures, including the *Redbooks*, which are free, downloadable, book-length explanations of various computer topics. These range in difficulty from beginner to highly technical. Intel.com (for the x86 series) and sun.com (for the SPARC architecture) are other useful brand-specific websites.

Instruction sets, instruction formats, and addressing are discussed at length in every computer architecture textbook. The book by Patterson and Hennessy [PATT07] covers the topics of Chapters 7 and 8 thoroughly, and has the additional benefit of being highly readable. A more advanced treatment, by the same authors, is found in [HENN06]. Good discussions of multiprocessing are also found in Patterson and Hennessy and in Tanenbaum. Two readable websites introducing the Cell processor are Gschwind, et. al. [GSCH06] and Moore [MOOR06].

A different approach to this material is to compare the architectures of various machines. The book by Tabak [TABA95] looks at several different CPUs in detail. Most of these CPUs are obsolete, but the comparison between different architectures is useful. There are textbooks and trade books devoted to the architecture of every major CPU. The most thorough discussion of the x86 architecture is found in Mueller [MUEL08]. I also recommend Brey [BREY08], Messmer [MESS01], and Sargent and Shoemaker [SARG95] for the Intel x86 series. The PC System Architecture series is a collection of short books describing the architectures of various parts of computers. Volume 5 [SHAN04] describes the evolution and architecture of the Pentium 4. The case studies provided in Supplementary Chapter 2 are additional information resources.

Stallings also includes an entire chapter on superscalar processors. Clear, detailed discussions of all aspects of CPU and memory design can be found in the two books by Patterson and Hennessy [PATT07, HENN06]. There are many additional references in each of these books. Specific discussions of the superscalar processing techniques for particular CPUs can be found in Liptay [LIPT92] for the IBM ES/9000 mainframe, in Becker and colleagues [BECK93], Thompson and Ryan [THOM94], Burgess and colleagues [BURG94], and Ryan [RYAN93] for the PowerPC, and "Tour of the P6" [THOR95] for the P6.

An alternative approach to the topics in this chapter can be found in any assembly language textbook. There are many good books on these topics, with new ones appearing every day. A website such as Amazon is a good resource for identifying the best currently available.

KEY CONCEPTS AND TERMS

branch history table	instruction set architecture	scalar processing
cache controller	(ISA)	simultaneous thread
cache line	instruction unit	multiprocessing (STM)
clock	locality of reference	speculative execution
code morphing layer	logical register	stall time
control dependency	logical storage elements	superscalar processing
data dependency	master-slave	symmetrical
disk cache	multiprocessing	multiprocessing (SMP)
execution unit	memory interleaving	tag
explicitly parallel	miss	threads
instruction computer	multiprocessor systems	tightly coupled system
(EPIC)	multicore processor	very long instruction word
fetch unit	n-way interleaving	(VLIW)
hazard	organisation	wide path memory access
hit	pipelining	write-back
hit ratio	register alias table	write through
instruction reordering	rename register	

READING REVIEW QUESTIONS

8.1   The x86 series is an example of a CPU *architecture*. As you are probably aware, there are a number of different chips, including some from different manufacturers even, that qualify as x86 CPUs. What, *exactly*, defines the x86 architecture? What word defines the difference between the various CPUs that share the same architecture? Name at least one different CPU architecture.

8.2 What is the major performance advantage that results from the use of multiple general-purpose data registers?

8.3 Explain how pipelining serves to reduce the average number of steps in the execution part of the fetch-execute cycle.

8.4 Which class of instructions can reduce performance by potentially invalidating the instructions in a pipeline? Identify two methods that can be used to partially overcome this problem.

8.5 Explain the advantage in implementing separate fetch and execute units in a CPU. What additional task is implemented in the fetch unit as a performance enhancement measure?

8.6 The use of multiple execution units can improve performance but also cause problems called *hazards* or *dependencies*. Explain how a hazard can occur. How can hazards be managed?

8.7 Most CPUs today are *superscalar*. What does that mean?

8.8 What is a *rename register*? What is it used for?

8.9 What performance improvement is offered by *memory interleaving*?

8.10 Describe how cache memory is organized. What is a *cache line*? How is it used?

8.11 Explain the *hit ratio* in cache memory.

8.12 What specific performance improvement is offered by the use of cache memory?

8.13 Explain what takes place when cache memory is full.

8.14 Explain the difference between cache *write-through* and cache *write-back*. Which method is safer? Which method is faster?

8.15 Explain the *locality of reference* principle and its relationship to cache memory performance and the hit ratio.

8.16 When a system has multiple levels of cache memory, L2 always has more memory than L1. Why is this necessary?

8.17 Modern computers are usually described as multicore. What does this mean? Under ideal conditions, what performance gain would be achieved using a four-core processor over a single-core processor?

8.18 Identify and briefly explain two different ways of configuring a multiprocessing system. Which configuration is more effective for general purpose computing? Which configuration is more effective for handling specialized processing tasks, such as those used in game applications?

EXERCISES

8.1 Consider a CPU that implements a single instruction fetch-decode-execute-write-back pipeline for scalar processing. The execution unit of this pipeline assumes that the execution stage requires one step. Describe, and show in diagram form, what happens when an instruction that requires one execution step follows one that requires four execution steps.

8.2   **a.**   Consider a CPU with two parallel integer execution units. An addition instruction requires 2 clock pulses to complete execution, and a multiplication requires 15 clock pulses. Now assume the following situation: the program is to multiply two numbers, located in registers R2 and R4, and store the results in R5. The following instruction adds the number in R5 to the number in R2 and stores the result in R5. The CPU does not stall for data dependencies, and both instructions have access to an execution unit simultaneously. The initial values of R2, R4, and R5 are 3, 8, and 0, respectively. What is the result? Now assume that the CPU does handle data dependencies correctly. What is the result? If we define wasted time as time in which an execution unit is not busy, how much time is wasted in this example?

b.   Now assume that a later instruction in the fetch pipeline has no data dependencies. It adds the value in R1, initially 4, to the value in R4 and stores the result in R5. Data dependencies are handled correctly. There are no rename registers, and the CPU retires instructions in order. What happens? If the CPU provides rename registers, what happens? What effect does out-of-order execution have upon the time required to execute this program?

8.3   Some systems use a branch prediction method known as static branch prediction, so called because the prediction is made on the basis of the instruction, without regard to history. One possible scenario would have the system predict that all conditional backward branches are taken and all forward conditional branches are not taken. Recall your experience with programming in the Little Man Computer language. Would this algorithm be effective? Why or why not? What aspects of normal programming, in any programming language, support your conclusion?

8.4   Suppose that a CPU always executes the two instructions following a branch instruction, regardless of whether the branch is taken or not. Explain how this can eliminate most of the delay resulting from branch dependency in a pipelined CPU. What penalties or restrictions does this impose on the programs that are executed on this machine?

8.5   Find a good reference that describes the x86 chip. Discuss the features of the architecture that make superscalar processing possible in this chip. What limitations does the Pentium architecture impose on its superscalar processing?

8.6   How would you modify the Little Man Computer to implement the pipelined instruction fetch-execution unit model that was described in this chapter? What would it take to supply multiple execution units? Describe your modified LMC in detail and show how an instruction flows through it.

8.7   **a.**   Suppose we are trying to determine the speed of a computer that executes the Little Man instruction set. The LOAD and STORE instructions each make up about 25% of the instructions in a typical program; ADD, SUBTRACT, IN, and OUT take 10% each. The various branches each take about 5%. The HALT instruction is almost never used (a maximum of once each program, of course!). Determine the average number of instructions executed each second if the clock ticks at 100 MHz.

b.   Now suppose that the CPU is pipelined, so that each instruction is fetched while another instruction is executing. (You may also neglect the time required to refill the pipeline during branches and at the start of program execution.) What is the average number of instructions that can be executed each second with the same clock in this case?

8.8 The goal of scalar processing is to produce, on average, the execution of one instruction per clock tick. If the clock ticks at a rate of 2 GHz, how many instructions per second can this computer execute? How many instructions would a 2 GHz superscalar processor that processes three instructions per clock cycle execute?

8.9 What is the purpose of the tag in a cache memory system?

8.10 Consider a cache memory that provides three hundred 16-byte blocks. Now consider that you are processing all the data in a two-dimensional array of, say, four hundred rows by four hundred columns, using a pair of nested loops. Assume that the program stores the array column by column. You can write your program to nest the loops in either direction, that is, process row by row or column by column. Explain which way you would choose to process the data. What is the advantage? Conversely, what is the disadvantage of processing the data the other way? What effect does choosing the incorrect way have on system performance?

8.11 Carefully discuss what happens when a cache miss occurs. Does this result in a major slowdown in execution of the instruction? If so, why?

8.12 Describe the trade-offs between the memory cache write-through and write-back techniques.

8.13 As you know, a single CPU processes one instruction at a time. Adding a second CPU (or *core*, in current terminology) allows the system to process two instructions at a time, simultaneously, effectively doubling the processing power of the system. A third core will offer triple the processing power of a single CPU, and so on. However, studies have shown that, in general, the expected increase in computing power starts to decline when the number of cores grows large, beyond eight or so. Why would you expect this to be the case? For what types of computing problems might this *not* be true?

8.14 Carefully describe the advantages and disadvantages of master-slave multiprocessing and symmetrical multiprocessing. Which would you select for fault-tolerant computing? Why?

8.15 Locate information about the Cell Processor. Describe the tasks performed by the various slave processors. What is the primary role of the master processor? Explain the advantages of master-slave multiprocessing over other forms of processing for this application. Can you think of some other types of computer problems that would benefit from this approach?

INPUT/OUTPUT

"Here comes the 64-bit local bus."

9.0 INTRODUCTION

Of course you're aware that no matter how powerful the CPU is, a computer system's usefulness ultimately depends on its input and output facilities. Without I/O there is no possibility of keyboard input, of screen output, of printout, or even of disk storage and retrieval. Although you might be inclined to think of I/O in terms of user input and output, there would be no computer network or Internet access either. To the CPU and its programs, all these devices require specialized input and output processing facilities and routines.

In fact, for most business programs and for nearly every multimedia application, I/O is the predominant factor. E-commerce applications offer an even bigger challenge: Web services generally require massive amounts of fast I/O to handle and process I/O requests as they occur. The speed at which most of these programs operate is determined by the ability of their I/O operations to stay ahead of their processing. With PCs rapidly increasing in CPU processing capability, but still somewhat limited in I/O processing, it has been greater I/O capability that has maintained, until recently, the advantage of mainframe computers over PCs for business transaction processing.

We handled input and output in the Little Man Computer by providing input and output baskets for that purpose. Each input instruction transferred one three-digit data number from the input basket to the calculator; similarly, each output instruction transferred one data number from the calculator to the output basket. If we wanted to input three numbers, for example, an input instruction had to be executed three times. This could be done with three separate input instructions or in a loop, but either way, each individual piece of data required the execution of a separate input instruction.

It is possible to transfer data between input and output devices and the CPU of a real computer in a similar manner. In the real computer, the in basket and out basket are commonly replaced by a bus interface that allows a direct transfer between a register within the CPU and a register within an I/O module that controls the particular device. Both input and output are handled similarly. The technique is known as programmed I/O.

There are a number of complicating factors in handling input/output processes (which we will normally simply call I/O) in a real computer. Although the method of transferring data one word at a time does really exist, and may be adequate and appropriate for some slow-operating I/O devices, the volume of data commonly transferred in I/O devices, such as disks and tapes, makes this method too slow and cumbersome to be practical as the only I/O transfer method in a modern high-speed machine. We need to consider some method of transferring data in blocks rather than executing an instruction for each individual piece of data.

The problem is further complicated by the fact that in a real computer, there may be many input and output devices all trying to do I/O, sometimes at the same time. There needs to be a way of distinguishing and separating the I/O from these different devices. Additionally, devices operate at different speeds from each other and from the CPU.

An inkjet printer may output characters at a rate of 150 per second, whereas a disk may transfer data at a rate of tens or hundreds of thousands, or even millions, of bytes per second. Synchronization of these different operations must be achieved to prevent data loss.

Finally, it should be noted that I/O operations take up a lot of computer time. Even if a block of data can be transferred between the CPU and a disk with a single instruction, much time is potentially wasted waiting for the completion of the task. A CPU could execute millions of instructions in the time it takes a printer to print a single character. In a large modern computer, the number of I/O operations may be very large. It would be convenient and useful to be able to use the CPU for other tasks while these I/O transfers are taking place.

In the computer, several different techniques are combined to resolve the problem of synchronizing and handling I/O between a variety of different I/O devices operating with different quantities of data at different speeds. In this chapter, we first consider the I/O requirements of some commonly used devices. This discussion, which appears in Section 9.1, leads to a set of requirements that the I/O-CPU interface should meet to optimize system performance. Next, in Section 9.2 we briefly review programmed I/O, the method used in the Little Man Computer, and consider its limitations. Section 9.3 addresses the important issue of interrupts, the method used to communicate events that need special attention to the CPU. Interrupts are the primary means for the user to interact with the computer, as well as the means used for communication between the CPU and the various I/O devices connected to the system. In Section 9.4 we look at Direct Memory Access, or DMA, a more efficient alternative technique used to perform I/O in the computer. DMA provides the ability to utilize the CPU more fully while I/O operations are taking place. Finally, Section 9.5 considers the I/O modules that provide the capability both to control the I/O devices and to interact with the CPU and memory.

9.1 CHARACTERISTICS OF TYPICAL I/O DEVICES

Before discussing the techniques that are used in the real computer for performing I/O, it will help to consider some characteristics of the devices that will typically be connected to the computer. In this chapter we are not interested in the inner workings of these devices nor with the interconnection of the various computer components and I/O devices that make up the whole computer system—these discussions we'll save for Chapters 10 and 11, respectively. For now, we are only interested in those characteristics of these devices that will affect the I/O capabilities of the computer, in particular the speed and quantity of data transfer required to use the computer efficiently and fully. This survey is intended to be intuitive: what must be true about the I/O, based on what you already know about the particular devices from your own practical experience. Although this discussion may seem like a digression, it is intended to establish a set of basic principles and requirements that will help you to better understand the reasons behind the methods that are used to perform I/O in computers.

Consider, for example, the keyboard as an input device. The keyboard is basically a character-based device. You are probably already aware that typing on the keyboard of your PC results in Unicode or ASCII input to the computer, one character at a time. Even mainframe terminals, many of which can send text to the computer a page at a time, only transmit a page occasionally, so the data rate for keyboards is obviously very slow compared to the speed at which the CPU processes the data.

Input from the keyboard is very slow because it is dependent on the speed of typing, as well as on the thought process of the user. There are usually long thinking pauses between bursts of input, but even during those bursts, the actual input requirements to the computer are very slow compared to the capability of the computer to execute input instructions. Thus, we must assume that if the computer is simply performing a single task, it will spend most of its time waiting for input from the keyboard.

It is also useful to note that there are two different types of keyboard input. There is input that is expected by the application program in response to a "read" statement of some kind requesting input data for the program. Then there are other times when the user wishes to interrupt what the computer is doing. On many computers, a character such as Control-"C" or Control-"D" or Control-"Q" can be typed to stop the program that is running. Control-"S" is used on some machines to stop the display from scrolling. Typing Control-Alt-Delete on a PC will stop normal processing and open an administrative window that can be used to kill a program or shut down the computer. These are examples of unpredicted input, since the executing program is not necessarily awaiting specific input at those times. Using the input method that we already described would not work: the unexpected input would not be noticed, possibly for a long time until the next input instruction was executed for some later expected input.

Finally, on a multiuser system, there may be many keyboards connected to a single computer. The computer must be able to distinguish between them, must not lose input data even if several keyboards send a character simultaneously, and must be able to respond quickly to each keyboard. The physical distances from the computer to these keyboards may be long.

Another input device that will generate unexpected input is the mouse. When you move the mouse, you expect the cursor to move on the screen. Clicking on a mouse button may serve as expected input to a program, or it may be unexpected and change the way in which the program is executing. In fact, unexpected input is fundamental to programs written in modern event-driven languages such as Visual Basic and Java. When the user selects an item on a drop-down menu or clicks on a toolbar icon, she expects a timely response. Again, data rates are slow.

Printers and display screens must operate over a wide range of data rates. Although most monitors and printers are capable of handling pure ASCII or Unicode text, most modern output is produced graphically or as a mixture of font descriptors, text, bitmap graphics, and object graphics, a page or a screen at a time, using a page description language. The choice of page description language and mixture of elements is determined by the capabilities of the printer or graphics card. Clearly, output to a printer consisting only of an occasional page or two of text will certainly not require a high data rate regardless of the output method used.

The output of high resolution bitmap graphics and video images to a monitor is quite a different situation. If the graphics must be sent to the graphics card as bitmap images, even in compressed form, with data for each pixel to be produced, it may take a huge amount of data to produce a single picture, and high-speed data transfer will be essential. A single, color image on a high-resolution screen may require several megabytes of data, and it is desirable to produce the image on the screen as fast as possible. If the image represents video, extremely high data transfer rates are required. This suggests that screen image updates may require bursts of several megabytes per second, even when data compression methods are used to reduce the transfer rate. It may also suggest to you why it is nearly impossible to transmit high quality images quickly over voice-grade phone lines using modems.

Contrast the I/O requirements of keyboards, screens, and printers with those of disks and DVDs. Since the disk is used to store programs and data, it would be very rare that a program would require a single word of data or program from the disk. Disks are used to load entire programs or store files of data. Thus, disk data is always transferred in blocks, never as individual bytes or words. Disks may operate at transfer rates of tens or, even, hundreds of megabytes per second. As storage devices, disks must be capable of both input and output, although not simultaneously. On a large system there may be several disks attempting to transfer blocks of data to or from the CPU simultaneously. A DVD attempting to present a full screen video at movie rates without dropouts must provide data steadily at input rates approaching 10 megabytes per second, with some transient rates and high definition video rates even higher. In addition, video and audio devices require a steady stream of data over long periods of time. Contrast this requirement with the occasional bursts of data that are characteristic of most I/O devices.

For both disk and image I/O, therefore, the computer must be capable of transferring massive amounts of data very quickly between the CPU and the disk(s) or image devices. Clearly, executing a single instruction for each byte of data is unacceptable for disk and image I/O, and a different approach must be used. Furthermore, you can see the importance of providing a method to allow utilization of the CPU for other tasks while these large I/O operations are taking place.

With the rapid proliferation of networks in recent years, network interfaces have also become an important source of I/O. From the perspective of a computer, the network is just another I/O device. In many cases, the network is used as a substitute for a disk, with the data and programs stored at a remote computer and served to the local station. For the computer that is acting as a server, there may be a massive demand for I/O services. User interfaces such as X Windows, which allow the transfer of graphical information from a computer to a display screen located elsewhere on the network, place heavy demands on I/O capability. With simple object graphics, or locally stored bitmap images, and with a minimal requirement for large file transfers, a small computer with a modem may operate sufficiently at I/O transfer rates of 3,000 bytes per second, but computers with more intensive requirements may require I/O transfer rates of 50 megabytes per second, or more.

A table of typical data rates for various I/O devices appears in Figure 9.1. The values given are rough approximations, since the actual rates are dependent on the particular hardware systems, software, and application. As computer technology advances, the high end data rates continue to increase at a rapid pace. For example, local area networks operating at 1 gigabit (or, equivalently, 125 megabytes) per second are increasingly common.

It should be pointed out that disks, printers, screens, and most other I/O devices operate almost completely under CPU program control. Printers and screens, of course, are strictly output devices, and the output produced can be determined only by the program being executed. Although disks act as both input and output devices, the situation is similar. It is the executing program that must always determine what file is to be read on input, or where to store output. Therefore, it is always a program executing in the CPU that initiates I/O data transfer, even if the CPU is allowed to perform other tasks while waiting for the particular I/O operation to be completed.

FIGURE 9.1

Examples of I/O Devices Categorized by a Typical Data Rate

Device	Input/Output	Data rate	Type
Keyboard	Input	100 bps	char
Mouse	Input	3800 bps	char
Voice input/output	Input/Output	264 Kbps	block burst
Sound input	Input	3 Mbps	block burst or steady
Scanner	Input	3.2 Mbps	block burst
Laser printer	Output	3.2 Mbps	block burst
Sound output	Output	8 Mbps	block burst or steady
Flash drive	Storage	480-800 Mbps read; 80 Mbps write	block burst
USB	Input or output	1.6-480 Mbps	block burst
Network/Wireless LAN	Input or output	11-100 Mbps	block burst
Network/LAN	Input or output	100-1000 Mbps	block burst
Graphics display	Output	800-8000 Mbps	block burst or steady
Optical disk	Storage	4-400 Mbps	block burst or steady
Magnetic tape	Storage	32-90 Mbps	block burst or steady
Magnetic disk	Storage	240-3000 Mbps	block burst

Adapted from Patterson, David A. and John L. Hennessy, (2005), *Computer Organization and Design, 3rd Edition*, Morgan Kaufmann Publishers, Inc, San Fransisco, CA

Some input devices must be capable of generating input to the CPU independent of program control. The keyboard and mouse were mentioned earlier in this context, and voice input would also fall into this category. Some devices, such as CD-ROMs and USB devices, can self-initiate by signaling their presence to a program within the operating system software. Local area networks can also generate this kind of input, since a program on a different CPU might request, for example, a file stored on your disk. In a slightly different category, but with similar requirements, are input devices for which input is under program control, but for which the time delay until arrival of the data is unpredictable, and possibly long. (You might consider regular keyboard input in this category, especially when writing a paper using your word processor.) This would be true if the data is being telemetered from some sort of measurement device. For example, the computer might be used to monitor the water level at a reservoir, and the input is water-level data that is telemetered by a measurement device once per hour. Provision must be made to accept unpredictable input and process it in some reasonable way, preferably without tying up the CPU excessively.

Additionally, there will be situations where an I/O device being addressed is busy or not ready. The most obvious examples are a printer that is out of paper or a DVD drive with no disk in it or a hard disk that is processing another request. It would be desirable for the device to be able to provide status information to the CPU, so that appropriate action can be taken.

The discussion in this section establishes several requirements that will have to be met for a computer system to handle I/O in a sufficient and effective manner:

1. There must be a means for individually addressing different peripheral devices.

2. There must be a way in which peripheral devices can initiate communication with the CPU. This facility will be required to allow the CPU to respond to unexpected inputs from peripherals such as keyboards, mice, and networks, and so that peripherals such as printers and floppy disk drives can convey emergency status information to the executing program.

3. Programmed I/O is suitable only for slow devices and individual word transfers. For faster devices with block transfers, there must be a more efficient means of transferring the data between I/O and memory. Memory is a suitable medium for direct block transfers, since the data has to be in memory for a program to access it. Preferably this could be done without involving the CPU, since this would free the CPU to work on other tasks.

4. The buses that interconnect high-speed I/O devices with the computer must be capable of the high data transfer rates characteristic of modern systems. We will return to this issue in Chapter 11.

5. Finally, there must be a means for handling devices with extremely different control requirements. It would be desirable if I/O for each of these devices could be handled in a simple and similar way by programs in the CPU.

The last requirement suggests that it is not practical to connect the I/O devices directly to the CPU without some sort of interface module unique to each device. To clarify this requirement, note the following conditions established from the previous discussion:

1. The formats required by different devices will be different. Some devices require a single piece of data, and then must wait before another piece of data can be accepted. Others expect a block of data. Some devices expect 8 bits of data at a time; others require 16, 32, or 64. Some devices expect the data to be provided sequentially, on a single data line. Other devices expect a parallel interface. These inconsistencies mean that the system would require substantially different interface hardware and software for each device.

2. The incompatibilities in speed between the various devices and the CPU will make synchronization difficult, especially if there are multiple devices attempting to do I/O at the same time. It may be necessary to buffer the data (i.e., hold it and release part of it at particular times) to use it. A **buffer** works something like a water reservoir or tower. Water enters the reservoir or tower as it becomes available. It is stored and released as it can be used. A computer buffer uses registers or memory in the same way.

3. Although the I/O requirements for most devices occur in bursts, some multimedia, video and audio in particular, provide a steady stream of data that must be transferred on a regular basis to prevent dropouts that can upset a user. I/O devices and the interconnections that support multimedia services must be capable of guaranteeing steady performance. This often includes network interfaces and high-speed communication devices as well as such devices as video

cameras, since networks are frequently used to supply audio and video. (Think of downloading streaming video from the Web.)

4. Devices such as disk drives have electromechanical control requirements that must be met, and it would tie up too much time to use the CPU to provide that control. For example, the head motors in a disk drive have to be moved to the correct disk track to retrieve data and something must continually maintain the current head position on the track once the track is reached. There must be a motor controller to move the print heads in an inkjet printer across the paper to the correct position to print a character. And so on. Of course, the requirements for each device are different.

The different requirements for each I/O device plus the necessity for providing devices with addressing, synchronization, status, and external control capabilities suggest that it is necessary to provide each device with its own special interface. Thus, in general, I/O devices will be connected to the CPU through an I/O module of some sort. The I/O module will contain the specialized hardware circuits necessary to meet all the I/O requirements that we established, including block transfer capability with appropriate buffering and a standardized, simple interface to the CPU. At the other interface, the I/O module will have the capability to control the specific device or devices for which it is designed.

The simplest arrangement is shown in Figure 9.2. I/O modules may be very simple and control a single device, or they may be complex, with substantial built-in intelligence, and may control many devices. A slightly more complex arrangement is shown in Figure 9.3.

The additional I/O modules require addressing to distinguish them from each other. The lower module will actually recognize addresses for either of the I/O devices connected to it. I/O modules that control a single type of device are often called **device controllers**. For example, an I/O module that controls disks would be a *disk controller*. We look at the I/O modules more carefully in Section 9.5.

FIGURE 9.2

Simple I/O Configuration

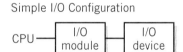

FIGURE 9.3

A Slightly More Complex I/O Module Arrangement

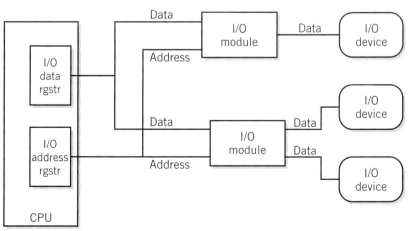

9.2 PROGRAMMED I/O

In the simplest method for performing I/O, an I/O module is connected to a pair of I/O registers in the CPU via a bus. The I/O data register serves the same role in the real CPU as the input and output baskets served in the Little Man Computer. Alternatively, one might view the I/O baskets as buffers, holding multiple inputs or outputs, with the I/O data register as the interface between the CPU and the buffer. The I/O operation is similar to that of the Little Man Computer. Input from the peripheral device is transferred from the I/O module or buffer for that peripheral device one word at a time to the I/O data register and from there to an accumulator register under program control, just as occurred in the Little Man Computer. Similarly, individual words of output data pass from an accumulator register to the I/O data register where they can be read by the appropriate I/O module, again under program control. Each instruction produces a single input or output. This method is known as **programmed I/O**.

In practice, it is most likely that there will be multiple devices connected to the CPU. Since each device must be recognized individually, address information must be sent with the I/O instruction. The address field of the I/O instruction can be used for this purpose. An I/O address register in the CPU holds the address for transfer to the bus. Each I/O module will have an identification address that will allow it to identify I/O instructions addressed to it and to ignore other I/O not intended for it.

As has been noted, it is common for an I/O module to have several addresses, each of which represents a different control command or status request, or which addresses a different device when a particular module supports multiple devices. For example, the address field in the Little Man input and output instructions could be used to address up to a combination of one hundred devices, status requests, or control commands. Figure 9.4 illustrates the concept of programmed I/O. Indeed, the LMC uses the address field to select the I-basket (901) or O-basket (902) as the I/O device within the 900 instruction.

The I/O data and address registers work similarly to the memory address register (MAR) and memory data register (MDR). In fact, in some systems, they may even be connected to the same bus. The CPU places a control signal on the bus to indicate whether the transfer is I/O or memory.

Programmed I/O is obviously slow, since a full instruction fetch-execute cycle must be performed for each and every I/O data word to be transferred. Programmed I/O is used today primarily with keyboards, with occasional application to other simple character based data transfers, such as the transmission of commands through a network I/O module or modem. These operations are slow compared with the computer, with small quantities of data that can be handled one character at a time. One limitation, which we shall address later in the chapter, is that with programmed I/O, input from the keyboard is accepted only under program control. An alternative means must be found to accept unexpected input from the keyboard.

There is one important application for programmed I/O: alternative methods of I/O use the I/O module to control I/O operations from outside the CPU, independent of the CPU, using memory as the intermediate site for the data transfer. Programmed I/O is used by programs in the CPU to send the necessary commands to the I/O modules to set up parameters for the transfer and to initiate I/O operations. We shall return to this topic in Section 9.4.

FIGURE 9.4

Programmed I/O

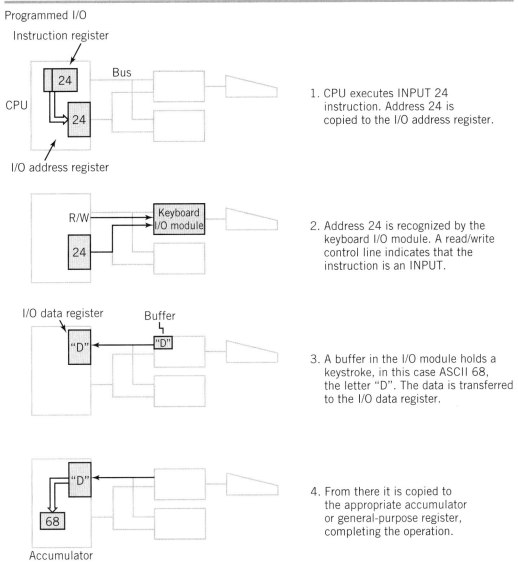

Instruction register

Bus

CPU

I/O address register

1. CPU executes INPUT 24 instruction. Address 24 is copied to the I/O address register.

R/W

2. Address 24 is recognized by the keyboard I/O module. A read/write control line indicates that the instruction is an INPUT.

I/O data register

Buffer

3. A buffer in the I/O module holds a keystroke, in this case ASCII 68, the letter "D". The data is transferred to the I/O data register.

4. From there it is copied to the appropriate accumulator or general-purpose register, completing the operation.

Accumulator

9.3 INTERRUPTS

As you know from our previous discussion, there are many circumstances under which it is important to interrupt the normal flow of a program in the computer to react to special events. An unexpected user command from the keyboard or other external input, an abnormal situation, such as a power failure, that requires immediate attention from the computer, an attempt to execute an illegal instruction, a request for service from a network controller, or the completion of an I/O task initiated by the program: all of these suggest that it is necessary to include some means to allow the computer to take special actions when required. Interrupt capabilities are also used to make it possible to time share the CPU between several different programs or program segments at once.

Modern computers provide interrupt capability by providing one or more special control lines to the central processor known as **interrupt lines**. For example, the standard I/O for a modern PC may contain as many as thirty-two interrupt lines, labeled IRQ0 through IRQ31. (IRQ stands for Interrupt ReQuest.) The messages sent to the computer on these lines are known as **interrupts**. The presence of a message on an interrupt line will cause the computer to suspend the program being executed and jump to a special interrupt processing program.

Consider, as an example, the following situation:

EXAMPLE

In a large, multiuser system there may be hundreds of keyboards being used with the computer at any given time. Since any of these keyboards could generate input to the computer at any time, it is necessary that the computer be aware of any key that is struck from any keyboard in use. This process must take place quickly, before another key is struck on the same keyboard, to prevent data loss from occurring when the second input is generated.

Theoretically, though impractically, it would be possible for the computer to perform this task by checking each keyboard for input in rotation, at frequent intervals. This technique is known as **polling**. The interval would have to be shorter than the time during which a fast typist could hit another key. Since there may be hundreds of keyboards in use, this technique may result in a polling rate of thousands of samples per second. Most of these samples will not result in new data; therefore, the computer time spent in polling is largely wasted.

This is a situation for which the concept of the interrupt is well suited. The goal is achieved more productively by allowing the keyboard to notify the CPU by using an interrupt when it has input. When a key is struck on any keyboard, it causes the interrupt line to be activated, so that the CPU knows that an I/O device connected to the interrupt line requires action. Interrupts satisfy the requirement for external input controls, and also provide the desirable feature of freeing the CPU from waiting for events to occur.

Servicing Interrupts

Since the computer is capable only of executing programs, interrupt actions take the form of special programs, executed whenever triggered by an interrupt signal. Interrupt procedures follow the form shown in Figure 9.5.

Specifically, the interrupt causes the temporary suspension of the program in progress. All the pertinent information about the program being suspended, including the location of the last instruction executed, and the values of data in various registers, is saved in a known part of memory, either in a special area associated with the program, known as the **process control block** (**PCB**), or in a part of memory known as the stack area. This information is known as the program's **context**, and will make it possible to restart the program exactly where it left off, without loss of any data or program state. Many computers have a single instruction that saves all the critical information at once. The

FIGURE 9.5

Servicing an Interrupt

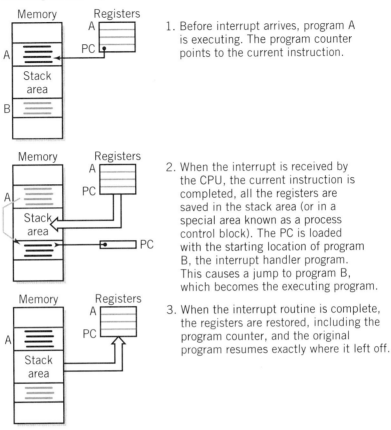

1. Before interrupt arrives, program A is executing. The program counter points to the current instruction.

2. When the interrupt is received by the CPU, the current instruction is completed, all the registers are saved in the stack area (or in a special area known as a process control block). The PC is loaded with the starting location of program B, the interrupt handler program. This causes a jump to program B, which becomes the executing program.

3. When the interrupt routine is complete, the registers are restored, including the program counter, and the original program resumes exactly where it left off.

memory belonging to the original program is kept intact. The computer then branches to a special interrupt handler program elsewhere in memory; the **interrupt handler** program is also known as an **interrupt routine**. The interrupt handler program determines the appropriate course of action. This process is known as **servicing the interrupt**. Since many interrupts exist to support I/O devices, most of the interrupt handling programs are also known as **device drivers**.

When the interrupt routine completes its task, it normally would return control to the interrupted program, much like a subroutine. Original register values would be restored, and the original program would resume execution *exactly* where it left off, and in its identical state, since all the registers were restored to their original values. There are some circumstances when this is not the case, however, since actions taken by the interrupt routine may make a difference in what the original program is supposed to do. For example, a printer interrupt indicating that the printer is out of paper would require a different action by the original program (perhaps a message to the screen telling the user to load more paper); it would not be useful for the program to send more characters!

Intuitively, the servicing of interrupts works just the way that you would expect. Suppose that you were giving a speech in one of your classes, and someone in the class interrupts you with a question. What do you do? Normally, you would hold your current thought and answer the question. When you finish answering the question, you return to your speech just where you left off, pick up the thought, and continue as though no interrupt had occurred. This would be your normal interrupt servicing routine. Suppose, however, that the interrupt is the bell ending class or the instructor telling you that you have run out of time. In this case, your response is different. You would *not* return to your speech. Instead, you might do a quick wrap-up followed by an exit.

In other words, you would react in a way quite similar to the way in which the interrupt servicing routines work.

The Uses of Interrupts

The way in which an interrupt is used depends on the nature of the device. You've already seen that externally controlled inputs are best handled by generating interrupts whenever action is required. In other cases, interrupts occur when some action is *completed*. This section introduces several different ways in which interrupts are used.

THE INTERRUPT AS AN EXTERNAL EVENT NOTIFIER   As previously discussed, interrupts are useful as notifiers to the CPU of **external events** that require action. This frees the CPU from the necessity of performing polling to determine that input data is waiting.

EXAMPLE

Keyboard input can be processed using a combination of programmed I/O and interrupts. Suppose a key is struck on the keyboard. This causes an interrupt to occur. The current program is suspended, and control is transferred to the keyboard interrupt handler program.

FIGURE 9.6

Using a Keyboard Handler Interrupt

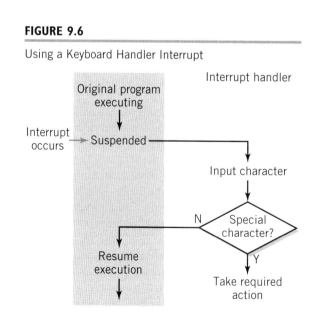

The keyboard interrupt handler first inputs the character, using programmed I/O, and determines what character has been received. It would next determine if the input is one that requires special action. If so, it would perform the required action, for example, suspending the program or freezing the data on the screen. Otherwise, it would pass the input data to the program expecting input from that keyboard. Normally, the input character would be stored in a known memory location, ready for the program to use when it is reactivated.

When the action is complete, that is, when the interrupt has been serviced, the computer normally restores the register values and returns control to the suspended program, unless the interrupt request specifies a different course of action. This would be the case, for example, if the user typed a command to suspend the program being run.

Figure 9.6 shows the steps in processing a keyboard input interrupt.

EXAMPLE

A real-time system is a computer system used primarily to measure external events that happen in "real time"; that is, the event, when it occurs, requires processing quickly because the data is of critical time-sensitive value.

As an example, consider a computer system that monitors the coolant temperature from the core of a power plant nuclear reactor. The temperature is transmitted once a minute by a temperature measurement transducer to the computer.

In this particular case, the transducer input is expected, and, when it occurs, requires immediate evaluation. It is reasonable to assume, however, that the computer system is to be used for other purposes, and it is not desirable to tie up the CPU in an input loop waiting for the transducer data to arrive.

This is a perfect application for interrupts. The transducer input is assigned to an interrupt. The interrupt service routine in this case is used to process the transducer input data. When the interrupt occurs, the interrupt routine evaluates the input. If everything is normal, the routine returns control to whatever the computer was doing. In an emergency, the interrupt routine would transfer control instead to the program that handles emergency situations.

THE INTERRUPT AS A COMPLETION SIGNAL   The keyboard and transducer examples demonstrate the usefulness of the interrupt as a means for the user to control the computer from an input device, in this case the keyboard or transducer. Let us next consider the interrupt technique as a means of controlling the flow of data to an output device. Here, the interrupt serves to notify the computer of the completion of a particular course of action.

EXAMPLE

As noted previously, the printer is a slow output device. The computer is capable of outputting data to the printer much faster than the printer can handle it. The interrupt can be used to control the flow of data to the printer in an efficient way.

The computer sends one block of data at a time to the printer. The size of the block depends on the type of printer and the amount of memory installed in the printer. When the printer is ready to accept more data, it sends an interrupt to the computer. This interrupt indicates that the printer has completed printing the material previously received and is ready for more.

In this case, the interrupt capability prevents the loss of output, since it allows the printer to control the flow of data to a rate that the printer can accept. Without the interrupt capability, it would be necessary to output data at a very slow rate to assure that the computer did not exceed the ability of the printer to accept output. The use of an interrupt also allows the CPU to perform other tasks while it waits for the printer to complete its printing.

By the way, you might notice that the printer could use a second, different interrupt as a way of telling the computer to stop sending data temporarily when the printer's buffer fills up.

This application is diagrammed in Figure 9.7. Another application of the interrupt as a completion signal is discussed in Section 9.4, as an integral part of the direct memory access technique.

THE INTERRUPT AS A MEANS OF ALLOCATING CPU TIME   A third major application for interrupts is to use the interrupt as a method of allocating CPU time to different programs or threads that are sharing the CPU. (Threads are small pieces of a program that can be executed independently, such as the spell checker in a word processing program.)

Since the CPU can only execute one sequence of instructions at a time, the ability to time share multiple programs or threads implies that the computer system must share the CPU by allocating small segments of time to each program or thread, in rapid rotation among them. Each program sequence is allowed to execute some instructions. After a certain period of time, that sequence is interrupted and relinquishes control to a dispatcher program within the operating system that allocates the next block of time to another sequence. This is illustrated in Figure 9.8.

FIGURE 9.7

Using a Print Handler Interrupt

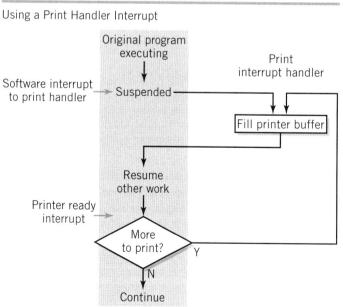

FIGURE 9.8

Using an Interrupt for Time Sharing

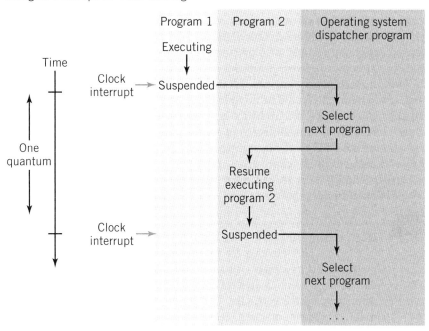

The system cannot count on an instruction sequence relinquishing control voluntarily, since a program caught in an infinite loop would not be able to do so. Instead, the computer system provides an internal clock that sends an interrupt periodically to the CPU. The time between interrupt pulses is known as a **quantum**, and represents the time that each program or thread will have allotted to it. When the clock interrupt occurs, the interrupt routine returns control to the operating system, which then determines which program or thread will receive CPU time next. The interrupt is a simple but effective method for allowing the operating system to share CPU resources among several programs at once.

Time sharing is discussed in more depth in Chapters 15 and 18.

THE INTERRUPT AS AN ABNORMAL EVENT INDICATOR   The fourth major use for interrupts is to handle **abnormal events** that affect operation of the computer system itself. Under certain conditions, we would like the computer to respond with a specific course of action, quickly and effectively. This usage is similar to that of other external input events, but in this case, the events are directed at problems or special conditions within the computer system itself.

One obvious example of an external event requiring special computer action is power failure. Most computers provide enough internal power storage to save the work that is being performed and to shut down gracefully, provided that the computer has quick notification of the power failure. A power line monitor that connects to the interrupt facility provides this capability. The interrupt routine will save the status of programs that are in memory, close open files, and perform other housekeeping operations that will allow the computer to restart without any loss of data. It will then halt the computer.

Another important application of the abnormal event interrupt is when a program attempts to execute an illegal instruction such as a *divide by 0* or a nonexistent op code, or when a hardware error is detected, such as a memory parity error. When the error occurs it is not possible to complete the executing program. Yet it is important that the system attempt to recover from the error and that the appropriate personnel be notified. It is not acceptable simply to halt the computer. Particularly in modern multitasking computer systems this would be undesirable since it would also stop other executing programs that might not be affected by the error and would affect other users if the system is a multiuser system. Instead, an interrupt routine can notify the user of the error and return control of the CPU to the operating system program. You should notice that these interrupts are actually generated from inside the CPU, whereas the other interrupts that we have discussed so far are generated externally. Internal interrupts are sometimes called **traps** or **exceptions**.

EXAMPLE

Most modern computers have a set of instructions known as **privileged instructions**. These instructions are intended for use by an operating system program. The HALT instruction generally is a privileged instruction. Privileged instructions are designed to provide system security by preventing application programs from altering memory outside their own region, from stopping the computer, or from directly addressing an I/O device that is shared by multiple programs or users. (Suppose, for example, that two programs sharing the computer each sent text out to a printer. The resulting printout would be garbage, a mixture of the outputs from each program.) An attempt by a user's program to execute a privileged instruction would result in an illegal instruction interrupt.

You might assume from the examples above that abnormal event interrupts always result from critical errors or catastrophic failures within the computer system, but this not necessarily the case. *Virtual storage* is a memory management technology that makes it appear that a computer system has more memory than is physically installed in the computer. (There is a detailed discussion of virtual storage in Chapter 18.) One particularly important interrupt event occurs as an integral part of the design and operation of virtual storage. Other internal and external events also make use of the interrupt facility. The table in Figure 9.9 shows a list of the built-in interrupts for the IBM System z family of computers.

SOFTWARE INTERRUPTS In addition to the actual hardware interrupts already discussed, modern CPU instruction sets include an instruction that simulates an interrupt. In the Intel x86 architecture, for example, this instruction has the mnemonic INT, for INTerrupt. The IBM System z uses the mnemonic SVC for SUPERVISOR CALL. The interrupt instruction works in the same way as a hardware interrupt, saving appropriate registers and transferring control to an interrupt handling procedure. The address space of the INT instruction can be used to provide a parameter that specifies which interrupt is to be executed. The **software interrupt** is very similar to a subroutine jump to a known, fixed location.

FIGURE 9.9

Table of Interrupts for zSeries Family

Priority	Interrupt class	Type of interrupts
Highest	Machine check	Nonrecoverable hardware errors
	Supervisor call	Software interrupt request by program
	Program check	Hardware-detectible software errors: illegal instruction, protected instruction, divide by 0, overflow, underflow, address translation error
	Machine check	Recoverable hardware errors
	External	Operator intervention, interval timer expiration, set timer expiration
	I/O	I/O completion signal or other I/O-related event
Lowest	Restart	Restart key, or restart signal from another CPU when multiple CPUs are used

Software interrupts make the interrupt routines available for use by other programs. Programs can access these routines simply by executing the INT instruction with the appropriate parameter.

An important application for software interrupts is to centralize I/O operations. One way to assure that multiple programs do not unintentionally alter another program's files or intermingle printer output is to provide a single path for I/O to each device. Generally, the I/O paths are interrupt routines that are a part of the operating system software. Software interrupts are used by each program to request I/O from the operating system software. As an example, a software interrupt was used in Figure 9.7 to initiate printing.

Multiple Interrupts and Prioritization

As you have now seen, there may be many different input and output devices and event indicators connected to interrupt lines. This means that there may be many different events vying for attention. Inevitably, multiple interrupts will occur from time to time.

There are two questions that must be answered when an interrupt occurs. First, are there other interrupts already awaiting service, and, if so, how does the computer determine the order in which the interrupts get serviced? And, second, how does the computer identify the interrupting device?

Two different processing methods are commonly used for determining which device initiated the interrupt. Some computers use a method known as **vectored interrupt**, in which the address of the interrupting device is included as part of the interrupt. Another method provides a general interrupt that is shared by all devices. The computer identifies the interrupting device by **polling** each device. These two methods are illustrated in Figures 9.10 and 9.11, respectively. The vectored interrupt method is obviously faster, but requires additional hardware to implement. Some systems use different interrupt lines for each interrupt; others use a method called "daisy chaining," which places the interrupts onto a single interrupt line to the CPU in such a way that highest priorities are recognized first.

FIGURE 9.10

Vectored Interrupt Processing

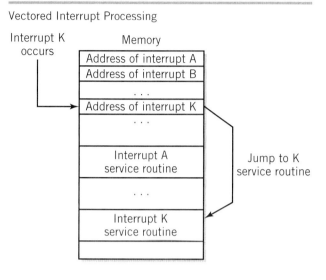

Multiple interrupts can be handled by assigning **priorities** to each interrupt. In general, multiple interrupts will be handled top priority first. A higher-priority interrupt will be allowed to interrupt an interrupt of lower priority, but a lower-priority interrupt will have to wait until a higher-priority interrupt is completed.

This leads to a hierarchy of interrupts, in which higher-priority interrupts can interrupt other interrupts of lower priority, back and forth, eventually returning control to the original program that was running. Although this sounds complicated, this situation is actually quite common, and is fairly easy to implement. Figure 9.12 shows a simple example of this situation. In this figure, interrupt routine C is the highest priority, followed by B and A.

Most computer systems allow the system manager to establish priorities for the various interrupts. Priorities are established in a logical way. The highest priorities are reserved for time-sensitive situations, such as power failure or external events that are being time measured. Keyboard events are also usually considered high-priority events, since data loss can occur if the keyboard input is not read quickly. Task completion interrupts usually take lower priorities, since the delay will not affect the integrity of the data under normal conditions.

Depending on the system, priorities may be established with software or with hardware. In some systems, the priority of I/O device interrupts is established by the way their I/O module cards are physically placed on the backplane. The daisy chain interrupt line can

FIGURE 9.11

Polled Interrupt Processing

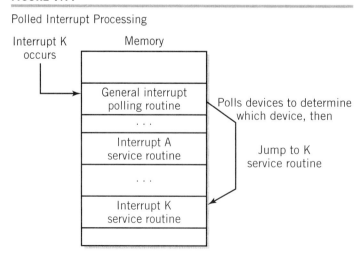

FIGURE 9.12

Multiple Interrupts

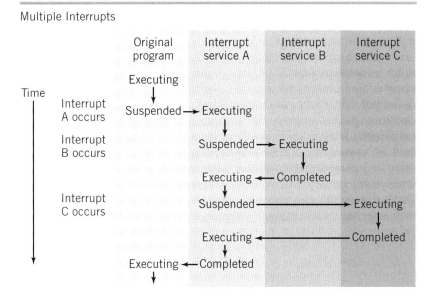

be used for this purpose: the highest-priority devices are placed closest to the CPU and block the signals of lower-priority devices that are farther down the line. In other systems, priorities are established by assigning a priority number to each interrupt.

Most interrupts can be temporarily disabled by program instructions when a program is performing a critical task that would be negatively affected if an interrupt were to occur. This is particularly true of time-sensitive tasks. In many systems, interrupts are **maskable**; that is, they can be selectively disabled. Certain interrupts, such as power failure, that are never disabled are sometimes referred to as *nonmaskable interrupts*. Most modern computer systems save interrupts that occur when interrupts are disabled, so that when the interrupts are reenabled, the pending interrupts will be processed.

EXAMPLE

In the IBM System z architecture, interrupts are divided into six classes, with the priorities shown in Figure 9.9. All the different interrupts within each class are handled by the interrupt service routine for that class. Each interrupt class has two vectored addresses permanently associated with it. The first of these is a space reserved for the Program Status Word of the current program, known in IBM jargon as the OLD PSW. The Program Status Word is a 64-bit word that includes the program counter and other significant information about the program. The second vectored address contains a pointer to the interrupt routine. This address is known as the NEW PSW. The method used to switch from the original program to a service routine and back is illustrated in Figure 9.13.

When an interrupt occurs, the PSW for the current program is stored automatically in the OLD PSW space, and the NEW PSW is loaded. The effect is a jump to the location in memory pointed to by the NEW PSW, which is the location of the interrupt service routine for that class of interrupts. Incidentally, note that this procedure does not save other registers. Each interrupt service routine saves and restores the registers that it uses.

FIGURE 9.13

Processing an Interrupt in the IBM zSeries

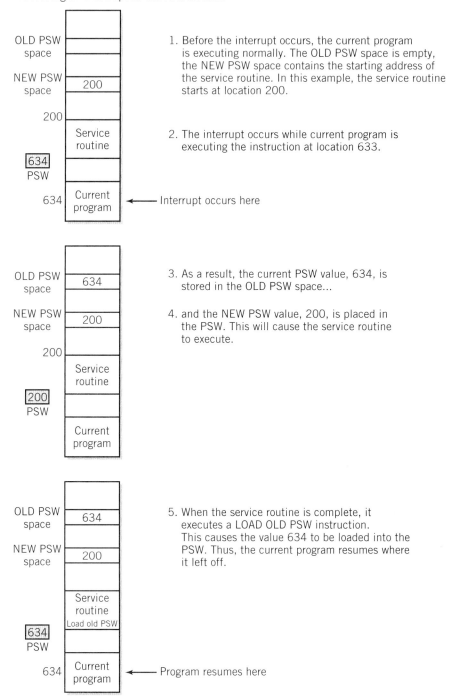

1. Before the interrupt occurs, the current program is executing normally. The OLD PSW space is empty, the NEW PSW space contains the starting address of the service routine. In this example, the service routine starts at location 200.

2. The interrupt occurs while current program is executing the instruction at location 633.

Interrupt occurs here

3. As a result, the current PSW value, 634, is stored in the OLD PSW space...

4. and the NEW PSW value, 200, is placed in the PSW. This will cause the service routine to execute.

5. When the service routine is complete, it executes a LOAD OLD PSW instruction. This causes the value 634 to be loaded into the PSW. Thus, the current program resumes where it left off.

Program resumes here

The Z-architecture CPU has an instruction LOAD OLD PSW. When the interrupt service routine is completed, it simply uses this instruction to return to the original program. Interrupts of lower priority are masked, but higher-priority interrupts are allowed to interrupt the lower priority service routine while it is executing. Most important, interrupts belonging to the same class must be masked. Since there is only a single address space available for storing the OLD PSW for each class, a second interrupt of the same class would destroy the return address to the original program. Worse yet, the second interrupt would store the current address being executed in the OLD PSW space. Since that address is itself within the service routine, this would result in an infinite loop. To see this, look again at Figure 9.13. Pick a location inside the service routine, say, 205, and cause an interrupt to occur at that point. Now, follow through the diagram, and notice the results.

The preceding example demonstrates one way of providing return access from interrupts. An alternative method is used in x86 series computers. The x86 interrupt structure is also vectored, but the context is stored on an interrupt stack. Using a stack in this way is essentially analogous to the way in which subroutine jumps and returns work. These were discussed in detail in Chapter 7. Stack storage for interrupts makes interrupts reentrant, although such a condition would seem to be extremely rare.

Interrupts are normally checked at the completion of each instruction. That is, interrupts are normally checked *after* one instruction is finished and *before* another begins. This assures that conditions won't change *in the middle* of an instruction that would affect the instruction's execution. Certain long System z instructions can be interrupted in the middle of their fetch-execution cycle, however. These instructions use the general-purpose registers for their intermediate values, so it is important that the general-purpose registers be stored during an interrupt for later retrieval; otherwise, some instructions could not be restarted properly. The System z computer does not automatically store registers when an interrupt occurs. It is therefore important that the interrupt programs be written carefully so that the interrupted instruction doesn't crash when the routine is restarted. In the x86 computer, the registers are also generally stored on a stack, which makes retrieval simple even if the interrupt routine itself is interrupted. Virtual storage also requires the ability to interrupt in the middle of an instruction.

9.4 DIRECT MEMORY ACCESS

For most applications, it is impractical to transfer data to the CPU from a peripheral device using programmed I/O, even with interrupts. Indeed, the data from disks and tapes are transferred only in blocks, and it does not make sense to execute a separate instruction for each piece of data in the block. It is also more reasonable to transfer blocks of data directly between a device's I/O module and memory, since most processing will also take place in blocks. This suggests bypassing the CPU registers, if possible, and then processing the block of data as a group, from memory.

As a simple example, consider a program that sorts a block of numbers. To operate efficiently, the entire block of numbers must be stored in memory for the sort operation to take place, since instructions in the CPU can operate only on data in memory. Thus, it makes sense to move the entire block from disk to memory at once.

For this purpose, computer systems provide a more efficient form of I/O that transfers block data directly between the I/O module and computer memory, under control of the I/O module. The transfer is initiated by a program in the CPU, using programmed I/O, but the CPU can then be bypassed for the remainder of the transfer. The I/O module will notify the CPU with an interrupt when the transfer is complete. Once this has occurred, the data is in memory, ready for the program to use. This technique of I/O–memory data transfer is known as **direct memory access**, or more commonly, simply as **DMA**.

In Little Man terms, direct memory access could be viewed as providing data for the Little Man by loading data directly into the mailboxes through a rear door, bypassing the Little Man I/O instruction procedures. To reemphasize the fact that this operation only takes place under program control, we would have to provide a means for the Little Man to initiate such a transfer and a means to notify the Little Man when the data transfer is complete.

For direct memory access to take place, three primary conditions must be met:

1. There must be a method to connect together the I/O interface and memory. In some systems both are already connected to the same bus, so this requirement is easily met. In other cases, the design must contain provisions for interconnecting the two. The issue of system configuration is discussed in Chapter 11.

2. The I/O module associated with the particular device must be capable of reading and writing to memory. It does so by simulating the CPU's interface with memory. Specifically, the I/O module must be able to load a memory address register and to read and write to a memory data register, whether its own or one outside the I/O module.

3. There must be a means to avoid conflict between the CPU and the I/O module. It is not possible for the CPU and a module that is controlling disk I/O to load different addresses into the MAR at the same instant, for example, nor is it possible for two different I/O modules to transfer data between I/O and memory on the same bus at the same instant. This requirement simply means that memory can only be used by one device at a time, although, as we mentioned in Chapter 8, Section 8.3, some systems interleave memory in such a way that the CPU and I/O modules can access different parts of memory simultaneously. Special control circuits must be included to indicate which part of the system, CPU or particular I/O module, is in control of the memory and bus at any given instant.

DMA is particularly well suited for high-speed disk transfers, but there are several other advantages as well. Since the CPU is not actively involved during the transfer, the CPU can be used to perform other tasks during the time when I/O transfers are taking place. This is particularly useful for large multiuser systems. Of course, DMA is not limited to just disk-to-memory transfers. It can be used with other high-speed devices. And the transfers may be made in either direction. DMA is an effective means to transfer video data from memory to the video I/O system for rapid display, for example.

The procedure used by the CPU to initiate a DMA transfer is straightforward. Four pieces of data must be provided to the I/O controller for the particular I/O device to initiate the transfer. The four pieces of data that the I/O module must have to control a DMA transfer are

1. The location of the data on the I/O device (for example, the location of the block on the disk)
2. The starting location of the block of data in memory
3. The size of the block to be transferred
4. The direction of transfer, read (I/O → memory) or write (memory → I/O)

Normally, the I/O module would have four different registers, each with its own I/O address available for this purpose. In most modern systems, normal programmed I/O output instructions are used to initiate a DMA transfer. On some systems, a fifth programmed I/O instruction actually initiates the transfer, whereas other systems start the DMA transfer when the fourth piece of data arrives at the I/O module.

IBM mainframes work a bit differently, although the principle is the same. A single programmed I/O START CHANNEL instruction initiates the process. A separate **channel program** is stored in memory. The I/O module uses this channel program to perform its DMA control. The four pieces of data are a part of the channel program and are used by the I/O module to initiate the DMA transfer. The concept of I/O channels is considered in more detail in Chapter 11.

Once the DMA transfer has been initiated, the CPU is free to perform other processing. Note, however, that the data being transferred should not be modified during this period, since doing so can result in transfer errors, as well as processing errors.

If, for example, a program should alter the number in a memory location being transferred to disk, the number transferred is ambiguous, dependent on whether the alteration occurred before or after the transfer of that particular location. Similarly, the use of a number being transferred into memory depends on whether the transfer for that particular location has already occurred.

This would be equivalent to having the Little Man read a piece of data from the area of memory being loaded from the rear of the mailboxes. The number on that piece of data would depend on whether a new value loaded in from the rear came before or after the Little Man's attempt to read it. Clearly, this is not an acceptable situation.

It is thus important that the CPU know when the transfer is complete, assuring that the data in memory is stable. The interrupt technique is used for this purpose. The program waiting for the data transfer is suspended or performs other, unrelated processing during the time of transfer. The controller sends a completion signal interrupt to the CPU when the transfer is complete. The interrupt service routine notifies the program that it may continue with the processing of the affected data.

Finally, note that it takes several programmed output instructions to initiate a DMA transfer. This suggests, correctly, that it is not useful to perform a DMA transfer for very small amounts of data. For small transfers, it is obviously more efficient to use programmed I/O. It is also worth pointing out that if a computer is capable only of performing a single task, then the time freed up by DMA cannot be used productively, and there is little advantage in using DMA.

It is worth interrupting the discussion at this point (yes, the pun was intentional) to remind you that in reality an application program would not be performing I/O directly, since doing so might conflict with other programs that are also performing I/O at the same time. Instead, the application program would request I/O services from the operating system software by calling a procedure within the operating system that performs the I/O operations described here. The I/O instructions and interrupt procedures are, of course, privileged: only the operating system software is allowed access to these instructions and procedures.

EXAMPLE

Consider the steps required to write a block of data to a disk from memory. The executing program has already created the block of data somewhere in memory.

First, the I/O service program uses programmed I/O to send four pieces of data to the disk-controlling I/O module: the location of the block in memory; the location where the data is to be stored on disk; the size of the block (this step might be unnecessary if a fixed disk size is always used on the particular system); and the direction of transfer, in this case a write to disk.

Next, the service program sends a "ready" message to the I/O module, again using programmed I/O. At this point, the DMA transfer process takes place, outside the control of the CPU, the I/O service, or the program that requested I/O service. Depending on the design of the operating system programs, the current application program may resume execution of other tasks, or it may be suspended until the DMA transfer is complete.

When the transfer is complete, the I/O module sends an interrupt to the CPU. The interrupt handler either returns control to the program that initiated the request or notifies the operating system that the program can be resumed, depending on the design of the system.

This example shows how the programmed I/O, DMA, and interrupt methodologies work together in the most important and common way of doing I/O. The technique is diagrammed in Figure 9.14.

9.5 I/O MODULES

In the example shown in Figure 9.14, a major role is played by the disk controller. The disk controller is an example of an I/O module. The I/O module serves as an interface between

FIGURE 9.14

DMA Initiation and Control

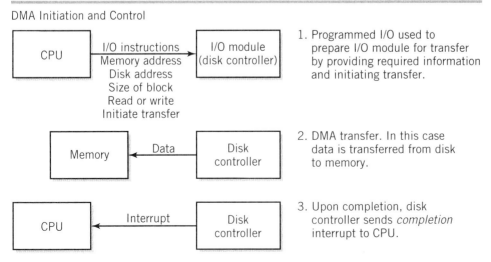

the CPU and the specific device, in this case a disk drive, accepting commands from the CPU on one side and controlling the device on the other. In this example, the I/O module provides the following functions:

- The I/O module recognizes messages addressed to it and accepts commands from the CPU establishing what the disk drive is to do. In this case, the I/O module recognizes that a block of data is to be written from memory to disk using DMA.

- The I/O module provides a buffer where the data from memory can be held until it can be transferred to the disk.

- The I/O module provides the necessary registers and controls to perform a direct memory transfer. This requires that the I/O module have access to a memory address register and a memory data register separate from those of the CPU, either within the I/O module or as a separate DMA controller.

- The I/O module controls the disk drive, moving the head to the physical location on the disk where data is to be written.

- The I/O module copies data from its buffer to the disk.

- The I/O module has interrupt capability, which it uses to notify the CPU when the transfer is complete. It can also interrupt the CPU to notify it of errors or problems that arise during the transfer.

It is desirable to offload tasks specific to I/O operations from the CPU to a separate module or modules which are designed specifically for I/O data transfer and device control. In some cases, the I/O module even provides a processor of its own to offload I/O related processing from the system CPU.

The use of separate I/O modules offers several benefits:

- The module can be designed to provide the specialized control required by a particular device.

- The module frees the CPU to perform other tasks while the much slower I/O operations are taking place.

- The presence of I/O modules allows control of several different I/O devices to occur simultaneously.

- A processor-based module can provide specialized services that would otherwise overload the system CPU with time-consuming CPU-intensive work. For example, a high-end graphics display I/O controller can decode compressed and encrypted MPEG video or adjust images for lighting and shading effects.

As seen in Figure 9.15, I/O modules perform two different functions. At the CPU interface, the module performs CPU interfacing tasks: accepting I/O commands from the CPU, transferring data between the module and the CPU or memory, and sending interrupts and status information to the CPU. At the device interface, the I/O module supplies control of the device— moving the head to the correct track in a disk drive and rewinding tape, for example. Most I/O modules provide buffering of the data to synchronize the different speeds of the CPU and the various I/O devices. Some modules must also have the capability of receiving requests from a device independently from the

FIGURE 9.15

I/O Module Interfaces

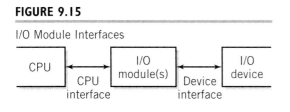

computer, and must be able to pass the request in the form of an interrupt to the computer. This is true for any device that can cause an unexpected interrupt, including devices that can be installed or removed during computer operation, (sometimes known as *hot-swappable* or *plug-and-play*), devices with removable media, and network modules.

An I/O module or control unit module used to control a peripheral device is known as a **device controller**, or sometimes as a **device card**. Often, the device is named–the module in the preceding example would be referred to specifically as a *disk controller*, a network module would be called a *network interface controller* or *network interface card*. And, of course, you're probably already familiar with *graphics cards*. A device controller accepts I/O requests and interacts directly with the device to satisfy those requests. The device controllers are individually designed to provide the specialized built-in circuitry necessary for control of a particular type of device. This ability is important, because there is such a variety of requirements for different peripheral devices. A tape drive must be turned on and off and switched between fast forward, play, and rewind. A disk head must be moved to the correct track. A display screen requires a steady transfer of data representing each point on the screen and special circuitry to maintain the correct position on the screen for the display of each point. (Operation of a display controller is discussed in Chapter 10.)

It would be difficult to program the CPU to provide the correct types of signals to operate these and other types of I/O devices, and the CPU time required to control these devices would significantly reduce the usefulness of the system. With a device controller, simple CPU I/O instructions can be used to control quite complex operations. Multiple devices of the same kind can often be controlled with a single controller.

In a small system, most of the I/O modules are device controllers that serve as direct interfaces between a general system bus and each of the system's peripheral devices. There may also be I/O modules that act as an additional interface between the system bus and other modules that then connect to the device. In a typical PC, for example, the disk controller is normally mounted inside the PC case and connects directly to a system bus. The printer, on the other hand, is controlled indirectly. One I/O module connects to the system bus and terminates in a parallel bus or USB port; the actual print controller is inside the printer, at the other end of the bus.

In general I/O modules simplify the task of interfacing peripheral devices to a CPU. I/O modules offload a considerable amount of work from the CPU. They make it possible to control I/O to a peripheral with a few simple I/O commands from the CPU. They support DMA, so that the CPU may be free to perform other tasks. And, as we have already noted, device controllers provide the specialized circuitry required to interface different types of peripherals to the computer.

Much of the power in modern computers comes from the ability to separate out CPU operations from other, more individualistic, I/O peripheral functions, and allowing the processing of each to progress in parallel. In fact, the more powerful the computer, the more essential is the separation of I/O to the satisfactory operation of the system as a whole.

SUMMARY AND REVIEW

This chapter describes the two methods used for input/output, programmed I/O and DMA, and introduces the various components and configurations that make both methods possible. After a brief description of the I/O requirements of the most common peripherals, the text describes the process of programmed I/O, and describes the advantages and disadvantages of this technique. In general, the use of programmed I/O is limited to slow devices such as keyboards and mouses that are not block oriented.

Next, we introduced the concept of an interrupt, a means of causing the CPU to take special action. We described various ways in which an interrupt could be used, including as notification of an external event that requires attention, as a completion signal for I/O, as a means of allocating CPU time, as an abnormal event indicator, and as a way for software to cause the CPU to take special action. We explained the method used by the interrupt to attract the CPU's attention and the ways in which the interrupt is serviced by the CPU. We considered the situation in which multiple interrupts occur and discussed the prioritization of interrupts.

As an alternative to programmed I/O, direct memory access allows the transfer of blocks of data directly between an I/O device and memory. We discussed the hardware requirements that make DMA possible and showed how DMA is used. We explained how DMA works in conjunction with interrupts.

We concluded with a discussion of the I/O modules that serve to control the I/O devices and act as an interface between the peripheral devices, the CPU, and memory. The I/O modules receive messages from the CPU, control the device, initiate and control DMA when required, and produce interrupts. The I/O modules in a channel architecture also serve to direct I/O requests to the proper channel and provide independent, intelligent control of the I/O operation.

FOR FURTHER READING

Detailed discussions of I/O concepts and techniques, including the concepts of interrupts and DMA, can be found in the engineering textbooks previously mentioned, particularly those by Stallings [STAL05] and Tanenbaum [TAN05]. An outstanding treatment of I/O in the IBM mainframe architecture can be found in Prasad [PRAS94] and in Cormier and others [CORM83]. PC I/O is discussed in a number of excellent books, among them Messmer [MESS01] and Sargent [SARG95]. Somewhat less organized, but still valuable, is the treatment found in Henle [HENL92].

KEY CONCEPTS AND TERMS

abnormal event	exception	priority
buffer	external event	privileged instruction
channel program	interrupt	process control block
context	interrupt handler	(PCB)
device card	interrupt lines	programmed I/O
device controller	interrupt routine	quantum
device driver	interrupt service	software interrupt
direct memory access	maskable	trap
(DMA)	polling	vectored interrupt

READING REVIEW QUESTIONS

9.1 Name at least two devices that can generate unexpected input.

9.2 In terms of the nature of the data, how does a keyboard differ from a hard disk as an input device?

9.3 Explain the purpose of a buffer.

9.4 When an interrupt occurs, what happens to the program that is currently executing at the time?

9.5 The book lists four primary uses for interrupts. State and explain at least three of them.

9.6 What kind of interrupt occurs when a user's program tries to execute a privileged instruction?

9.7 What is a *context*? What does it contain? What is it used for?

9.8 Explain the reasons why programmed I/O does not work very well when the I/O device is a hard disk or a graphics display.

9.9 What does DMA stand for? What capability does DMA add to a computer?

9.10 What are the three primary conditions that are required for DMA to take place?

9.11 What data must an I/O controller have before a DMA transfer takes place? How is this data sent to the controller?

9.12 What is the purpose of a completion interrupt at the conclusion of a DMA transfer?

9.13 Name at least three benefits that are provided by I/O modules.

9.14 A graphics card is an example of an I/O controller. I/O controllers have (at least) *two* interfaces. What are the two interfaces of a graphics card connected to?

EXERCISES

9.1 DMA is rarely used with dumb computer terminals. Why?

9.2 Why would DMA be useless if the computer did not have interrupt capability?

9.3 What is the advantage of using a disk controller to control the hard disk? How else could you do the job that the disk controller does?

9.4 What is an interrupt vector?

9.5 Consider the interrupt that occurs at the completion of a disk transfer.

    a. "Who" is interrupting "whom"?

    b. Why is the interrupt used in this case? What would be necessary if there were no interrupt capability on this computer?

    c. Describe the steps that take place after the interrupt occurs.

9.6 What is polling used for? What are the disadvantages of polling? What is a better way to perform the same job?

9.7 Suppose you wish to send a block of data to a tape drive for storage using DMA. What information must be sent to the tape controller before the DMA transfer can take place?

9.8   Describe a circumstance where an interrupt occurs at the beginning of an event. Describe a circumstance where an interrupt occurs at the completion of an event. What is the difference between the types of events?

9.9   In general, what purpose does an interrupt serve? Stated another way, suppose there were no interrupts provided in a computer. What capabilities would be lost?

9.10   Describe the steps that occur when a system receives multiple interrupts.

9.11   What is the difference between polling and polled interrupt processing?

9.12   The UNIX operating system differentiates between block-oriented and character-oriented devices. Give an example of each, explain the differences between them, and explain how the I/O process differs for each.

9.13   Consider the interface between a computer and a printer. For a typical printout it is clearly impractical to send output data to the printer one byte or one word at a time (especially over a network!). Instead data to be printed is stored in a buffer at a known location in memory and transferred in blocks to memory in the printer. A controller in the printer then handles the actual printing from the printer's memory.

   The printer's memory is not always sufficient to hold the entire printout data at one time. Printer problems, such as an "out of paper" condition, can also cause delays. Devise and describe, in as much detail as you can, an interrupt/DMA scheme that will assure that all documents will be successfully printed.

9.14   To use a computer for multimedia (moving video and sound), it is important to maximize the efficiency of the I/O. Assume that the blocks of a movie are stored consecutively on a CD-ROM. Describe the steps used to retrieve the blocks for use by the movie display software. Discuss ways in which you could optimize the performance of the I/O transfer.

CHAPTER 10

COMPUTER PERIPHERALS

"I DIDN'T MIND HIS POCKET COMPUTER, BUT NOW THAT HE'S ADDED A CD-ROM, AN EXTERNAL HARD DRIVE, AND A PORTABLE INKJET PRINTER, IT'S GOTTEN A BIT OUT OF HAND."

Thomas Sperling. Adapted, courtesy of David Ahl, Creative Computing.

10.0 INTRODUCTION

The typical personal computer system described in an advertisement consists of a CPU, memory, a DVD or CD read-write drive, a hard disk drive, a keyboard, a mouse, wireless and wired network interfaces, USB ports, sound and video system components, usually a modem, perhaps parallel, FireWire, and serial ports, and a monitor. Additional available components include scanners of various types, printers, plotters, TV tuners, floppy disk drives, and tape drives. Internal to the computer there is also a power supply that converts wall plug power into voltages suitable for powering a computer. All the items mentioned, except for the CPU, memory, and power supply, are considered peripheral (that is, external) to the main processing function of the computer itself and are known, therefore, as **peripherals**. Some of the peripherals use the USB, parallel, and serial ports as their interconnection point to the computer. Others have their own interface to internal system buses that interconnect various parts of the computer.

The peripherals in a large server or mainframe computer are similar, except larger, with more capacity. Large numbers of hard disk drives may be grouped into arrays to provide capacities of tens or hundreds of terabytes (TB). One or more high-speed network interfaces will be a major component. The capability for handling large amounts of I/O will likely be a requirement. Means of implementing large-scale, reliable backup will be necessary. Conversely, fancy displays, high-end graphics and audio cards, and other multimedia facilities may be totally unneeded.

Despite different packaging and differences in details, the basic operations of these devices are similar, regardless of the type of computer. In previous chapters we have already looked at the I/O operations that control devices that are external to the CPU. Now we direct our attention to the operation of the devices themselves. In this chapter we study the most important computer peripheral devices. We look at the usage, important characteristics, basic physical layouts, and internal operations of each device. We will also briefly consider the interface characteristics for these devices.

Peripheral devices are classified as input devices, output devices, or storage devices. As you would expect, input data is data *from* the outside world *into* the CPU, and output data is data moving *from* the CPU *out to* the outside world. Storage devices are, of course, both input and output devices, though not at the same time. If you recall the concept of input process-output from Chapter 1, programs require input, process it, and then produce output. Using a storage device, data output is stored, to be used as input at a future time. In a transaction processing system, for example, the database files are stored on line. When a transaction occurs, the transaction processing program will use input from the new transaction together with data from the database to update the appropriate database records as output. The updated database remains in storage for the next transaction.

Because of the importance of storage, we will begin with a discussion of storage devices. Following that, we will consider various input and output devices.

It should be noted that the technologies used for many peripheral components are very sophisticated; some would even say that these devices operate by magic! You may agree when you see the descriptions of some components. It is not uncommon to have more sophisticated control and technology in a peripheral component than in the computer itself. Perhaps you have wondered how these devices work. Here's your opportunity to find out!

We have not attempted to provide a detailed explanation of every possible peripheral device in a computer system. Instead, we have selected several interesting devices that are representative of a number of technologies.

At the completion of this chapter, you will have been exposed to every important hardware component of the computer system, with the exception of the pieces that tie the components of the computer systems together, and furthermore extend the systems themselves together into networks. You will have seen the role and the inner workings of each component that we have discussed, and you will have seen how the different components fit together to form a complete computer system. You will have a better understanding of how to select particular components to satisfy specific system requirements and of how to determine device capacities and capabilities.

10.1 THE HIERARCHY OF STORAGE

Computer storage is often conceptualized hierarchically, based upon the speed with which data can be accessed. The table in Figure 10.1 shows this hierarchy, together with some typical access times.

At the top of the hierarchy are the CPU registers used to hold data for the short term while processing is taking place. Access to registers is essentially instantaneous, since the registers are actually a part of the CPU. Cache memory, if present, is the fastest memory outside the CPU. You recall from Chapter 8 that cache memory is a small fast memory that is used to hold current data and instructions. The CPU will always attempt to access current instructions and data in cache memory before it looks at conventional memory. There may be as many as three different levels of cache. The CPU accesses the data or instruction in conventional memory if cache memory is not present. Next in the hierarchy is conventional memory. Both conventional and cache memory are referred to as **primary**

FIGURE 10.1

The Storage Hierarchy

Device	Typical access times
CPU registers	0.25 nsec
Cache memory (SRAM)	1-10 nsec
Conventional memory (DRAM)	10-50 nsec
Flash memory	120 μsec
Magnetic disk drive	10-50 msec
Optical disk drive	100-500 msec
Magnetic tape	0.5 and up sec

Increasing storage capacity

Increasing access times

memory. Both provide immediate access to program instructions and data by the CPU and can be used for the execution of programs. The data throughput rate of memory is determined primarily by the capability of the bus and interfaces that connect memory to the CPU. Rates well in excess of 1 GB/sec are common in modern computers.

Below the level of conventional memory, storage in the hierarchy is not immediately available to the CPU, is referred to as **secondary storage**, and is treated as I/O. Data and programs in secondary storage must be copied to primary memory for CPU access.[1] Except for flash memory, access to secondary storage is significantly slower than primary storage. Disks and other secondary storage devices are mechanical in nature, and mechanical devices are of necessity slower than devices that are purely electronic. The location of the desired data is usually not immediately accessible, and the medium must be physically moved to provide access to the correct location. This requires a *seek time*, the time needed to find the desired location. Once the correct data is located, it must be moved into primary memory for use. The throughput rate in Figure 10.1 indicates the speed with which the transfer of data between memory and the I/O device can take place. Most of the access time specified for secondary storage devices consists of seek time. As a result of this access time, even the fastest disks are only about one-millionth as fast as the slowest memory. It should be apparent that a *lot* of CPU instructions can be performed while waiting for a disk transfer to take place.

One important advantage of secondary storage, of course, is its permanence, or lack of volatility. As noted in Chapter 7, RAM data is lost when the power is shut off. Flash memory uses a special type of transistor that can hold data indefinitely without power. The magnetic media used for disk and tape and the optical media used for DVD and CD disks also retain data indefinitely. Secondary storage has the additional advantage that it may be used to store massive amounts of data. Even though RAM is relatively inexpensive, disk and tape storage is much cheaper yet. Large amounts of **online secondary storage** may be provided at low cost. Current hard disks store data at a density of nearly 40 Gbits per square centimeter!

Tape, most flash memory devices, optical disks, and many magnetic disks are designed for easy removal from the computer system, which makes them well suited for backup and for **off-line storage** of data that can be loaded when the data is needed. This provides the additional advantage that secondary storage may be used for offline archiving, for moving data easily from machine to machine, and for offline backup storage. For example, a flash memory card may be used to store digital camera photographs until they are moved to a computer for long term storage; similarly, a removable hard disk can be used to move large amounts of data between computers.

As an increasingly common alternative, data and programs may be stored on a secondary storage device connected to a different computer and accessed through a network connection between the computers. In this context, the computer with secondary storage is sometimes known as a **server** or a **file server**. In fact, the primary purpose of the server may be to act as a storage provider for all the computers on the network. Web services are a common application of this type. Optical disks require little space and can

---

[1] In the earliest days of computing, secondary storage devices, particularly rotating drums (forerunner of the disk), were actually used as memory with direct access to the CPU. To run efficiently, programs had to be designed to minimize the number of rotations of the drum, which meant that the programmer would always attempt to have the next required location be just ahead of where the drum head was at that instant. Those were interesting days for programmers!

store large amounts of data for archiving and installation purposes, with rapid mounting for retrieval when required. A few high-capacity optical disks could store all the medical records and history for a large insurance company, for example. Most modern programs are supplied on DVD or CD-ROM.

Of the various secondary storage components, flash memory and disk devices are the fastest, since data can be accessed randomly. In fact, IBM refers to disks as **direct access storage devices** (**DASDs**). With tape, it may be necessary to search sequentially through a portion of the tape to find the desired data. Also, the disk rotates continuously, while the tape will have to start and stop, and possibly even reverse direction and rewind to find the desired data. These factors mean that tape is inherently slower unless the data is to be read sequentially. This makes tape suitable only for large-scale offsite backup storage where the entire contents of a disk are transferred to tape to protect the data from a potential catastrophe or to meet legal long term data retention requirements. Although magnetic tape storage had large inherent cost and storage capacity advantages in the past, that is no longer the case, and the use of tape is decreasing as businesses replace their equipment with newer technology.

10.2 SOLID STATE MEMORY

Flash memory is nonvolatile electronic integrated circuit memory, similar conceptually to the read-only memory discussed in Chapter 7, but different in technology. The difference makes flash memory suitable for use in situations where traditional ROM would be impractical. Whereas traditional ROM must be read, erased, and written in large blocks of addresses, it is possible to read individual bytes or small blocks of flash memory when necessary. This makes flash memory useful for applications that require random access, particularly those applications where most accesses are reads.

Although read accesses and certain simple overwrite accesses are relatively fast, flash memory must be erased in blocks, so that most write accesses require an additional step that rewrites the unchanged data back to the block. Furthermore, the erase-and-rewrite operation is very slow compared to the read access. Although there is research into other types of nonvolatile memory that might solve this problem, flash memory is generally considered to be impractical as a replacement for conventional RAM, at least for now.

Because of its small size, flash memory is frequently the secondary storage of choice for the memory cards that plug into portable devices such as cell phones, portable music players, and digital cameras. It is also well suited for small, portable "thumb drives" that plug directly into a USB port. These drives are useful for moving files and data from one machine to another and also serve as an inexpensive and convenient backup medium.

Flash memory is more expensive than disk storage at this writing. However, its capacity is rapidly increasing and its price falling. As a result, large capacity flash memory units called "solid-state drives" have appeared on the market and are starting to supplant disk drives as the long-term storage device of choice in computers where less weight, low power consumption, and small size are important. "Solid-state drives" have the additional advantages of being relatively immune to failure due to physical shock and vibration (since they have no moving parts), and generate little heat and no noise. Solid-state drives have not yet reached the huge storage capacities of large disk drives, but their capacity is continually expanding, and is already adequate for many applications.

10.3 MAGNETIC DISKS

A magnetic disk consists of one or more flat, circular platters made of glass, metal, or plastic, and coated with a magnetic substance. Particles within a small area of the magnetic substance can be polarized magnetically in one of two directions with an electromagnet; an electromagnet can also detect the direction of polarization previously recorded. Thus, magnetic polarization can be used to distinguish 1s and 0s. Electromagnetic read/write heads are used for this purpose.

A drive motor rotates the disk platter(s) about its central axis. On most drives, the motor rotates the disk at a fixed speed. An arm has the read/write head mounted at the end. The arm makes it possible for the head to move radially in and out across the surface of the disk. A head motor controls precisely the position of the arm on the disk.

Most **hard disk drives** contain several platters, all mounted on the same axis, with heads on each surface of each platter. The heads move in tandem, so they are positioned over the same point on each surface. Except for the top and bottom, each arm contains two read/write heads, which service the surfaces of two adjoining platters.

With the head in a particular position, it traces out a circle on the disk surface as the disk rotates; this circle is known as a **track**. Since the heads on each surface all line up, the set of tracks for all the surfaces form a **cylinder**. Each track contains one or more blocks of data. On most disks the surface of the disk platter is divided into equally sized pie shape segments, known as **sectors**, although the disks on some large computers divide up the track differently. Each sector on a single track contains one **block** of data, typically 512 bytes, which represents the smallest unit that can be independently read or written. Figure 10.2 shows the layout of a hard disk.

If you assume that the number of bytes in a sector is the same anywhere on the disk, then you can see from the layout that the bits on the disk are more closely packed on the inner tracks than they are on the outer tracks. Regardless of the track, the same angle is swept out when a sector is accessed; thus, the transfer time is kept constant with the motor rotating at a fixed speed. This technique is called **CAV**, for **constant angular velocity**. CAV has the advantage of simplicity and fast access.

It is possible to increase the capacity of the disk by utilizing the space at the outer tracks to pack more bits onto the disk. But this would result in a different number of bytes per sector or a different number of sectors per track depending on which track is being

FIGURE 10.2

A Hard Disk Layout

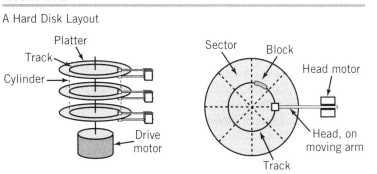

accessed. This would make it more difficult to locate the required sector. Notice, too, that with a constant speed motor, the time to move the head over a pie-shaped sector at the edge is the same as that near the center. If there were more bits packed into the outer tracks, the data would be transferred faster at the edge than at the center. Since the disk controller is designed to expect data at a constant speed, it would seem to be necessary to design the motor so that it would slow down when the head was accessing the outer tracks to keep the data transfer speed constant. In this case, the motor speed would be adjusted such that the speed *along the track* would be constant regardless of the position of the head. This approach is called **CLV**, for **constant linear velocity**. The capacity of a CLV disk with the same diameter and bit density is approximately double that of an equivalent CAV disk. Although CLV technology is commonly used with CDs and DVDs, the design makes it more difficult to access individual blocks of data rapidly, so it is rarely used for hard disks.

As a compromise, modern disk drives divide the disk into a number of zones, typically sixteen. This approach is shown in Figure 10.3. The cylinders in different zones have a different number of sectors but the number of sectors within a particular zone is constant.

FIGURE 10.3

Multiple-Zone Disk Configuration

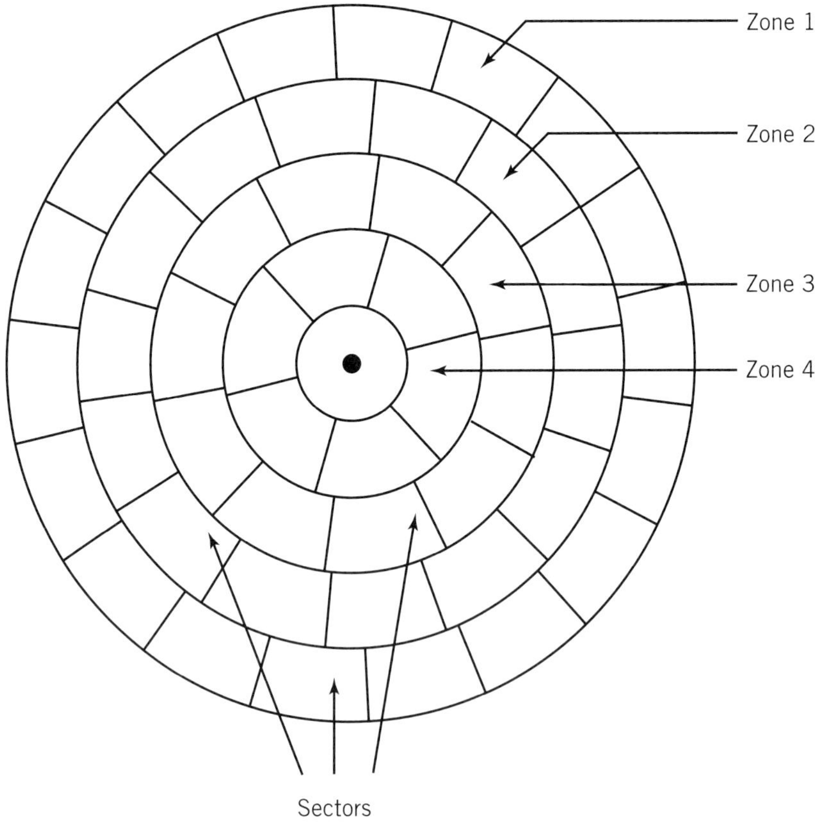

Sectors

Obviously, the largest number of sectors will be in the zone containing the outermost cylinders, Instead of adjusting the motor speed, the disk controller buffers the data rate so that the data rate to the I/O interface is constant, despite the variable data rate between the controller and the disk. Different vendors call this technique **multiple zone recording**, **zone bit recording** (**ZBR**), or **zone-CAV recording** (**Z-CAV**).

The platter on a hard disk drive is made of a rigid material and is precisely mounted. The heads on a hard disk do not touch the surface; rather, they ride on a bed of air a few millionths of an inch above the surface. The location of the heads radially is tightly controlled. This precision allows the disk to rotate at high speed and also allows the designers to locate the tracks very close together. The result is a disk that can store large amounts of data and that retrieves data quickly. A typical hard disk rotates at 5400 revolutions per minute (rpm), 7200 rpm, or even 10,800 rpm.

A photograph of a hard disk assembly showing a disk platter, arm, and read/write head is shown in Figure 10.4. This particular hard disk drive contains three platters and six heads. Only the topmost platter and head are fully visible. The entire assembly is sealed to prevent dirt particles from wedging between the heads and the disk platter, since this situation could easily destroy the drive. Even a particle of cigarette smoke is much larger than the space between the head and the disk. When the disk is stationary, the head rests in a **parked** position on the edge of the drive. The head has an aerodynamic design, which causes it to rise on a cushion of air when the disk platter spins.

Figure 10.5 shows the operation required to locate an individual block of data. First, the arm moves the head from its present track until it is over the desired track. The time that is required to move from one track to another is known as the **seek time**. Since the distance between the two tracks is obviously a factor, the **average seek time** is used as a specification for the disk. Once the head is located over the desired track, the read/write

FIGURE 10.4

A Hard Disk Mechanism

Courtesy Western Digital Corporation.

FIGURE 10.5

Locating a Block of Data: (a) Seek Time, (b) Latency Time, (c) Transfer Time

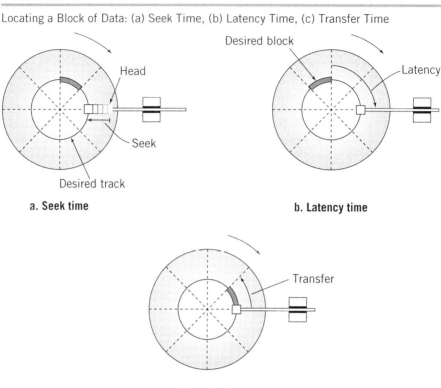

a. Seek time   b. Latency time

c. Transfer time

operation must wait for the disk to rotate to the beginning of the correct sector. The time for this to occur is known as the **rotational latency time**, or sometimes as **rotational delay** or simply **latency time**. The latency time is obviously variable, depending on the position of the disk. As a best case, the head is just about to enter the sector, and the rotational latency time is 0.

At the opposite extreme, the head has just passed the beginning of the sector, and a full rotation is required to reach the beginning of the sector. This time can be calculated from the rotational speed of the disk. Both situations are equally probable. On average, the disk will have to rotate half way to reach the desired block. Thus, the average latency time can be calculated from the rotational speed of the disk as

$$\mathtt{average\ latency} = \frac{1}{2} \times \frac{1}{\mathtt{rotational\ speed}}$$

For a typical hard disk rotating at 3600 revolutions per minute, or 60 revolutions per second, the average latency is

$$\mathtt{average\ latency} = \frac{1}{2} \times \frac{1}{60} = 8.33\ \mathit{milliseconds}$$

Once the sector is reached, the transfer of data can begin. Since the disk is rotating at a fixed speed, the time required to transfer the block, known as **transfer time**, is defined by the number of sectors on a track, since this establishes the percentage of the track that is used by a single data block. The transfer time is defined by

$$\text{transfer time} = \frac{1}{\text{number of sectors} \times \text{rotational speed}}$$

If the hard drive in the example contains 30 sectors per track, the transfer time for a single block would be

$$\text{transfer time} = \frac{1}{30 \times 60} = 0.55 \, milliseconds$$

Figure 10.6 shows a table of typical disks of different types, comparing various characteristics of the disks.

Since the total time required to access a disk block is approximately the sum of these three numbers, a typical disk access might require 20 to 25 msec. To put these speeds in perspective, consider that the typical modern computer can execute an instruction in less than 1 *nanosecond*. Thus, the CPU is capable of executing *millions* of instructions in the time required for a single disk access. This should make it very clear to you that disk I/O is a major bottleneck in processing and also that it is desirable to find other work that the CPU can be doing while a program is waiting for disk I/O to take place.

An expansion of part of a track to show a single data block is shown in Figure 10.7. The block consists of a header, 512 bytes of data, and a footer. An **interblock gap** separates the block from neighboring blocks. Figure 10.8 shows the layout of the header for a Windows-based disk. The track positions, blocks, and headers must be established before the disk can be used. The process to do this is known as **formatting** the disk. Since the header identifier must be a unique pattern of 1s and 0s, the data being stored must be checked by the disk controller to assure that the data pattern does not accidentally match the header identifier. If it does, the pattern stored on the disk is modified in a known way.

The entire track is laid down as a serial stream of bits. During write and read operations, the bytes must be deconstructed into bits and reconstructed.

Because the transfer speed of the disk is not the same as that required to transfer the block to memory, buffering is provided in the disk controller. The buffer is a first-in, first-out buffer, which receives data at one speed and releases it as required at the other speed. Buffer memory also makes it possible to read a group of blocks in advance so that requests for subsequent blocks can be transferred immediately, without waiting for the disk. Most modern disks provide substantial buffers for this purpose.

It is important to realize that the layout of the disk as discussed here does not take into account the structure of the files stored there, nor does it naturally provide a filing system. There is no direct relationship between the physical size of the block and the logical size of the data block or file that it contains, other than that the data must fit into the physical block or provisions made to extend the data to another block. It is also possible to store multiple logical blocks in a single physical block, if they fit.

File organization issues and the allocation of physical blocks for storage are within the domain of the operating system software, not the disk controller. File storage and allocation issues are discussed extensively in Chapter 17.

Before leaving the subject of disks, it will be useful to review briefly some of the material from Chapter 9 to give you an overview of the typical disk I/O operation. You will recall that the CPU initiates a request to the disk controller and that the disk controller does most of the work from that point on. As you now know from this chapter, the disk controller identifies

FIGURE 10.6

Characteristics of Typical Disks

Disk type	Platters/ heads	Cylinders	Sectors per track	Block size	Capacity	Rotational speed	Avg. seek time read/write	Latency	Sustained transfer rate
Professional SCSI	4/8	74,340	avg. 985	512 Bytes	300 GB	15,000 RPM	3.5–4 msec	2 msec	var. 75–120 MB/sec
Desktop	3/6	est. 102,500	variable	512 Bytes	1 TB	7200 RPM	8–9 msec	4.2 msec	115 MB/sec
DVD-ROM	1/1	spiral	variable	2352 Bytes	4.7–9.4 GB	variable, 570–1600 RPM (1x)	100–600 ms	variable	2.5 MB/sec (1x)
Blu-ray DVD	1/1	spiral	variable	2352 Bytes	24–47 GB	variable, 820–2300 RPM (1x)	variable	variable	4.5 MB/sec (1x)

Notes: (1) Hard disk data courtesy of Seagate Technology
(2) (1x) represents standard DVD speed, higher speeds and data rates are possible

FIGURE 10.7

A Single Data Block

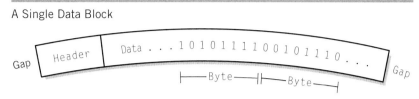

FIGURE 10.8

Header for Windows Disk

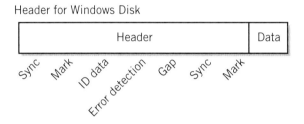

the disk block to be located, moves the head to the correct track, then reads the track data until it encounters the header for the correct block. Assuming that it is performing a read, it then transfers the data from the disk to a buffer. From the buffer, the data is transferred to conventional memory using DMA. Once the DMA transfer is complete, the disk controller notifies the CPU with a completion interrupt.

Disk Arrays

In larger computer environments, with mainframe computers or large PCs that provide program and data storage facilities for a network, it is common to group multiple disks together. Such a grouping of two or more disk drives is called a **disk array** or a **drive array**. A disk array can be used to reduce overall data access time by sharing the data among multiple disks and also to increase system reliability by providing storage redundancy. The assumption made is that the number of blocks to be manipulated at a given time is large enough and important enough to justify the additional effort and additional space requirements. One useful type of disk array is known as **RAID**, which stands for **Redundant Array of Inexpensive Disks**. (Some people say "Redundant Array of Independent Disks").

There are two standard methods of implementing a disk array. One is known as a **mirrored array**, and the other as a **striped array**.

A mirrored array consists of two or more disk drives. In a mirrored array, each disk stores exactly the same data. During reads, alternate blocks of the data are read from different drives, then combined to reassemble the original data. Thus, the access time for a multiblock read is reduced approximately by a factor equal to the number of disk drives in the array. If a read failure occurs in one of the drives, the data can be read from another drive and the bad block marked to prevent future use of that block, increasing system reliability. In critical applications, the data can be read from two, or even three, drives and compared to increase reliability still further. When three drives are used, errors that are not detected by normal read failures can be found using a method known as **majority logic**. This technique is particularly suitable for highly reliable computer systems known as **fault-tolerant computers**. If the data from all three disks is identical, then it is safe to assume that the integrity of the data is acceptable. If the data from one disk differs from the other two, then the majority data is used, and the third disk is flagged as an error.

The striped array uses a slightly different approach. In a striped array, a file segment to be stored is divided into blocks. Different blocks are then written simultaneously to different disks. This effectively multiplies the throughput rate by the number of data disks in the array. A striped array requires a minimum of three disk drives; in the simplest configuration, one disk drive is reserved for error checking. As the write operation is taking place, the system creates a block of parity words from each group of data blocks and stores that on the reserved disk. During read operations, the parity data is used to check the original data.

There are five well-defined RAID standards, labeled RAID 1 through RAID 5, and a number of additional proprietary and nonstandard varieties, including one labeled RAID 0. The most common of these are RAID 0, RAID 1, and RAID 5.

RAID 1 is a mirrored array as described above. RAID 1 provides protection by storing everything at least twice, but offers a substantial performance gain, particularly under heavy data read usage. RAIDs 2, 3, and 4 are arrays that are striped in different ways. Each uses a separate disk for error checking. Since data on every disk must be checked, this can create a roadblock on the single disk that is used for error checking. RAID 5 eases the roadblock by spreading the error-checking blocks over all of the disks.

RAID 0 is not a true RAID, because it provides no redundancy and no inherent error checking. Data is striped across all of the disks, primarily for fast access. However, the lack of redundancy means that a failure of *any* single disk block in the array corrupts all of the data in the system. However, this shortcoming can be overcome with proper backup and with certain types of journaling file systems, which we will discuss in Chapter 17. It is also possible to "nest" RAIDs. For example, we can use a pair of RAID 0 groups inside RAID 1 to achieve mirrored redundancy. The combination is known as RAID 0+1. With or without the additional protection, RAID 0 is sometimes attractive as a low-cost method of achieving high data transfer rates when they are required.

A number of vendors provide RAID controller hardware. particularly for large RAID 5 systems. With RAID controller hardware, RAID processing takes place within the array controller. The array appears as a single large disk drive to the computer. It is also possible to create a RAID using conventional, off-the-shelf disk controllers and operating system software. Although this uses CPU processing time, modern computers have enough spare power to make this a practical solution in many instances. It also reduces the possibility that a single RAID controller can cause the entire array to fail.

10.4 OPTICAL DISK STORAGE

An alternative to magnetic disk storage is optical storage. Optical storage technologies include various types of CDs and DVDs, in read-only, write-once, and read/write forms. Optical disks are portable and are capable of packing a relatively large amount of data into a convenient package. For example, an inexpensive CD-ROM, 12 centimeters in diameter, stores approximately 650 MB, while a Blu-Ray DVD of the same physical size can hold more than 50 GB of data. (There is also a standard for a new optical disk, called HVD, for Holographic Disk, that, when fully developed, is expected to hold more than 1.6 TB, but presently the cost is too high for most uses.) Optical storage serves a different purpose from magnetic disk storage. While magnetic disk storage serves primarily to store, read, and write data for current use, optical storage is intended more for offsite archiving, as well

Layout of a CD-ROM versus a Standard Disk

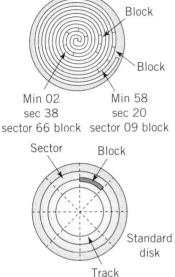

Block

Block

Min 02
sec 38
sector 66 block

Min 58
sec 20
sector 09 block

Sector   Block

Standard
disk

Track

as program and file distribution, although the latter use has declined somewhat due to the growth of the World Wide Web.

CDs and DVDs used for data storage use the same basic disk format as their audio and video equivalents. Within certain file structure limitations, personal computer CD and DVD drives can read and write audio and video CDs and DVDs that will play on home media equipment and vice versa.

Conceptually, **CD-ROM** data storage is similar to magnetic disk: data is stored in blocks on the disk. The blocks can be arranged in files, with a directory structure similar to that of magnetic disks. The technical details are very different, however. Figure 10.9 compares the layout of a CD-ROM to that of a sectored magnetic disk. Rather than concentric tracks, data on a CD-ROM is stored on a single track, approximately three miles long, which spirals from the inside of the disk to the outside. Instead of sectors, the data is stored in linear blocks along the track. It should be remembered that the CD design was originally intended primarily for audio applications, where most data access is sequential, from the start of a musical selection to its finish; thus, a single spiral track was a reasonable decision.

Since the CD format was designed for maximum capacity, the decision was made to pack the bits on the disk as tightly as possible by making each block the same length along the spiral track, regardless of location on the disk. Thus, the disk is read at a constant linear velocity (i.e., CLV), using a variable speed motor to keep the transfer rate constant. Since the angle of a block is smaller on the outer tracks, the disk moves more slowly when outside tracks are being read. This is easily observable if you have access to a portable CD player that allows you to observe the disk as it rotates.

A CD-ROM typically stores 270,000 blocks of data. Each block is 2352 bytes long and holds 2048 bytes of data. In addition, there is a 16-byte header, which provides 12 bytes to locate the start of a block and 4 bytes for block identification. Due to the difficulty of the manufacturing process, errors can occur, so the CD-ROM provides extensive means for correcting the errors. Therefore, each block also provides 288 bytes of an advanced form of parity known as cross-interleaved Reed-Solomon error correcting code. This code repairs not only isolated errors but also groups of errors that might result from a scratch or imperfection on the disk. The resulting total data capacity of a single CD-ROM is approximately 550 MB. The error correction is occasionally omitted for applications where errors can be tolerated, such as audio, which increases the capacity of a CD-ROM to about 630 MB.

Blocks on a CD-ROM are identified by a 4-byte identification code that was inherited from the audio origins of the medium. Three bytes, stored in binary-coded decimal (BCD) format, identify the block by minute, second, and sector. There are 75 sectors per second and 60 seconds per minute. Normally, there are 60 minutes, although this number can be increased to 70 minutes if necessary. This increases the disk capacity to about 315,000 blocks. The fourth byte identifies a mode of operation. Mode 1, the normal data mode, provides the data as we've described, with error correction. Mode 2 increases the capacity by eliminating the error correction. Other modes are provided for special audio and video features. It is possible to mix data, audio, and video on the same disk. Data blocks on CD-ROMs are sometimes called *large frames*.

Data is stored on the disk in the form of pits and lands. These are burned into the surface of the master disk with a high-powered laser. The disk is reproduced mechanically, using a stamping process that is less expensive than the bit-by-bit transfer process required of magnetic media. The disk is protected with a clear coating. Figure 10.10 shows a basic diagram of the read process. A laser beam is reflected off the pitted surface of the disk as a motor rotates the disk. The reflection is used to distinguish between the pits and lands, and these are translated into bits.

On the disk itself, each 2352-byte data block, or large frame, is broken up into 98 24-byte small frames. Bytes are stored using a special 17-bit code for each byte, and each small frame also provides additional error correcting facilities. Translation of the small frames into more recognizable data blocks is performed within the CD-ROM hardware and is invisible to the computer system. The bit-encoding method and additional error correction built into the small frames increases the reliability of the disk still further.

DVD technology is essentially similar to CD-ROM technology. The disk is the same size, and is formatted similarly. However, the use of a laser with a shorter light wavelength (visible red, instead of infrared) allows tighter packing of the disk In addition, the laser can be focused in such a way that two layers of data can be placed on the same side of the disk, one underneath the other. Finally, a different manufacturing technique allows the use of both sides of a DVD. Each layer on a DVD can hold approximately 4.7 GB. If both layers on both sides are used, the DVD capacity is approximately 17 GB. The use of a blue laser extends this capability even further, to approximately 50 GB.

WORM, or **write-once-read-many-times**, disks were originally designed to provide an inexpensive way for archiving data. WORM disks provide high-capacity storage with the convenience of compact size, reasonable cost, and removability. As the name indicates, WORM disks can be written, but, once written, a data block cannot be rewritten. The inability to tamper with the data on a WORM disk has taken on importance in business, where the permanence of many business data archives is required for legal purposes. When a file is updated, it is simply written again to a new block and a new directory entry is provided. Thus, a complete audit trail exists automatically. When the disk is filled, it is simply stored away and a new disk used.

WORM disks work similarly to a CD or DVD. The major difference is that the disk is made of a material that can be blistered by a medium-power laser. Initially, the entire disk is smooth. When data is to be written, the medium-power laser creates tiny blisters in the

FIGURE 10.10

CD-ROM Read Process

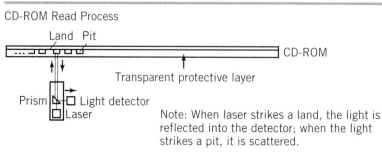

Note: When laser strikes a land, the light is reflected into the detector; when the light strikes a pit, it is scattered.

appropriate locations. These correspond to the pits in a normal CD-ROM. The WORM disk is read with a separate low-power laser in the same way as a CD-ROM.

This blister technology is used in various CD and DVD formats, called CD-R, DVD-R, and DVD+R. Additionally, there are rewriteable versions of this technology. These are known as CD-RW, DVD-RW, DVD+RW, DVD-RAM, and DVD+RAMBD-RE. There are file compatibility issues between the different WORM and rewriteable CD and DVD formats. Some drives will read every format; others will only read some of the formats.

10.5 MAGNETIC TAPE

Magnetic tape is used by many companies for backups and archives in large computer systems. Like other magnetic media, tape is nonvolatile, and the data can be stored indefinitely. Note that tape is a sequential medium, which makes it impractical for random access tasks. Generally, full system backups are made to tape and moved to offsite locations for long term storage.

There are several basic tape layouts, but all current formats are cartridge-based mechanisms. Regardless of type, the tape cartridge is removable from the tape drive for offline storage. When the tape is in the tape drive, ready for operation, it is said to be **mounted**. Tape cartridges have the major advantage of convenience. They are easy to mount and dismount, and small and easy to store. Current tape cartridges can store as much as 1.6 TB of compressed data or 800 GB of uncompressed data. Cartridges with uncompressed capacities as large as 4 TB are currently in development.

There are two main categories of data cartridge formats in use. The LTO (*linear tape open*) formats are representative of **linear recording cartridges**. An LTO format data cartridge is shown in Figure 10.11. The LTO format typically holds up to 820 meters of

FIGURE 10.11

Tape Cartridge with Top Removed

Image from Wikipedia, http://en.wikipedia.org/wiki/File:LTO2-cart-wo-top-shell.jpg

FIGURE 10.12

Data Cartridge Formats

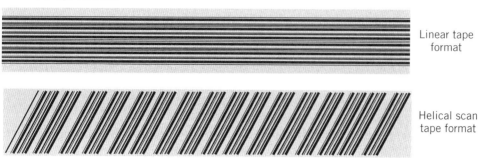

Linear tape
format

Helical scan
tape format

one-half inch wide tape in a 102 mm × 105 mm × 21.5 mm cartridge. The technique used for storage and retrieval is called **data streaming**. The cartridge tape is divided longitudinally into many tracks, currently as many as 886. The tape mechanism writes and reads the bits longitudinally, along the length of one group of tracks. At each end, the tape reverses, and the next group of tracks are written or read. Data is usually stored on the tape starting with the centermost track and moving outward toward the edge of the tape. Error correction is built into the system, and WORM archiving is also available as an option.

An alternative data cartridge format is based on the technology that was originally developed for videotape. These are called **helical scan cartridges**. The data on helical scan cartridges is very tightly packed, using a read/write head that rotates at a high speed to pack the tape more tightly with data. This results in a track that is made up of diagonal lines across the width of the tape. There are two different helical scan cartridges in common use. The smaller AIT (*advanced intelligent* format) uses 8-mm wide tape in tape lengths of up to 246 meters, with a current maximum uncompressed capacity of 400 GB in a cartridge 95 mm × 62.5 × 15 mm. The larger SAIT (*super-AIT*) cartridge contains up to 640 meters of one-half inch wide tape, with a current maximum uncompressed capacity of 800 GB. The SAIT cartridge is the same size as the LTO cartridge, but the two types of cartridge are not interchangeable.

Figure 10.12 shows the track layouts for both types of cartridges.

10.6 DISPLAYS

As viewed by the user, a display is an image made up of thousands of individual **pixels**, or picture elements, arranged to make up a large rectangular screen. Each pixel is a tiny square on the display. The layout for a display is shown in Figure 10.13. Older display screens have a horizontal to vertical ratio of 4:3. More recent displays are typically 16:9, described as "widescreen". A typical 4:3 screen is made up of 768 rows of 1024 pixels each, known as a 1024 × 768 pixel screen. Screens with resolutions of 1280 × 1024 pixels, or higher have also become common, especially on physically larger screens. Typical 16:9 screens are 1280 × 720 or 1920 × 1080.

Displays are specified by their screen sizes are measured diagonally. Figure 10.14 shows the relationship between the horizontal, vertical, and diagonal dimensions. The **resolution** of the screen is specified either as the size of an individual pixel or as the number of pixels per inch. The pixel size for a typical 15.4-inch wide laptop screen with 1280 × 720 pixel

FIGURE 10.13

Layout for a Display

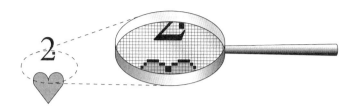

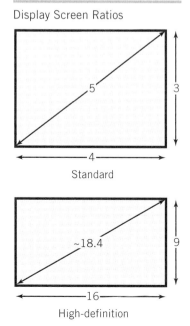

resolution is approximately 0.01 inch square, or about 100 pixels per inch resolution. Since the resolution essentially specifies the minimum identifiable object size capability of the monitor, the larger the number of pixels per inch, the better.

As we noted in Chapter 4, each individual pixel represents a shade of gray (on a monochrome screen) or a color. A color pixel is actually made up of a mixture of different intensities of red, green, and blue (RGB). We could represent a black-and-white image with 1 bit per pixel (for example, on for white, off for black), but, more typically, a color display would present at least 256 colors, and normally many more. It takes 2 bytes per pixel to represent a 65,536-color image, considered the minimum acceptable for Web use. A more sophisticated system would use 8 bits per color, or 24 bits in all. Such a system can present 256 × 256 × 256, or more than 16 million, different colors on the screen and is sometimes described as a **true color** system. There are even a few 30-bit and 36-bit systems.

FIGURE 10.14

Display Screen Ratios

Even 16 bits per pixel requires a substantial amount of video memory. To store a single 1024-pixel by 768-pixel graphic image requires 1.55 MB of memory. A 24-bit-per-pixel image of the same size would require over 2.3 MB.

With 8 bits, there is no way to divide the bits to represent reds, blues, and greens equally. Instead, 256 arbitrary combinations of red, blue, and green are chosen from a larger palette of colors. The 256 colors might be chosen by the artist who created the image. More commonly, a default color scheme is used. Originally designed by Netscape for its Web browser, the default color scheme presents a reasonably uniform selection of colors ranging from black to white. Each selected color is represented by a red value, a green value, and a blue value that together will present the selected color on the screen. Most commonly, the system will use 1 byte for each color, providing an overall palette of sixteen million colors to choose from.

Each pixel value is represented by a value between 0 and 255, representing the color for that pixel. A color transformation table, also known as a palette table, holds the RGB values for each of the 256 possible colors. A few rows of a color transformation table are shown in Figure 10.15. To display a pixel on the screen, the system transforms the pixel color to a screen color by reading the RGB values that correspond to the particular pixel value from the table. The RGB colors are

FIGURE 10.15

Use of a Color Transformation Table

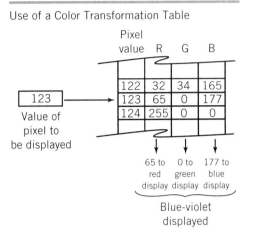

then sent to the screen for display. Although this transformation requires an extra step, the task is performed in special circuitry on the video card and is not difficult to implement.

Transformation is also required for a display of sixty-four thousand colors, which uses 16 bits per pixel, however, a 24-bit color can be divided equally into three bytes, one for each color, so no transformation table is required.

In a modern system nearly all output, including text data, is presented graphically. For graphical output, values for each pixel on the screen are produced by a program, then stored in a display memory. Usually, the display memory is separately associated directly with a graphics display controller. On inexpensive personal computers, video memory is sometimes allocated as part of the regular memory.

The actual display is produced by scanning and displaying each pixel, one row at a time, from left to right, top to bottom. This method of displaying all the pixels is known as a **raster scan**. It is essentially identical to the way that television pictures are generated. When one row has been displayed, the scanner returns to the left edge and scans the succeeding row. This is done for each row, from top to bottom. This process is repeated more than thirty times a second. Most display monitors scan each row in turn, row 1, row 2, row 3, and so on. Some monitors **interlace** the display, by displaying the odd rows, row 1, row 3, row 5, and so on, and then coming back and displaying the even rows. Interlacing the rows is less demanding on the monitor, since each row is only displayed half as often, but results in flickering that is annoying to some users. Figure 10.16 shows the difference between interlaced and noninterlaced displays. Noninterlaced displays are also

FIGURE 10.16

Interlaced versus Progressive Scan Raster Screen

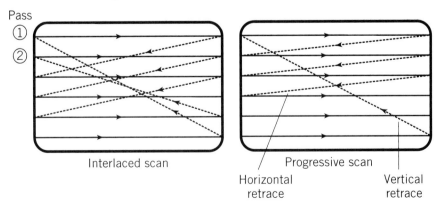

sometimes called **progressive scan displays**. Although some TV displays are interlaced, most computer display monitors are noninterlaced,

An alternative to raster scan is **vector scan**, in which pixels are displayed in whatever order is necessary to trace out a particular image. Vector scan could trace a character, for example, by following the outline of the character. Vector scan is obviously not suitable for bit map graphics, but can be used with object graphics images, such as those used for CAD/CAM applications. Generating vector scan images on a display screen is electronically much more difficult and expensive than producing raster scans, consequently, raster scans are used almost universally today for display. Vector scans are sometimes used when printing object graphics-based drawings to a plotter.

Figure 10.17 is a simplified diagram of the process that is necessary to produce a raster scan image. Each value to be displayed is read from the appropriate location in video memory in synchronization with its appearance on the screen. Although a palette table is shown in the figure, a 3-byte value would be read directly from video memory to the RGB display inputs when 24-bit color is used. A scan generator controls both the memory scanner and the video scanner that locates the pixel on the display screen. For normal images displayed graphically on a noninterlaced monitor, the values are stored consecutively, row by row, so that each traverse through memory corresponds to a single complete scan of the image. Video memory is designed so that changes in the image can be made concurrently by the CPU while the display process is taking place. The display process is illustrated with a simple example.

FIGURE 10.17

Diagram of Raster Screen Generation Process

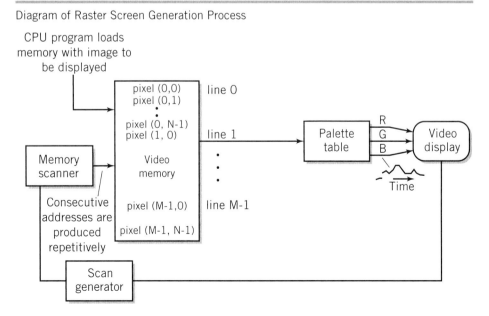

EXAMPLE

Suppose our system has a 7-pixel by 5-pixel display monitor. On that monitor we wish to display an "X". The desired output is shown in Figure 10.18a. The different pixels on the "X" are to be colored as shown in the figure.

To support the display, our system provides 35 bytes of video memory. Each byte corresponds to one location. Since each location holds 1 byte, the system supports up to 256 different colors. The display memory is shown in Figure 10.18b. The memory is the usual type of linear memory, but we have redrawn it so that you can see more easily the relationship between the memory and the display. If you look carefully, you can see the "X" in this figure. Initially, the video memory was set to all zeros, where zero represents the background color. Presumably, a program in the CPU has since entered the data that represents the figure "X" to be currently displayed.

The table in Figure 10.18c represents the color translation palette for this example. The table has a red, blue, and green column for each entry. In our system, each RGB entry in the table holds a 6-bit number. This means that this system can produce $64 \times 64 \times 64 = 256K$ different colors. The RGB value (0, 0, 0) would produce black, the value (63, 0, 0) would produce pure red (i.e., maximum red, no green, no blue), and (63, 63, 63) would produce white. In this case, you can see from the table that the background color for the screen is white.

The display controller reads each memory location in turn, looks up the three values in the palette table, and displays the corresponding pixel on the screen. This process repeats indefinitely. The red, blue, and green signals that go to the video system as a result of the display operation are shown in Figure 10.18d. This pattern will be repeated over and over again, at least thirty times a second, until the display is changed. Notice that the red and blue signals are identical, since red and blue always appear together in maroon and are both totally absent from green.

As noted, the method just described is used for graphical images. Since characters are also represented by displaying pixels, most modern computers also treat character output graphically; the popularity of what-you-see-is-what-you-get (WYSIWYG) output requires the ready availability of different fonts and flexibility in layout on the screen. Both these requirements are easily met with the graphical techniques already described.

Some systems, particularly older systems, provide an additional method for dedicated character output. In this method, usually called **text mode**, the pixels of the display screen are divided into blocks, often twenty-five rows of eighty, although other values are often also provided. Each block will display a single ASCII character. Instead of storing individual pixels, the video memory is used to store the ASCII values of the characters to be displayed. Many PCs start up in text mode.

Pixels are displayed on the screen in the usual way. To convert the characters to a raster scan line, the display controller provides a set of character-to-pixel tables, stored in ROM. As each character is read from memory, the appropriate pixels are pulled from the table and output to the screen. Most controllers limit the display output to the fonts that are provided in ROM. Some controllers also provide video memory that can be used to download additional character conversion tables. Most systems also include an ASCII extension set that provides simple graphical shapes for drawing lines and boxes, as well as facilities for creating underlines, blinking characters, and color changes of the character or the block. Note that in text mode it is not possible to alter individual pixels. All addressing of the screen must be performed by block.

FIGURE 10.18

Display Example: (a) Desired Display, (b) Video Memory
Contents, (c) Color Palette Table, (d) Color Signals

a. Desired
display

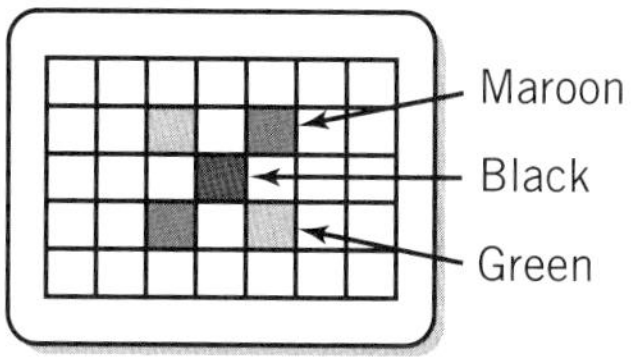

— Maroon

— Black

— Green

b. Video
memory
contents

0	1	2	3	4	5	6	Address
0	0	0	0	0	0	0	Value

7	8	9	10	11	12	13	Address
0	0	17	0	123	0	0	Value

14	15	16	17	18	19	20	Address
0	0	0	255	0	0	0	Value

21	22	23	24	25	26	27	Address
0	0	123	0	17	0	0	Value

28	29	30	31	32	33	34	Address
0	0	0	0	0	0	0	Value

c. Color
palette
table

Pixel value	Red	Green	Blue
0	63	63	63
...			
17	0	63	0
...			
123	31	0	31
...			
255	0	0	0

d. Color
signals

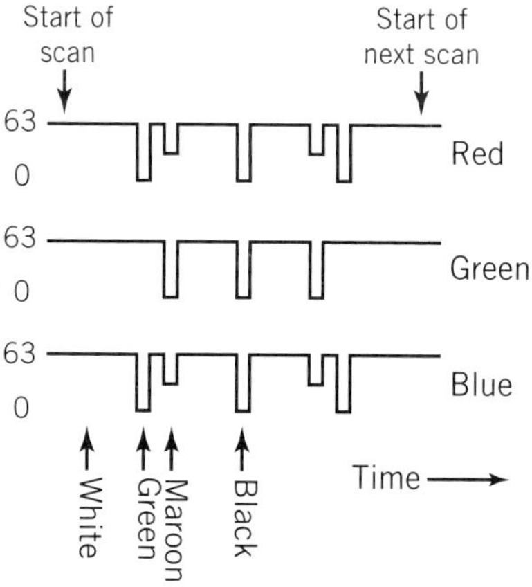

Start of
scan

Start of
next scan

63

0

Red

63

0

Green

63

0

Blue

White
Maroon
Green
Black

Time →

Every pixel in a graphics display must be stored and manipulated individually; therefore, the requirements for a graphic display are much more stringent than those for a character display. Also, text mode display has the advantage that it requires significantly less memory than does graphics mode. As the price of memory has declined rapidly, this has become less of an issue. Text mode has one important additional advantage, however. Text data can be transmitted to a terminal located remotely from the computer much more compactly and efficiently in text mode than in graphics mode. It is obviously easier to transmit a single character than the dozens of pixels that make up the image of that character. Because of this, some terminals are still character based, particularly in business environments where most of the data is alphanumeric.

A compromise between the simplicity of text mode and the elegance of graphics mode is to transmit the data using an object-based description language such as PostScript. Fonts described in this way are known as **outline fonts**. By contrast, those fonts that are described by laying out the detailed pixel diagram for the characters are known as **bitmapped fonts**. Outline fonts and graphics described by page description languages have the additional advantage that they may be scaled easily to different sizes and rotated to different angles. The graphic image is then reconstructed at the terminal by translation software that is built into the display controller. This method is particularly amenable to printers and to Postscript displays used for precision graphical and layout work. The methods of managing graphical images are explored more fully in Chapter 16.

Liquid Crystal Display Technology

Although CRT display technology is still in use, liquid crystal display technology has become the prevalent means of displaying images. A diagram of a **liquid crystal display (LCD)** is shown in Figure 10.19. A fluorescent light or LED panel, located behind the display, produces white light. A polarizing filter in front of the light panel polarizes the

FIGURE 10.19

Liquid Crystal Display

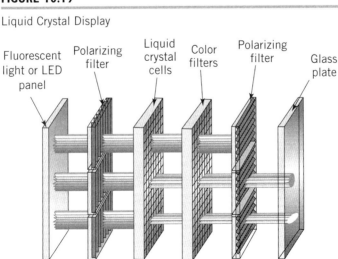

light so that most of it is polarized in one direction. The polarized light then passes through a matrix of liquid crystal cells. In a color display, there are three cells positioned properly for each pixel. When an electrical current is applied to one of these cells, the molecules in the cell spiral. The strongest charge will cause the molecules to spiral 90 degrees. Since the light is passed through the crystal, its polarization will change, the amount depending on the strength of the electrical current applied.

Therefore, the light coming out of the crystal is now polarized in different directions, depending on the strength of the current that was applied to the crystal. The light is now passed through a red, blue, or green color filter and through a second polarizing filter. Because a polarizing filter blocks all light that is polarized perpendicular to its preferred direction, the second filter will only pass through the light that is polarized in the correct direction. Therefore, the brightness of the light is proportional to the amount of polarization twist that was applied by the liquid crystal's spiral.

There are several different ways of applying the electric current to the crystal. In an **active matrix** display, the display panel contains one transistor for each cell in the matrix. This guarantees that each cell will receive a strong charge, but is also expensive and difficult to manufacture. (Remember that even one imperfect cell will be apparent to the viewer!) A less expensive way provides a single transistor for each row and column of the matrix and activates each cell, one at a time, repetitively, using a scan pattern. This type of panel is known as a **passive matrix** display. The charge is applied for less time and is therefore lower. The result is a dimmer picture. Most modern LCD displays use the active matrix approach.

LCD panels have the advantage of bright images, no flicker, low power consumption, and thinness, so they are ideal for laptop computers. They are also used in most desktop displays. Because they are essentially flat, they can be placed anywhere. The same technology is also used for large-screen computer projectors.

CRT Display Technology

With CRT technology, the image is produced on the face of a **cathode ray tube (CRT)**, using a methodology similar to that used for older television receivers. A diagram of a color cathode ray tube is shown in Figure 10.20. Three **electron guns** within the tube shoot beams of electrons from the back of the tube. There is a gun for each of the primary colors, red, blue, and green. A high voltage applied to the inside of the face of the tube attracts the beams to the face. The face of the tube is painted with tiny dots or thin stripes of **phosphors**, which glow when struck by electrons. There are phosphors that glow red, blue, and green. A **shadow mask** in the tube is designed such that electrons from each gun can strike only phosphors of the matching color. The strength of the beams varies depending on the color and brightness of the point being displayed. The stronger the beam for a particular color, the brighter that color appears on the screen.

The three beams of electrons are *deflected* both horizontally and vertically by a pair of electromagnetic coils, so that the beam scans across the screen and top to bottom, to form the scan pattern that you already saw in Figure 10.16. Monochrome video monitors work identically, except that only a single gun is required, the phosphor is white, yellow, or green, and no shadow mask is required.

FIGURE 10.20

Diagram of a CRT

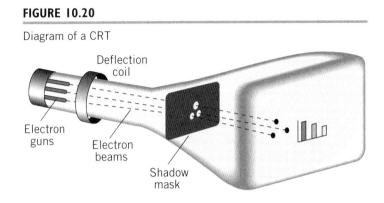

OLED Display Technology

OLED (Organic Light-Emitting Diode) technology is a new screen technology that is poised to supplement or replace LCD technology in display monitors. OLED technology offers an image that is brighter, with colors that are more vivid and with vastly improved contrast. Despite the improved image, the OLED panel consumes less power, with a package that is even thinner than current flat screen monitors. LCD technology is *passive* in the sense that light is generated by a backlight; the light is selectively blocked by the LCD cells in the panel. Leakage in the cells limits the level of darkness that can be achieved and the maximum brightness is limited by the brightness of the backlight.

In contrast, OLED technology is *active*. OLED technology consists of a thin display panel that contains red, green, and blue LEDs for each pixel with transistors for each LED that generate electrical current to light the LED. The light output is produced directly by these LEDs. The brightness of a pixel is determined by the amount of current supplied by the transistor, which in turn is determined by an input signal indicating the desired level of brightness. The simplicity of the panel, combined with the lack of need for a backlight, result in the thinness of the panel. Sony and Samsung have both demonstrated OLED panels less than 3 mm thick.

10.7 PRINTERS

Earlier printers were derived from typewriters. They used formed characters that were mounted at the ends of arms, on wheels shaped like a daisy, on chains, or on spheres. Printing resulted from the hammer-like physical impact of the character through an inked ribbon onto paper. These printers were difficult to maintain and were incapable of generating any character or graphical image that was not provided in the set of formed characters. Later **impact printers** used pins that were selectively employed to generate dot matrix representations of the characters on the page. These printers were known as *dot matrix* printers; in addition to the standard characters, they were also capable of printing simple geometric shapes. Impact printers have mostly disappeared from use.

Except for some commercial printing of items such as books, magazines, and newspapers, nearly all modern printing is done using nonimpact technologies. This is true

FIGURE 10.21

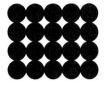

Creating a Gray Scale

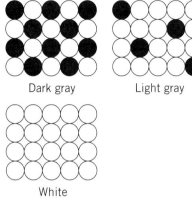

| Black | Dark gray | Light gray |

White

regardless of the size of the system, the quantity of printing, or the capacity of the printer.[2] Single-color (usually black and white) printers normally use **laser**, or **inkjet** printing technology. Low-cost color printing also uses inkjet technology. More expensive color printing uses **thermal wax transfer** or **dye sublimation**, inkjet, or laser technology.

The impression on the paper is sprayed at the paper or laid down on the paper. Like displays, printer output can be character based or graphics based. Most printers have built-in character printing capability and can also download fonts. Nonetheless, much of the output from modern computers is graphics based, even when text is being printed, since graphics output produces more flexibility. The output to many printers takes the form of graphical bitmaps that represent the required pixels directly. Some printers have built-in computing capability and can accept data in the form of a page description language, predominantly Adobe **PostScript** or *PCL*, an industry standard print command language originally developed by HP. The controller in the printer can then convert from the page description language to the bitmap within the printer itself. Memory is provided within the printer to hold the bitmapped image while it is being printed.

Nearly all modern computer printers produce their output as a combination of dots, similar in style to the pixels used in displays. There are two major differences between the dots used in printers and the pixels used in displays. First, the number of dots per inch printed is generally much higher than the number of pixels per inch displayed. The number of pixels displayed usually ranges between about 70 and 150 per inch. Typical printers specify 600, 1200, or even 2400 dots per inch.

This difference in resolution is partially compensated for by the second major difference: the dots produced by most printers are either off or on. A few printers can vary the size of the dots somewhat, but, in general, the intensity, or brightness, of the dots is fixed, unlike the pixels in a display, which can take on an infinite range of brightnesses. Thus, to create a gray scale or color scale, it is necessary to congregate groups of dots into a single equivalent point and print different numbers of them to approximate different color intensities. An example of this is shown in Figure 10.21.

Laser Printers

Today, the prevalent form of printing for most applications is laser printing. Laser printing is derived from xerography. The major difference is that the image is produced electronically

---

[2]Even most modern commercial printing uses a nonimpact technique called *offset printing* that is based on contact between a rubber mat containing a print image and the paper, a method similar in many respects to laser printing. The impact printing press technology that you see in old movies is called *letterpress* printing.

FIGURE 10.22

Operation of a Laser Printer

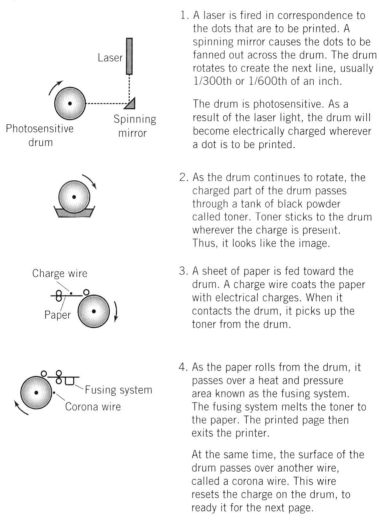

1. A laser is fired in correspondence to the dots that are to be printed. A spinning mirror causes the dots to be fanned out across the drum. The drum rotates to create the next line, usually 1/300th or 1/600th of an inch.

   The drum is photosensitive. As a result of the laser light, the drum will become electrically charged wherever a dot is to be printed.

2. As the drum continues to rotate, the charged part of the drum passes through a tank of black powder called toner. Toner sticks to the drum wherever the charge is present. Thus, it looks like the image.

3. A sheet of paper is fed toward the drum. A charge wire coats the paper with electrical charges. When it contacts the drum, it picks up the toner from the drum.

4. As the paper rolls from the drum, it passes over a heat and pressure area known as the fusing system. The fusing system melts the toner to the paper. The printed page then exits the printer.

   At the same time, the surface of the drum passes over another wire, called a corona wire. This wire resets the charge on the drum, to ready it for the next page.

from the computer using a laser or light-emitting diodes, rather than scanning a real image with a bright light, as in a copy machine. A description of the steps in the operation of a laser printer is shown in Figure 10.22. Color images are produced by printing the sheet four times with different colored toners.

Inkjet Printers

Inkjet printers operate on a simple mechanism that also has the advantages of small size and economy. Despite their simplicity, inkjet printers with high-quality inks are capable of photographic quality color output. Mechanically, the inkjet printer consists of a print cartridge that moves across the page to print a number of rows of dots, and mechanical rollers that move the page downward to print successive rows.

The inkjet print cartridge contains a reservoir of ink and a column of tiny nozzles, so that several rows can be printed at once. Each nozzle is smaller than the width of a human hair. A dot is produced by heating the ink behind a nozzle. When the ink is boiled it sprays a tiny droplet of ink toward the paper. The volume of each droplet is about one-millionth the volume of the drop from an eyedropper of water! Some printers use a vibrating piezo-crystal instead of heat to produce the ink droplets. Multiple reservoirs of ink make it possible to print multiple colors.

Thermal Wax Transfer and Dye Sublimation Printers

For the highest quality color images, more specialized methods are required. The preferred methods are thermal wax transfer and dye sublimation. The mechanisms for both types are similar. The paper is fed into the printer and clamped against a drum. A print head provides a row of dot-sized heating elements. Between the paper and the print head, the printer feeds a roll of film that is impregnated with either colored wax or dye. The film is made up of page-sized sections of magenta, cyan, and yellow colors; sometimes an additional section of black is also included. Each rotation of the drum exposes the paper to a different color. The heat from the print head melts the wax or dye onto the paper.

Thermal wax can be applied to ordinary paper. To improve quality, some printers precoat the paper with clear wax. This compensates for slight imperfections in the paper so that the wax may be applied more uniformly. Different colors are produced in the same way that black-and-white printers produce gray scales.

The dye sublimation technique differs slightly, in that transparent dyes diffuse in the paper, so that the dots of color actually blend. Furthermore, it is possible to control the amount of dye by adjusting the temperature of individual print head elements. Thus, dye sublimation can print continuous color tones. Unfortunately, the dye sublimation technique also requires higher temperatures, therefore, special paper must be used.

10.8 USER INPUT DEVICES

Keyboards and Pointing Devices

Users use a variety of devices to interact with the computer, but most commonly, the modern user interface is based upon a keyboard and a pointing device. Keyboards consist of a number of switches and a keyboard controller. The keyboard controller is built into the keyboard itself. There are several different types of switches in use, including capacitive, magnetic, and mechanical. In most environments, the type of switch used is not important. Different types of switches feel differently when used. Some switches are more suitable than others for environments where dust or electrical sparks or the need for ultra-high reliability are a problem. When a key is pushed, a signal called a scan code is sent to the controller. A different scan code is sent when the key is released. This is true for every key on the keyboard, including special keys such as *Control, Alt*, and *Shift* keys. The use of two scan codes allows keys to be used in combination, since the controller is able to tell whether a key is being held down while another key is struck. The controller can also determine when a key is to cause a repeated action.

If the keyboard is part of a terminal, the scan codes are converted to ASCII, Unicode, or EBCDIC (see Chapter 4 if you need a reminder) and sent to the computer, usually via a serial port. Keyboards local to a computer such as a PC interrupt the computer directly. The scan codes are converted to ASCII or Unicode by software in the computer. This latter method allows more flexibility in remapping the keyboard for different languages and keyboard layouts.

Modern graphical user interfaces also require the use of a pointer device as input to locate and move a cursor on the display screen. The best known pointer device is a mouse, but there are other pointer devices in use, including light pens, touch screens, and graphics tablets, as well as the special pointer devices used for interfacing with computer games.

The simplest device is the mechanical mouse. As the mouse is moved across a surface, the roller ball protruding from bottom of the mouse also moves. Two wheels, mounted at a 90-degree angle from each other, touch the roller ball, and move with it. These wheels are called **encoders**. As the encoders move, they generate a series of pulses. The number of pulses corresponds to the distance that the mouse was moved. One encoder records movement forward and backward; the other records sideway motion. The pulses are sent to a program in the computer to interpret the current location of a cursor. Some encoders use a tiny light and sensor to create the pulses, others use a tiny mechanical switch, but the method used is not important. Desktop game pointing devices and trackballs work similarly. Space-based game controllers, such as the Nintendo Wii remote, use accelerometers to detect movement in all three dimensions; software in the game console then uses that information to perform the appropriate action upon the object of interest.

Light pens are used differently and work differently. A light pen is pointed at the screen to identify a position on the screen. By moving the pen around the screen, a cursor can be made to follow the pen. The light pen can be used to point to a target, such as a control button on the screen, and can also be used as a drawing tool. The light pen is not actually capable of telling the system its position. Instead, the software program that is used with the light pen rapidly generates pixels of light on the display screen at known locations in the area where the light pen is believed to be pointing. The light pen has a photodetector that can respond to the point of light on the screen, so when the point on the screen that corresponds to the light pen is lit, the light pen is activated, which notifies the program that the current location is correct.

Graphics tablets use a variety of techniques, including pressure-sensitive sensors, optical sensors, magnetic sensors, and capacitive sensors to determine the location of a pen on the pad. Some techniques require the use of a special pen, which is attached to the tablet, while others allow the use of any pointed object, such as a wooden pencil, with or without lead, or even a finger. The resolution and accuracy of graphics tablets depends on the technique employed. Graphics tablets can be used as mouse replacements, but are particularly suited for drawing. A similar mechanism is used for the touch pads commonly found on laptop computers.

Touch screens provide a capability similar to that of graphics tablets, but with the sensing mechanism attached directly to the display screen, allowing the user to point directly to an object on the screen. Touch screens are particularly popular on devices such as PDAs, cell phones, portable game consoles, and portable music and video players. They are also available on many commercial devices that require user interaction with the public, such as store self-checkout machines and information kiosks, as well as some personal computers. A number of different technologies can be used to detect the point of touch.

These technologies differ in cost, accuracy, and durability. Common technologies include resistive, capacitive, and surface acoustic wave. Some touch screens are capable of detecting multiple touch points.

Scanners

Scanners are the primary means used to input paper images. Although video frame grabbers and television cameras can also be used for this purpose, scanners are generally less expensive and more convenient.

There are three primary types of scanners, flatbed scanners, sheet-fed scanners, and handheld scanners, but all three work similarly and differ only in the way the scan element is moved with respect to the paper. In a flatbed scanner, the paper is placed on a glass window, while the scan element moves down the page, much like a copy machine. In a sheet-fed scanner, a single page of paper is propelled through the mechanism with rollers; the scan element is stationary. Handheld scanners are propelled by the user over the page.

Regardless of which means is used, the basic operation is the same. The scanning mechanism consists of a light source and a row of light sensors. As the light is reflected from individual points on the page, it is received by the light sensors and translated to digital signals that correspond to the brightness of each point. Color filters can be used to produce color images, either by providing multiple sensors or by scanning the image three times with a separate color filter for each pass. The resolution of scanners is similar to that of printers, approximately 600–2400 points per inch.

Multimedia Devices

Despite its importance in modern systems, not much needs to be said about this topic. Most modern personal and workstation computers provide input ports with an audio analog-to-digital converter for microphones and other audio input equipment, as well as an output converter and speakers and headphone jacks for audio output. USB ports can also be used for this equipment and for computer-compatible video cameras, TV tuners, and other multimedia devices.

10.9 NETWORK COMMUNICATION DEVICES

It is impossible to overemphasize the fact that, from the perspective of a computer, a network is simply another I/O device, a device that, like a disk, offers input to applications on the computer and receives output from applications on the computer. Like other I/O devices, there is a controller, in this case a **network interface unit (NIU) controller** or **network interface card (NIC)** that handles the physical characteristics of the connection and one or more I/O drivers that manage and steer input data, output data, and interrupts.

There are a number of different types of network interfaces, with different network interface controllers for each. On large mainframe systems, there may be network interface controllers for a variety of different network connections, including various flavors of Ethernet, FDDI fiber, token-ring, and other types. On most systems, the standard connection is to an Ethernet network. Nearly every current computer system is supplied with one or more Ethernet network interface cards as a basic part of the system. Wireless Ethernet and Bluetooth network interface cards are also commonplace.

The interface between a computer and a network is more complicated than that for most other I/O peripherals. Data must be formatted in specific ways to communicate successfully with a wide range of application and system software located on other computers. The computer also must be able to address a large number of devices individually, specifically, every other computer connected to the network, whether connected directly to the local network, or indirectly connected through the Internet. Unlike many device controllers, NICs must be capable of accepting requests and data from the network, independent of the computer, and must be able to provide interrupt notification to the computer. Security of communication is an important concern, whereas local devices normally require only minimal security considerations. Many of these concerns are handled with protocol software in the operating system. The NIC is responsible only for the electrical signals that connect the computer to the network, either directly or through a communication channel, and for the protocols, implemented in hardware, that define the specific rules of communication for the network. These protocols are called **medium access control** protocols, or **MACs**. We note in passing that every NIC and network device throughout the world has a unique address called a MAC address that can be used to identify the specific device and its characteristics. The MAC address is sometimes used by cable and DSL vendors to restrict network access to a specific device.

The hardware aspects of the network interface are considered more fully in Chapter 14. A deeper look at the fundamentals of networking infrastructure, including types of networks, the nature of communication channels, media, the movement of data across a network, protocols, and the operation of the Internet, is described in Chapters 12 and 13.

SUMMARY AND REVIEW

This chapter provides an overview of the workings of the most common computer peripheral devices. Peripheral devices are classified as input devices, output devices, and storage devices. We began by demonstrating that storage can be thought of hierarchically, with registers the most immediately available form of storage, followed by memory, and then the various peripheral devices. We discussed the trade-offs that make each form desirable for some purposes.

Following this general introduction, we introduced flash memory, and discussed its applications, strengths, and weaknesses.

Next, we showed the layout and explained the operation of various forms of disk, including hard magnetic and optical. We showed how the performance factors, capacity and various speed measures, are obtained. For each device we showed how a block is identified and located. We noted the difference between the concentric tracks used on magnetic disks and the spiral tracks used on many optical disks. We explained the difference between CAV and CLV operation. The discussion of disks is followed by a similar discussion for magnetic tape.

The display is the most important output device. We explained the process used to produce a display, from the bytes in memory that represent individual pixels or characters to the actual output on a screen. We showed that there are two different forms of output, character and graphic. We showed how colors are determined for the display. We also showed the basic technology for the two methods that are used to produce an image, video on a CRT, and liquid crystal display.

There are a number of different technologies used in printers. We introduced laser printers, inkjet printers, and thermal transfer printers as representative of the most important current technologies.

The chapter continues with a brief discussion of keyboards, various pointer devices, scanners, and multimedia devices that are used for input. We conclude with a brief consideration of the network as an input/output device, a discussion to be expanded greatly in later chapters.

FOR FURTHER READING

Much of the discussion in this chapter reviews material that you have seen before, probably in an introduction to computers course. Any good introductory textbook will also serve as a further reference for this chapter. In addition, there are several good books that describe I/O devices. White [WHIT05] provides straight-forward explanations of many I/O devices. Mueller [MUEL08] contains comprehensive treatments of memory, disk storage, optical disks, video hardware, and more.

KEY CONCEPTS AND TERMS

active matrix (LCD)
average seek time
bitmapped fonts
block (of data)
cathode ray tube (CRT)
CD-ROM
constant angular velocity (CAV)
constant linear velocity (CLV)
cylinder
data streaming
direct access storage devices (DASDs)
disk array
DVD
drive array
dye sublimation
electron guns
encoders
fault-tolerant computers
file server
flash memory
formatting
graphics tablet
hard disk drive

helical scan cartridge
impact printer
inkjet printer
interblock gap
interlace
laser printer
latency time
light pen
linear recording cartridge
liquid crystal display (LCD)
majority logic
medium access control (MAC)
mirrored array
mounted
multiple zone recording
network interface card (NIC)
network interface unit (NIU) controller
off-line storage
OLED (organic light-emitting diode) display
online secondary storage

outline fonts
parked (position)
passive matrix (LCD)
peripherals
phosphors
pixels
PostScript
primary memory
progressive scan display
raster scan
redundant array of inexpensive disks (RAID)
resolution
rotational delay
rotational latency time
secondary storage
sectors
seek time
server
shadow mask
striped array
text mode
thermal wax transfer
touch screen
track

transfer time	WORM (write-once-	zone bit recording (ZBR)
true color	read-many-times)	zone-CAV recording
vector scan	disks	(Z-CAV)

READING REVIEW QUESTIONS

10.1 Peripheral devices can be categorized into three classes. What are the three classes? Give an example of each.

10.2 State at least three reasons why storage in a computer is organized hierarchically.

10.3 What is the advantage of flash memory over RAM? What is the advantage of RAM over flash memory? What is the advantage of flash memory over magnetic hard disk?

10.4 Draw a circle representing one platter surface of a hard disk. On your drawing show an example of a track, of a sector, and of a block.

10.5 Draw a sector representing one platter surface of a hard disk with sixteen sectors. On your drawing show a track, the sectors, and a single block. Place a magnetic head somewhere on your drawing. Show on your drawing the seek time, latency time, and read time for the block that you drew on the disk.

10.6 Suppose a disk is rotating at 7200 rpm. What is the minimum latency time for this disk? What is the maximum latency time for this disk?

10.7 What is a *disk array*? What advantages does a disk array offer over those of a single disk?

10.8 How does the layout of a typical optical disk differ from that of a magnetic disk? How many tracks does a standard single-layer CD-ROM contain?

10.9 What does *WORM* stand for when it is used to describe an optical disk?

10.10 What are the advantages and disadvantages of magnetic tape as compared to other peripheral storage devices?

10.11 What do the numbers 1920 × 1080 represent when describing a display?

10.12 How many pixels are there in a 1024 × 768 display? What is the picture ratio of this display?

10.13 Explain how a raster scan works.

10.14 What is true of the red, blue, and green pixel values if the color of the pixel is white? What if it's black?

10.15 What is the difference between interlaced scan and progressive (or noninterlaced) scan?

10.16 What are the advantages of LCD technology over CRT technology?

10.17 What does OLED stand for? How does OLED technology differ from LCD technology?

10.18 What is the measure used to indicate the resolution of a printer?

10.19 What are the two types of printers in primary use today?

10.20 Name at least three user input devices in common use.

10.21 What does NIC stand for?

EXERCISES

10.1   The average latency on a disk with 2200 sectors is found experimentally to be 110 msec.

    a.   What is the rotating speed of the disk?

    b.   What is the transfer time for one sector?

10.2   A multiplattered hard disk is divided into 1100 sectors and 40,000 cylinders. There are six platter surfaces. Each block holds 512 bytes.

    The disk is rotating at a rate of 4800 rpm. The disk has an average seek time of 12 msec.

    a.   What is the total capacity of this disk?

    b.   What is the disk transfer rate in bytes per second?

    c.   What are the minimum and maximum latency times for this disk? What is the average latency time for this disk?

10.3   What are the advantages of flash memory over hard disk storage? What are the advantages of hard disk over flash memory storage? What are the advantages of both hard disk and flash memory storage over RAM? What is the major advantage of RAM over other types of storage?

10.4   An optical disk consists of two thousand concentric tracks. The disk is 5.2 inches in diameter. The innermost track is located at a radius of 1/2 inch from the center. The outermost track is located 2 1/2 inches from the center. The density of the disk is specified as 1630 bytes per inch along the track. The transfer rate is specified as 256,000 bytes per second. The disk is CLV. All blocks are of equal size.

    a.   The innermost track consists of ten blocks. How many bytes are contained in a block?

    b.   How many blocks would the outermost track contain?

    c.   The capacity of the disk is approximately equal to the capacity in bytes of the middle track times the number of tracks. What is the approximate capacity of the disk?

    d.   What is the motor rotation speed when reading the innermost track? the outermost track?

10.5   Old fashioned twelve-inch laser video disks were produced in two different formats, known as CAV and CLV. The playing time of a CLV disk is approximately twice that of a CAV disk, although the number of tracks, track width of the tracks on the disk, and amount of data per video frame is the same. Explain why this is so.

10.6   Explain why it is easy to perform read and write in place on a disk but not on a tape.

10.7   There is a current proposal to cut the size of an individual bit in a DVD-ROM in half so as to increase the capacity of the disk. This would cut both the width of the track and the track length required per bit in half. If the current capacity of a DVD-ROM is approximately 4.7 GB, what would be the capacity of the new "high-density" DVD-ROM?

10.8 Why is the average seek time for a hard disk much shorter than for a CD-ROM or DVD-ROM?

10.9 A 1024 × 768 image is displayed, noninterlaced, at a rate of thirty frames per second.
   a. If the image is stored with 64K-color resolution, which uses 2 bytes per pixel, how much memory is required to store the picture?
   b. How much video memory is required to store the picture as a "true color" image, at 3 bytes per pixel?
   c. What is the transfer rate, in bytes per second, required to move the pixels from video memory to the screen for the "true color" image?

10.10 For a motion picture image it may be necessary to change every pixel in the image as many as thirty times per second, although usually the amount of change is somewhat smaller. This means that without data compression or other tricks that a large number of pixel values must be moved from main memory to video memory each second to produce moving video images. Assume a video image on the screen of 1 1/2″ × 2″, with a pixel resolution of seventy-two dots per inch and a frame rate of thirty per second. Calculate the required data transfer rate necessary to produce the movie on the screen. Do the same for an image of 3″ × 4″.

10.11 A 1600-pixel by 900-pixel display is generated on a 14-inch (diagonal) monitor.
   a. How many dots per inch are displayed on this monitor?
   b. What is the size of an individual pixel? Would a .26 mm pixel resolution monitor be sufficient for this display?
   c. Repeat (a) and (b) for a 1280 × 720 display.

10.12 The cost of a monitor increases rapidly with increasing bandwidth. The bandwidth of a monitor is measured roughly as the number of pixels displayed on the screen per second.
   a. Calculate the bandwidth of a 640-pixel by 480-pixel display operating in an interlace mode. One-half of the image is generated every 1/60th of a second.
   b. Do the same for a 1920-pixel by 1080-pixel display operating in noninterlace mode. One entire image is generated every 1/60th of a second.

10.13 A high-quality photographic image requires 3 bytes per pixel to produce sixteen million shades of color.
   a. How large a video memory is required to store a 640 × 480 image during display? A 1600 × 900 image? A 1440 × 1080 image?
   b. How many 1024 × 768 non-compressed color images will fit on 4.7 GB DVD-ROM?

10.14 A text display displays 24 rows of 80 characters on a 640-pixel by 480-pixel 15-inch monitor. Assuming four spaces for horizontal space between each row of characters, how big are the characters in inches? In pixels? How big would a character of the same pixel size be if the display is increased to 800 × 600? How many rows of characters could be displayed in this case?

10.15 A typical published page consists of approximately forty lines at seventy-five characters per line. How many published pages of 16-bit Unicode text would fit on a typical 600 MB CD-ROM? How many published pages of text would fit on a netbook computer with an 80 GB flash memory?

10.16   Explain the difference between pixel graphics and object graphics, and discuss the advantages and disadvantages of each.

10.17   What are the limitations of typewriter-type (formed character) printers that caused them to fade from popularity?

10.18   What is the actual resolution of a gray scale picture printed on a 600-dot-per-inch laser printer if the gray scale is created with a 3×3 matrix?

10.19   Explain the difference in the method used to generate characters between graphics mode and character mode display.

10.20   In printer jargon, ''replaceables'' are the items that are used up as part of the printing process. What are the replaceables in a laser printer? In an inkjet printer? In a dot-matrix impact printer?

CHAPTER 11

MODERN COMPUTER SYSTEMS

"He wants a system with lots of memory, but without a mouse."

11.0 INTRODUCTION

It's time to put all the pieces together!

In the last five chapters, we carefully explored the various fundamental components of computer systems. We explained in detail the operation of the computer CPU and introduced some of the many variations on the basic CPU design found in different systems. You learned that there is a fundamental group of instructions that make up the repertoire of the computer and that each instruction is performed in a series of simple steps known as a fetch-execute cycle. You have seen variations in instruction sets and memory addressing techniques that differentiate computers from one another and extend the flexibility of the basic architecture. We explored various CPU architectures, memory enhancements, and CPU organizations that expand the processing power of the CPU. We also considered various techniques used to perform I/O operations. We explored the advantages of adding additional CPUs in the form of multiprocessing and of off-loading operations into additional processors built into I/O modules. In addition, we presented the workings of various peripheral devices. You have also seen some of the interactions between the various components in the computer system. You've learned that various buses tie everything together.

The primary goal of this chapter is to complete our discussion of computer system hardware by showing you how all these pieces fit together in real modern computer systems. Considering the system as a whole will also give us the opportunity to study some of the ways in which computer designers are meeting the demand for more computing power.

Today's software places tremendous demands on all components of a computer system. Forty years ago, an IBM mainframe computer was supplied with a maximum of 512 KB of primary memory. The performance of this machine was measured at 0.2 millions of instructions per second (MIPS). Today, a *personal* computer or personal digital assistant with that level of performance would be considered unusable for most applications. It wouldn't even be adequate for a cell phone! Graphics and multimedia applications, in particular, require performance far in excess of previously acceptable levels. Most modern computers perform at levels of a billion instructions per second or more. Supercomputers can perform *trillions* of instructions per second! There is a continuing demand for higher and higher levels of performance, driven by the desire to solve complex problems that require more computer power, as well as by market needs and by competition. As you'll see, we've even learned to tie computers together into massive networks and clusters and grids to accumulate even more computer power for the massive problems that require ever-increasing computer capability: sophisticated problems in physics, weather analysis, searches for medical cures, complex financial, economic, and business analyses, even the search for extraterrestrial intelligence.

Obviously, individual components—CPU, memory, I/O modules, and the connections between them—have been optimized to maximize computer system performance. Considering the system as a whole allows further advances in performance, which result from system integration. Individual components are designed to work together in such a way that overall performance is enhanced beyond the performance of each component. This concept is known as **synergy**.

Much of the discussion in this chapter is devoted to innovations in computer system design resulting from a synergistic approach to system integration. An important consideration in this discussion is the means used to interconnect the various components to achieve effective integration. This chapter introduces bus and channel computer system architectures that attempt to optimize interconnectivity goals, as well as maximize I/O throughput and fast storage capability.

Some of the new techniques in computers are improvements in technology, design, and implementation: improved materials, manufacturing techniques, and circuit components and better ways of performing the same task that enhance the operation of a particular system component. Others are architectural changes: new features and implementation methods that change in a fundamental way the design of the system.[1] Many of the innovations and enhancements that are used to achieve high performance are a fundamental part of modern systems. The terminology that names and describes these techniques is a basic part of the vocabulary of computing. To analyze, purchase, and manage modern business systems intelligently, it is important to understand these techniques.

In Chapters 7, 8, 9, and 10 we provided the conceptual framework for a computer system, and analyzed the operations and methods used by the individual components. In this chapter we focus on the modern computer system as a whole. Section 11.1 puts together everything that we've discussed up to this point and shows you the organization of complete, modern, high-performance computer systems. Perhaps surprisingly, the model presented is relatively independent of system size or CPU type; it applies across the board, from the embedded system found in a car, to the cell phone or game controller or PC laptop, to the mainframe system used in the largest businesses.

Although computer power has increased tremendously, one continuing challenge is the ability to support the massive amounts of input/output, including networking, as well as storage requirements that accompany modern computer usage. There are a number of different approaches in use. Enhanced traditional bus approaches are suitable for smaller systems, particularly with specialized high-speed buses, such as USB and FireWire, designed for this purpose. Larger systems, particularly mainframe computer systems, supplement their I/O capability with specialized I/O processors that offload much of the I/O processing to separate I/O equipment to achieve extremely high I/O data transfer rates. The best known of these is IBM's channel architecture, a technology that has been continually updated to achieve ever-increasing I/O capability. In Section 11.2 we present discussions of the various means used to support current I/O and storage requirements.

Many modern computer systems satisfy the demand for computing power by integrating multiple processors. In Chapter 8, Section 8.5, we introduced multiprocessing as one possible solution. In Section 11.3 we briefly present an overview to coupling entire computer systems together as an alternative approach. Section 11.4 introduces clustering as one means to couple individual computer systems together to provide more power.

---

[1] It is useful to note that computer science establishes the ultimate theoretical capability of a computer to solve a particular problem. None of the developments in computer architecture have changed the fundamental capability of the computer in this regard.

Multiprocessing and clustering are often used together to provide the tremendous computing power offered in many large scale modern systems, including supercomputer systems. In fact, modern large-scale computers are predominantly designed as carefully integrated combinations of multiprocessing and clustering technology.

In Section 11.5 we consider briefly special purpose methods used to achieve even more computing power. The primary method used for this purpose utilizes spare CPU capability available when individual computers on a large network facility, such as the Internet, are working at less than full capacity. This technique, gradually increasing in importance, is known variously as grid computing or cloud computing.

Interestingly, despite the previous discussion, it is sometimes not practical to utilize the available CPU capability of a system effectively. A programmer may wish to test a program, for example, that presents a security or failure risk to the production work of the system. Or there may be a need for systems to support a number of tasks in a facility where it may be more cost effective to provide and support a single large system rather than a number of smaller systems. One important solution to situations such as these is a technique called **virtualization**, in which an individual computer system is used to simulate multiple computers, all sharing the same CPU and I/O facilities. The simulated machines are known as **virtual computers**. Each virtual computer runs its own operating system and programs. Special hardware and software is designed to assure isolation between the various virtual computers, to prevent unwanted interactions, such as security breaches. Many organizations consider virtualization an important tool in building large, cost effective, system solutions. We mention virtualization here because, in a sense, it is the opposite side of the coin—now that all this computing power is available, how do we put it to use? An introduction to the concept of virtualization is presented in Chapter 18.

Of course, there are other parts of the system we have yet to consider, in particular the operating system software and the interconnection of individual computing systems into larger systems using network technology. But, hey, it's not possible to discuss everything all at once! Those discussions take place in later chapters.

11.1 PUTTING ALL THE PIECES TOGETHER

At this point we have explored the various components that make up a computer system: one or more CPUs, primary storage, I/O modules, various I/O devices, and the buses that connect everything together. You have seen how the CPU processes instructions, and the kinds of instructions that are executed. You have seen the different methods that are used to transfer data between an I/O device and memory for use by the CPU. You've seen that the use of DMA and a completion interrupt is an effective and efficient way to move large blocks of data quickly. You've also seen that programmed I/O is more effective for small amounts of data, particularly when speeds are extremely slow. You've seen how interrupts can be used together with programmed I/O to keep a pipeline of slow, character-based I/O data moving, for example, from a program to a modem.

In this section we are concerned about the blocks and interconnections that make up the organization of a computer system. There are various ways to interconnect the CPU, memory, and I/O peripherals, each with their own advantages and disadvantages.

The blocks that make up the essential components of a personal computer or workstation are shown as a simplified diagram in Figure 11.1. The major components in

FIGURE 11.1

A Basic Personal Computer System

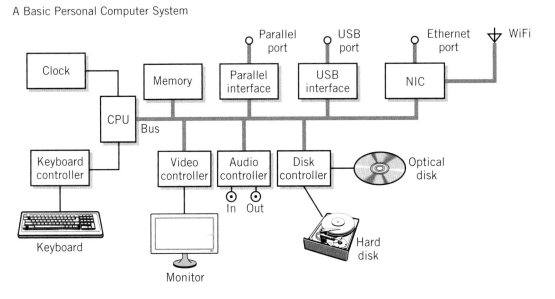

this model are a CPU, memory, optical disk drive, one or more hard disks, (or, perhaps, solid-state disks), the keyboard, and built-in video and audio capability.

The unit typically also provides USB, parallel, Ethernet, WiFi, and modem interface controllers and ports (perhaps FireWire, also, and maybe even Bluetooth). These ports can be used for network connections, printers, modems, mice, and other devices. The package also includes plug-in connectors for additional option boards that will interface to the master bus.

For comparison, Figure 11.2 shows the block diagram of a processor unit for a large mainframe computer system. The main components in this system are one or more CPUs, memory, and a variety of disks and other I/O devices, connected to the processor with an I/O channel system. In this diagram, the processor unit includes the CPUs, memory, and I/O interface components. Specialized internal buses interconnect the various parts of the processor unit. The keyboard and video display connected to the processor unit are used only for control of the system. Other terminals and workstations are connected to the processor indirectly, through the I/O system or by network. In addition, multiple processor units may be coupled together to form a large, integrated computer facility that can share programs and data.

A diagram showing more detail of a typical personal computer's components is shown in Figure 11.3. Although early PCs used separate integrated circuits for each of the various functions, today most of the functions shown in the diagram are combined into just a few **very-large-scale integrated circuits (VLSIs)** (usually just called *chips* or *support chips*).

The block diagram in Figure 11.3 connects together many of the important concepts familiar to you from previous chapters. The PC is driven by one or more CPUs, which interface to memory and to the various I/O peripherals and ports by one or more buses.

FIGURE 11.2

A Mainframe Computer System

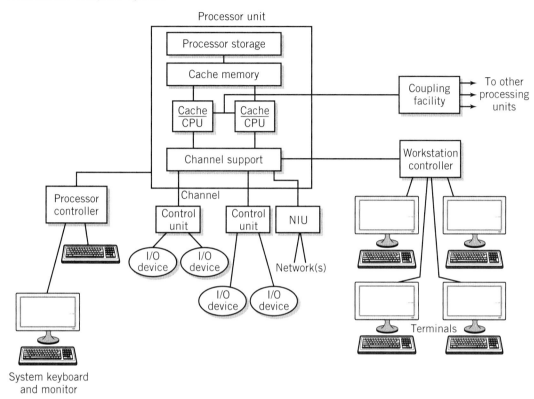

FIGURE 11.3

Major PC Systems Components

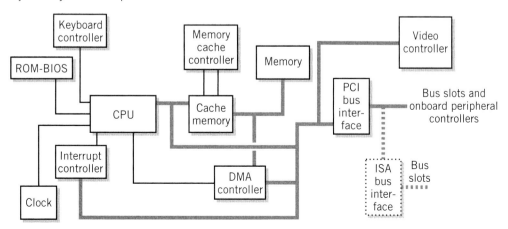

A clock controls the operation of the CPU. Interrupt and direct memory access (DMA) capabilities are provided to enable rapid and efficient I/O processing. L1 and L2 cache memory for each CPU is included within the same integrated circuit as the CPU for most modern processors. Older systems also include an Industry Standard Architecture (ISA) bus or its 8-bit predecessor on the IBM PC, or the NuBus on an Apple Macintosh system. Today, the ISA bus is nearly obsolete, and multiple buses are used, to maximize data transfer rates between components.

Figure 11.4 shows the layout of a typical desktop PC, including the motherboard, case, and other components. The wiring for the primary buses that interconnect the CPU and its peripheral components is printed on the motherboard. Connectors on the motherboard

FIGURE 11.4

The Components in a Typical Desktop PC

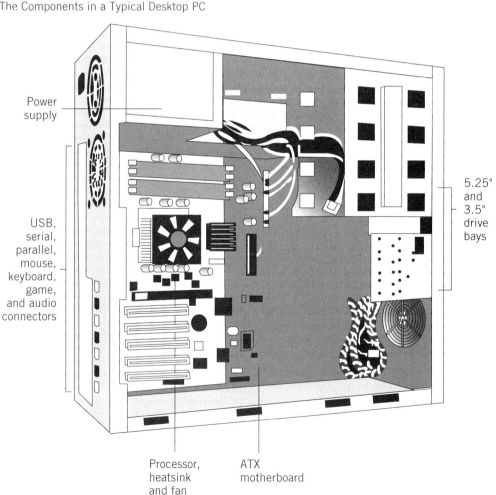

Power supply

USB, serial, parallel, mouse, keyboard, game, and audio connectors

5.25" and 3.5" drive bays

Processor, heatsink and fan

ATX motherboard

FIGURE 11.5

Basic CPU-Memory-I/O Pathway

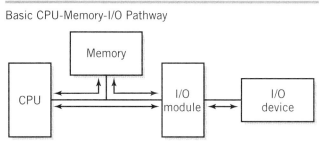

Source: From *PCI Local Bus Specification Production* Version 2, Copyright © 1993, by PCI Special Interest Group, pg. 9. Reprinted by permission.

combine with the frame of the case to hold the motherboard and plug-in peripheral cards in place, and, of course, the connectors on the motherboard provide the electrical connections between the peripherals and the buses. The mainframe computer is packaged differently, since the mainframe computer is much larger physically, as well as operationally. Still, the essential components and operations are similar to those of the personal computer.

Figure 11.5 illustrates the basic pathways required in a CPU-memory-I/O system. There are five basic components involved in the interfaces between the CPU, memory, and the I/O peripherals:

1. The CPU or CPUs.

2. The I/O peripheral devices.

3. Memory. Except for single pieces of input or output that can be transferred directly from a register, data from input or intended for output is normally stored at least temporarily in memory, where it can be accessed by the appropriate program, even for situations preferring programmed I/O.

4. I/O modules. The I/O modules act as interfaces between the CPU and memory and one or more I/O devices. As you recall from Chapter 9, an I/O module receives commands from the CPU and provides the control of the I/O device or devices so as to execute those commands. It also responds to requests from devices and provides interrupt service to the CPU to process those requests.

5. The buses connecting the various components together. The buses may be an integral part of the architecture of the system or may simply be a point-to-point connection between other components, depending on the architectural design.

The pathways include a required connection between the CPU and the I/O module to enable the CPU to issue programmed I/O commands to the I/O module and also for the I/O module to provide service request, special condition, and completion interrupt signals to the CPU. The connection from the I/O module to the device or devices is required both for I/O module control of the devices and as a passageway for the data. There must be a connection between the I/O module and memory for DMA to take place.

Although the illustration implies that these pathways represent actual direct connections between the various component blocks, this is not actually true. The connections could be direct or they could be electronic switches that provide the connections at the time they are required. For example, memory and the I/O modules could each be attached to different buses that are connected together when DMA takes place, or the I/O module could be attached by separate connections both to memory and to the CPU. These differences constitute different computer system architectures, representing different vendors, different goals, and different design philosophies.

In nearly every system, one or more buses form the backbone for connection of the various components, memory and I/O, to the CPU. In simplest form, a single **system bus** could connect the CPU to memory and to all the various modules that control I/O devices. Of course this approach would subject the overall performance of the system to the limited bandwidth of a single bus. More commonly, the system bus in a bus architecture connects through one or more bus interface circuits to a number of different interconnected buses.

A more realistic general bus interface configuration is shown in Figure 11.6. The bus organization of a PC, for example, often consists of the system bus, a video display bus, a PCI-Express and/or PCI bus, a serial or parallel ATA bus for the disk drives, probably a Universal Serial Bus, and sometimes an ISA bus or other buses. The system bus, which is the primary interface with the CPU, is sometimes referred to as the **front side bus (FSB)**. The bus interfaces are known by a variety of different names, including *expansion bus* interfaces or *bus bridges* or *bus controllers*.

Bus interfaces expand the flexibility of the system bus architecture by converting the format of the bus signals from one bus to another so that different types of buses can be used together. These other bus types can then be used to connect to specific devices, such as disks or terminals. The ability to interconnect buses makes it possible for the system designer to optimize each I/O function for maximum speed and flexibility, as well as to maximize overall system performance. It also makes possible the design and use of

FIGURE 11.6

General Bus Interface Configuration for a Modern Personal Computer

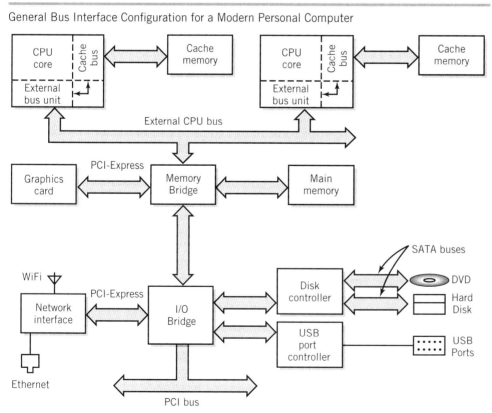

industry standard buses on equipment of different vendors. The use of standard system buses generally simplifies the purchase, setup, and proper operation of peripherals from multiple vendors by allowing the connection of I/O devices that have been standardized across a wide range of equipment types and manufacturers. This is a major aspect of the concept of **open architectures**.

In most computer systems, the CPU, memory, and other major components are mounted to wiring on a printed circuit board known as a **motherboard**. Figure 11.7 is a photograph of a recent motherboard. The wiring on the motherboard interconnects all of the peripheral cards that are plugged in to connectors, together with circuitry that steers I/O to the CPU and memory. In general, this arrangement is known as a **backplane**. A predominant example of a backplane bus is the *PCI-Express* bus, used to plug in various peripherals in a personal computer. Each peripheral has its own address. The wiring in this configuration carries data, addresses, control signals, and power for the peripheral cards.

FIGURE 11.7

A Personal Computer Motherboard

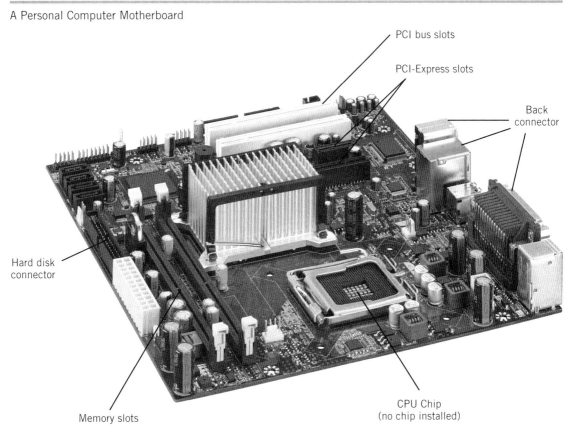

PCI bus slots

PCI-Express slots

Back connector

Hard disk connector

CPU Chip (no chip installed)

Memory slots

For example, numerous manufacturers produce various I/O modules mounted on printed circuit cards that plug into the PCI-Express bus that is provided on the backplane of nearly every current "PC-compatible" model. (PCI bus interface capability is also available on most midsize and mainframe computers, including recent IBM mainframes.) Most PC models also support plug-in cards for older PCI slots. Bus interface switching circuitry in the PC connects memory and the PCI-Express bus together during DMA transfers, which provides the required CPU-memory-I/O link. PCI and PCI-Express cards provide graphic display support, audio capability, serial and parallel ports, modem connections, Ethernet interfaces, and many other functions, demonstrating the advantages of standardization. Although Intel originally designed the PCI backplane, it and its PCI-Express successor have become standards through common use and agreement.

The ability to interconnect buses also provides flexibility for the future; as bus designs evolve, new bus interfaces can be implemented to add the capabilities of new and improved buses to the system. As Figure 11.6 shows, there can even be multiple levels of bus control. Notice from Figure 11.6 that an interconnection of two buses also suggests that memory and I/O devices will often be connected to different buses. The bus interface includes the necessary connections to allow DMA, interrupt, and control capability.

Except for issues of performance, it is not important to understand the details of a particular bus. What is important to note is how similar buses are, in essence, differing mostly in details and implementation. Each bus provides the necessary data and address lines, lines for interrupts, and lines to control timing, reads and writes, and so on. The major differences, other than specifications, actual pin assignments, and physical differences, lie in the way the control signals are implemented. For example, the ISA bus is defined by its data width as a "16-bit" bus. The PCI bus can be used to support either a 32-bit or 64-bit data width. The ISA bus has separate data and address lines. As noted earlier, addresses and data are multiplexed on the PCI bus. The PCI bus is designed to transfer several pieces of data in a rapid sequence called a **burst** once a starting address is established.

For most current personal computer motherboard designs, the PCI-Express has assumed predominance as the master bus of choice. PCI-Express is gradually replacing an older bus, called simply *PCI*. PCI-Express is a serial I/O bus that was designed to replace the parallel PCI bus that long dominated backplane design. PCI-Express is designed to be data and signal compatible with components designed for the PCI bus. The original PCI bus is a "32- or 64-bit" (meaning 32 or 64 bits of data at a time) backplane bus that provides plug-in capability for various I/O modules that control external serial and parallel ports, sound cards, network cards, and the like. The PCI bus provides 32 or, optionally, 64 lines that are used for both addresses and data, labeled AD00 through AD31 or AD63, plus various control and power lines. The power lines provide required power for the plug-in peripheral interface cards. The control lines control timing, handle interrupts, arbitrate between different devices seeking to use the bus, and perform other similar functions. All lines, other than the power lines, carry digital signals. A connection diagram of the PCI bus, which is still provided as an I/O interface in most PCs and many other computers, is shown in Figure 11.8.

Unlike the parallel PCI bus, however, the PCI-Express is made up of a bundle of thirty-two serial, bidirectional point-to-point buses. Each bus consists of two simplex lines that carry data, addresses, and control signals simultaneously in both directions at a current maximum rate of 1 GB per second in each direction. Each two-way bus is called a *lane*.

FIGURE II.8

PCI Bus Connections

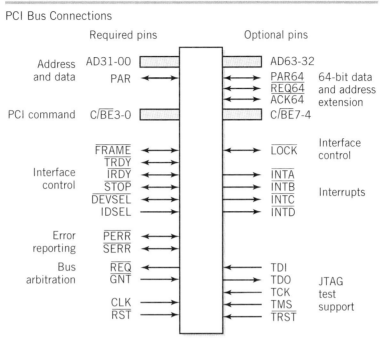

Source: Copyright © PCI Pin List/PCI Special Interest Group, 1999.

One end of each lane is connected to an I/O device controller, or perhaps to a controller for another bus. The other end of each lane is connected to a shared switch that is capable of connecting any two pairs of lanes together. The controller also provides connections between the serial lanes, the system bus, and the memory bus, converting the format as necessary between serial and parallel. The controller can use multiple lanes to achieve higher data rates where necessary. The switch is similar to those used in networking. Many new computer systems are adopting this technology to achieve the high throughput being demanded by today's customers, particularly in the area of video display.

11.2 INPUT/OUTPUT SYSTEM ARCHITECTURES

Modern computer systems are highly dependent on fast, reliable I/O. Even small systems must be capable of managing the large amounts of I/O data that are required for storing and retrieving large files on disk, communicating with a high speed network, and managing a high resolution display. In business use, a system must manage large databases, satisfy client requests for Web services, manage customer accounts, and print large numbers of invoices, to name just a few of the many I/O intensive tasks.

There are two basic I/O system architectures in common use: bus architecture and channel architecture. The bus architecture is used in almost all personal computers, workstations, and in some mainframe computers. The channel architecture is found primarily in IBM mainframe computers. The newest IBM mainframes use a combination of both.

I/O Bus Architecture

Recall that in Chapter 9 we introduced the concept of an I/O device controller, a module that serves as an interface between an I/O device and a system bus to facilitate communication between the device, memory, and the CPU. Devices that are physically mounted within the system are generally connected to I/O device controllers that are either plugged into a system bus connector on a motherboard or permanently wired to the bus. As Figure 11.4 shows, buses and network connections also provide a means for devices external to the system buses to communicate with the system. Such I/O devices are commonly called *peripherals* or *peripheral devices* because they are connected peripherally to the system.

Keyboards, mice, printers, and many other devices are often designed to operate from a standard port. (A reminder from Chapter 7: a *port* is simply a connector at the end of a bus into which a device can be plugged.) General control for the port is provided by a port controller. The port controller connects to a standard bus, such as a PCI or ISA bus. Specific device control is built into a controller within some devices and into the computer software programs that control I/O from these devices. These programs are called **device drivers**. Device drivers are either built into the computer's operating system, or they are installed into the operating system as supplements to the system. Other devices are controlled by controllers and device drivers associated with the particular bus port. In this case, the controllers also convert the bus signals between the form that is used on the main bus and the form required at the port where the alternative bus is to be connected. Until recently, most printers, modems, and mice were connected to computer systems through general I/O bus ports called *parallel* and *serial* ports. Today, these devices, plus disk drives, DVD-ROMs, graphics scanners, video cameras, and other devices are more commonly connected to the computer system through one of several high-speed general interface bus ports or through a network connection. Interface buses in common use for this purpose include **USB**, **SCSI**, **SATA**, and **IEEE 1394** buses. USB stands for Universal Serial Bus; SCSI stands for Small Computer System Interface. SATA stands for Serial Advanced Technology Attachment; it replaces an older standard, IDE (Integrated Drive Electronics), and is used primarily as an interface for magnetic and optical disk storage devices. A variation, eSATA, extends the SATA bus to support external storage drives. The IEEE 1394 bus is officially named after the specification that describes it, but is more often called **FireWire** or, less commonly, *ilink*.

The Universal Serial Bus was created to offer a simple, effective way to plug external devices into a computer as they are required. USB-2 is capable of a data transfer rate up to 480 megabits per second, which makes it suitable for use with a wide range of devices. A proposed new standard, USB-3, would increase the data transfer rate to 4.8 gigabits per second using a mix of fiber optic cable and standard copper wire. Globally, USB can be viewed as a multipoint bus. Multiple devices can be connected to USB. USB uses a hierarchical connection system, in which **hubs** are used to provide multiple connection points for I/O devices. Although the host controller is aware of the location of each of the hubs, the hubs simply pass data through, so that it appears that each I/O device is directly connected to the bus at the host controller. The USB topology is illustrated in Figure 11.9. Devices can be added and removed at any time without powering down the system. Removal of a hub removes all of the devices attached to the hub. Data is transferred

FIGURE 11.9

USB Topology Example

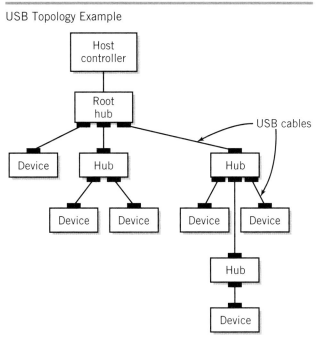

over the USB in packets. Each packet contains a device identifier and a small set of data, representing all or a portion of the data to be transferred by that device. Thus, a single device cannot tie up the system. The USB protocol allows packets to be scheduled for delivery at regular time intervals. This technique is known as **isochronous data transfer**. This assures that a device transmitting data such as audio or video at a regular rate will receive sufficient bus time to prevent data dropouts, as long as the aggregate requirement of all the devices connected does not exceed the maximum data transfer rate of the bus. The USB supports up to 127 devices. A system can support multiple USB host controllers to increase this number even further.

The USB cable holds four wires. Two lines make up a single data pair to carry the data, as well as address and control information. The other two lines can be used to provide power to devices connected to the bus. USB connectors at each end of a cable are polarized to force a hierarchical structure emanating from the host controller.

Like USB, FireWire is a serial, multipoint bus specification. FireWire is designed for extremely fast data transfer. The latest version of FireWire will support a projected data transfer rate of up to 3.2 gigabits per second, which is suitable for the transfer of full motion video with sound, for handling video conferencing data, and for other applications with high-speed data transfer requirements. FireWire has many of the characteristics of a network: FireWire devices can be daisy-chained or connected together with hubs; network components such as repeaters, splitters, and bridges can be used to segment and extend the FireWire bus to support longer distances and additional devices. FireWire connections can be made using either copper or fiber optic cable. Each segment of the bus can handle up to sixty-three devices. Like USB, I/O devices may be connected or removed during operation, and, like USB, a packet protocol that can guarantee performance for isochronous data transfer is used for data transfer and control. One major difference between USB and FireWire is that each device controller in a FireWire connection is independent, so that no host bus controller is required. Thus, devices can communicate with each other via FireWire without the presence of a computer. However, FireWire control capability must be built into every I/O module connected to a FireWire bus. An example of a FireWire application is shown in Figure 11.10. FireWire uses a cable made up of two data pairs and an optional pair of power lines.

The SCSI bus is an older parallel bus designed for "universal" I/O interfacing. It is rarely found on current personal computer systems, but is still in use on larger systems. SCSI devices include disk drives, optical drives, tape drives, scanners, and other I/O devices. The SCSI bus is designed to be "daisy-chained". The SCSI bus provides addressing for each device. Each device on the bus is plugged into the previous device, as shown in Figure 11.11. The final device on the daisy chain has a terminator, which prevents signals from echoing

FIGURE 11.10

Typical FireWire Configuration

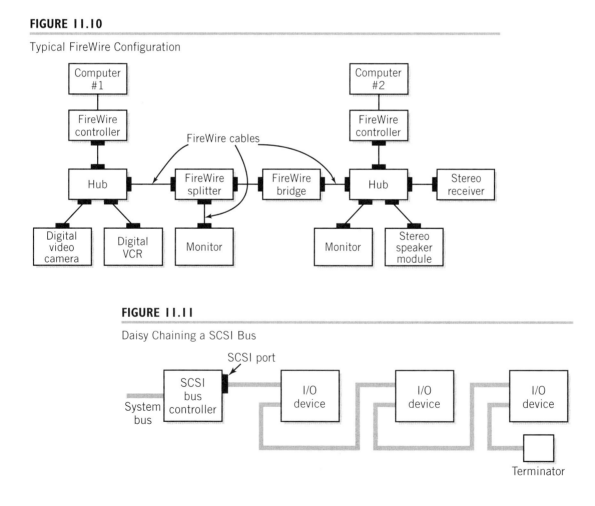

FIGURE 11.11

Daisy Chaining a SCSI Bus

back down the bus in the wrong direction. There is also a terminator in the SCSI bus controller. The I/O devices each contain their own specific built-in device controller.

A large number of modern I/O devices, particularly network-attached hard disks and printers, are designed to connect to a network, rather than to an individual computer. This allows users to share use of the device among multiple computers. Network-attached, large-capacity storage devices serve to store large files, such as video downloads, and to provide system backup.

Channel Architecture

An alternative I/O architecture is used by IBM in all their mainframe computers since the late 1970s. The channel architecture in the z10, IBM's most recent mainframe system as of this writing, can handle I/O data at rates of hundreds of gigabits per second. The basic architecture, known as *channel architecture*, is shown in Figure 11.12. The channel architecture is based on separate I/O processors known as a **channel subsystem**. The I/O processor acts as a separate computer just for I/O operations, thus freeing the computer CPU for other tasks. The channel subsystem executes its own set of instructions, known as **channel control words**, independent of the CPU. Channel control words are stored as "programs" in memory, just like other computer instructions.

The channel subsystem is made up of **subchannels**, each of which is connected through a *control unit* module to an individual device by one or more *channel paths*. The control unit module serves the same role as a device controller. The design allows multiple channel paths between the channel subsystem and a control unit, so that if one is busy another can be selected. Up to eight different channel paths can exist for a particular I/O device. Channel paths can also be used to interconnect computers into a cluster. Information about the characteristics of each subchannel and its corresponding device are stored in memory. Each subchannel is operated by executing a channel program, also stored in memory, made up of channel command words. The primary purpose of channel programs is to transfer data using DMA between an I/O device and memory.

Several different channel programs are available to perform different I/O functions, such as read a block, write a block, and so on, for each type of device on the system. The channel subsystem manages all I/O, independent of the CPU, and also supplies the appropriate interrupts and status information to the CPU upon completion of an I/O operation or if a problem occurs. The channel subsystem can perform several I/O functions simultaneously.

A CPU program initiates an I/O operation by issuing a START SUBCHANNEL command to the channel subsystem. The START SUBCHANNEL command specifies the subchannel number, which identifies the device, and the particular channel program to be executed. The channel subsystem attempts to identify an available

FIGURE 11.12

I/O Channel Architecture

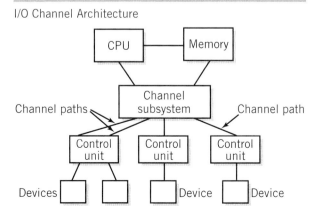

FIGURE 11.13

Simple Channel Program

Instruction	Comment
CONTROL	SEEK operation, to place head over correct track
SEARCH ID	Read ID of record on track and compare with specified ID
TRANSFER IN CHANNEL	Branch if unequal, back to previous instruction to look at next record
READ	Read the record, DMA into memory

Source: From *IBM Mainframes*, 2nd Ed., N. Prasad and J. Savit, Copyright © 1994, by McGraw-Hill Companies. Reprinted by permission.

channel path and initiates data transfer. If there is no available channel path, the channel subsystem simply holds the request until a path becomes available. In this way, the channel subsystem frees the CPU from having to keep track of the status of the I/O operation. The IBM architecture also provides I/O instructions to halt the subchannel operation, to resume the subchannel operation, to test subchannels, and to configure the subchannels. There are six different types of channel control word instructions:

- Read
- Write
- Read backward (used for tape)
- Control (used for controlling a device, such as rewinding a tape or positioning a disk head)
- Sense (used to determine the status of a device)
- Transfer in channel (equivalent to a JUMP instruction)

Although these instructions are used specifically for I/O, in other respects they are similar to other computer instructions. Each instruction has its own op code and address field. Each instruction results in the execution of a fetch-execute cycle by the channel subsystem. A simple channel program appears in Figure 11.13. This program performs a disk read operation. The channel control word instructions are designed in such a way that a single I/O operation can transfer a number of blocks. The blocks do not have to be contiguous on the disk or tape, nor do they have to be contiguous in memory. This feature provides a lot of flexibility.

Physically, the channel subsystem is connected to the CPU by a bus, and the various control units and I/O devices are also connected by buses. Conceptually, the channel architecture is very different, however, and the buses connecting the various parts of the I/O system are not identified as such.

Blurring the Line

It is worth observing that there has been a recent significant blurring of the line that distinguishes between I/O buses, I/O channels, and networks. PCI-Express, USB and

FireWire are all examples of recent I/O buses that have many of the characteristics of networks. PCI-Express uses a switch similar to that found in Ethernet networks to connect lanes together. PCI-Express, USB and FireWire all break messages into packets for transmission across the bus, and protocols that provide the capability to access the bus, to identify and reconstruct messages, and prevent conflict. Although USB is built on a hierarchical, hub-based structure that clearly identifies a single host, FireWire devices share the bus, in a manner similar to a network. There may be multiple hosts. The FireWire protocol establishes means for multiple hosts to access the bus without conflict. The FireWire protocol standard defines physical, data link and transaction layers, as well as a bus configuration manager that bears resemblance to a shared session layer. These are network features that will be presented in the next chapter. FireWire also supports network-type components, such as hubs, repeaters, and bridges. This blurring reflects an important tendency to adapt and combine the use of various architectural features and components in computer system and data communication technology in an ongoing effort to provide ever more system power and capability.

An interesting example of convergence between I/O and networking is a protocol, *Ficon over IP*, that enables IBM mainframe computers to extend access to I/O devices over a network. *Ficon* is an IBM fiber optic high-speed channel component used to connect IBM peripheral devices to an I/O channel processor. The protocol allows a user to connect a Ficon-based I/O device anywhere there is a network connection and control it from an IBM mainframe I/O processor at the user's location.

11.3 COMPUTER INTERCONNECTION: A BRIEF OVERVIEW

In Chapter 8, we first introduced the concept of multiprocessing. Multiprocessing systems are also known as tightly coupled systems. In multiprocessing we increase processing speed by introducing multiple CPUs, or cores, to share the processing load. Each core shares access to memory and to I/O resources.

As an alternative approach, it is possible to build systems in which the computers are tied together loosely. By this we mean that each computer is complete in itself, each with its own CPU, memory, and I/O facilities. Data communications provide the link between the different computers. Such systems of computers are called **loosely coupled systems**. Some authors refer to these systems as **multicomputer systems**. Loosely coupled systems enable program and data sharing and exchange between complete computers.

Some loosely coupled systems share a disk resource or a small amount of memory that can be used to communicate between the different computers. The determining factor that distinguishes a loosely coupled system is the autonomy of each computer within the system complex or network.

There are two basic methods of connecting loosely coupled computers. Clustered computers are connected directly together with a dedicated communication channel or link that passes messages between machines. The cluster is designed to operate as a single autonomous system sharing a workload. Networked computers operate more independently. The data communication channel between machines is used to exchange and share data and external resources, rather than to share the actual processing. Our focus in this chapter is on clusters. Networks are discussed in the next part of this book.

11.4 CLUSTERS

Overview

A **cluster** is a group of loosely coupled computers configured to work together as a unit. Unlike the tightly coupled multiprocessing system, each computer in a cluster is a complete unit, with its own CPU, memory, and I/O facility. In fact, the individual computers in a cluster may, themselves, be multiprocessing systems. Each computer in the cluster is called a **node**. Unlike a network, the computers in a cluster are intended to appear to users as though they are a single machine. The clustering is transparent to the users.

IT experts identify four primary, interrelated reasons for creating clusters of computers:

1. Clustering is used to increase the available computing power by combining the power of the individual systems. Since each computer can process data independently, the increase is approximately proportional to the number of nodes in the cluster. Brewer [BREW97] and others have noted that clusters are inherently scalable, both incrementally and absolutely. An installation can add nodes incrementally as additional computing power is needed. Furthermore, it is possible to create a cluster with a large number of nodes. Such a cluster will have more computing power, at lower cost, than would be possible using even the largest single machine. Clustering is a fundamental technology in the design of high performance computing systems. The processing of problems that are amenable to parallel processing can be broken into subtasks and distributed among different nodes and solved in parallel.

2. Clustering is used to create fault tolerant systems. Since each computer in the cluster is capable of standalone operation, a failure in one node will not bring down the entire system. Instead, the software controlling the cluster can simply switch processing to other nodes in the cluster, an operation called **failover**. A single point of failure is defined as a single component in a system that, upon failure, prevents further operation of the system. It is possible to design a cluster in which there is no single point of failure. This can be an extremely important advantage in systems that perform critical applications.

3. Clustering is used to create high-availability systems. The computers in a cluster can be geographically disbursed over a wide area. A user would normally access the closest computer system in the cluster, creating a natural balancing of loads between the different nodes in the cluster. Software can attempt to balance the processing workload evenly between different nodes even further. The failure of a system in one area, due to an area power failure, perhaps, simply shifts the load to other computers in the cluster. Backup is also simplified.

4. Clustering is used for load-balancing systems with large workloads. For example, the email accounts for a large organization can be divided up alphabetically and assigned to different machines for storage and processing.

Classification and Configuration

There are two primary models used for clustering, the **shared-nothing** model, and the **shared-disk** model. Both models are shown in Figure 11.14. As you can see from

FIGURE 11.14

Cluster Models

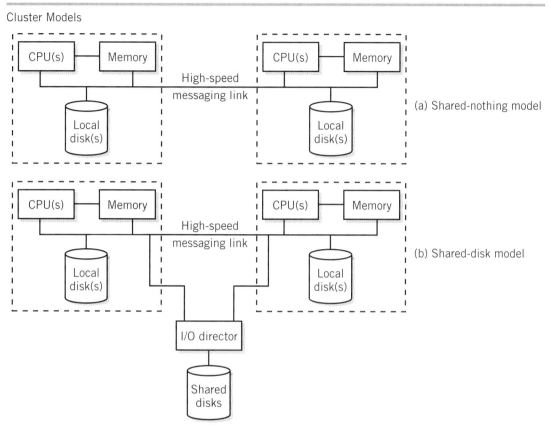

(a) Shared-nothing model

(b) Shared-disk model

Figure 11.14(a), the shared-nothing model bears resemblance to a point-to-point network connection between two computers. Each computer has its own disks. The critical difference is the presence of a high-speed messaging link between the nodes, plus software that controls the behavior of each node and the interaction between nodes. At least one of the nodes will provide access to the outside world and manage the cluster. The link is used to pass messages and data between nodes. It can also be used to repartition the disks as conditions change. The workload is divided by partitioning the data between the nodes so that requests made of each node will be approximately equal. This method has the advantage that little communication is required between nodes because each node is essentially independent. The primary difficulty with this configuration is that it is not always possible to plan for and predict accurately the partitioning. As a result, individual nodes may be over-utilized or under-utilized, and the efficiency of the cluster as a whole suffers.

The alternative, shared-disk model is shown in Figure 11.14(b). In this model, data may be shared between cluster nodes because of the presence of disks that are accessible to every node. This model offers the advantage of easy dynamic workload balancing and, with careful design, high availability, and fault tolerance. Availability is enhanced on many systems by the use of RAID technology for the shared disks. (See Chapter 10 if you need a reminder.) Although these benefits make shared-disk clusters attractive, there is a cost in software complexity. The software that controls the cluster must be capable of maintaining coordination and synchronization of the data that is being processed by different nodes, to prevent corruption of the shared data and to assure accurate retrieval.

For example, suppose that one node attempts to retrieve data that has been modified in memory, but not yet stored on the shared disk, by another node. This type of activity must be controlled. (If this doesn't seem too problematic to you, consider the following example: you make two ATM transactions in quick succession and they are processed on different nodes of a cluster. Without synchronization, your deposit could be wiped off the record!)

Different nodes of a cluster may be located in the same physical cabinet or may be located miles apart, provided there is a way to interconnect the high speed messaging link, and, if applicable, the shared-disk links. In fact, creating a cluster with widely separated nodes can also serve to protect the overall system and its data from catastrophe at a single location, particularly if the shared disks are also available at both locations. Clusters can even be configured to operate over the Internet.

Despite the additional complexity and planning effort, clustering has grown in importance in the last few years, because it provides a scalable and reliable way to attain large amounts of computer power at relatively low cost.

Beowulf Clusters

Beowulf clusters are simple, highly configurable clusters designed to provide high performance at low cost. Beowulf clusters consist of multiple computers connected together by a dedicated, private Ethernet, which serves as the link between the computers in the cluster. The cluster can be configured either as a shared-nothing or shared-disk model. Each node contains a CPU, memory, an Ethernet connection, and, sometimes, hard disks, floppy disks, and other peripherals. Beowulf clusters are generally configured with one of two types of computer components.

- **COTS**, or **commodity-off-the-shelf** components are simply inexpensive computers connected together to form a Beowulf cluster. In many cases the COTS components are older PCs scavenged from the scrap pile, and connected together to do some useful work.

- **Blade** components are computers mounted on a board that can be plugged into connectors on a rack, in much the same way peripheral cards are plugged into a PC motherboard. The backplane of the rack provides power and the dedicated Ethernet connection to each blade. The blades themselves are built from standard off-the-shelf parts.

Figure 11.15 shows photographs of a blade and the rack that together comprise the components of a Beowulf cluster in use at Los Alamos National Laboratory. Each blade contains a Crusoe processor, 256 MB of memory, a 10 GB hard disk, and three 100-MB/sec Ethernet interfaces.

The network connection between the nodes is not accessible from outside the cluster, which eliminates security concerns other than the authentication required to maintain

FIGURE 11.15

Blade and Rack of Beowulf Cluster

Source: W. Feng, M. Warren, and E. Weigle, "The Bladed
Beowulf: A Cost-Effective Alternative to Traditional Beowulfs,"
Advanced Computing Laboratory, Los Alamos National
Laboratory, Los Alamos, NM, 2002. Used with permission.

cluster integrity. Instead, a Beowulf cluster generally has a single front-end gateway server that manages the nodes in the cluster and provides connectivity to the outside world. It also provides a monitor and keyboard to be shared among all of the nodes in the cluster. Each node is configured with its own hardware, its own operating system, and its own Beowulf clustering software. In a COTS system, it is common to see a variety of hardware from different vendors in use at different nodes, but blade systems tend to be more uniform. Linux is generally the operating system of choice because of its flexibility. In addition to its own configurability, Linux provides the tools needed to configure the cluster to include all the features of a powerful distributed system. Beowulf clusters are ideal for use as Web servers because blades can be added or removed as required to maintain performance levels under varying loads. Most systems allow this operation to take place without powering down or rebooting the cluster. With their distributed processing capability, Beowulf clusters can also be used effectively for shared or parallel processing, where a single large task is divided into subtasks that can be processed simultaneously by different computers within the cluster.

11.5 HIGH-PERFORMANCE COMPUTING

Many interesting and important problems are not amenable to normal computer solution, either because the problem is so complex computationally or because the volume of data to be processed is prohibitively large. Example problems include the analysis of weather patterns, the behavior of physics particles, models of the effects of various factors on global warming, and prediction of the economic and social effects of a particular political policy.

The field of high-performance computing, sometimes called **supercomputing**, arose in an attempt to meet the challenge of solving difficult problems that require massive amounts of computing power. There have been a number of different approaches to high-performance computing, but recently developed systems tend to fall loosely into one of two architectural categories:

- Systems that are built from clusters of powerful machines or larger Beowulf blade clusters. These were discussed in the previous section.
- Systems that use the spare processing capacity of computers connected to a network. Each computer is given a small portion of the task to process in its spare time. This technique is called **grid computing**.

Grid Computing

Research by David Gelernter [MAR92] and others demonstrated that it was possible to produce supercomputer performance for processing large problems by distributing the problem and using the spare processing time of personal workstations connected to a network. Much additional research on grid computing has been done since then. Issues include effective division of the workload, scheduling work, preventing interference with local processing, effective use of the results, and security and privacy for the client machines. There have been a number of projects that are attempting to solve large-scale problems using grid computing. One interesting project is the SETI@home project, which is a systematic search for extraterrestrial intelligence organized by the Space Science Laboratory of the University of California at Berkeley [KORP00]. A radio telescope at Arecibo, Puerto Rico scans the sky for signals. An entire sky survey returns about 39 TB of data for processing.

The processing algorithms allow the data to be broken into tiny chunks for analysis. More than half a million active volunteers from all over the world receive chunks of data over the Internet. Application software built into a screen saver analyzes the data when the client's system is idle and returns the results to the collection system at Berkeley, where the results are stored in a giant database for analysis.

On a smaller scale, grid computing is moving into a number of large financial enterprises to provide more processing capability for their employees by harnessing the combined unused processing power of their servers and their end-user workplace computers to augment their own machines for the fast solutions of large financial applications (Schmerken [SCHM03]).

SUMMARY AND REVIEW

We started by showing how the components of a computer are interconnected to form a complete computer system.

Two different methods are commonly employed as architectures to connect the CPU, memory, and I/O. The I/O channel method is used by IBM on its mainframe computers. The bus method is used on most computers smaller than a mainframe. In the text we explain both methods. We expand on the discussion of buses in Chapter 7 to include buses used for I/O, including PCI-Express, USB, FireWire, and SCSI. We show the layout for an I/O channel and discuss how it is used in practice. We noted the growing convergence between I/O bus technology and network technology.

The emphasis in modern computers is on increasing amounts of power and capability. To that end, computer designers have resorted to a variety of techniques to increase the amount of capability in a computer system. In addition to increasing the raw power of individual components, current technology relies on the high-speed interconnection of computers to achieve the capabilities required of modern systems.

A number of autonomous computer systems, each with its own memory and I/O, can be loosely coupled into a cluster or a network. Clusters represent a form of loosely coupled system in which computers are interconnected with high-speed messaging links. A cluster consists of multiple computers acting as one. Shared-nothing clusters utilize separate disks and data partitioned and distributed among the systems in the cluster. Shared-disk systems provide multiple system access to one or more shared disks that hold the data to be processed by all.

High-performance computing utilizes large numbers of interconnected CPUs or computers to provide large amounts of computing power. The two primary technologies are clustering and grid computing.

FOR FURTHER READING

Mueller [MUEL08] and Messmer [MESS01] have both long provided an ''indispensable'' and thorough discussion of PC hardware, with all its bells and whistles. Unfortunately, Messmer is now dated, but one can only hope that a new edition will appear at some point. Mueller continues to publish a new edition every year. The best discussion of IBM mainframe architecture appears in Prasad [PRAS94]. This discussion includes a detailed explanation of I/O channels. The cases in Supplementary Chapter 2 present the features of the x86, POWER, and IBM zSeries system architectures.

There are a number of different buses, both internal and external, used to connect components together. Discussions of the USB can be found in McDowell and Sager [McD99] and Anderson [AND01]. FireWire is presented in Anderson [AND98]. PCI-Express is discussed in Anderson [AND03]. Much additional information may be found on the Web. Simple explanations of FireWire can be found at www.skipstone.com/compcon.html or at www.1394ta.org. The USB specification is available at www.usb.org. PCI-Express bus developments are presented at www.pcisig.com.

Good discussions of clustering can be found in Pfister [PFIS98], Brewer [BREW97], and Nick, et al. [NICK97]. The ''Green Destiny'' Beowulf cluster is described in [FENG02]. The SETI@Home project is the best known example of grid computing. This project is discussed in Korpela [KORP01]. Three readable introductions to grid computing are IBM Redbooks by Jacobs, et. al. [JAC05], Joseph [JOS04] and Berstis [BERS02].

KEY CONCEPTS AND TERMS

backplane	grid computing	shared-nothing
Beowulf cluster	hub	Small Computer System
blade	IEEE 1394 bus	Interface (SCSI)
burst	isochronous data transfer	subchannel
channel control word	loosely coupled system	supercomputing
channel subsystem	motherboard	system bus
cluster	multicomputer system	synergy
commodity-off-the-shelf	node	Universal Serial Bus (USB)
(COTS)	open architectures	very-large-scale integrated
device driver	Serial Advanced	circuit (VLSI)
failover	Technology Attachment	virtual computer
FireWire	(SATA)	virtualization
front side bus (FSB)	shared-disk	

READING REVIEW QUESTIONS

11.1   What are the five basic hardware components that make up a computer?

11.2   Explain what you expect to find on a motherboard.

11.3   What is the purpose of a bus interface or bus bridge?

11.4   What is the predominant master bus found on modern personal computers? What advantages does this bus offer over other buses?

11.5   What are major similarities and differences between the PCI-Express bus and the PCI bus?

11.6   Explain what is meant by *synergy*.

11.7   What is a topology? Describe the basic USB topology.

11.8   What are the advantages of USB as a means to connect peripheral devices to the computer?

11.9   What are the advantages offered by I/O channel architecture, such as that used on mainframe computer systems, over bus architecture?

11.10 What is a "loosely coupled" computer system? How does it differ from a "tightly coupled" system?

11.11 Define *cluster*.

11.12 Briefly explain each of the four reasons for creating a cluster. Give an example of each reason if you can.

11.13 What is a *shared-nothing* cluster?

11.14 Explain grid computing.

EXERCISES

11.1   Find a current computer ad similar to the one in Figure 1.1 of this text. Identify each of the featured items in the ad, show its position in the system block diagram of Figure 11.1, explain how it operates, and define its purpose in the system.

11.2   Carefully explain the purpose of a bus interface.

11.3   What are the trade-offs in using a serial bus versus a parallel bus to move data from one place to another?

11.4   Figure 11.6 shows that a typical computer system is interconnected with a number of different buses, both internal and external. The diagram includes multiple cache buses, an external CPU bus, PCI-Express buses, a parallel PCI bus, SATA buses, USB ports, and more. What are the advantages of providing multiple buses rather than connecting everything together with a single bus?

11.5   PCI-Express, SATA, USB, FireWire, and Serial Attached SCSI (SAS) are all serial buses used to connect external devices to a computer system. Locate the specifications or descriptions of each type. Compare the features of each type. Compare the speeds of each type.

11.6   As described in the text, the PCI-Express bus consists of thirty-two "lanes." As of January, 2009, each lane is capable of a maximum data rate of 500 MB per second. Lanes are allocated to a device 1, 2, 4, 8, 16, or 32 lanes at a time.

Assume that a PCI-Express bus is to be connected to a high definition video card that is supporting a 1920 × 1080 true-color (3 bytes per pixel) progressive scan monitor with a refresh rate of 60 frames per second. How many lanes will this video card require to support the monitor at full capability?

11.7   How many PCI-Express lanes are required to support a 10 Gb per second Ethernet card?

11.8   Why is a multilane PCI-Express bus not subject to the same problem of skew as an equivalent parallel bus?

11.9   Explain how the three primary conditions required for DMA described in Chapter 9 of the text are met by the I/O channel architecture.

11.10   Discuss the major differences, advantages, and disadvantages between bus I/O and channel I/O.

11.11   Clearly and carefully discuss each of the advantages of clustering.

11.12   Describe how you might use a cluster to provide fault-tolerant computing. Describe the trade-offs between your solution and a single multiprocessor-based computer system solution.

11.13   Describe how you might use a cluster architecture to provide rapid scalability for a Web-based company experiencing rapid growth.

11.14   Obtain information and compare the features, capabilities, performance, and operational methods between Windows Server, Linux, and IBM zSeries clustering techniques.

11.15   How does a Beowulf cluster differ from other types of clusters?

11.16   Clusters and networks are both categorized as loosely-coupled systems, but they serve different purposes. Explain the differences in purpose between clusters and networks.

11.17   *Cloud computing* is a recent technology being marketed and used as a means to provide off-site computing power to an organization. Locate information about cloud computing and compare cloud computing with grid computing. In what ways are they similar? How do they differ?

11.18   Find a current example of a large-scale grid computing project and describe it in as much detail as you can. What is the purpose of the project? What is the problem being addressed? How is grid computing being used to implement a solution to the problem?

PART FOUR

It is almost impossible to find a piece of computer-based equipment operating by itself, without connection to other computers. This is true of laptop and desktop computers, PDAs, cell phones, automobile computers, even satellite TV receivers and other computer-embedded devices. Computer networks are an essential part of the infrastructure of modern systems. Indeed, it would be fair to say that the Internet is an essential part of modern society as a whole. The three chapters that make up Part 4 of this textbook consider different aspects of the technology of data communication and networking.

Chapter 12 presents a careful, detailed overview of the essential features of networking. We consider the basic requirements for communicating data through a network. Topics include the definition and nature of communication channels; the two layered models: TCP/IP and OSI, which together with Ethernet are the basis for nearly all networking; the various types of addresses—port numbers, domain names, IP addresses, and MAC addresses—that are used to make global communication possible; and the various types of networks, including local area, metropolitan area, and wide area networks, and the Internet.

NETWORKS AND DATA COMMUNICATIONS

Chapter 13 expands on the concepts presented in Chapter 12. This chapter reviews the fundamental concepts of TCP/IP and Ethernet from Chapter 12. For each layer, there are issues of importance and interest—how are domain names translated into IP addresses? how are IP addresses constructed? what is DHCP all about?—that are explained in detail. We also look very briefly at three special topics: quality of service, security, and some alternatives to TCP/IP and Ethernet that are in use.

Chapter 14 introduces the basic technology that is used for data communication: analog and digital signaling techniques, the methods used for sharing networks; and the characteristics and use of different media: wire, fiber optic cable, and radio. This chapter concludes with a detailed introduction to the foundations of wireless Ethernet.

The material in these three chapters could fill a book. In fact, it does even more than that—it fills *many* books! It's impossible to tell you everything you should know about networks, but at least we've tried to give you a good head start!

CHAPTER 12

NETWORKS AND DATA COMMUNICATIONS

12.0 INTRODUCTION

In Chapter 10, we observed that a network connected to a computer could be viewed from the perspective of the computer simply as another I/O device. Indeed, for many purposes, this is an attractive and appropriate choice. As users, we don't really care if a file that we are using is stored on a local disk drive or on a network server located halfway 'round the world, provided the file is readily accessible. As long as we can retrieve our printouts conveniently, it is not important to us that our printer is actually an office printer being shared by others. In Chapter 2, Figure 2.6, shown again in Figure 12.1, we viewed the network as a cloud. To each computer in the figure, the cloud is simply another source of I/O.

As an alternative point of view, the network represents an essential component of modern technology infrastructure, offering the ability to interconnect computers, storage devices, computer peripherals, cellular telephones, personal digital assistants, video and audio devices, and, most importantly, other networks, to share resources and services, to share and exchange data and knowledge, and even to communicate and socialize. From this perspective, a computer is simply another device connected to the network. In this view, for example, a computer connected to a network might be masquerading as a telephone or a display device for videos or a source of music, using the network as the medium of communication.

Both views are important and useful at different times. Often, viewing a network connection as an I/O device is a very useful approach to system design and problem solving, particularly if your goal as a user is simply to obtain data from a database stored on a server somewhere on a particular network. On the other hand, if your job is to design and implement, or maintain and administer a network, you must thoroughly understand the design issues from the perspective of the technology and infrastructure of the network itself.

FIGURE 12.1

Basic Client-Server Architecture

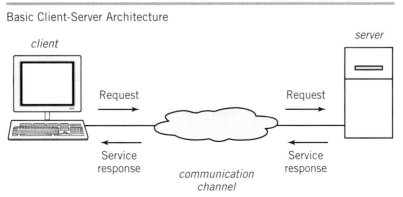

In this chapter, we are interested in the latter view. We will "open the cloud", so to speak, and study the basic concepts and infrastructure of network technology. As has been the case throughout this text, our primary focus in this chapter is on broad fundamental concepts, rather than the specifications and details of a particular type of network or methodology. In a field as fast-changing as network technology, specifications can and will change. Basic concepts are more stable and evolutionary. Even so, most of our specific examples in this chapter and the next are based on TCP/IP and Ethernet, the prevalent implementations of network technology at present and for the foreseeable future.

Section 12.1 discusses the importance of networking as a major impact on modern business processes and user access to knowledge. Networking makes collaboration and cooperation between organizations possible and practical. It provides new marketing, research, and sales channels. There are many who would argue that the Internet is the most important social and business tool ever created. As such, networking is an essential element in the study of computer system infrastructure.

Section 12.2 introduces three simple examples of network models, offering a first look at some of the criteria and requirements that form the basis for networking.

Section 12.3 serves as an overview to the fundamental concepts of data communication and networking. It introduces the general requirements and considerations that a network must meet to be effective and useful, as well as common components and common terminology that are basic to network technology.

Section 12.4 expands the discussions of Sections 12.2 and 12.3 to explore communication models with the capability to manage multiple nodes, support and provide transparent conversion for a variety of channel technologies, share channel resources, and provide international network addressing capability. This discussion focuses primarily on the TCP/IP model that defines nearly every modern network, and the Internet as well. There is also a somewhat briefer introduction to the OSI reference model and a comparison between the two models.

Section 12.5 provides an overview of different types of networks, including local area networks, metropolitan area networks, wide area networks, and backbone networks. It also introduces the tools, devices, and methods used to interconnect various types of networks, ultimately leading to an introduction of the technology of the Internet.

Last, but not least, Section 12.6 provides a brief introduction to the standards organizations, and to the specific protocols and other standards that serve as the basis for modern global interconnectivity and pervasive computing.

12.1 THE IMPACT OF NETWORKING ON BUSINESS PROCESSES AND USER ACCESS TO KNOWLEDGE AND SERVICES

Although it is easy to think of a specific need for a communication between your system and some particular source of data, the concept of networking is much bigger than that. Even if we wanted to, it would be impossible to store all the information that we use daily on a single machine. There is simply too much information "out there", and our requirements and needs for information change on a minute-to-minute basis. We would not have the expertise to understand and store all of it knowledgeably, accurately, and intelligently. Instead, data is stored and supplied on a distributed basis. Networks provide access to this data wherever and whenever it is needed. Note that we use the word "data" in the broadest possible sense of the word, to include programs, as well as traditional data, e-mail, music, streaming video, instant messaging, network-based telephony—indeed, anything that can be communicated with bits and bytes.

This capability to store and access data across a vast network facility has revolutionized our access to knowledge and has had major impact on both individual quality of life and on business processes and capabilities. At the personal level, we check our bank accounts and pay our bills online. We socialize on facebook.com or myspace.com and network our careers at linkedIn.com.

At the organizational level, we access files and databases to accomplish our daily work. More generally, we rely on new types of organizations that use a mix of traditional business practices and network access to create products and services that were difficult to locate and obtain just a few years ago. Companies such as Amazon and eBay have built their business models around the ability of users to access a vast array of goods on their online stores through general network capability. Companies such as Ford and Toyota use networking to communicate and collaborate (or synchronize their business processes) with their suppliers, dealers, and customers, and use the results to improve their production and their products. Music and video are downloaded from media services, and stored and played on miniature portable devices that can be carried anywhere. Goods that were available only in limited areas are now readily available everywhere internationally. Marketing and advertising can be localized to meet an individual's needs and location. Information is located and obtained from information resources such as Wikipedia and Google.

The same is true of interpersonal communication: e-mail, instant messaging (IM), social networking, voice-over-IP Internet telephony, Internet multiplayer games, collaborative work tools, real-time video conferencing, and more convert the computer from a high power calculator to a ubiquitous communication device; all of these capabilities are dependent on computing devices with ready access to networking.

Thus, we can't consider modern information system infrastructure without including data communication technology as a fundamental component of the equation.

Despite the complex interactions implied by modern computing, most of the complexity results from the large number of simple messages that are sent between the various computers involved in the operations, rather than any inherent complexity in the basic process of communication itself. Indeed, it is possible to reduce the basic ideas of networking to a few simple basic ideas. (In a sense, the issue is analogous to the way in which complex programs are constructed out of the simple instructions that make up basic computer program operations.)

No matter how complex the overall communication, the communication ultimately reduces to a series of individual "messages", each of which is a communication between a source computing device and one or more receiving computing devices.

12.2 A SIMPLE VIEW OF DATA COMMUNICATIONS

From the simplest perspective, it is natural to compare data communication by its similarity to the I/O methods that we have already considered. In each case, the computer sends data to or receives data in the form of "messages" from another device. For example, the "messages" in the Little Man Computer were three-digit numbers that were "communicated" with the user using the input and output baskets as a communication channel. The communication in this case consisted of two factors: the messages (the three-digit numbers) that were sent to or received from the application program that was being executed and the medium of exchange (the I/O baskets.) One important assumption that we made is that both the user and the program understood the "protocol", specifically the meanings of the three-digit numbers that represented the "messages".

Another hint at the origins of data communication can be deduced from POTS, the acronym for Plain Old Telephone Service. Again, the goal is communication of "messages" between two end users. The messages in this case are conversations between the users. Of course, the medium in this case is more complex. Assuming that you have "land-line" service, copper wires (or, perhaps, fiber-optic cables) connect your phone to a central office. Switching mechanisms at the central office connect your wire to the wire of the party with whom you plan to communicate. Although there is additional complexity in the communication channel due to the switching required to serve the large number of potential users that may wish to communicate at a given time, the principal conceptual components are the same: messages to be shared by users and a communication channel to transport the messages between users. There is an implied "protocol" in this case also; namely, the assumption that both users share a common language which they both can speak. For this example, there are also more subtle protocols that determine how the connection is made and standards that establish the identities of the users in the form of "addresses" on the telephone network—or to be more specific, telephone numbers.

Although these two examples seem superficial and simplistic, they do establish three essential ingredients for data communication: first, the data being passed between sender and receiver represents messages that are to be shared among the parties to the communications, second, there must be a communication channel that can capably and reliably transport the messages, and third, there must exist protocols that establish accurate and appropriate meaning to the messages that are understood by both senders and receivers. The second example also raises the issues of connectivity methods and addressing.

As a more realistic example of real-world data communication, consider the communication between a Web browser and a Web server. In this case, the message sent by the browser is a request for a Web page to be sent by the server. Assuming that everything works correctly, the response message by the server is a Web page to be displayed on the browser. The standard protocol used for this communication is *HTTP, hypertext transfer protocol*. Figure 12.2 shows the format of this communication.

The request from the Web browser consists of the key word *GET* (in ASCII or Unicode, of course) followed by the location of the web server on the host computer, as derived from the Universal Resource Locator (*URL)*, in this case /webapps/Login/. The request also contains the version of HTTP used by the browser *HTTP/1.1*, and the URL of the host, blackboard.bentley.edu, where the server resides. The HTTP request also provides the date and time of the request, the name of the browser, and, if the request comes from a link, the name of the referring URL that provided the link. (The referrer field in this case is omitted because the user typed the URL directly into the browser URL field.) An optional section to the request can also offer additional information, such as responses to questions on a Web form, for example. These are usually the data that appear on the URL request line following a question mark. The last line of the request closes the communication.

FIGURE 12.2

An HTTP Request and Response

<u>HTTP <u>message</u> <u>sent:</u></u>

```
GET /webapps/login/ HTTP/1.1
Host: blackboard.bentley.edu
Date: Wed, 23 Jul 2008 22:01:44 GMT
User-Agent: Mozilla/5.0 (Windows; U; Windows NT 5.1;
  en-US; rv:1.8.1.16) Gecko/20080702 Firefox/2.0.0.16
Connection: close
```

<u>HTTP <u>response</u> <u>received:</u></u>

```
HTTP/1.1·200·OK(CR)(LF)
Date:·Wed,·23·Jul·2008·22:01:46·GMT(CR)(LF)
Server:·Apache/1.3.37·(Unix)·mod_ssl/2.8.28
  OpenSSL/0.9.8d·mod_jk/1.2.21(CR)(LF)
X-Blackboard-product:·Blackboard·Academic·Suite&#8482;
  7.2.383.23(CR)(LF)
Pragma:·no-cache(CR)(LF)
Cache-Control:·no-cache(CR)(LF)
Set-Cookie:·session_id=@@C296D067A2A703542F0C959C25\
  314FFE(CR)(LF)
Set-Cookie:·JSESSIONID=0115BEF92808AF234DD8843E\
  509AD2BD.root;·Path=/webapps/login(CR)(LF)
Connection:·close(CR)(LF)
Transfer-Encoding:·chunked(CR)(LF)
Content-Type:·text/html;charset=UTF-8(CR)(LF)
(CR)(LF)
<HTML content>
```

In its response message, the Web server identifies the version of HTTP that it is using and a status code. The status code is accompanied by a brief explanation of the code, in this case, "OK". The server message also includes a date and time, the name and version of the server, and information about the content. (Note, for example, that this website sets a cookie.) Under normal conditions, this header data is followed by actual Web page content, most commonly specified in HTML, a standard markup language.

There are a number of useful observations to be made about this example, which is far more representative of a real data communications situation than the previous examples.

- This example clearly represents a client-server model, as we defined it in Chapter 2. The Web browser client requests services from the Web server in the form of Web pages. In fact, most data communications are client-server based.

- The Web browser request requires an addressing method for the identification and location of the Web server, since the request specifies the Web server only by its URL.

- The nature of the communication channel connecting the sender and receiver nodes is unspecified for this example, but possibly far more complex than those of the previous examples. Although details of the channel must be resolved for the communication to take place, you can see that the physical connection is independent of the messaging. This suggests that a networking model must support at least two independent means of communication: a message-sharing "connection" between corresponding applications at the sender and receiver computers, and also a physical connection with signaling that represents the messages being transported. In reality, addressing individual nodes out of the many that are typically available in a large multinetworked system, communication line sharing, and other issues require a number of additional layers of communication management that will be presented in Section 12.4.

As we just indicated, these examples do not attempt to present a full picture of the requirements for effective data communication. We chose to omit many important factors in order to clarify the basic communication process. Some of the factors that we must consider include the characteristics of the communication channels; the nature and formats of the interfaces with the sender and receiver end points, usually referred to as **hosts** or **nodes**; the nature and contents of the messages; the means of transporting messages where the distances between sender and receiver are large and the routes complex; the association of network addresses with their physical location; the means of sharing channel resources efficiently; methods for dealing with heavy network traffic and congestion; providing network security when required; maximizing network reliability and minimizing errors; providing timely network response; and more.

12.3 BASIC DATA COMMUNICATION CONCEPTS

Figure 12.3 shows a model that constitutes the essential elements of data communication. Two nodes, or hosts, are connected by a communication channel. An interface connects each node with the channel. The channel carries signals that represent messages between the nodes. Protocols define the ground rules for the channel signals and for the messages.

FIGURE 12.3

Model of a Communication Channel

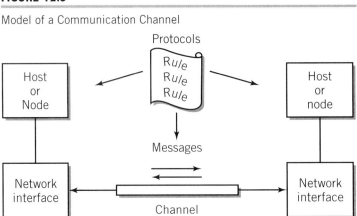

To get a better understanding of this model, let us consider each of the elements in turn.

Messages

The **message** is the primary purpose of the communication. It can take many forms. It may be data in the traditional sense of the word. It may also be a program or a file or a snippet of personal conversation or a request or status information or a stream of audio or video or some other agreed-upon purpose. For our discussion, we will assume that it is represented digitally, as a series of bits, in the sense of the data formats presented in Chapter 4. Since data communication is predominantly serial, we usually describe the data as a **byte stream**. Regardless of form or content, the message is a communication between cooperating applications at each node. The meaning of the message is established by the protocols recognized by the cooperating applications. Thus, the HTTP keyword "GET" used by the web browser in the third example in Section 12.2, above, is recognized by the cooperating Web server application as a request for a Web page as the appropriate response. The use of standard protocols by the application is not required as long as the cooperating applications agree on the meaning of the messages (some applications choose to use their own, nonstandard protocols for various reasons). However, the use of standard protocols such as HTTP makes the operation and administration of large networks much easier. There are definitions for a large number of standard applications, with standard protocols, designed for many of the most common communication tasks.

As you may have noticed, one of the major limitations of the use of messages as a communication tool is that the message length may vary widely from application to application. Without some form of control, a streaming video download, for example, could tie up a communication channel indefinitely. This situation is obviously intolerable if there are other messages that need to share use of the channel. (Note the similarity between this situation and that of traditional telephone switching, by the way. Any time there is a pause in the conversation, the capability of the communication lines used for the call is wasted.) The demand for channel capacity is large, therefore, full utilization of the channel is a desirable and reasonable goal.

Packets

To solve the related problems of channel availability and maximum utilization, there must be a way to break long messages into smaller units. These units are called **packets**. Packets can take turns using the channel, allowing sharing of the channel for different messages. Packets are used for most data communications. A packet consists of data of some kind encapsulated by information about the packet. A packet is equivalent to an envelope containing pages of data. Like envelopes, packets come in different shapes and sizes. A description of the packet, the designated receiver and source addresses, and information about the data enclosed is provided in a preamble or header, followed by the data. The amount of data depends on the type and length of the messages, the design of the packet, and the requirements of the channel. Some packets require a fixed amount of data, others allow a variable amount within some maximum limit. Some packet designs also include a trailer or footer at the end of the packet. The packet design used for a communication installation reflects the protocol suite in use. We will look at some specific packet formats in Chapter 13.

The use of packets offers a number of important advantages in data communication:

- *The use of packets simplifies operations and increases communication efficiency.* It reduces communication overhead by making it possible to transmit a large block of data while requiring only a single block of overhead information to identify the destination and meaning of the enclosed data.

- *It represents a reasonable unit for the routing of data.* This factor is particularly important in wide area networks, where a packet of data may be passed through many different networks and communication channels before it reaches its destination. (We discuss the routing of packets later in this section. Wide area networking is presented in Section 12.5.)

- *Packets offer an alternative to dedicating a channel for the entire length of a message.* This increases utilization and availability of a channel by allowing packets from several sources to access and share a single channel.

- *The use of packets presents a productive way to use a communication channel.* A channel can be switched to route data packets to different destinations in such a way that each sender-receiver pair appears to have a channel to itself.

- *The receiving computer is able to process a block of data all at once, instead of a character or a byte at a time.* Furthermore, it is usually easier to organize the data, since there are fewer individual blocks of data to deal with.

- *It simplifies synchronization of the sending and receiving systems.* Packets provide a clearly delineated burst of data, with an identifiable start and stop point.

There are different types of packets defined for different situations. Some types of packets go by specific names, such as *frame* or *datagram*, which identify their purpose. For long messages, there may be many packets. To recover the message, it is sometimes necessary to number the packets, so that they may be reassembled in their original order at the receiving node. In addition to data transmission, packets can also be used for control of the network itself. To do so, the data is replaced by control messages that specify the action to be taken. Packets are a fundamental unit of communication.

General Channel Characteristics

The **communication channel** provides the path for the message between the two communicating nodes in the model. Although the model in Figure 12.3 represents the channel as a direct point-to-point connection between the nodes, this is not generally the case. In reality, the channel can take many different forms. In the simplest case, it might be a direct connection between nodes in a local area network. More typically, the communication channel is actually divided into segments, called **links**, with intermediate nodes between the links that forward packets from one link to the next. Data originates at one end point and passes through each link to reach the destination end point. As an example, consider Figure 12.4. In this example, data (perhaps a Web request) originating from a home computer connects wirelessly through a router to a DSL modem. From there, the data passes through the DSL link to an Internet Service Provider, then through many additional connections to a computer somewhere on the Internet.

FIGURE 12.4

A Multi-Link Channel

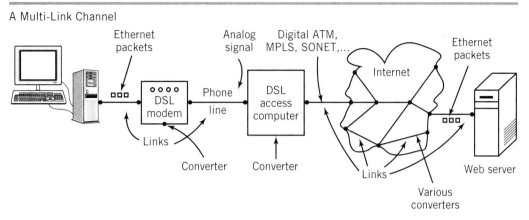

In other words, the communication channel between your Web browser and the Web server on the Internet may be divided into many links, each with its own characteristics. This is true in general of most communication channel connections. Conversely, there may be many nodes sharing the use of a single channel or channel link. Thus, a channel or channel link may be required to carry several messages from different sources and bound for different destinations simultaneously. The requirements for data communication must include the ability to share the channel elements among many different sender-receiver pairs and to direct messages to their correct nodes, wherever those nodes might be located.

One way to view the channel is to consider the connection between the end point sender-receiver pair as the communication channel for that pair. If our prime objective is to consider the overall characteristics of the channel as a conduit for messages being sent between that pair, this view may be useful and sufficient. We noted in the previous paragraph, however, that the channel between two end points may actually consist of a number of links, with intermediate nodes connecting the links. Each link has its own characteristics of interest. In a more limited sense, each link can also be described as a communication channel.

Since the channel may be made up of multiple links, the interfaces at each end of the connection may differ from each other and the characteristics of the end-to-end channel may differ from, and depend upon, those of the individual links. For example, the computer initiating a message might be connected to a network using a telephone modem, which transmits messages one byte at a time using audio tones as a signaling method. The receiving computer might be connected to the network using Ethernet, which expects messages formatted as digital packets consisting of many bytes of data, together with additional bytes that define the specific characteristics of the particular packet. Again, there are protocols and standards that define the makeup of the packets. The network must be capable of converting the message from one format to another at the intermediate nodes when required. The points where conversion is required for the previous example are noted in Figure 12.4.

Not only do the characteristics of each link obviously impact the overall capability of the end-to-end connection, they also affect the technical and business decisions that must be made when the channel and its affiliated networks are designed, implemented, modified, and upgraded. Consider, for example, the effect on the users of an organizational network that is connected to its external resources with a link of severely limited capacity.

Thus, we must accept some ambiguity in the way we define a particular communication channel, depending on the purpose that we have in mind. As we study data communications we will be concerned with the characteristics of different types of channels, as well as the nature of the interconnections between them. In this text, we shall be careful to indicate what kind of channel we are discussing at a particular time, end-to-end, or link.

As shown in Figure 12.3, each end node has an interface to the end-to-end communication channel. Our primary concerns for an end-to-end connection are the interface characteristics of the end points and the rate of speed with which data can be moved successfully through the channel, usually measured in bits per second and known as the **bit rate** or **bandwidth**[1] of the overall channel. "Successfully" in this case means that any noise or errors incurred during the passage through the channel can be removed and that the message can be accurately recovered at the receiving end. For example, if the channel connects a Web browser with a Web server, we are most interested in how quickly and accurately we can download the Web pages and data of interest. The same definition of bit rate or bandwidth also applies to individual links.

Note, however, that the characteristics of the end-to-end communication channel are determined by the characteristics of individual links. For example, the modem in the first link of the channel described above limits the overall speed of the channel, regardless of the speed in the remaining links.

Each link channel may be individually characterized by the type of medium it uses, by the signaling method and data formats used to carry its messages, by the directionality of signals supported by the channel, by its interfaces with the end nodes and with other links, by its bandwidth, by restrictions on the length of the channel, by the time delay between the time the channel receives data from its incoming node and the time it releases the data to its outgoing node, by the number of connections sharing the channel, by the noise characteristics of the channel, by the way in which packets are steered through the channel from link to link (see the next part of this section), and by the electrical or optical properties of the channel. Note that there are numerous similarities between communication channels and buses. The following is a brief description of some of the more important characteristics that apply to link channels:

MEDIUM A communication channel medium can be either **guided** or **unguided**. Radio waves transmitted from an antenna are unguided. They may be received by any radio receiver tuned to the corresponding radio frequency within the range and directionality of the transmitting antenna. Unguided media include cellular phone, broadcast radio, microwave, wireless networking, infrared light, and satellite technologies. Laser signals that are not confined to an optical cable are also generally considered unguided, although the field of view is extremely narrow. Note in particular that unguided communication channels are inherently insecure, since they can be intercepted easily by anyone within the field of view of the channel. Wireless networking is particularly vulnerable to interception because the transmitting antenna is generally omnidirectional.

---

[1]Bit rate and bandwidth are actually somewhat different, but are directly related as measures of channel capacity.

Guided media limit communications to a specific path constrained to a cable of some sort. Guided media can be either electrical or optical and include various forms of wire and fiber optic cables.

DATA TRANSMISSION DIRECTIONALITY Like the buses discussed earlier in Section 7.5 of Chapter 7, channels can also be characterized by the direction in which the messages can flow. A channel that carries messages in only one direction is known as a **simplex channel**. Television broadcasting stations use a simplex channel. Programs are sent from a transmitting antenna to television receivers, but the receivers do not respond with messages or data back to the broadcasting station. A channel may carry messages in both directions, but only one direction at a time. This channel is known as a **half-duplex channel**. If the computer at point B wants to send a message to point A, it must wait until point A has stopped transmitting to do so. Most walkie-talkies are half-duplex communication devices. Channels which carry signals simultaneously in both directions are called **full-duplex channels**. Traditional telephone lines are full-duplex channels. Both parties can speak simultaneously, and each can hear the other. Some channels are made up of separate lines for each direction. Some practitioners characterize these as full duplex; others refer to these as *dual-simplex* channels. The PCI-Express bus specification calls them *lanes*, a term that is likely to catch on within the network community.

NUMBER OF CONNECTIONS Like buses, a communication channel can be point-to-point or multipoint, although the choice is often predetermined by the nature of the medium. Wireless networking, for example, is, of necessity, multipoint, because there is no realistic technological way to limit the number of radio signals in a given space. Conversely, fiber optics are usually point-to-point because of the difficulty of tapping into a fiber optic cable. Note that even a point-to-point channel can be shared by packets arriving at its input node from different sources.

Some channel characteristics are determined innately by the medium. For example, unguided messaging must be carried by an analog signal: radio transmission is based intrinsically on sine waves, which are **analog**. Signaling is achieved by varying certain properties of the radio wave at the transmitter and detecting the variations at the receiver. This process is called **modulation** and **demodulation**. (A modem works on the same principle.) The signals in guided media may be either analog or digital, although digital is usually preferred because of its better immunity to noise and the ease with which the medium can be shared by multiple messages. We will expand on these ideas in Chapter 14. Recall from Chapter 4 that the conversion of data between analog and digital is often required because of the nature of the data that we are processing. Audio and video are analog in nature, but are converted to digital and processed digitally in the computer.

Today, the most common end-node interface to a channel is a local area network connection, usually either wired or wireless Ethernet. Nonetheless, there are other possible interfaces to consider: Bluetooth, WiMax, DSL or cable link, various forms of cell phone technology, older types of network connections, and, to a more limited extent, telephone modem. Each technology has its own requirements. We will consider a few of these in Chapters 13 and 14. Regardless of the characteristics of the end-to-end communication channel and of its links, we must re-emphasize the fact that the message must ultimately arrive at its destination node in a form expected and recognized by the application receiving it.

FIGURE 12.5

An End-to-End Channel with Many Possible
Paths through Intermediate Nodes

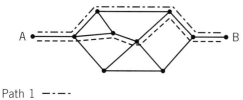

Path 1 ‒‒·‒·
Path 2 ‒‒‒‒

Packet Routing

In the previous section, you saw that the typical communication channel is made up of a series of intermediate nodes, connected together by links. Packets are passed along the links from node to node. We next consider how the path is selected.

Figure 12.5 illustrates a simplified version of an end-to-end channel with some of its intermediate nodes. In some cases, the movement of data from node to node is obvious: there is only a single path. In many cases, however, there may be several choices. Figure 12.5 shows two possible channel paths out of many between end nodes A and B. Overall, in a large interconnection of networks, a so-called internet (with a small *i*), there may be thousands of possible paths connecting end nodes A and B.

There are two basic techniques for selecting the path through a channel: circuit switching and packet switching. A third technique, virtual circuit switching, is an important alternative to ordinary packet switching that also operates on packets.

Traditional telephony uses **circuit switching**. Circuit switching dedicates a path for the exclusive use of the sender-receiver pair for the entire length of time of the connection. The previous discussion of POTS in Section 12.2 was an example of circuit switching. The telephone circuits are dedicated to the individual lines for the length of the phone call. Circuit switching is inefficient and is rarely used today, even for telephony.

A **virtual circuit** is a channel path that is set up when a connection is established for communication between two end nodes, and maintained until the connection is closed. Data is sent through the channel in packets; each packet follows the same channel links. However, the links and intermediate nodes are shared with other connections, making the use of the channel more effective. Figure 12.6 shows the use of two virtual circuits, one connecting end nodes A and B, another connecting end nodes C and D. These two circuits share intermediate nodes *k*, *n*, and *p*, as well as the path between *n* and *p*. The use of virtual circuits simplifies the routing of packets and also assures that packets will arrive in the correct order, since all packets follow the same path. However, congestion at an intermediate mode or through an intermediate channel segment that is used by several different virtual circuits can affect the overall performance of the network.

Some network protocols use virtual circuit technology as the basis for packet flow. **ATM** (**asynchronous transfer method**, not the bank machine!) is one example. ATM uses very small packets (53 bytes) and careful path selection to control traffic. The fact that packets always arrive in correct order makes ATM effective for streaming data, such as video. The use of extremely small packets minimizes time delay through the ATM network, assuring that video will traverse the network in a timely and consistent fashion.

FIGURE 12.6

Virtual Circuits in a Network

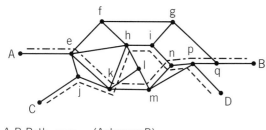

A-B Path ‒‒·‒· (AekmnpqB)
C-D Path ‒‒‒‒ (CjkhinpD)

Ordinary **packet switching**, usually called **datagram switching**, assumes that each packet is routed from node to node independently, based on such criteria as the shortest path to the packet's destination and traffic conditions, At each intermediate node, the next link is determined by the node's switch or router at the time the packet arrives. TCP/IP uses datagram switching exclusively for all of its routing decisions.

Now consider the most common network scenario, illustrated in Figure 12.7. In the figure, the makeup of the cloud from Figure 12.1 is viewed as a large network of networks. In this scenario, each end node is linked to an intermediate node that is part of a network, most commonly a local area network. (We will describe the details about local area networks later, in Section 12.5 and in Chapter 13.) The intermediate links connect nodes belonging to various networks together. A component at each intermediate node **routes** the packet to the next appropriate node. It also converts the data format of the packet to the format required for the next link, if necessary. The component may be a computer programmed to do routing, but it's more likely to be a **router** or a **gateway**. Routers and gateways are specialized devices used to interconnect networks and pass packets from one network to the other. Depending on the network protocols in use, either ordinary packet switching or virtual circuit switching will be used to guide the decisions made at each router or gateway as the packet is forwarded from node to node through the system. This same explanation also describes the functioning of the Internet (with a capital *I*).

As you've just seen, routers and gateways are used to set the path that each packet takes to move through the channel. A simplified diagram of a router is shown in Figure 12.8. The router consists of one or more input ports, one or more output ports, a switch mechanism, and a processor with memory. The input ports and output ports are connected to links.

FIGURE 12.7

Connecting End Points through Links and Networks

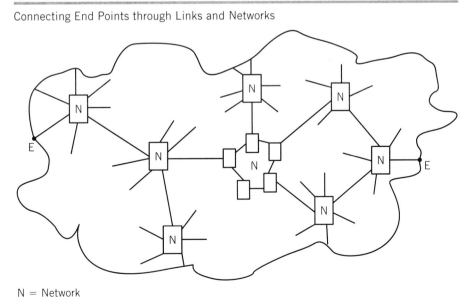

N = Network
E = Endpoint

FIGURE 12.8

Block Diagram of a Router

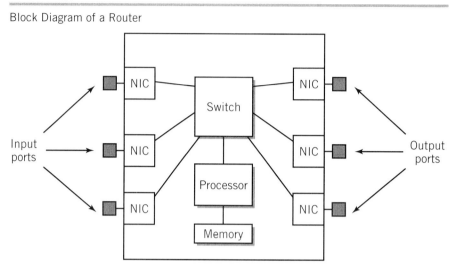

Routing protocols are sent to the router processor and stored, using packets with control information. The basic operation of a router is simple. When a packet arrives at an input port, the processor makes a decision on where the packet is to be directed and sets the switch to direct the packet to the correct output port. Routers are used wherever the incoming networks and outgoing networks operate on the same set of network protocols, although the physical characteristics of the links might be different. For example, a router could be used to switch packets between wireless and wired Ethernet networks.

Gateways operate similarly, but are intended for use when two dissimilar networks are connected together. The router operation is the same; the major difference is that the gateway is able to convert the packet headers that arrive at the input ports to meet the requirements of the different types of networks at the output ports. Traditionally, gateways have been thought of as complex routing devices that converted (in both directions) between TCP/IP networks and the older network protocols that were common on large mainframe systems. Since most modern mainframes also operate predominantly using the TCP/IP protocols, the use of this type of gateway is now relatively rare. Gateways are sometimes used to interconnect TCP/IP networks with Frame Relay network links that are supplied by some vendors for connection to computers beyond the local area. Similarly, although we rarely think about DSL and cable modems as routing equipment, it is worth noting that they do fit the technical definition of a gateway.

EXAMPLE

The technique of routing can perhaps be clarified with a simple example. The delivery of packets through a system of networks can be compared to a delivery system that delivers packages by train. See Figure 12.9. Suppose you live in Freetown and wish to send a birthday present to your Aunt Margaret DuMont in Sylvantown. You hand the present to the agent at the Freetown railroad station (the initial link from you to the network), who places it on the train headed towards Sylvania.

FIGURE 12.9

Delivery of a Package to Aunt Margaret's House

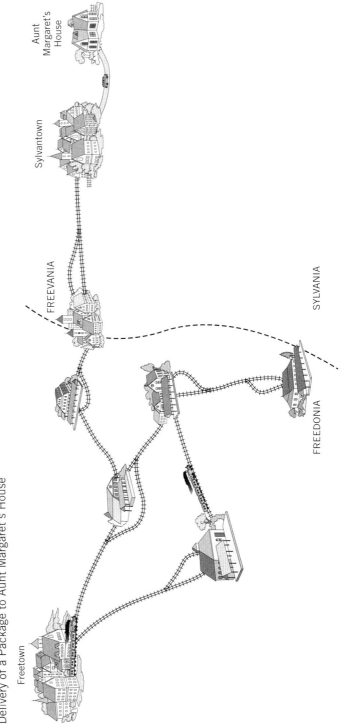

The train passes through a number of stations on the way to Sylvania. At each station, there are switches on the railroad tracks that direct the train towards Sylvania. Obviously the switches will be set differently for trains headed for other destinations. (Note, by the way, that the tracks are *shared*.) The track switches are equivalent to the routers in the packet switching model.

When the train reaches the border town of Freevania, the package must be passed to a different train, because the gauge of the railroad tracks from Freevania to Sylvantown is narrower, so the Freedonia train can't use them. Instead, the agent at Freevania removes the package from the Freedonia train and places it on another train to Sylvantown. The package has just passed through a gateway. The package is removed from the train at Sylvantown and delivered by van (the link to the end node) to your Aunt Margaret's house.

12.4 TCP/IP, OSI, AND OTHER COMMUNICATION MODELS

Overview

We remind you that in simplest and most general terms, the goal of data communication is to provide a means of reliable and efficient data communication between two end nodes or hosts. The communication takes the form of a message or a group of messages between an application or service at one end node and a corresponding application or service at a second end node. The message may be discreet or a continuous stream of data.

It is possible to implement the simplest forms of data communication with nothing more complicated than a message format that both ends agree on and a means to access the channel. Realistically, this simple approach is inadequate in most real-world situations.

Suppose that two or more computers are to communicate via a communication channel. What are the requirements for them to communicate successfully? As we already noted, they must agree on the signaling methods and the means used to access the connecting channel, but in addition there is much more. Even the format of the message is more complicated than it first appears. How long is the message? Which part of the message is actual data and which part is overhead information such as the address of the sender and the address of the recipient? How are errors to be detected by the receiver, and what will be done about them? How does the receiver know that it has received a complete message, and how does it reassemble a message that was sent in parts, possibly with the parts arriving in the wrong order? Each end of the communication must recognize all of the commands and requests of the other and be able to respond in a reasonable way. For example, if one computer speaks ASCII and the other speaks Unicode or some other code, successful communication will not occur unless they are aware of the difference and are prepared to perform the translations back and forth. E-mail messages will become garbled or not reach their destination if there isn't agreement on the meaning of the name and address on the "envelope". What if there is no obvious communication path between the sender and receiver or one link of the path is missing? How does the message get relayed appropriately? There are many more such issues, and it's easy to see that communication is not trivial.

Indeed, a substantial number of ground rules are required to satisfy all the conditions necessary to communicate successfully.

The key to successful communication is a set of protocol standards that agree upon hardware and software rules that will allow computers to establish and maintain useful communication at various levels, from the rules that govern messages to the hardware protocols that define the physical nature of the channels themselves. International protocol standards exist for communication by modem, for local area networks, for connection between local area and wide area networks, for Internet and other wide area network communications, and for many other purposes.

The ability to communicate between dissimilar computing and channel resources, the efficient use of channel resources, the ability to identify, associate, and locate specific addresses to which the messages are to be sent, and the ability to deliver messages through a complex system of channels are essential requirements for a successful message delivery system.

Two slightly different, but overlapping, standard models address these goals and concerns. The **Open Systems Interconnection Reference Model (OSI)** is a theoretical model, developed over many years as a standard by the International Standards Organization (ISO). **TCP/IP** is an older and more practical model, independently developed to meet the needs of the original Internet design, and regularly modified and updated to meet current needs. Each model is conceived and implemented as a hierarchical **protocol stack**, in which each layer of the stack at the sender node contributes information that will be used by the corresponding **peer**, layer at the receiver node. (You can see the similarity between the behavior of a protocol stack and the last-in, first-out nature of other types of computer stacks that we have already discussed and that you've also seen in programming courses.) As you will see, there are many similarities between the OSI and TCP/IP models, despite the fact that they were developed independently.

In each model, there are different protocols for different aspects of the communication. Each protocol is responsible for a particular set of tasks. As long as the interfaces between tasks are well defined, it is possible to separate the tasks. Separating the tasks involved in communication adds flexibility, simplifies design of the protocols, makes it possible to modify protocols or substitute alternative protocols without affecting unrelated tasks, and allows a system to select only the protocols that it needs for a particular application.

The TCP/IP Network Model

The prevalent collection of protocols that are designed to work together and guide all aspects of network communications is called the TCP/IP protocol suite. Although the name suggests two protocols, TCP/IP is actually a name encompassing an integrated suite consisting of numerous protocols that control various aspects of data communication, including modem communication, communication through a gateway, error reporting, address resolution, and many other functions. There are also a number of perhaps familiar application protocols, including HTTP, telnet, ftp, smtp, and many more.

The TCP/IP model consists of five layers.[2] Each layer represents an attempt to isolate a single factor that is relevant to communication between computers and other devices.

---

[2] Strictly speaking, the lowest two of the five layers in the model are not part of the "official" TCP/IP protocol suite, although their operations are required and directly related to the overall data communication procedure. We will clarify this issue later in the chapter, but the difference is unimportant to our present discussion.

FIGURE 12.10

The Layers of the TCP/IP Network Model

Application layer	HTTP FTP DNS ... SMTP SSH POP3
Transport layer	TCP UDP SCTP
Network layer	IP ICMP DHCP ARP
Data link layer	Depends on underlying network
Physical layer	Depends on underlying network

Figure 12.10 identifies the five layers in the model, along with some of the major protocols found at each layer. In addition to the layer names, each layer is also identified by a layer number, starting from 1 at the lowest layer. Figure 12.11 shows the operation of the TCP/IP model. As you can see from Figure 12.11, operation of the model is hierarchical. Each layer of the model is implemented to fulfill a specific function in the communication process. Each layer at the sending node performs its services, and adds additional data to the message, usually in the form of a header that encapsulates the data from above. (A few protocols also require a trailer.) The result is then passed to the next lower layer. This is also shown in the diagram. Each layer relies on the layers below it to provide all the additional functionality necessary to fulfill the communication function. At the receiving node, the peer layer interprets and removes the information provided for it by the sender, then passes the remainder upwards, layer by layer, until the original, reassembled message finally reaches the application layer.

The independence of each layer means that an individual layer needs to be concerned only with the interfaces of the layers immediately above it and below it. Ideally, the

FIGURE 12.11

Operation of the TCP/IP Model

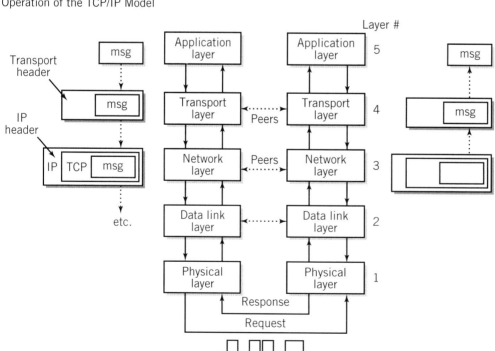

operation of a particular layer is transparent to other layers and could be modified or replaced without affecting other layers, provided that the layer continues to provide its required services to the communication process and that there is agreement between the equivalent, or peer, layers at the sender and receiver end nodes.

Not surprisingly, the message to be sent through the communication channel gets larger and larger as it passes down the chain, since each layer in the sender must add its own component to the message from the previous layer. There is an obvious advantage in eliminating layers, whenever they are not needed, to reduce message traffic and overhead. If a message is being sent point-to-point directly between a sender and the ultimate user of a message (i.e., the message is not being forwarded), for example, there is no reason to specify an address for the receiver. Therefore, the five layers specified in the protocol suite actually represent a maximum.

In an earlier, 2001, edition of his book, Fitzgerald [FITZ07] likened the layered model to a pair of office buildings, where the people on each floor are responsible for a specific set of business tasks. The TCP/IP buildings are each five stories tall. The people on the fifth floor of one building put a message for the other building into an envelope, seal the envelope, and send it down to the fourth floor. Each floor adds its own message and puts the previous envelope plus the new message into another, somewhat larger, envelope.

When the package reaches the first floor, a messenger person (this is the physical layer) carries the package across the street to the other building, where the people on each floor retrieve their messages and pass the remaining envelopes back up the hierarchy, until the final message, actually the original, reaches the fifth floor.

Now consider briefly the function of each layer in the model. (We will expand on the role of each layer in Chapter 13.)

APPLICATION LAYER (LAYER 5)   The procedure begins at the application layer, where the message is created. The TCP/IP suite offers protocols that support a wide assortment of applications, including Web resources, e-mail, instant messaging, RSS news feeds, network management tools, file transfer capability, remote login (SSH and telnet), and lots more. The application layer also provides utilities and tools, such as domain name system services, that support use of the TCP/IP suite itself. The application layer passes its messages to the transport layer as a stream of bytes, together with its intended destination address and other relevant information about the message.

As an interesting side note, there is no requirement that applications must be "official" members of the TCP/IP protocol suite. As long as an application provides software that can communicate successfully with the transport layer, it can be used. For this purpose, operating systems provide an interface called a **socket**, which makes it easy to add to the communication services provided by the TCP/IP suite. The concept of sockets originated with BSD UNIX. Sockets provide the interface between the application layer and the transport layer. Sockets are used by applications to initiate connections and to send messages through the network. You can picture a socket as a sort of software doorway through which bytes can flow. This allows new applications simply to "plug in" software that adds to the communication services available from the system. Sockets also provide a means for adding new protocols and keeping the network facilities current in their offerings. This capability offers some interesting possibilities. For example, it is possible to use TCP/IP to extend a different protocol over a TCP/IP-based network. The example below illustrates this option.

EXAMPLE

SCSI is an I/O bus protocol used for connecting hard disks and other devices to a computer. By using a computer interface with an application layer program that converts the SCSI bus protocol to a message that can be transmitted over a TCP/IP network it is possible to locate and operate a hard disk drive anywhere on any network that is reachable from the original site. The hard disk has a similar interface that translates the message back to its SCSI form. This type of application is usually named "XYZ over IP", where XYZ is the name of the original protocol. In this case, the application is called *iSCSI* or *SCSI over IP*. Note that this example again illustrates the duality of I/O and networking. See Figure 12.12.

There are many examples of this technique in the literature.

TRANSPORT LAYER (LAYER 4)   The purpose of the transport layer is to provide services that support reliable end-to-end communications. It is responsible for receiving a message from an application at the source node and delivering it to a corresponding application at the destination node. In a wide area network, a message is passed from node to node to get from its source to its destination. The message will often pass through a large number of intermediate nodes. In effect, each node forwards the message to the next. The three lower layers provide communication services between nodes that are immediate neighbors. The transport layer is responsible for generating the final address of the destination and for all end-to-end communication facilities, including establishing a connection with the destination, flow control, data assurance, reordering of packets, if necessary, error recovery, and termination of the connection. The transport layer is the layer responsible for **packetization** of the message, that is, the breaking up of the message into packets of reasonable size.

The ultimate destination address is established at the transport layer, although the network layer is the layer responsible for the routing of packets through the intermediate nodes to the destination. The message headers and control messages of the application

FIGURE 12.12

SCSI over IP

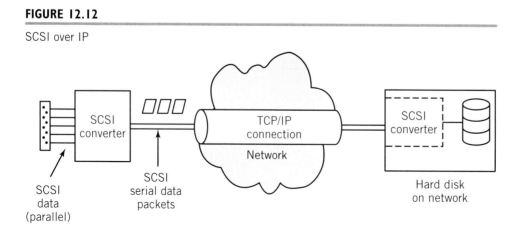

and transport layers make it possible for end nodes to communicate fully without regard or concern for the nature of any intermediate nodes, and conversely, the end-to-end communication is essentially transparent to the intermediate nodes.

The transport layer is implemented with three different standard protocols: TCP, UDP, and SCTP. When a message reaches the transport layer, one of these three is selected, based on the characteristics and requirements of the particular type of message. Each of the transport layer protocols works slightly differently. **Transmission Control Protocol (TCP)** is known as a **connection-oriented** service. Before data packets are sent to the receiving node, TCP at the sending node establishes a connection with TCP at the receiving node by exchanging control packets. TCP also uses sockets as the interface for this purpose. To establish a connection, the sending and receiving TCP each create a socket; the connection is made by connecting the sockets together. Ignoring the lower layers of the model for a moment, this conceptually results in a stream of bytes leaving the sender's application and flowing into the receiver's application. The connection made is full-duplex: packets can flow in both directions. The use of sockets allows a single TCP service to create multiple connections that operate simultaneously simply by creating additional sockets as they are needed.

Once the connection is made, TCP divides the message into packets, numbers them, and sends them to the network layer for transmission. TCP requires that an acknowledgment message be sent from the receiving node back to the sender to verify the receipt and acceptability of each packet in the message. If a packet is not acknowledged, TCP resends it. This capability is enhanced by the full-duplex connection that TCP establishes: data packets and acknowledgment packets can flow through the channel simultaneously. Thus, TCP offers a **reliable delivery** service. When the communication is complete, TCP closes the connection. In a way, TCP is like a pipe that opens to pass data in the form of a byte stream from an application at the sending node to the corresponding application at the receiving node, without regard for the details of the underlying mechanism (i.e., the lower layers). The pipe is called a **logical connection** because it operates independently of the actual physical characteristics of the network. Figure 12.13 illustrates this idea.

Note that the path that the packets take is not established by TCP; routing is the responsibility of the network layer. The network layer uses datagram switching, therefore the packets may each be routed differently. This creates the possibility that packets may arrive at the receiving node out of order. Numbering the packets allows the receiving node transport layer to reorder the packets, if necessary, to recreate the original message. TCP packets are called **segments** by some network practitioners, because their data content is part of an ordered sequence of bytes that is maintained across an entire packetized message.

An alternative protocol, **UDP**, for **User Datagram Protocol**, is used for some applications instead of TCP. UDP is a **connectionless service**. Unlike TCP, there is no communication between the sender and receiver nodes to set up a connection in advance. UDP packets are known as **user datagrams**. A UDP packet contains the message exactly as delivered from the application, thus it is the responsibility of the application to divide the message into smaller pieces, if necessary. Every datagram is sent independently. UDP is faster and simpler, but does not guarantee delivery. There is no acknowledgment of receipt by the receiving node. UDP is useful for communications in which the retransmission of a lost, out of order, or error-containing packet is not practical or in which the loss of a packet is relatively inconsequential. Streaming video is an example of this situation.

FIGURE 12.13

A "Logical Connection" View of TCP

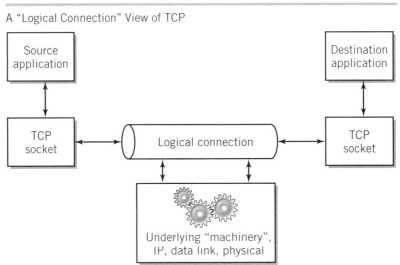

The newest alternative, **SCTP**, for **Stream Control Transmission Protocol**, offers features similar to TCP, with additional features that improve fault tolerance and enable multiple messages (in the form of byte streams—hence the name) to be transported simultaneously through the same connection Although SCTP could theoretically replace TCP, its current use is limited primarily to new applications, primarily those used with IP telephony and multimedia applications.

NETWORK LAYER (LAYER 3)   The network layer is responsible for the addressing and routing of packets to their proper final destination. The TCP/IP network layer is also called the internetworking layer or IP layer. IP is the single standard protocol for this layer, although there are several additional support protocols for matching IP addresses to the physical addresses that are used by the data link layer, for error reporting, for making information requests, and other auxiliary tasks.

For communications confined to a local area network, the task is usually simple. IP appends a header with a node-specific physical address to each packet (these are now referred to as **IP datagrams**), and passes the datagrams on to the data link layer. There is no routing to do, since all the nodes on a local area network are connected together and directly addressable. If the message address is in the form of an IP address, the software looks up the corresponding physical address in a table.

When the message is being sent to a node outside a local network, for example, to the Internet, the network layer is responsible for moving the message from sender to receiver, packet by packet, from one intermediate node to another through router packet switches. At each intermediate node, the network layer removes the current node address and establishes an address for the next node, using various tables and algorithms. The new address is added to the packet and the packet is passed to the data link layer, which handles the actual connection between nodes. It is not possible to store the address of every location at each node. Instead, the network layer has access to tables at various sites that assist in routing the message. Because routing takes place at the network layer, routers and gateways are sometimes called **layer 3 switches** to indicate the layer at which routing takes place.

Remember that the IP datagram may pass through different types of links. For certain types of physical layer connections, it is necessary to further divide the IP datagrams into smaller packets before they are delivered to the data link layer. IP has this capability, although it is rarely needed in modern systems, where the vast majority of linkages are based on Ethernet. These smaller packets are called **fragments**. IP datagram fragments are reassembled by IP when the final destination is reached, using header information that is stored with each fragment.

Although IP attempts to route every datagram to its final destination, it is a connectionless, packet switching service. Every IP datagram is routed independently. IP is an *unreliable*, **best-effort delivery service**: it does not guarantee delivery nor check for errors. Those tasks are the responsibility of the TCP layer, which takes responsibility for the entire message. Services similar to those of TCP are also available in the data link layer for reassembling and correcting packet errors that occur at the node-to-node level, although the services offered by the data link layer are rarely used since they mostly duplicate the services performed by TCP.

The intention of the original TCP/IP designers was to provide universal connectivity, with connection-independent protocols at the network layer. Thus, the TCP/IP standard does not "officially" address the data link and physical layers at all, although it recognizes the existence of these two layers as a necessity. As we noted earlier, these layers are generally addressed by a mixture of hardware and software that is directly tied to the needs of each particular type of communication channel. Nonetheless, there are clear relationships between the IP network layer and the data link layers, as described below.

DATA LINK LAYER (LAYER 2)   The data link layer is responsible for the reliable transmission and delivery of packets across the communication link between two adjacent nodes. Because the data link layer must be specific to the characteristics of the network or link and medium to which the node is attached, there are many different standards in use. The most common of these are the Ethernet standards, but there are many others.[3]

Most data communication practitioners divide the data link layer into two separate sublayers: the hardware medium-access control sublayer, which defines procedures for accessing the channel and detecting errors, and a software logical link control sublayer, which provides error correction and manages IP datagram/frame conversions, flow control, retransmission, and packet reconstruction.

If necessary, packets from the network layer are resized for compatibility with the medium-access control protocol used by the particular network or link. Packets at the data link layer are called **frames**. In most cases, the data link layer simply encapsulates the incoming IP datagram without change, and adds a data link layer header, and in some cases, a trailer, to create a frame.

---

[3]The author's favorite is a proposed standard for "IP over Avian Carrier," specifically, for carrier pigeons. The standard proposes that IP datagrams be written out on small sheets of paper and attached to the legs of carrier pigeons. The concept was implemented and successfully tested in Norway using the *ping* application. See the references in For Further Reading at the end of the chapter.

The **logical link control sublayer** provides appropriate error detection for each frame. Most data link protocols offer a means for requesting and retransmitting a frame that has not been received successfully. Since some communication conditions make it possible that frames will be received in the wrong order, the data link layer also numbers the frames and reorders the received frames if necessary to recreate the original message. Frames may be received in the wrong order if they are separately routed over communication paths of significantly different path lengths (it takes longer to get a message from Los Angeles to San Diego if it is routed via Alaska and Hawaii, for example) or if a frame has to be resent due to an error. As we noted above, the transport layer also provides these services, therefore the services of the logical link control layer are usually bypassed.

The **medium-access control (MAC) sublayer** is responsible for providing orderly access to the physical medium. Because there are a variety of media and signaling techniques in use, the standards define a number of different protocols and frame headers, each corresponding to a particular physical medium and signaling method. The protocol is responsible for such services as data encoding, collision handling (when multiple computers try to access a multipoint connection at the same time, for example), synchronization, and multiplexing. We will defer further consideration of this sublayer to Section 12.5 and Chapter 13.

PHYSICAL LAYER (LAYER 1)   The physical layer is the layer at which communication actually takes place. Communication at the physical layer consists of a bare stream of bits. The physical access protocol includes definition of the medium, the signaling method and specific signal parameters, voltages, carrier frequencies, lengths of pulses, and the like; synchronization and timing issues; and the method used to physically connect the computer to the medium. An example of a physical access protocol is the specification describing the specifics of the communication between an 802.11n wireless network card and a corresponding access point. The physical layer protocol defines the frequency of the carrier signal, data modulation and demodulation technique, bandwidth, strength of the transmitted signal under different conditions, and more. Physical communication between computers, routers, and other devices takes place only at the physical layer. The physical layer is implemented primarily in hardware by a **network interface controller (NIC)**[4], which generates the particular voltages, light pulses, radio waves, clock and synchronizing signals, and the like appropriate to a particular specification. More on this topic will be found in Chapter 14.

Figure 12.14 illustrates the use of the various layers in a simple end-to-end communication with an intermediate node that is used for routing The transport layer controls the flow of packets from the source to the destination. For each link, the network, data link, and physical layers are established according to the rules for the immediate communication. At the intermediate node, the lower three layers are stripped from the message-at-large and recreated according to the rules for the next link. For the first link, the network layer delivers the packets to the address of the router; the second link delivers the packets to the physical address that corresponds to their destination. The upper layers, consisting of the message

---

[4]NIC originally stood for "Network Interface Card" because the networking hardware was on a separate card that plugged into a bus on a computer. Today, the interface is often integrated into the motherboard, so the word "card" is a bit outdated, but "NIC" is firmly established as the name of the unit. Hence, "Controller".

FIGURE 12.14

Passing a Message through an Intermediate Node

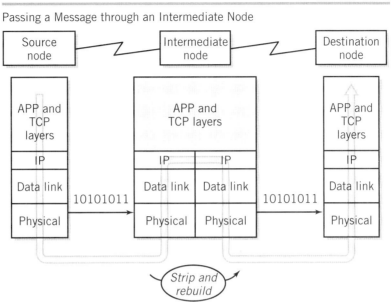

encapsulated in transport layer packets, pass through intermediate nodes untouched until the packets reach their destination. At that point, the transport layer opens the packets, performs error checking, and delivers the message to the designated application. If TCP or SCTP services are used, it also assures that all the pieces of the encapsulated message are present and reassembled correctly before delivery.

The OSI Network Model

As we noted above, the Open Systems Interconnection Reference Model or, more familiarly, the OSI model, represents an important theoretical attempt to present a complete protocol standard. The OSI model identifies all the factors that must be standardized in order for two computers to communicate completely and successfully at every possible level. The OSI standard was created by the International Standards Organization (ISO) after many years of study. Originally, the intention was to create a single protocol standard that would be used internationally for all computers. Although the OSI protocol suite itself has not been widely accepted and used for actual communication, the model is considered conceptually important as a means of identifying the factors involved for different types of communications and for comparing the performance and capabilities of different protocols. It is generally not viewed as an implementable alternative to the TCP/IP model. Figure 12.15 is a diagram comparing some of the more important protocols in the TCP/IP suite to the OSI reference layer model.

The OSI model consists of seven layers, instead of five. The most important difference between TCP/IP and OSI is that the functions of the application layer of the TCP/IP

FIGURE 12.15

A Comparison of OSI and TCP/IP

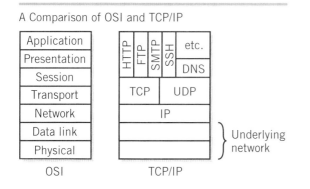

model are essentially divided among three OSI layers. The capabilities and features of the additional two layers, the presentation layer and the session layer, are almost entirely subsumed into the TCP/IP application layer. However, a few services of the session layer in the OSI model are actually part of the TCP/IP transport layer. There are only minor differences in the other layers. Since the other layers have already been described as part of the TCP/IP model, we only explain the additional two OSI layers.

SESSION LAYER The upper three layers of the OSI model assume that a successful end-to-end connection is established and maintained at the transport layer. These layers are concerned with the flow of data and control between applications on the communicating nodes.

A session is the dialogue between two cooperating applications or processes at the ends of the communication link. The session layer is responsible for establishing the session between the applications, controlling the dialogue, and terminating the session. Remote login and spooling operations would use the services of the session layer to assure successful login and to control the flow of data to the remote printer, for example.

PRESENTATION LAYER The presentation layer provides common data conversions and transformations that allow systems with different standards to communicate. The presentation layer includes services such as data compression and restoration, encryption and decryption, ASCII-Unicode conversion, data reformatting, and the like. The fundamental purpose of the presentation layer is to present data at the destination with the same meaning and appearance as it would have at the source.

There are a number of different protocol suites in use that operate similarly to the OSI reference model, or implement parts of it. In addition to TCP/IP, these include the IBM Systems Network Architecture (SNA), Novell IPX/SPX, and Appletalk, among others. In the past few years, the TCP/IP protocol suite has become the network connectivity protocol of choice for a huge number of installations. TCP/IP has been closely associated with connection to local area networks and to the Internet in people's minds. While the association is accurate, TCP/IP is also popular for general communication at all levels of network connectivity, from the smallest local area networks to the largest wide area networks, even for modem connections to networks through the telephone system. (PPP, Point-to-Point Protocol, may be familiar to you as it is used for dial-up modem, DSL, and cable access to the Internet.) TCP/IP is included for nearly every modern operating system. TCP/IP is reliable and mature.

Addressing

The ability to tie multiple network devices into a network require addressing standards that are implemented for every device attached to the network. When the network is interconnected with other networks, the requirements for addressing are even more stringent, and the addressing standards must apply globally. TCP/IP is typical of network models in this respect. TCP/IP requires addresses to specify the applications responsible for message communication, the addresses of the sender and receiver nodes plus all intermediate nodes involved in a communication, and finally, a physical address that selects a particular node within a network.

A user creates a message at the application layer. Like any messaging system, the user must also specify the address of a receiver for the message. The message could be a print server request, a Web request, an e-mail message or any other application-based message. The user will normally specify this address as a *user-friendly* address: a URL such as www.youtube.com, or an e-mail address such as somebody@yahoo.com, or perhaps even the name of a printer on the local network. User-friendly addresses allow a user to work with addresses that are familiar and understandable.

To be effective, user-friendly addresses must be global in scope if they are to exist outside the confines of an isolated network. There must also be no possibility of duplicates. The use of a standard global **domain name** system with required name registration provides these assurances and provides a hierarchical system for name creation and registration and tools for locating and identifying specific names.

TCP/IP requires addresses to be specified numerically in the form of **IP addresses**. IP addresses are also called **logical addresses**. There are two standards for IP addresses. The older system, IPv4, specifies 32-bit addresses. To make these easier for humans to read, they are generally separated into 8-bit groups called **octets**, delimited by dots. Each octet is written as a decimal number from 0 to 255. A typical address might be written as 208.80.152.2 (it's Wikipedia), for example. IPv6, which is intended to supplant IPv4, specifies 128-bit addresses. These are expressed as eight groups of four-digit hexadecimal numbers separated by colons. To simplify the written description somewhat, leading zeros and zero values in one or more consecutive groups can be eliminated. A typical IPv6 address might look like this: 6E:2A20::35C:66C0:0:5500. (This one is tricky: there are two consecutive groups of 0 between the empty colons in this example, but the :0: is required to avoid ambiguity. Otherwise, you would not be able to tell which pair of empty colons had the two groups of 0.) Needless to say, user-friendly names take on even more importance when working with IPv6!

Before a message is sent by an application to the transport layer for data transmission, the address is translated, if necessary, from user-friendly to IP address using an application-support program that utilizes a global domain name directory service. We will expand our discussion of DNS, the domain name system service in Chapter 13.

In addition to the message and the IP address to whom the message is being sent, the transport identifies the application that created the message and the application that is to receive the message with **port addresses,** or more commonly, **port numbers**.[5] Port numbers are sixteen bits in length. The first 1024 numbers are called **well-known ports**. These are standard addresses specified for most common applications. You are probably

---

[5]Network port numbers are different than I/O ports. They are created and used in software, as opposed to I/O ports, which are hardware based.

FIGURE 12.16

Some Well-Known Port Numbers

ftp	20	file transfer
ssh	22	secure login
smtp	25	simple mail transfer
nicname	43	"who is" request
finger	79	info about system
http	80	Web
kerberos	88	encryption
pop3	110	post office protocol
sqlserv	118	SQL services

FIGURE 12.17

The Different Addresses Used
in a Network

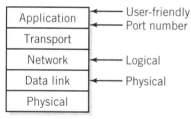

familiar with port number 80, which is commonly used for Web services. Figure 12.16 shows the port numbers for some of the familiar applications.

Port numbers can be modified by an application. A large number of user-defined port numbers are available for this purpose. To accommodate this option, the application of the sender can specify the port number of the application to which the message is being sent. For example, if a user knows that the Web server being addressed is on port 8080, instead of port 80 (a common trick used to hide a Web server from users who do not have access privileges), she can specify the port number by appending it to the URL with a colon thus: www.somewhere.org/hidden Server:8080.

As noted previously, the application sends its message to the transport layer, together with sending and receiving port addresses and sending and receiving IP addresses. The transport layer and network layers perform the tasks we described earlier. The port addresses will not be looked at again until the message reaches the transport level at the receiver.

The network layer uses IP addresses to forward datagrams to the receiving node. This is not the whole story, however, because the data link and physical layers require **physical addresses** to identify the nodes to which they are attached. Physical addresses are associated with individual devices connected to a network. IP addresses are converted to physical addresses by an address resolution protocol at the network layer. The details of this process are left for Chapter 13. Both physical and IP addresses are required because devices can be moved from one network to another and because IP addresses can be assigned dynamically.

The physical addressing of individual devices attached to a network is part of the standard for that type of network. By far the most common type of physical address in use, however, is the **medium-access control (MAC) address**. Every manufactured device that may connect to a network anywhere in the world is supplied with a permanent, unique MAC address. A MAC address is 48 bits in length described as six two-digit hexadecimal numbers separated by colons. For example, the Ethernet adapter for the computer upon which this text is being typed has MAC address 00:C0:9F:6C:F9:D0.

Figure 12.17 shows the positions of all of the different addresses used in networking.

12.5 TYPES OF NETWORKS

There are numerous ways to categorize networks: by medium (coaxial cable, wireless, fiber, for example), by protocol group (TCP/IP, Frame Relay, FDDI, ATM), by standard specification number (802.3, 802.11, X.25), by usage (Web server, database server, peer-to-peer, storage area network), or by range of service (Bluetooth, LAN, MAN, WAN) to name a few.

The most familiar, and often most practical and useful, of these is to categorize networks by their geographical range of service. A common approach is to categorize them hierarchically. From smallest range to largest, the major categories are local area networks, backbone networks, metropolitan area networks, and wide area networks. We will also include Internet backbones and the Internet. These designations are somewhat arbitrary, and more a matter of style and architecture than of rigid rule, but they are helpful as a starting point for visualizing and designing networks. We will also mention briefly some special cases: virtual local area networks, intranets, extranets, personal area networks (also known as piconets), and virtual private networks, that do not fit neatly into the standard categories.

Network Topology

Before we describe each type of network, we need to provide a brief introduction to the concept of network topology. **Network topology** describes the fundamental layout of a network. Topology is a characteristic of all networks, large and small. It defines the path, or paths, between any two points in the network, and therefore affects the performance of the network, particularly in terms of availability, speed, and traffic congestion. If you picture the packets in a network as tiny automobiles (actually, this is *often* a useful way to think about networks), there is an obvious similarity to automobile traffic. Figure 12.18 illustrates a few of the potential issues.

Figure 12.18(a) shows one common approach to road traffic design. A single main road runs through a small city, with side roads intersecting the main road at regular intervals. There is only a single road from one end of the city to the other. Traffic lights control the flow of traffic along the main road, but of course, they must allow the lines of traffic on the side streets to enter the main road from time to time. If traffic is sufficiently light (think 4 a.m.), this layout works adequately; at rush hour, it's a nightmare!

Figure 12.18(b) shows an alternative approach. In this case, there are a number of main streets running from one end of town to the other, with cross streets that allow traffic to move from one main street to another. Traffic will distribute itself along different routes,

FIGURE 12.18

Traffic Scenarios

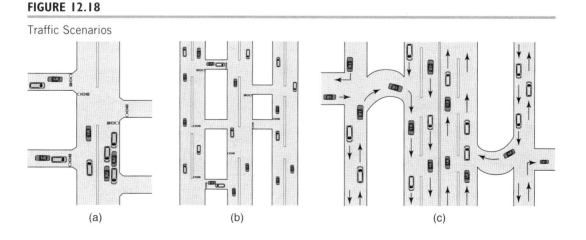

(a)   (b)   (c)

depending on each driver's preferences and destination. Traffic in general will probably flow more smoothly, although there could be congestion at certain intersections.

Figure 12.18(c) shows a third approach. In this case a superhighway runs alongside the city, with ramps at strategic locations that connect into the main streets. For short distances, the average driver will use the city streets because it is easier: the distances are shorter and the overall travel time is normally less. For longer distances, the superhighway is the way to go.

Figure 12.19 shows the four basic topologies used for networks. Each topology has its tradeoffs, advantages, and disadvantages. In given circumstances, a particular topology is often more natural or appropriate for the application. The art of network design is about selecting the right combination to attain the mixture of features, performance, network availability, maintenance, cost, and convenience to meet a given set of requirements or needs.

Figure 12.19(a) shows a **mesh network**. Mesh networks provide multiple paths between end nodes. The failure of an individual intermediate node will slow, but not stop network traffic as long as an alternative path is available. As you will see shortly, large networks are

FIGURE 12.19

Four Network Topologies

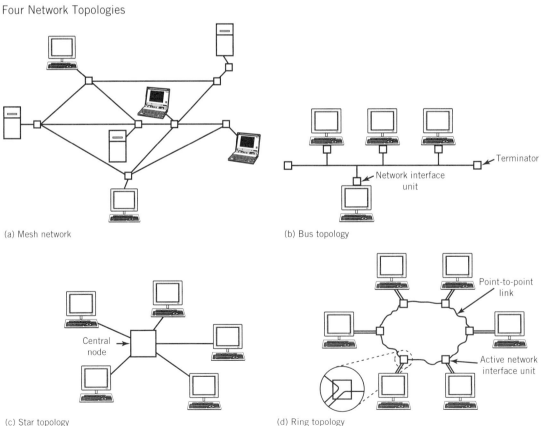

(a) Mesh network

(b) Bus topology

(c) Star topology

(d) Ring topology

FIGURE 12.20

A Five-Node Full Mesh Network

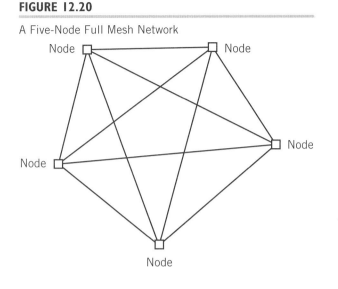

usually made up of a mixture of local area networks, links, and connecting nodes, with switches and routers connecting the different networks and links together. By default, the result is usually a mesh network. It is also possible to create a mesh network intentionally, by design. ATM, mentioned earlier in Section 12.3, is an example of a mesh network of this type.

The "best" configuration for connecting a number of end nodes would be to provide a direct point-to-point channel connecting each pair of nodes. This scheme, known as a *full* mesh network, is not practical for most installations, however, because the number of lines required increases too rapidly as the number of nodes increases. Furthermore, each node requires an interface for each connecting line. Figure 12.20 shows a mesh network with five nodes. Even this simple case requires ten connections to provide full connectivity. Since each node is connected to four others, the network also requires four interfaces for each node, for a total of twenty interfaces. Simply increasing the number of nodes to twenty increases the number of connections to 190 and requires 380 interfaces. For 500 computer nodes, we would require nearly 125,000 interconnecting cables! In general, the number of connections for a fully connected mesh network with N nodes is the sum of all integer values from 1 to $N-1$. Fortunately, this reduces to a simple formula:

$$\text{number of connections} = (\text{nodes}) \times (\text{nodes} - 1)/2.$$

More realistically, most mesh networks are *partial* mesh networks. One rare exception is the use of full mesh networks to connect a small number of major corporate centers for a large organization in a metropolitan or wide area network, particularly when the network traffic between centers is heavy and relatively evenly distributed.

Figure 12.19(b) shows a **bus topology**. Note the obvious similarity to the multipoint buses described in Chapter 7. With a bus topology, each node is tapped into the bus along the bus. To communicate, a sending node "broadcasts" a message which travels along the bus. Every other node receives the message, but, because each node matches its address to that of the message, the message is ignored by every node except that of the desired recipient. Each end of the bus is equipped with a terminator to prevent signals from echoing. Branches can be added to a bus, expanding it into a tree. Messages are still broadcast through the tree. Terminators are placed at the ends of each branch in the tree.

Bus topology is the easiest to wire. It is only necessary to run a single pair of wires from one end of the network space to the other. Bus topology also has the advantage of low cost, however, traffic congestion is a major issue with bus topology. Compare this figure with that of Figure 12.18(a) and the reason becomes clear. Bus topology is still in use for legacy and local area networks and some backbone networks, but is now rarely used for new designs. Because of the unguided nature of radio waves, some form of bus topology is a requirement for wireless networking.

Figure 12.19(c) shows a **star topology**. This topology is used primarily for local area networks, although it is sometimes used in metropolitan and wide area networks to connect individual centers of activity to a central office. In this configuration, all nodes are connected point-to-point to a central device. Nodes communicate through the central device. Switching in the central device connects pairs of nodes together to allow them to communicate directly and steers data from one node to another as required. Most modern switches allow multiple pairs of nodes to communicate simultaneously.

Figure 12.19(d) shows a **ring topology**. A ring topology consists of a point-to-point connection from each node on the network to the next. The last node on the network is connected back to the first to form a closed ring. Each node retransmits the signal that it receives from the previous node to the next node in the ring. Packets are placed on the loop at a node, and travel from node to node until the desired node is reached. Although the ring is inherently unidirectional (data passes through it in one direction), it is possible to build a bidirectional ring network.

Ring networks were popular in the past because they provided a controlled way in which to guarantee network performance. This was an important issue when increased network capacity incurred a large incremental cost. Today, that is no longer the case. It is often cheaper and easier to increase capacity than it is to try to wring the last bit of performance out of a network. Nonetheless, there are legacy token-ring local area networks and FDDI fiber optic backbone and metropolitan area networks still in service.

When we consider topology—any topology—it is important to understand that there is a difference between physical topology and logical topology. **Physical topology** describes the actual layout of the wiring for the network. **Logical topology** defines the operational relationship between the various network components. The physical topology is unimportant when trying to understand how a network works, but very important to a network designer trying to figure out where to place the wires in a room. However, our focus in this text is on the logical topology only.

Local Area Networks

A **local area network (LAN)** is a network that connects computers and other supporting devices over a relatively small localized area, typically a room, the floor of a building, a building, or multiple buildings within close range of each other. Usually, most of the computers in a local area network are personal computers or workstations, although sometimes there may be larger server computers present. Supporting devices might include printers, external storage devices, and routers. Routers, and perhaps gateways, will be used to connect the LAN to other networks.

Some LANs are further limited in geographical scope by the particular medium in use. Wireless Ethernet, commonly identified by its trade name, Wi-Fi, for example, is limited to a maximum range of a few hundred feet under ideal conditions by the usable strength of the radio signal that is used to carry the data. Walls and other obstructions will limit the range of the signal even more.

Since *all* communication channels are limited in the amount of data that they can carry, it is sometimes useful to design a LAN to minimize extraneous traffic on the network where possible. One common way to do this in business is to create separate LANs for different business functions or departments. Traffic between the different LANs is enabled by connecting the LANs together with a backbone network, as described later in this section. For example, there would be a LAN for the accounting department, a LAN for the marketing department, and so on. The interconnection between networks allows the different departments to communicate with each other, as well as to access data stored on central company servers. This was the approach shown in Figure 1.4 of Chapter 1.

There are different kinds of local area networks, each defined by its network protocols, particularly the data link and physical layers, maximum bit rate, connecting media, topology (the physical and logical layout), and various features. Most modern local area networks are based on a set of standards and associated protocols called **Ethernet**. They are also identified by their IEEE standards (see Section 12.6). The standards define Ethernet at the data link and physical layers. Although Ethernet comes in a number of "flavors", three are prevalent: switched Ethernet (IEEE 802.3), Wi-Fi (IEEE 802.11), and hub-based Ethernet (also IEEE 802.3). The Ethernet protocols are designed to make It is possible to mix different flavors in a single network. There are a number of variations on each flavor. Figure 12.21 describes the features of some of the prevalent Ethernet standards.

As an example of how Ethernet units operate together, consider a home network with a router that also provides a wireless access point and an Ethernet switch. The router uses Ethernet to connect to a DSL or cable modem for Internet access, an Ethernet cable

FIGURE 12.21

Some Common Ethernet Standards

Standard	Medium	Speed	Max span	Topology
10 BASE-T	2-UTP	10 Mbps	100 meters	hub or switch
100 BASE-TX "Fast Ethernet"	2-UTP or STP or CAT-5	100 Mbps	100 meters	hub or switch
100 BASE-FX	2-Fiber optics	100 Mbps	100 meters	-
1000 BASE-T "Gigabit Ethernet"	CAT-5 UTP	1 Gbps	100 meters	switch
1000 BASE-SX, LX	2-Fiber optics	1 Gbps	550 meter, 5 km	
10G BASE-X "10-Gigabit Ethernet"	2-Fiber optics	10 Gbps	300 m, 10 km, 40 km	
Under development				
40G BASE-X	2-Fiber optics	40 Gbps	100 m, 10 km	
100G BASE-X	2-Fiber optics	100 Gbps	100 m, 10 km, 40 km	

Key: UTP unshielded twisted pair
     STP shielded twisted pair
     CAT-5 four UTP in a cable

FIGURE 12.22

A Typical Home Network

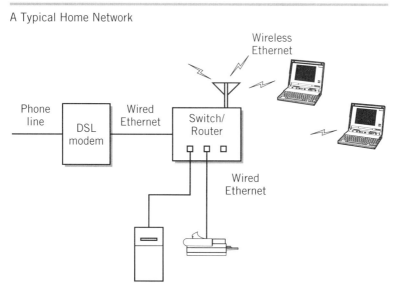

connects a printer directly to the switch, and one or more computers use wireless Ethernet to connect wirelessly. See Figure 12.22.

FIGURE 12.23

Hub-Based Ethernet

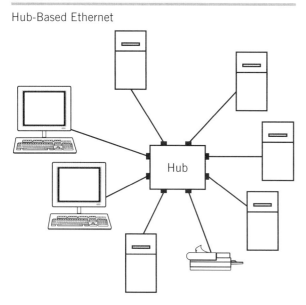

As shown in Figure 12.23, **hub-based Ethernet** is based on a the bus topology shown in Figure 12.19(b). A **hub** is a passive central connection device used to simplify wiring and maintenance. A hub is a layer 1 physical layer device. All of the connections at the hub are simply tied together inside the hub. The word "passive" means that the hub performs no operation or modification of the signals as they arrive at the hub. Signals arriving at the hub are simply **broadcast** in their original form to every other device connected to the hub. In other words, logically the hub is basically a "squeezed-down" version of a multipoint bus topology. Network interface units from various computers, computer peripherals, and other network support devices such as routers are connected to the hub and share the "bus". The signals, of course, represent frames. Since each frame has a destination address, the NICs simply ignore the broadcast data for any frame whose destination address does not match that of the NIC.

Because every device connected to the hub is sharing the bandwidth of the network, the

FIGURE 12.24

Switch-Based Ethernet

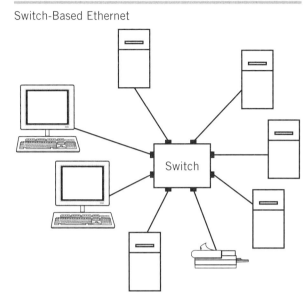

bandwidth available to individual connections decreases at least proportionally to the number of units using the network. When traffic is heavy, there may be many devices contending for use of the bus. A medium access control protocol called **CSMA/CD** (Carrier Sense Multiple Access with Collision Detection) is used to manage access to the bus, but, like the main street in Figure 12.18(a), traffic jams can occur, and the performance of hub-based Ethernet deteriorates rapidly when traffic is heavy.

Hubs are used primarily in local area networks, but are also sometimes seen in backbone networks. However, the use of hubs is declining because better performance can be obtained from other devices that can isolate and operate on individual nodes, particularly switches, discussed next.

Figure 12.24 shows an alternative topology called **switched Ethernet**. Switched Ethernet is based logically on a star topology. Each node of the network is connected to a central switch that is capable of connecting any two nodes together. When a node on the network wishes to communicate with another node, the switch sets up a direct connection between the two. Standard Ethernet cables contain at least two pairs of wires, which are used to make the connections full-duplex. Multiple pairs of nodes can communicate at full bandwidth through the switch simultaneously. For wired local area networks, switched Ethernet is the prevalent method in use today.

Wireless Ethernet, or **"Wi-Fi"** is a radio-based, compatible extension to the Ethernet standard. Wi-Fi is based around a central **access point** that is somewhat equivalent to a hub. However the access point is an active node, since it must transmit and receive radio waves to communicate with the nodes.

There are a number of different versions of the Wi-Fi standard, operating at different radio frequencies and with different bit rates. Only those operating at the same radio frequency are compatible with each other, however Wi-Fi components that operate at higher bit rates can slow their data rate for compatibility with slower speed units. Some access points and NICs support multiple radio frequencies. Figure 12.25 compares the features of the current Wi-Fi standards.

Like hub-based Ethernet, the "radio space" must be shared; only one unit can

FIGURE 12.25

Wireless Ethernet Characteristics

Standard	Carrier band	Max. data rate	Claimed typical max. range
802.11a	5 GHz	54 Mbps	60 feet
802.11b	2.4 GHz	11 Mbps	300 feet
802.11g	2.4 GHz	54 Mbps	300 feet
802.11n[*]	5, 2.4 GHz	248 Mbps[**]	600 feet

[*] Unofficial as of December 2008
[**] Possible future theoretical max. data rate of 600 Mbps.

transmit at a time. Therefore, the bit rate of Wi-Fi is dependent both on the specified maximum speed and the number of simultaneous users. Twice the users means half the speed.

Nodes on a Wi-Fi LAN attempting to transmit simultaneously are more difficult to manage with Wi-Fi than with hub-based Ethernet, particularly because it is possible for units to have radio signals that are strong enough to communicate with the access point but still be far enough apart to be unaware of each other's presence. The Wi-Fi standard provides a number of medium access protocols to handle possible interference between nodes. These protocols are proactive. They are designed to avoid collisions, unlike the hub protocol, which is designed simply to detect and correct for collisions.

Traditionally, multiple access points have been linked by wire. A new standard introduces the concept of **mesh points**, which extends the range of a wireless network by creating a wireless mesh network of access points. Mesh points operate at the medium-access control layer (layer 2) and are essentially invisible to the upper layers of the network. This new standard effectively adds backbone capability to wireless networking. Figure 12.26 shows a simple wireless mesh network.

FIGURE 12.26

Wireless Mesh Network

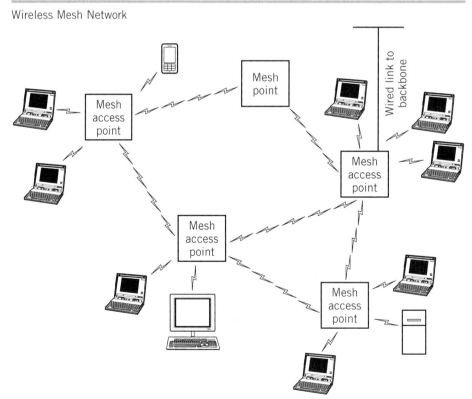

More information about Ethernet local area networks will be found in Chapter 13. Information about Wi-Fi and wireless networking in particular will be found in Section 14.4 of Chapter 14.

Backbone Networks

Backbone networks are used to interconnect local area networks. A backbone can tie several local area networks together to provide for the passage of data between the individual networks and from the networks to the Internet or other external network resources. A primary motivation for a backbone network is to improve overall performance of a larger network by creating separate local area networks for groups of users who communicate primarily with each other. Network traffic can be isolated into small areas of usage, replacing one large heavily used local area network with a number of smaller, isolated LANs. The backbone enables communication between the individual LANs when it is required. For example, a college campus might have LANs built around dormitory areas, plus wireless access points in classrooms, study areas, libraries, dining halls, and various other points around the campus where people congregate. A backbone network would provide the interconnections between all of these LANs. The backbone network also makes it possible to extend the overall range of the combined networks well beyond that of a single LAN. In this case fiber optic cables in the backbone combined with the use of switches makes coverage of a large geographical area, such as a large college campus, feasible.

One simple way to view a backbone network is to picture it as a large local area network where each node is, itself, a local area network. Figure 12.27 shows an example of such an Ethernet-based backbone network implementation. In this example, we have assumed that the interLAN traffic would be light, so a hub-based form of Ethernet is used. If traffic were heavy, or if the length of the connections between the hub and the individual LANs is long, switched Ethernet would be used instead, that is, the hub would be replaced by a switch. The longer cables and interconnections with heavier traffic might also be connected with fiber optic cable instead of copper wire to improve overall performance. Since the backbone network shown in Figure 12.27 is obviously hierarchical, the concept can be extended to another hierarchical level, if desired. Some network designers actually call this backbone network layout **tiered Ethernet**.

There are two additional features to observe in the backbone network shown in Figure 12.27. First, is the presence of a server. Since it is located directly on an arm of the backbone it is readily available from every LAN. The other feature is a router or gateway that will connect the backbone to other networks through a common carrier. This feature will enable the capabilities of metropolitan and wide area networking that we discuss below and will also provide access to the Internet.

One important use for backbone networks is to extend the availability of wireless Ethernet access beyond the limited range of an individual access point. Instead, multiple access points are distributed over a large area to provide a wider range of coverage. A backbone network provides the interconnection between the access points. This method also improves the speed for individual users, since fewer users are sharing any single access point. This is a particularly common application of backbone network technology on college campuses. Although the current discussion is focused on wired or fiber optic backbone networks, and although most access point backbones are currently based on wire

FIGURE 12.27

A Backbone Network

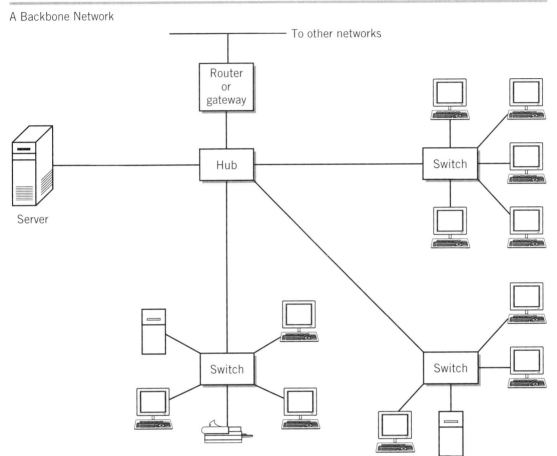

or fiber, we have already mentioned wireless mesh networks as a new alternative backbone technology.

Backbone networks are well suited for small intranets. An **intranet** is an organizational network where the user interfaces and applications are based primarily on Web services. Its use is restricted to authorized users within the organization. Some network practitioners refer to it as a "private Internet". Intranets for larger organizations require the connectivity of metropolitan area networks or wide area networks. As we discuss next, the primary limiting factor in larger networks is the ability to connect separate locations over intervening public and private property.

It is worth mentioning that it is possible to design a backbone area network with switches in such a way that the network can be reconfigured dynamically. Specifically, individual hosts can be moved from one local area network to another by changing the settings in the switches. This feature allows the network administrator to tailor the traffic load on various parts of the network to optimize performance. Such a network is called a **virtual local area network**. Further discussion of virtual networks is beyond the scope of this text.

Metropolitan Area Networks

A **metropolitan area network** (**MAN**) is usually defined as a network larger in geographical scope than a local area network, but generally within a range of less than 30 miles or 50 kilometers. A MAN would be used to connect several buildings in an area together or, perhaps, connect a company's buildings in a city or region together. Some communities have built or plan to build MANs, both for their own use, and as a service utility for their residents and businesses.

When the area is relatively small, it may be possible to implement a MAN almost entirely with a combination of local area networks and one or more backbone networks, plus some easy-to-manage form of Internet access such DSL. More commonly, there is a desire to create network links to connect properties over areas that would require **right-of-way access**, that is, permission to run wires through somebody else's property. When this is the case, a company generally requires services from a **service provider** (**SP**) or other public carrier, and the infrastructure of the MAN begins to resemble that of a wide area network. A service provider is a company that provides the equivalent of a link or links between nodes that are not directly accessible to simple forms of connection, like wire or fiber optic cable. A connection to a provider occurs at an access point on the customer's premises. The access point is usually connected to the company networks with a switch, a router, or a gateway, depending on the type of connection. The connection is often referred to as an **edge** connection, because it sits at the "edge" of the local network. Thus, a router at the access point would be called an **edge router**.

Figure 12.28 illustrates the features of a medium-sized MAN. This business operates a small chain of stores, together with a related, company-operated website. Most of the business and IT operations in this company take place at company headquarters; those needs are satisfied by an intranet consisting of local area networks connected with an on-site backbone. On the outskirts of the city, however, are three additional offices with links that connect to the backbone system at company headquarters.

The office that hosts the Web service is connected to the Internet with a high-speed optical fiber link to an **Internet Service Provider** (**ISP**). (All connections to the Internet are made through an ISP—more about that later.) The Web server is located here because the ISP has a **point of presence** in the immediate vicinity that provides the required connection. The office is connected to company headquarters with a point-to-point Metro Ethernet link; Metro Ethernet is a relatively new approach, in which a service provider provides Ethernet access to each site, creating a logical connection between the two sites. The literature refers to this link as an *Ethernet Virtual Connection*. Standard Ethernet switches at the access points connect the company's backbone network to the service at the headquarters and to a local area network at the satellite office.

A brief comment about the carrier providing the Metro Ethernet service offers a worthwhile opportunity to expand your perspective on the protocol layers in the network models. We noted earlier in the chapter, in Section 12.4, that the network model makes it possible to substitute protocols for a given layer (in the example, SCSI over IP), provided the interfaces between layers are suitably maintained. The network within the service provider itself, then, has a number of options that are transparent at the access points. Some provider networks are based entirely on Ethernet, from end to end, but many use alternative protocols within their own networks, for various reasons including bandwidth

FIGURE 12.28

A Metropolitan Area Network

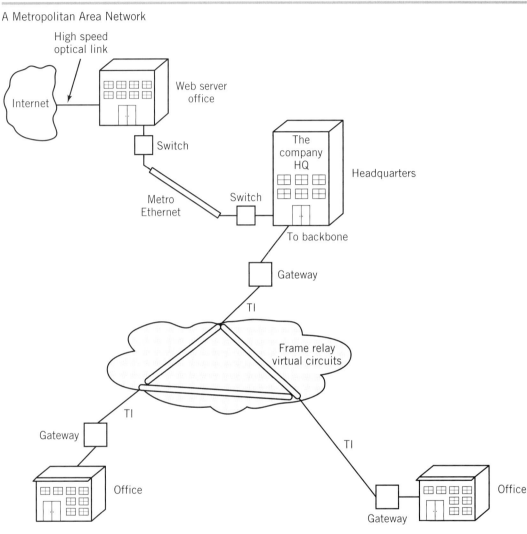

control, protection of service privacy, reliability, scalability, and legacy (i.e., the system was already in place). Common alternatives include (Ethernet over) MLPS, ATM, Sonet, and SDH. (A brief overview of these protocols will be found in Chapter 13.) Metro Ethernet was developed specifically with metropolitan area networks in mind.

The other two offices communicate with each other and with headquarters using a virtual network created by a carrier using T1 lines and a Frame Relay supplied by the telephone company. T1 and Frame Relay are more traditional approaches to carrier connectivity. Gateways are required to convert between the various office networks in this case.

This figure illustrates a number of fundamental features of metropolitan area networking. Most important, notice that the carrier-provided service links and the links in the outlying offices form an integral part of the overall company network, just as though they were all located on the same premises with the main backbone network. With this understanding, you can see that the design is based on traffic requirements between the different offices and between each office and headquarters, just as the backbone network was designed to optimize traffic with each LAN and between the various LANs.

The role of the service provider is to supply network links that are transparent to the overall topology of the network. There are a number of different options available. We will expand on the various types of service connections in the discussion of wide area networking.

Some network specialists also define a network type between LAN and MAN, which they call a *campus area network (CAN)*. A campus area network consists of a number of interconnected local area networks operating over a limited geographic region consisting of several buildings clustered together, such as would be found on a college campus, military base, or multi-building company setting. Campus area networks are commonly implemented as backbone-based networks with high-speed optical fiber interconnections that are topologically similar to MANs, but without the requirements of a service provider. One or more edge gateways or routers connect the campus area network to the Internet and perhaps to other facilities, as well. Connections to other facilities would, of course, create a more MAN- or LAN-like configuration.

Wide Area Networks (WAN)

Wide area networks are networks designed to facilitate communications between users and applications over large distances—between the various corporate offices of an international organization that are located in cities all over the world, for example.

There are two primary compelling reasons for designing and building wide area network capabilities:

- An organization requires data communication links between widely spread facilities and between an organization and its business partners, customers, and suppliers.
- An organization requires fast access to the Internet, either as a consumer or as a provider of Internet services, or both.

These two requirements, may, of course, overlap substantially. For example, an **extranet** is a connection between a business and its business partners, used for the exchange of information and services, and for collaboration, coordination and planning. The Internet is generally preferred as the medium for extranet activities.

The main distinguishing feature that characterizes the wide area network concept is the extensive reliance on service providers to supply the required connectivity between the various locations of the network nodes. The distances are too large to connect directly with a network owner's own resources and it is impractical to obtain rights of access to all of the intervening property, public or private. Plus, it just isn't practical for a company to lay its own cable across the Pacific Ocean! Wide area networks require the use of resources that are within the sphere of **public switched telephone networks (PSTNs)**, large cable companies, and other common carrier service providers. A company builds its network at each location out to an edge access point, usually a gateway or router, at which point it is connected to the carrier's facilities with a leased line to the carrier's nearest point of presence.

Despite the distances between nodes, it is still possible to view the networks as a whole in the same way as we have viewed other, much smaller networks. Local area networks and backbone networks, and, perhaps even metropolitan area networks, are linked to form a large wide area network. However, it is common to represent the services provided by the carrier as a "black box." (Actually, they are usually represented as a cloud!) Our interest in the details of the carrier network are generally limited to the edge connections and to the performance of the network as a whole. For clarity, the carrier network is sometimes represented as a collection of **private virtual circuits**, within the cloud which reflect the logical connections of the wide area network as a whole.

Most wide area networks are classified topologically as partial mesh networks, but occasionally you may see examples of full mesh topology and star topology at the visible and logically connected top level of a wide area network. Figure 12.29 shows two examples of wide area network configurations. Figure 12.29(a) shows an example of a star-configured wide area network. In this example, all of the logical connections within the carrier network connect between individual regional research and educational centers and the main center in Amsterdam. There are no direct connections between the branches. Figure 12.29(b) shows a more typical partial-mesh configuration.

There are a number of different options to provide the carrier connections for a wide area network These can be classified into three categories, according to the layer of the network selected for access: physical, data link, or network. The table in Figure 12.30 shows some of the more popular options.

Internet Backbones and the Internet

In theory, it should be possible to link any two computers or computer-based devices in the world using nothing but the routing capabilities of interconnected networks, TCP/IP, routers and gateways, plus appropriate data link layer software and physical connections. And indeed, the Internet is a gigantic partial mesh network, connecting a high percentage of all the computers in the world. In practice, though, the number of intermediate nodes, measured as **hops** between nodes, would make this scheme impractical. The connections would be too slow, the order of arrival of packets too erratic, and the traffic too heavy, to sustain the effort for long. Although the Internet concept postulates that such connections can occur, it is more practical to provide fast connections between distant points to reduce the time it takes to traverse long distances, to reduce the number of hops to just a few, and to reduce the traffic on the local connections. The Internet can be compared to a structure of roads and highways. We travel on long distance, high-speed, limited access superhighways for the longest legs of a journey and use the local roads for initial access to the highways and for the final access to our destination. There might even be a middle tier of medium-speed highways that provide a means to get from the nearest superhighway exit to the network of local roads. In the United States, for example, Interstate highways provide the long legs of the journey, national and state highways the connections to the local roads of cities and towns, and local roads to start and finish our journeys.

FIGURE 12.29

Two Real-World Wide Area Networks

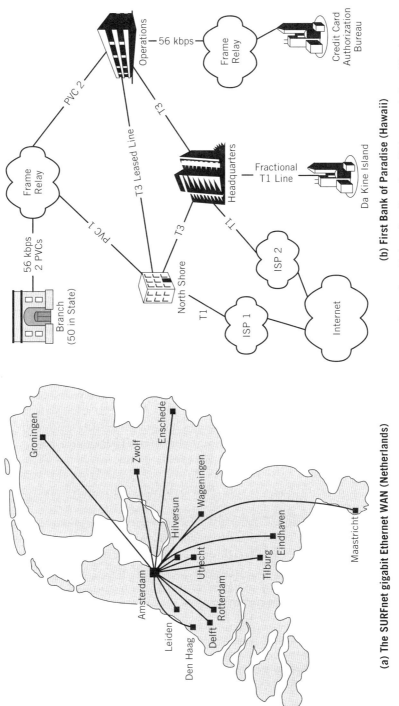

(b) First Bank of Paradise (Hawaii)

Source: From *Business Data Networks and Telecommunications*, 7th ed.,
R. Panko, Copyright © 2008, by Prentice Hall p. 305.
Reprinted with permission.

(a) The SURFnet gigabit Ethernet WAN (Netherlands)

Source: From *Business Data Communications and Networking*, 9th ed.,
J. Fitzgerald and A. Dennis, Copyright © 2006, by John Wiley & Sons, p. 331.
Reprinted with permission.

FIGURE 12.30

Wide Area Network Carrier Options

Layer	Name	Description	Speed range	Media
1 (Physical)	T-1, T-2, T-3, T-4, E-1, E-3; (fractional T-1)	Traditional telephone co. T-lines, E-lines; known as Digital Service (DS-1, etc.)	1.5 Mbps–275 Mbps (< 1 Mbps)	data-grade UTP or fiber optic
	OCn/STMn	SONET/SDH Optical fiber network	50 Mbps–40 Gbps	fiber optic
2 (Data Link)	DSL (HDSL, HDSL2, SHDSL)	Digital Subscriber Line, business class	384 Mbps–2.3 Mbps	voice-grade UTP
	Frame Relay	Public Switched Data Networks (PSDN)	1.5 Mbps–45 Mbps	depends
	ATM	Asynchronous Transfer Mode	155 Mbps–650 Mbps std., several Gbps unofficial	any
3 (Network)	Internet	Use the Internet, usually with VPN for security	depends on ISP connections	depends on ISP
	IP carrier network	Similar to Internet, but private; used for corporate; carrier may use MPLS, ATM, Ethernet, SONET, ...	depends on carrier	depends on carrier

Although there is no official central backbone for the Internet and no official guidance for its development, the Internet has developed similarly. All access to the Internet is provided by ISPs—Internet Service Providers. The arrangement is approximately hierarchical. A small number of large ISPs, known as national or international service providers, have built high-speed fiber optic **Internet backbones** that carry traffic between large cities throughout the world. The speeds of these backbones generally range from 45 to 625 GBps, with faster backbones on the way. Interchanges between these backbones occur at **network access points** (**NAPs**). Smaller ISPs, known as regional ISPs, receive their Intenet access from one or more national service providers. In addition to their interconnection with the national service providers, most regional ISPs also interconnect among themselves. Local ISPs receive their service from the regional ISPs. Most of us are customers of local ISPs, although large businesses and others with stringent requirements may connect directly to the regional or, even, national service providers. We connect to the Internet at one or more service provider's points of presence. Figure 12.31 shows a comparison between the road system and the Internet.

Piconets

Piconets, or **personal area networks** (**PANs**) are a different category than the other networks previously discussed. These are networks created for the personal use of an individual. They generally have ranges of thirty feet or less, sufficient for an individual to interconnect his personal computing devices. Connections between different cooperating users are possible, but rare. Bluetooth is the primary medium for personal area networks.

FIGURE 12.31

A Comparison of Internet and Highway Architecture

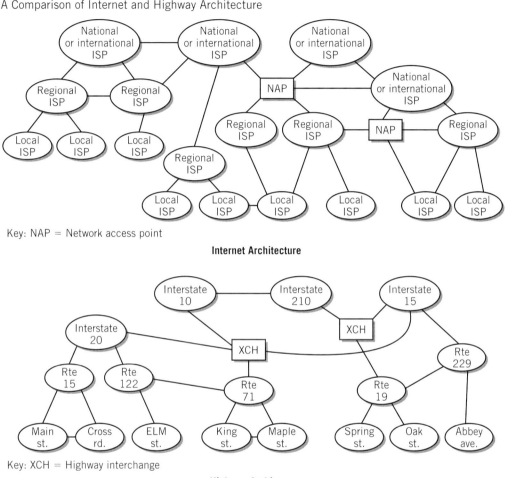

Key: NAP = Network access point

Internet Architecture

Key: XCH = Highway interchange

Highway Architecture

Bluetooth is used for such purposes as the interconnection between a cell phone or GPS and a car radio or hands-free speaker/microphone device, or for transferring and synchronizing pictures and other data between a cell phone and a computer.

12.6 STANDARDS

The need for data communication standards is evident throughout this chapter. Amusingly, there is no single standard or standards organization for creating standards. Instead, there are a number of different government agencies, technical groups, trade groups, and industry organizations, each of whom are responsible for particular areas of standardization. Occasionally, this has resulted in competitions and conflicts, but for the most part this technique has worked pretty well.

The major organizations that participate in the creation of standards for data communications, networks, and internetworks include ISO, the International Organization for Standardization, an agency made up of standards-setting organizations from many countries (www.iso.ch); the International Telecommunications Union Telecommunications Group (ITU-T), a UN agency made up of various major players from other standards organizations, government agencies, and industry representatives; the Institute for Electrical and Electronics Engineers (IEEE), a technical organization that oversees most local area networking standards (www.standards.ieee.org); and the Internet Engineering Task Force (IETF), a large volunteer group of network designers, network operators, industry representatives, and researchers, operated under the auspices of the Internet Society, a nonprofit corporation (www.ietf.org).

ISO is probably best known to network engineers for its development of the OSI Reference Model, but it has also published more than 17,000 international standards on a wide variety of topics, ranging from steel to sewing machines to telecommunications.

Among other technical standards, IEEE is responsible for the standards that define most local area and metropolitan area networking, including Ethernet (802.3), Wi-Fi (802.11), Bluetooth (802.15), and WiMax (802.16).

IETF is concerned with the evolution of the Internet architecture and the smooth operation of the Internet. IETF standards are based on a large published list of **requests for comments (RFCs)**, that define every aspect of TCP/IP and the Internet. There are more than 5000 RFCs, representing information, proposed standards, and accepted standards.

There are various other groups who monitor very specific areas. Of particular interest to us are ICANN and IANA. The Internet Corporation for Assigned Names and Numbers (ICANN) is a private, nonprofit corporation responsible for IP address allocation, domain name registration, and protocol parameter assignment, as well as management of domain name and root server systems (www.icann.org). ICANN also maintains a list of registrars accredited to assign domain names to individuals, groups, and corporations. ICANN also operates the Internet Assigned Numbers Authority (IANA), which is responsible for registering application layer port numbers, as well as the specific parameter values used in the headers of various Internet protocols and other similar tasks (www.iana.org).

SUMMARY AND REVIEW

Chapter 12 introduced many different aspects of networking. Networking is ubiquitous—it is hard to find a computer of any kind that is totally unconnected from a network. Organizations rely on networks for their daily work and to interact with customers, collaborators, and suppliers. Individuals use networks to locate information, make purchases, and for interpersonal communications: e-mail, instant messaging, social networking, and more.

Networks work by passing messages over a channel between end nodes. The channel may be divided into links, made up of local area networks and point-to-point connecting links between intermediate nodes. Individual links may differ in data format and medium. Switches, routers, and gateways steer messages from one node to another, converting the data format as necessary at each node.

The basic unit of data communication is the packet. Messages are broken into packets for transmission through the network. The prevalent transmission media are fiber optic cable, copper wire, and radio.

Packets are routed using either packet switching or virtual circuit switching. With packet switching, each packet is routed individually. With virtual circuit switching, all packets in a message follow the same path through the network.

Management of packets is performed by protocol suite software. The most common suite is TCP/IP. TCP/IP tasks are divided into five layers: application, transport, network, data link, and physical. Most messages are created at the source application layer, are converted to packets, and pass through the other layers, adding header information at each layer along the way. At the destination, the process is reversed; each layer strips off its header, until the message is finally delivered to the corresponding application.

There are four types of addresses used in networking. Port numbers identify the application. IP, or logical, addresses are used for the source and destination. Physical addresses identify each hardware component. User-friendly addresses, such as domain names, make it easier for users to interact with the network.

Topology describes the physical and logical layout of a network. The common topologies include bus, start, mesh, and ring.

Networks are loosely categorized by range as local area networks, backbone networks, metropolitan area networks, and wide area networks. The Internet is a large wide area network. There are also personal area networks, of which Bluetooth is the best-known example.

FOR FURTHER READING

Chapter 12 presents a general overview of networking. There are many excellent network/data communications textbooks that can support and expand your understanding of networks. The ones listed here are just a sampling that reflect my personal preferences at the time of this writing. New data communications textbooks appear frequently; the recommendations and personal reviews at amazon.com may be helpful in sorting through the many possibilities. My current basic preferences, based primarily on the appropriateness of level of difficulty, readability, breadth, and accuracy, are Stallings [STAL09], Kurose [KUR08], Dumas and Schwartz [DUM09], and Panko [PANK09]. At a more advanced level, Forouzan [FOR07] is also excellent. The *IP Datagrams on Avian Carriers* rfc mentioned in the text can be found at www.ietf.org/rfc/rfc1149.txt; the test, with pictures and comments, is located at www.blug.linux.no/rfc1149.

There are a number of books devoted specifically to TCP/IP. One appropriate choice is Comer [COM05]. Parker [PARK02] is another. Parker presents TCP/IP in a very straightforward, self-teaching way. The specifics of ATM are discussed in great depth in a special issue of the Communications of the ACM for February, 1995.

KEY CONCEPTS AND TERMS

access point	best-effort delivery	Carrier Sense Multiple
analog	service	Access with Collision
asynchronous transfer	bit rate	Detection (CSMA/CD)
method (ATM)	broadcast	circuit switching
backbone networks	bus topology	communication channel
bandwidth	byte stream	connectionless service

connection-oriented service
datagram switching
demodulation
domain name
edge
edge router
Ethernet
extranet
fragment
frame
full-duplex channel
gateway
guided medium
half-duplex channel
hop
hosts
hub
hub-based Ethernet
Internet backbone
Internet Service Provider
    (ISP)
intranet
IP address
IP datagram
layer 3 switches
links
local area network (LAN)
logical addresses
logical connection
logical link control
    sublayer
logical topology

medium-access control
    (MAC)
MAC address
mesh network
mesh point
message
metropolitan area network
modulation
network access point
    (NAP)
network interface controller
    (NIC)
network topology
nodes
octet
Open Systems
    Interconnection
    Reference Model (OSI)
packet
packetization
packet switching
peer
personal area network
    (PAN)
physical address
physical topology
piconet
point of presence
port address
port number
private virtual circuits
protocol stack

public switched telephone
    network (PSTN)
reliable-delivery service
requests for comments
    (RFCs)
right-of-way access
ring topology
route
router
segments
service provider (SP)
simplex channel
socket
star topology
Stream Control
    Transmission Protocol
    (SCTP)
switched Ethernet
TCP/IP
tiered Ethernet
Transmission Control
    Protocol (TCP)
unguided medium
user datagrams
User Datagram Protocol
    (UDP)
virtual circuit
virtual local area network
well-known port
wide area network (WAN)
Wi-Fi
Wireless Ethernet

READING REVIEW QUESTIONS

12.1 Offer at least three examples that show the importance of data communications in your daily life.

12.2 Explain briefly the communications between a Web browser and a Web server in fulfilling a Web page request.

12.3 What is a *message* in the context of data communications?

12.4 State at least three reasons why messages are broken into packets for transmission through a network.

12.5 What is the physical or logical connection between a sender and a receiver called? This connection is usually broken into several parts. What are those parts called? What are the connection points between parts called?

12.6   State three major general characteristics that define a *channel*.

12.7   What is routing? Explain the difference between circuit switching and virtual circuit switching. What is a third, more common, alternative? How does it differ from the other two?

12.8   TCP/IP is arguably the most important example of a protocol *suite*. Why is it called a suite? Name another protocol suite that could be used for networking.

12.9   Including the layers that are not "officially" part of TCP/IP, how many layers are there in the TCP/IP network model? Name and briefly describe each layer. Offer at least one specific example of a protocol at each of the layers that is an official part of the TCP/IP standards. At what layer does HTTP reside?

12.10   What is the major advantage of layering in the network model?

12.11   What is the relationship between neighboring layers in the TCP/IP model? What is the relationship between corresponding layers at the sender and receiver nodes?

12.12   How many layers are there in the OSI model? What are the layers that are not found in TCP/IP called? What is their relationship to the layers in TCP/IP?

12.13   What is a socket?

12.14   Explain the major differences between TCP and UDP.

12.15   IP is described as a "best-effort delivery service". What does this mean?

12.16   What layer simply delivers a stream of bits from one node to another?

12.17   Explain the use of port numbers or port addresses.

12.18   What is the more common name for a logical address?

12.19   What is a MAC address?

12.20   What is the difference between a physical topology and a logical topology?

12.21   Identify and briefly explain the four fundamental topologies used in networks.

12.22   What are the advantages of switched Ethernet over hub- or bus-based Ethernet?

12.23   It is common to characterize networks by their range or area of coverage. What are the major categories of networks based on this criterion?

12.24   What is the major difference in implementation between a LAN and a MAN or WAN?

12.25   What is an *edge connection* in a MAN or WAN?

12.26   What is the purpose of a backbone network?

12.27   Explain *intranet*.

12.28   Who owns *Internet backbones*?

12.29   What is a *point of presence*?

EXERCISES

12.1   Explain the differences between virtual circuits and packet switching.

12.2   Explain the differences between circuit switching and virtual circuit switching.

12.3   Discuss the trade-offs between circuit switching, packet switching, and virtual circuit switching.

12.4 Packages and high priority mail are handled by The Typical Large Corporation (TyplCorp) in a way that is typical of large corporations. Each company building has a centralized mailroom where packages are received from personnel from various departments. Packages destined for other offices in the same building are delivered directly by the mailroom to those offices. Other packages are picked up by a van driver for OPS (Other Parcel Service) for handling and delivery by OPS.

The OPS driver delivers the packages to a local district OPS office where packages are sorted for shipment to different areas. Packages with addresses within the district are delivered directly by the local OPS drivers. Other packages are trucked to the nearest OPS central air shipping facility. At OPS air shipping facilities, packages are normally each shipped to a facility near their destination, trucked to a district office, and delivered. However, during peak seasons or bad flying weather, some packages may be shipped more indirectly, by truck or air, through multiple central facilities and district offices, before they reach their final destination.

Network professionals would argue that the OPS model is nearly identical to the TCP/IP model conceptually. Carefully describe the similarities between these two models.

12.5 Describe clearly, step by step, and layer by layer, the operation that takes place when passing a datagram through an intermediate node in a switching network.

12.6 Is it possible to build a network that can recognize more than one protocol? If so, explain how this could be done.

12.7 Locate and read the proposed standard and test report for the "IP over Avian Carrier" proposed standard. Explain how this proposed standard fulfills the requirements of the TCP/IP model.

12.8 Explain the relationship between corresponding layers at the source and destination nodes of a TCP/IP communication connection.

12.9 The TCP/IP protocol suite appears to have no equivalents to the OSI session and presentation layers. How are the services provided by those layers handled in TCP/IP? Be as specific as you can when you refer to the particular services provided by those layers.

12.10 Using the operations of UDP and TCP as a basis, carefully explain the difference between connectionless and connection-oriented communication.

12.11 IP is described as a "best-effort delivery service". What exactly does this mean? What happens if the "best effort" is not good enough?

12.12 Locate protocol information for the IBM System Network Architecture (SNA) model. Compare the operation of SNA with that of TCP/IP.

12.13 In the text, we identify four different "addresses" that are normally used during the passage of a message from source to destination using TCP/IP and Ethernet. These include a "user-friendly" address, a port number, an IP address, and a physical address. For each "address", state which layer or pair of layers uses that address and explain carefully how the address is used.

12.14 Describe, as precisely as you can, the tasks that must be performed by a NIC connected to a network.

12.15   A short-circuit failure is a failure in which the connection point signal line is electrically shorted to ground. Although NIC short-circuit failures are extremely rare, they do occur occasionally. What is the effect on a bus-based network if a short-circuit failure occurs? How would a repair person locate the source of the problem? What is the effect of an open-circuit failure?

12.16   Suppose that you are trying to design a network that would be suitable for a company that is located in several buildings scattered around a town. No building is more than a 1/4 mile from another building, but direct wire connections between all buildings are not possible due to roads, houses, and other obstacles. Propose a network configuration for this company, and justify your proposal.

12.17   Carefully explain the difference between the physical topology of a network and the logical topology of a network.

12.18   Each of the input and output ports on a router have a separate physical address. Why is this an important requirement for the operation of a router in a network?

12.19   Your cousin has asked you to help her to design a small home network for her own use.

    a.   What are the important questions that you will need to ask as you start to consider your design?

    b.   What are the critical components that you will need to specify in your design?

12.20   Suppose you own a widespread chain of turkey tartare and sushi fast-food joints. Your stores are scattered all over the mainland United States and Canada. There are also a few stores in Western Europe. The computers in each store must communicate with the central operation in Texas on a regular basis, but not with each other. Design a network that would meet the requirements of your company.

12.21   Draw a six-node full mesh network. How many connections did your drawing require? Does this agree with the formula in the text? (If not, fix your drawing!) How many connections would a fifty-node full mesh network require?

12.22   Locate, download, and install a copy of *traceroute* or *tracert* software. Use the software to ping an IP address at least 2000 miles from your location. Do this several times and record the paths that your packets take. Assuming that you're not unlucky enough to have all your packets use the same route, draw a diagram of the portion of the mesh network revealed by your results.

12.23   Consider the e-business system of a large automobile manufacturer such as Ford. List at least a dozen mission-critical ways that this system would be used to communicate between its various locations, between itself and its suppliers, and between itself and its dealers. For each item, indicate the benefit that results from the networking capability of such a system.

CHAPTER 13

ETHERNET AND TCP/IP NETWORKING

Illustration by Jeff Moores

13.0 INTRODUCTION

Although there are other types of networks and network protocol suites, the combination of TCP/IP and Ethernet represents the vast majority of network connectivity and use today. Chapter 12 presented a careful introduction to the basic concepts of networking, and introduced TCP/IP and Ethernet. In Chapter 13, we expand the discussion to clarify many areas of importance and interest in the implementation of TCP/IP and Ethernet networks. The goal in Chapter 12 was to help you to achieve a basic understanding of networking. The goal of Chapter 13 is to add richness and color to the overall picture of how your e-mail and Web surfing and IMing retrieves your Web pages successfully most of the time and gets your messages to the right place.

This chapter focuses particularly on TCP/IP and Ethernet protocols that solve some of the more interesting and important problems—domain name translation, the formats of the packets, address resolution between IP and physical addresses, and the like. We also expand our discussion of TCP/IP and the Ethernet to improve your understanding of the overall process of moving packets of data from one place to another.

For this chapter, we have taken a different approach. In Chapter 12 you studied the overall operation of the five layers of a TCP/IP-Ethernet network transaction, starting at the application layer of a source end node with a data request and working down to the lower layers, through a number of intermediate nodes, to the destination end node. In this chapter, we review the overall process, stopping to raise various issues of interest along the way.

Section 13.1 briefly reviews the application layer as background for the remaining discussion.

Section 13.2 raises the first important issue of interest: the method used to extract the domain name from the URL and convert it to an IP address using DNS.

After obtaining the IP address from DNS, the application sends its request to the transport layer. Section 13.3 discusses some of the features of the transport layer.

Section 13.4 addresses several issues that arise in the networking layer: the nature of IP addresses, DHCP, and ARP, the address resolution protocol.

Section 13.5 is concerned with the operation of the medium access control portion of the Ethernet data link layer.

In the final sections of the chapter, we briefly address two additional issues: quality of service and network security, and also provide brief overviews of other important technologies that are alternatives to TCP/IP and Ethernet.

13.1 INTRODUCING THE PROCESS—THE APPLICATION LAYER

The TCP/IP protocol offers a large number of applications for use on a network. These include voice over IP telephoning, video conferencing, instant messaging (IM), remote login, RSS news feeds, file transfer, remote program execution, and much more. Nonetheless, three applications: Web services, e-mail, and peer-to-peer music and video sharing account for the vast majority of the traffic on the Internet.

We remind you at the outset that a typical communication requires lots of little operations. Each operation is, in itself, fairly simple, but they all add up to a powerful and elegant set of tools for communication. At the same time, trying to view the whole picture at once can be somewhat intimidating. As you read through the description that runs through this chapter, be sure that you always keep the simplicity in mind!

For this purpose, we assume that a user sitting at his computer types a URL into his Web browser. The URL consists of a domain name. In Chapter 12, Figure 12.2 we showed you the format of an HTTP message that is sent by the Web browser HTTP client application to an HTTP server application in response to a user's request for a Web page. As you are already aware from the previous chapter, the HTTP client initiates the process with a request to the TCP socket to establish a logical connection with the HTTP server at the destination site. Before it can do so, however, the HTTP client must first obtain the IP address of the computer that holds the Web server. For this purpose, the HTTP client will request the services of a domain name service application. This is the first step in the process of sending the HTTP message to the Web server.

13.2 DOMAIN NAMES AND DNS SERVICES

Domain Name System Directory Services

As a user you know that domain names serve as user address identifiers for most of your network transactions. Domain names are used throughout the Internet, as well as on local area networks, intranets, and extranets. As we noted in Chapter 12, network navigation within the network itself relies on numeric IP addresses and physical addresses. The inventors of the Internet understood that the average user would have difficulty remembering the number groupings that are used as IP addresses, and created a hierarchical system of domain names as an alternative. The decision to offer translation from domain names to IP addresses as a basic Internet service is one of the cleverest and most successful aspects in the original development of the TCP/IP protocol suite.

When an application requests services from TCP, UDP, or SCTP at the transport layer, it must supply a numerical IP address. TCP/IP provides a support application that fulfills the role of the **Domain Name System** (**DNS**) protocol, to translate domain names into IP addresses. The DNS application uses a massive distributed database organized as a directory system of servers to obtain the required information. Each entry in the database consists of a domain name and an associated IP address (plus some other information about the entry that is not of concern to us here.)

The directory system that is used to translate domain names into IP addresses is organized as a tree structure, very similar to the directory structure of a computer operating system, except that there is a separate server at each node on the tree. Figure 13.1 shows the structure of the tree. Each directory node on the tree provides name-to-IP address services corresponding to its position on the tree. There are three primary levels of interest. Below that, individual domain name owners can extend the number of levels down as far as they wish for convenience of organization and clarity.

FIGURE 13.1

Domain Name System Server Hierarchy

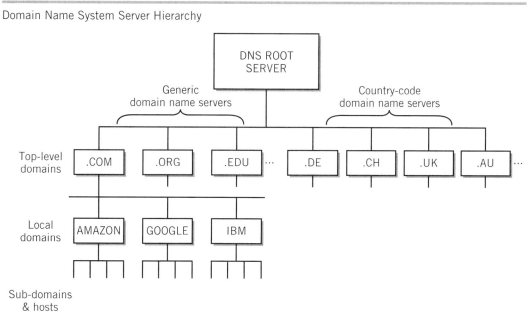

At the top of the tree is the root directory, called the **DNS root server**. Actually, there are thirteen of these servers, scattered all over the world, and each of them is actually a cluster consisting of many computers, also disbursed widely. As you will see shortly, the DNS root servers must handle a large number of queries, more than 50 billion a day as of June 2008. Disbursing the root servers geographically reduces the amount of long distance traffic by providing nearby access for as many queries as possible. The DNS root servers have entries for all of the so-called **top-level domains**. There are **country-code top-level domain name servers (ccTLDs)** for every identifiable country in the world plus a number of authorized commercial and noncommercial *type* domains. The non-country-code domains include .com, .edu, .org, .net, and many more. In mid-2008, a decision was made to allow the creation of additional top-level domains. Figure 13.2 shows a table of some of the leading top-level domains in current use. As of June, 2008, there were more than 160 million domain name registrations, according to the *Domain Name Industry Brief* [Domain2008].

Domain names below the top-level domains are registered for a small fee by users with one of a number of registrars. ICANN (see Chapter 12, Section 12.6) assumes overall responsibility for the millions of registered names on the Internet. Domain names at this level are called **local domains**. The name must, of course, be unique; there can be no duplicates anywhere in the world. Once the domain name is registered, it can be used to assign names of individual nodes or hosts within that domain, and matched to one or more assigned IP addresses. Domain names are read left to right, from the lowest subdomain to the top level domain. See Figure 13.3 for an example.

Each local domain must register the IP address of a domain name service of its own to identify its hosts and subdomains, if any. This server is called an **authoritative domain name server**. In the simplest case there are no subdomains. Rather than complicate matters,

FIGURE 13.2

Top Domain Name Registrations

GENERIC*		COUNTRY CODE**	
TLD	NO.IN MILLIONS	TLD	NO. IN MILLIONS
.com	75.3	.de (Germany)	13.7
.net	11.4	.cn (China)	11.4
.org	6.7	.uk (Britain)	7.1
.info	5.0	.nl (Netherlands)	3.5 (est.)
.biz	2.0	.eu (European Union)	3.1

*Source: Zooknic (http://www/zooknic.com), Apr 2008
**Source: Verisign (http://www.verisign.com/static/043939.pdf) Jun 2008

simple domains usually rely on the authoritative domain name service of the Internet Service Provider to fulfill this requirement. Larger domains provide their own authoritative DNS servers. The authoritative domain name servers are the third tier in Figure 13.1.

Each top-level domain maintains multiple servers with tables containing entries for all of the registered names; each name entry contains the IP address of its authoritative domain name server. As you can imagine, the tables for .com are huge! These tables are updated continually. Multiple servers are required to handle the volume, for redundancy, and to protect the integrity of the Internet domain name system against attacks. These servers are also widely disbursed geographically. Each table is updated and synchronized periodically, using a process called **replication**.

Now, consider a slightly simplified step-by-step description of the translation process that takes place when a user types a URL into her Web browser application. The translation process is known as domain name **resolution**. The steps are diagrammed in Figures 13.4 and 13.5. Figure 13.4 is a simple pointer diagram showing each of the steps. Figure 13.5 is a traditional flow diagram showing the same information in a different way. Both are included to make it easier for you to follow the steps.

1. The HTTP application extracts the domain name from the URL and requests resolution of the name from the DNS support application. The DNS support application is a client program residing on the same host as the HTTP application, so this is a simple program call. The DNS client issues a query packet with the name to a **local DNS server** for resolution.

FIGURE 13.3

The Elements of a Domain Name

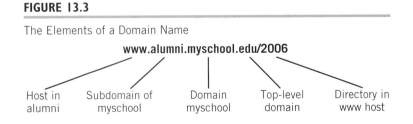

FIGURE 13.4

Resolving a Domain Name to its IP Address

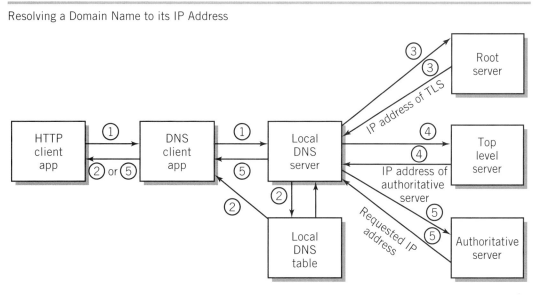

The local DNS server is not part of the domain name server hierarchy. It could be on the host machine requesting service, or elsewhere. More commonly it is located elsewhere, on the same LAN as the host or at an ISP's site. Regardless of where it is located, its IP address is already known by the DNS client application. Its task is simply to respond to requests from the DNS application with the IP address requested. Note that the DNS client request must follow the usual path through the layers of the network model. Since DNS request packets are simple and small, UDP datagrams are used for packet transport.

2. The local DNS server table generally contains the addresses of its own subdomains. It also frequently contains the addresses of commonly used domain names, such as www.google.com and www.yahoo.com, as well as addresses for various top-level servers. It also stores, on a more temporary basis, the names and IP addresses resulting from other recently issued requests. If the information is in the local DNS table, the information is returned to the DNS client by the local DNS server as a response to the query (again through all five layers, using UDP as the transport mechanism.) The DNS client passes the IP address to the HTTP application. The DNS application's job is done.

3. If the local DNS server does not have the information in its own table, the process continues. Unless the local server already has an IP address for the appropriate top-level DNS server, it must query one of the DNS root servers seeking that address. In that case, the root server responds with the IP address of a nearby top-level server.

4. Next, the local DNS server issues a query to the DNS top-level server, requesting the IP address of the authoritative DNS server associated with the requested domain name.

FIGURE 13.5

Resolving a Domain Name - Flow Diagram

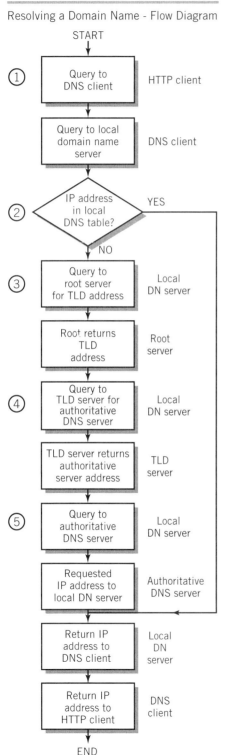

5. Finally, the authoritative DNS server responds with the requested IP address. The local DNS server returns the address to the DNS client on the host machine making the original request. The IP address is delivered to the HTTP application. We're done!

DNS offers useful services beyond the basic one-to-one name-to-IP address translation service described above. Two of these are mentioned here:

- The domain name system permits the use of alias names that share the same IP address. This is particularly useful when the actual host is deep within a subdomain and is hard to remember. Its name can be aliased with a simpler name. DNS can determine the actual name and IP address from the simpler name. This aliasing capability even extends to the use of the same alias for both Web and mail applications.

- DNS can also perform load balancing for organizations that require multiple replicated servers to handle large request loads. An obvious example of such an organization is google.com, whose websites receive billions of communications every year. Recall that we mentioned in Chapter 2 that google.com has a large number of Web server sites all over the world for handling search queries. Each site is connected to a different part of the Internet and each site has its own IP address. However, one domain name, google.com is associated with all of these sites. DNS includes all of the IP addresses associated with that name in its database. DNS will return the entire list of potential IP addresses in response to a query; however, it modifies the order of the listing each time a query is made. DNS clients normally select the first IP address on the list, therefore the requests are distributed approximately evenly among the different sites. This has the additional advantage of equalizing the traffic load over different parts of the Internet.

13.3 NEXT STEPS—TCP AND THE TRANSPORT LAYER

Once the HTTP application has obtained the IP address, it is ready to pass the request to the transport layer for transmission through the network. HTTP issues a request asking TCP to open a connection to the desired website. Sockets (see Chapter 12 if you forgot what these are) are used for this purpose. Sockets are equivalent to an open door through which messages can pass. The use of sockets makes it possible to create multiple open connections through which data can flow simultaneously without losing track of which is which. Obviously, a Web server must be able to handle many requests simultaneously. The HTTP request includes the IP address of the site and the port number of the server application at the destination, presumably port 80 in this case.

As we already discussed in the previous chapter, TCP sends a packet (through the usual network layers) to TCP at the Web site, requesting a connection; this results in a brief back-and-forth series of requests and acknowledgments known as **handshaking**. See Figure 13.6. If the negotiation is successful, a connection is opened. This connection

FIGURE 13.6

Three-Way TCP Connection Handshake

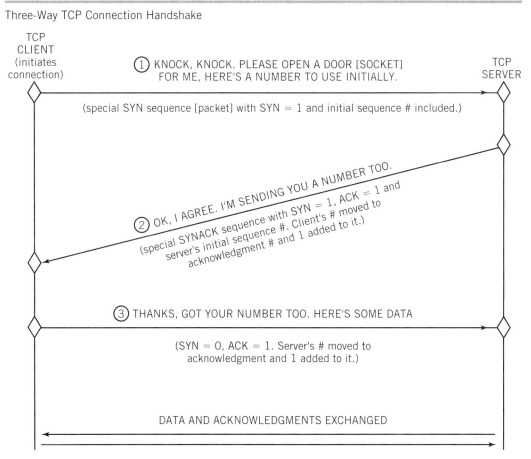

FIGURE 13.7

TCP Segment Format

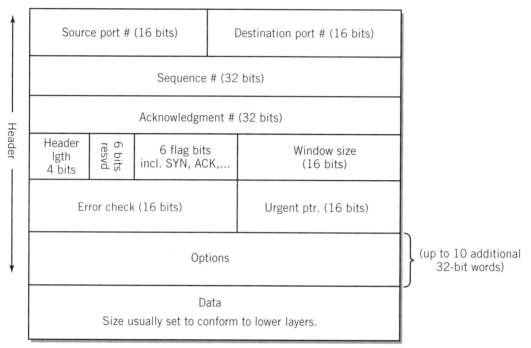

is logically a full-duplex connection, both because Web page requests from the browser application at one end node will result in file transfers from the Web server at the other, and because TCP requires an acknowledgment packet be sent in return for every packet received.

Figure 13.7 shows the format of a TCP packet. The same format is used at both ends of the connection. Notice that the packet format cleverly facilitates two-way communication by allowing the inclusion of a data packet together with an acknowledgment for a packet received. The packet specifies both the source and destination port numbers, but does not require IP addresses because the connection is already established, and thus is known. The sequence number and acknowledgment number are cleverly designed both to number the packets in order and to indicate the amount of data present in the data field of the packet. Since the packet format provides a field for options, the packet must also contain a header size field. The header is twenty bytes long if there are no options.

13.4 THE NETWORK LAYER, IP ADDRESSES, AND ARP

You are already aware, from Chapter 12, that the network layer, specifically the IP protocol, is responsible for relaying packets from the source end node through intermediate nodes to the destination end node. This task is performed using datagram packet switching and logical IP addresses. We also remind you that IP is a *best-attempt* unreliable service.

FIGURE 13.8

IPv4 IP Datagram Format

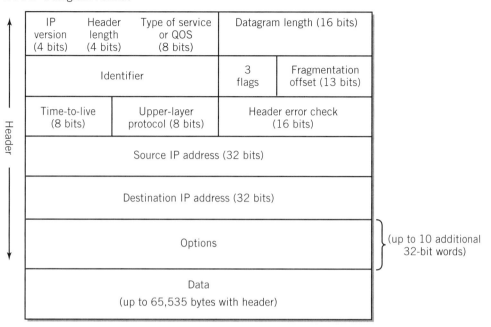

The format for an IP datagram is shown in Figure 13.8. The total size of an IP datagram can range from 20 to 65,536 bytes, although the total size is usually determined by the capability of the data link that will be carrying the data. This avoids the need for datagram fragmentation. (See Chapter 12 if you need a reminder.) The header size is between 20 and 60 bytes; the rest is available for data from the transport layer. The header identifies the source and destination IP addresses, as well as the transport protocol and the version of IP in use. It also provides the total length of the datagram and an error checking field. There are several additional fields and options.

IP Addresses

You know that DNS translates domain names into IP addresses. You also know that IP addresses and domain names are registered and allocated by ICANN. This section provides more information about the IP addressing system used with IPv4. IPv6 is outside the scope of our discussion.

An IPv4 address is 32 bits long. Every node on the Internet has a unique address. As you are aware, the 32 bits are divided into four octets for easier reading; in the earlier days of the Internet, these octets also identified the assignee to some extent, however that is less true today. Nonetheless, IP addresses are still assigned in blocks. The addresses in a block are contiguous, and the number of addresses in a block must be a power of two. A block is assigned by specifying a given number of bits, from left to right; the remaining bits represent addresses in the block.

FIGURE 13.9

IP Block Addresses

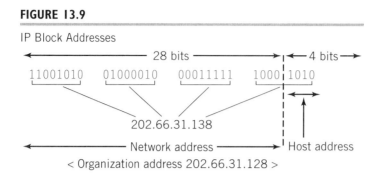

Look at Figure 13.9. For example, if your organization is issued a block starting with the 28 bits to the left of the dividing line in the figure, the four remaining bits would provide a block of sixteen addresses for computers within your organization. Your organization could allocate these sixteen addresses any way it wishes. The first address in the block is defined as the network address for your organization; it is used for routing.

Traditionally, most blocks are larger than sixteen addresses, and IP addresses are usually divided into three levels, and in some cases four or more. Figure 13.10 shows an IP address divided into three levels; the top level is, of course, the network address. The remaining bits are divided into subnetworks, or **subnets**. Each subnet has a number of hosts (or nodes). **Masks** are used to separate the different parts of the address. A mask consists of a number of 1s followed by 0s. When the mask is suitably combined with the IP address using Boolean algebra, individual components of the address can be identified. A mask is specified by placing a slash mark with the number of 1s at the end of the IP address. Alternatively, it can be specified in dotted decimal notation. Both notations are shown in the figure.

A number of IP addresses are reserved for private use. These IP addresses may not be used on the Internet, but they are suitable for networks which are not directly exposed to the Internet. There is also a universal broadcast address consisting of all 1s that addresses all nodes on a subnet. The private addresses are listed in Figure 13.11.

FIGURE 13.10

IP Hierarchy and Subnet Mask

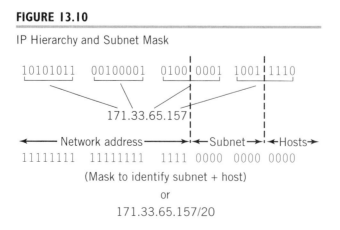

FIGURE 13.11

Reserved Private and Broadcast IP Addresses

Address range	Total number of addresses		
	Binary	Decimal	
10.0.0.0 – 10.255.255.255	2^{24}	≈ 16 million	Private addresses
172.16.0.0 – 172.31.255.255	2^{20}	≈ 1 million	
192.168.0.0 – 192.168.255.255	2^{16}	≈ 64,000	
255.255.255.255		Broadcast address	

Dynamic Host Configuration Protocol (DHCP)

For some time, people have been aware that the total number of possible IPv4 addresses available is inadequate to meet the needs in the near future. Although IPv6 has the potential to solve this problem in the long term, its adoption to date has been limited. The potential shortage of IP addresses is further exacerbated by the block numbering design of the IPv4 addressing system, in which organizations are often assigned more IP addresses than they need. There are two alternative methods that are presently used to distribute IP addresses more efficiently:

1. Small organizations with limited Internet gateway access can place their networks behind a router that keeps the addresses private and use the private IP addresses that are designed for this purpose. Private IP addresses are not recognized as valid on the Internet. The source address of IP packets originating on the private network is modified to conform to the public IP address. Conversely, IP packets from the outside are readdressed with the private destination address when they pass through the router from the outside into the private network. There are two difficulties with this approach:

   ■ Traffic passing through the router to the outside, for example Web requests, must be carefully tracked by the router, so that responses from the outside are routed to the correct private address on the inside. For a small network, this is relatively manageable. The task becomes far more challenging when the number of privately addressed computers is large and traffic through the interface is substantial. The correct routing of e-mail is particularly challenging.

   ■ An organization with multiple local area networks connected with a backbone network must configure the private networks in such a way that traffic between the various private local area networks can be managed successfully. One possible solution is to use a single private IP addressing scheme for all networks attached within the backbone, with translation at the edge router. Again, the problem of translation becomes large and difficult to manage.

2. The second alternative is to maintain a bank of available IP addresses, and assign them dynamically to computers for use during the time that the computers are connected to the network. This is the approach generally taken by large

organizations and by DSL and cable service providers. DHCP is used for this purpose.

Dynamic Host Configuration Protocol (DHCP) is an application layer protocol used to assign and reclaim IP addresses from a pool of addresses when a computer is connected to or removed from a network. The DHCP client resides on the computer or other device that is being connected. The client communicates with a DHCP server. The IP addresses are a block of addresses reserved for this purpose.

When a computer is connected to a network, the DHCP client broadcasts a query to every computer on the network, in order to locate the DHCP server. The DHCP server responds with a lease, which includes an IP address, and other configuration parameters, including the domain name of the network, the IP address of a local DNS server, a subnet mask to identify other nodes on the local area network, and the default IP address of the Internet gateway. Some DHCP servers also include the addresses of other useful services, such as a time server. The lease is issued for a fixed period of time. Most systems allow the DHCP client to renew the lease before it expires. This allows the client computer to maintain the same IP address while it is actively connected to the network.

Because the IP address is allocated at the time of connection, most computers connected using DHCP are not used to provide services to other computers on the network because there is no consistent domain name–IP address link for the computer. A companion protocol, Dynamic Domain Name Service, DDNS, can provide this link by updating the local DNS server. DDNS is a documented part of the DNS protocol. However, DDNS is rarely used.

The Operation of IP

IP performs two major functions:

1. It routes datagrams from node to node until they reach their destination end node.

2. It translates IP addresses to physical addresses before it passes the packets to the data link later for delivery.

The topic of datagram routing is dependent on a number of different mathematical algorithms and sophisticated statistical techniques that are outside the scope of this text. We will not consider this topic further.

You will recall from Chapter 12 that the network layer bases its addressing on IP addresses. Before IP sends a datagram from the source to the data link layer, it must identify the physical address of the destination node on the network it is attached to. IP address-to-physical address translation is performed in conjunction with a support protocol, **Address Resolution Protocol (ARP)**. ARP is implemented at the network layer.

Once IP has determined the address of the node where the datagram is to be sent, it uses ARP to determine the corresponding physical address. The destination node may be a router on an intermediate node or it may be the node of the final destination for the datagram. ARP sends a broadcast packet with the IP address to every node on the local network. The matching node responds with its physical address; in the case of Ethernet, the physical address is the MAC address of the destination node. The physical address is then sent in a frame to the data link layer. At each intermediate node, this process is repeated until the final destination is reached; the current destination MAC address is stripped from the frame and replaced with the new address. At the final destination, the packet is passed up to the transport layer for deployment to the application layer. ARP maintains a cache of recently used IP address–physical address pairs to simplify the process. Only the first packet in a set of packets headed for the same destination requires use of the broadcast process.

13.5 THE DATA LINK LAYER

The task of the data link layer is to transmit the packet from the current node to the next node. In Chapter 12, we presented a brief overview of the Ethernet protocols. In this section we take a closer look at the medium access protocol for wired Ethernet.

Node access for a particular network is defined by the medium access control protocol. The purposes of a medium access protocol are to steer data to its destination, to detect errors, and to prevent multiple nodes from accessing the network simultaneously in such a way that their messages become mixed together and garbled. Such an event is called a **collision**. As you already know, the predominant medium-access protocol for local area networks is Ethernet. MAC protocols are implemented primarily in hardware in the NIC.

Local area networks are defined generally in the IEEE Standard 802 suite. Ethernet is defined in Standard 802.3. In Chapter 12, we introduced two different forms of wired Ethernet, based on hubs and switches. Technically, Ethernet is called the **Carrier Sense Multiple Access with Collision Detection** (**CSMA/CD**) protocol. Ethernet is a trade name for this protocol. The trade name belongs to Xerox Corporation, who did the original development on the protocol. Ethernet was originally based on bus topology. The name CSMA/CD reflects that fact. Switched Ethernet, which is defined in the same specification, does not actually implement the CSMA/CD protocol, because connections are point-to-point and collisions are not possible. The 802.3 specifies many variations, which differ in the type of wiring or fiber optic cable used, in the method used to connect to the physical medium, in the signaling method used, and in the speed of operation. The address for each node on an Ethernet network is called a MAC address. It is set in the hardware. Addresses are permanently assigned by the IEEE organization to the manufacturers of Ethernet-attached equipment.

Every node on the network has equal access to the bus and is normally in "listening" mode; that is, each node is listening for messages addressed to it. Remember that messages on the bus are broadcast; every node receives every message, but a node will ignore messages that are not addressed to it. The bus is silent when no node is transmitting.

The standard Ethernet packet is a frame. The format of an Ethernet frame is shown in Figure 13.12. The frame consists of a preamble, used for timing synchronization between the sender and receiver, a start frame delimiter to indicate the beginning of the frame contents, the destination and source addresses, specified as MAC addresses, a data length field to indicate the amount of data in the frame, the data field itself, and a field that is used to confirm the integrity of the frame. The data field requires a minimum of 46 bytes, with padding if necessary; this value was originally selected to guarantee that collisions on the original Ethernet bus could be detected before the frame was accepted by the receiver. The maximum data field is 1500 bytes. Although the destination field is specified

FIGURE 13.12

Standard Ethernet Frame

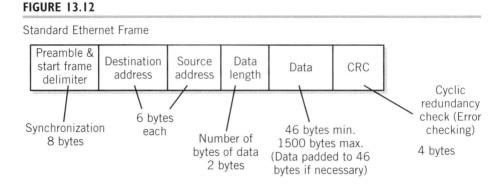

as a MAC address, there are special addresses that allow a frame to be delivered to a group of receivers simultaneously. The ability to broadcast a frame to every receiver is required as part of the ARP protocol. A destination address consisting of all 1s is used for this purpose.

Hub-Based Ethernet

Ethernet was originally based on a bus topology. Hub-based Ethernet provides a simple means of wiring a bussed Ethernet together, but the hub does not affect the operation logically. Any node may use the bus to send a message to another node any time the bus is not in use; there is no specific timing control on the bus. When a node has a message to send, it listens to see if the bus is in use. If not, it begins to send its packet. If the bus is already in use, the node waits until the bus is available. This is the "CSMA" part of CSMA/CD.

CSMA/CD does not try to prevent the occurrence of collisions. As the node sends its frame, it continues to listen to the bus. If network traffic is light, the node will usually complete sending the frame and will then return to listening mode. Occasionally, two (or more) nodes may sense that the bus is free and initiate transmission simultaneously. A collision occurs, and the message on the bus becomes scrambled, due to the interference between the two signals. Since each node continues to listen as it transmits, it can recognize that the message is scrambled—the signal on the bus is not the same as the message it is transmitting. When a node detects a collision, it immediately stops transmitting, waits a short time, then returns to listening mode, and tries again when the bus is free. The amount of time each node waits after a collision is random for each node. If both nodes waited the same length of time, collisions would continue to recur indefinitely.

It might seem to you that collisions would occur very rarely, especially on a network with sparse traffic. There is an additional factor to consider, however. Signals on the bus require a small but finite (and, as it turns out, sometimes significant) amount of time to travel down the bus. Signals on a bus travel at approximately three-fourths the speed of light, or roughly 9 inches per nanosecond. This may seem like a very small number, but if two nodes on the bus are 500 feet apart, it will create a window of about 5/8 microseconds after one node begins transmitting before the second node is aware that the bus is in use. In other words, the probability of collisions is higher than one would first assume. Particularly if bus traffic is heavy, a node may have to try several times before it sends a packet successfully. The amount of time that it takes for a packet to get from one end of the network is called the **network propagation delay**.

Hub-based Ethernet is adequate for networks with light traffic, because of its simplicity. Every node is independent. Nodes may be added simply by plugging them into the hub. No central network control is required. However, Ethernet is unsuitable for networks with widely separated nodes, due to the increase in the probability of collisions. Similarly, as traffic increases, the number of collisions and retransmissions also increases and Ethernet performance deteriorates, making Ethernet less suitable also for networks that frequently carry heavy traffic.

Switched Ethernet

The desire to operate local area networks at higher speed and with longer ranges also makes hub-based Ethernet unusable in many circumstances. Instead, switched Ethernet permits the point-to-point connection of any pair of nodes. Multiple pairs can be connected simultaneously. Modern switches even provide a buffer to hold frames destined for a receiver already in use. Switching thus prevents collisions, and there is no need to implement CSMA/CD in switched Ethernet systems. Switched Ethernet has two additional advantages: (1) it is possible to connect nodes together in full-duplex mode, which is not possible with a single bus connection, and (2) each pair of connections can operate at the maximum bit rate of the network.

Wireless Ethernet is similar to hub-based Ethernet because of the nature of the medium. A variation on CSMA/CD is used for Wi-Fi. Wi-Fi protocols are presented in Chapter 14.

13.6 QUALITY OF SERVICE

Certain types of data are dependent on reliable end-to-end transport where packets arrive at the receiving host in order, with sufficient throughput, with minimum, or at least, consistent, delay, at precise, even time intervals, and with a low probability of errors and missing packet failures. These necessary qualities are particularly important for streaming audio and video applications, such as IPTV and VoIP, and for online gaming and virtual reality applications. In contrast, IP offers unreliable, best-effort service that provides limited support for any of these qualities. Similarly, the basic Ethernet specifications do not indicate any level of quality support, although a number of alternative data link layer protocols do include such methods and measures in their specifications. These include Frame Relay, ATM, and MLSP, among others, as well as certain variants on Ethernet.

There is no simple, effective measure of the quality of packet switched delivery. Instead, **Quality of Service (QoS)** focuses on two parameters: (1) methods to reserve and prioritize channel capacity to favor packets that require special treatment, and (2) service guarantees from contracted carrier services that specify particular levels of throughput, delay, and jitter. Throughput is important to assure that the network can deliver the entire stream at the required data rate. (Picture a favorite song that gets slower and slower as you listen to it—not entirely accurate, but you get the idea.) **Jitter** is defined as the variation in delay from packet to packet. It is a particularly important parameter in the transmission of video and audio because jitter causes large fluctuation in the image and sound. Note that a large amount of jitter can actually cause the packets to arrive at the receiver in the wrong order. Delay is somewhat less important, but only provided that the delay itself is constant. Generally, if there is substantial delay, it is due to network congestion, and the throughput and jitter will also suffer.

With the growing prominence of multimedia on the Internet the need for effective QoS has taken on increased importance. Various partial solutions have emerged. IP provides a 6-bit field in its header which has been adapted for this purpose. This field is called the **differentiated service (DS)** field, usually abbreviated to DiffServ. (DS is actually an 8-bit field, but the other 2 bits do not concern us here.) The DS field serves as an index into a table that defines various classes of service. For a particular set of packets, the DS field is set by the application at the sender or by the first node. Modern routers, sometimes called *DiffServ capable nodes*, can then prioritize and route packets based on the packet class. Interestingly, there are no ground rules on the basis for setting the DS field, nor for the way the routers make decisions based on the class of service, but it is generally agreed that routers prioritize streaming multimedia if they can do so without creating major congestion at the router's node and beyond.

Currently, the DiffServ approach appears to be the most successful in practice. However, its success is contingent on a number of factors; the major factor is sufficient network capacity to minimize congestion at router nodes.

QoS is a complex topic with many nuances and implications for the design and use of networks. There are references to QoS in a number of networking specifications, and many books and articles written about various facets of QoS. A few of these are indicated in the *For Further Reading* section at the end of this chapter.

13.7 NETWORK SECURITY

The words "network security" are an oxymoron. Networks are inherently insecure. Therefore, strong security measures must be taken independently of the network to protect the components of the network as well as the data flowing through the network. Security measures are an essential part of any system, large or small. The issue of computer system and network security is a broad and extensive topic; it is often taught as a separate course. We shall only touch the surface in this discussion. Our focus is upon issues related specifically to network security measures that are an essential part of the design of any network infrastructure.

Network-related security issues are often placed into one or more of five categories, with specific types of measures required for each category:

- Intrusion—Keeping network and system resources intact and free from the results of intrusion. Intrusion includes the ability of an intruder to modify the system for future access, destroying system data and program files, injecting viruses, and more. The primary measures required are physical and circuit protection of the network to the extent possible; firewalls on individual components, including routers, where appropriate; and protection of passwords that traverse the network with encryption.

- Confidentiality—Keeping the content of data traversing the network and information about the communication taking place private. Encryption measures are required for this purpose.
- Authentication—verifying the identity of a source of data being received. This is similar to the concept of **electronic signatures**. Special encryption features are used for this purpose.
- Data integrity and nonrepudiation—Protecting the content of data communication against changes and verifying the source of a message. Special encryption features are also used for this purpose.
- Assuring network availability and access control—Restricting access to network resources to those permitted to use them and keeping network resources operational and available.

Although there is obvious overlap between these requirements, the measures to be taken fall into three primary categories: physical and logical access to systems, firewalls (which are a type of logical access restriction), and encryption technology.

Physical and Logical Access Restriction

There are numerous ways to intrude into a networked system. The tools for **packet sniffing** are free and readily available to anyone. Packet sniffing is defined as the reading of the data in a packet as it passes through a network. With wired networks, packet sniffing can be achieved by physically tapping into the network itself or by reading packets as they pass through a node. Hub-based networks are particularly vulnerable because anyone connected to the "bus" at any point can read every packet that uses the bus. Wireless networks are even worse. Anyone within range of a radio signal can receive the signal.

In general, it is safest to assume that it is possible to intercept and read any packet passing through a network. This makes passwords that travel through a network unencrypted useless at protecting a network and its computers from intrusion.

The Internet provides an additional means of intrusion access. Any system on any network that is publicly accessible from the Internet is susceptible to probing attacks that seek IP address/port numbers combinations that will accept data packets. Specially constructed packets can then be used to access and modify the host machine.

A number of measures are used to protect systems and networks from intrusion. Physical eavesdropping on local area networks is minimized by limiting access to network wiring and network equipment to personnel who are responsible for the equipment. Logical access is limited with intelligent firewall design that blocks public access where it is not required and robust network applications that drop or repel packets that might be invasive. Intelligent firewall design includes making port numbers that are not in active use unavailable, evaluating every packet according to a set of acceptability criteria, blocking or hiding local IP addresses and computers from the Internet, and more.

Logical access is also limited with the use of private networks. These make it difficult for intruders to identify individual machines within the firewall/router that protects the network.

Public MAN and WAN carrier networks are secured by using protocols that hide and separate a user's packets from other users. Stringent password policies are enforced and passwords are never transmitted over unencrypted networks.

Encryption

Encryption provides security beyond that of other measures, provided that the security is strong and effectively applied. Encryption in various forms is used to prevent intrusion, to protect privacy, for authentication, and to assure data integrity and nonrepudiation. There are a number of different algorithms for encryption, but they generally fall into one or both of two categories. **Symmetric key cryptography** requires that the same key be used for both encryption and decryption. This means that both users must have access to the same key, which is often difficult to achieve securely. The second category is called **public key–private key cryptography**, in which two different keys, one publicly available, the other private, are used together in various ways to achieve the different goals mentioned above.

The reader is referred to a number of excellent books dealing with the details of this topic.

13.8 ALTERNATIVE PROTOCOLS

Although this chapter is focused primarily on TCP/IP and Ethernet, there are a number of important alternative technologies in use, particularly by carriers providing wide area network services, and also for specialty purposes, such as Internet backbones and storage area networking. New developments in this area occur frequently and rapidly. At this writing, the prevalent alternatives include Multi-Protocol Label Switching (MPLS), Asynchronous Transfer Mode (ATM), Sonet/SDH, and Frame Relay.

Each of these protocols can be implemented at different layers of the OSI or TCP/IP models, and each can serve as a carrier mechanism for IP datagrams and Ethernet frames. In typical use, wide area network service providers connect a TCP/IP or Ethernet gateway to their service at the customer's edge point. The alternate technology carries the packets to another edge point where they are converted back to their original form.

What follows is a brief description of each. More information on these and other protocols can be found in various network text books and on the Web.

MPLS

The goal of **MPLS (Multi-Protocol Label Switching)** is to improve the forwarding speed of IP datagrams by creating virtual circuit capability over traditional packet switched networks, such as Ethernet. MPLS operates at the data link layer. MPLS is a relatively recent, but fast growing, technology. MPLS inserts a small, 32-bit fixed-length header between the layer 2 and layer 3 headers in a packet. In the case of a TCP/IP-Ethernet frame, the header would be situated between the Ethernet header and the embedded IP header. The MPLS header contains a label that identifies a virtual circuit path. The label is added initially by a *label edge router* when it enters the network and removed by a corresponding edge label router at the exit point.

MPLS requires routers that are capable of reading and acting on the MPLS header. Such a router is called a *label-switched router*. The label-switched router can route IP datagrams through the virtual circuit without the overhead of returning to the network layer, thereby simplifying routing speed. MPLS is sometimes called a layer 2.5 protocol because it works with existing networks between the two layers.

ATM

ATM (Asynchronous Transfer Mode) is a partial-mesh network technology, in which data passes through the network in cells. Data enters an ATM network at an *ATM adaption layer*. There, the data (which could be, for example an Ethernet frame or IP datagram) is combined with a header and broken into cells. The combination is called a protocol data unit, and assigned a 28-bit virtual circuit number called a *virtual circuit identifier* that is used throughout the network for routing. Cells are 53-byte packets, containing a 5-bit header and 48 bits of data. At the exit point, a matching adaption layer recombines the cells into their original form.

ATM is well-suited for the transmission of multimedia because the combination of mesh networking and small cell size makes it easier to control congestion and the quality of service. Interestingly, the physical layer of ATM is loosely defined. ATM is used with different media, including both wire and fiber-optic cable, and with different technologies. It was originally designed to operate over SONET/SDH (see below) as its physical layer. It is capable of extremely high performance, and is used for Internet backbones. To some extent it is being supplanted by MPLS, but ATM will probably be in use for some time to come.

SONET/SDH

SONET (Synchronous Optical Network) and **SDH (Synchronous Digital Hierarchy)** are related protocols and architectures that are designed to take advantage of fiber optic technology. The intention of both standards was to create wide area networks capable of extremely high bit rates over long distances. The differences between the two standards are minor. We shall refer to both as SONET for the remainder of this discussion. SONET is based on networks that are synchronized globally to a single clock. Electrical signals from different sources are converted to light, then synchronously multiplexed and added and removed from nodes by *add/drop* multiplexers as required to optimize the speed of each packet. To extend the distance, *regenerators* are built into the network. These recreate the signal as it is attenuated within the fiber, to extend its range. SONET networks are constructed as meshes, or rings, or point-to-point links.

SONET is frequently employed as a physical layer carrier, supporting other higher-level protocols. The technology, frame formats, and details of operation of SONET are complex. Further information is beyond the scope of this text.

Frame Relay

Frame Relay is a relatively slow, wide area network standard. It is included because it is still in common use as an inexpensive on-ramp to wide area networks and to the Internet through service providers, especially large telephone companies. Like the other protocols discussed here, Frame Relay relies on edge connections to convert data between other protocols and frame relay frames for transmission over the network.

Frame Relay operates at the data link and physical layers, using its own switch design to forward frames through virtual circuits. Frame Relay allows the use of *permanent virtual circuits*. These are circuits that route all packets between a source and destination by the same route, which is advantageous for some private wide area network links. At the physical layer, Frame Relay operates over a variety of networks.

SUMMARY AND REVIEW

In Chapter 13, we described each of the TCP/IP and Ethernet layers in more detail, focusing on specific areas of interest.

The domain name system translates, or *resolves*, user-friendly names into their corresponding IP addresses. The domain name addressing system is hierarchical, with a root, generic and country-code top-level domains, local domains, and, sometimes, subdomains. DHCP is a protocol that allows the dynamic assignment of IP addresses on a short-term lease basis.

The interface between the TCP/IP network layer and Ethernet data link layer requires translation between IP addresses and physical addresses. This task is performed by the Address Resolution Protocol.

Local area Ethernet networks are either switched or hub-based. CSMA/CD manages collisions in a hub-based network.

Two issues of interest when discussing modern networks are quality of service and network security. Quality of service attempts to measure and provide packet routing with speeds and reliability sufficient for tasks such as multimedia. Network security identifies the problems that must be overcome to provide adequate protection, and the tools that are used for this purpose.

FOR FURTHER READING

For the most part, the suggestions made in Chapter 12 apply to Chapter 13, as well. There are also a number of special topics in this chapter that deserve extra attention. Although the QoS concept is vague, reasonable discussions of quality of service (usually abbreviated QoS) can be found in the white paper by Hartmann [HART04] and in the QoS chapter of Cisco's Internetworking Technology Handbook [INT08]. Two well-regarded books are by Armitage [ARM00] and Ferguson and Huston [HUST98]. Stallings [STAL09], Kurose [KUR08], and Forouzan [FOR07] all provide substantial coverage of network security. Forouzan is the most technical, offering detailed explanations of encryption techniques. There are numerous books devoted exclusively to network security. One of many readable choices is Cheswick [CHES03].

KEY CONCEPTS AND TERMS

Address Resolution
Protocol (ARP)
ATM (Asynchronous
Transfer Mode)
authoritative domain name
server
Carrier Sense Multiple
Access with Collision
Detection (CSMA/CD)
protocol
collision
country-code top-level
domain name server
(ccTLD)
differentiated service (DS)
field

DNS root server
Domain Name System
(DNS)
Dynamic Host
Configuration Protocol
(DHCP)
electronic signature
handshaking
local DNS server
local domain
mask
MPLS (Multi-Protocol
Label Switching)
network propagation delay
packet sniffing

public key–private key
cryptography
Quality of Service (QoS)
replication
resolution (of domain
name)
SDH (Synchronous Digital
Hierarchy)
SONET (Synchronous
Optical Network)
subnet
symmetric key
cryptography
top-level domain

READING REVIEW QUESTIONS

13.1   What is a domain name? How is it used on the Internet?

13.2   What does TLD stand for? What is a ccTLD? What other kinds of TLDs are there? What is the function of a TLD?

13.3   What task is performed by a DNS root server?

13.4   What function is performed by a local domain name server? What two kinds of addresses would you expect to find stored in a local domain name server table?

13.5   What two major tasks are performed by IP?

13.6   What does ARP stand for? What task does an ARP perform?

13.7   Briefly explain CSMA/CD. What common name does this protocol go by? What topology does CSMA/CD apply to?

13.8   Explain how an Ethernet frame provides synchronization between sender and receiver nodes.

13.9   What is meant by *data nonrepudiation*?

13.10   What does the expression *Quality of Service* mean?

13.11   What types of security problems does a firewall try to prevent?

EXERCISES

13.1   Name at least four different application layer protocols other than HTTP. For each, describe the purpose of the protocol, and give a brief overview of the methodology of its operation.

13.2 The DNS database is described as "a directory system of servers". Based upon your understanding of DNS from the text, explain the meaning of this description.

13.3 What service is provided by a *DNS root server*? To whom is this service provided?

13.4 Explain the purpose of an *authoritative domain name server*. How does its purpose differ from that of a local DNS server.

13.5 Explain the technique that is used by DNS to distribute the load of large websites.

13.6 How does someone obtain a URL?

13.7 Explain carefully the purpose and use of the sequence number and acknowledgment number in connection-oriented communications. Create a multi-packet example that illustrates exactly how these packets are used by TCP.

13.8 Explain the concept of a DHCP lease. How is it obtained? How is it used? What does it provide?

13.9 What is the purpose of an IP address mask? Suppose an IP address is identified as 222.44.66.88/24. What is the network address in this case? What is the host address? How many hosts can this network address support? Repeat this exercise for the IP address 200.40.60.80/26.

13.10 Why does the IP datagram require separate fields for the header length and the total datagram length, instead of combining both into a single value?

13.11 Prior to the invention of Ethernet, researchers at the University of Hawaii proposed a broadcast radio network called ALOHANet as a means to provide wireless links between the Hawaiian islands. Each node had a radio transmitter which could be used to send data packets. When two stations attempted to transmit simultaneously, a collision occurred, and like Ethernet, each station would wait a random period of time, then try again.

Compare ALOHANet with Ethernet. What are the similarities? What are the differences? What are the major factors contributing to the differences? What effects do the differences have upon performance? Under what conditions would you expect ALOHANet to perform satisfactorily? Less satisfactorily?

13.12 Discuss the trade-offs between bus-based and switched Ethernet. State the various conditions under which one or the other would be preferred and explain why.

13.13 Explain the operation of the Address Resolution Protocol.

13.14 The chapter notes that the physical layer is only concerned with the transmission of a sequence of bits from one point to another. Suppose that the sequence 110010011 is used as a synchronization sequence preamble to a data packet. Propose a method that can be used to allow the channel to distinguish the synchronization sequence from an identical data sequence within the packet. In what layer of the TCP/IP model would you implement your solution? Why?

13.15 Before effective Ethernet switching existed, some network designers used an alternative bus collision avoidance protocol known as the *token bus* protocol. With the token bus protocol, a "token" made up of a short, standard string of 1s and 0s was circulated constantly in a round robin fashion among the NIUs attached to the bus. NIUs did not hold the token; they simply passed it without delay to the next NIU in the chain. An NIU was only allowed to place a message on the bus when it possessed the token. After the message was delivered, the token was again put into circulation. No NIU was allowed to use the token again until the token had circulated to every other NIU at least once.

Under what conditions would this protocol perform more satisfactorily than CSMA/CD? Explain. Under what conditions is CSMA/CD preferable? Explain.

13.16 Consider again the network described in Exercise 12.20. For each of the links in this network, describe a technology (medium and signaling method) that would be suited to this application.

13.17 Find and read a good article that describes ATM in more detail than is provided in this text. Compare ATM methodology with the other networking topologies that we have discussed. What characteristics of ATM make it capable of high performance compared to other networking techniques?

13.18 Explain the differences between TCP and UDP in the context of ordering a number of items from an online seller such as amazon.com.

13.19 What are the specific so-called "qualities" that *quality of service* attempts to measure and achieve? Describe the two methods that are normally used as an attempt to achieve this quality.

13.20 The governments of Freedonia and Sylvania need to set up data communications to prevent the possibility of war. Discuss the security implications of fiber optic versus coaxial wire versus satellite as a means of communication.

13.21 Explain the purpose of *repudiation*. How does repudiation differ from *authentication*? Create a business scenario that illustrates the importance of each.

13.22 Locate, download, and install a packet-sniffing software package, such as Wire-Shark (formerly known as Ethereal). Experiment with this software until you understand how it works and the range of its capabilities. Write a brief paper describing several of its most important capabilities and the potential security dangers that those capabilities create.

COMMUNICATION CHANNEL TECHNOLOGY

14.0 INTRODUCTION

In Chapter 12, we introduced the concept of a communication channel. We noted that communication channels are fundamental to modern technology, whether we are discussing wired networks, wireless networks, a backbone of the Internet, cell phones, satellite television, or even your TV remote control. The discussion of channels in Chapter 12 presents features of the channel, introduces channel media and shows how communication channels and channel segments—or links—are interconnected to build networks. Chapter 14 extends the discussion by introducing the fundamental technology of communication channels. After we have introduced the technology, we will apply the technology to offer an understanding of wireless data communication.

First, in Section 14.1, we review some of the characteristics and features of the channel that are governed most directly by the technology. We have carefully differentiated between end-to-end channels and channels that are links. Since the technology can differ from link to link, we note that the emphasis in this chapter is almost entirely on channels that are individual links. The major topics of interest include the signaling methods used to represent data, interaction between the signaling methods and the choice of media, and the characteristics of channels.

Fundamental signaling techniques and the general characteristics of channels are covered in Section 14.2. As you hopefully recall from Chapter 4, data comes in many forms, both analog and digital. Similarly, there are both analog and digital signaling methods in use. Section 14.2 introduces the fundamental characteristics of both analog and digital signals and shows how the channel manages different kinds of data with both kinds of signaling. It also considers the tradeoffs between different combinations of data and signaling.

In Section 14.3, we look more closely at the nature of transmission media, identify specific media that are commonly used, and discuss the relationship between the selection of a communication channel medium and a signaling method.

One of the most important technological concepts explained in this chapter is the use of radio as a medium for the transmission of digital data. Section 14.4 discusses wireless data communication methods.

A note: Overall, our focus is specific to networks and network interconnectivity. There are other types of communication channels, those used in traditional telephony, for example, which are basically similar to those used in networks, but differ in the details. While these are occasionally mentioned to clarify some of the concepts in the chapter, they are generally outside the scope of the discussion in this chapter.

14.1 COMMUNICATION CHANNEL TECHNOLOGY

You will recall that a communication channel consists of a NIC transmitter that places a signal from a sending node onto the channel and a receiver that transfers the signal from the channel to the NIC of the receiving node, a transmission signaling method, and a medium to carry the signal. This is, of course, equally true for any type of

FIGURE 14.1

Model of a Communication Channel

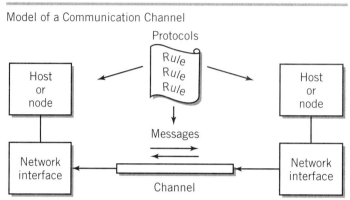

channel. To refresh your memory, Figure 14.1 reproduces the model of a communication channel shown previously in Figure 12.3.

At this point, we remind you that the view of a end-to-end communication channel is conceptual. In reality, the signal coming from one end node may pass through a number of different channel links, each with its own medium, signaling method, and channel characteristics, and connected by intermediate nodes that consist of switches, routers, and other devices, before reaching the other end node. In order to discuss the technology of a particular medium with a particular signaling method, we must treat each channel segment as an independent channel. We use the word "channel" in this chapter to mean the smallest link with a pair of nodes, whether end or intermediate. Our focus in this chapter is on the data link and physical layers of the TCP/IP-OSI models.

For a particular channel, the transmission signaling method used depends not only on the channel medium but also on other factors such as the distance between nodes, the application, and other technical, physical, and economic considerations. The network interface units at each node connect to a computer or router or some other connecting device and may also be required to convert the data into a form suitable for the signaling method used, and for compatibility with other equipment connected to the channel. The channel may pass data in one direction only, or it may be used to transmit and receive data in both directions. We have already noted that a channel may be point-to-point or may be shared and that, with rare exception, a channel carries data serially. At any given instant, the computers or other devices using the channel may be sending, receiving, or both. All the transmitters and receivers connected to a channel must agree on the signaling method to be used on that channel.

As an example, recall the end-to-end channel presented in Chapter 12, Figure 12.4, reprinted here as Figure 14.2. This example uses various combinations of media and signaling technologies to relay a Web request from a home computer to a Web server somewhere on the Internet. The data in this example originates at a computer, is converted to an Ethernet-based radio signal by a NIC in the computer, transmitted to a router, converted back to wired Ethernet and passed to a DSL modem, converted again, this time to a DSL format then passed through various routers, backbone networks, and other Internet devices until it is ultimately directed to a network with the Web server. Some of

FIGURE 14.2

A Multi-Link Channel

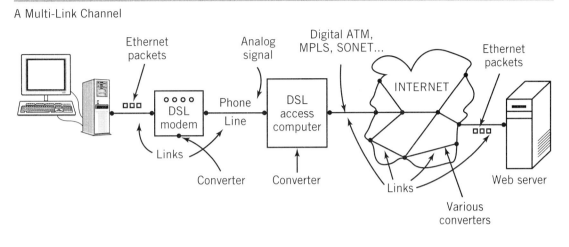

these links will be wires, some fiber optic cables, perhaps even a microwave or satellite link along the way. The data signals in this example take the form of radio waves, electrical pulses, and perhaps, light pulses at various points along its journey.

Although there are a number of data conversions along the way in this example, it is not untypical of modern communication applications. We selected it to show you some of the different possible forms that the data might take as it passes from one end of the end-to-end channel to the other. Conceptually, the channel is an Ethernet connection carrying digital signals between two computers. Physically, the data passes through several different communication channel forms, with signal format converters at each node, but the intermediate operations are invisible to the nodes located at each end of the conceptual channel.

A communication channel is characterized primarily by the signaling transmission method used; by its bandwidth or bit rate capacity; by the direction or directions in which signals can flow; by its noise, attenuation, and distortion characteristics; by the time delay and time jitter imposed by the channel and node connections; and by the medium used.

There are many different signaling methods in use, but the most important consideration is whether a signaling method is analog or digital. Analog transmission uses a continuously varying waveform to carry data. Digital transmission carries data in digital form, using two different values of electrical voltage or current or an on/off light source.[1] The choice of digital or analog transmission signaling depends upon a number of factors. Some media are only suitable for one or the other. Where either is suitable, the choice is made on the basis of other factors such as noise characteristics, the application, the bandwidth requirements, and other uses for which the channel is to be shared.

---

[1]To be strictly accurate, technically, switched light is a digital signal superimposed on an analog waveform of extremely high frequency, using a modulation technique called amplitude shift keying (ASK).We will introduce modulation and amplitude shift keying later in this section. ASK imposes some technical conditions on the use of light as a transmission signaling method that are beyond the scope of our discussion. Practically speaking, we can treat light transmission as if it were digital.

Except where analog transmission is required by the medium, there is a strong tendency toward digital transmission in most circumstances. Digital transmission has the advantage that it is less susceptible to noise and interference, which means a higher likelihood that the original data can be reproduced exactly, error-free, at the receiving end of the channel. Digital transmission is also simpler, more efficient and more economical. When a digital signal is to be transmitted on an analog channel, it is necessary to convert the digital signal into a form suitable for analog transmission. The converse is also true. The methods of conversion, and resulting limitations, are discussed in Section 14.2.

It is also possible to share a channel among multiple sender-receiver pairs, using one of several **multiplexing** techniques. Digital channels use time division multiplexing (TDM). Analog channels can also use time division multiplexing, but most use frequency division multiplexing (FDM) instead. There are several important variations on these two primary methods, as well. Again, digital technology has an advantage: digital multiplexing is easier to implement than analog multiplexing, is less expensive, and requires less maintenance. Multiplexing techniques are also discussed in Section 14.2.

14.2 THE FUNDAMENTALS OF SIGNALING TECHNOLOGY

Signals are the means used to communicate data. A signal is carried on a communication channel as an electrical voltage, an electromagnetic radio wave, or a switched light. Data is represented by changes in the signal as a function of time. The signal may take on a continuous range of values, in which case it is known as an **analog signal**, or it can take on only discrete values, in which case it is known as a **discrete signal**. A *binary* discrete signal is usually called a **digital signal**. A representation of a signal shown as a function of time is called a **waveform.** Figure 14.3 shows an analog signal and a digital signal. We are primarily interested here in analog and digital signals, although we note in passing that the "analog" video signals going to a display from a computer video card takes on only specific

FIGURE 14.3

Analog and Digital Waveforms

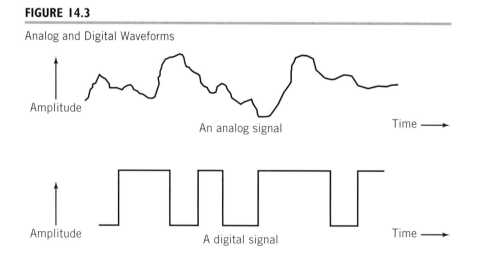

values, 16 or 256 or some different number of values depending on the video adapter used, and are therefore more accurately considered to be discrete rather than analog or digital. (We shall not consider discrete signals further here, although discrete signals are used in certain cases to increase the bandwidth of a channel. For example, discrete signals are used to increase the speed of a modem beyond its basic bit rate.)

Computer data is fundamentally digital in nature. A digital waveform on a channel might represent a sequence of bits of data representing a text file, for example. Sound is analog. The loudness of sound coming from a stereo speaker would be represented by a continuously changing waveform. It is important to know that the electromagnetic waves used for radio transmission are also analog.

It is often necessary or desirable to be able to transform a digital signal into some analog equivalent representation or vice versa. For example, analog sound is stored digitally in an MP3 player. To listen to the audio on the player requires that the bits of data be converted to analog waveforms. Headphones reproduce the waveforms as sound. Conversely, to transmit computer data on an ordinary voice-grade phone line requires that the computer data must be represented by an analog signal, since the phone line is designed to carry sound. A modem is used to perform the conversion. (Actually, to be more accurate, the phone line carries analog electrical voltage signals that *represent* the sound wave, which are converted back to actual sound at the earpiece of the phone receiving the signal.)

Ideally, the transformation between digital and analog should be reversible. That is to say, if we transform a digital waveform into an analog representation and then transform it back, the resulting digital waveform should be identical to the original. For digital waveforms, this is theoretically achievable. In practice, all systems, both digital and analog, are subject to noise, attenuation, and distortion, and it is often necessary to provide compensation in the form of error correction. Nonetheless, under most conditions, it is possible to recover the original digital data exactly. When analog data is converted into digital form, however, a small amount of information is lost during the transformation, and it is not possible to recover the original analog waveform exactly, although the error can be reduced to the point that it doesn't matter.

The medium itself may require transformation of a signal from analog to digital (A-to-D) or vice versa if the signal is to be transmitted through a medium that can carry only one or the other. Wires can carry either digital or analog signals, but as we already noted, normal residential phone lines carry analog signals. Radio signals, known as radio waves, require another type of analog signal, with the digital signal embedded within.

Analog Signaling

Although digital transmission is favored for most use these days, analog transmission methods are required for wireless media, such as radio and sound, for wireless networking, and for other forms of wireless data communication. Radio transmission methods include satellite, cellular phone, wireless networking, and microwave communications. Radio waves can also be converted to equivalent electrical signals and used with wire media and may be preferred when a mixture of digital and analog data is being transmitted through the cable, such as cable TV with a digital Internet feed, though most cable TV is now digitally distributed and converted, if necessary, to analog at the customer's site.

FIGURE 14.4

A Sine Wave

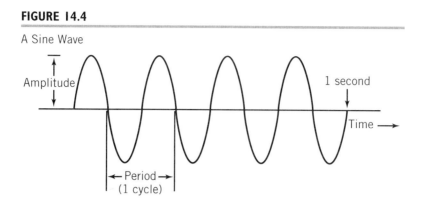

The basic unit of analog transmission is a **sine wave**. A sine wave is shown in Figure 14.4. A sine wave has a peak **amplitude** A, or size, and a **frequency,** measured as the number of times the sine wave is repeated per second. The instantaneous value of the sine wave varies with time, ranging from 0 to amplitude A, back to 0, to value −A, and back to 0 again. The value may measure voltage, or loudness, or the mechanical movement of the metal in a bell, or the movement of air in an organ pipe, or some other quantity. The **period** of a sine wave is the amount of time it takes to trace out one complete cycle of the wave. Thus, the frequency, f, is defined as the number of periods per second, or mathematically,

$$f = 1/T \quad \textit{or conversely,} \ \ T \ = \ 1/f$$

where T is the period, measured in seconds.

The amplitude and period are shown in the diagram. For this particular sine wave, the period is one-quarter second, and the frequency is four cycles per second, or more commonly, 4 Hertz. **Hertz,** usually abbreviated Hz, is the unit used to measure frequency. One Hertz corresponds to one cycle per second. Note from the diagram, also, that since the sine wave is symmetric about the center axis, its amplitude is measured from the center axis to either peak, not from negative peak to positive peak.

Sometimes it is useful to view a sine wave from a slightly different perspective: what is the physical length of a sine wave that is traveling in space at the speed of light? This parameter is known as the **wavelength** of the sine wave. It is usually designated by the Greek letter lambda (λ). It should be apparent to you that at a higher frequency the wavelength of a single sine wave will be shorter because the waveform will not have time to travel as far before the wave is complete. In fact, the wavelength of a sine wave signal is inversely related to its frequency as follows:

$$\lambda = c/f \quad \textit{where c is the speed of light.}$$

For calculation purposes, the speed of light in a vacuum is approximately 300 million meters per second or one foot per nanosecond. (This latter figure might surprise you.) You may be unconsciously aware of one interesting application of this formula: perhaps you have noticed that when the frequency of a radio wave is higher, the antenna is shorter. The size of an antenna is based on the wavelength of the signal that one is trying to receive.

Why a sine wave? Sine waves occur naturally throughout nature. Sound, radio waves, and light are all composed of sine waves. Even ripples on a pond are sinusoidal. Although

FIGURE 14.5

Circle and the Sine Wave

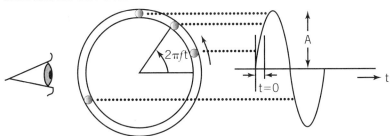

the sine wave may seem an odd waveform to occur so commonly, the sine wave is related in a simple way to a circle. Picture a marble rolling around a circle at constant speed. If you view the circle edgewise, the marble will trace out a sine wave in time. This is illustrated in Figure 14.5. For this reason, points on the sine wave are often designated in degrees. The sine wave begins at $0°$ and ranges to $360°$ and then repeats from $0°$ again. At any given instant in time, the amplitude of the wave is given by the position of the marble for the specified angle. Mathematically, that value is represented by the equation

$$v[t] = A \ \sin[2\pi ft + \varphi]$$

where A is the maximum amplitude, corresponding to the radius of the circle, and f is the number of times that the marble rolls around the circle per second. For mathematical reasons unimportant to us here, the angle is usually given in **radians**, rather than degrees. When $t = T$, the marble has rolled around the circle once, therefore 2π radians is equal to $360°$. A radian is therefore approximately $57.3°$. φ (the Greek letter *phi*), represents the angle of the marble when we begin our viewing, i.e., when $t = 0$. For the view shown in the figure, $\varphi = 0$.

FIGURE 14.6

Phase-Shifted Sine Waves: (a) Reference Waveform, (b) Phase-Shifted 90°, (c) Phase-Shifted 180°

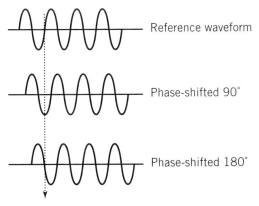

To show you the practical aspect of this illustration, electricity is generated by the rotor of an electrical generator rotating in a circle at the rate of sixty revolutions per second. The electrical output (in many countries) is a standard 117-volt 60-cycle (more accurately Hertz) alternating current sine wave. The instantaneous output of the sine wave corresponds to the angular position of the rotor as it rotates. (Incidentally, the actual peak amplitude of a 117-volt sine wave is approximately 165 volts. The technique used to measure AC voltage is based on a special kind of averaging of the sine wave voltage over a period of time.)

In addition to the amplitude and frequency, it is possible to measure the position of a sine wave with respect to a reference sine wave. The difference, measured in degrees, is known as the **phase** of the sine wave. This measurement is shown in Figure 14.6.

An important characteristic of sine waves is that mathematically *all* waveforms, regardless of shape, both analog and digital, can be represented as the sum of sine waves of different frequencies, phases, and amplitudes. For example, Figure 14.7 shows the construction of a square wave from the first few of its sine wave constituents. The constituent frequencies that make up a signal are known as the **spectrum** of the signal. The **bandwidth** of a channel is the range of frequencies that are passed by the channel with only a small amount of attenuation. (Yes, there is a direct mathematical relationship between the bandwidth defined here and that defined earlier in terms of bits per second, but it's a detail that we shall not go into. Suffice it to say that a wider range of frequencies allows more bits per second to flow through the channel.) Other frequencies are blocked by the channel. To reproduce a signal faithfully, the spectrum of the signal must fall within the bandwidth of the channel, and conversely the bandwidth of the channel must be wide enough to pass

FIGURE 14.7

Creating a Square Wave from Sine Waves

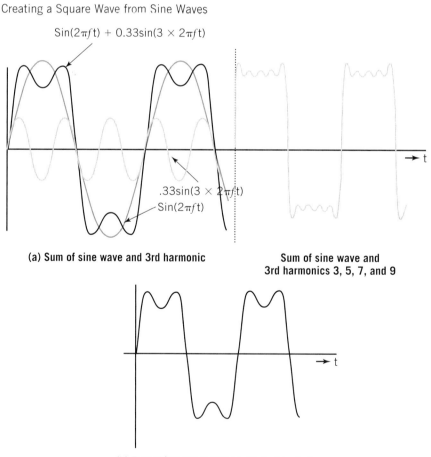

Sin(2πft) + 0.33sin(3 × 2πft)

.33sin(3 × 2πft)

Sin(2πft)

(a) Sum of sine wave and 3rd harmonic

Sum of sine wave and
3rd harmonics 3, 5, 7, and 9

(b) Everything above 3rd harmonic blocked

all the frequency components of desired signals. Note that the waveform in Figure 14.7(b) is the way that the square wave would appear if the frequencies above three times the fundamental sine wave frequency were blocked. In many cases, it is appropriate to limit the bandwidth intentionally to prevent interference from other signals. There are electronic means to control the bandwidth of a channel, using a process called **filtering.** As we will show later, filtering is also used to separate the bands in frequency division multiplexing.

Sound waves use frequencies between approximately 20 Hz and 20,000 Hz, although some animals can hear sounds outside this range. A dog whistle produces a sine wave of approximately 25,000 Hz. Most stereo systems have a bandwidth of at least 20–20,000 Hz, for the faithful reproduction of sound. Telephones have a bandwidth of only about 20–4000 Hz, which makes them unsuitable to carry high-fidelity sound but adequate for voice. The ordinary telephone bandwidth limits the speed that data can be transmitted through a conventional phone line, however additional bandwidth is actually available for the use of DSL technology, discussed later in this chapter. Sound waves are produced by vibrating molecules and require a medium such as air or water. A microphone converts sound to an identical analog electrical signal for transmission through the wires of a phone line, or stereo amplifier, or whatever.

Radio waves are electromagnetic in nature. Radio waves can be transmitted at frequencies as low as 60 Hz, although radio waves of frequencies this low are not useful for most purposes. Currently, radio waves can use frequencies up to about 300 GHz or 300 billion Hertz. To give you some reference points, the standard AM radio band occupies the range between 550 KHz and 1.6 MHz in most countries, the standard FM band from 88 MHz to 108 MHz (what is the frequency of your favorite station?), television from 54 MHz to about 700 MHz, and cellular telephones, Wi-Fi wireless networks, and other devices occupy several bands between 800 MHz and 5.2 GHz. The bandwidth required for different types of signals depends on the application. AM radio stations, for example, use a bandwidth of about 20 KHz, centered about the dial frequency of the station. TV stations require a bandwidth in excess of 4.5 MHz. Each TV channel provides a 6-MHz bandwidth in a different part of the frequency spectrum. In North America, for example, channel 2 uses the frequency range 54–60 MHz, and channel 3 uses 60–66 MHz. By limiting the bandwidth of the TV receiver's tuner, we are able to tune in separate stations. (As you will see later, this is also the principle used by frequency division multiplexing for sharing channels.) A general map of the useful frequency spectrum indicating various familiar sound and electromagnetic wave regions is shown in Figure 14.8.

Electromagnetic waves use space as a medium, although many materials are nearly transparent to the wave at some frequencies, so that the wave passes right through the material with little or no attenuation. Air, for example, is transparent at all frequencies. Most other materials are more transparent at low frequencies than at high frequencies. AM radio band waves will pass through reasonable thicknesses of solid stone, for example, whereas FM radio band waves are attenuated more. The result is that your AM/FM car radio works better on AM when you're in a tunnel, because the AM radio band uses lower frequencies than the FM radio band. Leaves and thick rain clouds can block a satellite TV signal. Light is also made up of electromagnetic waves, with frequencies in the region of 100 thousand billion Hz. There are only a few materials that are transparent to light. Materials that are not transparent can be used to guide or reflect a wave. A satellite dish, for example, works by reflecting radio waves from the dish to a single point, where they are concentrated

FIGURE 14.8

Useful Frequency Spectrum

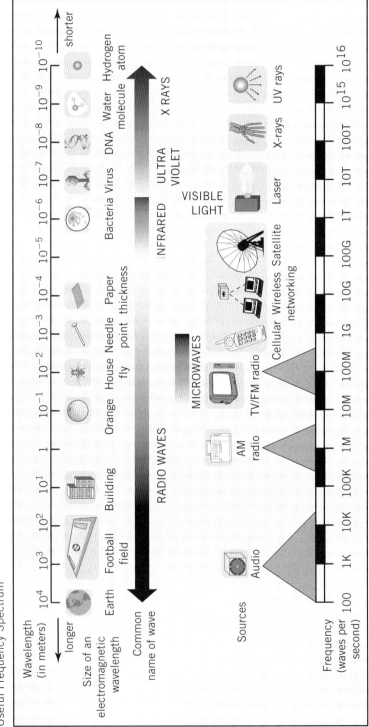

FIGURE 14.9

Amplitude Modulations:
(a) Data Waveform, (b) Carrier,
(c) Modulated Waveform

Data waveform   Carrier

Modulated waveform

and collected by a sensitive receiver. Similarly, fiber-optic cables maximize the light at the receiving end of the cable by guiding the light through the cable.

In practice, the sine waves that we have discussed are of limited use by themselves. A sound made up of a sine wave produces a single, pure tone. A 440-Hz sine wave produces the tone called "A," for example. There is not much useful information value (or musical interest) in a pure sine wave tone. Instead, sine waves are used as **carriers** for the data that we wish to transmit. We **modulate,** or *change*, one or more of the three characteristics of the sine wave, amplitude, frequency, or phase, to represent the signal that is to be transmitted. Thus, an AM, or **amplitude-modulated**, radio station at 1100 KHz would use a sine wave carrier of 1100 KHz. The music broadcast on that station would modulate the amplitude of the carrier to correspond to the sound of the music. The AM station uses only one type of modulation. You should be able to guess what kind of modulation is used by an FM station! To restore the original waveform that was used to modulate the carrier, we use a **demodulator** or **detector.** An example of a carrier amplitude modulated by another analog signal is shown in Figure 14.9. Note that amplitude modulation is symmetric with respect to the center of the carrier sine wave.

For digital signals, the carrier signal is modulated with only two possible values, the value representing a "0" and the value representing a "1." In this case, the modulation technique is called **amplitude shift keying (ASK), frequency shift keying (FSK),** or **phase shift keying (PSK).** Examples of each are shown in Figure 14.10.

FIGURE 14.10

ASK, FSK, and PSK

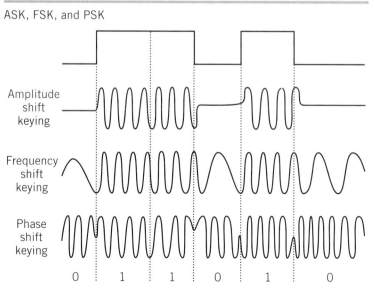

The spectrum of frequencies used for a modulated signal depend on the frequency of the carrier used and will include the carrier frequency itself. The bandwidth of the modulated signal depends on the type of modulation. The bandwidth of an amplitude-modulated wave is approximately double the highest frequency in the waveform being modulated. In other words, the 20-KHz bandwidth of an AM radio station is suitable for transmitting audio frequencies up to about 10 KHz; FM bandwidth requirements are somewhat larger. The 400-KHz bandwidth of an FM station can carry audio frequencies up to approximately 45 KHz.

When considering the bandwidth required for a single FM station, think about what would happen if the FM station were placed instead on the AM radio band. The spectrum of the entire AM band is only 1050 KHz wide (550–1600 KHz) so there would only be enough bandwidth for two stations! The point to be made is that at higher frequencies more bandwidth is available; at higher frequencies, the bandwidth is a smaller percentage of the frequency. From Chapter 12, you are aware that fiber-optic cable is a preferred medium for carrying data. As you can see from the frequency spectrum shown in Figure 14.8, the frequency of light is extremely high, allowing very wide bandwidths, and hence high bit rates.

When we modulate a particular signal with a sine wave carrier of different frequencies the modulated signal will require the same amount of bandwidth but will move the spectrum by changing the basic frequency about which the bandwidth of the signal occurs. This means that, by modulating different data signals with different carrier frequencies, it is possible to carry multiple signals on the same channel, if the overall channel bandwidth is wide enough to include the spectra for each signal. Filtering can separate the different data signals at the receiving end. This technique is called **frequency division multiplexing (FDM).** It can be used to carry several phone conversations on long-distance phone lines, for example, or to provide multiple channels for wireless Ethernet (Wi-Fi). Ultimately it uses the bandwidth more effectively to increase the capacity of the channel. An Illustration of FDM is shown in Figure 14.11.

The same technique can be applied to the light transmitted through a fiber-optic cable. Light of different colors have different frequencies. Viewed from the perspective of ASK analog signaling, it is possible to increase the bit rate of data transmitted optically by combining lights of different color, with filters on the receiving end of the cable to separate the different color signals. This procedure is essentially identical to that of frequency division multiplexing, although the implementation is actually somewhat easier. To differentiate optical multiplexing from lower frequency radio multiplexing, we give the process a different name: **wavelength division multiplexing (WDM).** This name reflects the fact that light is usually identified by its wavelength, rather than by its frequency. As of this writing, there are claims that current optic technology can support bit rates of 8 Tbps over distances of 2500 km using a dense form of WDM called DWDM. As we noted earlier, most users think of the signals in fiber-optic cables as digital.

Both wired and wireless analog signals are particularly susceptible to noise and attenuation and other forms of distortion in a channel because the distortion created cannot be detected and reversed. There is also interference from other signals operating nearby in the same spectrum. **Attenuation,** or signal loss, is the reduction of a signal that occurs in a medium as a function of the physical length of the channel. Attenuation limits the possible length of a channel. Signal loss can also occur if there are taps or splitters along the channel. These are devices that remove some of the energy of the signal for

FIGURE 14.11

Frequency Division Multiplexing

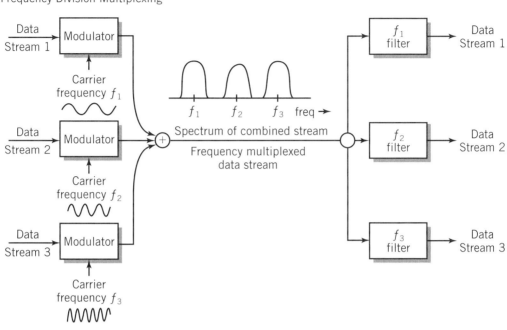

use, for example, to implement multipoint connectivity. **Amplifiers** can be used to restore the original strength of the signal. All channels generate some noise internally, and as the signal gets weaker, the noise becomes more predominant with respect to the signal. In this case, amplification does not help, since the noise is amplified also. Maintaining a high signal-to-noise ratio is important in maintaining the integrity of an analog signal. Minimizing external noise, such as electrical noise from other devices and from such natural sources as lightning, is also important. External noise, of course, can change the basic shape of the signal, and may make it impossible to recover the original signal. If the noise falls within the same frequency range as the signal, there is no way to separate the noise from the signal. See Figure 14.12.

In addition, analog signals are susceptible to distortion of the waveform that results from variations in attenuation and phase shifts that occur across the channel spectrum. Slight distortion is, unfortunately, common in real-world systems. Consider the situation shown in Figure 14.13. If the signal is made up of sine waves of frequencies from different parts of the spectrum, say, at the points marked f_1 and f_2, then the composite signal at the output of the channel is distorted, since the different sine wave components have been attenuated by different amounts. The channel will also change the phase of some components more than others, which also contributes to the distortion. To some extent, filtering can compensate for these variations, but realistically, signal distortion is always present in a channel. The goal, then, when working with analog signaling, is to design a system in which noise, attenuation, and spectral distortion do not prevent recovery of the original data to the degree required.

FIGURE 14.12

The Effects of Noise on a Signal

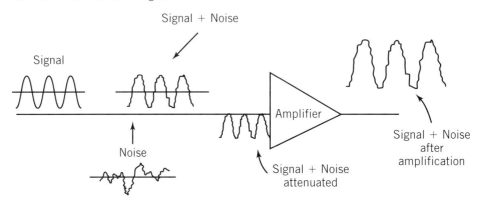

FIGURE 14.13

Effects of Attenuation

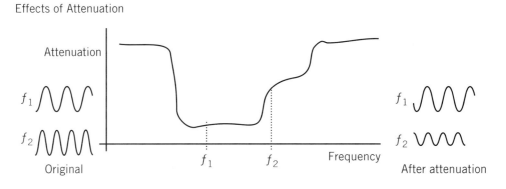

Digital Signaling

Digital data being carried by a digital communication channel is already in correct format, so theoretically no conversion is necessary. In practice, the situation is somewhat different. Since there is no carrier present on the channel, there may be no way to detect a string of bits at the receiving end of the channel for some signals. The signal in Figure 14.14, for example, consists of a string of twelve zeros, but there's no way to tell. A "0" is represented by a value of 0 volts, and the state of the line when no signal is present is also 0 volts. Obviously, there is no way to determine the presence of this signal.

This example shows one difficulty in coordinating digital data that is transmitted from one node to another. One obvious way to solve this problem is to use a different value for the "0" bit, say, −5 volts. This solution helps somewhat, but we still can't tell one bit from another in the data stream.

FIGURE 14.14

A Problematic Digital Signal

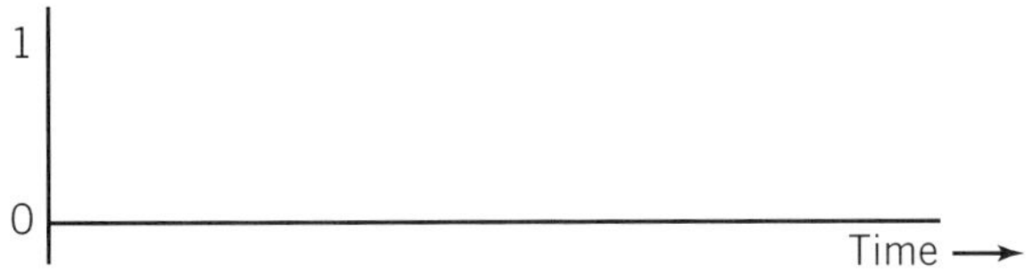

1

0

Time ⟶

As another example, consider a related problem, a steady stream of bits across a communication channel from one computer to another. Suppose that each group of 8 bits forms a byte. If the stream is continuous, how does the receiving computer know how to group the bits into bytes?

Some method of synchronizing digital signals between the sending computer and the receiving computer is always necessary, to be able to identify the position of each bit successfully at the receiver. The basic problem is that the sending computer may opt to transmit data at any time, and the receiving computer has no way of knowing when data will actually be sent. The difficulty of synchronization is compounded by likely slight differences in timing in each system, so that the receiver may sample the data at a slightly different rate. If the sequence of bits is long, the receiver may ultimately sample the wrong bit, creating an error. Figure 14.15 illustrates this situation. In this illustration the timing difference is somewhat exaggerated, for clarity.

There are a number of different ways of synchronizing the two systems. For modems, which transmit data one byte at a time, the solution is to provide clear start and stop signals for the data and to resynchronize the timing between the transmitter and receiver for each byte of data, so that the receiver knows exactly when each bit is expected to occur. This approach is somewhat inefficient, because two extra bits (the start and stop signals) must be sent for each byte of data. This technique is called **asynchronous transmission.**

For longer bit sequences, the solution is to convert the data into a signaling method that provides clocking as part of the data. Consider a signaling method that say, generates a $0 \rightarrow 1$ transition whenever the bit is a *one*, and a $1 \rightarrow 0$ transition whenever the bit is a *zero*. This technique guarantees at least one transition per bit of data sent through the channel. The transitions can be used for clock synchronization. Look at the example in Figure 14.16. The required transitions are shown as heavy arrows within the resulting

FIGURE 14.15

Reception Errors Resulting from Timing Mismatch Between Sending and Receiving Computers

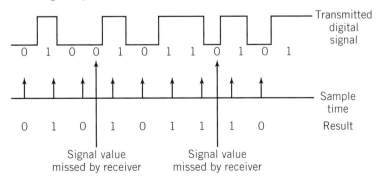

FIGURE 14.16

Manchester Encoding

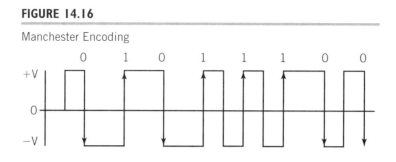

waveform. Note that the fourth and fifth bits both require 0 → 1 transitions. To accomplish this, there must be an additional downward transition to make the second 0 → 1 transition possible, however the extra downward transition occurs between the data points and is ignored. This particular method is called **Manchester encoding**. It is one of several possible **self-synchronization** techniques. Manchester encoding is used in 10 Mbps Ethernet transmissions. For practice, you might wish to create the waveform for the original example shown in Figure 14.14: the case of twelve zeros.

FIGURE 14.17

4B/5B Block Coding

4-bit data sequence	5-bit code		
0000	11110	1000	10010
0001	01001	1001	10011
0010	10100	1010	10110
0011	10101	1011	10111
0100	01010	1100	11010
0101	01011	1101	11011
0110	01110	1110	11100
0111	01111	1111	11101

a. 4B/5B encoding table

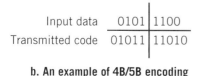

b. An example of 4B/5B encoding

An alternative encoding methodology is called **block coding**. Block coding adds additional bits to small blocks of data; it then converts each block to a different block of data that supplies the required self-clocking. At the receiving end, the blocks are converted back to the original data. Block coding is often used to compensate for shortcomings of other methods. A simple example will clarify the idea. 4B/5B is a block coding algorithm that compensates for a shortcoming of a method called NRZ-I that loses synchronization if the data contains a lot of zeros. 4B/5B converts 4-bit groups into 5 bits for transmission using the conversion table shown in Figure 14.17 (a). Figure 14.17 (b) shows the resulting encoding. Block encoding has the additional advantage that it can detect certain errors. There are sixteen unused 5-bit blocks. If any of these blocks appear at the receiver, the system knows that there is an error. There are a number of different block codes in use. The block coding shown in this example is used for most 100 Mbps Ethernet transmissions.

In addition to self-synchronization, there must be a means to synchronize the data so that the receiver knows the boundaries of each byte. Ethernet frames use an 8-byte preamble for this purpose. The pattern 10 is repeated twenty-eight times, followed by a *start frame delimiter* with the pattern 10101011.

As you know, digital signals can also be used to represent analog waveforms. We have already mentioned the iPod as an example. Other examples include the digital signals that represent video in a direct satellite TV system and the digitization of sound that can be used to store telephone voice mail in a computer.

One way of converting analog data into digital form is shown in Figure 14.18. This method is called **pulse code modulation** (**PCM**). There are three steps in the process. In step 1, the analog waveform is sampled at regular time interval, as shown in Figure 14.18a. In Figure 14.18b the maximum possible amplitude of the waveform is divided into intervals

FIGURE 14.18

The A-to-D Conversion Process

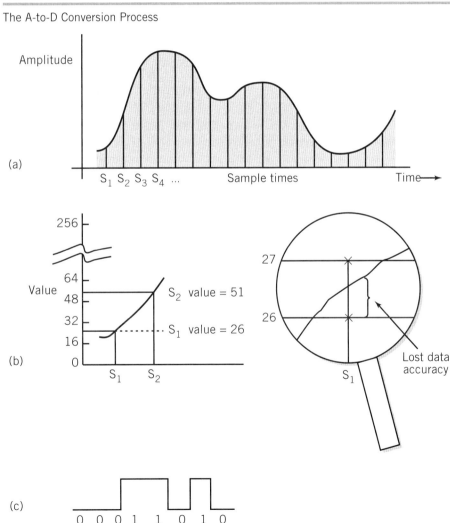

FIGURE 14.19

Use of a Repeater

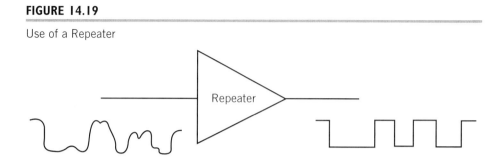

corresponding to a range of binary numbers. This example uses 256 levels, which will result in 8 bits per sample. This intermediate step is called **pulse amplitude modulation (PAM)**. PAM can be used directly, to provide a discrete signal signal, if desired. More commonly, the sampled values are each converted into their corresponding number value. The result is PCM. Incidentally, the information lost in converting data from analog to digital can be seen in this step: it consists of the difference between the actual value of the sample and the value corresponding to the nearest available number. Finally, in Figure 14.18c, the number is reduced to its binary equivalent. The device that performs this conversion is called an **A-to-D converter**.

Digital signals are susceptible to noise, attenuation, and distortion, just as analog signals are. However, it is only necessary to distinguish between two levels, so much more distortion and noise in the channel can be tolerated. It is also possible to recreate the original signal at intervals along the channel, since the original shape is limited to ones and zeros. **Repeaters** are used for this purpose. Repeaters make it possible to transmit digital signals over long distances. Error correction techniques can also be used to repair data. Error correction can be particularly effective in the presence of bursts of noise. Figure 14.19 illustrates the operation of a repeater.

Digital signals can also be multiplexed to allow different signals to share a channel. **Time division multiplexing (TDM)** is normally employed for this purpose. Figure 14.20 illustrates a time division multiplexer being used to share a communication channel among three digital signals. We've used the idea of a rotary switch to illustrate the operation of the multiplexer, although the switch is actually electronic. Each signal is sampled in turn, at a rate high enough to assure that no data is lost. The number of bits in each sample depends on the application. The data is combined and transmitted over the channel. At the other end of the channel the process is reversed. Each sample is sent to its respective destination. TDM has one potential shortcoming. If there is a lot of data in one incoming channel and very little in another, TDM is inefficient. There will be empty slots from the lightly used channel while data is backlogged in another. An alternative form of TDM, called **statistical TDM**, solves this problem by adding a small header to each slot of data that identifies its channel. In this way, every slot can be filled when the data load requires it.

The bandwidth of a channel is also important for digital transmission. Remember that even digital signals can be represented as a sum of sine waves of different frequency. The higher the data rate, the higher the frequencies of the sine waves that make up the

FIGURE 14.20

Time Division Multiplexing (TDM)

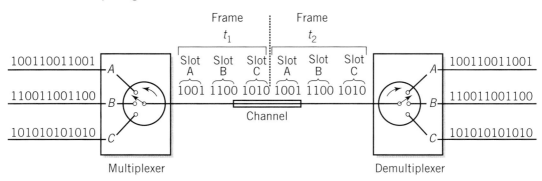

signal. Thus, a channel of wider bandwidth can carry data at a higher data rate, effectively increasing the data capacity of the channel.

Modems and Codecs

Home-to-service-provider network connections commonly rely on telephone or cable service to provide connectivity. In some areas, service providers offer fiber direct delivery to the home, supplying telephone service, TV, and Internet connectivity digitally on a single fiber-optic cable. In older systems, **modems** (**mo**dulator/**dem**odulators) convert Ethernet signals from a computer or router to analog signals for transmission over the phone line or cable system and vice versa. Speeds of 10 Mbps and more are possible under some conditions with DSL and cable services. DSL technology uses FDM to separate a traditional phone line into a traditional voice component and two or more data components. The data components use a mixture of ASK and PSK for the transmission of data between the user and the telephone switching center. At the switching center, a *DSL access multiplexer* packetizes the data component for transmission to the Internet. See Figure 14.21.

FIGURE 14.21

DSL

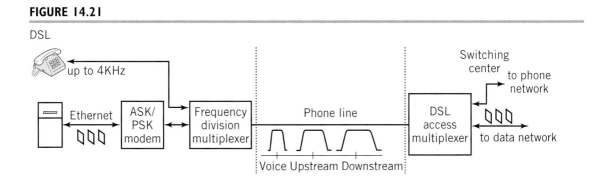

14.3 TRANSMISSION MEDIA AND SIGNALING METHODS

A transmission medium is defined as the means used to carry the signal being transmitted from one location to another. Data may be transmitted using electrical signals on wires, with light signals on fiber-optic cable, or wirelessly, using radio waves or, less commonly, light or sound. A transmission medium is characterized by its physical properties, by the signaling method(s) that it supports, by its bandwidth, and by its sensitivity to outside interference, or **noise.**

Transmission media that confine the signal physically to a cable of some kind are called **guided media.** Media that broadcast the signal openly using radio waves, light, or sound are called **unguided media.** Unguided media do not confine the signal to a particular area, but the signal may be focused in a particular direction.

You have already seen that the bandwidth and noise affect the capability of a channel to transmit data. Although the effect is more obvious with analog signaling, the same is true for both analog and digital signaling. Communication theory shows that the data capacity of a channel increases as the bandwidth of the channel increases. Noise in a channel is measured relative to the size of the signal. The measurement is called the **signal-to-noise ratio.** As you would expect, a higher signal-to-noise ratio for a given bandwidth increases the data capacity of a channel.

Consider the characteristics and general capabilities of each media type in turn:

- Electrically based media require a complete **circuit** consisting of two wires, one to carry the signal, the other as a return. This is perhaps most familiar to you from the electrical wiring in your house. (Some electrical wiring uses a third wire, which is connected to the ground to protect you from shocks, but the third wire is not actually part of the circuit.)

  Electrically based media are often referred to as *wired* media, or just *wire.* Wire carries the signals in the form of changing electrical voltage or current. Analog or digital signaling methods may be used. Wired media are the natural choices in many instances because the signals to be transmitted are already in electrical form and will be used in electrical form at the receiving end, so no conversions are necessary. Wire is inexpensive and easy to use. Wire channels are easily interconnected to extend a channel, to form networks, and to pass signals from one channel to another.

  The most common electrical transmission medium is **twisted pair.** Twisted pair is used for standard telephone and most local area network wiring. Twisted pair consists of two wires twisted together. One wire acts as the signal carrier, the other is the ground return. Twisting the two wires together reduces noise interference somewhat because the same noise presumably occurs in both wires, which cancels the noise to some extent. Groups of twisted pairs are frequently **bundled** together in a larger cable. There are a number of standardized types of twisted pair wiring. There are also some wire pairs that are **untwisted**.

  Coaxial cable consists of a wire surrounded by insulation. The second "wire" consists of a copper shield that surrounds the insulation. The shield acts as a signal return, but also prevents external noise signals from interfering with the signal carried by the inner wire.

Coaxial cable is capable of high bandwidths. It can be used for high-speed transmission of digital signals, at rates of up to 100 million bps, or even more. It can also carry wide-bandwidth analog signals. The cable used to carry cable TV is usually coaxial cable, although fiber optic cable (see below) is gradually replacing coaxial cable. Analog cable TV uses frequency division multiplexing to carry dozens of channels of television at 6 MHz of bandwidth per channel. Coaxial cable bandwidths in excess of 500 MHz are possible. Similarly, the cable can also be used to carry a large number of data compressed time division multiplexed digital TV signals. Coaxial cable is far less susceptible to noise than twisted pair, and is well suited for relatively long distance connections, however its cost is significantly higher than twisted pair, and its bandwidth is small compared to fiber, so its use is fading.

- **Fiber-optic cables** carry signals in the form of light. Optical signals are produced by using the electrical data signal to turn a light on and off very rapidly. A laser or light-emitting diode is used as the light source. It is not possible to use a conventional light bulb, because a light bulb cannot be switched on and off rapidly enough. An optical detector at the other end of the cable converts the light signal back to electrical form. The cable itself consists of one or more strands of glass fiber specially designed to carry waves of light. Each strand is thinner than a human hair and may be tens or hundreds of miles long. The bundle of fibers is surrounded by a plastic sheath, called cladding, to protect the fibers. Fiber-optic cables are often grouped together in bundles, which are further protected by an additional tough plastic jacket. Light is confined to the fibers, and attenuation is very low. Since light is an electromagnetic wave, turning a light on and off is technically a form of ASK. Most users tend to think of fiber-optic transmission as a digital signaling method, for practical purposes. Since light waves are of such high frequency, fiber-optic cable provides an extremely wide bandwidth. A single fiber can carry information at rates of hundreds of millions of bits per second. Fiber-optic cable is nearly invulnerable to most forms of noise, since the signal is optical, not electrical. It is also difficult to tap into a fiber-optic cable, which offers some measure of security. At the nodes, signals are readily converted between light and electrical for interconnection with other media types.

  Its huge data-carrying capacity makes fiber-optic technology highly desirable in many situations. Entire communities are being "rewired" with fiber-optic cables to provide improved communication capability for the future.

- **Electromagnetic wave** transmissions do not require a specific physical medium, but simply propagate through space or through any material that is relatively transparent to the waves. For signaling purposes, the medium is space; radio waves are the carriers. Electromagnetic waves having frequencies above 1 GHz but below the frequencies of light are generally referred to as microwaves. Microwaves are the most common form of wave transmission carrier although lower-frequency radio waves are also used. Microwaves are unguided, but they can be tightly focused and used point-to-point between microwave antennas or between a microwave antenna and a satellite. Lower-frequency radio waves are less directional and harder to focus and require much larger antennas. (Recall that the size of an antenna is inversely proportional to its frequency.) They also provide less bandwidth. Conversely, higher-frequency waves are more susceptible to attenuation within the physical medium that the wave travels through. A heavy rainstorm can make microwave communication difficult, whereas low-frequency radio waves are sometimes used as a communication channel under water.

Microwave communication applications include large-scale Internet backbone channels, direct satellite-to-home television, cellular telephony, and 802.11 ("Wi-Fi") wireless networking.

It is usually necessary to convert between electrical and electromagnetic media formats. However, this technology is well developed and relatively inexpensive. One difficulty with the use of radio waves is interference between different communications using the same carrier frequencies. Although the frequency spectrum seems large, it is heavily used for many different purposes in most areas of the spectrum where communication is practical. (Consider the interference between a microwave oven and a cordless phone, for example.) Higher frequencies are somewhat more available because of the ability to focus the wave in a particular direction. The highest usable frequencies are, of course, light waves. There are wireless networks and direct computer-to-computer channels that use infrared light as a medium.

14.4 WIRELESS NETWORKING

Wireless networking uses radio wave technology as a transmission medium. Like wired networking, wireless networking tends to fall into categories based on range. For typical short-range, local area networking, **wireless Ethernet**, more commonly called **Wi-Fi** is the standard. For longer ranges there are two contenders, **WiMAX** and cellular telephone technology, although as of this writing neither technology has achieved the standardization, degree of deployment, or use to determine its long-term success. At the personal level, Bluetooth is the generally accepted standard. As we mentioned in Chapter 12, there is also a recent development of technology and standards to interconnect wireless Ethernet into a wireless mesh network using wireless technology that can link many Wi-Fi areas into a larger network.

Wireless data communications must deal with a lot of difficult issues that are not present with standard networking. These include signals whose strengths vary widely, buildings, trees, and other structural signal blocks, and interference from other wireless devices, including both devices designed for wireless data communication and devices with other purposes, such as microwave ovens and standard cordless phones. There is the additional problem that mobile users may move from one signal source to another during their communication, with the expectation that there will be no interruption in data flow. Finally, the bandwidth of wireless systems is limited, with the number of users who want to share the bandwidth increasing rapidly. This has required the development of sophisticated signaling techniques to maximize the use of the bandwidth.

Cellular and WiMAX data communication technologies are complex and not well-standardized as of the time of this writing. We focus here solely on wireless Ethernet. Other technologies are beyond the scope of this text.

Wi-Fi

The most common use of wireless networking is defined by IEEE Standard 802.11. There are several different versions of Wi-Fi. As of this writing, these are known as 802.11a, 802.11b, 802.11g, and 802.11n. A table in Figure 12.25 compared the various versions of Wi-Fi. The basic configuration of a Wi-Fi local area network is shown in Figure 14.22. Each wireless unit is connected by radio to a base station **access point**, which serves as a hub to enable data communication between the various wireless devices and also as a router to enable communication between a wireless device and a wired network. As the figure shows, it is common for an installation to have multiple base stations for wireless access.

All nodes communicate with the access point. The access point forwards the packet to the destination station. Packet forwarding is a necessity because there is no guarantee that nodes can "hear" each other. As Figure 14.23 shows, it is possible for stations to be out of range or blocked by buildings or other obstacles from each other, however all stations can communicate with the access point. This is sometimes referred to as a *hidden node condition*.

The Wi-Fi standard also includes an ad hoc mode where wireless units can communicate with each other without the use of a base station. This mode is almost never used. We won't discuss it further.

The Wi-Fi standard divides the total bandwidth into overlapping channels; the number depends on the type of wireless and the bandwidth permitted within a particular country. For example, in the United States, the 2.4 GHz band is divided into eleven channels. However, interference between channels requires that channels being used simultaneously must be separated by at least four channels to communicate successfully. This means that

FIGURE 14.22

Configuration of a Wi-Fi Network

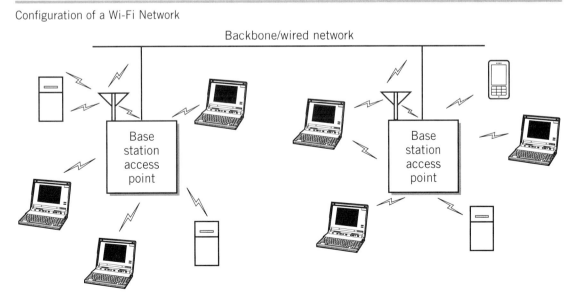

FIGURE 14.23

Examples of a Hidden Node Condition and Out-of-Range Conditions

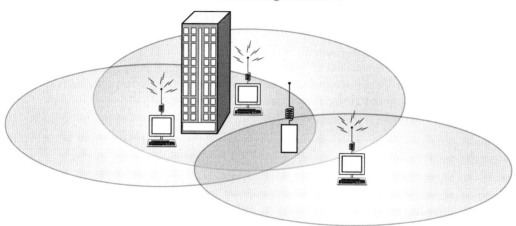

there is only a single group of three channels that can be used simultaneously, channels 1, 6, and 11. (A nearby access point that is nearly out of range might be configured to use channels 3 and 8 though.)

Since the medium effectively has the characteristics of a hub, collision handling is required. The standard specifies two techniques, one mandatory, one elective. Collisions in a wireless network are harder to detect than in a wired network and the consequences are greater. It is much more difficult to receive a signal from another station while transmitting a signal. In addition, the hidden node condition means that is is possible that some stations can never detect collisions from each other. Furthermore, once a sender begins to transmit a frame, it will be transmitted to its conclusion, even if a collision has occurred, meaning the delays due to collisions are much longer than those on a wired hub.

Instead, the 802.11 standard specifies the use of a collision *avoidance* MAC protocol, **CSMA/CA**. As with CSMA/CD, a station is always listening. When a station wishes to transmit a packet it waits until the channel is clear, plus an additional short random amount of time. It then transmits its frame. The wireless Ethernet frame contains a field that states the time duration of the packet, which assists other stations in knowing how long a transmission will take. When the frame reaches its destination, the receiver checks for errors, then sends a short acknowledgment packet to indicate satisfactory receipt of the frame. The requirement for receivers to acknowledge the receipt of frames is the reason for the extra delay in starting transmission. The acknowledgment is the only sure way to know that a collision has not occurred.

An optional enhancement uses a reservation system to improve collision avoidance between hidden nodes. Instead of transmitting a frame, a sender will send a short "request to send" (RTS) packet to the access point, including the time duration that it needs to send a frame. If the channel is clear, the access point will return a "clear to send" (CTS) packet, at which time the sender begins transmission of its frame. Even if a node cannot receive the RTS packet, it will be able to receive the CTS packet that was sent from the access point.

SUMMARY AND REVIEW

Communication between loosely coupled computers consists of messages passed over a communication channel. A communication channel is characterized by the transmission medium; the signaling transmission method; the channel capacity or bandwidth; the direction(s) of message flow; and the noise, attenuation, and distortion factors. Realistically, a channel may be made up of several subchannels, each with its own characteristics. The overall channel is defined primarily by the characteristics measured and observed at its access points.

The signaling method may be either analog or digital depending on the medium, the requirements of the sender and receiver stations, and a number of other factors. There are three primary types of medium in use: wires, fiber optics, and electromagnetic radiation. Wires can pass analog and digital signals. Fiber optics use light signals. Electromagnetic radiation media include radio and microwaves and require analog waveforms. Wire and fiber optics are guided media; electromagnetic radiation is unguided.

It is possible to transform data between analog and digital signaling methods; however, there is a small amount of unavoidable data loss in the analog-to-digital transformation process. Digital signals (and some analog signals) are transformed into electromagnetic waves by the process of modulation. Modulation works by varying the amplitude, frequency, or phase of the sine wave that acts as a carrier for the signal carrier.

Currently, the most important wireless data technology is wireless Ethernet, also known as Wi-Fi. There are several different types of Wi-Fi. A Wi-Fi network consists of an access point and a number of wireless stations. Collision avoidance is important; CSMA/CA and RTS/CTS protocols are used to minimize collisions.

FOR FURTHER READING

Any of the books recommended in Chapter 12 are also useful references for the material in Chapter 14. The most thorough discussion of the topics discussed in Chapter 14 is found in Forouzan [FOR07].

KEY CONCEPTS AND TERMS

access point	bundled twisted pair	frequency
A-to-D converter	carriers	frequency division
amplifier	circuit	multiplexing (FDM)
amplitude	coaxial cable	frequency shift keying
amplitude modulation	CSMA/CA protocol	(FSK)
amplitude shift keying	demodulation	guided media
(ASK)	detector	Hertz (Hz)
analog (signal)	digital signal	Manchester encoding
asynchronous transmission	discrete signal	modem
attenuation	electromagnetic wave	modulation
bandwidth	fiber-optic cable	multiplexing
block coding	filtering	noise

period	signal	unguided media
phase	signal-to-noise	untwisted pair
phase shift keying (PSK)	ratio	waveform
pulse amplitude	sine wave	wavelength
modulation (PAM)	spectrum	wavelength division
pulse code modulation	statistical TDM	multiplexing (WDM)
radian	time division multiplexing	Wi-Fi
repeaters	(TDM)	WiMAX
self-synchronization	twisted pair	Wireless Ethernet

READING REVIEW QUESTIONS

14.1   List at least four properties that characterize a communication channel.

14.2   Which layers of the network model are specifically concerned with communication channel media and signaling technology?

14.3   What determines the choice of analog or digital signaling?

14.4   Which, analog signals or digital signals, are more susceptible to noise? Justify your answer.

14.5   What is the purpose of *multiplexing*? Briefly explain time division multiplexing. Briefly explain frequency division multiplexing.

14.6   What is the basic unit of analog signaling?

14.7   What is a *waveform*?

14.8   Explain the relationship between frequency, period, and wavelength in a sine wave.

14.9   What is *modulation*? Is the image in Figure 14E.1 an example of AM, FM, or PM?

FIGURE 14E.1

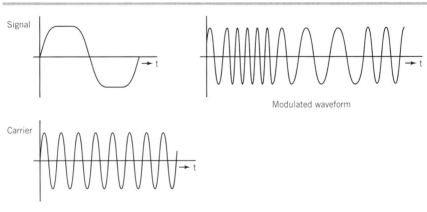

14.10   What is the *spectrum* of a signal? What is the relationship between the spectrum of a signal and the bandwidth of a channel?

14.11   When attenuation occurs in an analog signal, what hardware device is used to restore the original signal? When attenuation occurs in a digital signal, what hardware device is used to restore the original signal?

14.12   What problem does Manchester encoding address? What alternative to Manchester encoding is also discussed in this chapter?

14.13   What potential shortcoming of TDM is addresses by statistical TDM?

14.14   Name a guided medium. Name an unguided medium.

14.15   Coaxial cable, twisted pair, and untwisted pair are examples of what type of medium?

14.16   What factors contribute to the high data capacity of fiber-optic cable?

14.17   What is the relationship between the data capacity of a channel and its signal-to-noise ratio?

14.18   What is an *access point*?

14.19   What are the major differences between CSMA/CD and CSMA/CA? Which is used in Wi-Fi wireless networking? What properties of wireless networking necessitate the use of this approach?

EXERCISES

14.1   Draw a pair of sine waves that are $45°$ out of phase.

14.2   As indicated in the chapter text, any wave can be represented as a sum of sine waves of various frequencies, amplitudes, and phases. This problem explores the effects of channel bandwidth, shape of the spectrum, and phase distortion on the shape of a waveform. A square wave is made up of sine waves according to the following equation:

$$S = \sin(2ft) + 1/3 \; \sin(3 \times 2ft) + 1/5 \; \sin(5 \times 2ft) + \ldots$$

It is difficult to plot sine waves with any accuracy. Instead, we will use a triangular waveform shape as an approximation for the sine wave.

a.   On a sheet of graph paper, carefully construct a triangular wave that starts at 0, rises to a maximum value of 15, falls to a minimum value of -15, then returns to 0. Your waveform should extend over 15 units on the time scale. Now construct a second triangle wave with an amplitude of 5 and a time span of 5. Your second waveform should start at 0. Add the amplitudes of the new waveform and the previous one to produce a new waveform which is the sum of the two. What do you observe?

b.   Now create a third waveform of amplitude 3 and time span 3, and add it to the previous result. What do you observe? If the bandwidth is limited so that only the first two waves can pass through the channel, what is the effect on the waveform?

c.   Next, start with a fresh sheet of graph paper. Draw the fundamental triangle wave. Draw the second triangle wave, but this time shift the phase $90°$, so that the positive peak of the second wave coincides with the initial zero position of the fundamental. Add the two waveforms. What effect did the phase shift have on the summed waveform shape?

d.   On another fresh sheet of graph paper, draw the fundamental waveform one more time. Draw the second waveform, this time with a height of 3 instead of 5. Also draw the third waveform with a height of 4 instead of 3. All waveforms start at 0, that is, with no phase shift distortion. Add the three waveforms. What effect did the altered spectrum shape have on the waveform?

    e. Based on the original amplitudes of the waves and the modified amplitudes used in part (d), draw the spectrum of the channel.

14.3 A waveform travels in space at a rate of approximately 300 million meters per second. The *wavelength* of a sine wave is the actual distance in space that is used by one sine wave as it travels. What is the wavelength of a 100-MHz sine wave? What is the wavelength of a 500-MHz sine wave? Antennas to send and receive electromagnetic waves are often sized to be one-half of the wavelength for the particular wave being used. Compare your previous calculations to the size of VHF and UHF television antennas. How large would a 1/2 wavelength antenna have to be to transmit a 60-Hz wave?

14.4 What is the carrier frequency of your favorite radio station? Is the station amplitude modulated or frequency modulated? How do you know? What is the bandwidth of this station? (Hint: what is the carrier frequency of the next nearest possible station on the dial?)

14.5 **a.** The *Doppler effect* is the varying frequency of the sound made by a train whistle as the train approaches and then moves away from you. The Doppler effect is also used to measure the speed of stars in space relative to the earth. Explain this effect on the basis of what you know about the relationship of wavelength (see Exercise 14.12), speed of light or sound, and frequency.

    b. On a cold day, the speed of sound decreases. What effect would that have on the sound of the train whistle?

14.6 What effect would you expect a wider bandwidth to have on the noise in a channel?

14.7 **a.** A simple TV cable converter converts the TV signal of a channel on the cable to channel 3 for reception on the TV set. A clever viewer notices that she can pick up the adjacent channel that is normally blacked out by tuning her TV set to channel 4. What does this tell you about the way channels are carried on the cable?

    b. The converter on a direct broadcast satellite also converts TV signals to channel 3 for reception. However, changing the TV set to channel 4 does not result in reception of the adjacent channel. Why not? How are the different TV signals carried on the channel?

14.8 On a sheet of graph paper, draw an FSK waveform that represents the following waveform. The carrier frequency of a 0 is 1000 Hz, and that of a 1 is 2000 Hz. The data rate is 500 bps.

14.9 Consider a message that is made up of a sequence of bits as follows:

$$0111001011010110\ldots$$

Suppose that we transmit this message using a combination of FSK and ASK. Draw waveforms that would represent each pair of bits, then use your representations to draw a complete waveform that represents the entire message.

14.10 Describe the advantages that repeaters have over amplifiers.

14.11   Consider a communication system that converts a digital signal to analog form for transmission, then recovers the digital signal at the receiving end. Another system starts with an analog signal, which it then converts to digital form for transmission, and recovers the analog signal at the receiving end. Both systems require both A-to-D and D-to-A conversion, yet one system is considered more reliable than the other. Which one? Why? Compare the A-to-D-to-A communication system with one that is entirely analog. What are the important factors affecting the performance of each system?

14.12   What effect does time division multiplexing have on the bandwidth requirements of a channel?

14.13   In recent years, much of the storage and communication of data has been in digital form, even if the source data is actually analog. Even most television is now transmitted digitally. What benefits and advantages are gained by using digital storage and signaling?

14.14   Many phone companies are replacing the wire in their phone systems with fiber optic cable. What do they expect to gain from doing so?

14.15   Discuss the trade-offs between coaxial wire and fiber optics in a network made up of fifty computer stations all located within 1000 feet of each other.

14.16   Discuss the trade-offs between fiber optic and satellite communication in terms of costs, signal capacity, signaling method, interference, likelihood of failure and repair issues, multipoint capability, reconfiguration capability, and noise.

14.17   Carefully draw a diagram that represents the binary sequence 00101110100010. Now, below your original diagram, draw the Manchester encoded representation of the same sequence.

14.18   Identify the binary sequence that is represented by the Manchester encoded sequence shown in Figure 14E.2.

FIGURE 14E.2

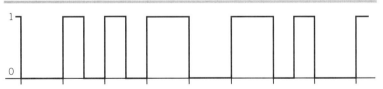

14.19   What is the 4B/5B encoding for the binary sequence 1101000011001101?

14.20   **a.**   What is the binary sequence represented by the 4B/5B encoded sequence

   `11110011111101111110`?

   b.   What is the binary sequence represented by the 4B/5B encoded sequence

   `10101010101010101011`?

14.21   Describe the differences between CSMA/CD and CSMA/CA. Explain the reasons why CSMA/CA is used instead of CSMA/CD for wireless networks. Would the use of CSMA/CA improve the performance of bus-based Ethernet? Why or why not?

PART FIVE

The bare bones computer system described in Chapters 6 through 11 cannot, by itself, meet the needs of today's computer users. Since the job of the hardware is simply to execute the instructions given to it in the form of programs, the ultimate task is the responsibility of software.

Without software, there is no easy way to load programs into memory, no user interface, no means for controlling the various peripheral devices connected to the system, no means for storing, retrieving, or manipulating files, and no way to manage concurrent multiple programs or multiple users.

Of course, we could insist that each application program provide its own tools and facilities, but this would be inconvenient and inefficient. It would also severely limit use of the system. It is obviously useful to provide a set of programs that perform basic functions as an integral part of the computer system.

These programs control the hardware, load and start application programs, provide file services, implement communication between systems, and support a user interface to the computer. This *system software* provides a complete environment in which the user can concentrate on the problem to be solved rather than deal with the nuances of the computer itself. The user interface allows system access to users of different skill levels, and the file and hardware control modules effectively isolate the user from internal computer operations.

Most of this system software is grouped into a set of programs known as an operating system. You are probably most familiar with the operating systems known as Windows, but there are many other important operating systems. Linux, z/OS, and Mac OS X are just a few that may come to mind.

In the next four chapters, we will devote our attention to a study of system software and *operating systems*. We begin in Chapter 15 with an overview of operating systems. In this chapter we introduce the various tasks to be performed by the operating system software. We show the various ways in which the operating system software interacts with the user and with application programs. We show how the operating system is implemented to allow the sharing of resources, so that a user may execute more than one program at a time. It also enables multiple users to share the system.

THE SOFTWARE COMPONENT

The remaining chapters in this section offer more detailed discussions of various parts of the operating system, following the natural hierarchy of the operating system, as described in Chapter 15. In Chapter 16, we look at the interface between user and computer. We consider the various types of commands that are required or desired and the different types of interfaces that are provided on different systems to initiate commands and control the system. We also discuss the concept of *command languages*, powerful ways of combining system commands and utilities that allow the user to perform sophisticated computer tasks with a minimum of effort.

File management is so important that it merits a chapter of its own. Database management systems are at the core of most large modern information technology systems. File management provides the storage facility that makes database management possible. It also provides the capability that allows you to access files by name on your personal computer.

In Chapter 17 we discuss the methods used to store, retrieve, and manipulate files. We look at the methods used for accessing files and consider how the files are stored on various peripheral devices. We study the methods used to implement file directory systems, and consider why some file access methods work better than others under different conditions.

Chapter 18 explores some of the most important algorithms and methods used internally to implement various aspects of the operating system. We begin with a discussion of a simple system that includes the key components required to implement a multitasking system. The remainder of the chapter focuses on primary and secondary storage scheduling, and memory management. The discussion of memory management includes a thorough discussion of virtual storage. We show how the operating system and computer hardware work together synergistically to provide powerful primary storage management capability. Other operating system issues are considered briefly. The chapter concludes with a discussion of virtualization, a topic of considerable importance in modern computer usage.

At the completion of this section, you can expect to have a good understanding of the four major components that make up a computer system: the data, the hardware, the software, and the communication facilities that connect systems together into powerful information resources at both corporate and international levels.

CHAPTER 15

OPERATING SYSTEMS: AN OVERVIEW

15.0 INTRODUCTION

In Chapter 2, we introduced the modern computer system as a synergistic set of components that work together to make the computer accessible and productive to the user. The **operating system (OS)** software component provides the basic functionality of the system by offering programs that operate, control, and support the fundamental resources of the computer. Those resources include both CPU and peripheral hardware, network services, application programs, short-term program and data storage for use while a program is executing, time in which to execute programs, and overall access to the system. The operating system programs make system resources available to the user(s), the user's application programs, and to other application programs running on the computer. The operating system also provides and controls access to other, interconnected systems through its networking and clustering capabilities. Although the operating system programs are tailored to the specific hardware provided on a particular system, it is possible to offer different operating systems on a particular hardware platform and to offer the same operating system on different hardware platforms.

The hardware and the operating system operate together architecturally to form a complete working individual computer environment. The operating system has two fundamental purposes: to control and operate the hardware in an efficient manner and to allow the "users" powerful access to the facilities of the machine by providing a variety of facilities and services. (For this discussion, we will define "users" loosely to include server requests from networked clients on other machines as well as users directly accessing the machine.) These services are available both directly to the users and to the programs that the users execute. In addition, the operating system expands the capability of the computer system to allow for the concurrent processing of multiple programs and support for multiple users, both local and networked, as well as other specialized tasks that would not be possible otherwise. The operating system also makes possible the synergistic implementation of specialized hardware that is designed to improve system performance and capability. The primary example of this, virtual storage, is introduced in Chapter 18.

This chapter provides an overview of the various components, facilities, and services of the operating system. We explore the services that an operating system can provide and show how the operating system integrates these services into a unified working environment. We introduce the tasks that the operating system performs and show how these tasks are interrelated and work together to make it possible for users to get their work done more efficiently.

There are many different types of operating systems, reflecting different purposes and goals, and many different methods of organizing operating systems. These differences are indicated by the way in which the user interacts with the system—an idea that is often surprising to the user who has worked with a single system. This chapter discusses various types of systems and organizations. It notes the different ways in which work is accomplished on a computer system and the different services that are provided.

Although the focus of this book is on IT systems, we note at the outset of this discussion that the use of computer-based operating systems is not limited to business systems or other obvious computer-based devices. Mobile phones, home theater systems, TV sets and DVD players, automobiles, digital cameras, electronic toys, even many household appliances, all rely on computers with their associated operating systems to provide their functionality. The material in this chapter applies, to lesser or greater extent, to all of these. Interestingly enough, the convergence of these diverse areas has, itself, had a major impact on the design and use of business systems.

15.1 THE BAREBONES COMPUTER SYSTEM

Consider once again the Little Man model that we introduced in Chapter 6. To use this model, a single program was stored in memory. The Little Man executed the program by executing each instruction in turn until he encountered a HALT instruction, which stopped the computer. For simplicity, the Little Man scenario was designed to ignore several issues that must be considered in a real computer.

First, we assumed that the program was already loaded into memory, without considering how it got there. In a real computer, the contents of RAM are destroyed when power is shut off. When power is again turned on, the contents of memory are initially unknown. Means must be provided to load a program when the machine is turned on. Remember that the CPU simply executes whatever it finds in memory as instructions, so there must be a program in memory before the computer can even begin to execute instructions. After the computer is on, there must be a method to load a program into memory any time a new program is to be executed.

Second, there must be a means to tell the computer to start executing the instructions in a program. The Little Man began executing instructions whenever the location counter was reset to zero.

Third, the barebones computer has no user interface except for the I/O routines that are provided with the executing program. This means that common program requirements such as keyboard and screen I/O, file operations, interrupt capability and other internal facilities, and printout must be created and supplied as a part of every program written. It would be dangerous for programs to share disks because there would be no way to establish and protect ownership of particular space on a disk.

The most important consideration to remember is that once the computer is running, it will continue to execute instructions until a HALT instruction is encountered or until power is removed. Halting a program at its conclusion means restarting the computer. This suggests that it is highly desirable that there be an additional program in memory that is always available to execute instructions whenever no other program is being run. This would allow programs to complete execution without halting the machine. Instead, a program would terminate with a jump instruction to the alternative program. The alternative program could be used to accept user commands and to provide a memory loader for the execution of other programs.

As a final consideration, notice that the barebones computer is limited to one program at a time. To run multiple programs concurrently, each program must be in memory and there must be a method in place for sharing the time to execute instructions in the CPU. Since the barebones computer offers no provisions for the functions required to handle the memory management and time scheduling needed, multitasking—the execution of multiple programs concurrently—is not possible. Sharing of the computer by multiple users is also not possible, for the same reason. In Chapters 8 and 9 you were made aware of the CPU time wasted during I/O transfers that could be used by other programs. An even more important waste of time occurs as a program waits for user input. The barebones computer is not capable of using the CPU productively during these intervals.

Behind these considerations is the realization that ultimately the purpose of the computer is to help the user to get work done. Obviously, modern computers are not meant to be operated in a barebones fashion like the Little Man. The user should be able to start and operate the computer easily, should be able to choose programs to load and execute, should be able to communicate with others users and other systems, and should be able to perform these operations in a convenient, flexible, and efficient manner. Larger computer systems should be able to share the resources among many users. What is required is additional programs that can provide services to make these expanded capabilities possible.

15.2 THE OPERATING SYSTEMS CONCEPT: AN INTRODUCTION

The solution to the limitations of a barebones system is to include programs with the computer system that will accept commands from the user and that will provide desired services to the user and to the user's programs. These included programs are known collectively as an operating system. The operating system acts as a system manager, controlling both hardware and software and acting as an interface between the user and the system. The operating system itself consists of a collection of programs that work together collectively to accomplish these tasks.

An operating system may be defined as

> a collection of computer programs that integrate the hardware resources of the computer and make those resources available to a user and the user's programs, in a way that allows the user access to the computer in a productive, timely, and efficient manner.

In other words, the operating system acts as an intermediary between the user and the user's programs and the hardware of the computer. It makes the resources available to the user and the user's programs in a convenient way, on the one hand, and controls and manages the hardware, on the other.

Intuitively we think of a user as a human interacting with a computer system; however, there are situations in which the "user" is actually another computer or a mechanical or electronic device of some sort. A common example of this situation is one in which an application program on one computer requests services from an application program or system service on another machine, for example a Web server application requesting data from a back-end database server. Another example would be a situation in which a user on a client machine requests file or printer services on a server machine.

In serving as an intermediary between the users of computer services and the computer's resources, the operating system provides three basic types of services:

1. It accepts and processes commands and requests from the user and the user's programs and presents appropriate output results.
2. It manages, loads, and executes programs.
3. It manages the hardware resources of the computer, including the interfaces to networks and other external parts of the system.

The relationship between the various components of a computer system is shown schematically in Figure 15.1.

In its intermediary role, the operating system makes it possible for users and programs to control the computer hardware transparently without dealing with the details of hardware operation. Programs can be executed and controlled with mouse clicks and keyboard commands and other types of input. When programs are completed or interrupted, control returns to the operating system, enabling the user to continue to operate without restarting the computer.

Effectively, the operating system provides a complete working environment, making the system convenient for the user by providing the services necessary to get work done.

The easiest way to think of an operating system is to consider it as a master "program" that accepts requests from the user, the user's programs, or other sources, and then calls its own programs to perform the required tasks. At the same time, it also calls programs to control and allocate the resources of the machine, including the use of memory, the use of I/O devices, and the time available to various programs. Thus, if the user issues a command to load a program, a program loader is executed, which then loads the desired program into memory and transfers control to the user's program to run. That program can then issue its own requests, for example to produce output to a printer or to send a message through the Internet to a Web server somewhere.

If you like, you could picture a command-interpreter-and-program-loader program sitting at the high end of the Little Man Computer memory. When a particular value is received as input, say, 999, that corresponds to the user's command to load a program, the loader performs a loop that inputs the instructions one at a time from the input box

FIGURE 15.1

The Modern Integrated Computer Environment

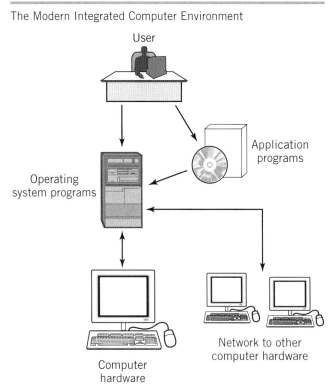

into lower memory and then jumps to mailbox 00 to execute the new program. (See Exercise 15.14.)

In a real computer, the operation is more complex, of course. There are many different I/O devices to be controlled, for one thing. There will usually be more than one program sharing the hardware resources, for another. To accept a command from a user, the operating system must first service mouse clicks and input keystrokes from the keyboard. It must interpret these actions, for example, as a command that requests that a program be loaded and executed. It must provide a file system that can interpret the name of the program being requested and determine the location of the file, first by determining the secondary storage device to be used and then by locating the file on the device. It must read the appropriate blocks from the device into memory. Only then can the operating system transfer control to the program being executed.

Modern computer systems enable users to work with more than one program at the same time as a way to improve their efficiency. A user can be listening to music on the Web while word processing a document (which is what the author is doing at this moment). A programmer can be editing one program while compiling another. Nearly every modern system provides means and support for manipulating multiple programs, even on a system with only a single CPU. This technique is known as **multitasking** or **multiprogramming**.[1] Since a system may be manipulating many tasks on a computer with one or a few CPUs, the operating system must support **concurrency**, which simulates the simultaneous execution of multiple programs to provide multitasking and multiuser support. To support concurrency there will be additional requirements: programs to allocate memory and other computer resources to each program, programs to allot the CPU time in an equitable way to each program, programs to direct input and output appropriately, and programs to maintain the integrity of each program, to name a few.

Multitasking also enables multiple users to share the computer resources of a single system. Such a system, known as a **multiuser** system, would still have to be multitasking, of course, because each user on the system would be running at least one program, and might even be running several programs concurrently.

This suggests that most operating systems will include additional services that augment the basic operating system services to be provided. These additional services include one or more interfaces that simplify the user's ability to interact with the system and standardize the system's I/O operations. Modern operating systems also provide the necessary tools to facilitate the sharing of the system services and resources among multiple programs, computers, and users. Typically, an operating system provides most or all of the following capabilities:

- The operating system provides interfaces for the user and also for the user's programs.
- It provides file system access and file support services.
- It provides I/O support services that can be used by every program.

---

[1]Note that even though operating systems commonly refer to executing programs as processes, multiprogramming is not the same as multiprocessing. The latter refers to the presence of multiple CPUs within the system.

- It provides a means for starting the computer. This process is known as **bootstrapping** or **Initial Program Load (IPL)**. The word *bootstrapping* is often abbreviated simply to *boot* or *booting*. (An explanation of bootstrapping is provided in Chapter 18, Section 18.2)

- It handles all interrupt processing, including error handling and recovery, as well as I/O and other routine interrupts.

- It provides services for networking. Most modern systems also provide services to support symmetric multiprocessing, clustering, and distributed processing. Where necessary, the operating system may also provide support for special features of the system. For example, the operating system for a Sony Playstation 3 must support the asymmetric multiprocessing that is a principal feature of the Cell multiple CPU processor used within.

- The operating system provides services that allocate resources, including memory, I/O devices, and CPU time to programs as they need them.

- It provides security and protection services: specifically, program and file control services to protect users' programs and files from each other and from outsiders, as well as to make communication between programs possible, when desired.

- It provides information and tools that can be used by the (human) system administrator to control, tailor, and tune the system for appropriate behavior and optimum performance.

Figure 15.2 is a simplified diagram showing the relationships between the different components of an operating system. The diagram focuses on the interactions among the most user-visible services. Specific multitasking and bootstrapping components are not shown. These are part of the core services, which also include process and thread management, resource allocation, scheduling, memory management, security, and interprocess communication. Also not shown on the diagram, many operating systems allow programs to call the command interface directly to execute commands. Thus, a C++ program operating under Linux could issue a Linux command as part of its processing.

The diagram also shows the command interface as part of the operating system. In some systems, this is not quite the case. Instead, the command interface is viewed as a **shell** outside of the operating system per se. As you will see, this view can result in increased user flexibility by allowing the user to select different shells for different types of tasks.

Since the programs that make up the operating system occupy space in memory that might be needed for application programs, the operating system is commonly divided into resident and nonresident parts. Some operating system services are critical to the operation of the system and must be resident in memory all the time. Others can be loaded into memory only when they are needed, and executed just like other programs.

The critical programs are loaded into memory by the bootstrap loader at start-up time and will remain resident as long as the computer is running. The bootstrap for most modern computers is stored in read-only memory; on some computers, part or all of the resident operating system will also be contained in ROM, so that it is permanently resident in memory and always available for use. This is particularly true for operating systems embedded into electronic devices such as mobile phones or DVD players.

The memory resident components of an operating system are commonly known as the **kernel** of the operating system. For example, the operating system program that accepts user commands must always be present whenever the machine is operative, as

FIGURE 15.2

A Simplified Diagram of Operating System Services

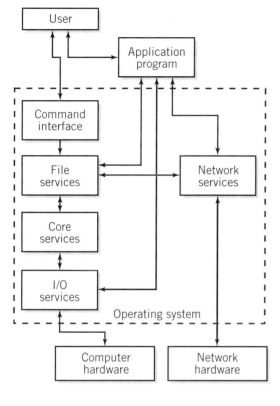

must the routines that handle interrupts and manage commonly used resources in a multitasking system. On the other hand, an operating system command that formats a new disk is only used occasionally; it can be loaded and executed only when it is required.

Most people assume that the operating system software for a conventional computer system is stored on a disk that is connected directly to the computer, but this is not necessarily true. If the computer is attached to a network, it may obtain its programs, including the operating system, from another computer on the network. This has led to the concept of the **diskless workstation**, a personal computer that, once booted, relies completely on the network for its data and program storage and access. Diskless workstations are also known as **thin clients**.

The size of the kernel and the particular services provided within a kernel vary from operating system to operating system, depending on the organization and capabilities of the system, as well as by the type of system. Some operating system vendors define the kernel more narrowly than others, precluding from memory residency some components that are deemed less critical to the basic operation of the system. Thus, the kernel in one system may be small, with only the most critical components included, and another might be large, with a tremendous range of services.

There are many different types of operating systems, some tailored for very specific purposes, but general-purpose computing systems can be loosely divided into categories, as follows:

- Single-user, single-tasking systems (this category is essentially obsolete)
- Single-user, multitasking systems
- Mainframe operating systems
- Operating systems for mobile devices
- Distributed systems
- Network servers: Web servers, database servers, application servers, and the like
- Embedded systems, such as those found in medical instruments, basic cellphones, automobile control systems, marketplace kiosks, household appliances, DVD players and TVs, electronic toys, and the like
- Real-time systems, used for instrumentation where system responses are time sensitive

Not surprisingly, these categories are somewhat arbitrary and are not mutually exclusive. Indeed, there is a lot of overlap between the various categories. For example, the embedded computer system that controls the braking system for an automobile must obviously be capable of real-time response when the driver of the car slams on the brakes in an emergency.

Systems can also be categorized by the degree of activity between the user and the system during program execution. As a student, you are probably most familiar with **interactive systems**. When the system is interactive, the user interacts directly with the program to provide input data and guidance during program execution. Interactive systems are sometimes known as **conversational systems**. Most personal computing is done interactively.

Many business tasks are performed more effectively in a batch, where the data input for the program is collected together into a file on disk or tape. It does not make sense to have a user enter data one record at a time if an entire set of data is to be processed into monthly credit card bills, for example. Instead, the user *submits* the program(s), or **job(s)**, to the computer for processing. This type of processing is known as **batch processing**. The user does not interact with the program during batch processing. Large-scale billing, payroll, and other similarly data intensive systems are usually processed this way.

We remind you that a CPU can execute only one instruction at a time; therefore, time used by the operating system on a single CPU system is not available for the execution of user programs. In general, the time used by the OS program is considered overhead. In reality, though, the operating system actually saves time for the users in most situations:

- In a single-user system, the operating system program creates minimal overhead. While the OS program is available to the user at any time, the executing user programs have priority; the OS program runs only to distribute CPU time among executing programs, or to handle interrupts, or if the users' programs request its services.

- The operating system program performs tasks directly for the user that would otherwise have to be performed, with more difficulty, by the user. This includes the various commands available to the user and I/O services to the user's programs. Most important, this includes the loading and execution of programs. When a user program is not being executed, the OS is always available to the user for these purposes.

- The OS user interface provides a means for the user to get work done more quickly and efficiently. This is especially true for the user interface found on modern operating systems. The best modern operating systems combine graphical simplicity with sophisticated text command input capability and output display of results to provide the user with powerful access to the facilities of the computer.

- Under most conditions, the computer system operates well below full capacity. The CPU sits idle while waiting for I/O transfers to occur. A user sits thinking at the keyboard. Multiuser and multitasking operating systems make it possible for many users or tasks to share the computer resource, providing fuller utilization of the system.

- The operating system extends the capability of the computer to include features that require special coordinated hardware and software that is invisible to the user. These features include virtual memory, cache memory, multiprocessing, vector processors, and networking.

■ The operating system provides powerful tools to the user's programs that improve the quality of the programs and make the user's work easier. For example, modern OS tools allow work to be easily transferred between applications through a clipboard, or make it possible to embed a spreadsheet into a word processing document. System services are provided by an **API**, or **Application Programming Interface.** The API provides file and I/O services, tools that create and support the graphical user interface, even tools to embed a spreadsheet into a word processing document.

We say that the operating system is **event driven**. This means that the operating system normally sits idle and executes only if some event occurs that requires operating system action. Events may result from interrupts or from **service requests** by a program or a user. Events include file requests, I/O, keyboard inputs from users, memory requests from programs, messages sent from one program to another, clock interrupts that allow the operating system scheduler program to dispatch programs during time sharing operation, network requests, and much, much more. In reality, the operating system on a large computer has quite a bit of work to do. Service requests and interrupts are a fundamental means of communication with the operating system.

Computer designers attempt to integrate the computer hardware and operating system, so that each supports the features of the other in such a way as to create a powerful environment for the users and for the users' programs. Such an environment is called symbiotic. This would seem to suggest that each type of computer hardware would require its own proprietary operating system. In fact, this is not necessarily the case. Most modern hardware vendors do not provide their own brand of operating system at all. Instead, their systems are supplied with a standard operating system such as Linux or Windows XP or Vista.

Linux and Windows Vista are both examples of operating systems that operate on a variety of different hardware platforms. There is a strong advantage at providing a standard operating system that works on different hardware. Such a system provides program portability, as well as file portability, and also allows users to move comfortably from one machine to another by providing a recognizable interface and command structure.

Portable operating systems are designed in such a way that they may be tailored for different hardware by changing only the small portion of the operating system program code that interacts directly with the hardware. Most of the operating system is written in high-level language, which can be ported easily to a new machine by recompiling the high level code. The portion of the operating system that must be built for the individual machine is written in a mixture of high-level language and assembly language. Languages such as C++ and Java are ideal **system languages**, because they provide facilities that make it possible to interact with the hardware with very little need for assembly language. In fact, the language C was originally designed specifically for this purpose. The portability of Linux, and other modern operating systems, stems directly from this capability.

While it is true that a single operating system can be ported to operate with different hardware, it is also true that a particular hardware platform can support different operating systems. Thus, the user or system designer can select an operating system that provides the desired facilities for the particular use of the system. Although x86-based personal computers have traditionally been provided with some version of Windows, there are other operating system options available that a user could select. An unsophisticated user on a stand-alone system might run Windows XP or Vista for its familiarity and ease of use, but a more sophisticated user with particular needs might prefer Apple MacIntosh OS X for its excellent tools and applications or Linux for its additional power. Particularly, if the machine is supporting multiple users, an X Windows-based Linux or UNIX operating system might be more appropriate.

15.3 SERVICES AND FACILITIES

Section 15.2 provided an overview of the various services and components that make up an operating system. In this section we consider the fundamental building blocks of an operating system in more detail. There are ten major blocks to be considered, not all of which will necessarily be found in any particular operating system:

- The command processor, application program interface, and user interface
- The file management system
- The input/output control system
- Process control management and interprocess communication
- Memory management
- Scheduling and dispatching
- Secondary storage management
- Network management, communication support, and communication interfaces
- System protection management and security
- Support for system administration

Some systems also provide a program known as a system manager, commonly known as a **monitor** or **supervisor**, which handles competing requests or conflicts, and which acts as a general controller and arbiter for the entire system. There are other system functions, such as accounting and error handling, that are sometimes handled as separate blocks but frequently appear within the blocks already listed.

In different types of operating systems, some of these components may be combined, or even absent. An embedded system may not require a file system or memory manager if all its programs are permanently resident in ROM, for example, but the listed components represent a collection of the most general operating system requirements.

Some of these modules, particularly the command interface and file system modules, are quite visible to the user. The other modules are primarily used for internal control of the system, controlling and optimizing use of the hardware resources, and maximizing program throughput and efficiency. Most modules also make their services available to user programs through the API.

In this section, we present an overview of the services provided by each of these operating system components. Individual components are discussed in more detail in other chapters, the capabilities and operation of the user interface and related services in

Chapter 16, and the file management services in Chapter 17. Details of the most important internal components and operations of the operating system are discussed in Chapter 18.

User Interface and Command Execution Services

To the user, the most important and visible service provided by the operating system is the user interface and the capability that it provides to execute commands.

Some systems do not consider the user interface and command processor to be a part of the operating system kernel, even though much of it is likely to be memory resident. Instead, these systems consider the user interface as a separate shell that is provided with the operating system and that interacts with the kernel to provide the necessary user command capabilities. Theoretically, a different shell could be used that provides different command capabilities. In Linux, for example, two different GUI shells, *KDE* and *Gnome*, and three different text-based shells, *bash, csh,* and *zsh* are in common use, and many other shells for Linux are available. Each of these shells provides different features and command structures and capabilities.

Different types of user interfaces exist. The most common are the **graphical user interface** (**GUI**), and the **command line interface** (**CLI**). The graphical user interface accepts commands primarily in the form of icons, drop-down menus or tabbed ribbons, mouse movements, and mouse clicks. Some GUI interfaces are also sensitive to touch or to hand motion in the vicinity of the screen. The command line interface relies on typed commands. Underneath the very different appearances of these interfaces, however, similar commands are being executed.

Regardless of the user interface provided, the command interface provides direct access to various other modules within the operating system. The most often used commands access the file system for file operations and the scheduler for program loading and execution. On some systems, commands may also provide direct access to the I/O system, protection services, network services, and process control services. On other systems, these commands may be processed indirectly, using built-in operating system utilities intended for the purpose.

A few systems even provide commands and built-in utilities for access to memory and to secondary storage. Generally, use of these commands is restricted to users with special access needs, such as the people who control and maintain the system. UNIX and Linux, for example, refer to these individuals as "superusers."

Some commands are built directly into the operating system. They remain in memory for immediate access. These are known as **resident commands**. Other commands are loaded only as they are needed. These are called **nonresident commands**.

Most modern operating systems provide some capability for combining computer commands into pseudo-programs, commonly called **shell scripts**. Batch-oriented systems also make it possible to combine individual commands into a sequence of **control statements**, which will be interpreted and executed one at a time without user intervention to control the processing of a multistep "job." Each step in the job performs an individual task. On large IBM systems, for example, the set of commands used for this purpose form a language known as **Job Control Language (JCL)**.

In addition to the standard operating system commands, shell scripting languages typically provide branch and loop commands and other computer language features. Shell scripts can be executed as though they were actual programs. Other common features include:

- A means for redirecting I/O data to a device different from that ordinarily used, to a disk file instead of the screen, for example
- A way to combine commands using a technique called piping, so that the output from one command is automatically used as the input for another
- A means for providing additional parameters to the script that can be entered by the user at the time the program is executed

More sophisticated command languages provide larger command sets with a more extensive and powerful set of options and with more extensive control structures that allow the creation of shell scripts with more flexibility, both in design and in run-time execution. Some command languages even provide special powerful commands that can eliminate normal programming effort. UNIX and Linux are particularly notable in this regard, providing commands that can search, select, edit, sort, enumerate, and process data from files in a way that rivals many programming languages.

The simplest Windows scripts are based on a command set that evolved from MS-DOS. These scripts are commonly called **.BAT files**. Recent versions of Windows also include a more powerful scripting facility called **Windows PowerShell**. PowerShell is based on an object-oriented language similar to C# and can manipulate both text and graphical objects.

There are a number of scripting languages that are designed to work independently of the particular operating system in use. The most popular of these include *perl, python, PHP, Ruby*, and *JavaScript*. Command and scripting languages extend the power and flexibility of the operating system and simplify use of the system for less sophisticated users.

File Management

The concept of a file is central to the effective use of a computer system. A file is generally loosely defined as a collection of related information. Defined in this way, a file is a rather abstract concept; indeed, the contents of the file only have meaning in the context of their particular internal description and use. Thus, the sequence of bytes in a file might represent a program, or a graphical image, or maybe the alphanumeric text data for a book, to be used within a word processor. A file may be organized internally into records or it may simply be a stream of bytes. A file constitutes a *logical unit* of storage, that is, logical to the person or program using the file. The logical unit may or may not correspond to the physical storage characteristics of the I/O device where it is stored.

The **file management system** provides and maintains the mapping between a file's logical storage needs and the physical location where it is stored. The file management system identifies and manipulates files by the names provided by their users. It determines the physical requirements of the file, allocates space for it, stores it in that space, and maintains the information about the file so that it may be retrieved, partially or in full, later. The file management system keeps track of the available space on each device connected to the system. The user and the user's programs need not be aware of the underlying physical storage issues. Users and programs simply access the files by name, and the file management system handles the details.

The file management system provides a consistent view of files across different I/O devices. This view even extends to files located elsewhere, on devices accessible from a network. To the user, file requests operate in the same way independent of the device, even between devices of different characteristics. Thus, it is not necessary to know the physical differences between, say, disk and tape, to move a file from one to the other. A program can request file services without knowing the file structure of the device being addressed, indeed without even knowing what kind of device the file is stored on.

The file management system provides and maintains

- Directory structures for each I/O device in the system and tools to access and move around these structures. The directory structure allows the retrieval and storage of files by name, keeps track of the mappings, allocates and frees space, allows the mounting and unmounting of file structures, and provides other functions required to maintain the structures of the file system. Provisions are made to move easily from one structure to another.

- Tools that copy and move files from one I/O device to another and from one directory to another, merge files, create and delete files and directories, and undertake other basic file manipulations.

- Information about each file in the system and tools to access that information. Typically, information about a file might include its name, type of file, size, date and time of creation, date and time of the most recent update, and protection and backup characteristics.

- Security mechanisms to protect files and control and limit file access to authorized users. Most modern systems also provide encryption protection and **journaling**, a technique which assures the currency and integrity of files when system failures occur during file changes.

Some file management systems also provide advanced features, including auditing, backup, emergency retrieval and recovery mechanisms, file compression, and transparent network file access.

File management systems are particularly important in systems in which secondary storage devices are shared in common by multiple users, since they provide a directory system that assures that there is no duplicate use of physical storage. Without this facility, it is likely that users would unintentionally overwrite each other's files. And, of course, we already noted that the file management system also provides file access protection between the different users. The file management system is discussed more fully in Chapter 17.

Input/Output Services

In Chapter 9, we introduced the concept of interrupts and showed the various techniques for handling I/O. Programs that implement these concepts are known as I/O device drivers. It would be awkward to require each program to provide its own **I/O services**. I/O device drivers are important because they are available to serve every program that will be executed on the system and provide a standard methodology for the use of each device. Even more important, the use of standard I/O drivers within the operating system limits access and centralizes control of the operations for each device.

The operating system includes I/O device driver programs for each device installed on the system. These drivers provide services to the file management system and are also available, through the API, to other programs for their use. The I/O device drivers accept I/O requests and perform the actual data transfers between the hardware and specified areas of memory.

In addition to the I/O device drivers provided by the operating system, modern systems provide certain I/O drivers with minimal functionality in ROM, to assure access to critical devices, such as the keyboard, display, and boot disk during the system startup process. The ROM-based drivers are replaced or integrated with other I/O drivers during normal system operation. On IBM-type PCs, these drivers are stored in the system **BIOS (basic input/output system)**.

Device drivers for newly installed devices are added and integrated into the operating system at the time of installation. On some systems, the process is manual. On many systems, the Apple Macintosh, for example, this process is completely automatic. In Windows, this capability is known as **plug-and-play**. Many modern systems even make it possible to add and modify devices on the fly, without shutting down the system. USB and FireWire both provide this capability.

Every operating system, large or small, provides input/output services for each device in the system. The use of one set of I/O services for each device assures that multiple programs will not be competing for the device and assures that the use of each device will be managed through a single point of control. Multiple access can cause serious conflict in multitasking systems. For example, a user would not be pleased to discover that parts of the printouts from two different programs were intermingled on the pages, even more so if the outputs belonged to two different users! The operating system assigns and schedules I/O devices appropriately to each process to eliminate this problem.

Process Control Management

Briefly, a **process** is an executing program. It is considered the standard unit of work within a computer system. *Every* executing program is treated as a process. This includes not only application programs, but the programs within the operating system itself. The process concept considers the program, together with the resources that are assigned to it, including memory, I/O devices, time for execution, and the like. When admitted to the system, each program is assigned memory space and the various resources that it initially requires to complete its work. As the process executes, it may require additional resources, or it may release resources that it no longer needs. The operating system performs various functions with processes, including scheduling and memory management, by providing the various services that we have discussed in this chapter. Processes must often be synchronized, so that processes sharing a common resource do not step on each other's toes by altering critical data or denying each other needed resources. Systems also provide communication capability between different processes. Processes may cooperate with each other by sending messages back and forth using **interprocess messaging services**. Other services include functions such as setting process priorities and calculating billing information.

Process control management keeps track of each process in memory. It determines the state of each process: whether it is running, ready to run, or waiting for some event, such as I/O to be completed, in order to proceed. It maintains tables that determine the current program counter, register values, assigned files and I/O resources, and other parameters for each process in memory. It coordinates and manages message handling and process synchronization.

Many modern systems further break the process down into smaller units called **threads**. A thread is an individually executable part of a process. It shares memory and other resources with all other threads in the same process, but can be scheduled to run separately from other threads.

Memory Management

The purpose of the memory management system is to load programs and program data into memory in such a way as to give each program loaded the memory that it requires for execution. Each program that is being executed must reside in memory. For multitasking to occur, multiple programs will occupy memory simultaneously, with each program in its own memory space.

The memory management system has three primary tasks. It attempts to perform these tasks in a way that is fair and efficient to the programs that must be loaded and executed.

1. It keeps track of memory, maintaining records that identify each program loaded into memory together with the space being used and also keeps track of available space. It allocates additional space for running programs as required. It prevents programs from reading and writing memory outside their allocated space, so that they cannot accidentally or intentionally damage other programs.

2. If necessary, it maintains one or more queues of programs waiting to be loaded into memory as space becomes available, based on such program criteria as priority and memory requirements. When space is available, it allocates memory to the programs that are next to be loaded.

3. It deallocates a program's memory space when it completes execution. The deallocated space is made available for other programs.

Older systems used a variety of algorithms to divide up the available memory space. Except for special-purpose embedded systems, every modern computer system provides **virtual storage**, a method of utilizing memory which includes hardware support for sophisticated memory management capability. Virtual storage creates the illusion of a memory space that is potentially much larger than the actual amount of physical storage installed in the computer system; its development was a major breakthrough in system capability. Where virtual storage is available, the memory management module of the operating system works directly with the hardware and provides the software support to create an integrated memory management environment that takes maximum advantage of the features of virtual storage. Virtual storage is explained in detail in Chapter 18, Section 18.7.

Scheduling and Dispatch

The operating system is responsible for the allocation of CPU time in a manner that is fair to the various programs competing for time, as well as maximizing efficient utilization of the system overall.

There are two levels of scheduling. One level of scheduling determines which jobs will be admitted to the system and in what order. Admission to the system means that a job will be placed into a queue, based on some order of priority, and ultimately assigned memory space and other resources, which will allow the program to be loaded into memory and executed. (Some operating systems divide this operation into two separate tasks, one for admittance to the system, the other to assign memory.) This scheduling function is sometimes known as **high-level scheduling**. The other level of scheduling is known as **dispatching**. Dispatching is responsible for the actual selection of processes that will be executed at any given instant by the CPU. The dispatch component of the operating system makes concurrency possible by allocating CPU time in such a way as to make it appear that several processes are executing simultaneously. For those systems that allow the division of processes into threads, dispatch is done at the thread level, instead of at the process level.

In modern systems, with their extensive facilities and capabilities, high-level scheduling is relatively straightforward. Most of the time, new processes will simply be admitted to the system and given memory space if it is available, or held until space is available, then admitted.

Selecting the appropriate candidate for CPU time at any given instant is much more important and difficult, since the capability of the dispatcher directly affects the ability of the users to get their work done. A single program cannot be allowed to "hog" the machine; therefore, the dispatcher must interrupt whatever process is running periodically and run itself to determine the status of the machine's resources and to reassign CPU resources to assure that every user and task is receiving what it needs.

Since a single CPU can process only one instruction at a time, the simultaneous execution of two or more programs is obviously impossible with a single processor. Instead, the dispatcher acts as a controller to provide concurrent processing. There are various ways in which multitasking can be achieved with concurrent processing, but mostly these methods take advantage of two simple strategies:

1. While one program is waiting for I/O to take place, another can be using the CPU to execute instructions. This strategy is shown in Figure 15.3. In Chapter 9 we demonstrated that I/O could be performed efficiently without tying up the instruction executing capability of the CPU. We further showed that most of the time, the CPU was idle, since I/O represents such a large percentage of a typical

FIGURE 15.3

Sharing the CPU During I/O Breaks

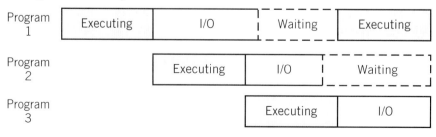

program's execution. This suggests that the idle time can be used to execute other programs, as an effective way to increase utilization of the CPU.

2. The CPU may be switched rapidly between different programs, executing a few instructions from each, using a periodic clock-generated interrupt. This method was discussed in Chapter 9, Section 9.3, and diagrammed in Figure 9.8, redrawn here as Figure 15.4. This strategy will slow down execution of each program, since each program must split its time with other programs. There is also some operating system overhead, as a dispatcher must be invoked at each interrupt to select the next program to receive CPU time. In most cases the CPU is so powerful compared to the requirements of the programs that the slowdown is not even noticeable. This technique is called **time-slicing**.

The algorithms used by the dispatcher combine these two methodologies, taking into account such issues as fairness to each program, the priorities of the different programs, quick response for critical situations, such as displaying a user's cursor movement or displaying streaming video, the number of CPUs available for dispatching, and other criteria.

Different processes have different requirements. Some processes require extensive amounts of CPU time; such processes are considered to be **CPU bound**. Others are mostly I/O operations, with very little CPU processing; these are known as **I/O bound**. Immediate response time is important under some conditions, for example, when echoing cursor movement to a screen and unimportant in others, such as producing printed output from a batch job that will not be picked up by the user until later in the day. It is obviously desirable to dispatch processes in such a way that the system is used effectively. Various dispatching algorithms are used to meet these different requirements, and there are various criteria for measuring how well the dispatcher is doing its job. Generally, interactive processes require faster response than do batch processes. Processes that must control instrumentation in real time require the fastest response of all.

The dispatcher is also responsible for the actual transfer of control to the process that is being dispatched. This responsibility includes preservation of the previous running program's program counter, register values, and other parameters that represent the state of the program at the time it was stopped, as well as restoration, if necessary, of the exact previous state of the program being dispatched. This operation is called **context switching**.

The operation of the dispatcher is dependent on the nature of the system and on the nature of the programs that the system is running. The dispatcher can be **preemptive** or **nonpreemptive**. The dispatcher for a nonpreemptive

FIGURE 15.4

Time-Sharing the CPU

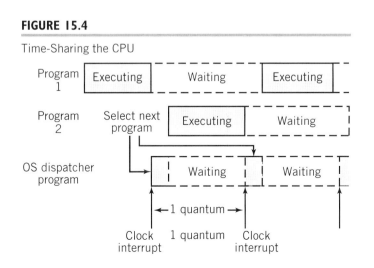

system replaces an executing program only if the program is blocked because of I/O or some other event or if the program voluntarily gives up the CPU. When necessary, the executing program may be suspended momentarily, so that the CPU can handle interrupts, but when the interrupting task is complete, control is returned to the same program. (This exception is necessary for several reasons. Without it, there would be no way to stop a runaway program, for example, a program with an infinite loop in it. It is also necessary to prevent losing keystrokes from user keyboards and to echo keystrokes back to users' screens.)

Preemptive multitasking uses the clock interrupt, as described earlier, to preempt the executing program and to make a fresh decision as to which program executes next.

In general, nonpreemptive dispatching algorithms apply mostly to older, batch-oriented systems. Modern dispatchers are predominately preemptive. However, most provide a mechanism to dispatch individual programs nonpreemptively, for programs that must execute to completion without unnecessary interruptions. Linux uses nonpreemptive dispatching to protect certain operating system operations from interrupts that could destroy the integrity of operating system data, for example.

A more detailed explanation of process creation can be found in Chapter 18, Section 18.3. Scheduling and dispatching are discussed further in Chapter 18, Section 18.5.

Secondary Storage Management

The file management system keeps track of free secondary storage space and maintains the file system and its directories. The input/output control system provides device drivers that actually control the transfer of data between memory and the secondary storage devices.

On large multitasking systems there may be many programs requesting I/O services from a secondary storage device at one time. The order in which these requests are fulfilled affects the ability of the different programs to get their work completed, since the programs must usually stop and wait for their I/O requests to be completed before proceeding. Although it would be simplest to process I/O requests in the order received, it may be more efficient to process the requests out of order, particularly if the blocks requested are scattered all over the disk. This is true because the disk seek time (i.e., the time to move from track to track) is long compared to other times within the system.

The secondary storage management system attempts to optimize the completion of I/O tasks by using algorithms that reorder the requests for more efficient disk usage. For example, it might attempt to read all the requested data blocks from the tracks in one area of the disk before going to read data on tracks at the other end of the disk. In some large modern systems, optimization is provided by a combination of I/O hardware and operating system software. Further details of secondary storage management appear in Chapter 18, Section 18.8.

Network and Communications Support Services

With the exception of some specialized embedded systems, nearly all computers today are interconnected, directly or indirectly, into networks. (There is even a trend toward networking embedded computers: modern automobile computers routinely report maintenance problems to the service technician when you bring your car in for service—some cars even report problems wirelessly from the road to a service representative. And you may have heard of the refrigerator that calls an order in to an Internet grocery delivery service when food stocks are low.) The network and communications support facilities within the operating system carry out the functions required to make the system perform seamlessly in a networked and distributed environment.

Most modern communications services rely on the TCP/IP protocol suite, together with its IP-based applications. TCP/IP provides the facilities to locate and connect to other computer systems, to pass application data in packet form from one system to another, to access files, I/O devices, and programs from remote systems, to provide error checking and correction when appropriate, and to support the requirements of distributed processing. Network and communication services within the operating system provide the communication software necessary to implement the features and facilities of TCP/IP. Most systems also implement a substantial set of TCP/IP applications and extensions, including e-mail, remote login, Web services, streaming multimedia, voice over IP telephony (VoIP), secure networking across the Internet (called a **virtual private network**, or **VPN**), and more. Some systems also offer support for alternative communication protocols, for example, Novell IPX/SPX and IBM Systems Network Architecture.

Communications services within the operating system also provide the interface between the communication software and the OS I/O control system that provides access to the network. The I/O control system includes the software drivers for modems, network interface cards, wireless communication cards, and other devices that are used to connect the computer physically and electrically to the network or networks.

Larger computers used for server applications often require the capability for additional growth and reliability to serve the needs of their clients. These capabilities are sometimes referred to as **system scalability** and **fail-safe operation** respectively. In addition to networking support, the operating systems for such machines often include clustering software, so that these computers can be clustered together and viewed transparently by clients and users as a single, high-powered system. The clustering software provides single-point logins, single-point user and client requests, request steering, failure detection and cutover, and system load balancing between the individual nodes within the cluster.

Security and Protection Services

It is certainly no surprise to anyone that modern systems require security and protection services to protect the operating system from user processes, to protect processes from each other, and to protect all processes from the outside world. Without protection, a buggy or malicious program, for example, could unintentionally or intentionally modify or destroy the program code or data in the memory space belonging to the operating system or to another process. It is also important to protect the system and user processes from unauthorized entry to the system, and against unauthorized use of the system, even by authorized users.

In most modern systems, executing processes are limited to the execution of instructions and access to data within their own memory space. All other services, such as file management and I/O, must be requested by the process from the operating system, using the service requests provided by the OS for that purpose. This methodology is fundamental to the security of the system. In this way, the operating system, the file system, and other processes are protected from unauthorized use or operations, protecting the integrity of the system as a whole. Interprocess messaging services are usually provided by the operating system to allow processes to communicate with each other without compromising the system. Critical parts of the operating system execute in a specially protected mode of operation provided as part of the CPU design. In protected mode, the operating system can prevent programs from executing certain instructions and from accessing parts of memory specified by the operating system, for example, parts being used by other programs.

Each module in the operating system includes provisions that protect its assets. Thus, the file management system would not allow a process to store data on a part of a disk that is being used by another file. Nor would process management allow the assignment of an I/O resource that would prevent another process from completing its task. Since all services are requested from the operating system, the OS has the capability to determine that requests will not damage other processes or the system itself.

The operating system also provides login and password services that can help to prevent entry from unauthorized users and access control facilities that allow users to protect their individual files at various levels of availability to other users and outsiders. The modern operating system includes firewall protection, which, artfully administered, can make it more difficult for outsiders to penetrate the system, but is not foolproof; the need for security must be carefully balanced with the needs of the users to get their work done. Despite all the protection offered by a modern system, bugs, viruses, and vulnerabilities within the operating system, poor configuration of firewalls and other security features, and poor user management policies such as weak password enforcement can make a system vulnerable to attack by outsiders. The design and deployment of effective security and prevention services is an important ongoing concern in operating system design. A number of research projects that show promise are attempting to design OS security mechanisms that prevent infiltrators from moving beyond the actual program that they invaded into other areas of the operating system.

System Administration Support

The **system administrator**, or **sysadmin**, for short, is the person who is responsible for maintaining the computer system or systems. In a large organization, the sysadmin may support hundreds, or even thousands, of computers, including those of the employees. Some of the important administrative tasks managed by a system administrator include:

- System configuration and setting group configuration policies
- Adding and deleting users
- Controlling and modifying user privileges to meet the changing needs of the users
- Providing and monitoring appropriate security
- Managing, mounting, and unmounting file systems
- Managing, maintaining, and upgrading networks
- Providing secure and reliable backups
- Providing and controlling software, installing new software, and upgrading software as required
- Patching and upgrading the operating systems and other system software

- Recovering lost data
- Tuning the system for optimum availability and performance
- Monitoring system performance and recommending system modifications and upgrades when necessary to meet user requirements

These and other important tasks must be applied both to central server systems and to client machines and other desktop computers on a network to coordinate and maintain a reliable and useful system. Modern operating systems provide software to simplify these tasks.

On small personal computers, the user is often the administrator as well. The major administrative tasks of the user are to install and upgrade software, to reconfigure the system and the desktop from time to time, to maintain network connections as required, and to perform regular file backup and disk maintenance and defragmentation. For user administration of this type, simple tools are sufficient. Indeed, the goal of a desktop operating system might be to *hide* the more sophisticated tools from the typical user. For example, Windows operating systems store the system configuration within a registry that is normally hidden from the user, and provide, instead, a variety of simple tools specifically for tailoring the system to user preferences and performing maintenance tasks. The Windows operating system supplies default configuration parameters for many tasks that suit the needs of most users, with tools to modify the parameters to meet specific user requirements. The simplest tools are sufficient for most users to perform routine system administration. Knowledgeable users can also manipulate the system registry directly, when necessary. On desktop computers connected to a larger system within an organization, central administration tools allow the application of group policies and configuration to individual desktop computers without user involvement.

On larger systems, administration is much more important and much more complex. The hardware and software to be managed is far more extensive, and there are numerous users requiring accounts and service. Installation of new equipment on large systems is common, and in some cases, the system must be reconfigured to use the new equipment. IBM calls this process sysgen, for system generation. It is one of the most important tasks of system administration on large systems. Modern systems provide software for simplifying common system administration tasks. Large mainframe operating systems provide tools for performing all the major system administration requirements. They also provide tools that allow the administrator to tailor the system to optimize its performance, for example, to optimize throughput or the use of resources. This is done by modifying system parameters and selecting particular scheduling and memory management algorithms. Among the parameters that can be adjusted on various systems are the amount of memory allocated to a program, user disk space allocation, priorities, assignments of files to different disks, the maximum number of programs to be executed concurrently, and the scheduling method employed. IBM z/OS even includes a Workload Manager, which attempts to optimize system resources automatically, without administrator intervention.

The system administrator on a traditional UNIX/Linux system, for example, can log in to the system as a *superuser*, with privileges that override all the restrictions and security built into the system. The superuser can modify any file in the system. (However, the new security mechanisms mentioned above might make it much more difficult to override the security, thereby protecting a system from a hacker who manages to infiltrate the kernel.) More important, the UNIX system provides tools that simplify the tasks of system administration. These tools take the form of commands that can be executed only by the superuser and text-based configuration files that can be modified with any text editor.

For example, UNIX/Linux systems typically provide a menu-driven or graphical *adduser* program for administering user accounts. This program provides a simple procedure for performing all the tasks required to add a new user to the system, including setting up the user name and ID number, building entries to the appropriate user and group tables, creating the user's home directory, assigning login shells, and establishing user initialization files (corresponding to the user's particular terminal hardware, prompt preferences, and the like).

Other typical UNIX/Linux administration commands include a partition tool for partitioning hard disk drives; *newfs* for building a file system; *mount* and *umount* for mounting and unmounting file systems; *fsck* for checking and repairing the file system (similar in concept to, but much more complex and thorough than, CHKDSK on Windows systems); *du* and *df* for measuring disk usage and free space; *tar* for collecting files into archives; and *ufsdump* and *ufsrestore* for creating backups and recovering damaged files. *config* is used to build the system. There are many additional tools available to the UNIX/Linux sysadmin.

Like other large systems, server-based versions of Windows provide a full suite of tools for measuring system performance and managing the system, including the ability to control and configure client systems remotely.

Most systems provide a variety of statistical information that indicates the load on the system and the efficiency of the system. This information is used by the system administrator as a basis for tuning the system. Part of a typical system status report appears in Figure 15.5. This particular report comes from a Linux system. The report indicates the load on the system as a function of time, shows CPU and memory usage, identifies the most CPU-intensive processes, together with the name of the user and the percent of CPU and memory resources consumed, shows the efficiency of virtual storage, and provides many other useful system parameters. It even provides an analysis of the data shown. Although the typical user might not find a report such as this very useful in terms of what steps to take as a result of the information presented, a skilled system administrator can make valuable use of the information in determining ways in which to improve system performance. A consistently heavy load on a particular disk might suggest splitting the most used files on that disk onto two separate disks, so that they might be accessed in parallel, for example. Or heavy use of the CPU by a particular user during peak hours might suggest lowering the priorities for that user at those times.

SYSTEM GENERATION   One of the most important system administration tasks to be performed is the creation of an operating system tailored to the specific needs of a particular installation. The process of building a system is called a **system generation**, or more familiarly, a **sysgen**. The result of a sysgen matches the operating system to the characteristics and features of the hardware provided and includes the desired operating system features and performance choices. Two primary means are used to tailor the system:

- By selecting the operating system program modules to be installed. Typically, an operating system provides a large number of modules that might be used under different circumstances. Only those modules that are relevant to the installation

FIGURE 15.5

A Typical System Status Report

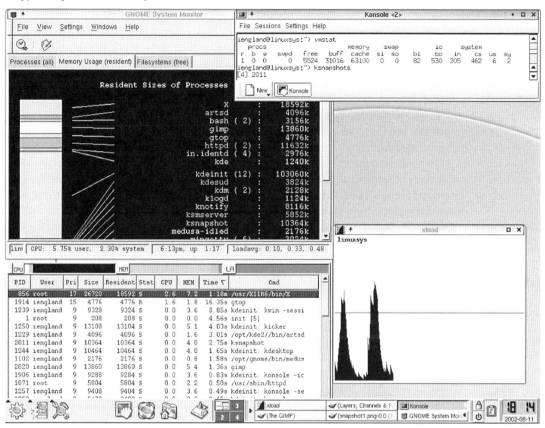

are selected. As an example, a particular installation has an individualized selection of I/O devices. Only those device drivers that are required for the installed I/O devices would be included in the tailored system.

- By assigning values to parameters of the system. Parameters are used to provide the details of an installation. On a Windows-based PC system, for example, devices are assigned to specific, numbered interrupt channels known as IRQs; memory locations for each device interrupt driver are also specified. Another example of a parameter would be the number of concurrent users permitted on a multiuser system. On some systems, a parameter might be used to determine whether a module is memory resident or is loaded on demand. Most large systems also provide parameters that tailor the system scheduling mechanism and adjust the behavior of other resource control modules. These and other parameters must be determined by the system administrator to meet the needs of the installation.

Some systems provide a lot of flexibility, with many options. Other systems may provide only a minimal amount of selection, perhaps no more than a selection of I/O device drivers.

The method used to perform a sysgen depends on the operating system. Some systems provide the operating system modules in source code form. Modules and parameters are selected, and the operating system is assembled or compiled and linked to form the loadable binary operating system. A barebones operating system with the appropriate compilation tools may be provided to enable the sysgen procedure to take place on the target system, or the procedure may be executed on a different machine. Other operating systems use an installation program to determine which modules should be included in the operating system, and parameters are selected during the installation procedure. On these systems, the various modules are already provided in binary form and need only be linked during the sysgen procedure.

On many systems, the sysgen procedure is provided as a series of menu selections and parameter entry forms that guide the operator through the procedure. On some systems, the procedure is entered as a script or batch file. Most systems also allow some degree of dynamic configuration, which makes it possible to build changes into the system without rebuilding the entire system. We noted earlier that in Linux configuration script files are used for this purpose.

15.4 ORGANIZATION

There is no standard model for the organization of an operating system. Some systems were developed in a deliberate and carefully planned manner, while others grew topsy-turvy over a long period of time, adding new functions and services as they were required. Thus, the programs that make up an operating system may be relatively independent of each other, with little central organization, or they may form a formal structure.

Overall, the organization of most operating systems can be described generally by one of three configuration models. These are commonly referred to in the literature as the **monolithic configuration**, the **layered** or **hierarchical configuration**, and the **microkernel configuration**. Within a configuration, individual programs can be categorized in different ways. As we noted earlier, operating system programs can be memory resident or nonresident, depending on their function. Of the resident programs, some will operate in a protected mode, often called **kernel mode**, others in a conventional user mode.

FIGURE 15.6

A Simplified Representation of UNIX

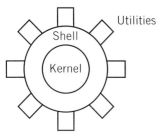

As an example of a monolithic configuration, UNIX is commonly described by the model shown in Figure 15.6. In this model, the various memory resident operating system functions are represented by a monolithic kernel. There is no specific organization. The operating system programs simply interact as required to perform their functions. The critical functions within the kernel operate in protected mode, the remainder, in user mode. The shell is separate from the kernel and serves as an interface between the users, utilities, and user programs with the kernel. Thus, the shell can be replaced without affecting kernel operations. (UNIX organization is considered in more detail as a case study in Supplementary Chapter 2.)

The major difficulty with a monolithic configuration is the stability and integrity of the system as a whole. Any defect in a program within the kernel can crash the entire system, as can unexpected interactions between different programs in the kernel. Thus, the addition of a new device driver, for example, could compromise the entire system. Nonetheless, with proper design and control, it is possible to build a secure and stable system, as evidenced by Linux.

An alternative operating system organization is built around a *hierarchical* structure. A simple representation of a hierarchical operating system organization is shown in Figure 15.7. This representation shows the operating system divided into layers. The upper layers are the ones that are visible to the user; the middle layers comprise the major kernel operations. The lowest layers are the I/O device drivers that interact with the hardware.

In this model, each layer is relatively independent of the other layers. Thus, the file management layer determines the location of a file identified by logical name and interprets the nature of the request, but does not attempt to access the hardware directly. Instead, it makes a request to the kernel. Local requests are then passed on to the I/O device driver level for access to the hardware. Network requests are passed on to the I/O device drivers on the machines providing the services.

The hierarchy is arranged so that access to the various layers of the operating system is from the top. Each layer calls the next lower layer to request the services that it needs. Most computer systems today provide appropriate hardware instructions that allow the operating system design to enforce this procedure. This provides security, as well as a clean interface between the different functions within the operating system.

FIGURE 15.7

A Hierarchical Model of an OS

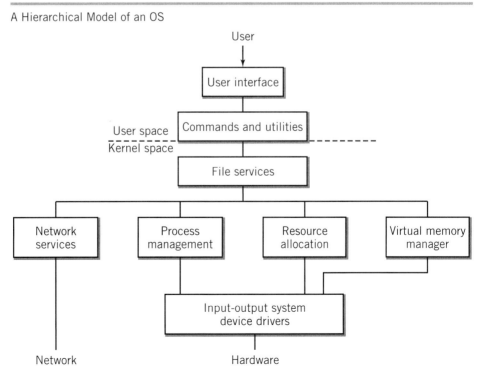

Layered operating systems must be designed carefully, because the hierarchy requires that services be layered in such a way that all requests move downward. A program at a particular layer must never require services from a higher layer because this could compromise system integrity. Another disadvantage of the layered approach is the time required to pass the request through intermediate layers to receive services from the lowest layers. In contrast, a program in a monolithic operating system could request the service directly from the program that supplies the service, resulting in much faster operation. The obvious advantage of the layered approach is the stability and integrity that result from a well-structured modular design.

Still another approach to operating system design is the microkernel. An illustration of a microkernel configuration is shown in Figure 15.8. The microkernel configuration model is based on a small protected kernel that provides the minimum essential functionality. The definition of "minimum essential functionality" differs from system to system. The Mach operating system kernel includes message passing, interrupt processing, virtual memory management, scheduling, and a basic set of I/O device drivers. It is possible to build a microkernel with nothing but message passing, interrupt processing, and minimal memory management, although the practical advantage of doing so has not been shown.

The microkernel configuration constitutes a client-server system, where clients and servers reside on the same system. Operating system services outside the essential functionality are performed by programs in user mode. Each program acts as a server that performs specific operating system tasks upon request of application programs as well as other operating system programs, the clients in this model. Clients request services by sending messages directly to the microkernel. The microkernel passes the messages to the appropriate server, which performs the required function, and replies to the request by sending a message back to the client. The reply is also passed through the microkernel. System security and integrity is maintained, because all communication must pass through the microkernel.

One of the advantages of the microkernel configuration is that it is possible to create different operating system designs simply by changing the service programs that reside outside the microkernel, while maintaining the security and stability of the microkernel. For example, Macintosh OS X is one of many operating systems built on the Mach microkernel.

FIGURE 15.8

Microkernel Architecture

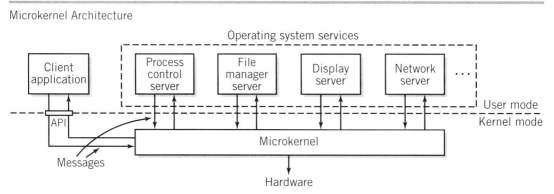

The microkernel approach offers reliability, flexibility, extensibility, and portability. It is particularly amenable to object-oriented design. New features can be added easily without compromising the system. The extensive message-passing required in a microkernel configuration can result in a performance penalty over other types of designs, but practical applications of the model have shown that, with care, the potential disadvantage of this approach can be minimized.

15.5 TYPES OF COMPUTER SYSTEMS

Modern computer system hardware is essentially similar regardless of the type of system. Therefore, the differences among computer systems are set primarily by the operating system software. The operating system software is selected to meet desired requirements and goals.

As we outlined briefly in Section 15.2, there are many different types of operating systems, each designed to meet a particular set of requirements and needs. Some of the factors that influence operating system design/architecture are the primary type of user base, whether the system is intended for direct user access or behind-the-scenes server access, or whether the system is to be used for a specific purpose, such as embedded electronic control or mobile use.

For example, one computer might be designed for business end users, another for programmers and engineers, and other high-technology specialists. The Macintosh, for example, is well designed for the inexperienced user (and for other users too, of course!) Windows is adequate for a user with simple needs; a more sophisticated user might choose a system with Linux instead. The PC is adequate for many single users, but a large mainframe type system might be more appropriate for use as a large server, or, perhaps, a network- or cluster-based system is more appropriate for a particular server application. Special-purpose applications that require specialized designs might include embedded control applications (such as automotive and microwave oven applications), CAD/CAM graphics, multimedia (the Pixar computer is a special system designed specifically for motion picture animation and special effects), and real-time control applications. An operating system designed for mobile computing may have to operate with limited resources, particularly in the areas of power consumption, network connectivity, memory size, and display. Each of these systems has different needs and requirements that are met by the operating system design.

There are, of course, costs associated with increasing sophistication in operating system software. As more features are added, more memory is required for the operating system. The original version of MS-DOS ran successfully in 64 KB of memory. The IBM MVS operating system for the IBM S/370 family required more than 6 MB of memory even before any applications were considered. Some computer experts have recommended a minimum of 2 GB of memory for Windows Vista and its applications. The overhead time required for the operating system to perform its functions becomes a sizable fraction of the overall time. One hopes that the overhead is worthwhile in terms of increased efficiency and ease of use. For example, graphical user interfaces and multimedia support consume a high percentage of system resources on personal computers. On a computer used primarily as a Web server, those resources might be better utilized in providing faster Web access or supporting more users.

Within the context of the previous discussion, we can loosely categorize computer systems into seven types: single-user systems and workstations; mainframe systems; operating systems for mobile devices, network server systems; real-time systems; embedded control systems; and distributed systems. (We noted earlier that systems capable of only a single task at a time, while historically important, are essentially obsolete.)

- The predominant systems in current use are single-user, multitasking systems. These are the systems found on laptop and desktop computers, workstations, tablets, personal digital assistants, "smart phones", and other similar devices. Common examples include various versions of Windows, Macintosh OS X, Linux, and Sun Solaris. A GUI is usually a key feature of these systems since it allows the user easily to run several processes at the same time, maximizing overall productivity. Windowing interfaces allow output presentations from several tasks to appear on the screen simultaneously, and provide methods for easy task switching. (Note, however, that a windows environment is not a requirement for multitasking. Some single-user systems allow an individual user to multitask from a command line interface. Linux, Sun Solaris, and other UNIX-based systems, in particular, allow users to specify that processes are to execute in the "background." Background processes can present output to the screen, but only the foreground process can accept input from the keyboard. The operating system provides commands that allow the user to select which process is in the foreground at any particular time.) Workstations generally provide single-user multitasking operating systems, although most workstations have the capability to be configured for multiuser or server operation.

- Mainframe operating systems are designed to manage large-scale computing resources, particularly in major enterprise environments, where large numbers of transactions requiring extensive I/O capability are the norm. Mainframe systems were originally created to to allow hundreds of users to share the computing power of a central facility, as well as to support batch data processing operations such as billing and credit card processing. Today, mainframe operating systems manage typical mainframe computer hardware made up of clusters of multi-processor units, all designed to work together as a single processing unit, with hundreds of gigabytes of memory, femtobytes of disk storage and I/O and networking capabilities of hundreds of gigabytes per second. Mainframe operating systems differ from smaller multitasking systems in the variety of features that they offer, in the versatility with which they can be configured, with the level of security that they supply, with the degree of control that they offer the system administrator(s), and in the overall amount of power and capability that they offer.

- Network server systems are similar to single-user multitasking systems in most respects. However, the major focus of system use is shifted from meeting the needs of the direct user to the support of clients connected to the server through a network. The server may have no direct user facilities of its own, other than those required for management of the system. The server is designed to provide Web services, file services, print services, application services, and/or database services to the clients, as determined by the particular requirements of the system application. It may also provide some program execution services for clients, including support for client system start-up, particularly on networks with thin clients. Network servers often work together in clusters. For these applications, one would expect the network server OS to provide improved security and system integrity protection, high reliability file management and backup with large file capability, strong support for clustering and multiprocessing, improved mechanisms for failure prevention, automatic cutover to alternative systems when failures occur, and failure recovery, as well as strong system administration capability.

■   Mobile operating systems are operating systems designed for small hand-held devices, such as personal digital assistants (PDAs) and smart phones. These systems must provide the basic capabilities and features of traditional single-user multitasking systems within the constraints of electrical power limitations, limited memory, lower CPU execution speed, slower network capability, and file storage that is generally limited to small stationary nonvolatile memory devices, along with some special features that would not be required in a larger system, such as touch screen capability, special keyboard handling, careful management of battery power consumption, support for special I/O devices such as global positioning and telephony mechanisms, features for synchronizing data with other systems, and handwriting recognition.

■   **Real-time systems** are systems in which one or more processes must be able to access the CPU immediately when required. Real-time systems are used for applications in which one or more programs are measuring or controlling I/O devices that must respond within specific time restraints. A real-time system might be used to control instrumentation, such as the control rockets on a space flight, or to measure time-sensitive data, such as the periodic measurements of the temperature in a nuclear reactor. Although some real-time systems are created special for the particular application, most are general-purpose multitasking systems that have been designed so that they can be used for other tasks except when the time-sensitive application is being executed. A real-time system could be viewed as a multitasking system in which the interrupts that cause execution of the real-time program or programs have very high priority, but in many cases, special effort is made to assure that the real-time program can operate within its required time restraints.

■   **Embedded control systems** are specialized systems designed to control a single piece of equipment, such as an automobile or microwave oven. The software for embedded control systems is usually provided in ROM. Nonetheless, many functions of the operating system may still be found in these systems. The computer that controls an automobile, for example, requires most of the features of a multitasking system. There are many measurement sensors representing CPU input on a car and many different control functions to manage. The service technician must be able to connect an I/O terminal to the system for car analysis. Effectively, an embedded control system is a real-time system that is dedicated to the particular application.

■   Finally, **distributed systems** are rapidly growing in prominence and importance. In a distributed system, processing power is distributed among the computers in a cluster or network. Even the Internet can be used as a distributed system. Programs, files, and databases may be also be dispersed. Programs may be divided into functional pieces, with execution distributed throughout the network. Alternatively, program components may be stored on different systems, and executed in place upon remote request. .NET and CORBA, discussed briefly in Chapter 16, are two standards designed to expedite this process. Regardless of which method is used, the operating system or systems require additional complexity to handle the distribution of tasks or instructions within a process, the sharing of memory and I/O, and the intercommunication of data and control that are required of these systems. Many modern computing systems include additional operating system modules to make distributed processing feasible and practical. **Distributed Computing Environment (DCE)**, is an OpenGroup standard that establishes a set of features for a distributed computing operating system. (OpenGroup is an organization that promotes open computing by setting standards and certifying products in a number of major areas of computing. UNIX is arguably the best known OpenGroup standard.) The DCE standard is supported and incorporated into the operating systems of a number of major vendors, including Microsoft, Sun, and IBM.

There are, of course, other ways of categorizing computer systems. One way of describing systems that is sometimes useful is to consider the intent and philosophy of the designers of the system. This description can sometimes provide a lot of insight into the strengths and weaknesses of a system. For example, the IBM mainframe operating system, z/OS, is an offshoot of an operating system that was originally designed primarily for large, batch-oriented business transaction processing systems. As business users moved their operations online, predecessors of z/OS were provided with capabilities to handle large numbers of online transactions. This would suggest that the modern z/OS is well equipped to handle routine Web transactions from hundreds or thousands of network clients concurrently. At the same time, it might suggest that z/OS is not particularly user-friendly to individuals doing their own independent work on the system. Development tools are more difficult to use on z/OS than on many other systems. Most people would agree that these statements describe z/OS fairly well.

As a different example, the Apple Macintosh system was designed to make tasks as easy as possible for the average, minimally trained computer end user. As a result, much of the design effort for the Macintosh system has continually gone into the user interface. The operating system provides powerful interface and graphical resources to the user and to the user's programs. Other operating system facilities, such as time sharing and memory management, became secondary to the stated purpose. Indeed, these functions in OS X are implemented with a kernel built from a UNIX variant called FreeBSD.

Finally, consider an operating system whose primary design goal is to be capable of open system operation. The primary features that define an open system are as follows:

- The system should be capable of operating on many different hardware platforms.
- Communication between systems should be simple and straightforward. Commands that access remote systems should perform nearly identically to those performing local operations and should appear as transparent as possible to the user or the user's programs. Thus, a COPY command that copies files between

systems should operate essentially the same as one copying files between different points on a single system.

■   Shell programs should behave identically, regardless of platform. Source level application programs should operate identically, once compiled on the new platform.

These features dictate an operating system with considerable thought given to networking, as well as to a system with minimum dependency on the particular hardware being used. This suggests an operating system with a small kernel, with powerful networking facilities built in, and with the hardware-specific part of the system concentrated into a single part of the kernel, isolating all other parts of the system from the platform. FreeBSD is an example of such a system, which makes it an ideal basis for the MacInosh OS X design.

There have been many attempts to build operating systems whose activities are truly distributed across a network. Some of the best known of these are Mach, Amoeba, Locus, and Chorus.

SUMMARY AND REVIEW

Chapter 15 presents a comprehensive overview of the operating system. The operating system software is a collection of programs that extend the power of the computer hardware by providing a user interface to the computer, plus control and support for the computer's resources, plus other facilities that make it easier to manage and control the computer system. Many operating systems also make possible the sharing of computer resources concurrently among multiple users and among multiple tasks for each user.

The operating system provides one or more user interfaces, file support, control for I/O devices, network support, and management of the computer resources, including memory, the various I/O devices, and the scheduling of time. The operating system is event driven. It performs these tasks in response to user commands, program service requests, and interrupts. We noted that although the operating system represents overhead, under most conditions the overall computer system performance is improved and enhanced by the presence of the operating system. Some operations, particularly concurrency, would be difficult or impossible without the operating system.

In our discussion of the various operations performed by an operating system, we identified ten of the major services and facilities provided within an operating system and described each. These included the user interface and command execution, the file system, the I/O control system, process control, memory management, scheduling and dispatch, secondary storage management, network management, security, and system administration facilities.

The programs that provide these services must be organized in some way. There is a considerable amount of interaction between the different program modules that make up an operating system. Many operating systems use a hierarchical model to organize the various modules. This model has the advantage of a significant amount of protection, since it is easy to control access and the flow of information between modules using a hierarchy. Other models in use include the monolithic model and the microkernel model.

The chapter concluded by presenting various types of computer systems in use and compared the operating system facilities required for each. We noted that these categories are somewhat arbitrary, with substantial overlap between them.

FOR FURTHER READING

There are a number of excellent textbooks that describe operating systems in detail; recommended are books by Silberschatz and others [SILB08], Deitel [DEIT03], Tanenbaum [TANE07], Davis and Rajkumar [DAVI04], McHoes and Flynn [McHO08], and Stallings [STAL08]. Davis, in particular, presents a very practical, hands-on view of operating systems, with many examples. McHoes and Flynn is also quite practical and readable. The others tend to be deeper and more theoretical. For particular topics in operating systems, see the references at the back of this textbook and references in any of the other books. There are also numerous trade books that discuss particular topics in operating systems and specific operating systems. Henle and Kuvshinoff [HENL92] provides a satisfying low-level introduction to desktop computer operating systems.

KEY CONCEPTS AND TERMS

application programming
   interface (API)
basic input/output system
   (BIOS)
.BAT file
batch processing
bootstrapping
command line interface
   (CLI)
concurrent processing
context switching
control statements
conversational systems
CPU bound
diskless workstation
dispatching
Distributed Computing
   Environment (DCE)
distributed system
embedded control system
event driven
fail-safe operation
file management
   system

graphical user interface
   (GUI)
hierarchical configuration
high-level scheduling
Initial Program Load (IPL)
interactive systems
interprocess message
   servicing
I/O bound
I/O services
Job
Job Control Language (JCL)
Journaling
kernel
kernel mode
layered configuration
microkernel configuration
monitor
monolithic configuration
multiprogramming
multitasking
multiuser system
nonpreemptive dispatch
nonresident commands

operating system (OS)
plug-and-play
preemptive dispatch
process
real-time system
resident commands
service request
shell
shell scripts
supervisor
system administrator
   (sysadmin)
system generation
   (sysgen)
system languages
system scalability
thin client
threads
time-slicing
virtual private network
   (VPN)
virtual storage
Windows PowerShell
Windows Scripting Host

READING REVIEW QUESTIONS

15.1   The definition of an operating system specifies two primary purposes served by the operating system. What are they?

15.2   Explain the major error in the following sentence: "One of the major tasks performed by the operating system program is to load and execute programs."

15.3   What are the memory resident parts of an operating system called? When are these parts loaded into memory?

15.4   What does API stand for? What is the purpose of an API?

15.5   Operating systems are said to be *event driven*. Explain what this means.

15.6   Explain *concurrent processing*. Briefly describe at least two services that an operating system must provide to support concurrent processing.

15.7   What is the difference between multi*programming* and multi*processing*?

15.8   The basic role of a file management system is to provide a mapping service. Between what and what?

15.9   Briefly describe at least three of the four major services provided by a file management system.

15.10   What tasks are performed by *device drivers*?

15.11   Explain the concept of a *process*. How does a process differ from a program?

15.12   Explain *dispatching*. Describe the two basic methods that are used by operating systems to implement dispatching.

15.13   Explain what is meant by *preemptive* and *nonpreemptive* scheduling.

15.14   Describe at least two primary tasks performed by the memory management component of an operating system.

15.15   What is a *diskless workstation* or *thin client*?

15.16   What is true of system administration on small personal computers that is usually *not* true of larger systems or of personal computers within an organization?

15.17   Identify at least four different tasks performed by a *sysadmin*.

15.18   What is the purpose of system generation?

15.19   Describe the organization of a hierarchically structured operating system.

15.20   The UNIX kernel is described as a *monolithic* organization. What does this mean? What are the major challenges presented by a monolithic organization?

15.21   How do real-time systems differ from other types of operating systems?

EXERCISES

15.1   What are the specific limitations of a computer system that provides no operating system? What must be done to load and execute programs?

15.2   An operating system is described as an event-driven program. What is meant by event driven? Explain how the dispatching operation fits this description.

15.3   Concurrency, of course, is a requirement for modern operating systems. What are the major challenges that an OS designer faces in supporting efficient concurrency that she would not face if the operating system could just run one program at a time?

15.4   Describe the two methods that are used to provide concurrent operation of multiple processes on a single CPU. What are the advantages of each method? What is the advantage of providing concurrent operation?

15.5   For each of the most popular commands in Windows (or Linux if you prefer), identify the type of operating system service that is being provided, and identify the basic module or modules that are involved. Which commands would you assume are memory resident and which loaded as required? Explain your assumptions.

15.6   You are probably familiar with the standard Windows interface. Suppose you could replace the Windows shell with a different interface shell. What might be the advantages and disadvantages of selecting a different command shell as a replacement for the standard Windows interface?

15.7   What are the limitations of providing a BIOS in ROM?

15.8   Nearly every operating system separates the file system from the I/O services. What is the advantage in doing so?

15.9   What is the difference between the logical description of a file and the physical description?

15.10   Early versions of Windows did not support true preemptive multitasking. Instead, the designers of Windows provided something they called ''cooperative multitasking'' in which each program was expected to give up control of the CPU at reasonable time intervals, so that the Windows dispatcher could provide execution time to another waiting program. Describe the disadvantages of this method.

15.11   Discuss the similarities and differences between memory management fragmentation and disk fragmentation.

15.12   One approach to operating system design is to provide as small a kernel as possible and to make all other modules optional. What are the minimum services that must be provided in such a miniature kernel?

15.13   Write a Little Man bootstrap loader that will reside permanently in high memory for the Little Man Computer. The reset button will automatically cause the Little Man to start executing the first instruction of your bootstrap loader. Assume that the application program to be loaded will be input one instruction at a time through the input basket and will be loaded into consecutive locations of memory. The last instruction of the application program will be a 999. When your loader sees this slip of paper, it will cause the Little Man to start executing the program.

15.14   Windows hides most of its configuration in a binary file called the registry. Special Windows tools must be used to read and modify the registry. What are the advantages and disadvantages of this approach versus the use of text-based configuration files?

15.15   If you have access to the system administrator of a large system, find out the steps that are required to perform a sysgen on the system. Also, determine the options that are available for that system.

15.16   **a.**   Of what use is the list of active processes shown in Figure 15.5? What changes might a system administrator make in the system on the basis of this information?

     b.   What does the average number of processes data tell you about the way that this system is normally used?

     c.   Compare the three graphs in the figure.

15.17   Clearly explain the differences between multiprogramming, multiuser, and multiprocessing.

15.18   Based on the system status report shown in Figure 15.5, describe some of the ways in which the system could be tailored, and explain how the various items in the report would influence your tailoring decisions.

15.19   What are the conditions and restrictions that you would want to impose on a multitasking system that is being used with real-time processes?

15.20   What operating system functions would you expect to find in the computer that is built in to control your automobile, and which functions would be omitted? Justify your answer.

CHAPTER 16

THE USER VIEW OF OPERATING SYSTEMS

16.0 INTRODUCTION

In Chapter 15, we introduced you to two different views of the role of the operating system as part of the overall computer architecture. Specifically, we looked at the operating system both as a means of delivering services to the user and as a way of controlling and operating the system facilities. In this chapter, we take a closer look at the operating system from the perspective of service to the user.

Much of the material in this chapter is at least superficially very familiar to you. You have worked closely with at least one type of computer system and quite possibly with more than one. You are familiar with some of the tasks, services, and capabilities that are provided for you by the system or systems that you have worked with. You are familiar with the different types of interfaces that you have used to perform those tasks and with the commands and the command structure that are built into the system for you.

In this chapter we are interested in two aspects of the operating system as it pertains to the user. First, we will consider the services that are provided to the user, and second, we will consider the medium for delivery of those services, namely, the type and appearance of the user interface that the system provides. You will see the standard tasks that a user interface is expected to perform, various ways in which those tasks can be implemented, and the advantages and disadvantages of different implementations. You will be able to observe that the services provided are relatively independent of the means used to access them.

As for the interface, we are more interested in the *concepts* of a user interface than in the specific commands, syntax, appearance, and usage of a particular interface. You will understand that different design approaches to the interface meet different goals and achieve different ends and are often aimed at different classes of users. You will see additional features that are frequently built into an operating system to make the system more "user-friendly", or more powerful, or more efficient. Some of these represent additional services; many are simply ways to make access to the services easier, or more powerful, or more efficient. You will see that one interface may not be powerful enough for some tasks, while another interface requires too much effort to accomplish the common tasks that are required on a regular basis.

User services are a fundamental purpose for the existence of an operating system, and the user interface is essential to the access of those services. Nonetheless, some systems elect to view the user interface, and even many user services, as outside the realm of the operating system. Instead, these services and the user interface are treated as a shell that itself interfaces the operating system. There are strong arguments for this point of view. It makes possible different shells, each with their own services, capabilities, and work styles. If you don't like the shell that is provided, you simply exchange it for another. As we noted in Chapter 15, operating systems based on UNIX and its variants are the strongest proponents of this view—operating systems such as Linux are routinely supplied with several different shells offering different capabilities; in many cases, the user can change shells with a single command. The counterargument to this point of view is that building the user interface and services into the operating system provides standardization, consistency, and much improved integration of services. Apple Macintosh systems take this approach.

There is a third approach to the user interface, namely to hide the system user interface and to use a Web browser model to serve as the interface for the applications that the user works with. Limited access to system utilities can also be supported through the Web interface.

This chapter takes a detailed look at the issues we've just raised. It explains and justifies the different types of user services that are provided with an operating system. It discusses and illustrates and shows the rationale for the various types of user interfaces, and it considers the trade-offs between them. It shows how user services are accomplished with each type of interface. Our primary goal in this chapter is to expand your ability to use your systems effectively and to understand the alternative methods available to you for using the operating system to achieve higher productivity. We hope that the chapter will also provide you with a better understanding of what happens internally within the system when you use your computer.

16.1 PURPOSE OF THE USER INTERFACE

The primary purpose of the user interface is to make the facilities of the computer system accessible to the user by providing the necessary services and commands and means of access to allow the user to get her work done conveniently and efficiently. We emphasize that it is not the intention of the user to interact with the operating system per se. Rather, the operating system exists to help the user to use the computer system productively. In modern operating systems, a secondary purpose has arisen that is almost as important: the operating system provides user interface services to application programs that assure that different programs have user interfaces that operate in the same way. This simplifies use of different applications on the system and reduces the user's learning curve for new programs. We identify programs that use the operating system to provide similar interfaces as having the same (**common**) **look and feel**.

Although the operating system can support a common look and feel across the applications on a particular type of system, there is an important, steady trend toward the use of Web browsers to provide a common look and feel for applications across *all* types of systems. Because the World Wide Web is familiar to a large range of users, an organization can simplify the training requirements and enhance its productivity by using Web-based application interfaces as the predominant means of communication with its personnel. A Web-based approach is also attractive to the programmers that create the applications, because Web page creation is well understood and reasonably well standardized across different computer platforms. The use of internal corporate Internet-like **intranets** to provide information resources throughout an organization is an example of this trend, as is the capability of location-independent Web-based access to e-mail. In addition to the processing and display of data, documents, images, audio, and video, there is even a growing use of Web-based productivity tools such as word processors and spread sheet applications.

We note in passing that the Web interface is particularly effective when the "user" is not a person, but another machine. The standard languages shared across the Web, particularly XML and HTML, make it relatively easy to create Web-based interfaces that can coordinate work between systems.

A well-designed interface can enhance the user's experience of the system and make use of the computer system a pleasure. This will allow the system to provide maximum benefit to its users. Conversely, a system with a poor user interface will be used reluctantly, and its potential value to its users will be diminished. Different classes of users are likely to define the concept of a good interface differently.

The operating system provides a variety of services to the user and to the user's programs. The user interface provides access to these services using three different approaches. These are:

- A command interface of some type that accepts commands in some form directly from the user interface. Most commonly, the interface is either graphical (GUI) or command line (CLI).

- A command language that accepts and executes organized groups of commands as a form of program. Most command languages include capabilities for branching and looping, prompted user input, and passed arguments. Command languages are also referred to as **scripting languages**.

- An interface that accepts and performs requests for operating system services directly from the user's programs (the API).

Modern operating systems provide all three of these capabilities. There are even a number of scripting languages that support portability between different operating systems.

The user services provided by an operating system typically include:

- Loading and execution of program files
- Retrieval, storage, and manipulation of files
- User I/O services, in the form of disk commands, printer spooling, and so on
- Security and data integrity protection
- Interuser communication and shared data and programs, on multiuser and networked systems
- Information about the status of the system and its files
- I/O and file services plus other specialized services for user programs

Many systems also provide utilities that can be used in place of programs to manipulate the data within files and programs. These utilities can be used to sort data and to retrieve data selectively from within files. Frequently, utilities can be combined into "programs" using the command programming language to perform powerful and useful tasks. Linux is particularly strong in this regard. The choice of user services provided is dependent on the original focus and goals of the operating system designers.

Finally, modern systems expand on the concept of I/O service to provide libraries of specialized service routines that can be used by programs to generate graphics, control a mouse, create and manipulate user **windows**, generate and control menus, and perform other sophisticated functions. These make it easy for application programmers to supply a common-look-and-feel interface to their programs.

The difference in skills and interests among the various users on a system affects the design of an operating system user interface in two major areas:

- It affects the choice of services to be provided. For example, powerful programming services may not be needed by the typical user, but may be extremely useful to a system programmer. Conversely, tools that allow the end user easier access to the system may actually hinder the system programmer.

■ It affects the design of the actual interface. The sophisticated user may be more comfortable with a more powerful, but difficult to use, interface. The typical user does not want to, and should not have to, learn a special and difficult operating system lingo just to use the computer.

The operating system must ultimately serve both groups of users, but a particular operating system may be tailored toward one or the other. An operating system that was designed with the goal of supporting engineers may be difficult for a graphic layout artist or secretary to use. Conversely, an engineer may not be able to work effectively on a system that the secretary finds ideal. An alternative is to provide two (or even more) different interfaces, intended for different user groups. If the command interface is implemented as a shell independent of the remainder of the operating system, this is easy to do. The normal user can work with an interface that provides a menu or windowing interface. The more technically sophisticated user can use the GUI for typical tasks, but bypass the windowing shell and enter commands directly to a command interface, when necessary or convenient.

16.2 USER FUNCTIONS AND PROGRAM SERVICES

In Section 16.1 we listed seven major groups of user functions and program services that are provided by most operating systems. Now we'll consider these functions more specifically.

Program Execution

The most obvious user function is the execution of programs. Most operating systems also allow the user to specify one or more **operands** that can be passed to the program as arguments. The operands might be the name of data files, or they might be parameters that modify the behavior of the program.

To the typical end user, the smooth loading and execution of programs are nearly the sole purpose for the operating system. Many operating systems treat program execution the same as they treat nonresident operating system commands. The name of the program is treated as a command; loading and execution begin when the command is typed or, equivalently for a windowing system, when the mouse double-clicks on the graphical icon. Alternatively, the user may click on a data file **icon**. The program associated with the data file is executed with the data file as an operand.[1]

Since the operating system treats application and user programs in the same way as it treats nonresident commands, it is conveniently impossible to tell the difference. Most of the programs that you have used are not part of the operating system, but since they are initiated the same way, you cannot tell the difference. This provides a consistency that is convenient to the user. Microsoft Excel, Quicken, Firefox, and Adobe Acrobat, to name

---

[1] If you are not used to graphical system terminology, an icon is a small graphical representation of a program or data file. "Double-clicking" involves clicking a button on the mouse twice in rapid succession.

just a few, are all independent, nonoperating system programs that share this common behavior, look, and feel.

Application programs perform their operations on a user-specified data file. Spreadsheet programs, for example, require a file of spreadsheet data; word processors use a file of formatted text. The command interface provides a method for specifying the data file to be used when the program is executed. In a command line system, the data file may be specified as an operand typed on the same line with the command. In a graphical system, data files may be associated with a particular application. This association is set up automatically by the operating system when the data file is created, or it may be manually established by the user. Once the association is set up, the application can be initiated automatically by selecting the data file. On most computers, for example, each data file has an icon associated with it; the application is launched with the particular data file by double-clicking the mouse on the data file icon. In Microsoft Windows, the same result can also be achieved by double-clicking the mouse on the name of the data file within the Windows Explorer.

To expedite the execution of programs, the system also provides a means for moving around the system between different peripheral devices and between different storage areas on those devices. Most operating systems embed these operations in a logical device and directory structure and provide commands for moving around the structure. In a command line system, commands provide the ability to attach to different devices and to change one's attachment from one directory to another with a command such as *cd*, for change directory. Graphical interfaces provide file folders as the equivalent to achieve the same purpose.

Although you are probably most familiar with running your programs interactively, most operating systems also allow a program or sequence of programs to be run noninteractively, in a batch mode. The operating system allows the user to specify conditions under which the execution is to take place, for example, the priority of the programs, the preferred time when they should be executed, the stored location of the programs and the particular data files that are to be used. For example, the system can be told to perform a partial backup at a given time every night, with a full backup on Sundays.

File Commands

The second, and most familiar, category of user services are commands for the storage, retrieval, organization, and manipulation of files.

From the perspective of the user, the file management system is what "makes it all possible". Four factors account for the importance of the file management system to the user:

- The ability to treat data and programs by logical file name, without regard to the physical characteristics of the file or its physical storage location
- The ability of the file management system to handle the physical manipulation of the files and to translate between logical and physical representations
- The ability to issue commands to the operating system that store, manipulate, and retrieve files and parts of files
- The ability to construct an effective file organization utilizing directories or file folders to organize one's files in a meaningful way

FIGURE 16.1

Common Windows and UNIX/Linux File Commands

Windows	UNIX/Linux	
dir	ls	List a directory of files or get information about files
copy	cp	Copy a file from one place to another
move	mv	Move a file from one place to another
del or erase	rm	Delete (remove) a file
type	cat	Type a file out to the screen (or redirected to a printer)
mkdir	mkdir	Attach a new subdirectory to the tree at this tree junction
rmdir	rmdir	Delete a subdirectory

The file management system is so important that we have devoted the entirety of Chapter 17 to it. Of interest to us here, as users, is the fact that most of the user commands in the operating system are directly used to manipulate files and file data. This is evident if you consider the commands that you use in your regular work with the computer. The brief partial list of Windows and UNIX/Linux CLI commands in Figure 16.1 typifies the commands that you would probably consider to be most important to you. Other operating systems provide essentially identical commands, although the commands might appear quite different, depending on the user interface. Graphical user interfaces provide equivalent operations for each of these commands. On a Macintosh computer, for example, you move a file by dragging its icon with the mouse from its current location to the desired location. You create a new directory by moving an empty file folder into the window that represents the desired attachment point.

Many additional features built into the command structure reflect the importance of a flexible file structure to the user. These include

- The ability to change from one device and one directory or subdirectory to another without otherwise modifying the file
- The ability to redirect input and output to different devices and files from their usual locations

Disk and Other I/O Device Commands

In addition to the file commands, the operating system provides commands for direct operation on various I/O devices. There are commands for formatting and checking disks, for copying entire disks, for providing output directly to the screen or to a printer, and for other useful I/O operations. Some systems also require the **mounting** and **unmounting** of devices. This effectively attaches and detaches the directory structure of a device to the already existent directory structure as a means of adding devices to the system.

Most operating systems also provide a queuing system for spooling output to a printer. The printer is generally much slower than other computer facilities. The spooler works by copying the output text into a buffer in memory and then printing as a separate task. This allows programs to proceed as though printing had already taken place.

Security and Data Integrity Protection

Every operating system provides security protection for files. Generally, individual provisions are made to protect files from being read, written to, or executed. Some operating systems also provide protection from deletion. A few operating systems provide additional security, requiring a correct password to be typed before a disk can be used in the system, or a keyboard unlocked.

Systems with network multiple user access, of course, must provide much more protection. The system as a whole must be protected from unauthorized access. Files must be protected, so that the owner of the file can control who has access to the file. The owner can also protect the file from himself or herself by specifying read-only or execute-only access.

Many operating systems also allow controlled access from other users. UNIX provides three levels of security for each file, consisting of read, write, and execute access privileges for the owner, for associates of the owner (known as *groups*), and for anybody with access to the system. Windows offers share privileges to control file and device access between users on a network. Many large systems also provide **access control lists**, or **ACLs** (pronounced ack-ulls), that allow the system administrator to control access to program and data files on an individual user/file pair basis. In addition to file protection, every operating system with multiple user access provides a login procedure to limit access on the system to authorized users. Commands exist to allow the user to modify the access rights on a file and to change the user's password. Networks also require the use of a login procedure that limits the user to the appropriate computers and facilities.

Interuser Communication and Data Sharing Operations

Modern systems generally provide means for multiple users to share data files and programs. Most systems also provide a means to pass data between programs and to communicate between users. Application programs like Lotus Notes, instant messaging, and videoconferencing can extend this capability of users to work collaboratively in a powerful way to both small and large networks of computer systems.

The simplest form of program sharing on a single system is to place the shared programs in a common memory area where all users can reach them. This is done for editors, compilers, general utilities, and other system software that is not part of the operating system. Many operating systems even allow several different levels of control over such shared programs. For example, the Little Man Computer simulator used at Bentley College is accessible to all computer majors, but other users must have permission to access it.

Data file sharing is an important resource when using databases, because it makes it possible for multiple users to access the same data in a way that the integrity of the data is protected. Needless to say, the system must provide tight security to limit data file access to those who should have it. An additional use for data file sharing is when two or more users work as a group on a document. All these users have access to the document. Some can only read it, while others can modify it. Some systems provide means for attaching notes to the document for other users to see. As with program sharing, it is possible to set several levels of data file sharing.

Modern networks routinely provide operating system message passing services in the form of e-mail and newsgroup support, file transfer (ftp), simple terminal facilities for connecting to a different system (telnet or ssh), Web support (http), instant messaging, and audio and video conferencing. Some systems also provide an internal messaging service for rapid communication between users logged on to the system, either directly or through a network.

Operating systems also provide internal services that allow programs to communicate with each other during execution. Modern systems go one step farther and extend this concept to allow the user to control interprogram communication as a means of extending the capabilities of individual programs.

The simplest example of this is the PIPE command available in many systems for taking the output from one program and using it as the input to another. More sophisticated techniques allow a user to link two programs together so that a spreadsheet, for example, can appear in a word processing document. Double-clicking the mouse on the spreadsheet actually launches the spreadsheet program from within the word processor program, so that the spreadsheet can be modified. The most sophisticated systems actually allow the user to work with different application programs *transparently*, that is, without even being aware that an operation has launched another program. For example, modification of the spreadsheet would take place right within the word processing document; the user would not even be aware that a spreadsheet application program was being executed at the time.

This approach relies heavily on the operating system to support communication between different programs in a fashion invisible to the user. The user is not even aware of which application is executing at any given instant. This technique views the document as the center of focus, instead of the applications that are being executed.

System Status Information

As previously seen in Chapter 15, most operating systems provide status information that can be useful to a user who knows how to interpret the data. This data is usually more important to the people who operate and maintain the computer system, but sometimes status information can be useful to programmers and users in optimizing their work.

Commands commonly exist to determine the amount of available disk space, the amount of available memory, the number of users on the system and who they are, the percentage of time that the CPU and I/O channels are busy, and many other statistics.

As an example of how this data might be useful, consider an application program that does the billing for a large electric utility company. Such a program might require many hours of CPU time to complete a month's billing. A small change in the program could cut the CPU time by a significant percentage. The measurement of CPU time used is essential to assess the improvement. This data might also be important to a user who is being billed for her time.

The names of other users on the system might be used to establish a phone-type conference or to send a quick message to another user.

Many systems provide a logging facility that maintains a file of all keyboard and screen I/O. With a log file the user can determine at a later time what commands were typed and what modifications made to programs and data.

The examples given here are only a few of the possible uses for system status and information. There are many other possibilities. Status information can be particularly important to personal computer users who must maintain their own systems. For example, status information allows the user to ascertain the condition of a disk: to determine the number of bad blocks on the disk or to analyze and reduce the fragmentation that is present on the disk. For example, Windows provides the SCANDISK and DEFRAG commands for this purpose.

Program Services

One of the most important user functions provided by the operating system is actually invisible to the user. The operating system provides a variety of services directly to the user's programs. The most important of these are the I/O and file services. Also important are requests for the use of system resources that a program needs, such as additional memory or larger blocks of time and GUI services that support "common look and feel".

Typical program services can be used to retrieve a file, to save a file, or to locate the individual blocks of a file. The program services can read one or a few particular blocks of a file into a designated user area of memory. Most program service facilities can keep track of several files at once.

Typical program services also allow an application program to bypass the file system under certain conditions and to perform I/O directly to disk and other I/O devices. For example, the program could request a service that retrieves a particular block on the disk. This type of service might be important to a program that attempts to repair damaged data files, for example. Most operating systems control these services in such a way as to prevent damage to the system or to other users' files and resources. As another example, output to a screen is performed directly to I/O, rather than through the file system, on many computer systems. These I/O services allow programs to write text and graphics to the screen without compromising the system.

Services to programs also include services that are less apparent to the user, but important nonetheless. Interprocess message passing allows programs to synchronize their actions to protect data integrity, to share and exchange data, and even to distribute program processing among different machines on a network. **DCOM (Distributed Component Object Model)**, its extension **.NET**, and **CORBA (Common Object Request Broker Architecture)** are two standards that allow programs to locate and share objects, either on a system or across a network. **Remote Procedure Call (RPC)** allows a program to call a procedure at a remote location across a network.

.NET and other equivalent operating system tools also ease a programmer's task at creating new programs by providing commonly required program objects and allow computers on a network to share the processing load. Particularly in modern systems, where elegant user interfaces and graphics are the norm rather than the exception, the operating system provides a library of powerful service routines for implementing user interfaces and graphics for individual programs. On most modern workstations and personal computers, it is only necessary for a program to call a series of these routines to maintain control of windows, drop-down menus, dialog boxes, and mouse events. The routines also include powerful system calls for drawing complex graphic shapes on the screen.

To use the program service routines, the user's program makes requests to the operating system through the **application programming interface (API)**. In most systems, the API consists of a library of service functions that may be called by a program.[2] The call and required parameters are passed to the selected service function, using whatever method is implemented for the given machine. Most commonly, a simple call is used, with a stack used to pass the parameters. The service function is responsible for communication with appropriate routines within the operating system that perform the requested operation. A software interrupt or service request instruction is used for this purpose. The service routine returns required results, if any, to the calling program. On some systems, the calling program uses a software interrupt directly to access the API. Windows *win32*, the standard API on every Microsoft Windows system, provides hundreds of service functions to programs.

The use of operating system program services provides convenience for a program developer. More important, providing a single gateway through which all I/O must pass assures the integrity of files and other I/O. If each program placed its files on the disk independently, there would be no way to assure that the files didn't destroy each other. The integrity of the system is even more important if the system is multiprogramming and/or multiuser. As an example of what could go wrong, consider a printer being addressed directly by two different programs. The output would be a garbled mix of the output to be printed from the two programs, obviously useless to anyone. Early, single-user systems allowed programs to bypass the operating system and do their own I/O. Doing so increases the risk that data may be destroyed. Furthermore, bypassing the I/O services of the operating system may make the program incompatible with other, similar (such as clone) computers that may use different internal addresses for the I/O device functions. Finally, the I/O services provided are convenient. They make it possible to simplify the task of writing programs by providing the difficult I/O and file functions automatically.

A properly designed multiprogramming operating system will not allow programs to perform their own I/O; the operating system services must be used. It is the role of the system services to properly queue I/O requests and to perform them in such a way as to protect the data. No current machine allows a user program to bypass operating system services.

16.3 TYPES OF USER INTERFACE

There are two types of user interface in common use. One of these is the **command line interface (CLI)**, which is seen on a wide variety of operating systems, including the command prompt in Windows. Although this is historically the most common interface, the **graphical user interface (GUI)** has supplanted the CLI for most routine day-to-day use. GUIs are seen on the Apple Macintosh, Windows-based PCs, Sun workstations, most Linux desktop systems,[3] and a variety of other devices such as PDAs and mobile phones.

---

[2]The concept of an API also applies to applications that allow other applications to "piggyback" or "plug in" to their services. For example, Web browsers provide API services to their plug-ins, as do several Google tools.

[3]Many Linux servers have only a CLI, no GUI, because the GUI consumes so many computer resources that might be better used to provide a higher level of client services.

Although Web browsers are not actually part of the operating system, there are many computer people who believe that a Web browser (together with its tools) is viable as an adjunct or alternative to the standard GUI in many circumstances. It is possible to use the Web browser to perform many common tasks, such as file management. (As an experiment, try using file:///C: as a URL on any Web browser in Windows and notice that you can drag a file to the desktop, for example. Or double-click on a file icon in the browser to launch it.) There is even a Linux shell that promotes the use of a customized Web browser for most operations.

As already noted, the type of interface seen by the user depends on the focus of the operating system. A batch system requires a different interface than a system primarily intended for interactive use. A system designed primarily for inexperienced end users will differ from one designed for sophisticated technical users. Today, most users are reasonably comfortable at a computer screen, the purely batch system is in declining use, and the primary user interface with a computer is interactive, using a keyboard, mouse, and video display. Furthermore, the graphical user interface and Web browser are rapidly becoming the predominant user interfaces for most work.

The Command Line Interface

The command line interface is the simplest form of user-interactive interface. The operating system command shell provides a prompt; in response, the user types textual commands into the keyboard. The command line is read serially, character by character, into a keyboard buffer, where it is interpreted by the command interpreter and executed. Commands are entered and executed one line at a time, although most interpreters provide a means for extending a command onto multiple lines. The command line interpreters for most operating systems use a standard format for their commands. The command itself is followed by operands appropriate to the particular command, as shown:

```
command operand1 operand2...
```

The operands are used to specify parameters that define the meaning of the command more precisely: the name of a particular file to be used with the command, a particular format for listing data, or a detail about how the command is to be performed. Many times, some or all of the operands are optional; this simply means that a default condition is to be used if the operand is not specified.

In some circumstances, the command itself may be preceded by a logical path name that specifies the particular device or file location where the command is to be found. However, most operating systems maintain an internal list where most commands can be found. This list is often referred to as **path variable**.

As an example, the Linux command

```
ls -lF pathparta/pathpartb
```

consists of the command ls and the two operands -lF and pathparta/pathpartb. This command requests a directory listing from the subdirectory with path name pathparta/pathpartb. Without the optional operand pathparta/pathpartb, the command lists the current directory (or file folder, if you prefer), wherever that happens to be. An additional operand might redirect the output to a file or printer, for example, instead of to the screen. The Linux command to store the directory list in putfilea (presumably for later printing) would look like this:

```
ls -lF pathparta/pathpartb >putfilea
```

The equivalent command at a Windows command prompt would look like this:

```
DIR PATHPARTA\PATHPARTB>PUTFILEA
```

In each of these cases, many other optional operands are possible; these operands would be used to modify the facts listed and the format of the directory listing. The additional operand -lF in the Linux command tells the system to list the directory in a specific "long" format, one file to a line (the "l"), with subdirectories indicated (the "F").

Operands are either **keyword** or **positional**. In some systems, the operands may be both. Positional operands require the operand to be located in a particular position within the line. For example, in the Windows command

```
COPY SOURCE-FILE DESTINATION
```

the first operand, SOURCE-FILE, positionally specifies the path name of the file to be copied. the second operand, DESTINATION, which is optional, specifies either a new name for the file or the path name of a directory to which the file is to be copied. If the second operand is absent, the directory to which the user is currently "attached" is used. The importance of the position of these positional operands is obvious: some older operating systems specified the destination operand first; reversing the position could destroy the file to be copied.

Keyword operands are identified by the use of a particular keyword. In many systems, the keyword is accompanied by a modifier symbol that identifies the operand as a keyword as opposed to a file name. The keyword identifies the purpose of the operand. Keyword operands are frequently used as optional operands, sometimes with a particular positional value attached. In some systems, keyword operands and modifiers can be placed anywhere after the command without affecting the positions of positional operands. In other systems, the keyword operands, if present, must be placed in a particular position. The slash mark (/) in Windows and hyphen (-) in Linux are examples of modifier symbols. Keyword operands are sometimes known as **switches** or **modifiers**.

The Windows command

```
MODE COM1 BAUD=2400 PARITY=N DATABITS=8
```

uses the positional operand COM1 to identify a particular communications port or other device. BAUD, PARITY, and DATABITS are all examples of keyword operands. Each has its own positional operand that selects a particular option, but the order of the keywords is immaterial.

Similarly, the command

```
DIR /P/A:DH PATHNAME
```

uses the /P and /A switches to specify that files are displayed on a screen one page at a time, and to modify the list of path name directory files that will be displayed. Command line interpreters also include other provisions designed to increase the flexibility of the command. The most important provisions include the ability to redirect input and output, the ability to combine commands using pipes, and the ability to combine commands into shell scripts or, as they are sometimes incorrectly called, **batch programs**. (You are already aware of the correct usage of this term. In this book we will always differentiate between shell scripts and batch programs.) Another important capability is the use of the wild card, a character symbol or symbols that can substitute for one or more unspecified letters in an operand. Use of a wild card in a command can make possible a search, or can cause a command to be repeated with several different arguments.

Although they work somewhat differently, both Linux and Windows use the question mark symbol (?) to replace a single character and an asterisk (*) to replace a group of 0 or more characters. Linux has additional wild card possibilities, shown in the Linux case in Supplementary Chapter 2. For example, the Linux command

```
ls -l boo.*
```

would search the current directory for all files that have the name boo. This command might result in the following output:

```
-r--r--rwx  1  irv  cisdep   221  May  16   7:02  boo.dat
---x--xrwx  1  irv  cisdep  5556  May  20  13:45  boo.exe
-r--rw-rw-  1  irv  cisdep    20  Jun   5   2:02  boo.hoo
```

In the Windows command,

```
COPY ABC* B:
```

all files whose names begin with ABC are copied to the drive B: master directory. In this case, the wild card is used to expand the command to repeat the copy process for several different files.

In addition to **wild card** provisions, some operating systems allow the user to back up and repeat a previous command using the cursor keys on the keyboard. Such systems usually allow the user to edit the command, as well.

Command line interfaces are well suited to experienced users who are comfortable with the system and who want the power and flexibility that a CLI offers them. Command line interfaces are generally the hardest to learn. The range of possibilities and options that accompany many commands often make it difficult to figure out the particular syntax that is required for a desired operation. Manuals and online help are particularly useful in working with command line interfaces. Online help is available for all Linux commands using the "man commandname" command.

Batch System Commands

Batch systems use an interface that is similar to the command line interpreter in many respects, but the purpose is different. Commands specify the location of programs to be executed and data to be used, using a Job Control Language. Job control commands use a format similar to that of the command line interpreter:

```
command operand1 operand2...
```

Batch command operands also are either of keyword or positional type. The most familiar language of this type is IBM zOS/Job Control Language. Batch jobs consisting of one or more programs are "submitted" to a system for execution and are generally executed with no human interaction. Since direct human interaction with the batch system is not possible, all steps must be carefully planned out, including actions to be taken when errors occur. Batch programs are well suited for routine transaction processing applications, such as credit card billing and payroll.

As we noted above, command line interfaces also provide the ability to "batch" commands together to form pseudoprograms, known as **shell scripts**, or just **scripts**, that will be executed as a unit. These are not true batch programs, as they are still intended for interactive use. Nonetheless, Windows users sometimes refer to these programs as *batch programs* or, more commonly, as *bat files*. Most command line interfaces provide additional commands that are intended especially for the creation of powerful scripts. The overall command structure is then referred to as a **command language**, or scripting language. The topic of command languages is considered further in Section 16.5. There is an example of a JCL procedure in Supplementary Chapter 2.

Graphical User Interfaces

The mouse-driven, icon-based graphical user interface, or GUI (pronounced gooey) has, for all practical purposes, replaced the command line interface as the prevalent interface between user and computer. The GUI has been implemented in many forms. The best-known implementations are the user interfaces present on the Apple Macintosh computer and on IBM-type PCs that are equipped with the Microsoft Windows interface. Most other computer systems offer a similar interface. Figure 16.2 is a picture of a typical Windows XP screen. The screen of a Linux computer running the KDE shell appears in Figure 16.3. Notice the similarities between the two. The graphical user interface provides the convenience of a desktop metaphor. The user can arrange the desktop to his or her own preferences, can easily move around the desktop to perform different tasks, and can see the results in WYSIWYG (what-you-see-is-what-you-get) form.

Windowing systems from different vendors take on different appearances, but share similar elements. Normally, a graphic interface consists of one or more **screens** or **desktops**, each of which contains one or more windows. A window is a portion of the screen that is allocated to the use of a particular program, document, or process. Windows contain **gadgets** or **widgets** for resizing the windows, for moving the windows around the screen, for scrolling data and images within a window, and for moving windows in front of or behind other windows on the screen. Windows usually also contain a **title bar** that identifies the window. There is also at least one **menu bar** on the screen. On some systems, a single menu bar on the screen is always associated with the active window (discussed shortly). On other systems, each window has its own menu bar. Each item on the menu bar can be used to activate a hierarchical set of pull-down menus, used for selecting options within the program being executed. Windows and Linux screens also provide a **task bar** for rapid program start-up, task switching, and status information.

On many modern systems, Windows can be configured to look and act in different ways. As we already noted, one important option is the Web interface, which provides the look and feel of a Web browser for all operations within the window.

Many systems allow windows to be iconified, tiled, overlapped, or cascaded. Iconifying a window means reducing it to the size of an icon, even though the window is still open.

FIGURE 16.2

A Typical Windows Vista Screen

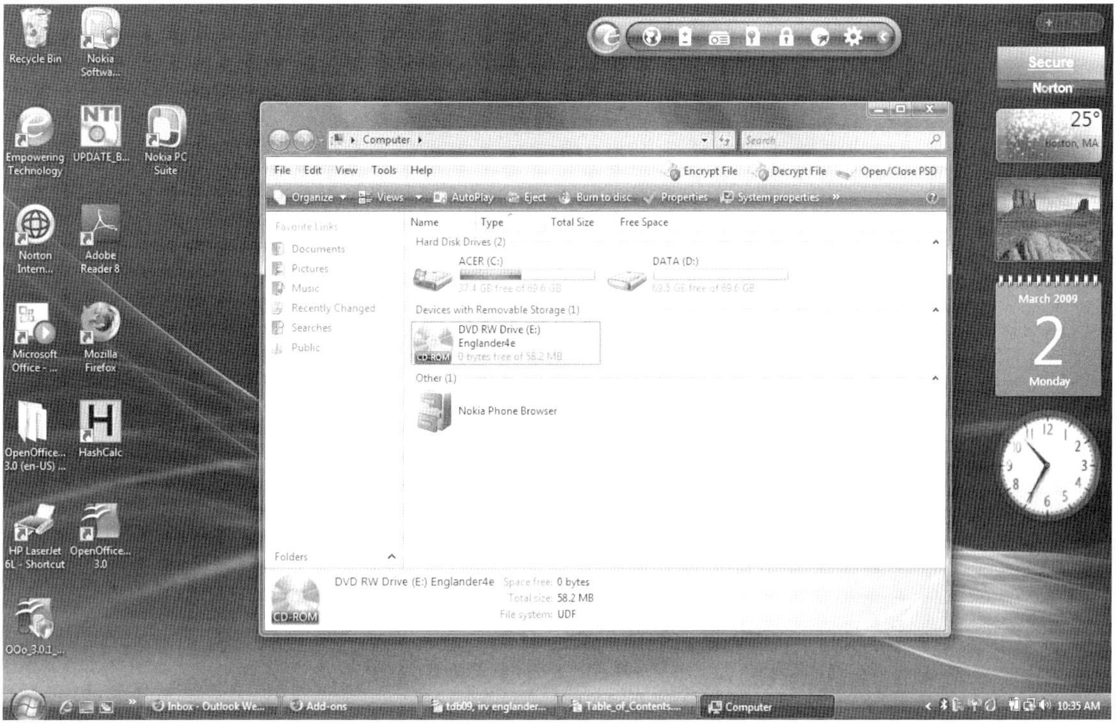

This allows screen space to be saved. The window is reexpanded by clicking on it. Tiled windows are lined up on the screen in such a way that they do not overlap and use all the available space on the screen. Overlapping windows is the normal situation, with windows located where placed by the system or by the user. Cascaded windows are a version of overlapped windows where the windows are overlapped in such a way that the title bar and one other border of each window can be seen. Some of the newest systems use transparent windows and miniaturized windows to ease the user's task of keeping track of everything on her desktop. A less common, but creative, approach used on certain systems "rolls up" the windows like a windows shade, showing only the title bar.

On systems that allow multiple screens, a group of windows is attached to a particular screen. Individual screens, together with their associated windows, can be minimized or can be moved forward or behind other screens, but are not usually resizable. When multiple screens are allowed, each screen represents a separate user interface. Four desktops are indicated in the task bar in Figure 16.3. A new, somewhat gimmicky, approach places the different screens on the sides of a cube that can be rotated to reveal the desired workspace. The future of this approach is (hopefully) uncertain.

FIGURE 16.3

A Linux Computer Running the KDE Shell

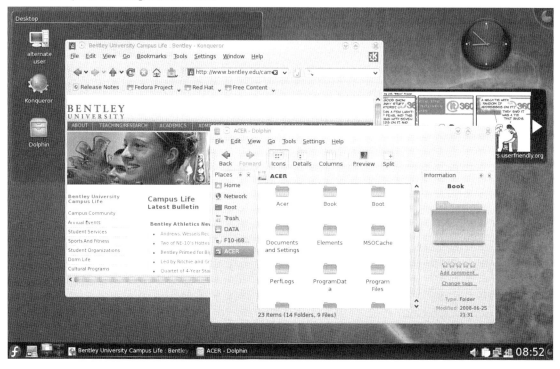

To the user, the window is a box that is used for the input of text and commands to a program and the graphical or text output resulting. Placing multiple windows on the screen provides a convenient way to implement a multiprogramming interface with separate input and output for each program. At any given time, one window is active, meaning that it will respond to the keyboard and mouse. The color or appearance of the title bar is frequently used to indicate which window on the screen is currently active. On some systems, moving the mouse cursor into a window activates the window. This method is known as **mouse focus**. In other systems, the window must be activated by clicking the mouse while the cursor is inside the window or by opening the window. This is known as **click to focus**.

Depending on the GUI design, data and program files can take the form of text or of graphical symbols called icons. On most systems, icons can be animated. Icons that are in use change shape or color. Icons can be moved around the screen with a mouse. Some systems also allow the use of a light pen or a tablet or a pressure pen, or even, a finger, for this purpose. Pressure pens are commonly used as the pointing device on personal digital assistants such as the Palm Pilot. The pressure pen itself is just a piece of plastic. The actual pointing signal is produced when the system detects the physical pressure at a particular location on the screen or senses the position and movement of a finger near the screen.

Many commands are issued to the operating system by moving the mouse and manipulating a button on the mouse at the appropriate time. For example, a program is initiated by pointing the mouse cursor at the icon for the program and clicking the mouse button twice. A copy command involves holding the mouse button down while the user **drags** the icon from its original position to a position on top of the desired destination directory icon or window, then **drops** it by releasing the button. A delete command is performed by dragging the icon to an icon that represents the picture of a trash can. Other commands use the mouse together with pop-up or pull-down menus.

Both program and data files are stored in folders, and folders may be nested. Double-clicking on a folder opens a window that shows the contents of the folder. In other words, folders are equivalent to a file directory structure. The **active window** corresponds to the current directory attachment point.

Requestor boxes can be used for commands that require textual input, such as a new file name. Additional gadgets, such as push buttons and sliders, exist for other types of control of the interface.

Most window-interfaced operating systems also allow the use of special keys on the keyboard to duplicate commands that use the mouse-icon-menu method.

EXAMPLE

The Macintosh OS X interface consists of a single screen known as the desktop. The desktop can be used to hold various items, such as a trashcan, folders, and data that is being worked on. A typical Macintosh OS X screen is shown in Figure 16.4. The desktop consists of icons representing each **volume** on the system, a menu bar, the **dock**, and a trash icon. A volume consists of a disk or partition of a disk.

Clicking the mouse on a volume or dock icon opens a window. On the Macintosh, icons can represent folders, applications, and documents. Clicking on an application will **launch** (load and execute) the program. Clicking on a document icon will open the **associated application** program and load the indicated data. Some windows may also be opened from the menu bar.

The dock serves as a convenient receptacle for applications, folders, documents, files, and volumes that are accessed often. It also holds icons for minimized open applications. Mac OS X does not distinguish between applications which are open and minimized from those that are permanently placed on the dock for convenience. If you look at the figure carefully, you will see that the dock is divided by a vertical line into two sections. The left section holds applications. The right side of the dock holds folders, documents, and the like.

Names for the icons on the dock are hidden; they appear when the mouse pointer is positioned on the icon. Some dock icons also sprout pop-up menus. Drag-and-drop is used to add icons to the dock. Icons are removed by dragging them out of the dock. The dock can be hidden, shrunk, or rotated into a new position on the desktop.

Two windows are open in the figure. The open windows provide a title bar that contains the usual gadgets, known on the Macintosh as **controls**. These are used to close the window, to expand the window to full screen size, to minimize the window, to resize the window to a desired size, and to provide scrolling left and right, up and down to expose the underlying

FIGURE 16.4

A Typical Macintosh OS X Screen

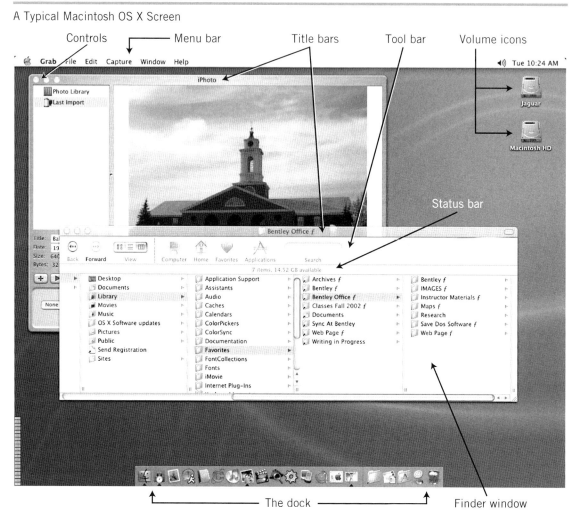

parts of the window. The mouse can also be used to move the window around the desktop. Some windows also offer a tool bar and a status bar.

The Macintosh desktop uses a single menu bar that is shared by the active window and the desktop. The mouse can be moved over the menu bar to cause pull-down menus to appear. Many of the items on pull-down menus are standard no matter what the user is doing. Those that are inappropriate at a particular time are "grayed out", that is, represented in a lighter color. These items do not respond to the mouse. This standardization makes the interface easier to learn and to use. Some menu bar items change to represent possible actions that are unique to a particular situation.

Numerous windows can be open at once, each with its own work, and it is possible to cut or copy and paste data between different windows by marking the desired data using the mouse and using the cut, copy, and paste menu functions. Only one window is active at a time. The user selects the active window by clicking the mouse anywhere inside it. Even though windows can overlap, the active window will always be brought to the front and displayed in full. Once a window is active, the user can manipulate the window and the data within it. During program execution, buttons, dialog boxes, and pull-down menus are used to control the program and to enter data, simplifying interaction between the user and the program.

In the figure, iPhoto is an application. The other open window is a special **Finder** window. The Finder window is used to navigate the system. It contains a tool bar that works similarly to a web browser and panels that represent a hierarchy of folders and their contents. The tool bar can be modified for a particular user's preferences. Applications can be launched and documents opened directly from the Finder.

Besides ease of use, what is important about the Macintosh interface is its consistency. Throughout the interface, every operation works the same way. This enhances ease of use and quick learning, as well as user comfort. A powerful library of graphics software routines within the operating system is used to enforce this consistency.

It should be noted that the graphical interface is totally committed to the user end of the user interface. Internally, the commands are executed by the operating system in essentially the same way as that of any other interface. We mention this so that you can see the value of separating the various layers of the operating system conceptually. Modification or change of one layer does not have to affect other layers, as long as the interface between layers is self-consistent.

Trade-offs in the User Interface

It might seem obvious to you that the ease of use of a graphical interface makes this the ideal interface for most users. For the typical end user, the graphical interface is indeed an attractive choice. It is easy to learn and easy to use. Little training is required, and the basic operations are intuitive. It therefore meets the most important criterion of the user interface: it is effective in allowing the user to get work done. The graphical interface has a second, less obvious, advantage as well. With a graphical interface, it is easy to implement a multitasking system in which the user can control every task by placing each executing task in a separate window. Although some command line systems provide a way to execute programs "in the background", the method is much more awkward: switching between tasks is not convenient, displayed output is mixed together, and it is difficult to separate and interact with both programs.

In addition, the GUI reflects current computer usage. Modern computers are used routinely to display graphics, photos, and video. The interface is simply more consistent with this type of usage than the CLI would be. The common use of the Web browser on devices such as cell phones, in addition to its use as a primary application tool on computers, provides further support for the GUI as a primary interface for the average user.

The graphical interface is not without disadvantages, however. The graphical interface is much harder to implement and much more demanding in its hardware and software requirements. This interface works best with a powerful graphic video capability. It requires a lot of memory, just to store the pictures as well as to hold the programs. The software is complex, although visual and object-oriented languages and API services simplify the coding of such programs.

In contrast, the command line interface is simple and straightforward. It is text oriented, and input to the command interpreter can be treated as a simple serial character stream. The command line interface also has more inherent flexibility and power. Many experienced users consider the graphical interface to be slow and clumsy. They prefer to type a command to get their work done. Arguments and operands are easy to use and to specify. It is easier to work with wild card commands when an operation is to be repeated many times or when a specialized search is to take place. It is more difficult to combine commands or to use piping techniques using a graphical interface.

Even though the graphical I/O built into user programs is easy to use, the development of graphical I/O for user programs is more difficult, and the programs are larger and slower, because of the numerous details that must be handled by service routines. It is obviously easier to read and write a stream of text than it is to draw windows, handle menus, and identify mouse movements and actions.

Finally, it is more difficult to combine a series of graphical actions into a working script of commands, especially when branches and loops are required, although Windows is attempting to move in that direction with Windows PowerShell. One of the powers of the command line interface is the ability to "program" the commands.

Despite these difficulties, the graphical user interface is convenient and useful for most users in most circumstances. It is the primary interface on most personal computer systems and is relatively common on mainframe computers as well.

Gradually, too, the disadvantages of this interface are being solved. Most systems now provide an alternative command line interface, such as the command prompt in Windows, for example, for use in situations where the graphical interface is inconvenient or weak. Application programs now exist to help the program developer with the creation of windows and other tasks required for the program interface. And of course the Web browser offers simple tools to create application interfaces that are both inherently graphical and easy to develop.

Standards exist that allow different computers and terminals to share the same graphical interface, even though the individual hardware and software is different. Such capability is important in networked and distributed computing environments, where display elements from one system must be displayed faithfully on a different system. As we have already noted, one obvious choice for this capability is the use of Web technology—Java applets, scripting languages, HTML, and XML and the like—to create the required display.

An attractive alternative in many instances is **X Window**, which allows various computers that use various forms of UNIX, Linux, and certain other operating systems to work together graphically. X Window provides a language that describes the graphical interface; each individual computer implements the language within its own operating system to produce the desired result. The X Window system was developed at MIT in 1986 and has been accepted by most manufacturers as a way of furthering the idea of a standard graphical interface regardless of hardware. X Window is discussed further in Section 16.4. In many instances, Web browsers can serve in this role, using Java applets, scripting languages, HTML, and XML to create the required display.

Software Considerations

The programs that control the user interface must perform two primary functions:

- Maintain the appearance of the user interface on the screen
- Translate user requests into user services and initiate the programs that will provide those services

Of course, if the interface is a command line, maintaining the appearance of the interface on the screen is trivial, since it is necessary only to print a prompt and wait for a response. CLI interfaces are text based; therefore, any necessary remote display over a network, for example, is not a problem.

Similarly, translation of CLI commands into the appropriate services is simple. It is necessary only to compare the text typed by the user to that of known commands or file names and execute the command as typed by the user. If the command is internal, it is executed within the operating system. If it is external, it is loaded and executed. The operands on the line are passed to the command procedure as arguments.

Windowing interfaces are more difficult. The windowing software is responsible for drawing and maintaining the appearance of the screen; for creating pull-down menus and dialog boxes; for reacting to requests made by the user in the form of mouse clicks; for maintaining the positions of different objects on the screen; for opening, closing, moving, and resizing windows when requested; and for accomplishing many other tasks.

Even a task as conceptually simple as moving an object on the screen, say, the cursor or an icon or a window or a slider control, requires a considerable effort in terms of programming. (Picture trying to write the program to do it using the Little Man Computer machine language!) As the user moves the mouse, the mouse generates interrupts to the CPU. The mouse interrupt program determines the direction and distance that the mouse has moved. It calculates the new X and Y coordinates of the object on the screen by geometrically adding the move to the present position of the object. Then it redraws the object at the new location, by storing a picture of the object in display memory. When it does so, it must also store the shadow of the image stored "behind" the new position of the object and restore the image of whatever was hidden by the object in its previous position. This operation is depicted in Figure 16.5.

(We note that in modern desktop computer systems and workstations, the software required to perform tasks such as the image shadowing just described is actually built into some graphics display controllers. The division of labor between the controller and the operating system is established by the

FIGURE 16.5

Moving an Object on the Screen

Created by Larry Ewing lewing@isc.tamu.edu

device driver software used with a particular graphics controller. Either way, the task must be performed.)

In addition to display maintenance and handling, the interface program must also interpret the commands and request the appropriate services. Double-clicking on a document icon, for example, requires the software to identify the icon from its location on the display screen, determine the associated application program, load and execute the application, and load the document data. The command interpreter is thus somewhat more complicated for a windowing system. Note that requesting a service will also require use of the display services, since it will be necessary for the new application to open one or more windows of its own, set up its own menus, and so on.

Finally, it is useful to consider the display of objects within a window, such as images in a photograph processing application, or formatted text in a word processor, or a page in a Web browser. Responsibility for each of these displays lies within the particular applications. The output to be displayed in a window will take the form of objects and bitmaps, as described in Chapter 4. The applications use the API facilities within the operating system to produce the actual display. In turn, the operating system will then create the overall screen display using a combination of its own software with that of the graphics display controller.

Overall, you can see that the graphical user interface software is considerably more complex than the corresponding CLI or menu interface software.

16.4 X WINDOW AND OTHER GRAPHICS DISPLAY METHODOLOGIES

Graphical user interfaces are attractive, convenient, and relatively straightforward when the computer and display are located together, such as in a personal computer or workstation. When the display terminal is separated by a distance from the computer the graphical interface is more difficult to achieve. Such a situation might occur, for example, if a user is trying to operate her computer across a network, using the local display and mouse facilities on a remote computer. The difficulty is the large amount of data that must be transmitted from one location to the other to transmit graphic images. In Chapter 9 we observed that a single bitmapped graphical image might contain thousands or millions of bytes of information. Clearly, it is not practical to transmit the screen display as a bitmapped image across the network on a continual basis.

The X Window standard represents one successful attempt to solve this problem. X Window works by separating the software that actually produces the display image on the screen from the application program that creates the image and requests the display into a somewhat unusual client-server arrangement. The program that produces the image on the screen is known as a **display server**. We remind you that in data communications terminology a server is a program that provides services for other programs. In this case, the server provides display services for one or more client application programs. (We have assumed that the client application programs are running on computer systems located remotely from the display, although, as you will see shortly, this is not a necessary assumption.) The display server is located at the display terminal, computer, or workstation where the image is to appear. The display server can draw and control windows. It provides gadgets, dialog boxes, and pull-down and pop-up menus. It can create and display various fundamental shapes, such as points, rectangles, circles, straight and curved lines, icons, a cursor, and text fonts. In conjunction with a mouse and keyboard located on the same terminal the display server can move, resize, and otherwise control these windows. The mouse can also move the cursor under display server control, that is, local to the terminal. It has only to notify the application as to the final position of the cursor.

Thus, much of the work in creating a graphical window interface is performed local to the display itself and does not have to be transmitted from the computer system that is running the application program. The application program uses the display services to produce its desired images by interacting with the display server. Again, in data communication terminology, the application program acts as a client, requesting display services that it needs from the display server. The program may request that a pull-down menu be displayed, for example; the display server draws the menu on the screen at the appropriate location, as determined by its knowledge of the size and location of the window. If the user at the terminal clicks a mouse on a particular menu entry, the server notifies the application that this event has occurred. Figure 16.6 illustrates the operation of an X Window application with a display server.

Although it is unavoidable that the application must still transmit actual image data to the display, the amount of data to be transmitted is considerably reduced. Essentially, the display server can perform many of the basic display operations with very little communication required. WYSIWYG text, for example, requires only that the choice of font, the

FIGURE 16.6

The X Window Client-server Relationship

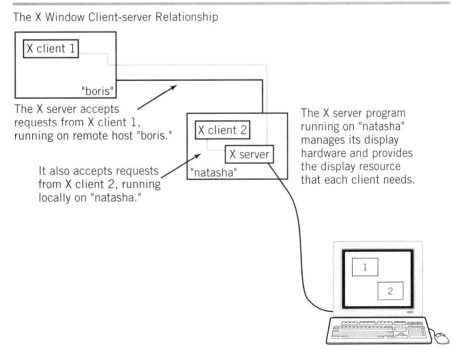

The X server accepts requests from X client 1, running on remote host "boris."

It also accepts requests from X client 2, running locally on "natasha."

The X server program running on "natasha" manages its display hardware and provides the display resource that each client needs.

display location, and the actual text data be transmitted. The font data is stored at the display server. The server also provides a library of all the basic tools and widgets to draw windows, provide drop-down menus, present control buttons, respond to mouse clicks, and many other functions. This method requires far less data communication between the program and the display than if the transmission of actual text images and windows were required.

X Window places no restrictions on the location of the client application; therefore, the application program could reside on the same computer system as the display server or remotely on a different system. Furthermore, the display server can process requests from several different client applications concurrently, each in its own window. You would expect this to be true, since a graphical user interface can have several open windows at one time. This leads to an interesting and exciting possibility: that different windows on a single display could be communicating with application programs on different machines! Indeed, this is the case. The picture in Figure 16.7 illustrates this situation. The window in the upper-left corner is communicating with a program located on the same PC with the display. The PC is running an X Window server under Microsoft Windows. The other windows on the screen are connected to various systems located remotely: a (now ancient) VMS system connected to a local area network and a Sun UNIX workstation connected

FIGURE 16.7

A Multicomputer X Window Display

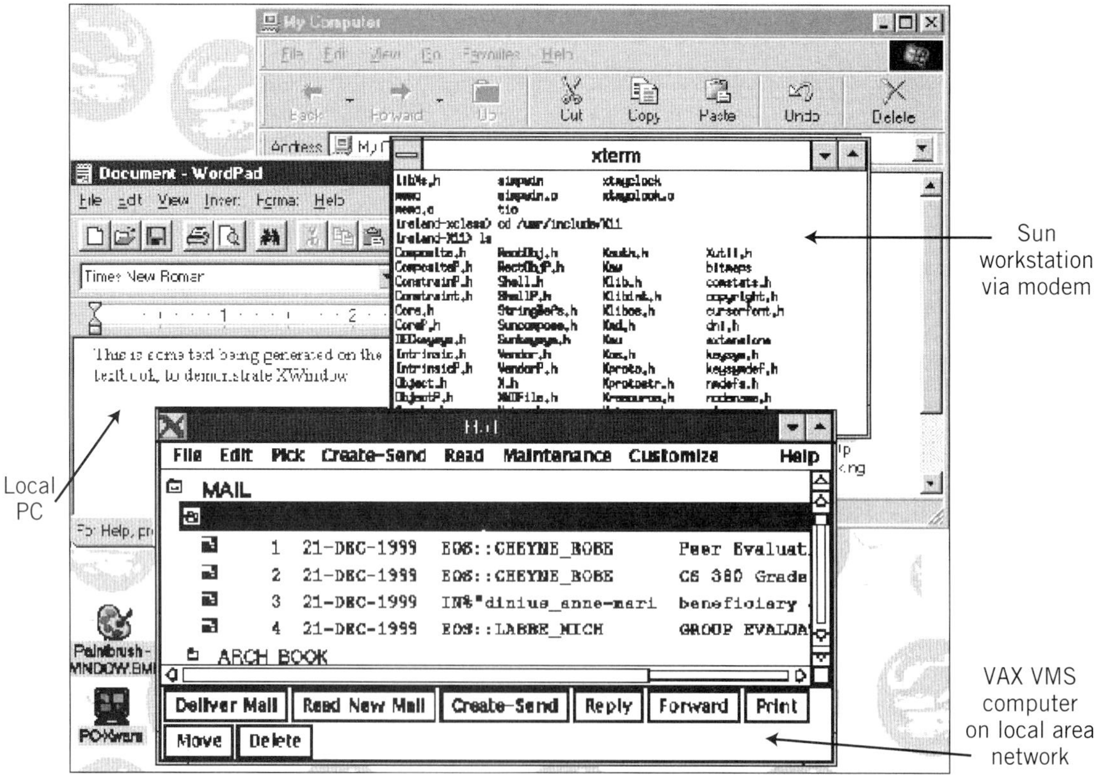

via telephone and modem. This image was taken many years ago, but the X Window technology that created it has changed only in minor details.

As in other windowing systems, the location of the cursor is used to determine the active window.

Notice that the operating system at the display need not be the same as the operating systems where the application programs are running, as long as display server software is available for the particular operating system in use at the display terminal. X Window display server software is available for most operating systems, including UNIX, Linux, Windows, the Macintosh OS, and many others. In fact, an X Window server can even be built into a bare bones display terminal and used with a central processor located elsewhere.

Systems similar to the X Window system also exist at the application level for services such as the Web-based services mentioned previously. Although these systems operate somewhat differently, the concept is quite similar: to produce as much of the display as possible using software located at the display and to minimize the amount of image data to be transmitted. These services provide software, display standard formats such as PNG, PDF, and SVG, and communications protocols, particularly HTML and XML for this purpose, and also store commonly used images and display features at the display site.

16.5 COMMAND AND SCRIPTING LANGUAGES

In early batch systems it was necessary to submit all pieces of a program at one time, including the data and any other programs that were required as part of the operation. Generally, punched cards were used for this purpose.

Suppose you had a COBOL program (it *would* have been COBOL in those days!) that was to be compiled and executed. Your submittal to the computer required the cards that made up the COBOL compiler, the COBOL program itself, perhaps a library of binary math routines that will be called by the program when it is executed, and finally some data for the program. Your submittal also contained commands to the computer telling it what to do with all these cards. (Some of the commands were actually more informational, like "load the following group of cards, which are data for the program that you are running.") The entire submission was known as a *job*.

Later on, the COBOL compiler and math routines became part of the software that was permanently stored on disk within the computer system, but the system still needed to be told what to do, what programs (e.g., the COBOL compiler) to call from the disk, where to find the data, and where to print the results.

As noted, the commands to the computer took the form of punched cards that contained the required information. These cards were called job control cards because they told the computer system how to control the job. The different types of commands made up a sort of language, called **job control language** or, more commonly, **JCL**. In other words, a job consisted of a series of commands in JCL intermixed with the appropriate programs and data.

The best known of these languages is IBM zOS/JCL, but you should be aware that other vendors have their own JCL languages. Generally, there is no compatibility between JCL languages from different vendors, and in fact, there are several different incompatible versions of "IBM JCL". (By the way, you might note that the expression "JCL language", which is in common use, is redundant.) The use of JCL continues to this day. JCL statements are entered into the system with a screen editor and are stored in the system as a file of **card images**, so called because each statement is still laid out as though it were stored on an 80-column card. These card images are usually batched together as a file of commands that is executed in the same way that a program is, except that each line of the "program" is actually a command to the operating system. Operands in each JCL command specify the appropriate files and other details that are required. Both positional and keyword operands are used.

The commands that you use on your computer are not very different from the ones that make up a job control language. After all, a computer is a computer, and the tasks that you do are not really very different from those that are done as part of a batch job. Although you commonly perform command operations one at a time, you can probably think of times when it would have been convenient to combine a group of commands that you could have done all at once. In fact, you may already be aware that there is a way to do this.

As we previously have noted, operating systems provide a way to group commands into a single file that can be executed as if it were a program. The file may itself even contain executable programs. In addition to the usual commands, the operating system provides additional commands that are used specifically for this purpose, commands that allow branching and looping, for example. Figure 16.8 is an example of a Windows command language script that prepares backup for a text file by copying an old version to a flash drive (E:), creating a new backup on hard disk, and then opening the word processor program. The name of the text file is given as an operand when the command file is executed. "%1" is a placeholder for the operand.

Most modern operating systems provide command languages. Perhaps the most elegant implementation of this concept belongs to UNIX. In addition to the usual commands, the UNIX and Linux shells contain a set of powerful utility commands and other features that allow the creation of very sophisticated command programs. In UNIX and Linux, shell scripts are a fundamental way of getting work done. Shell scripts can be executed just as if they were programs, and in fact, due to the power of the shell script language, it is frequently possible to avoid writing a normal program by using a shell script instead.

FIGURE 16.8

Windows Program DOWP

```
@echo
if '%1' == '' go to error
if not exist %1 goto error
if not exist %1.txt goto newtxt
if exist %1.old copy %1.old e:\%.arc
copy %1.txt %1.old
wordproc %1.txt
goto end
:newtxt
echo This is a new file. Opening word processor....
wordproc
goto end
:error
echo proper command format is 'dowp filname'
echo with no extension.
:end
```

FIGURE 16.9

The Linux Airport Distance Shell Script

```
export city state lat long port
grep -i "$1 $2" townfile ¦ read city state lat long port
if [ -z "$city" ] then
    echo "this city is not in the file"
elif [ "$port" = "y" ] then
    echo " $city $state has its own airport"
else
    awk '
    BEGIN {close = 10000}
    $5 == "y" {dist = ($3 - '$lat')*($3 - $lat')+($4 - '$long')*($4 - '$long')
        if (dist < close) {
            close = dist
            ccity = $1
            cstate = $2 } }
    END   {print ( "the nearest airport is in " ccity, cstate)
        print ( " approximate distance is " 60* sqrt (close) " miles")
        } ' townfile
fi
```

A typical line in townfile:

```
Boston MA 42.3333 71.083 y
```

You've already seen an example of a Windows command language script that assists the user in performing a routine computer task. Many Linux operating system operations are, in fact, shell scripts. Shell scripts often can be used in place of a conventional program, as well. The example shown in Figure 16.9 is a UNIX Bourne shell program that determines the nearest major airport to an arbitrary city entered by the user.

Scripting languages are expanded forms of command languages, often encompassing features well beyond those found in a standard command language. Some scripting languages even provide portability between different operating systems. Perl, Javascript, PHP, and Python are examples of portable scripting languages.

The Elements of a Command Language

Like any programming language, there are certain elements in a command language that affect the usefulness of the language. The choice of commands and utilities is an important consideration, but it is not the only consideration. There are other features that enhance the value of a language. These are some of the most important features of a command language:

- The ability to print messages on the screen and to accept input from the user into the script.
- The ability to specify variables and a method to assign and change the value for those variables.

- The ability to branch and loop. Notice that the ability to change variable values is important as a means of controlling branches and ending loops.
- The ability to specify arguments with the command that executes the program and to transfer those arguments into parameters and variables within the program. The command script in Figure 16.8 uses this technique to allow the user to specify the name of the file to be backed up.
- The ability to detect an error that results from a command and recover from it in a graceful way. If the operating system attaches numerical values to its errors, the command program can make decisions and branch based on the level of error. This could be used to determine if a particular file or a particular hardware component exists, for example.

The Command Language Start-up Sequence Files

A major use for a command language is the system start-up file. Most modern operating systems allow the execution of specific command files at system start-up and also when a user logs in to the system. Two types of start-up files exist. One type is used to configure the basic operating system, as we discussed in Chapter 15. Start-up configuration files are only modified by the system administrator.

The second type of start-up file is used to tailor the system to the user's preferences. User start-up commands can be used to set various parameters, such as the preferred places to look for files, the type of terminal that the user is working with, the selection of a **command shell**, and the appearance of the command line prompt. On a system shared by many users, the user start-up command file can be tailored to each individual user. It is executed whenever a user logs in. Login start-up files for a UNIX system depend on the default shell being used for the system. The Bourne shell start-up script is called *.login;* the C-shell script is called *.cshrc*. Since these files are text files, they can be easily communicated across a network to provide uniform capability to all users on the network. This allows a system administrator to change every user's profile with the modification of a single file.

16.6 SERVICES TO PROGRAMS

Most of the discussion in this chapter has centered around the user interface and methods of controlling and using the interface, but we would be remiss if we did not say a few additional words about services provided by the operating system to application programs that support and affect the user interface. As we noted in Chapter 15, operating systems have long provided services to application programs in the areas of file management, I/O processing, and system resource management. A few operating systems, particularly the Macintosh OS, have provided services such as the ToolBox that extend these capabilities to include the graphical user interface. Services outside the operating system, but not quite applications either, such as X Window, extend graphical capabilities to other systems.

Windows provides similar services through the Win32 API. These services reflect the trend to expand the role of the operating system generally to include services and support to application programs and users that provide many capabilities that were formerly within the applications themselves. As we noted earlier, these services enable the system to provide a standard look and feel for different applications extending, even, to the Web interface. They simplify and extend the graphic capabilities of application programs, they improve the capability of programs to communicate with each other and to pass data from one application to another, they provide the ability to launch an application program from within another, they provide e-mail and other communication capabilities, and they provide document and graphical storage services at a more sophisticated level than was found previously in traditional OS file management facilities.

By integrating these capabilities into the operating system, the system can assure that every application program responds in similar ways to user actions. Integration also provides smooth and seamless interaction between the different applications. Just as the file manager assures a consistent representation and interface for file manipulation across different devices, so these new services provide the user with a more powerful and easier to use way to access his program applications. The overall effect is an increased emphasis on the user interface and new ways of working that are more oriented toward the work to be accomplished and less to the launching and manipulation of application programs. Although many of these tools are found in a "shell", they are more tightly integrated into the operating system than was true of previous shells.

The addition of new operating system services is intimately tied to improved programming methods, particularly object-oriented programming. These services commonly take the form of libraries of objects that application programs request via the usual call mechanisms. Several standards continue to evolve for these services. Standards are necessary so that applications may be developed with the assurance that the services required will be available. The most important of these standards include DCOM, .NET, and CORBA. The dividing line between the operating system and the application programs has become increasingly unclear, as the operating system moves into a realm that has traditionally been part of the application programs themselves. The use of the Web browser as a primary user interface provides a common look and feel that extends all the way from local file management to Web-based business applications to the services of the Web. Perhaps these services will be considered part of a new OS layer, called application program services, or perhaps the operating system itself will be divided differently, into user services and a kernel that provides just the basic internal services. Some researchers and operating system designers envision a model consisting of a small operating system extended by objects that support the user's applications. This approach suggests the growing operating system emphasis on the user environment and on application integration.

Overall, the effect on the user's interaction with the computer has changed dramatically in the last few years and promises to change even more profoundly in the future. Presently, the user performs her work by opening applications and working within those applications. The concepts of *suites* of applications, at the application program level, and of object linking, at the system level, extend this capability to allow the applications to communicate, to share data, and to perform operations within an application by launching another application. The additional capabilities envisioned for software at the system level, whether considered part of the operating system or another type of interface shell, will expand this process and ultimately can be expected to shift the user's focus almost entirely to the document, data set, or other work entity, with applications launched invisibly as they are required to accomplish a particular task.

SUMMARY AND REVIEW

Modern operating systems provide an interface that is used by programs and by the user to interact with the system. The interface provides a variety of user and program services, including a user interface with command capability, program execution and control capability, I/O and file services for programs and for users, command languages for building programs of commands, system information, security features, and interuser communication and file sharing capability. An application programming interface (API) provides a standard set of services that application programs use to access the operating system and to provide a common look and feel to their user interfaces. In this chapter we considered each of these services.

Most systems are primarily interactive. For this purpose there are currently two primary types of user interface, the command line interface and the graphical user interface, each with its own advantages and disadvantages. Similar operations can be performed with each, although the method employed is different for each. For users with limited needs, a Web-based interface is often a more suitable and productive means of access to the system.

X Window is an important graphical display methodology, particularly in networked and distributed environments. X Window is an attempt to provide windowing capability while partially solving the difficulty of transmitting large quantities of graphical data from one location to another. X Window is built around a client-server architecture.

Command languages allow a user to build more powerful functions out of the command set. Most command languages provide looping and selection capability, as well as interactive input and output. Some command languages are intended for batch processing. IBM's zOS/JCL is an important example of a batch language.

FOR FURTHER READING

A general book that discusses the user interface in great detail is Sharp [SHAR07]. Marcus and colleagues [MARC95] provide an easy-to-read discussion and comparison of graphical user interfaces. There are several others listed in the references, including Weinschenk [WEIN97], Tidwell [TIDW06], and Tufte [TUFT90]. There are also numerous books on Web design, a related topic not included here. The general operating system aspects of the user interface and program services can be found in any of the operating system texts identified in Chapter 15. The X Window system is introduced well in Christian and Richter [CHRI94] and presented in much more detail in many books, including Mansfield [MANS93] or Jones [JONE00].

KEY CONCEPTS AND TERMS

access control list
   (ACL)
active window
application association
application program
   interface (API)

batch program
card image
click to focus
command language
command line interface
   (CLI)

command shell
common look and feel
controls
CORBA (Common Object
   Request Broker
   Architecture)

DCOM (Distributed
     Component Object
     Model)
desktop
display server
dock
drag-and-drop
Finder
gadget
graphical user interface
     (GUI)
icon
intranet

job control language (JCL)
keyword operand
launch
menu bar
modifier
mount a device
mouse focus
.NET
operand
path variable
positional operand
Remote Procedure Call
     (RPC)

screen
scripting language
(shell) script
switch
task bar
title bar
unmount a device
volume
widget
wild card
window
X Window

READING REVIEW QUESTIONS

16.1   What is the primary purpose for a user interface?

16.2   What is the advantage of offering the same user interface for applications, user programs, and commands?

16.3   Discuss the major tradeoffs between a command line interface and a graphical user interface.

16.4   What effect does the quality of a user interface have on the use and productivity of a computer?

16.5   Describe the format of a CLI command. What is an *operand*? What is the difference between a *keyword* operand and a *positional* operand?

16.6   Describe the user interface provided by a CLI command shell.

16.7   What is the purpose of a *command language* or *scripting language*?

16.8   In addition to the commands themselves, command languages provide additional capabilities that are important when a user is not directly involved in the control and execution of each command. Name at least three features that are necessary to make a command language useful.

16.9   Sketch or "print screen" a typical GUI screen. Label each of the major components on the screen.

16.10   Although Web-based user interfaces are somewhat limited when compared to CLIs and GUIs, their use in organizations has grown and continues to grow. What advantages do Web interfaces offer over CLIs and GUIs?

EXERCISES

16.1   Discuss the advantages and disadvantages of providing the user interface as a separate shell, rather than as an integral part of the operating system.

16.2   List and explain some definite advantages to the use of a command line interface over other types of interfaces. Do the same for a graphical user interface. Do the same for a Web-based interface. What is the target audience for each type of interface?

16.3   There are some capabilities that are easy to achieve with a GUI, but much more difficult with a CLI. Describe a few of these capabilities.

16.4   If you have access to two or more command line interface shells, such as Windows and Linux *bash* or Linux *bash* and *tcsh*, compare the major commands that are available on each. Note the similarities and differences between them, particularly in their capabilities and in the way the command task is performed.

16.5   Explain the concept of redirection. Illustrate your answer with an example of a situation where redirection would be useful.

16.6   Consider the major commands in a command line interface system such as the Linux *bash* shell. Explain how each task would be performed on a graphical user interface system such as Windows or the Macintosh.

16.7   Explain piping. What additional capability does piping add to a command language?

16.8   The designers of the UNIX operating system described the ideal shell command language as one that is made up of a large set of simple commands, each designed to perform one specialized task well. They also provided various means to combine these simple commands to form more powerful commands.

    a.   What tools are provided to combine the commands?

    b.   What are the advantages of this approach over providing a smaller set of much more powerful commands? What are the disadvantages?

    c.   If you know something about the UNIX or Linux command set, discuss the characteristics of UNIX/Linux commands that make it easier to combine these commands powerfully.

16.9   What purpose do arguments serve in a batch file or shell script?

16.10   If you could design a "wild card" system with features beyond those normally provided in a CLI, what features would you add?

16.11   Use the batch file or shell script capability of your system to build a menuing interface that implements the most common commands that you use.

16.12   Identify the name and purpose of each of the components of the GUI that you use.

16.13   When people describe client-server architecture, they are usually referring to a system in which a large server is serving a client on a PC. With X Window, the reverse is frequently the case. Explain.

16.14   Describe the difficulties that exist in providing a GUI at a location remote from the computer that is creating the display. Describe the methods used by X Window to partially overcome these difficulties. Why is it not possible for X Window to totally solve these problems?

16.15   Discuss the advantages that result from the client-server architecture of the X Window system.

CHAPTER 17

FILE MANAGEMENT

Thomas Sperling

17.0 INTRODUCTION

Most direct interactions between the user and the computer involve significant use of the file management system layer of the operating system. From the perspective of the user, the file management system is one of the most important and visible features of the operating system. Most user commands, whether typed into a command line interface (CLI) or activated with a mouse, are operations on files. Many interactions between programs and the operating system are file requests. When a user retrieves a document file using the drop-down file menu in a word processor, the word processor program is using the services of the operating system file manager to retrieve the document file. Even the database management application software requires the services of the file management system to perform its file storage and retrieval operations. It is the file management system software that allows users and programs to store, retrieve, and manipulate files as logical entities, rather than as physical blocks of binary data. Because of its importance and visibility to the user, we have chosen to discuss the file management system separately from the rest of the operating system.

We begin this chapter by reviewing the differences between the logical, or user, view of a file and the physical requirements of its storage and retrieval. Next, we show how the file management system accomplishes its mission of providing a logical file view to the user and the user's programs. You will see how logical file system requests are mapped to physical files. You will see how files are physically stored and retrieved, and how the logical file commands that you issue to the operating system are implemented. You will see some of the trade-offs that must be made as a result of specific user and program requirements and the limitations of different file storage methods. You will understand how a directory system works and read about some of the different methods that are used by file systems to keep track of and locate files and directories. You will see how the file manager finds and allocates space for files, and how it reclaims and keeps track of space vacated when a file is moved or deleted.

We hope that, as a result of the discussion in this chapter, you will be able to use and manage computer file systems more effectively.

17.1 THE LOGICAL AND PHYSICAL VIEW OF FILES

Whether on computer or paper, a file is an organized collection of data. The organization of the file depends on the use of the data and is determined by the program or user who created the file. Similarly, the meaning of the data in the file is established by the program or user. A computer file may be as simple as a single data stream that represents an entire program to be loaded at one time or a collection of text data read sequentially, or as complex as a database made up of individual records, each with many fields and subfields, to be retrieved one or a few records at a time in some random order.

Nearly all data in the computer is stored and retrieved as files. Thus, files may take many different forms. Here are a few examples of common forms files might take:

- A program file consisting of binary data; the bytes of data in the file represent the sequence of instructions that make up a program. The file is stored on a device such as disk and is loaded sequentially into succeeding locations in memory for execution.

- A data file consisting of alphanumeric Unicode text that represents a program in source code form and will serve as "data" input to a C++ compiler.

- A data file consisting of a sequence of numbers stored in ASCII format and separated by delimiters that will be used as input to a program that does data analysis.

- A data file consisting of a mixture of alphanumeric ASCII characters and special binary codes that represents a text file for a word processor or spreadsheet.

- A data file consisting of alphanumeric Unicode characters representing records made up of names, addresses, and accounting information applicable to a business database.

- A data file configured in some special way to represent an image, sound, or other object. Several examples of these types of files were illustrated in Chapter 4.

- A directory file consisting of information about other files.

One common file representation views a file **logically** as a collection of **records**, each made up of a number of **fields**. A typical record-oriented file is shown in Figure 17.1. In this illustration, each record is made up of the same fields, and each field is the same fixed length for all records, but these restrictions are not necessarily valid in all cases. Some fields may not be required for certain records. The company personnel file shown in Figure 17.2 does not require the salary field for retired employees. This file also uses a field of comments. The comments field is a variable-length field, so that more comments can be added when necessary. This figure also shows that the file may appear differently, without affecting the record structure underneath. The layout shown in Figure 17.1 is sometimes called a **table image**, while the layout in Figure 17.2 is referred to as a **form image**.

Describing a file by its records and fields represents the file logically; that is, it represents the file the way the user views it. The logical view may or may not be related to the **physical view** of the file, the way in which the data is actually stored. Most commonly, the data

FIGURE 17.1

A Typical File

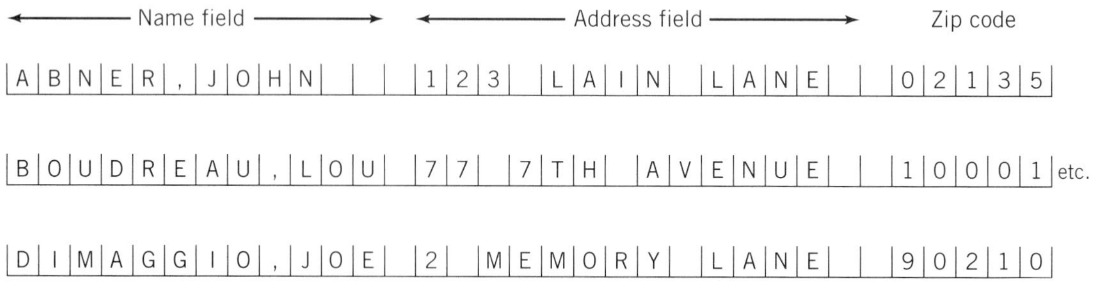

FIGURE 17.2

Database File—Form Image

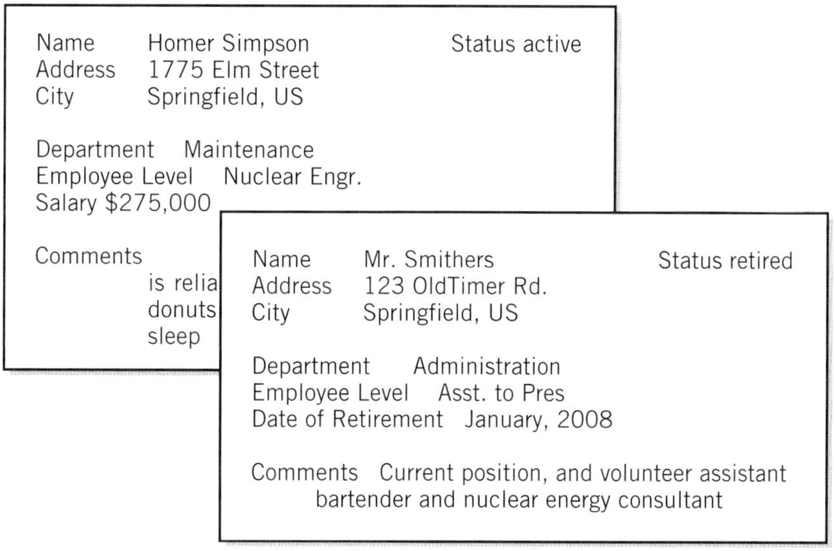

```
Name        Homer Simpson              Status active
Address     1775 Elm Street
City        Springfield, US

Department    Maintenance
Employee Level    Nuclear Engr.
Salary $275,000

Comments
            is relia
            donuts
            sleep

                    Name        Mr. Smithers              Status retired
                    Address     123 OldTimer Rd.
                    City        Springfield, US

                    Department      Administration
                    Employee Level    Asst. to Pres
                    Date of Retirement   January, 2008

                    Comments   Current position, and volunteer assistant
                                bartender and nuclear energy consultant
```

is stored in physical **blocks** on a disk. The blocks are of fixed size, say, 512 bytes. Just as there is no reason to assume that a paper record will fit exactly on a single sheet of paper, there is no reason to assume that the size of the logical records within the computer file corresponds to the physical in any particular way, although on some computer systems it may. This is an issue to which we shall return shortly.

Consider again, for example, the file shown in Figure 17.1. Another representation of this file, more akin to the means used physically for its storage, is shown in Figure 17.3. As another example, the program file mentioned earlier could be interpreted as a single-record, single-field logical file, with one long variable field in the record. Physically, the file might be stored as a sequence of physical blocks, accessed one after another to retrieve the program. Many word processors also treat files this way. Files of these types are frequently loaded entirely into memory as a single unit.

Different file management systems exhibit a range of capabilities in the ways in which they represent files logically. Some operating systems recognize and manipulate several different types of files and record structures, while others simply treat all files as streams

FIGURE 17.3

Yet Another File Representation

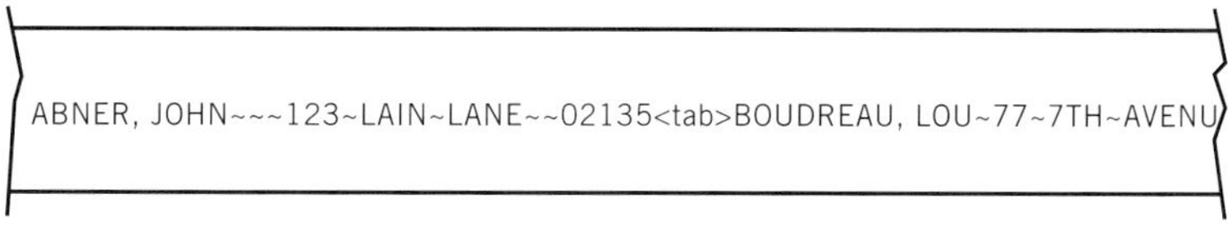

```
ABNER, JOHN~~~123~LAIN~LANE~~02135<tab>BOUDREAU, LOU~77~7TH~AVENU
```

of bytes and leave it to utility and application programs to determine the meaning of the data within the file. The file managers in Linux and Windows, for example, differentiate only between directories and byte stream files. On these systems, program and data files are treated identically by the file manager. You may have seen this as a result of using a command that displays the contents of a file on the screen, such as *cat* or TYPE or MORE, with a program file. Since the program file can contain any combination of bytes, including control characters, the result on the screen is gibberish. IBM z/OS represents the opposite extreme, providing detailed record management within its file management system.

There are good arguments for either approach. It would certainly be reasonable to interpret the program and word processing files mentioned above as a single stream of bytes, for example. Furthermore, we note that the structure of files can be complex, and every one is different. Treating all files in a similar way simplifies the file management programs, while at the same time adding flexibility to the application programs and utilities, since each application program can define the contents of its files in any way convenient to meet its own needs. Input and output redirection is simplified, since all data is treated in the same way, as a stream of bytes. The same is true for the use of program pipes, as described in Chapter 16.

Conversely, treating all files as a stream of bytes requires significantly more effort on the design of application and utility programs. Retrieval of data in the "middle of the stream", for example, is more difficult when the application program must keep track of its position in the file. A file management system that imposes well-designed standards on its files can simplify data storage and retrieval and simplify application program design, without severely limiting application flexibility.

As a practical matter, much of the data that is useful to a user is logically represented in record form. Data files whose records are always retrieved in sequence from the beginning of the file are known as **sequential files**. Some applications require that records be retrievable from anywhere in the file in a random sequence. These are known as **random access files**, or sometimes as **relative access files**, since the location is frequently specified relative to the beginning of the file. (We want the twenty-fifth record, for example.) One common method for retrieving records randomly from a file uses one field, known as the **key field**, as an index to identify the proper record. The key field in Figure 17.2 might be employee's name, since the file is alphabetized by name.

There are other methods of retrieving particular records from within a file. Some of these are discussed in Section 17.3. For now, it is only important that you be aware that, for certain types of files, it is necessary for either the file management system or the application program to be able to locate and access individual records from within the file.

In addition to the data within the file, it is convenient to attach attributes to the file that identify and characterize the file. The most important file attribute, obviously, is its name. The name itself may be specified in such a way as to allow identification with a particular type of file (usually known as a **file extension**); it may also be expanded to identify the file with a particular group of files or a particular storage device. In Windows, for example, the expanded name

```
D:\GROUPA\PROG31.CPP
```

identifies the file (if the user chose an appropriate name!) as a C++ program named PROG31, stored together in a group of files known as GROUPA, and located on the

DVD-ROM inserted into disk drive D:. The file extension may be important only to the user, or it may be required by the operating system or by an application program, to activate the correct application programs, for example. The extension .EXE, for example, notifies Windows that the file is an executable file. Similarly, the file extension may or may not be relevant to the file management system.

In addition to the name, the file can be characterized in various other useful ways. A file may be executable, as a program, or readable, as data. A file may be considered to be either binary or alphanumeric (although, of course, even alphanumeric characters are actually stored in binary form). The file may be characterized by the way data is to be retrieved. A file might be temporary or permanent. A file might be writeable or write-protected. There are other possibilities.

Files may also have such attributes as the date of origination, the most recent update, and information about who has the right to access, update, and delete the file. Some systems allow a data file to specify the program it is to be used with. This property is called an **association**. In such a case, calling the data file automatically loads and starts the associated program file. For example, Windows uses the file extension to create the necessary association. Other operating systems may store the association as a property of the data file.

The previous discussion has focused on the logical view of a file, the meaning of its contents and its attributes as viewed by the user, operating system utilities, and application programs. All the files, plus all the attributes and information describing those files, are stored, controlled, and manipulated by the file management system.

The physical view of a file is the way in which the file is actually stored within the computer system. We have already indicated that the physical view of a file may look very different from the file's logical view.

Physically, the file on nearly every system is stored and manipulated as a group of blocks. The blocks on a disk are normally of fixed size, typically 256, 512, or 1024 bytes. Some systems refer to a group of one or more blocks as a **cluster**.[1] The block or cluster will correspond to one or more sectors on a single track or cylinder. The block or cluster is the smallest unit that the file management system can store or retrieve in a single read or write operation.

There is, of course, no direct correlation between the logical size of a record and the physical block or cluster—the logical record size is designed by the programmer or user for the particular application and may actually be of variable size; the physical block is fixed as a part of the computer system design.

A file may fit entirely within a single physical block or cluster, or it may require several blocks or clusters. The file management system may pack the file into physical blocks without regard to the logical records, as shown in Figure 17.4a, or it may attempt to maintain some relationship between the logical records and physical blocks, as shown in Figure 17.4b. Logical records may be packed several to a physical record, or may be larger than a physical record and require several physical records for each logical record.

A minimum of one full block is required for a file, even if the file only contains a single byte of data. Depending on the file management system design, and perhaps on attributes of the file, the blocks that hold a particular file may be *contiguous*, that is, stored together, or may be scattered all over the disk or tape, *noncontiguously*.

---

[1] Note that a disk cluster is not related to a computer system cluster. Same word, totally different meaning.

FIGURE 17.4

The Relationship Between Logical and Physical Records

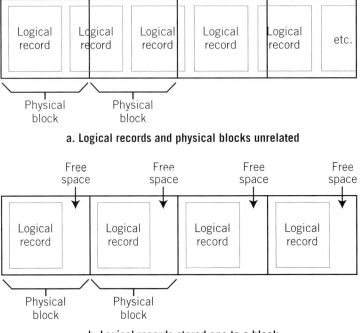

a. Logical records and physical blocks unrelated

b. Logical records stored one to a block

The physical block or cluster size is a compromise between file access speed and wasted space. If the blocks are too small, then most files will require several disk reads or writes to retrieve or store the data, as well as considerable space to keep track of usage of each block. Conversely, if the block size is too large, there will be a large amount of unused space at the end of many, perhaps most, blocks.

Note that it is the logical view that gives the data in a file meaning. Physically, the file is simply a collection of bits stored in blocks. It is the file management system that establishes the connection between the logical and physical representations of the file. Tape organization is somewhat different. Most tape systems use a variable size block, so it is possible to store a file exactly, with no internal fragmentation. Furthermore, some file management systems separate logical records into different blocks, making it possible to record individual records on tape.

17.2 THE ROLE OF THE FILE MANAGEMENT SYSTEM

The file management system is commonly called the **file manager**. In this text, we will primarily use the term "file manager", so please remember we are talking about a software program, *not a person*! The file manager acts as a transparent interface between the user's logical view of the file system and the computer's physical reality of disk sectors, tracks, and clusters, tape blocks, and other I/O vagaries. It provides a consistent set of commands and a consistent view of files to the user regardless of the file type, file characteristics, choice of physical device, or physical storage requirements. It translates those commands to a form appropriate for the device and carries out the required operation. To do so, it maintains **directory** structures for each device. These, too, are presented in logical form to the user and to the user's programs.

User file commands and program file requests are interpreted by the command shell, then passed in logical form as requests to the file manager. Program requests are made directly to the file manager. These requests commonly take the form of OPEN, READ, WRITE, MOVE FILE POINTER, RESET POINTER TO BEGINNING OF FILE, or CLOSE, and other similar procedure calls.

The file manager checks the validity of the requests and then translates the requests into the appropriate physical course of action. The directory system assists in the location and organization of the file. When required, the file manager makes specific I/O data transfer requests to the I/O device handler layer for execution of the transfer. Upon completion of the request, the directory is updated, if necessary, and control is returned to the command shell or program. A general view of the process is illustrated in Figure 17.5.

FIGURE 17.5

File Manager Request Handling

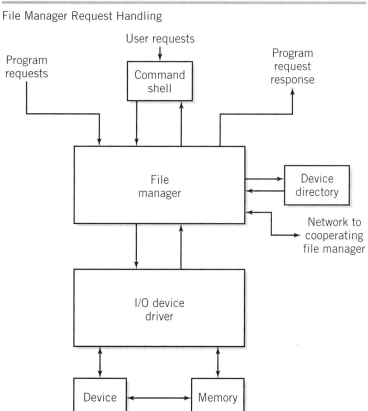

As a specific example of this process, consider what occurs within the operating system when the user of a typical system types the command

```
COPY D:\FILEX TO C:
```

(or moves the FILEX icon with a mouse to the C: drawer on a system with a graphical command interface—the operation is the same).

The following sequence of steps takes place. (Although this description seems long, the steps are reasonable and should not be too difficult to follow):

1. The command interface interprets the command and determines that a copy of FILEX on device D: is to be made and stored on device C:. The command shell passes the request to the file manager. Typically, the shell will request that the file manager open FILEX on D: and create FILEX on C:.

2. The file manager looks in the directory for device D: to find a file named FILEX. If it succeeds, the file manager reserves a block of space in memory, called a memory buffer, large enough to hold one or more physical blocks of data from the file.

3. Next, the file manager looks in the device C: directory to determine if there is enough free space to fit the file. If there is, the file manager adds FILEX to the directory and assigns enough blocks to the file for storage of the file.

4. The shell is informed that these requests succeeded. It now requests that the file manager read a block from D:FILEX. The file manager requests that the data from the first block or group of blocks from FILEX be read into the memory buffer. This request is addressed to the I/O device handler for device D:.

5. The device D: I/O device handler completes the transfer and notifies the file manager that the requested data is in the memory buffer.

6. The file manager now passes on a request that the data in the memory buffer be transferred to the first block or group of blocks that it assigned to C:FILEX. This request is addressed to the I/O device handler for device C:. (If device D: and device C: are the same type of device, both disks for example, the same I/O handler may service both devices.)

7. The last three steps are repeated until the file copy is complete. Some systems allow the user to specify the size of the memory buffer. Note that the use of a larger memory buffer can make the copy operation for a large file much faster by limiting the number of individual I/O transfers.

8. The file manager returns control to the command interface with an internal message to the command shell to indicate that the copy was successful.

If device D: is actually located somewhere on a network, rather than on the local machine, a number of additional substeps are required. The OS network services on both machines must be invoked to request services from the file manager on the machine where the file is located, the data is retrieved into a buffer on the remote machine using the I/O device driver, and the network drivers are used to move the data across the network to the buffer on the local machine; overall, these additional activities do not significantly alter the procedure decribed here, however.

The COPY operation is typical of requests made to the file manager. You are probably familiar with many others. Most user commands to the operating system are actually requests to the file manager.

Consider the operations on a file that a file management system would perform. These operations can be divided into three different categories of operations: those that work on the entire file, those that operate on data within the file, and those that actually manipulate the directory of the file without actually accessing the file itself.

The following examples of operations that work on the file as a whole are likely to be familiar to you as a user:

- Copy a file
- Load and execute a (program) file
- Move a file (assuming the move is to a different device)
- List or print a file
- Load a file into memory
- Store a file from memory
- Compile or assemble a file
- Append data from memory to a file

Fundamental to every file manager, both stream- and record-based, is the ability to manipulate the data within the file itself. The file manager provides a basic set of operations that are used for this purpose. These operations probably seem less familiar to you as a user. That is because they are usually requested by a program, rather than directly by the user.

- Open a file for reading or writing. This procedure provides a buffer for holding the data as it is read or written and also creates a pointer that moves through the data as it is read or written.
- Read a number of bytes from the file. The number of bytes can be specified as part of the request, or it may be indicated by a delimiter, such as a carriage return or comma, depending on the system.
- Write a number of bytes to the file.
- Move the file pointer a distance forward or backward.
- "Rewind" the pointer to the beginning of the file.
- Close the file.

A file management system that provides support for individual record storage and retrieval includes additional operations. The following are examples of record-based operations. These operations can be performed either sequentially or randomly, depending on the nature of the file, the capabilities of the file manager, and the particular application:

- Read (retrieve) a record
- Write (store) a record
- Add a record to a file
- Delete a record from a file
- Change the contents of a record

These operations manipulate the file directory, rather than the file itself:

- Delete a file
- Rename a file
- Append one file to another (known as concatenation)
- Create a new (empty) file. On some systems this operation will assign a block to the file even though the file is empty
- Move a file from one directory to another on the same physical device

It is often convenient to operate on a group of files together, for example, to copy all the files whose names begin with *assign* from your hard drive to a floppy disk for backup purposes. One way to do this is to organize your files in such a way that they are grouped into different areas of the disk. As we will discuss later, most systems provide a subdirectory structure for doing this.

An alternative method provided by most systems is the use of **wild cards** to identify a group of files. Wild cards are replacements for letters or groups of letters in a file name. When used with a command, they can identify a group of files whose names qualify when the wild card is substituted for some of the letters in the name. The most common wild cards in use are "?" which replaces any single letter in a file name, and "*" which replaces a group of zero or more letters that can be any letters that are legal in a file name. With one exception, the examples that follow work the same in UNIX or at a Windows command line prompt.

EXAMPLES

ASSIGN?.DAT will find files ASSIGN1.DAT and ASSIGNX.DAT, but will ignore ASSIGN.DAT, ASSIGN1.TXT, and ASSIGN12.DAT.

ASSIGN*.DAT will find ASSIGN.DAT, ASSIGNXQ.DAT, and ASSIGN12.DAT, but not ASSIGN2.TXT.

DE.DAT will find HOWDEDOO.DAT, ADAMBEDE.DAT, and DESIREE.DAT.

. will find every Windows file, even if there is no extension. It will find the UNIX file textfile., but not the file textfile, because the latter has no dot in it.

UNIX provides an additional wild card form, "[choices]". For example, [aeiou] would look for a file name with a single letter a, e, i, o, or u in the given position. [a-zA-Z]* would accept zero or more uppercase or lowercase letters, but no numbers, in the given position.

In addition, many systems provide file utilities within the command structure that call upon the file management system for support. Sort utilities sort the records within a file by key field or by some other positional indicator. Some sort utilities load the entire file into memory, while others retrieve and store records one by one. In both cases, the file management system is used to perform the actual file and record retrieval and storage. Other examples of utilities commonly provided include utilities to merge two files record by record and to compare two files record by record.

The file management system is directly responsible for all aspects of the maintenance of the file system. This requires the file system to perform five major functions:

- The file management system provides the connection between the logical file system with its physical implementation, allowing the physical view to remain essentially invisible. It creates a logical view for the user, masks the physical view, and provides the mapping between the two views. Stating this more informally, the user requests a file by name, and the file is retrieved; the user does not know where the file is actually stored, nor does he or she care.

- The file management system maintains the directory structure for each I/O device in use. It also maintains a record of available space for each device and assigns and reclaims physical space as required to meet the needs of file storage.

- The file management system supports manipulation of the data within the file. For some systems, it can identify, locate, and manipulate individual records or individual blocks within a file, possibly for several different methods of file access. For others, the manipulation is limited to reads, writes, and the movement of a pointer.

- The file management system acts as an interface for the transfer of data to and from the various I/O devices by requesting transfers from the I/O device driver level of the operating system. It also assigns buffer spaces in memory to hold the data being transferred. The actual transfer, and the interface between the physical device and the operating system, is handled by the appropriate I/O device driver.

- The file system manages file security and protection. It attempts to protect the integrity of files and prevent corruption. It provides a mechanism to control access to files. There are several different types of access control in use. These are discussed in Section 17.7.

Summing up the operation, the file manager receives requests from the utility/command layer of the operating system or from application programs, determines the course of action, and attempts to fulfill the request. In those cases that require data transfer to or from an I/O device, the file manager will issue a request to the appropriate I/O device driver in the next inner layer to perform the actual I/O transfer. The file manager specifies the physical block to be transferred, the direction of the transfer, and the memory location to be used, but the actual transfer is performed by the I/O device driver.

There are two powerful advantages in separating the file and I/O functions into different tasks.

1. When new I/O devices are added, or the device is changed, it is necessary only to replace the I/O driver for that device. The file system remains unchanged. The idea of changing an I/O device driver is familiar to you if you have ever installed a new printer, video card, or disk drive for your PC.

2. A command request to redirect data is easy to implement, since the file manager controls the file. The file manager simply directs the binary data to a different I/O driver.

In general, the file manager is responsible for, and assumes the chore of, organizing, locating, accessing, and manipulating files and file data and managing space for different devices and file types. The file manager takes requests as its input, selects the device, determines the appropriate format, and handles the request. It uses the services of the I/O device layer to perform actual transfers of data between the devices and memory.

17.3 LOGICAL FILE ACCESS METHODS

There are a number of different ways in which to access the data in a file. The method used reflects both the structure of the file and the way in which the data is to be used. For example, a program file made up of executable code will be read as a whole into memory. A file made up of inventory data records will often be accessed one record at a time, in some random order queried to the system. As we have already seen, some file management systems support a number of different formats, while others leave the structuring and formatting of data within a file to the application programs and utilities that use the file.

It is beyond the scope of this textbook to discuss file access methods in any detail. That material is better left to a file and data structures text. To an extent, however, the access method used affects the ways in which the file may be stored physically. For example, a file in which variable-sized records must be accessed in random order is not conveniently stored on tape, where the system must wind from the beginning of the tape to find the desired record. An overview of file access methods will serve to pinpoint the requirements of physical file storage.

Sequential File Access

Nearly every file management system supports **sequential file access**. Files that are accessed sequentially represent the great majority of all files. Sequential files include programs in both source and binary form, text files, and many data files. Information in a sequential file is simply processed in order of storage. If the file is record-oriented, records are processed as they are stored. A file pointer maintains the current position in the file. For read operations, the data is read into a buffer, and the pointer is moved forward into position for the next read. For write operations, the new data is appended to the end of the file. The pointer always points to the end. Most systems allow resetting the pointer to the beginning of the file. This operation is often referred to as *rewind*, because of its similarity to a tape operation. Some systems also allow the pointer to be moved a fixed amount. This operation is sometimes called *seek*. Sequential access is based on a tape model, since files on tape can only be read sequentially.

A file that is always read in its entirety is clearly accessed sequentially. Sequential access is fast, since no seek is required to find each succeeding record. Appending new records to the end of the file is also easy. On the other hand, it is not possible to add a record in the middle of a file accessed sequentially without rewriting at least all the succeeding records. This is a severe disadvantage in some situations.

Random Access

Random access assumes that a file is made up of fixed length logical records. The file manager can go directly to any record, in any order, and can read or write records in place without affecting any other record.

Some systems rely on the application to determine the logical block number where data is to be accessed. Others provide mechanisms for selecting locations based on a number of different possible criteria: for example, sequenced alphabetically on a key, sequenced in order of the time of entry, or calculated mathematically from the data itself. The most common method used is called **hashing**. Hashing is based on some simple mathematical algorithm that calculates a logical record number somewhere within the permissible range of record numbers. The range is based on the anticipated number of records in the file.

Hashing is very effective when the number of records is relatively small compared to the overall capacity of the file. However, hashing depends on the idea that the algorithm will result in a unique record number for each record. As the file fills, this becomes less and less probable. A **collision** occurs when two different records calculate to the same logical record number. Collisions must be detected by the file manager to prevent erroneous results. This is done by comparing the key used for hashing with that stored in the file. When a collision occurs, the system stores the additional record in an **overflow** area that is reserved for this purpose.

Once the logical record number is known, the file manager can locate the corresponding physical record relative to the start of the file. If there is an integer-to-one relationship between the logical and physical blocks, this calculation is almost trivial. Even at its most difficult, the translation requires nothing more than the use of a simple mathematical formula

$$P = \text{int } (L \times S_L / S_P)$$

where

P = the relative physical block number

L = the relative logical block number

S_L = the size in bytes of a logical block

S_P = the size in bytes of a physical block

Once the relative physical record is known, the actual physical location is located using information stored with the directory. Because physical records must be accessed a block at a time, the file manager provides a memory buffer large enough to hold the physical record or records that contain at least a single logical record. It then extracts the logical record from the buffer and moves it to the data area for the program requesting access.

Random access is also known as relative access, because the record number to be accessed is expressed relative to the start of the file. Most modern file management systems provide a way for an application to access files randomly. It is easy to simulate sequential access in a system that supports random access. The system simply reads the records in order. The reverse is not true. It is possible, but difficult, to simulate a random access file using sequential access. Random access is based on a disk model; the head on a disk can be moved immediately to any desired block.

Indexed Access

Indexes provide an additional means for accessing specific records in a file. A file may have multiple indexes, each representing a different way of viewing the data. A telephone list could be indexed by address, by name, and by phone number, for example. The index provides pointers that can immediately locate a particular logical record. Furthermore, an index is often small enough that it can be kept in memory for even faster access. Indexes are generally used in combination with sequential and random access methods to provide more powerful access methods.

Simple systems normally provide sequential and random access at the file manager level and rely on application programs to create more complex methods of access. Large systems provide additional access methods. The most common of these is the **indexed sequential access method** (**ISAM**). ISAM files are kept sorted in order of a key field. One or more additional index files are used to determine the block that contains the desired record for random access.

The IBM mainframe operating system z/OS provides six different access methods, and one of these, VSAM, is further divided into three different submethods. All these additional methods are built upon either random or sequential access or a mix of the two and use index files to expand their capability.

17.4 PHYSICAL FILE STORAGE

The file manager allocates storage based on the type of I/O device, the file access method to be used for the particular file, and the particular design of the file manager. There are three primary file storage methods used for random access devices, such as disks. For sequential access devices, particularly tape, the options are somewhat more limited. We shall deal with each type of device separately.

Consider the disk first. As you are already aware, disk files are stored in small, fixed-size blocks. This gives disks the important advantage that individual blocks can be read and written *in place*, without affecting other parts of the file. Many files require several blocks of storage. If the file is larger than a block, then the system needs to be concerned about an efficient storage method that allows for efficient retrieval of the file. If the file is accessed sequentially, then the file manager must be able to access all of it quickly. If the file is accessed randomly, the file manager must be able to get to the correct block quickly. As you will see, the methods that are most convenient for storage are not necessarily consistent with these requirements. There is no ideal solution to this problem. The physical allocation method chosen may depend on the way in which the file is to be logically retrieved. In particular, you will see that there is more flexibility in the physical storage method if the file is to be retrieved sequentially than if random access capability is required.

Three methods are commonly used to allocate blocks of storage for files. These are commonly known as *contiguous*, *linked*, and *indexed storage allocation*.

Contiguous Storage Allocation

The simplest method to allocate storage is to assign contiguous blocks sufficient to hold the file. Figure 17.6 shows a group of files of different sizes assigned using **contiguous storage**.

On the surface, this seems like the obvious way to allocate storage. Only a single directory pointer is required to locate the entire file. Since the file is contiguous, file recovery is quite easy. Retrieval is straightforward: the file manager can simply request a multiblock read and read the entire file in one pass. Relative file access is also straightforward: the correct block can be determined easily from the formula shown in Section 17.3 and then added to the pointer value that locates the beginning of the file.

There are some important difficulties with contiguous storage allocation, however.

■   The file system must find a space large enough to hold the file plus its anticipated growth.

FIGURE 17.6

Contiguous Storage Allocation

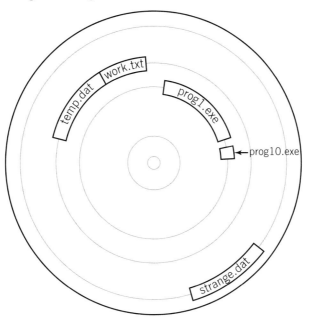

- Unless sufficient space is allocated initially, the file may grow to exceed the capacity of its storage allocation. In this case, the file may have to be moved to another area, or other files rearranged to make expanded room for the enlarged file.
- The use of contiguous storage allocation eventually leads to fragmentation of the disk. As files come and go there will occur small block areas between files, but none large enough to hold a new file unless the new file is small.

Fragmentation also occurs when a file is deleted or moved. Unless the space can be filled with a new file of the same size, there will be a space left over. Finding an exact replacement is unlikely: files are rarely exactly the same size, file space may be limited, a new, smaller file needs to be stored, and there is no alternative space available, so the space is used.

Allocation strategies can be used to try to minimize fragmentation. The **first-fit strategy** simply places the file into the first available space that the system finds. The **best-fit strategy** looks for the space that will most closely fit the file, thereby minimizing the external fragmentation. (At one time there was also a worst-fit strategy, which allocated file space from the largest available cluster. The idea was to leave as much room for another file as possible, but studies showed that it didn't work any better than the others.)

Ultimately, it becomes necessary to reorganize the space periodically to eliminate the fragments by collecting them together to form one new, usable space. This operation is called **defragmentation**, usually shortened to **defragging**. It is also sometimes called *compaction*. The time and effort required to defrag a disk is large, but pays off in faster disk access.

Noncontiguous Storage Allocation

A file system will normally attempt to allocate file storage space contiguously. When this is not possible, the file must be stored **noncontiguously** in whatever blocks are available. With noncontiguous storage, new blocks do not have to be assigned until they are actually needed. Fragmentation of the storage space cannot occur, although defragmentation may still be used to reduce the number of file accesses by maximizing the contiguous use of space.

The use of noncontiguous space requires that the file system maintain a detailed, ordered list of assigned blocks for each file in the system, as well as a list of free blocks available for assignment. For consistency, the file system will maintain ordered lists for all files, contiguous and noncontiguous.

There are two basic approaches to maintaining the lists of blocks allocated to each file:

1.   The block numbers for a file may be stored as a linked list, using pointers from one block to the next. This method is known as a **linked allocation**.
2.   The block numbers for each file may be stored in a table. This method is known as **indexed allocation**. Commonly, there is a separate table for each file.

LINKED ALLOCATION AND THE FILE ALLOCATION TABLE METHOD   At first it would seem that the system could simply place link pointers to the next block at the end of every file block. However, placing link pointers within the file blocks themselves is impractical, because it would be necessary to read each block from the beginning of the file, in sequence, to obtain the location of its succeeding block. This method would therefore be slow, awkward, and unsuitable for relative access files, where it is desirable to read or write *only* blocks containing relevant data.

A somewhat more practical method is to store the pointers as linked lists within a table. Windows still makes this available for small disks and solid-state storage devices, such as low-capacity flash drives and floppy disks. When this method is used, Windows provides a single table on each disk (or disk partition, since these systems allow a disk to be divided into partitions) on the system. This table is called a **file allocation table** or **FAT**. Each file allocation table holds the link pointers for every file stored on the particular disk or disk partition. These file allocation tables are copied to memory at system boot time or, in the case of removable devices, mount time, and remain in memory as long as the file system is active.

The FAT method is illustrated in Figure 17.7. It will help to "follow the trail" in the diagram as you read this description.

The directory for each file contains an entry that points to the first block of the file. Each entry in the FAT corresponds to a block or cluster on the disk. Each entry contains the link pointer that points to the next block in the file. A special value is used to indicate the end of a file. Any 0 entry in the FAT represents a block that is not in use. Therefore, it is easy for the system to locate free space when it is needed. To locate a particular block in a particular file, the file manager goes to the directory entry and finds the starting block for the file. It then follows the links through the FAT until the desired block is reached. Since the FAT is stored in memory, access to a particular block is fast.

For example, for the file STRANGE.DAT shown in Figure 17.7, the directory entry indicates that the first block of the file is stored in block number 42. Successive blocks of this file are stored in blocks 48, 70, and 16. Confirm your understanding of the FAT method by finding the third block of the file WORK.TXT in the figure.

FIGURE 17.7

File Allocation Table

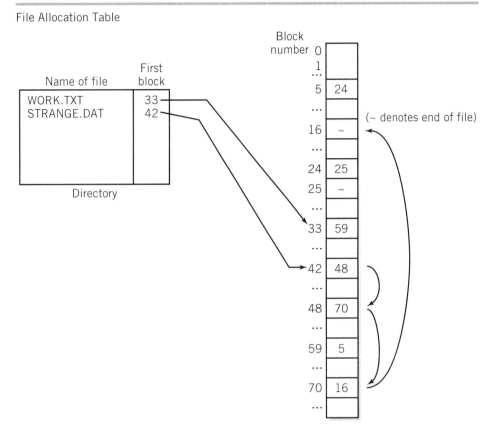

A major disadvantage of the FAT approach is that it becomes unacceptably inefficient for devices with large amounts of storage because the FAT itself requires a large amount of memory. Observe that the FAT table requires an entry for every block on the device, even if the block is unused. If a disk is broken into 2^{16}, or 65,536 clusters, with a corresponding 2-byte entry for each cluster, the FAT will require 128 KB of memory. A 1 GB disk would require a cluster size of 16 KB. If most of the files on the disk are small, then much of the capacity of the disk is wasted. A 1 KB file stored in a single cluster would waste more than 90 percent of the capacity of the cluster. Alternatively, the number of blocks in the table can be increased with a corresponding increase in the memory requirements to hold the table. FAT32 allows as many as 2^{28} or 256 million clusters. Each entry requires 4 bytes of storage. Of course, the actual number of clusters is set much smaller than that, because the size of such a table would require an outrageous amount of memory.

Neither of the above solutions is acceptable for modern, large capacity storage devices. The FAT technique appears to have reached the end of its useful life, but because it is still offered sometimes as an option when formatting devices, it is useful to understand the method and its shortcomings.

FIGURE 17.8

Index Blocks for Indexed Allocation of Linked Files Shown in Figure 17.7

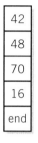

STRANGE.DAT

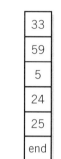

WORK.TXT

Indexed Allocation

Indexed allocation is similar to linked allocation, with one major difference: the link pointers for a file are all stored together in one block, called an **index block**. There is a separate index block for each file. Loading the index block into memory when the file is opened makes the link pointers available at all times for random access. Assuming the same linkages shown in Figure 17.7, the index blocks would look like those in Figure 17.8.

Since the only index blocks in memory are those for open files, indexed allocation represents a much more efficient use of memory.

One method used by some systems, including recent versions of Windows, to reduce memory usage even further is to allocate storage in groups of contiguous blocks as much as possible. Rather than store individual block links, this method allows the system to store a single link to the starting block of each group, together with a count of the number of blocks in the group. For files that grow in size gradually this may not be a useful strategy, but even for a file of known size that is to be stored on a disk that does not have a single contiguous space that is sufficient for the entire file, it may be possible to store the file in a small number of groups. Some modern file systems offer excess capacity when the file is created to allow for future growth in the size of the file. Although this would have been considered wasteful in earlier days, the large capacity of modern disks makes this solution feasible and practical today.

There are several possible options as to where the index block should be placed. As you will see in Section 17.6, the file management system maintains a directory structure that identifies and locates each file by name. Directory entries also store the attributes of the file that we mentioned earlier. Some systems store a single pointer to the index block in the directory entry as a way of locating the file. Other systems store link pointers in the directory entry itself.

The following examples show two of the most common approaches, the UNIX i-node method and the NTFS method.

UNIX and Linux use an indexed file allocation method, as shown in Figure 17.9. The directory entries in a UNIX system each contain just the name of the file plus a single pointer to an index block called an **i-node**. The i-node for a file contains the index pointers, and also the attributes of the file.

A typical i-node design allocates thirteen index pointers. The first ten pointers are links, just as we have described. This is adequate for small files. In fact, the needs of most of the files on the system are met this way. The last three entries in the table serve a special purpose. These are called the **single indirect**, **double indirect**, and **triple indirect block pointers**. The single indirect block pointer points to another index block. Additional links are found in that block. The number of links is determined solely by the size of a standard disk block. The double and triple indirect blocks are two and three steps removed, respectively. We have shown the single and double indirect blocks on the diagram. Using 4 KB clusters, this scheme is sufficient to access files in the hundreds of gigabytes. Actually, the limiting factor turns out to be the number of bits in each pointer.

FIGURE 17.9

Linux i-node File Storage Allocation

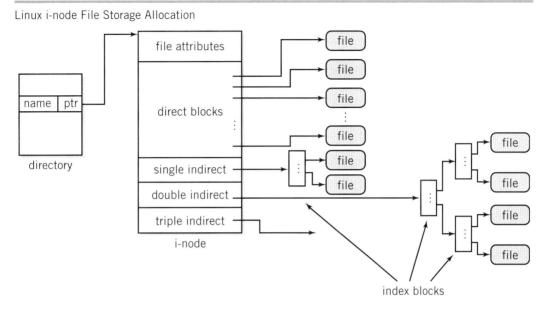

WINDOWS NTFS FILE SYSTEM The Windows **NT File System** (**NTFS**) was originally created to solve the shortcomings of the FAT file system, specifically to support large files and large disks, to provide file security, to reduce access times, and to provide recovery capability.

NTFS operates on volumes. In Windows NT volumes were determined solely by the layout of logical disk partitions. A volume in Windows NT was created by creating a logical disk partition, using the Windows NT fault-tolerant disk manager. Current versions of Windows continue to support the Windows NT disk manager for legacy volumes, but new volumes in Windows are created and managed by a disk manager, that allows the creation of volumes dynamically. Newer Windows volumes need not correspond to logical disk partitions. Dynamic volumes can be expanded or contracted to meet changing user needs while the system is online. Volumes may occupy part of a disk or an entire disk or may span multiple disks.

Like other systems, the NTFS volume allocates space in clusters. Each cluster is made up of a contiguous group of sectors. The NTFS cluster size is set when the volume is created. The default cluster size is generally 4 KB or less, even for large disks.

Figure 17.10 shows the layout for an NTFS volume. The core of each volume is a single file called the **master file table** (**MFT**). The master table is configured as an array of file records. Each record is 1 KB in size, regardless of the volume cluster size. The number of rows is set at volume creation time. The array contains one row for each file in the volume. The first sixteen rows contain metadata files: files that describe the volume. The first record stores attributes of the MFT itself. The second record points to another location in the middle of the disk that contains a duplicate of the metadata, for disk recovery.

NTFS file records are made up of **attributes**. An attribute is a stream of bytes that describes some aspect of the file. Standard attributes include the file name, its security

FIGURE 17.10

NTFS Volume Layout

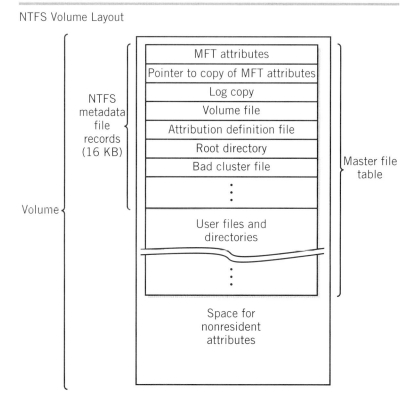

Source: Adapted from D. A. Solomon, *Inside Windows NT*, 2nd ed. (Redmond, WA: Microsoft Press, 1998).

descriptor, time stamps, read-only and archive flags, links, and data (i.e., the file's contents). Directory files have attributes that index the directory. Each attribute has a name or number plus a byte stream representing the value of the attribute. The primary data stream is unnamed, but it is possible to have named data streams in addition. Thus, there may be multiple data streams in a single file record.

Small files may fit within the MFT record itself. For larger files, the MFT record will contain pointers to clusters in an area of the disk outside the MFT. Attributes that extend beyond the MFT are called *nonresident attributes* (usually the data attribute, obviously). Nonresident clusters are called *runs*. If the attribute outgrows its space, the file system continues to allocate runs as needed.

Free Space Management

To allocate new blocks as they are required, the file management system must keep a list of the free available space on a disk. To create a new file or add blocks to an existing file, the file manager takes space from the free space list. When a file is deleted, its space is returned to the free space list. There are two methods commonly used for this purpose.

FIGURE 17.11

Free Space Bitmap

Block numbers

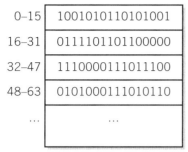

0–15	1001010110101001
16–31	0111101101100000
32–47	1110000111011100
48–63	0101000111010110
…	…

BITMAP METHOD   One method of maintaining a free space list is to provide a table with one bit for each block on the disk. The bit for a particular block is set to 1 if the block is in use and to 0 if the block is free. (Many systems also set defective blocks to 1 permanently to prevent their use.) This table is known as a **free space bitmap** or, sometimes, as a table of **bit vectors**. A **bitmap** is illustrated in Figure 17.11. A bitmap is usually kept in memory for fast access.

The bitmap method is an economical way of keeping track of free space, since only one bit is needed for each block on the disk. It has the further advantage that it is easy for the file manager to locate contiguous blocks or blocks that are nearby to those already allocated to a file. This allows the file manager to maintain files in a way that can minimize disk seeks during file access.

Although the bitmap must be stored 8 bits to a byte, CPU instruction sets provide bit manipulation instructions that allow efficient use of the bitmap. One disadvantage of the bitmap method is that there is some processing overhead in returning space from a large file with many blocks to the free space list. A second disadvantage is that once space has been returned to the bitmap, it may be immediately reassigned. There is no way of determining the order in which the space was returned. Therefore, the space used by a deleted file may be reused again immediately, eliminating the chance for file recovery.

LINKED LIST METHOD   An alternative method maintains all the free space on the disk in a **linked list**. A pointer to the first free block is kept in a special location on disk and also in memory. Each free block is then linked to the next. The file manager allocates blocks from the beginning of the list. The blocks from deleted files are added to the end of the list.

This method has considerable overhead in disk seeks if a large number of blocks are to be allocated, but is simple and efficient for small numbers of blocks. It is not practical with this method to identify blocks in particular locations for optimizing allocation to an individual file. One advantage of the linked list method is that file recovery is enhanced. The blocks in a linked free space list are stored in the order in which files are deleted. Since deleted files are placed at the end of the list, the data on those blocks will be recoverable until the blocks are needed for reuse.

Note that the data in deleted files is not truly deleted from disk unless special effort is made to clear or scramble all the bits in the blocks used by the file. This is a potential security risk. Special software, called **shredder software**, is available for the purpose of truly deleting files from disk in a way that they cannot be recovered. New systems are starting to offer this feature as "secure delete".

Tape Allocation

Tape allocation is simpler than disk allocation. The size of a block can be varied to fit the logical requirements of the file. It is usually not practical to reallocate space in the middle of a tape, so files that grow must be rewritten. If necessary, the tape can be compacted, but it is usually easier to do so by copying the tape to a new tape. Tape blocks can be linked, but, in general, files are stored contiguously whenever possible. Tape is convenient for sequential access, but not practical for random access. Random access files that are stored on tape are normally moved to disk as a whole before use.

CD, DVD, and Flash Drive Allocation

The file system used for various optical drives and flash drives is similar to those found on hard disks. The standard format is called UDF, for Universal Data Format. It can support up to 2 TB of data on a disk. The directory format is hierarchical., consistent with other file directory systems There are also extensions that make it possible to store a mixture of data, audio, and images on the same disk. The UDF system includes support for both High Definition and Blu-Ray DVD formats.

17.5 FILE SYSTEMS, VOLUMES, DISKS, PARTITIONS, AND STORAGE POOLS

Even a medium-sized computer system may store thousands or even millions of files. To locate and use files effectively there must be some organization that makes sense to the users of the system, as well as to the people responsible for administering the system. For a desktop system, the files may all be stored on a single disk drive. On a larger system, files may be stored on a number of different disks, either locally or on a network. Some disks may be fixed, others removable. Some may be set up as RAID drives. (Forgot what RAIDs are? Check Chapter 9.)

So how is the operating system to handle all of this effectively? From the perspective of the user, the goal is simplicity and convenience; for the system, the goal is efficiency. The system administrator looks for manageability.

Although operating systems manage the massive amounts of data in modern systems differently, most attempt to provide a structure that can divide the files, both logically and physically, into reasonable groupings that attempt to meet the goals of the different parties.

Even the definition of a file system is somewhat arbitrary. Think of all the different ways that you could use to organize and store all of your college research papers in file boxes. Your main concern would be your ability to locate the files you need with minimum effort. You might choose to create a single file system with the papers filed alphabetically by title. Or, you might create a number of file systems, where each file box contains the papers for a particular course sequence.

The computer file system works similarly. The user might face a single file system that hides all of the storage details. Alternatively, she may be working on a system where each I/O device is catalogued individually.

An important (and, it turns out, reasonable) assumption is that it is possible to group the logical view of the files differently from that of physical storage as a means to achieve an optimum solution. The file management component of the operating system provides the connectivity between the two. The primary methods used for grouping files are based on dividing and organizing file systems into disks, partitions, volumes, storage pools, and multiple, separate file systems. Some designers carry the concept of separate file systems even further into **virtual file systems**.

As an example, an inexpensive desktop computer might have a single disk and a CD drive or DVD drive. By default, Windows would treat this simple configuration as two file systems, one for each disk, probably labeled C: and D:, respectively. In this situation, each disk has a single file and directory system, logically facing the user, and a single I/O interface facing the disk controller for each device. This configuration is illustrated in Figure 17.12(a).

FIGURE 17.12

Partitions, File Systems, Volumes, and Pools

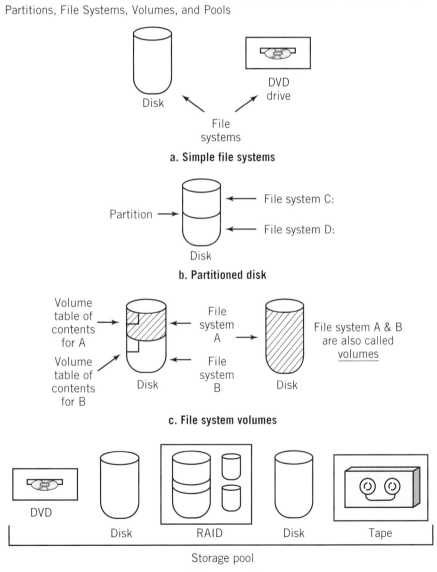

a. **Simple file systems**

b. **Partitioned disk**

c. **File system volumes**

d. **Storage pool**

Many systems also provide a means for dividing physical devices, particularly disks, into independent sections called **partitions**. Disks may be divided physically or logically. (Think the drawers of a file cabinet versus the dividers in a single drawer.) The partitions themselves can be further divided conceptually into *primary* and *extended* partitions. Each partition can have its own file system and directory structure. Figure 17.12(b) illustrates a disk partitioned into two separate file systems. Files located on other partitions are often invisible to the file system on an active partition. Each partition in a Windows system, for example, is assigned a different letter and has its own file system. A partition is selected by specifying the letter of the desired file system, followed by a colon. Of course, all of the file systems are accessible to the file manager, so that a user can open multiple windows, each representing its own file system, to move data from one to another, and to perform other operations requiring simultaneous access.

The partition concept includes the option of providing separate operating system facilities on different partitions, so that each partition may have its own bootstrap loader, operating system, and file management system. When this is the case, the file systems on different partitions may be incompatible with each other, so that it is not natively possible for one file system to read the directory or load the files from a different partition, even on the same physical disk. In most cases, utilities exist that allow conversions between different file formats. For example, utilities built into Linux systems can read and write to Windows FAT and NTFS file systems. Conversely, the freeware *ext2fs.sys* utility can be installed on Windows systems to enable Windows to read and write to Linux file systems.

(A brief historical note: disk partitioning was originally created because the file systems in early personal computers, particularly MS-DOS and early versions of Windows, were barely adequate to handle numbers large enough to address all of the blocks on the small disks of the era. As a means of extending the capability of the file system to address all of the blocks on larger disks, the disks themselves were partitioned. As the addressing capability of the file systems grew, disk partitioning was retained as a means of creating separate logical spaces for the user, as well as for making it possible to provide different types of file systems and/or different operating systems on a single disk.)

Figure 17.12(c) illustrates another possibility. On many systems, different disks or disk partitions from different disks and other devices can be combined into a single file system.

The file system must maintain a directory structure for each device or partition. In most cases, the directory for each device is stored on the device itself. In many computer systems, each file system is called a **volume**. On some of these systems, the directory is called a **volume table of contents**. The volumes are indicated for each file system organization shown in Figure 17.12. In particular, note that the volume concept is relatively independent of the actual physical disk configuration, but is instead tuned to the needs of the user(s) and the requirements of the system administrator(s).

On many systems, it is necessary to **mount** a volume, device, or partition before it can be used. Mounting a volume means that the directory structure for the volume is merged into an overall file structure for the system by attaching the directory structure of the volume to some point in the overall file structure. This point is known as the **mount point**. In some systems mounting is automatic. In others, mounting must be performed manually, using a MOUNT command. Volumes in the Macintosh system, for example, are mounted automatically if they are present when the system is booted. Flash drives, CDs, and DVDs are also mounted automatically when they are inserted into the drive. Other devices must be mounted manually. On older UNIX systems, all directories are mounted manually. Thus, it is necessary for the user to issue a MOUNT command when a CD is changed on a traditional UNIX workstation. The mount point also depends on the system. On a Macintosh, all volumes are mounted on the desktop; on UNIX and Linux systems, a volume can be mounted anywhere on the directory structure. The Linux file system design allows the mounting of multiple file system types for transparent access across partitions and, even, across networks. It also offers automatic mounting similar to that of the Macintosh.

An alternative file management model is implemented on the Sun Solaris 10 operating system. Solaris 10 is a UNIX-based system intended for use in medium to large computer installations. This model views disk storage as a single **storage pool**. The storage pool can be shared by multiple file systems, but allocation of file space is controlled by a single file manager. A major feature of this organization is that disks can be added to the pool dynamically as additional storage is required without modifying the file structure as viewed by the users. Because data can easily be stored by the file management system in multiple locations, the use of RAID drives, data backup, and data integrity measures can be built into the system as routine operations, handled invisibly by the system. Data and programs will also naturally spread fairly evenly over all of the avilable physical devices, resulting in faster average access times, especially in systems with heavy I/O requirements. Figure 17.12(d) illustrates the storage pool approach.

Although the storage pool design concept is recent, it was released by Sun to the open source community. It has already been adapted for the FreeBSD operating system and partially adapted for OS X; its use is likely to spread to other operating systems in the future.

17.6 THE DIRECTORY STRUCTURE

The directory system provides a means of organization so that files may be located easily and efficiently in a file system. The directory structure provides the linkages between logical files identified by their names and their corresponding physical storage area. Every stored file in a file system is represented in the directory for that system. The directory system serves as the basis for all the other file operations that we have already discussed. It also maintains records of the attributes for each file. Some of the important attributes for a file that are commonly found in a directory (or in the UNIX-style i-node) are shown in Figure 17.13.

A file system may support many different devices, including, often, multiple disks, as well as tapes, CD-ROMs, flash drives and cards, and devices elsewhere on a network. In many systems, the directory system conceals the physical differences from the user, providing logical consistency throughout the system. On others, the physical device on which the file resides may be represented by nothing more than a letter change preceding the file name, F: for the CD-ROM on a Windows system, perhaps, and M: for the network file server. On a system with a graphical interface, different devices may simply be represented by different disk or folder icons.

There are a number of possible ways in which a directory can be organized. The simplest directory structure is just a list. It is also known as a single-level, or flat, directory. All the files stored in the system, including system files, application programs, and user

FIGURE 17.13

Typical File Attributes

Name and extension	Name and extension, if any, stored in ASCII or Unicode form
Type	Needed if system supports different file types; also used for special attributes, such as system, hidden, archive; alphanumeric character or binary; sequential or random access required; and so on.
Size	Size of file in bytes, words, or blocks
Maximum allowable size	Size file will be allowed to grow to
Location	Pointer to device and to location of starting file block on device, or pointer to index block, if stored separate from file, or pointer to entry in FAT table
Protection	Access control data limiting who has access to file, possibly a password
Name of owner	User ID for owner of file; used for protection
Name of group	Name of group with privileges, in some protection systems
Date of creation	Time and date when file was created
Date of modification	Time and date of most recent modification to file; sometimes user identification is also maintained for audit purposes
Date of last use	Time and date of most recent use of file; sometimes user ID

files, are listed together in a single directory. The single-level directory system has some obvious disadvantages:

- There is no way for a user to organize his work into logical categories as all the files are of equal status in the directory.

- It is possible to destroy a file by mistake if the user isn't careful when naming files. This is particularly true because many of the files in the directory, notably the system and application program files, were not originally created and named by the user. There is even potential naming conflict between different commercial software packages. Installation of a software package could cause another package to fail at a later date, and it would be difficult to track down the problem.

- The single-level directory is unsuitable for a system with multiple users. There would be no way to differentiate which files belong to which user. Naming of files by the users would have to be done extremely carefully to prevent destroying another user's work. (How often have you named a program assignment "PROG1.JSP" or "ASSIGN3.C"? How many other students in your class would you guess also did so?)

- Implementation of a single-level directory system is simple. However, as the directory grows, the list will expand beyond its original space allocation and it will be necessary for the system to allocate additional space, with pointers to move between the spaces. Although this is also true of other directory systems, the single-level directory system does not provide any organization that will make it easier to locate file entries when the files are to be retrieved, so the search procedure must follow all the pointers until the file is located. This is somewhat akin to searching an unalphabetized address book from the beginning to find the name you want. On a large system, with many files, an undirected search of this kind could take a considerable amount of time.

As a result of these disadvantages, it is rare to see a single-level directory system in use today.

Tree-Structured Directories

A tree structure satisfies most file directory requirements and is in common use in modern computer systems. The directory in MS-DOS and older versions of Windows is a **tree-structured directory**. A variation on a tree-structured directory, the **acyclic-graph directory** structure is even more powerful, but introduces some difficulties in implementation. UNIX, Windows 2000, XP, and Vista, and Macintosh systems support an acyclic-graph directory structure. Nearly all modern computer systems provide one of these two structures.

An example showing part of a tree-structured directory, also known as a **hierarchical directory**, is represented in Figure 17.14. The tree structure is characterized by a root directory, from which all other directories stem. On most systems, the root directory contains few, if any, files. In this illustration, two files, AUTOEXEC.BAT and CONFIG.SYS, are found in the root directory. All other entries in the root directory are themselves directories, sometimes called **subdirectories** for clarity. The root directory and all its subordinate directories can contain files or other directories. Additional branches can stem from any directory. The root directory is stored in a particular location, known to the file system. Other directories are themselves stored as files, albeit files with a special purpose. This means that directories can be manipulated by the system like any other file.

The root directory, other directories, and files are all identified by names. Duplicates within a particular directory are not legal, but use of the same name in different directories is acceptable. Every file in the system can be uniquely identified by its **pathname**. The pathname for a file is the complete list of names along the path starting from the root and

FIGURE 17.14

Part of a Tree-Structure Directory

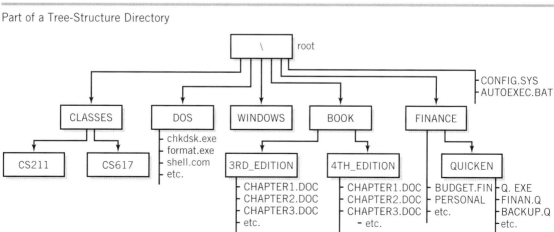

ending at the particular file. A **separator symbol** separates each name along the path. In many systems, the separator symbol is the same as the name of the root directory. This is true both for Windows, with a root named "\", and for UNIX, "/".

Although the visual appearance is considerably different, graphical interface systems support a similar structure. Folders have a one-to-one correspondence to directories. Starting from the desktop, you move through the tree structure by opening folders until you reach the folder containing the desired files.

On single-user systems, the hierarchy is established by the user, usually in response to a logical arrangement of his or her work. On systems that support multiple users, the main part of the hierarchy is established by the system administrator, usually in an arrangement that is consistent with a standard layout for the particular type of system. This makes it easier for users who must move between multiple machines. Generally, the system has a particular subdirectory that serves as the account directory for everyone on the system. Each user is assigned a tree branch that can be expanded below that subdirectory and a starting point, known as the initial **working directory**. On a single-user system, the initial working directory is established by the system. In Windows, it is C:\Users\yourusername. In the Macintosh, it is a subdirectory just below the root called the *desktop*.

From the current directory, the user can access files anywhere in the system. The file name or new working directory can be specified relative to the current working directory, or absolutely, from the root, by using a **relative** or **absolute pathname**, respectively. The difference is easily determined by the system, since absolute pathnames begin with the root name or symbol and relative pathnames don't. In Figure 17.14, the file called BACKUP.Q can be specified absolutely as \FINANCE\QUICKEN\BACKUP.Q. If the current working directory is FINANCE, then the file can be accessed relatively as QUICKEN\BACKUP.Q. Systems generally do not directly allow the use of a relative pathname above the current directory. Instead, these systems provide a special name that can be used for the node at the next level above the current working directory. In both Windows and Linux, this name is ".." (double dot). Thus, to open the file CHAPTER1.DOC in the directory 4TH_EDITION from a current working directory of 3RD_EDITION, you can specify the file with the absolute pathname \BOOK\4TH_EDITION\CHAPTER1.DOC. The same file can also be accessed relatively as ..\4TH_EDITION\CHAPTER1.DOC.

When a user requests a file from the system, the system looks for the file in the user's current working directory, or in the location specified by the pathname. Most systems also provide an **environmental variable** called *path* that allows the user to specify other path locations that are to be searched for the file if a pathname is not given and if the file is not found in the current working directory. There is a specified order to the search so that if there is more than one file that qualifies, only the first file found is accessed.

The user can also change his or her current working directory. The user moves around the tree using a CHANGE DIRECTORY command. An absolute or relative pathname can be used. To change the current working directory from directory 3RD_EDITION to directory 4TH_EDITION in the figure, for example, one could issue a CD ..\4TH_EDITION command or one could use the full path name, CD \BOOK\4TH_EDITION. On systems that do not allow relative pathnames above the current directory, the CD .. command provides a convenient way to move upward to the next-level node. The user can also add and remove branches from the tree with MAKE DIRECTORY and REMOVE DIRECTORY commands to provide a file organization that meets the user's requirements and desires.

In a graphical interface system, the current working directory is the folder that is currently open. Folders can be created and deleted, which is equivalent to adding and removing branches to the tree structure. Since there may be many folders open on the screen, it is easy to move from one current working directory to another on a graphical interface system.

The tree-structured directory system provides solutions to the problems described at the beginning of this section. The tree structure provides flexibility that allows users to organize files in whatever way they wish. The tree structure solves the problem of organization for a system with a large number of files. It also solves the problem of growth, since there is essentially no limit on the number of directories that the system can support. It also solves the problem of accessing files in an efficient manner. A directory is located by following the pathname from the current directory or from the root, one directory file at a time. One negative consequence of this method is that it may require retrieval of several directory files from different parts of the disk, with the corresponding disk seek times, but at least the path is known, so extensive searching is not necessary. Since duplicate names in a tree structure use different paths there is no confusion between identical file names, because each has a different pathname. For this textbook, for example, the author has two different sets of files named CHAPTER1.DOC, CHAPTER2.DOC, and so on. One set is located in a directory with the (relative) pathname BOOK\4TH_EDITION. The other set is in a directory called BOOK\3RD_EDITION. This provides protection for the author in case of a disk error. Similarly, each user on a system with multiple users starts from a different pathname, so the use of similar file names by different users is not a problem.

Acyclic-Graph Directories

The acyclic-graph directory is a generalization of a tree-structure directory, expanded to include **links** between separate branch structures on the tree. The links appear in the directory structure as though they were ordinary file or directory entries. In actuality, they serve as pseudonyms for the original file name. The link provides an alternative path to a directory or file. An example is shown in Figure 17.15. In this diagram there are two links, shown in heavy print. There is a link between the directory CURRENT, belonging to user imwoman, and the directory 2008, belonging to user theboss. This makes all the files in directory 2008 available to imwoman. There is also a link between directory MYSTUFF, belonging to user jgoodguy, and the file PROJ1.TXT. (Apparently, jgoodguy is working only on this one project.) The file PROJ1.TXT can be accessed by theboss from her current directory by using the pathname PROJECTS/2008/PROJ1.TXT. jgoodguy can access the same file using pathname MYSTUFF/PROJ1.TXT. imwoman uses pathname CURRENT/2008/PROJ1.TXT to reach the file. Note that it is also possible for imwoman to change her current directory to 2008 as a result of the link.

The ability to add links between branch structures in a tree makes it possible to create multiple paths, and pathnames, that lead to a single directory or file. From the perspective of users on the system, this adds the powerful capability of being able to share files among users. Each user has his path to the file with its own pathname. For a group collaborating on a document, for example, a subdirectory could be created with all the pertinent files and then linked to the working directories of each of the users. An individual user can even create multiple paths to a file, if so desired. This capability could be useful if the file is

FIGURE 17.15

An Acyclic-Graph Directory

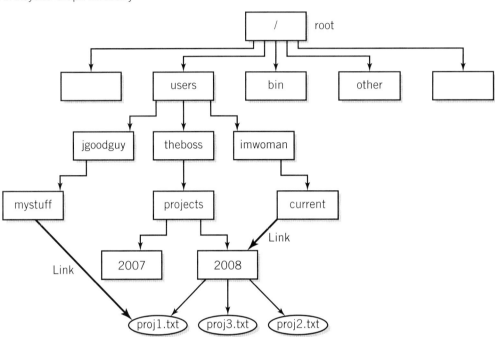

associated with two different directories, and the user would like to place it as an entry in both for more convenient access.

One difficulty with implementation of an acyclic-graph directory is assuring that the links do not connect in such a way that it is possible to **cycle** through a path more than once when tracing out the path to a file. Consider the situation in Figure 17.16. The links between current and projects and between projects and imwoman complete a cycle. Thus, the file name PROJ1.TXT can be reached by an infinite number of paths, including

```
IMWOMAN/CURRENT/PROJECTS/2008/PROJ1.TXT
IMWOMAN/CURRENT/PROJECTS/IMWOMAN/CURRENT/
    PROJECTS/2008/PROJ1.TXT
IMWOMAN/CURRENT/PROJECTS/IMWOMAN/CURRENT/
    PROJECTS/IMWOMAN/CURRENT/PROJECTS/ ...
```

and so on. This is obviously an unsatisfactory situation. When the file system is searching for files, it will encounter an infinite number of paths that it believes must be checked. The system must assure that the addition of a link does not create a cycle.

An additional difficulty is establishing a policy for the deletion of files that have multiple links. Removing a file without removing the links leaves **dangling links**, links that

FIGURE 17.16

Graph with a Cycle

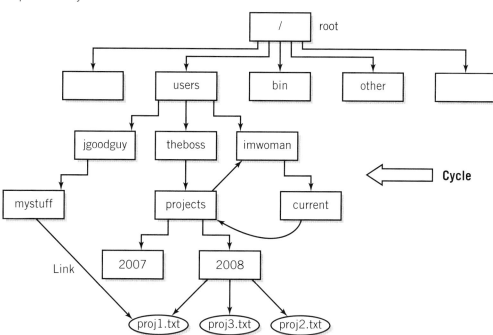

Source: Adapted from [CHR94]. Reprinted by permission of John Wiley & Sons, Inc.

point to nowhere. It is also possible on some systems to remove all links to the file, leaving file space that can't be reclaimed by the system.

There is also the necessity for setting rules about the modification of a file that is open by two different users at the same time. As an example, suppose that users 1 and 2 are both working on the same file. User 1 makes some modifications and saves the file with his changes. Then, user 2 makes other modifications and saves the file with her changes. Under certain conditions, the changes made by user 2 will destroy the changes made by user 1. A system for **locking** the file temporarily to prevent this type of error is required. Further discussion of locking is outside the scope of this textbook.

As you can see, there are difficulties and dangers in providing and using acyclic-graph directories. Many system designers feel that the advantages outweigh the disadvantages, however.

UNIX and the Macintosh both support acyclic-graph directories. Macintosh links are called **aliases**. The Macintosh uses a simple implementation. An alias is a **hard-coded link** that points to the original file. If the original file is moved or deleted, use of the link will cause an error. The Macintosh does not check for the presence of cycles; however, the visual nature of the Macintosh interface makes cycles less likely to occur and less problematic. The search operations that can cause loops are instead performed visually, and there is no reason for the user to continue opening folders beyond a point of usefulness. Windows implements links similarly with **shortcuts**.

UNIX provides two different kinds of links. The difference between them is shown in Figure 17.17. A hard link points from a new directory entry to the same i-node as another directory entry somewhere in the file system. Since both entries point to the same i-node, any changes made in the file are automatically reflected to both. The i-node has a field that keeps track of the number of directory entries pointing to it. Any time a link is added, the counter is increased by one. When a file is "deleted", the count is reduced by one. The file is not actually deleted until the count is zero. A major disadvantage of hard links is that some programs, such as editors, update files by creating a new file, then renaming it with the original name. Since the file creation results in a new i-node, the links now point to different i-nodes and different versions of the original file. In other words, the link is broken.

Symbolic links work differently. With a symbolic link, the new directory entry creates a file that holds a pointer to the original file's pathname. Then, when accessing the new entry, the symbolic link uses this file to identify the original pathname. Even if the original file is physically moved, the link is maintained as long as the original pathname exists. Of course, the link is broken if the original file is logically moved to a different directory, deleted, or renamed. In this case, an attempt to reference the file specified by the link will cause an error. UNIX does not attempt to keep track of symbolic links, as it does with hard links. An additional minor disadvantage of symbolic links is that the symbolic link also requires the existence of an additional file to hold the link pointer.

The UNIX system does not attempt to avoid cycles. Instead, it restricts access to the linking capability of the system. Normal users may only create hard links to files, but not

FIGURE 17.17

The Difference Between Hard and Symbolic Links

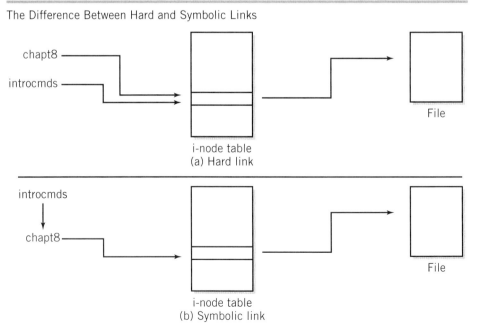

Source: Adapted from K. Christian and S. Richter, *The UNIX Operating System*, 3rd ed. New York: John Wiley, 1994.

to directories. This prevents the normal users from inadvertently creating cycles. Only the system administrators can create links between directories. It is their responsibility to assure that they do not create cycles.

17.7 NETWORK FILE ACCESS

One of the primary capabilities provided by networks is the access to files on other systems connected to the network. Depending on the method used, files may be copied from one system to another or may be accessed directly on the system holding the file. For the transfer of files from one system to another, the TCP/IP protocol family includes **ftp**, a standard file transfer protocol. ftp is implemented as a series of commands that can be used to move around and view directories on a remote system and to upload or download a file or group of files residing on that system. HTTP includes similar capabilities. However, ftp and HTTP do not include a facility for accessing and using the file remotely. It must be copied to the local system for use. For more general use, most operating systems provide a facility for using files from their remote locations, without copying them onto the local system. There are two different approaches. One technique, used primarily by Microsoft, is to identify with a name a connection point on each system that allows access, and to alias a local drive letter to that name. Files may then be manipulated using the drive letter as though the files were stored locally. For example, files stored in the USER/STUDENT/YOURNAME directory on the Icarus system might be aliased to drive letter M: on your personal computer. Then, you could perform any file or directory operation as though the files and directories were stored locally on drive M:. The M: drive icon would appear in your "My Computer" window if you were using Windows NT, XP, or Vista, for example. Notice that it is not necessary to copy the file to your local system to read or write it, but that you can do so if you wish, using the usual copy command or by dragging-and-dropping the file icon with the mouse.

The alternative method is to use the approach originated by Sun with the **Network File System (NFS)**. With NFS and similar systems, a remote directory is mounted to a mount point on the local system. Remote files and directories are then used transparently in the same way as local files. In fact, if the mount procedure was performed by the system as part of the network connection procedure, the user might not even be aware of which files and directories are local and which are remote. The NFS client/server manager is built into the operating system kernel, and operates as an alternative to the local file system manager, using the RPC (Remote Procedure Call) protocol. A typical NFS connection is shown in Figure 17.18. Linux and Macintosh OS X work similarly. To add a file system to a local directory tree, the user simply connects to a server and identifies a local mount point. File systems of different types are handled automatically by the local system.

More recently, steps have been taken to provide more generalized, distributed network directory services. These would be used for locating other types of information, in addition to file services. Such generalized services could identify the configuration of a system or information about employees in a business, for example. These systems are based on generalized naming schemes, such as the Internet Domain Name Service, and are designed to locate files and information uniquely wherever the information is located. A standard protocol, **LDAP (Lightweight Directory Access Protocol)**, exists for this purpose. Two examples of generalized network directory services are ActiveDirectory, supported by Microsoft, and Novell Directory Services.

FIGURE 17.18

Typical NFS Configuration

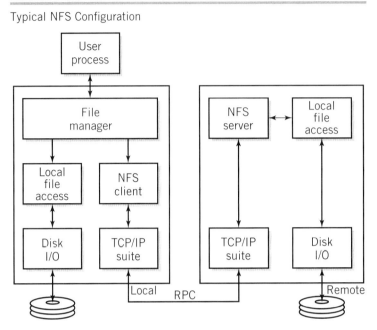

17.8 STORAGE AREA NETWORKS

Traditional network file access uses a client-server approach. Figure 17.19(a) shows this approach. To access a file, a user client requests service from a file server. Files are stored on hard disks and other devices attached to the server computer. In an organization, there may be many servers, with file storage attached to each.

In large enterprises, this approach is unwieldy. A user has to know on which server a desired file resides. The number of files in use is large. Synchronization of files that are stored on multiple servers is difficult and risky. Backup requires additional care and effort. Data warehousing and data mining applications are difficult because the data may be scattered over a large number of servers.

An alternative approach that is used by large enterprises is to store data in a **storage area network (SAN)**. Figure 17.19(b) illustrates the organization of a storage area network. In a storage area network, storage devices are stored together in a separate network that is accessible from all servers. A variety of different storage devices, hard disks, RAID, tape, and optical storage can all be used. Any server can access any storage device, with appropriate permission, of course. To a server, the network appears as a storage pool, similar to those that we discussed earlier. The technology of the network itself, as well as access to the network, is hidden within a cloud. SAN terminology refers to this cloud as the *fabric*. A storage network can extend over large distances using wide area network technology, allowing the use of devices at remote locations for backup.

Clients access files in the usual ways. Servers act as an intermediary, accessing the data from the SAN in the background, transparent to the client users.

There are standards and protocols in place for SAN technology, allowing products of differrent vendors to be mixed and matched. The most common network technology used

FIGURE 17.19

Alternative Approaches for Data Storage

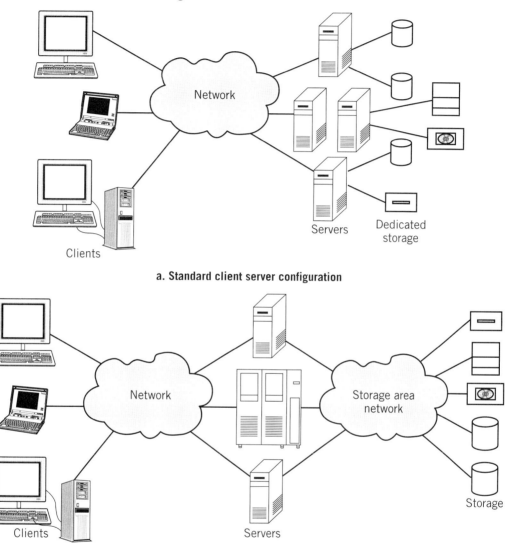

a. Standard client server configuration

b. Storage area network configuration

is **fibre channel**.[2] However, other technologies, including TCP/IP, ATM, SCSI, and Ficon can all interface directly with a fibre channel network.

For a deeper understanding of SAN, the reader is referred to Tate et al. [TATE06].

---

[2]The British spelling of *fibre* is intentional. The original network was designed for use with fiber optics. However, the standard includes options for the use of copper wire, so the decision was made to name the technology *fibre channel* instead.

17.9 FILE PROTECTION

Except in small, single-user systems, the system must provide file protection to limit file access to those who have authorization to use the file. File protection is provided on an individual file-by-file basis. There are several different forms that file protection might take. A user might be allowed to execute a file but not copy it, for example, or may be able to read it but not modify it. A file might be shared by a group of individuals, and the file protection system should make it convenient for group members to access the file, while protecting the file from others.

Although some systems provide additional forms of protection, most systems provide three types of protection on files:

- A file may be read or not be readable (**read protection**).
- A file may be written to or not accessible for writing (**write protection**).
- A file may be executed or not be executable (**execution protection**).

Although there are other, more specific, possibilities, these restrictions are sufficient for nearly every purpose and represent a good compromise for implementation purposes. For example, it might be important that a particular user not be able to delete a file. Write protection, although more restrictive, prevents deletion. If the user needs to modify such a file, the user can copy the file, provided he or she has read rights, and modify the copy. The ideal form of protection on a multiuser or server-based system would provide each file with an **access control list** (**ACL**) of users that may access the file for each of the three forms of protection. The list for a particular file would be maintained by the owner of the file. The amount of overhead required to maintain and use ACLs is tremendous. The system must provide utilities for maintaining the lists, storage space for the lists, and the mechanisms to check the lists whenever a file is accessed. If the number of users on the system is large, the ACL for each file might require a large amount of storage space. Since the system administrator is effectively the owner of all the system files, there is a tremendous responsibility on one person to maintain a large number of ACLs. Nonetheless, some systems do provide ACL protection.

A simpler, but more practical, protection method divides the user base of the system into three categories. For each file, the system defines an **owner**, a **group** associated with the file, and a **universe** that consists of everyone else. The file system maintains lists of groups. Each group has a name, and a user can be a member of more than one group. Generally, groups are administered by the system administrator, but on some systems, a group can be created by the owner of a file.

Under this protection method, each file provides nine protection flags, specifically, read, write, and execute permission for each of the three categories' owner, group, and universe. When a file is created, the system sets a default protection established by the system administrator. The owner of the file can then determine and set the protection differently, if so desired. In UNIX, there is a CHMOD command for this purpose. The nine protection flags can be stored in a single word within the directory. Figure 17.20 shows a typical UNIX directory listing. The leftmost flag in the listing simply indicates whether a file is a directory (*d*), a symbolic link (*l*), or an ordinary file (-). The next nine flags represent read, write, and execute privileges for owners, groups, and universe, respectively. The presence of a hyphen in the listing indicates that the privilege is turned off. The number

FIGURE 17.20

File Directory Showing Protection

```
$1s -1F
drwx------ 1 iengland csdept 36005 Feb 15 12:02 bookchapters/
-rw-r--r-- 1 iengland csdept  370 Sep 17  1:02 assignment1.txt
--wx--x--- 2 iengland csdept 1104 Mar 5 17:35 littleman*
-rwxrwx--- 1 iengland csdept 2933 May 22  5:15 airport shell*
drwxr--r-- 1 iengland csdept 5343 Dec 3 12:34 class syllabi/
```

of links to the file is next, then the name of the owner and the name of the group. The remainder of each row gives the name of the file and various file attributes.

Since directories are, themselves, files, most systems, including UNIX, provide similar protection for directories. You'll notice the same protection pattern listings for directories in Figure 17.20. A read-protected directory, for example, could not be listed by a user with no read access. It is not possible to save a file or delete a file to a write-protected directory. And a user without execute permission cannot change his or her current directory to an execute-protected directory.

A few systems provide an alternative form of file protection by assigning passwords to every file or to every directory. This method puts a burden on the user to remember the different passwords attached to each file or each directory.

No matter how file protection is implemented, file protection adds considerable overhead for the system, but file protection is an essential part of the system. In addition to the file protection provided by limiting file access to authorized users, most modern systems also provide file encryption capability, either for individual files and directories or to the file system as a whole. This additional layer of protection is particularly useful when the file is exposed to users (and, potentially, system invaders) on a network.

17.10 JOURNALING FILE SYSTEMS

For many business applications, the integrity of the file system is critical to the health of the business. Of course, the first line of defense against the file system failure is a well-defined set of proper system backup and file maintenance procedures. **Journaling file systems** extend this protection to include automated file recovery procedures in the event of a disk crash or system failure during file access operations.

Journaling systems provide a log file that records every system transaction that requires a write access to the file system. Before a file write operation actually occurs, the logging system reads the affected file blocks and copies them to the log, which is stored as a separate file. If a system fault occurs during the write operation, the journaling file system log provides the information necessary to reconstruct the file. Of course, there is a performance cost for journaling, due to the extra file block reads and writes that are necessary to support the log file.

Journaling file systems provide two levels of capability. Simple journaling file systems protect the integrity of the file system structure, but cannot guarantee the integrity of data that has not yet been written to the disk. The disk is simply restored to its pre-failure configuration. The Windows NTFS file system is a simple journaling file system. It is able to recover all of the file system metadata, but does not recover current data that had not yet been saved when the failure occurred.

A full journaling file system provides the additional ability to recover unsaved data and to write it to the proper file location, guaranteeing data integrity as well as file system integrity.

Current full journaling file systems include IBM JFS, Silicon Graphics XFS, and Linux ext3 and ext4.

SUMMARY AND REVIEW

The file management system makes it possible for the user, and for programs, to operate with files as logical entities, without concern for the physical details of file storage and handling. The file system opens and closes files, provides the mechanism for all file transfers, and maintains the directory system.

File systems vary in complexity and capability from the very simple, where all file data is treated as a stream and just a few operations are provided, to the very sophisticated, with many file types and operations. The simpler file systems require more effort within each program but, in trade, provide additional flexibility.

Files are accessed sequentially, randomly, or some combination of the two. More complex file accesses generally involve the use of indexes. To some extent, the method of storage depends on the required forms of access. Files may be stored contiguously or noncontiguously. Each has advantages and disadvantages. The pointers to the various blocks that allow noncontiguous access can be stored as links in the blocks themselves or in an index table provided for that purpose. Often the index tables are associated with individual files, but some systems store the indexes for every file in a single table, called a file allocation table. The file system also maintains a record of available free space, either as a bitmap or in linked form.

The directory structure provides mapping between the logical file name and the physical storage of the file. It also maintains attributes about the files. Most modern file systems provide a hierarchical directory structure, either in tree form or as an acyclic graph. The hierarchical file structure makes it possible for the user to organize files in whatever way seems appropriate. The acyclic-graph structure adds file-sharing capability, at the expense of more difficult maintenance of the structure.

Network file access is accomplished using files that are attached to servers or by using a storage area network. Files that are attached to servers are accessed either by aliasing a name or by mounting the directories locally. The server acts as an intermediary for files that are stored on an SAN.

The file system also provides file protection. Some file systems maintain access lists, which can establish privileges for any user on a file-by-file basis. Most systems provide a simpler form of security that divides users into three categories and affords protection based on category.

FOR FURTHER READING

General discussions of file management systems will be found in any of the operating systems texts that we have mentioned in previous chapters. Details about the file systems for particular operating systems can be found in books that describe the operating system innards for the particular system. For example, Glass and Ables [GLAS06] and Christian and Richter [CHRI94] describe the Linux and UNIX file systems. NTFS is described in Russinovich and Solomon [RUSS05]. There are many good books on file management systems. Among the best are those of Weiderhold [WEID87], Grosshans [GROS86], and Livadas [LIVA90].

KEY CONCEPTS AND TERMS

absolute pathname
access control list (ACL)
acyclic-graph directory
alias
association
attributes
best-fit strategy
bitmap
bit vectors
block
cluster
collision
contiguous storage
    allocation
cycle
dangling link
defragmentation
    (defragging)
directory
double indirect block
    pointers
environmental variable
execution protection
fibre channel
fields
file allocation table (FAT)
file extension
file manager
first-fit strategy

form image
free space bitmap
ftp (file transfer protocol)
group
hard-coded link
hashing
hierarchical directory
i-node
index block
indexed sequential access
    method (ISAM)
indexed storage allocation
journaling file system
key field
Lightweight Directory
    Access Protocol (LDAP)
linked list
linked storage allocation
locking
logical file
master file table (MFT)
mount
mount point
NFS (Network File System)
noncontiguous storage
    allocation
NT File System (NTFS)
overflow
owner

partition
pathname
physical view
random access files
read protection
records
relative access files
relative pathname
separator symbol
sequential access
sequential files
shortcut
shredder software
single indirect block
    pointers
storage area network (SAN)
storage pool
subdirectories
table image
tree-structured directory
triple indirect block
    pointers
universe
volume
volume table of contents
wild cards
working directory
write protection

READING REVIEW QUESTIONS

17.1 The file management system provides a connection between a logical view of files and a physical view of files. What is meant by a "logical view of files"? What is meant by a "physical view of files"?

17.2 Consider a data file made up of records. Invent a simple file, then draw a table image and a form image that each represent your file. In each of your drawings, identify a record and a field. Is your file a logical view or a physical view?

17.3 Give at least three examples of file operations that operate on the file as a whole.

17.4 Give at least three examples of file operations that manipulate the data within the file itself.

17.5 Give three examples of file operations that operate only on the directories, not on the files themselves.

17.6 A program file is always read in its entirety. Would this file be accessed sequentially or randomly or by indexed access? Explain.

17.7 What is a file *attribute*? Give two or three examples of a file attribute. Where would the file attributes of a particular file be found?

17.8 The physical block or cluster size of a device that holds a file is a tradeoff between access speed and wasted space. Explain.

17.9 Describe the challenges faced by a file system when attempting to store files contiguously.

17.10 What operation can a user perform to improve the ratio of contiguous to noncontiguous files in a system?

17.11 Briefly explain the concept of linked allocation, noncontiguous file storage. For a file that is stored in blocks 5, 12, 13, 14, 19, 77, and 90, show what a linked allocation might look like.

17.12 NTFS file records are made up of components which are also called *attributes*, although the word has a different meaning. What is an NTFS attribute? What are the contents of an NTFS *data* attribute?

17.13 Describe the contents and format of a free space bitmap.

17.14 What does it mean to *mount* a volume into a file system?

17.15 Windows and Linux use two different methods to identify files on a network. Briefly describe each method.

17.16 What is a *pathname*?

17.17 What is the difference between a relative pathname and an absolute pathname? How does the system know which one a user is specifying at a particular time?

17.18 You are given the directory tree in Figure 17E.1. Assume that you are currently located at the point indicated with the arrow labeled (A) in the diagram. What is the *relative* pathname for the file *ourfile.doc*? What is the *absolute* pathname for this file? Suppose you are user Joan, located at the point indicated by the arrow labeled (B). What is your relative pathname to the file *ourfile.doc*?

17.19 How does a storage area network differ from a client-server approach to storage?

EXERCISES

17.1 Explain why a MOVE operation from one device to another requires manipulation of the file itself, whereas a MOVE operation from one place to another on the same device involves manipulation only of the directory.

17.2 In many systems, the operations that work on a file as a whole are made up by combining the operations that manipulate the internal file data. Explain how you would copy a file from one location to another using the internal file operations.

FIGURE 17E.1

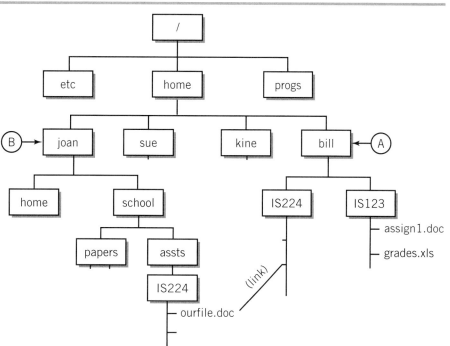

Does this method seem consistent with your experience of what happens when you copy a large file from one disk drive to another on your PC?

17.3   List a number of types of files that you would expect to be accessed sequentially. Do the same for files that you would expect would require random access.

17.4   Select a directory and list the files in that directory. For each file, determine how many blocks would be required if the block size were to be 512 bytes, 1 KB, 4 KB, and 8 KB. Calculate the internal fragmentation for each file and for each block size. How much disk space on your PC is wasted for each block size? Also give the answer as a percentage of the total block space used for that directory.

17.5   From a Windows command line prompt, do a DIR command. Carefully note how much space remains on your disk. Now open up NOTEPAD, and create a new file containing just a period with a carriage return. Call this file PROB174.TXT and return to the prompt. Do a DIR PROB174.TXT command. How much space does your new file take up? How much space remains on your disk? Explain what happened.

17.6   Explain the trade-offs between contiguous, noncontiguous linked, and noncontiguous indexed file allocation. In particular, note the effect on sequential and random access methods.

17.7   You have noticed that loading the programs from your hard disk seems to take longer than it used to. A friend suggests copying the files from your disk, one at a time, to a different device, and back to your disk. You do so and discover that the programs load much faster now. What happened? What alternative approach would achieve a similar result more easily?

17.8 What is the purpose of the open and close operations?

17.9 Consider a file that has just grown beyond its present space on disk. Describe what steps will be taken next for a contiguous file, for a linked noncontiguous file, and for an indexed file.

17.10 What does it mean to mount a disk?

17.11 Assume a UNIX i-node requires a block of 60 bytes. How many disk blocks can be accessed using just direct, single, and double indirect indexing, as shown in Figure 17.9?

17.12 What are the advantages of partitioning a disk, rather than using the entire disk as one partition?

17.13 What role does a path serve?

17.14 Explain the specific file privileges for each file in Figure 17.20. Who is the owner of these files? What is the name of the group that has access to these files?

17.15 The access control list for a file specifies which users can access that file, and how. Some researchers have indicated that an attractive alternative would be a user control list, which would specify which files a user could access, and how. Discuss the trade-offs of such an approach in terms of space required for the lists, and the steps required to determine whether a particular file operation is permitted.

17.16 **a.** Disk caching is a technique that is used to speed up disk access by holding blocks of disk in memory. Discuss strategies that could be used to improve system performance with disk caching.

b. The time of write back for files that have been altered depends on the system. Some systems write back a file immediately when it has been altered. Others wait until the file is closed or until the system is not busy or until activity on the particular file has stopped for a given period of time. Discuss the trade-offs between these different approaches.

CHAPTER 18

THE INTERNAL OPERATING SYSTEM

Thomas Sperling

18.0 INTRODUCTION

In Chapter 15 we presented an overview of the role of the operating system as a primary computer system component and observed that it is possible to represent the architecture of the operating system as a hierarchy, consisting of several layers of programs that interact with each other to handle the routine tasks of command processing, file management, I/O, resource management, communication, and scheduling. We continued the discussion in Chapter 16 by starting with the most familiar layer, the user interface. Chapter 17 moved inward to the next layer and presented the features and organization of the file management system. The file manager converts the logical representation of files as seen by the user or the user's programs to the physical representation stored and manipulated within the computer.

Now we are ready to examine major features of the remaining inner layers. These layers are designed primarily to manage the hardware and software resources of the computer and its interactions with other computers. In this chapter, we will look at how these internal operations are performed; we will consider how the operating system programs manage processes, memory, I/O, secondary storage, CPU time, and more for the convenience, security, and efficiency of the users.

We will briefly review the concepts from Chapter 15 first. Then we expand our focus to look at the various components, features, and techniques that are characteristic of modern operating systems. We will show you a simple example in which the different pieces have been put together to form a complete system.

A modern system must have the means to decide which programs are to be admitted into memory and when, where programs should reside in memory, how CPU time is to be allocated to the various programs, how to resolve conflicting requirements for I/O services, and how to share programs and yet maintain security and program and data integrity, plus resolve many other questions and issues. It is not uncommon for the operating system to require several hundreds of megabytes of memory just for itself.

In this chapter, we consider the basic operations performed by the operating system. We introduce individually the various tasks that are to be performed by the operating system and consider and compare some of the methods and algorithms used to perform these tasks in an effective manner. We discuss the basic procedure of loading and executing a program, the boot procedure, the management of processes, memory management, process scheduling and CPU dispatch, secondary storage management, and more.

As we have mentioned previously, the modern computer includes additional CPU hardware features that work in coordination with the operating system software to solve some of the more challenging operating system problems. Virtual storage is arguably the most important of these advances. Virtual storage is a powerful technique for solving many of the difficulties of memory management. Section 18.7 is devoted to a detailed introduction to virtual storage. It also serves as a clear example of the integration of hardware and operating system software that is characteristic of modern computer systems.

Other examples include the layering of the instruction set to include certain protected instructions for use only by the operating system, which we presented in Chapter 7, and memory limit checking, which the operating system can use to protect programs from each other.

The subject of operating systems can easily fill a large textbook and an entire course all by itself. There are many interesting questions and problems related to operating systems and many different solutions to the problem of creating a useful and efficient operating system. Obviously, we won't be able to cover this subject in a great amount of detail, but at least you'll get a feeling for some of the more important and interesting aspects of how operating systems work.

The many tasks that a modern operating system is expected to perform also expand the overhead required by the operating system, both in terms of memory and in the time required to perform the different functions. We will also look at some of the measures that are used to determine the effectiveness of an operating system. Finally, you'll have a chance to read about a few of the more interesting problems, especially those that can have a significant effect on the user.

18.1   FUNDAMENTAL OS REQUIREMENTS

Always keep in mind that the fundamental purpose of any operating system is to load and execute programs. This is true regardless of the specific goals, design features, and complexity of the particular operating system that you happen to be looking at.

With this fundamental idea in mind, look again at the various functions that are provided within the operating system. To assist with this task, the hierarchical model is shown again for your convenience in Figure 18.1.

Recall that to load and execute a program, the system must provide a method of getting the program from its storage location on some I/O device, such as disk, into memory; it must provide locations in memory for the program and its data; it must provide CPU time for the program to execute; and it must provide access to the I/O facilities that the program needs during its execution. Since multiple programs are normally sharing the system and its resources, it must do all this in a way that is fair and meets the sometimes conflicting requirements of the different programs.

The lower layers of the model provide programs that fulfill these requirements. The file manager layer translates logical file requests from the command shell or the user's programs into specific physical I/O requests that are then performed by the appropriate I/O device management programs. Resource allocation management is also provided in this layer to resolve conflicts between different programs that may require I/O services at the same time. The I/O device management and resource allocation programs are sometimes known collectively as an I/O control system, or more commonly, IOCS.

The memory management and scheduling operations within the resource allocation function determine if it is possible to load programs and data into memory, and, if so, where in memory the program is to be loaded. Once the program is in memory, the scheduler allocates time for the program to execute. If there are multiple programs in memory, the scheduler attempts to allocate time for each of them in some fair way.

FIGURE 18.1

A Hierarchical Model of an OS

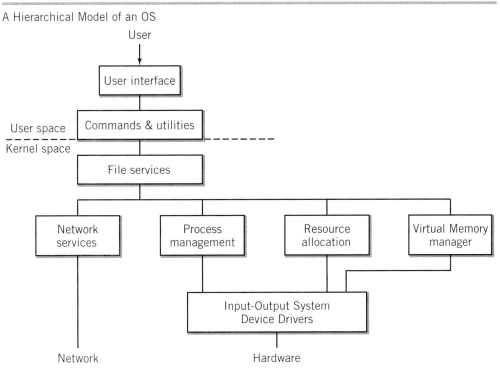

The monitor program, when included, provides overall control of the system. It establishes guidelines for the general management of the system based on goals provided by the human manager of the system. It watches for conflicts, breakdowns, and problems and attempts to take appropriate action to ensure smooth and efficient system operation. Some monitors can even reconfigure and reassign resources dynamically to optimize performance, particularly in clustered systems. These roles are handled by other operating system components in some systems.

To increase security, many operating systems construct these programs as a hierarchy in which each layer of programs in the model requests services from the next innermost layer, using an established calling procedure. Most modern computers provide special protected hardware instructions for this purpose. Recall from Chapter 15 that this is not the only possible architecture for an operating system. At the very least, the critical parts of the operating system will execute in a protected mode while other programs will execute in user mode. A well-designed operating system will repel attempts to penetrate the internal layers of the system by means other than established OS calling procedures. It must isolate and protect each program, yet allow the programs to share data and to communicate, when required.

There are many different ways of performing each of these functions, each with advantages and disadvantages. The trade-offs selected reflect the design goals of the particular system. To give you a simple example, a computer that operates strictly in a batch mode might use a simple CPU scheduling algorithm that allows each program to run without interruption as long as the program does not have to stop processing to wait for I/O. This strategy would not be acceptable on an interactive system that requires fast screen response when a user clicks the mouse or types something into the keyboard. In the latter case, a more sophisticated scheduling algorithm is clearly required.

Before we continue with discussions of the individual resource managers, you should be aware that these managers are not totally independent of each other. For example, if there are more programs in the memory of an interactive system, the scheduler must give each program a shorter period of time if satisfactory user response is to be achieved. Similarly, more programs in memory will increase the workload on a disk manager, making it more likely that there will be several programs waiting for disk I/O at the same time. A well-designed operating system will attempt to balance the various requirements to maximize productive use of the system.

Before proceeding to detailed discussions of each of the major modules in a multitasking operating system, it may provide some insight to introduce you to a simple example of a system, a sort of "Little Man multitasking operating system", if you will. The system discussed here does not run on the Little Man Computer, however. It was designed for a real, working computer system. This example illustrates many of the important requirements and operations of a multitasking system.

Example: A Simple Multitasking Operating System

The miniature operating system (hereafter referred to as MINOS) is an extremely small and simple multitasking system with many of the important internal features of larger systems. It is based on a real operating system that was developed by the author in the 1970s for a very early and primitive microcomputer that was used primarily to measure data in remote rural locations. Calculations were performed on the data and the results telecommunicated back to a larger computer for further processing. The original goals of the design were

- First and foremost, simplicity. Memory was very expensive in those days, so we didn't want to use much for the operating system. There was only 8 KB of memory in the machine.
- Real-time support for one very important program that was run frequently and had to operate very fast. This was the data measurement program. The system therefore features a priority scheduling system in choosing which program is to run.

The internal design of MINOS was of more interest and importance to the designers than the user interface or the file system. There was no disk on this computer, only an audio cassette tape recorder, modified to hold computer data, so the file system was simple. (Disks were too expensive, too large, and too fragile for this type of system back then!) There was a keyboard/printer user interface, but no CRT display interface. Security was not a concern.

The features of particular interest to us here are the operation of memory management, process scheduling, and dispatching. Despite their simplicity, the design of these modules is characteristic of the way current operating systems work. These were the important specifications for MINOS:

- Keyboard/printer command line user interface. To keep things simple, there were only a few commands, most of which could be entered by typing a single character. For example, the letter "l" was used to load a program from tape, the letter "s" to save a program to tape.

- Memory was divided into six fixed partitions of different sizes. A memory map is shown in Figure 18.2. One partition was reserved for MINOS, which was entirely memory resident. Partition P-1 was reserved for high-priority programs, most commonly the data retrieval program, since it had to retrieve data in real time. Partitions P-2, P-3, and P-4 were of different sizes, but all shared equal, middle priority. Partition P-5 was a low-priority area, which was used for background tasks, mostly internal system checking, but there was a simple binary editor available that could be loaded into the low-priority partition for debugging and modifying programs.

- The operating system was divided into three levels: the command interface; the I/O subsystem; and the kernel, which contained the memory manager, the communication interface, and the scheduler. The operating system kernel had the highest priority by default, since it had to respond to user commands and provide dispatching services. It could interrupt and preempt other programs. However, routine operations such as program loading were processed at the lowest priority level. A block diagram of MINOS appears in Figure 18.3.

Note again that MINOS did not support a file system or most other user amenities; it was primarily oriented toward program loading and execution. This limitation does not concern us, since the primary focus of this discussion is the internal operation of the system. The two major components of the kernel were the process scheduler/memory manager and the dispatcher.

MINOS was capable of manipulating up to five user programs at a time. The process scheduler handled requests for program loading. The header for a program to be loaded specified a priority level and a memory size requirement. Programs were loaded into the smallest available memory space of the correct priority level that would fit the program. Of course, there was only a single memory area available for each program of the highest and lowest priorities. If space was not available, the process scheduler notified the user; it was up to the user to determine which program, if any, should be unloaded to make room.

For each program in memory, there was an entry in a process control table, shown in Figure 18.4. Recall from Chapter 14 that at any instant in time, one process per CPU is running, while the others are ready to run or waiting for an event, such as I/O completion, to occur. The process control table shows the status of each program and the program counter location where the program will restart when it is next run. In MINOS, it also contained locations for storage and restoration of each of the

FIGURE 18.2

The MINOS Memory Map

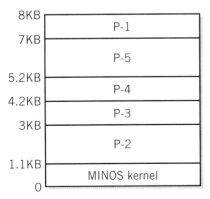

8KB	P-1	
7KB	P-5	
5.2KB	P-4	
4.2KB	P-3	
3KB	P-2	
1.1KB	MINOS kernel	
0		

FIGURE 18.3

Block Diagram, MINOS

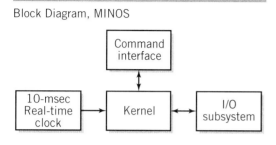

two registers that were present in the microcomputer that was used. There was also one additional register that kept track of which mid-priority process, partition 2, partition 3, or partition 4, was run most recently. We called this register the *mid-priority process run last*, or MPRL, register. Since there was one entry in the process table for each partition, the priority value for each program was already known by the operating system.

The most interesting part of MINOS was the program dispatcher. A real-time clock in the computer interrupted the computer every 1/100th of a second and returned control to the dispatcher. The dispatcher went through the process control table in order of priority and checked the status of each active entry. (An inactive entry is one in which there was no program loaded into the space, or in which the program in the space had completed execution and was not running.) If the entry was blocked because it was waiting for I/O to be completed, it was not available to run and was passed by. The highest-priority ready program was selected and control passed to it. If there were two or three ready programs of the same priority, they were selected in a round-robin fashion (program 2, program 3, program 4, program 2, program 3, ...), so that each got a turn. The MPRL register was used for this purpose.

The MINOS dispatching algorithm guaranteed that the high-priority real-time program always got first shot at the CPU and that the maximum delay before it could execute

FIGURE 18.4

MINOS Process Dispatch

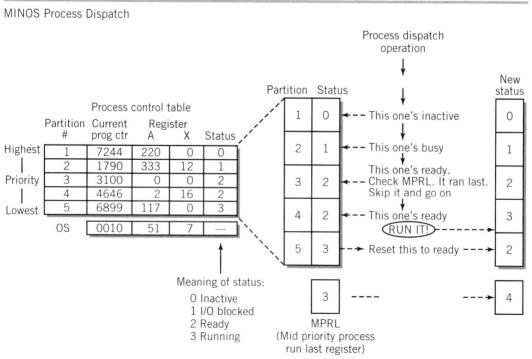

was 1/100th of a second. The ready bit for this program was actually set by a small interrupt routine controlled by the measuring device. Figure 18.4 illustrates the dispatching process.

The background task represented the lowest priority. By default, this partition contained software routines for testing various aspects of the hardware. Thus, when no other program was selected, MINOS defaulted to the hardware diagnostic routines.

With MINOS as a background, the next nine sections of Chapter 18 consider various aspects of a multitasking operating system in more detail. You may also wish to review Section 15.3 of Chapter 15, which introduces the various services and modules present in a modern multitasking system, before proceeding.

18.2 STARTING THE COMPUTER SYSTEM: THE BOOTSTRAP

As a first step, we need to consider what is required to get the computer started. You will recall that when the computer is first turned on, the contents of RAM are unknown. Furthermore, you know that there must be a program in memory for CPU execution to take place. These two considerations are contradictory; therefore, special means must be included to get the system into an operating state.

Initial program loading and start-up is performed by using a *bootstrap* program that is built permanently into a read-only part of memory for the computer. This bootstrap program begins execution as soon as the machine is powered up. The bootstrap program contains a program loader that automatically loads a selected program from secondary storage into normal memory and transfers control to it. The process is known as bootstrapping, or more simply, as *booting* the computer. IBM calls the process *Initial Program Load*, or *IPL*. Figure 18.5 illustrates the bootstrapping operation.

FIGURE 18.5

Bootstrapping a Computer

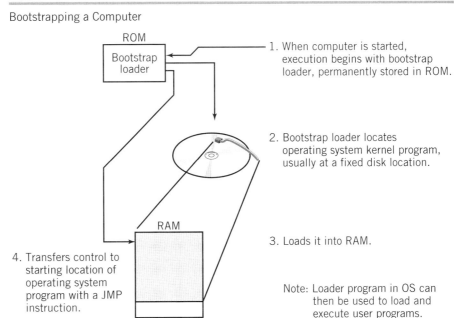

ROM

Bootstrap loader

1. When computer is started, execution begins with bootstrap loader, permanently stored in ROM.

2. Bootstrap loader locates operating system kernel program, usually at a fixed disk location.

RAM

3. Loads it into RAM.

4. Transfers control to starting location of operating system program with a JMP instruction.

Note: Loader program in OS can then be used to load and execute user programs.

Since the bootstrap is a read-only program, the program that it loads must be predetermined and must be found in a known secondary storage location, usually at a particular track and sector on a hard disk, although the bootstrap can be tailored to start the computer from another device, or even from another computer if the system is connected to a network. Usually the bootstrap loads a program that is itself capable of loading programs. (This is the reason that the initial program loader is called a bootstrap.) Ultimately, the program loaded contains the operating system kernel. In other words, when the boot procedure is complete, the kernel is loaded, and the computer is ready for normal operation. The resident operating system services are present and ready to go. Commands can be accepted, and other programs loaded and executed. The bootstrap operation is usually performed in two or more stages of loading to increase flexibility in the location of the kernel and to keep the initial bootstrap program small.

EXAMPLE

The PC serves as an appropriate and familiar example of the bootstrap start-up procedure. Although the PC uses a multistep start-up procedure, the method is essentially identical to that we have just described.

The PC bootstrap loader is permanently located in the system BIOS, read-only memory included as part of the computer, and introduced previously in Chapter 15. When the power switch for the computer is turned on, or when the reset button is pushed, control is transferred to the first address of the bootstrap loader program. The PC bootstrap begins by performing a thorough test of the components of the computer. The test verifies that various components of the system are active and working. It checks for the presence of a monitor, of a hard drive if installed, and of a keyboard. It checks the instructions in ROM for errors by calculating an algebraic function of the 1s and 0s, known as a checksum, and comparing that value with a predetermined correct value. It checks RAM by loading known data into every location and reading it back. Finally, it resets the segment registers, the instruction pointer, flags, and various address lines. (The 386, 486, P5, and P6 CPUs set many other registers as well.) The results of these tests appear on the monitor screen.

At the completion of this test, the bootstrap loader determines which disk is the system disk. This location is a setting stored permanently in a special memory, modifiable by the user at startup time. On modern PCs, the system may be booted from a hard disk, a floppy disk, a CD or DVD, or many USB-pluggable devices. The system disk contains a sector known as a boot record, and the boot record is loaded next.

The boot record now takes control. It also contains a loader, which is tailored to the I/O requirements for the particular disk. Assuming that Windows 2000, NT, or XP is to be loaded, the boot record then loads a sequence of files, including the kernel and executive program, NTOSKRNL.EXE; the registry; the hardware interface; various kernel, subsystem, and API libraries; and a number of other components. The items loaded are based on entries in the registry. The user has little control over this process while it is happening. Next, a logon program, WINLOGON.EXE is initiated. Assuming that the user is authorized and that the logon is successful, the kernel sets the user parameters defined in the registry, the Windows GUI is displayed, and control of the system is turned over to the user.

Different BIOSes vary slightly in their testing procedures, and some allow the user to change some PC setup settings when testing takes place. The user can also force the bootstrap to occur one step at a time to remedy serious system problems. Other than that, the user or system administrator controls the PC environment with standard tools provided by the operating system.

As noted, the procedure described here takes place when power is first applied to the computer. This procedure is also known as a cold boot. The PC also provides an alternate procedure known as a warm boot, for use when the system must be restarted for some reason. The warm boot, which is initiated from a selection on the *shutdown* menu, causes an interrupt call that reloads the operating system, but it does not retest the system and it does not reset the various registers to their initial values.

EXAMPLE

It is important to realize that basic computer procedures are not dependent on the size of the computer. The boot procedure for a large IBM mainframe computer is quite similar to that of a PC. IBM mainframe computers are bootstrapped using the Initial Program Load procedure. IPL works very similarly to the PC bootstrap procedure. Whenever power is applied to an IBM mainframe computer, the computer is in one of four operating states: operating, stopped, load, and check stop. The operating and stopped states are already familiar to you. The check stop state is a special state used for diagnosing hardware errors. The load state is the state corresponding to IPL.

The system operator causes the system to enter load state by setting load-unit-address controls and activating the load-clear or load-normal key on the operator's console. The load-unit-address controls establish a particular channel and I/O device that will be used for the IPL. The load normal key performs an initial CPU reset that sets the various registers in the CPU to their initial values and validates proper operation. The load-clear key does the same, but also performs a clear reset, which sets the contents of main storage and many registers to zero.

Following the reset operation, IPL performs the equivalent of a START I/O channel command, as discussed in Chapter 11. The first channel command word is not read from memory, since memory may have been reset to zero. Instead, a built-in READ command is used, which reads the IPL channel program into memory for execution. The IPL channel program then reads in the appropriate operating system code and transfers control to it.

18.3 PROCESSES AND THREADS

When considering a multitasking system, it is easiest to think of each executing task as a program. This representation is not inaccurate, but it is not sufficiently inclusive, precise, or general to explain all the different situations that can occur within a computer system. Instead, we may define each executing task more usefully as a process. A **process** is defined to include a program, together with all the resources that are associated with that program as it is executed. Those resources may include I/O devices that have been assigned to the particular process, keyboard input data, files that have been opened, memory that has been assigned as a buffer for I/O data or as a stack, memory assigned to the program, CPU time, and many other possibilities.

Another way of viewing a process is to consider it as a program in execution. A program is viewed passively: it's a file or a listing, for example. A process is viewed actively: it is being processed or executed.

In batch systems, a different terminology is sometimes used. A user submits a **job** to the system for processing; the job is made up of **job steps**, each of which represents a single **task**. It is not difficult to see the relationship among jobs, tasks, and processes. When the job is admitted to the system, a process is created for the job. Each of the tasks within the job also represent processes, specifically, processes that will be created as each step in the job is executed. In this book we tend to use the words job, task, and process interchangeably.

The difference between a program and a process is not usually important in normal conversation, but from the perspective of the operating system the difference may be quite significant and profound. For example, most modern operating systems have the capability of sharing a single copy of a program such as an editor among many processes concurrently. Each process has its own files and data. This practice can save memory space, since only a single copy of the program is required, instead of many; thus, this technique increases system capability. Crucial to this concept, however, is the understanding that each process may be operating in a different part of the program; therefore, each process maintains a different program counter value during its execution time, as well as different data. This concept is illustrated in Figure 18.6. By maintaining a separate process for each user, the operating system can keep track of each user's requirements in a straightforward manner.

Even in a single-user system, multiple processes may share program code. For example, the program code that produces the Windows interface will be shared by all the processes with open windows on a screen. Each process will have its own data: the coordinates of the window, pointers to the menu structure for that window, and so forth.

To the operating system, the basic unit of work is a process. When a process is admitted to the system, the operating system is responsible for every aspect of its operation. The operating system must allocate initial memory for it and must continue to assure that memory is available to the process as it is needed. It must assign the necessary files and I/O devices and provide stack memory and buffers. It must schedule CPU execution time for the process and perform context switching between the various executing processes. The operating system must maintain the integrity of the process. Finally, when the process is completed, it terminates the process in an orderly way and restores the system facilities and resources to make them available to other processes.

Processes that do not need to interact with any other processes are known as **independent processes**. In modern systems, many processes will work together.

FIGURE 18.6

Two Processes Sharing a Single Program

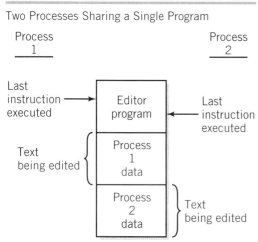

They will share information and files. A large task will often be modularized by splitting it into subtasks, so that each process will only handle one aspect of the task. Processes that work together are known as **cooperating processes**. The operating system provides mechanisms for synchronizing and communicating between processes that are related in some way. (If one process needs the result from another, for example, it must know when the result is available so that it can proceed. This is known as synchronization. It must also be able to receive the result from the other process. This is communication.) The operating system acts as the manager and conduit for these interprocess events.

To keep track of each of the different processes that are executing concurrently in memory, the operating system creates and maintains a block of data for each process in the system. This data block is known as a **process control block**, frequently abbreviated as **PCB**. The process control block contains all relevant information about the process. It is the central resource used by the various operating system modules as they perform their process-related functions.

In MINOS, the process control block was simple. It was only necessary to keep track of the program counter and a pair of register values so that processes could be suspended and restarted, plus the status and priority of the program. Since MINOS divided memory into partitions of fixed size, there was exactly one process and therefore one PCB per partition, so it was not even necessary for the operating system to keep track of the memory limits of a process.

In a larger system, process control is considerably more complex. There may be many more processes. Contention for the available memory and for various I/O resources is more likely. There may be requirements for communication between different processes. Scheduling and dispatch are more difficult. The complexity of the system requires the storing of much additional information about the process, as well as more formal control of process operations.

FIGURE 18.7

A Typical Process Control Block

Process ID
Pointer to parent process
Pointer area to child processes
...
Process state
Program counter
Register save area
...
Memory pointers
Priority information
Accounting information
Pointers to shared memory areas, shared processes and libraries, files, and other I/O resources

The contents of a typical process control block are shown in Figure 18.7. Different system PCBs present this information in different order and with some differences in the information stored, but these differences are not important for the purposes of this discussion.

Each process control block in Figure 18.7 contains a process identification name or number that uniquely identifies the block. In Linux, for example, the process identification number is known as a **process identifier**, or more commonly, a **PID**. Active processes are readily observable on the Linux system using the *ps* command.

Next, the PCB contains pointers to other, related processes. This issue is related to the way in which new processes are created. It is discussed in the next section. The presence of this area simplifies communication between related processes. Following the pointer area is an indicator of the process state. In MINOS, four

process states were possible: inactive, ready, blocked, and running. In larger systems, there are other possible states; processor states are discussed later in this section. The program counter and register save areas in the process control block are used to save and restore the exact context of the CPU when the process gives up and regains the CPU.

Memory limits establish the legal areas of memory that the process may access. The presence of this data simplifies the task of security for the operating system. Similarly, priority and accounting information is used by the operating system for scheduling and for billing purposes.

Finally, the process control block often contains pointers to shared program code and data, open files, and other resources that the process uses. This simplifies the tasks of the I/O and file management systems.

Process Creation

A little thought should make it clear to you that a process is created when you issue a command that requests execution of a program, either by double-clicking on an icon or by typing an appropriate command. There are also many other ways in which a process is created. Particularly on interactive systems, process creation is one of the fundamental tasks performed by the operating system. Processes in a computer system are continually being created and destroyed.

Since *any* executing program is a process, almost any command that you enter into a multitasking interactive system normally creates a process. Even logging in creates a process, since logging in requires providing a program that serves as your interface, giving you a prompt or GUI, monitoring your keystrokes, and responding to your requests. In many systems, this is known as a **user process**. In some systems, all processes that are not modules of the operating system are known as user processes.

It should also be remembered that the operating system itself is made up of program modules. These modules, too, must share the use of the CPU to perform their duties. Thus, the active parts of the operating system are, themselves, processes. When a process requests I/O or operating system services, for example, processes are created for the various operating system program modules that will service the request, as well as for any additional processes resulting from the request. These processes are sometimes known as **system processes**.

In batch systems, jobs are submitted to the system for processing. These jobs are copied, or spooled, to a disk and placed in a queue to await admission to the system. A long-term scheduler in the operating system, discussed in Section 18.5, selects jobs as resources become available and loads them into memory for execution. A process is created when the long-term scheduler determines that it is able to accept a batch job and admits it to the system.

For convenience, operating systems generally associate processes with the process that created them. Creating a new process from an older one is commonly called **forking** or **spawning**. The spawning process is called a **parent**. The spawned process is known as a **child**. Many systems simply assign priorities, resources, and other characteristics to the child process by **cloning** the parent process. This means creating a process control block that is a duplicate of itself. Once the child process begins to execute, it goes by way of its own path. It can request its own resources and change whatever characteristics it needs to.

As an example of process creation, a C++ program compiler might create child processes that perform the different stages of compilation, editing, and debugging. Each child process is created when the specific task is needed and killed when the task is complete. Incidentally, note the synchronization between processes that is suggested by this example. If the compile process encounters an error, for example, the parent is notified so that it can activate an editor process. A successful compile will result in a load process that will load the new program for execution. And so on.

Removing a parent process usually kills all the child processes associated with it. Since a child process can itself have children, the actual process structure may be several generations deep. Pointers are used within the process control block to help keep track of the relationships between different processes.

When the process is created, the operating system gives it a unique name or identification number, creates a process control block for it, allocates the memory and other initial resources that the process needs, and performs other operating system bookkeeping functions. When the process exits, its resources are returned to the system pool, and its PCB is removed from the process table.

Process States

Most operating systems define three primary operating states for a process. These are known as the **ready state**, the **running state**, and the **blocked state**. The relationship between the different process states is shown in Figure 18.8.

Once a process has been created and admitted to the system for execution, it is brought into the *ready* state, where it must compete with all other processes in the ready state for CPU execution time. Being in the ready state simply means that a process is capable of execution if given access to the CPU.

At some point in time, presumably, the process will be given time for execution. The process is moved from the ready state to the *running* state. Moving from the ready state to the running state is called **dispatching** the process. During the time that the process is in the running state, the program has control of the CPU and is able to execute instructions.

FIGURE 18.8

The Major Process States

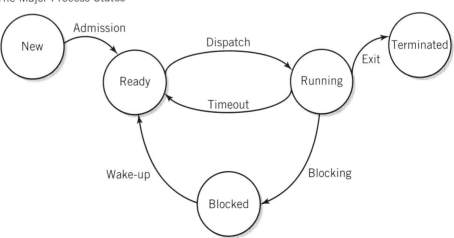

Of course, only one process can be in the running state at a time for a uniprocessor system. If there are multiple processors or a cluster under the operating system's control, the OS is responsible for dispatching a process to run in each available CPU. In a typical multitasking system, there may be many processes in *blocked* or ready states at any given time.

When I/O or other services are required for the continuation of program execution, the running process can no longer do any further useful work until its requirement is satisfied. Some operating systems will suspend the program when this occurs; others will allow the program to remain in the running state, even though the program is unable to proceed. In the latter case, most well designed programs will suspend themselves, unless the interruption is expected to be extremely brief. This state transition is known as **blocking**, and the process remains in a blocked state until its I/O requirement is complete. When the I/O operation is complete, the operating system moves the process from the blocked state back to the ready state. This state transition is frequently called **wake-up**. Blocking can also occur when a process is waiting for some event other than I/O to occur, for example, a completion signal or a data result from another process.

Nonpreemptive systems will allow a running process to continue running until it is completed or blocked. **Preemptive systems** will limit the time that the program remains in the running state to a fixed length of time corresponding to one or more quanta. If the process remains in the running state when its time limit has occurred, the operating system will return the process to the ready state to await further time for processing. The transition from the running state to the ready state is known as **time-out**.

When the process completes execution, control returns to the operating system, and the process is *destroyed* or *killed* or *terminated*.

Some operating systems provide one or more additional states, which are used to improve the efficiency of the computer system. Some processes make heavy demands on particular resources, say, a disk drive or a printer, or even the CPU, in such a way that other processes are unable to complete their work in an efficient manner. In this case the operating system may place a process in a **suspended state** until the required resources can be made available. When this occurs, the process is returned to a ready state. The transition from the *suspended* state to the ready state is known as **resumption**. Some operating systems also allow a user to suspend a process. On UNIX systems, for example, typing Control-z is one way in which to suspend a process. The process may be resumed by issuing the command *fg*, together with the process identification number of the process. Some operating systems will also swap out a suspended process from memory to secondary storage when the system becomes overloaded and will swap it back in when the load is lighter. Particularly in small systems, the use of **swap files** for this purpose is common. Even in large computer systems, transaction processing software often contains interactive processes that are used infrequently. These processes are often swapped out when they are not being used and returned to memory when they are activated by a user request. This technique is called **roll-out, roll-in**. The *suspend, resume*, and *swap* states have been left off the diagram for clarity.

Threads

It is common in modern systems to provide capability for a sort of miniprocess, known as a **thread**. A thread represents a piece of a process that can be executed independently of other parts of the process. (Think of the spell-checker in a word processor that checks words as you type, for example.) Each thread has its own context, consisting of a program counter value, register set, and stack space, but shares program code, and data, and other system resources such as open files with the other member threads in the process. Threads can operate concurrently. Like processes, threads can be created and destroyed and can be in ready, running, and blocked states. Context switching among threads is easier for the operating system to manage because there is no need to manage memory, files, and other resources and no need for synchronization or communication within the process, since this is handled within the process itself. This advantage suggests, however, that more care needs to be taken when the program is written, to assure that threads do not interact with each other in subtle ways that can create conditions that cause the program to fail. Note that there is no protection among the threads of a process, since all the threads are using the same program code and data space.

Some systems even provide a mechanism for context switching of threads independent of the process switching mechanism. This means that in these systems threads can be switched without the involvement of the operating system kernel. If a process becomes I/O blocked, it cannot proceed until the block is resolved. On the other hand, if a thread becomes blocked, other threads in the process may be able to continue execution within the process's allotted time, resulting in more rapid execution. Because the inner layers of the operating system are not even aware of thread context switching in these systems, thread switching is extremely rapid and efficient. Threads in these systems are commonly known as **user-level threads**.

Threads came about as a result of the advent of **event-driven programs**. In older programs with traditional text-based displays and keyboard input, there was a single flow of control. Event-driven programs differ in that the flow of control depends in a much more dramatic way on user input. With a modern graphical user interface, a user can pull down a menu and select an action to be performed at almost any time. Selecting an item from a menu or clicking a mouse in a particular place in a particular way is known as an **event**. The program must be able to respond to a variety of different events, at unknown times, and in unknown order of request.

Most such events are too small to justify creation of a new process. Instead, the action for each event is treated as a thread. The thread can be executed independently, but without the overhead of a process. There is no control block, no separate memory, no separate resources. The primary requirement for a thread is a context storage area to store the program counter and registers when context switching takes place. A very simple thread control block is adequate for this purpose. Threads are processed in much the same way as processes.

18.4 BASIC LOADING AND EXECUTION OPERATIONS

Since the CPU's capability is limited to the execution of instructions, every operation in a computer system ultimately arises from the fundamental ability to load and execute programs. Application programs do the users' work. Operating system programs and utilities manage files, control I/O operations, process interrupts, provide system security, manage the user interface, log operations for the system administrator to analyze, and much more. Except for programs that permanently reside in ROM, every one of these programs must be loaded into memory before it can be executed.

In general-purpose computer systems, the only programs permanently resident in ROM are usually just the few that are needed to boot the system. All other programs are loaded after the system is operational. Many of these programs are loaded into memory at start-up time and remain resident as long as the computer is on; others are loaded as they are requested or needed, but in either case, the program loading operation is central to system operation. Observing the steps in the loading process exposes the workings and interactions of many of the basic operating system components.

Incidentally, the program loader itself is a program that generally must be loaded; as we already noted in Section 18.2, this initial load occurs during the boot process. After that, the loader process remains resident in memory, ready for use.

In the previous section, you saw how processes are created from programs administratively by the process management component of the operating system. You are already aware, therefore, that requests for program loads are spawned from application or system programs that are already running. Now we take a brief look at the next step: what happens after the process is created but before it is loaded into memory and executed. This will prepare you for more detailed discussions of the memory management and scheduling issues that follow.

Figure 18.9 shows the basic steps required to load the program and ready it for execution.

18.5 CPU SCHEDULING AND DISPATCHING

CPU scheduling provides mechanisms for the acceptance of processes into the system and for the actual allocation of CPU time to execute those processes. A fundamental objective of multitasking is to optimize use of the computer system resources, both CPU and I/O, by allowing multiple processes to execute concurrently. CPU scheduling is the means for meeting this objective. There are many different algorithms that can be used for CPU scheduling. The selection of a CPU scheduling algorithm can have a major effect on the performance of the system.

As a way to optimize system performance, the CPU scheduling task is separated into two different phases. The **high-level**, or **long-term, scheduler** is responsible for admitting processes to the system. The **dispatcher** provides short-term scheduling, specifically, the instant-by-instant decision as to which one of the processes that are ready should be given CPU execution time. The dispatcher also performs context switching. Some systems also include a third, middle-level scheduler, which monitors system performance. When present, the middle-level scheduler can suspend, or **swap out**, a process by removing it from memory temporarily and replace it with another waiting process. This operation is known as **swapping**. Swapping is done to improve overall system performance. It would be used if a particular process were hogging a resource in such a way as to prevent other processes from executing.

High-Level Scheduler

The high-level scheduler determines which processes are to be admitted to the system. The role of the high-level scheduler is minimal for processes created in an interactive environment. Such processes are usually admitted to the system automatically. If a user

FIGURE 18.9

Loading and Executing a Process

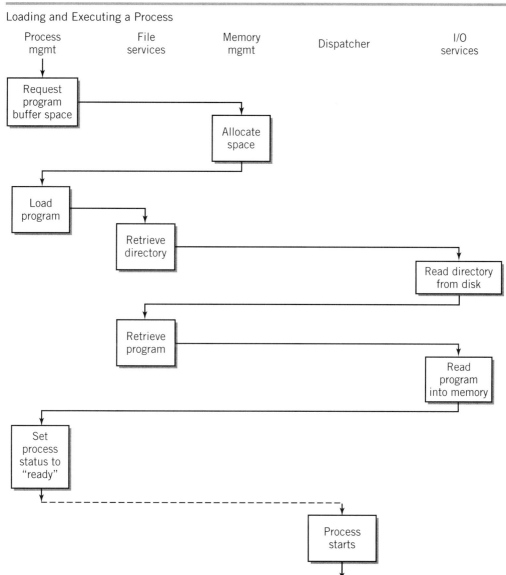

requests a service that requires the creation of a new process, the high-level scheduler *will*
attempt to do so unless the system is seriously overloaded. To refuse the user in the middle
of her or his work would be undesirable. The high-level scheduler will refuse a login process,
however, if it appears that doing so would overload the system. The high-level scheduler
will refuse admission to the system if there is no place to put the program in memory or if
other resources are unattainable. If the request is a user login request, the user will have to
wait until later to try again. Otherwise, requests are usually accepted, even though it may

slow down the system. You may have experienced such slowdowns when working with Windows. You may have even gotten an "out-of-memory" message if you tried to do too many things at once!

For batch processes, the high-level scheduler has a much more important role. Since most modern systems are predominately interactive, the use of batch processes is generally limited to processes with demanding resource requirements, for example, a monthly billing program for a large utility or department store chain, or an economics problem with huge amounts of data and complex calculations to be performed on the data. Processes of this type can make it difficult for regular users to get their work done if the process is executed during a busy time of day.

With batch processes, a delay in processing is usually acceptable to the user; therefore, the high-level scheduler has more flexibility in deciding when to admit the process to the system. The high-level scheduler can use its power to balance system resource use as an attempt to maximize the efficiency of the system and minimize disruption to the regular users.

Dispatching

Conceptually, the dispatching process is simple. Whenever a process or thread gives up the CPU, the dispatcher selects another candidate that is ready to run, performs a context switch, and sets the program counter to the program counter value stored in the process control block to start execution. In reality, dispatching is much more complex than it first appears. There are a number of different conditions that might cause a process to give up the CPU, some voluntary and some involuntary, as established by the operating system. Presumably, the goal of the dispatcher is to select the next candidate in such a way as to optimize system use. But, in fact, there are a number of different measurement criteria that can be used to define "optimum" system performance. Frequently, these criteria are in conflict with each other, and the characteristics of the candidates in contention as well as different conditions within the system can also affect the selection of a particular candidate for CPU execution at any given time.

Similarly, processes vary in their requirements. Processes can be long or short in their requirement for CPU execution time, they can require many resources, or just a few, and they can vary in their ratio of CPU to I/O execution time. Different scheduling algorithms favor different types of processes or threads and meet different optimization criteria. For example, an algorithm that maximizes throughput by consistently placing short jobs at the front of the queue is clearly not fair to a longer job that keeps getting delayed.

As a result, there are a number of different scheduling algorithms that can be used. The choice of scheduling algorithm then depends on the optimization objective(s) chosen, along with the expected mix of process types. Analysis requires consideration of a wide variety of process mix possibilities and dynamic situations. Some of the objectives considered are shown in the table in Figure 18.10. Of the various objectives in the table, the prevention of **starvation** is particularly noticeable. Some algorithms with otherwise desirable properties have a potential to cause starvation under certain conditions. It is particularly important that the algorithm selected not permit starvation to occur.

With operating systems that support threads, dispatching normally takes place at the thread level. As an additional criterion, the candidate selection decision can be made at

FIGURE 18.10

System Dispatching Objectives

Ensure fairness	The scheduler should treat every process equally. This means that every process should get a fair share of the CPU time.
Maximize throughout	The scheduler should attempt to maximize the number of jobs completed in any given time period.
Minimize turnaround time	The scheduler should minimize the time between submission of a job and its completion.
Maximize CPU utilization	The scheduler should attempt to keep the CPU busy as close to 100% of the time as possible.
Maximize resource allocation	The scheduler should attempt to maximize the use of all resources by balancing processes that require heavy CPU time with those emphasizing I/O.
Promote graceful degradation	This objective states that as the system load becomes heavy, it should degrade gradually in performance. This objective is based on the assumption that users expect a heavily loaded system to respond more slowly, but not radically or suddenly so.
Minimize response time	This objective is particularly important in interactive systems. Processes should complete as quickly as possible.
Provide consistent response time	Users expect long jobs to require more actual time than short jobs. They also expect a job to take about the same amount of time each time it is executed. An algorithm that allows a large variation in the response time may not be considered acceptable to users.
Prevent starvation	Processes should not be allowed to starve. *Starvation* is a situation that occurs when a process is never given the CPU time that it needs to execute. Starvation is also called *indefinite postponement.*

either the process or thread level. Some systems will select a candidate that meets criteria measured at the process level. A process is selected, then a thread within that process is dispatched. Other systems will select a thread for dispatch based on thread performance criteria without regard to the process to which they belong.

Some systems implement only a single algorithm, selected by the original system designers. Others provide options that can be selected by the administrator of the particular system installation. Other than preventing starvation, the most important consideration in selecting a scheduling algorithm is to determine the conditions under which dispatching is to be performed preemptively or nonpreemptively.

Early batch systems were predominately nonpreemptive. In a nonpreemptive system, the process assigned to the CPU by the dispatcher is allowed to run to completion, or until it voluntarily gives up the CPU. Nonpreemptive dispatching is efficient. The overhead required for the dispatcher to select a candidate and perform context switching in a preemptive system, particularly if the quantum time is short, becomes a substantial percentage of the overall CPU time available.

Nonpreemptive dispatching does not quite work in modern interactive systems. Some interrupts, particularly user keystrokes and mouse movements, demand immediate attention. **Response time** is an important criterion to a user sitting at a terminal waiting for a result. A long process executing nonpreemptively can cause the system to "hang" for a while. An additional disadvantage of nonpreemptive processing is that a buggy program with an infinite loop can hang the system indefinitely. Most nonpreemptive systems actually have a time-out built in for this purpose. A compromise position uses nonpreemptive processing for executing processes that do not require immediate responses, but allows critical processes to interrupt temporarily, always returning control to the nonpreemptive process. Earlier versions of Windows, through Version 3.1, presented another compromise that was dependent on the cooperation of the processes themselves. This position assumed that processes would voluntarily relinquish control on a regular basis, to allow other processes a chance to execute. To a large measure, this approach worked, although less well than true preemptive multitasking; however, it is subject to errors that may occur in individual processes that can prevent the execution of other processes.

Linux presents another compromise approach: user processes (i.e., regular programs) run preemptively, but operating system programs run nonpreemptively. An important requirement to this approach is that operating system processes run quickly and very reliably. The advantage to this approach is that critical operating system processes can get their work done efficiently without interruption from user processes.

The next section introduces a few typical examples of dispatching algorithms. There are many other possibilities, including algorithms that use combinations of these examples.

Nonpreemptive Dispatch Algorithms

FIRST-IN, FIRST-OUT   Probably the simplest possible dispatch algorithm, **first-in, first-out (FIFO)** simply assumes that processes will be executed as they arrive, in order. Starvation cannot occur with this method, and the method is certainly fair in a general sense; however, it fails to meet other objectives. In particular, FIFO penalizes short jobs and I/O-bound jobs, and often results in underutilized resources. As an illustration of the subtle difficulties presented when analyzing the behavior of an algorithm, consider what happens when one or more short, primarily I/O-based jobs are next in line behind a very long CPU-bound job in a FIFO queue. We assume that the scheduler is nonpreemptive but that it will allow another job to have the CPU when the executing job blocks for I/O. This assumption is essential to the full utilization of the CPU.

At the start of our observation, the long job is executing. While this happens, the short job(s) must sit and wait, unable to do anything. Eventually, the long job requires I/O and blocks. This finally allows the short jobs access to the CPU. Because they are predominately I/O-based jobs, they execute quickly and block, waiting to do I/O. Now, the short jobs must wait again, because the long job is using the I/O resources. Meanwhile, the CPU is idle, because the long job is doing I/O, and the short jobs are also idle, waiting to do I/O. Thus, FIFO can result in long waits and poorly balanced use of resources, both CPU and I/O.

SHORTEST JOB FIRST   The **shortest job first (SJF)** method will maximize throughput by selecting jobs that require only a small amount of CPU time. The dispatcher uses as its basis time estimates provided with the jobs when they are submitted. To prevent the user from lying, systems that use this algorithm generally inflict a severe penalty on jobs that run more than a small percentage over their estimate. Since short jobs will be pushed ahead of longer jobs, starvation is possible. When SJF is implemented, it generally includes a dynamic priority factor that raises the priority of jobs as they wait, until they reach a priority where they will be processed next regardless of length. Although SJF maximizes throughput, you might note that its **turnaround time** is particularly inconsistent, since the time required to complete a job depends entirely on the mix of the jobs submitted both before it, and possibly after it.

PRIORITY SCHEDULING   **Priority scheduling** assumes that each job has a priority assigned to it. The dispatcher will assign the CPU to the job with the highest priority. If there are multiple jobs with the same priority, the dispatcher will select among them on a FIFO basis.

Priorities can be assigned in different ways. On some systems that charge their users for CPU time, users select the priority. The fee is scaled to the priority, so that higher priorities cost more. In other systems, the priority is assigned by the system. Many factors can be used to affect performance, and the priorities may be assigned statically or dynamically. For example, a system may assign priority on the basis of the resources that the process is requesting. If the system is presently CPU-bound, it can assign an I/O-bound process a high priority to equalize the system.

Another variation on priority scheduling is basically nonpreemptive, but adds a preemptive element. As the process executes, it is periodically interrupted by the dispatcher, which reduces its priority, a little at a time, based on its CPU time used. If its priority falls below that of a waiting process, it is replaced by the higher-priority process.

Preemptive Dispatch Algorithms

ROUND ROBIN   The simplest preemptive algorithm, **round robin** gives each process a quantum of CPU time. If the process is not completed within its quantum, it is returned to the back of the ready queue to await another turn. The round-robin algorithm is simple and inherently fair. Since shorter jobs get processed quickly, it is reasonably good on maximizing throughput. Round robin does not attempt to balance the system resources and, in fact, penalizes processes when they use I/O resources, by forcing them to reenter the ready queue. A variation on round robin that is used by some UNIX systems calculates a dynamic priority based on the ratio of CPU time to total time that the process has been in the system. The smallest ratio is treated as the highest priority and is assigned the CPU next. If no process is using I/O, this algorithm reduces back to round robin, since the process that had the CPU most recently will have the lowest priority, and the priority will climb as it waits. The round-robin technique is illustrated in Figure 18.11.

MULTILEVEL FEEDBACK QUEUES   The **multilevel feedback queue algorithm** attempts to combine some of the best features of several different algorithms. This algorithm favors short jobs by providing jobs brief, but almost immediate, access to the system. It favors I/O-bound jobs, resulting in good resource utilization. It provides high throughput, with reasonably consistent response time. The technique is shown in Figure 18.12. The dispatcher provides a number of queues. The illustration shows three. A process initially enters the queue at the top level. The queue at the top level has top priority, so a new process will quickly receive a quantum of CPU time. Short processes will complete at this point. Since I/O-bound processes often require just a short amount

FIGURE 18.11

Round-Robin Scheduling

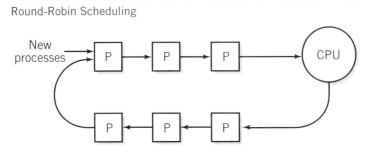

FIGURE 18.12

Multilevel Feedback Queue

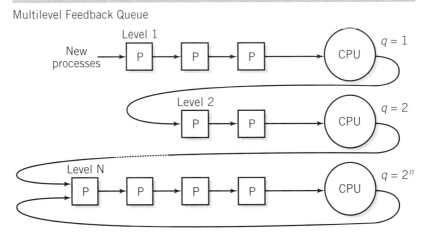

of initialization to establish their I/O needs, many I/O-bound processes will be quickly initialized and sent off for I/O.

Processes that are not completed are sent to a second-level queue. Processes in the second-level queue receive time only when the first-level queue is empty. Although starvation is possible, it is unlikely, because new processes pass through the first queue so quickly. When processes in the second level reach the CPU, they generally receive more time. A rule of thumb doubles the number of quanta issued at each succeeding level. Thus, CPU-bound processes eventually receive longer time slots in which to complete execution. This method continues for as many levels as the system provides.

The final level is a round robin, which will continue to provide time until the process is complete. Some multilevel feedback queues provide a good behavior upgrade to processes that meet certain criteria.

DYNAMIC PRIORITY SCHEDULING As noted above, the technique of **dynamic priority recalculation** can also be used as a preemptive dispatching technique. Both Windows 2000 and Linux use a dynamic priority algorithm as their primary criterion for dispatch selection. The algorithms on both systems adjust priority based on their use of resources. Details of the Windows and Linux dispatch algorithms are presented in Supplemental Chapter 2.

18.6 MEMORY MANAGEMENT

Memory management is the planned organization of programs and data into memory. The goal of memory management is to make it as simple as possible for programs to find space, so that they may be loaded and executed, together with the additional space that may be required for various buffers. A secondary and related goal is to maximize the use of memory, that is, to waste as little memory as possible.

Today, nearly all memory management is performed using virtual storage, a methodology that makes it appear that a system has a much larger amount of memory than actually exists physically. Virtual storage is discussed in Section 18.7.

Until the advent of virtual storage, however, effective memory management was a difficult problem. There may be more programs than can possibly fit into the given amount of physical memory space. Even a single program may be too large to fit the amount of memory provided. Compounding the difficulty, recall that most programs are written to be loaded contiguously into a single space, so that each of the spaces must be large enough to hold its respective program. Fitting multiple programs into the available physical memory would require considerable juggling by the memory management module.

In passing, we point out to you that there is also a potential relationship between scheduling and memory management. The amount of memory limits the number of programs that can be scheduled and dispatched. As an extreme example, if the memory is only large enough to hold a single program, then the dispatch algorithm is reduced to single tasking, simply because there is no other program available in memory to run. As more programs can be fit into memory, the system efficiency increases. More programs get executed, concurrently, in the same period of time, since the time that would be wasted when programs are blocked is now used productively. As the number of programs increases still further, beyond a certain point the resident time of each program starts to increase, because the available CPU time is being divided among programs that can all use it, and new programs are continually being added that demand CPU time.

Nonetheless within reason, it is considered desirable to be able to load new processes as they occur, particularly in interactive systems. A slight slowdown is usually considered preferable to a user being told that no resources are available to continue his or her work. As we have hinted a number of times, virtual storage provides an effective and worthwhile solution to the problem of memory management, albeit at the cost of additional hardware, program execution speed, disk usage, and operating system complexity. Before we explain the process of memory management using virtual storage, however, it is useful to offer a brief introduction to traditional memory management techniques to set the issues of memory management in perspective.

Memory Partitioning

The simplest form of memory management divides the memory space into a number of separate partitions. This was the method used prior to the introduction of virtual storage.

Today, it is used only in small embedded systems, where the number of programs running at a given time is small and well controlled. Each partition is used for a separate program.

Two different forms of memory partitioning can be used. **Fixed partitioning** divides memory into fixed spaces. The MINOS memory was managed using fixed partitioning. **Variable partitioning** loads programs wherever enough memory space is available, using a **best-fit, first-fit**, or **largest-fit algorithm**. The best-fit algorithm uses the smallest space that will fit the program. The first-fit algorithm simply grabs the first space available that fits the program. The largest-fit algorithm, sometimes called **worst-fit**, uses the largest space available, on the theory that this will leave the maximum possible space for another program. Figure 18.13 shows variable partitioning at work. Note that the starting positions of programs shift as space becomes available for new programs.

Realistically, partitionining is not suitable for modern general-purpose computing systems. There are two reasons for this:

- First, no matter which method is used, memory partitioning results in **fragmentation** of memory. This is seen in Figure 18.13. Fragmentation means that memory is being used in such a way that there are small pieces of memory available that, if pushed together, would be sufficient to load one or more additional programs. **Internal fragmentation** means that there is memory that has been assigned to a program that does not need it, but can't be used elsewhere. Fixed partitioning results in internal fragmentation. **External fragmentation** means that there is memory that is not assigned, but is too small to use. Variable partitioning will, after a while, result in external fragmentation, since the replacement of one program in an available space with another will almost always result in a bit of space left over. Eventually, it may be necessary to have the memory manager move programs around to reclaim the space. Internal and external fragmentation are shown in Figure 18.14.

FIGURE 18.13

Variable Partitioning of Memory at Three Different Times

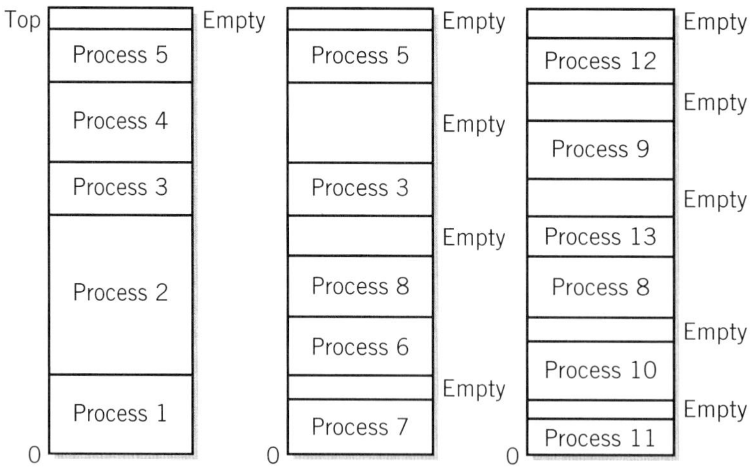

FIGURE 18.14

Internal and External Fragmentation

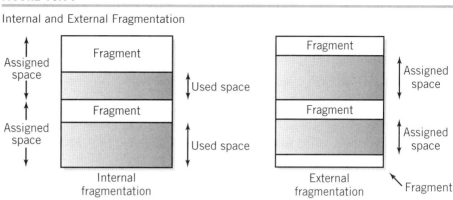

Although fragmentation is manageable when the number of programs to be loaded is small, and the size of each program known in advance, this is not the case for any general-purpose system.

■ Second, the size of most modern programs is sufficiently large that partitioning memory will make it even more difficult to find memory spaces large enough to accommodate all of the programs and data that the average user routinely expects to run concurrently. (You have already seen, in Chapter 17, similar fragmentation and partitioning problems that occur in the storage of files on disk.)

18.7 VIRTUAL STORAGE

Overview

There are three major problems inherent in the traditional (now outdated) memory management schemes described in the previous section:

1. As the system runs, fragmentation makes it harder and harder to find open spaces large enough to fit new programs as they are introduced into the system.

2. From Chapters 6 and 7, you should recall that Little Man programs, and indeed, all, programs, are coded on the assumption that they will be loaded into memory and executed starting from memory location 0. The address field in many, but not all, instructions points to an address where data is found or to the target address of a branch. Of course in reality, it is only possible to load one program at that location in memory. All other programs must be loaded into memory starting from some other address. That means that the operating system's program loader must carefully adjust the address field of all affected instructions to compensate for the actual addresses where the data or the branch target will actually be found.

3. There is often not enough memory to load all of the programs and their resources that we wish to execute at once.

Virtual storage (or **virtual memory**—the words are synonymous), is the near-universally accepted solution to the problems inherent in memory management. Virtual storage uses a combination of operating system software and special purpose hardware to simulate a memory that meets the management needs of a modern system. The primary method of implementing virtual storage is called **paging**.

Pages and Frames

To begin, assume that memory is divided into blocks. These blocks are called **frames**. Usually, all the frames are of equal size, typically 1 KB–4 KB. The exception, an alternative method called **segmentation** is used more rarely, and will be described later. The size of the blocks is permanently set as a design parameter of the particular hardware architecture, based on a number of factors. The most important criterion for the block size is that it must correspond exactly to a particular number of address bits. This guarantees that every address within the block is expressed by the same number of digits. In the Little Man Computer, for example, a block size of 10 would be the only reasonable choice, since every address within the block would be expressed with one digit (0–9). Similarly, in a real, binary-based computer, a 12-bit address can access an address space of exactly 4 KB.

The number of blocks depends on the amount of memory installed in the machine, but, of course, can't exceed the largest memory address possible, as determined by the architecture of the instruction set. We could install 60 mailboxes in the Little Man Computer, for example; this would give us six frames within the constraint that the address field of the LMC instructions limits us to a maximum of 100 mailboxes, or ten frames.

The blocks are numbered, starting from 0. Because the block size was selected to use a specific, fixed number of bits (or decimal digits for the Little Man Computer), an actual memory address consists simply of the block number concatenated with the address within the block. By selecting a frame size that corresponds exactly to a given number of digits, we can simply concatenate to get the whole address.

EXAMPLE

Suppose that a Little Man memory consisted of 60_{10} mailboxes, divided into 6 frames. Each frame is a one-digit block of size 10. The frames would be numbered from 0 through 5, and the address of a particular location within the frame would be a number from 0 to 9. Then, location number 6 in frame 3 would correspond to location 36 in memory. Similarly, memory address 49 would be in frame 4; the address would correspond to location 9 in that frame. Figure 18.15(a) illustrates this example.

EXAMPLE

Now consider a binary computer with 1 GB of memory divided into 4 KB frames. There will be 256 K, or approximately a quarter of a million, frames. (We divided 1 G by 4 K to get 256 K.) Another way to look at this is to realize that to address 1 GB of memory requires a 30-bit address. 4 KB frames will require 12 bits for addresses; therefore the number of frames will correspond to 18 bits, or 256 K frames.

For convenience, we will illustrate the example in hexadecimal. Remember that each hexadecimal digit represents 4 bits. Memory location $3A874BD7_{16}$ would then be located in

FIGURE 18.15

Identifying Frames and Offsets

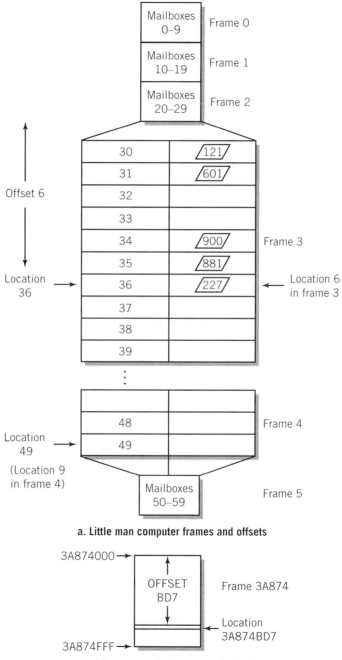

a. Little man computer frames and offsets

b. Binary computer frames and offsets

the frame block numbered $3A874_{16}$, and specifically found at location $BD7_{16}$ of that frame. Notice that the frame block number requires a maximum of 18 bits and that the location within the frame uses 12 bits. See Figure 18.15(b) for clarification. Similarly, location number 020_{16} within frame number $15A3_{16}$ corresponds to memory location $15A3020_{16}$.

Effectively, we are dividing each memory address into two parts: a frame number and the specific address within the particular frame. The address within the frame is called an **offset**, because it represents the offset from the beginning of the frame. (It should be clear to you that the first address in a frame, which is the beginning of the frame, is 0, with the correct number of digits of course, so address 1 is offset by 1 from the beginning, and so on.)

It is not immediately obvious why we are dividing memory into frame blocks, but the reason will become clear shortly. Here's a hint: note the similarity between the frame blocks that make up the memory space and the blocks that make up the space on a hard disk. Then, recall that we can find data within a file even if we store the files on a hard disk noncontiguously.

Suppose we also divide a program into blocks, where each block in the program is the same size as a frame. The blocks in a program are called **pages**. See Figure 18.16. The number of pages in a program obviously depends on the size of the program. We will refer to the instruction and data memory address references in a program as "logical" or "virtual" memory references, as opposed to the physical memory references that actually go out to memory and store and retrieve instructions and data. The words *logical* and *virtual* are used interchangeably.

Like frames, the number of pages is also constrained by the instruction set architecture, but, as we will show you later, it is not limited to the size of installed memory. Stated differently, a program can be larger than the amount of memory installed in a computer, and still execute successfully, although possibly slowly.

The key to this magical sleight-of-hand is a technique called **dynamic address translation (DAT)**. Dynamic address translation is built into the CPU hardware of every modern computer. The hardware automatically and invisibly translates every individual address in a program (the *virtual* addresses) to a different corresponding physical location (the *physical* addresses). This allows the operating system's program loader to place the pages of a program into any available frames of physical memory, page by page, noncontiguously, so that it is not necessary to find a contiguous space large enough to fit the entire program. Any page of any program can be placed into any available frame of physical memory. Since every frame is essentially independent, the only fragmentation will be the small amount of space left over at the end of the last page of each individual program.

For each program, the operating system creates a **page table**, which keeps track of the corresponding frame location in physical memory where each page is stored. There is one entry in the table for each page of the program. The entry contains the page number and its corresponding frame number.

FIGURE 18.16

Frames and Pages

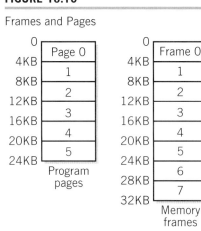

Since each page fits exactly into a frame, the offset of a particular address from the beginning of a page is also exactly the same as the offset from the beginning of the frame where the page is physically loaded. To translate a virtual address to a physical address, the virtual address is separated into its page number and an offset; a look-up in the program's page table locates the entry in the table for the page number, then translates, or *maps*, the virtual memory reference into a physical memory location consisting of the corresponding frame number and the same offset. We remind you again: this operation is implemented in hardware. Every memory reference in a fetch-execute cycle goes through the same translation process. The address that would normally be sent to the memory address register (MAR) is mapped through the page table and *then* sent to the MAR. It is also important to remember that the translation process is entirely invisible to the program. As far as the program can tell, every memory reference is exactly where the program says it is.

A simple example illustrates the translation process.

EXAMPLE

Consider a program that fits within one page of virtual memory. Placement of the program is shown in Figure 18.17a. The page for the program would be numbered 0, of course. If we assume a page size of 4 KB, then any logical memory location in this program would be between 0000 and 0FFF. Suppose frame 3 is available in which to place this program in physical memory. Then the physical addresses for this program to execute properly must all be between 3000 and 3FFF. We obtain the correct address in each case by changing the page number (0) to the frame number (3), keeping the offset the same as it was. A LOAD instruction, LOAD 028A, for example, would be translated to find its data in physical memory at 328A.

FIGURE 18.17(a)

A Simple Page Table Translation

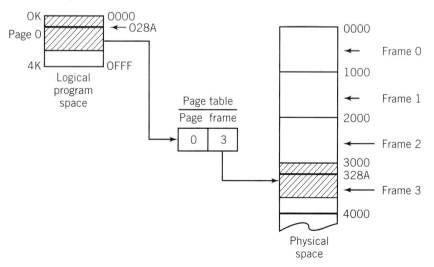

FIGURE 18.17(b)

The Page Translation Process

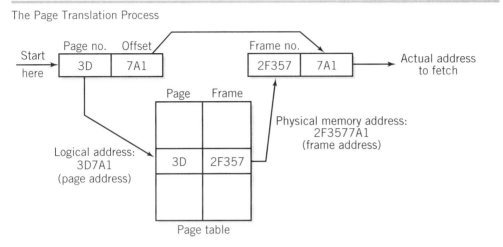

Another example, drawn differently to show the translation process more clearly, is presented in Figure 18.17b.

With virtual storage, each process in a multitasking system has its own virtual memory, and its own page table. Physical memory is shared among the different processes. Since all the pages are the same size, any frame may be placed anywhere in memory. The pages selected do not have to be contiguous. The ability to load any page into any frame solves the problem of finding enough contiguous memory space in which to load programs of different sizes.

Figure 18.18 shows a mapping for three programs located in memory. Note that each program is written as though it will load starting from address 0, eliminating the need for the loader to adjust a program's memory addresses depending on where the program is loaded. Since each program's page table points to a different area of physical memory, there is no conflict between different programs that use the same virtual addresses.

To complete this part of the discussion, let us answer two questions that may have occurred to you:

- Where do the page tables reside and how are they accessed by the hardware for address translation?
- How are memory frames managed and assigned to pages?

The simple answer to the first question is that page tables reside in memory, just like any other program or data. A page table address register in the CPU holds a pointer to the address in memory where the page table is located. The pointer is stored as part of the process control block; the address of the page table for the current process is loaded into the register as part of the context switching mechanism.

Although this answer is accurate, it is not quite complete. There are a few bells and whistles that improve performance, to be discussed later in this section under the paragraph title *Page Table Implementation*.

FIGURE 18.18

Mapping for Three Processes

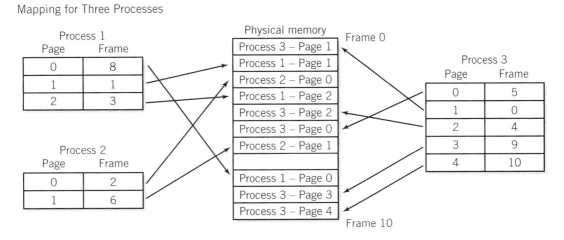

FIGURE 18.19

Inverted Page Table for Process Page Tables Shown in Figure 18.18

Frame	Process #	Page	
0	3	1	
1	1	1	
2	2	0	
3	1	2	
4	3	2	
5	3	0	
6	2	1	
7			Free page frame
8	1	0	
9	3	3	
10	3	4	

The answer to the second question is that physical memory is shared among all of the active processes in a system. Since each process has its own page table, it is not practical to identify available memory frames by accumulating data from all of the tables. Rather, there must be a single resource that identifies the entire pool of available memory frames from which the memory manager may draw, when required. There are two common approaches in use. One is to provide an *inverted page table*, which lists every memory frame with its associated process and page. This table shows the actual use of physical memory at every instant. Any frame without an associated page entry is available for allocation. Figure 18.19 illustrates an inverted page table. We'll leave it as a simple exercise for you to identify the available frames.

A second method maintains a list of available frames, usually as a simple linked list. When a process needs frames, it takes them from the top of the list. When a process exits, its frames are added to the end of the list. Since frame contiguity is unimportant, this is an effective way to manage the free frame pool.

The Concept of Virtual Storage

The first two issues of memory management that we raised initially are thus solved. But, as the TV infomercials say, "Wait—there's still more!"

As we noted before, the third major challenge for memory management is the limited total quantity of physical memory available. Even hundreds of megabytes of memory can only hold a few modern programs. Up to this point, we have assumed that there is a frame available for every page that needs one. While page-to-frame translation has eliminated the question of how to fit programs into existing memory space, the next step is more important and useful: we will show you how the concept of virtual storage allows the system to extend the address space far beyond the actual physical memory that exists. As you will see, the additional address space required to store a large number of programs is actually provided in an auxiliary form of storage, usually disk, although some systems now make it possible to use flash memory for this purpose.

So far we have assumed that all the pages of an executing program are located in frames somewhere in physical memory. Suppose that this were not the case—that there are not enough frames available to populate the page table when the program is loaded. Instead, only some pages of the program are present in physical memory. Page table entries without a corresponding frame are simply left empty. Can the program execute?

The answer depends on which pages are actually present in corresponding frames of physical memory. To execute a program instruction or access data, two requirements must be met.

- The instruction or data must be in physical memory.
- The page table for that program must contain an entry that maps the virtual address being accessed to the physical location containing the instruction or data.

These two requirements are related. The existence of a page listing in the page table implies that the required value is in memory and vice versa. If these two conditions are met, then the instruction can execute as usual. This suggests, correctly, that instructions and data that are *not* being accessed do not have to be in memory. At any given time in the execution of a program, there are active pages and inactive pages. Only the active pages require corresponding frames in the page table and in physical memory. Thus, it is possible to load only a small part of a program and have it execute.

Page Faults

The real question is what happens when an instruction or data reference is on a page that does not have a corresponding frame in memory. The memory management software maintains the page tables for each program. If a page table entry is missing when the memory management hardware attempts to access it, the fetch-execute cycle will not be able to complete.

In this case, the CPU hardware causes a special type of interrupt called a **page fault** or a **page fault trap.** This situation sounds like an error, but actually it isn't. The page fault concept is part of the overall design of virtual storage.

When the program is loaded, an exact, page-by-page image of the program is also stored in a known auxiliary storage location. The auxiliary storage area is known as a **backing store** or, sometimes, as a **swap space** or a **swap file.** It is usually found on disk, but some recent systems use flash memory for this purpose. Also assume that the page size and the size of the physical blocks on the auxiliary storage device are integrally related, so that a page within the image can be rapidly identified, located, and transferred between the auxiliary storage and a frame in memory.

When a page fault interrupt occurs, the operating system memory manager answers the interrupt. And now the important relationship between the hardware and the operating system software becomes clearer. In response to the interrupt, the memory management software selects a memory frame in which to place the required page. It then loads the page from its program image in auxiliary storage. If every memory frame is already in use, the software must pick a page in memory to be replaced. If the page being replaced has been altered, it must first be stored back into its own image, before the new page can be loaded. Page replacement algorithms are discussed later in this section. The process of page replacement is also known as **page swapping.** The steps involved in handling a page fault are shown in Figure 18.20.

FIGURE 18.20

Steps in Handling a Page Fault

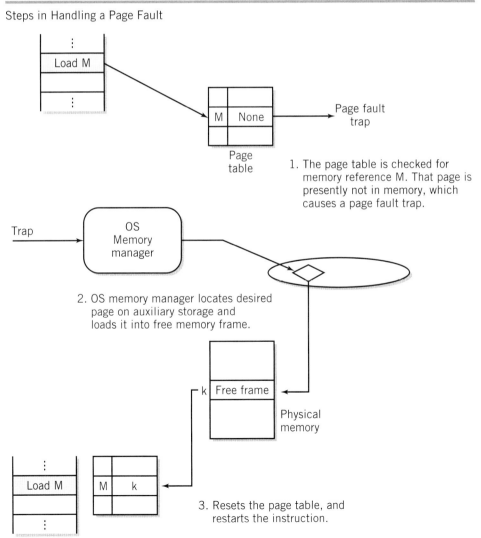

1. The page table is checked for memory reference M. That page is presently not in memory, which causes a page fault trap.

2. OS memory manager locates desired page on auxiliary storage and loads it into free memory frame.

3. Resets the page table, and restarts the instruction.

Most systems perform page swapping only when it is required as a result of a page fault. This procedure is called **demand paging.** A few systems attempt to anticipate page needs before they occur, so that a page is swapped in before it is needed. This technique is called **prepaging.** To date, prepaging algorithms have not been very successful at predicting accurately the future page needs of programs.

When the page swap is complete, the process may be started again where it left off. Most systems return to the beginning of the fetch-execute cycle where the page fault occurred, but a few systems restart the instruction in the middle of its cycle. Regardless of which way is used, the required page is now present, and the instruction can be completed. The importance of page swapping is that it means that a program does not have to be loaded into memory in its entirety to execute. In fact, the number of pages that must be loaded into memory to execute a process is quite small. This issue is discussed further in the next section.

Therefore, virtual storage can be used to store a large number of programs in a small amount of physical memory and makes it appear that the computer has more memory than is physically present. Parts of each program are loaded into memory. Page swapping handles the situations when required pages are not physically present. Furthermore, since the virtual memory mapping assures that any program page can be loaded anywhere into memory, there is no need to be concerned about allocating particular locations in memory. Any free frame will do.

Working Sets and the Concept of Locality

How many pages should be assigned to a new process just entering the system? It would seem that the more pages that are initially assigned to a process, the less likely it would be that a page fault would occur during execution of the process. Conversely, the more pages assigned to a process, the fewer the number of processes that will fit into memory. There is a lower limit on the number of pages to be assigned, which is determined by the instruction addressing modes used by the particular computer. Executing a single instruction in an indirect addressing machine, for example, requires at least three pages, the page where the instruction resides, the page where the indirect address is stored, and the page where the data is found. This assumes that each item is on a different page, but it is necessary to make the worst-case assumption to prevent instructions from failing in this way. Other instruction sets can be analyzed similarly.

More practically, experimentation performed in the early 1970s showed that during execution programs exhibit a tendency to stay within small areas of memory during any given period of time. Although the areas themselves change over time, the property continues to hold throughout the execution of the program. This property is called the **concept of locality.** An illustration of the concept at work is shown in Figure 18.21. The concept of locality makes sense intuitively. Most well-written programs are written modularly. During the initial phase of execution of a program, a small part of the program initializes variables and generally gets the program going. During the main body of the program, the likely operations consist of small loops and subroutine calls. These represent the different area of memory being executed at different times.

An effective compromise would allocate a sufficient number of pages to satisfy the locality of a particular program. This number of pages would be sufficient to run the

FIGURE 18.21

Memory Use with Time, Exhibiting Locality

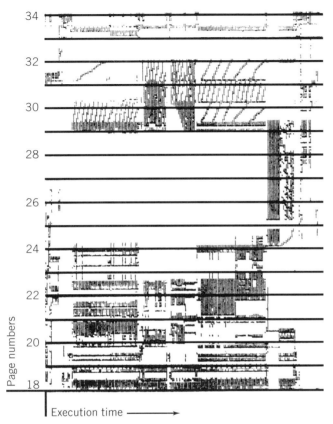

Source: Operating Systems 2/e by Stallings, W. © 1995. Reprinted by permission of Prentice-Hall, Upper Saddle River, NJ.

program normally. Page faults would only occur when the local area being used by the program moves to a different part of the program. The number of pages that meets the requirement of locality is called a **working set.** It differs somewhat from program to program, but it is possible to establish a reasonable page quantity that meets the needs of most programs without an undue number of page faults. Some systems go further and monitor the number of page faults that actually occur for each process. They then dynamically adjust the size of the working set for each process to try to meet its needs.

Page Sharing

An additional feature of virtual storage is the ability to share pages among different processes that are executing the same program. As long as the code is not modified, that is, the code is pure, there is no need to have duplicate program code stored in memory. Instead, each process shares the same program code page frames and provides its own work space for data. The page tables for each process will simply point to the same physical memory frames. This simplifies the management of multiple processes executing the same program.

Page Replacement Algorithms

There will be times on a heavily loaded system when every available page in memory is in use. When a page fault occurs, the memory manager must pick a page to be eliminated from memory to make room for the new page that is needed. The goal, of course, is to replace a page that will not be needed in the near future. There are a number of different algorithms that are used. As usual with operating system algorithms, each has advantages and disadvantages, so selecting an algorithm is a matter of trade-offs. Some systems select pages to be replaced from the same process. Others allow replacement from any process in the system. The former is known as **local page replacement**; the latter is called **global page replacement.** Global page replacement is more flexible, since there are a much larger number of pages to choose from. However, global page replacement affects the working set size of different processes and must be managed carefully.

As an additional consideration, some pages must never be removed from memory because doing so could eventually make the system inoperable. For example, removing the disk driver would make it impossible to swap in any new pages, *including the disk driver!* To prevent this situation, the frames corresponding to critical pages are locked into memory. These frames are called **locked frames.** An additional bit in each row of the page table is set to indicate that a frame is locked. Locked frames are never eligible for replacement.

FIRST-IN, FIRST-OUT PAGE REPLACEMENT   The simplest **page replacement algorithm** is a first-in, first-out algorithm. The oldest page remaining in the page table is selected for replacement. FIFO does not take into account usage of the page. Logically, a page that has been in memory for a long period of time is probably there because it is heavily used. The page being removed may be in current use, which would result in a second page fault and force the system to reload the page almost immediately. FIFO has a second, interesting deficiency. You would assume that increasing the number of pages available to a process would reduce the number of page faults for that process. However, it has been shown that under certain conditions, use of the FIFO page replacement algorithm results in more page faults with an increased number of pages, instead of fewer. This condition is known as **Belady's anomaly.** If you are interested, examples of Belady's anomaly can be found in the references by Deitel [DEIT03] and Silberschatz et al. [SILB08]. For these reasons, FIFO is not considered a good page replacement algorithm.

LEAST RECENTLY USED PAGE REPLACEMENT   The **least recently used (LRU) algorithm** replaces the page that has not been used for the longest time, on the assumption that the page probably will not be needed again. This algorithm performs fairly well, but requires a considerable amount of overhead. To implement the LRU algorithm, the page tables must record the time every time the page is referenced. Then, when page replacement is required, every page must be checked to find the page with the oldest recorded time. If the number of pages is large, this can take a considerable amount of time.

LEAST FREQUENTLY USED PAGE REPLACEMENT   Another possibility is to select the page that has been used the least frequently. Intuitively, this algorithm has appeal, since it would seem that a page not used much is more replaceable than one that has received a lot of use. The flaw with this algorithm is that a page that has just been brought into memory has not been used much, compared to a page that has been in memory for a while. Still, the new page was brought into memory because it was needed, and it is likely that it will be needed again.

NOT USED RECENTLY PAGE REPLACEMENT   The **not used recently (NUR) algorithm** is a simplification of the least recently used algorithm. In this method, the computer system hardware provides two additional bits for each entry in the page tables. One bit is set whenever the page is referenced (*used*). The other bit is set whenever the data on the page is modified, that is, written to. This second bit is called a **dirty bit.** Periodically, the system resets all the reference bits.

The memory manager will attempt to find a page with both bits set to 0. Presumably, this is a page that has not been used for a while. Furthermore, it is a page that has not been modified, so it is necessary only to write the new page over it. The page being replaced does not have to be saved back to the backing store, since it has not been modified. The second choice will be a page whose dirty bit is set, but whose reference bit is unset.

This situation can occur if the page has not been accessed for a while, but was modified when it was accessed, prior to the resetting of the reference bits. This page must be written back to the backing store before a new frame can be read into its spot. Third choice will be a page that has been referenced, but not modified. And finally, least desirable will be a page that has been recently referenced and modified. This is a commonly used algorithm.

One difficulty with this algorithm is that gradually all the *used* bits fill up, making selection difficult or impossible. There are a number of variations on this algorithm that solve this problem by selectively resetting used bits at regular intervals or each time a page replacement occurs. The most common approach pictures the process pages as numerals on a clock. When a page replacement must be found, the clock hand moves until it finds an unset used bit and the corresponding page is replaced. Pages with set used bits that the hand passes over are reset. The hand remains at the found replacement page awaiting the next replacement requirement. This variation on NUR is called the **clock page replacement algorithm**.

SECOND CHANCE PAGE REPLACEMENT ALGORITHMS   One second chance algorithm uses an interesting variation on FIFO, using a referenced bit similar to that of NUR. When the oldest page is selected for replacement, its referenced bit is checked. If the referenced bit is set, the bit is reset, and the time is upgraded, as though the page had just entered memory. This gives the page a second pass through the list of pages. If the referenced bit is not set, then the page is replaced, since it is safe to assume that it has not been referenced in some time.

Another second chance algorithm keeps a small pool of free pages that are not assigned. When a page is replaced, it is not removed from memory but, instead, is moved into the free pool. The oldest page in the free pool is removed to make room. If the page is accessed while in the free pool, it is moved out of the free pool and back into the active pages by replacing another page.

Both second chance algorithms reduce the number of disk swaps by keeping what would otherwise be swapped-out pages in memory. However, the first of these algorithms has the potential of keeping a page beyond its usefulness, and the second decreases the number of possible pages in memory by using some of those pages for the free pool.

Thrashing

A condition that can arise when a system is heavily loaded is called **thrashing.** Thrashing is every system administrator's nightmare. Thrashing occurs when every frame of memory is in use, and programs are allocated just enough pages to meet their minimum requirement. A page fault occurs in a program, and the page is replaced by another page that will itself be needed for replacement almost immediately. Thrashing is most serious when global page replacement is used. In this case, the stolen page may come from another program. When the second program tries to execute, it is immediately faced with its own page fault. Unfortunately, the time required to swap a page from the disk is long compared to CPU execution time, and as the page fault is passed around from program to program, no program is able to execute, and the system as a whole slows to a crawl or crashes. The programs simply continue to steal pages from each other. With local page replacement, the number of thrashing programs is more limited, but thrashing can still have a serious effect on system performance.

Page Table Implementation

As we mentioned previously, the data in the page table must be stored in memory. You should realize that data in the page table must be accessed during the fetch-execute cycle, possibly several times, if the fetch-execute cycle is executing an instruction with a complex addressing mode. Thus, it is important that the page table be accessed as quickly as possible, since the use of paging can negatively affect the performance of the system in a major way otherwise. To improve access, many systems provide a small amount of a special type of memory called **associative memory.** Associative memory differs from regular memory in that the addresses in associative memory are not consecutive. Instead, the addresses in associative memory are assigned to each location as labels. When associative memory is accessed, every address is checked at the same time, but only the location whose address label matches the address to be accessed is activated. Then the data at that location can be read or written. (Cache memory lines are accessed similarly.)

A mailbox analogy might be useful in helping you to understand associative memory. Instead of having mailboxes that are numbered consecutively, picture mailboxes that have those little brass inserts that you slide a paper label into. On each label is written the address of that particular box. By looking at all the boxes, you can find the one that contains your mail. For a human, this technique would be slower than going directly to a mailbox in a known location. The computer, however, is able to look at every address label simultaneously.

Suppose, then, that the most frequently used pages are stored in this associative memory. They may be stored in any order, since the address labels of all locations are checked simultaneously. The page number is used as the address label that is being accessed. Then, the only frame number that will be read is the one that corresponds to that page. A page table that is constructed this way is known as a **translation lookaside buffer** (TLB), table.

The number of locations available in a TLB table is small because associative memory is expensive. There must be a second, larger, page table that contains all the page entries for the program. When the desired page is found in the TLB table, known as a **hit,** the frame can be used without further delay. When the desired page is not found in the TLB table, called a **miss,** the memory management unit defaults to conventional memory, where the larger page table is stored. Access to the table in memory does, in fact, require an extra memory access, which will significantly slow down the fetch-execute cycle, but that can't be helped.

To locate the correct entry in the larger page table, most computers provide a special register in the memory management unit that stores the address of the origin of the page table in memory. Then, the nth page can be located quickly, since its address in memory is the address of the origin plus the offset. The process of page table lookup is shown in Figure 18.22. Figure 18.22a shows how the page is accessed when the page is found in associative memory; Figure 18.22b shows the procedure when the TLB does not contain the desired page.

FIGURE 18.22

Frame Lookup Procedures: (a) Page in TLB, (b) Page Not in TLB

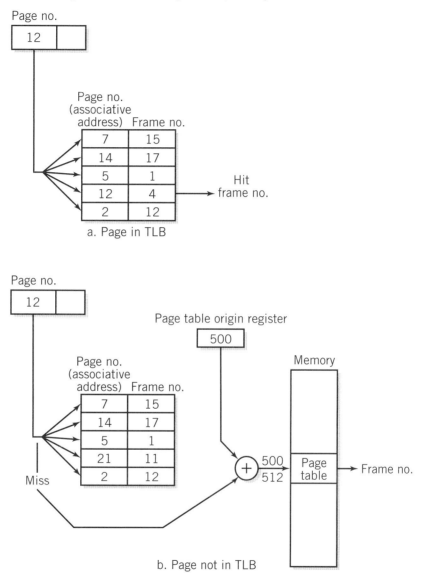

a. Page in TLB

b. Page not in TLB

Beyond the requirement that the frame or page size conform exactly to a fixed number of bits, the size of a frame or page is determined by the computer system designer as a fundamental characteristic of the system. It is not changeable. There are several trade-offs in the determination of page size. The page table for a program must contain an entry for every page in the program. The number of pages is inversely proportional to the page size, so as the page size is decreased, the number of page table entries required increases.

FIGURE 18.23

Internal Fragmentation

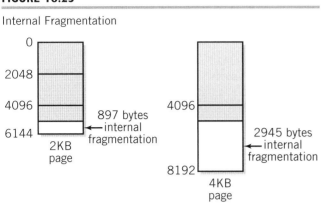

Program size: 5247 bytes

On the other hand, we have assumed that the size of the program corresponds exactly to the amount of memory occupied by the pages required for the program. This is not usually true. More commonly, the last page is partly empty. The wasted space is internal fragmentation. An example is shown in Figure 18.23.

Also, if the pages are small, memory will consist of more pages, which allows more programs to be resident. Conversely, smaller pages will require more swapping, since each program will have less code and data available to it at any given time. Experimentally, designers have determined that 2 KB or 4 KB pages seem to optimize overall performance.

Page tables on large machines can, themselves, require considerable memory space. One solution is to store the page tables in virtual memory. Page tables, or portions of page tables, in current use will occupy frames, as usual. Other portions or tables will reside only in virtual memory until needed.

Segmentation

Segmentation is essentially similar to paging conceptually, but differs in many details. A segment is usually defined as a logically self-contained part of a program, as determined by a programmer or by a compiler translation program. Thus, in most systems, segments can be variable in size. (A few systems define segments instead as large pages, of fixed size, but of 1 MB, 2 MB, or 4 MB, or even more. This definition does not interest us here, since the previous discussion of paging applies in this case. When a fixed size segment is further divided into pages, the program address is divided into three parts, a segment, a page, and an offset, and the mapping process takes place in two steps, but the procedure is otherwise identical to our previous discussion.) Program segments can represent parts of a program such as main routines and subroutines or functions, or they can represent program code and data, even separate data tables. The crucial difference between segments and pages is that due to their variability in size, the boundaries between segments do not fall on natural borders, as pages do.

Therefore, in the **segment table,** it is necessary to provide the entire physical address for the start of the segment instead of just a page number. It is also necessary to record the size or upper limit location of the segment, so that the system can check to make sure that the requested location does not fall outside the limit of the segment. Otherwise, it would be possible to read or write data to a location belonging to another segment, which would compromise the integrity of the system. This is not a problem with paging, since it is impossible for the offset to exceed the size of a page.

The program segment numbers are stored with each segment and are treated similarly to page numbers. For each segment number, there is an entry in the segment table containing the starting location of the segment in physical memory plus the limit of the segment. The physical address is calculated by adding the program segment offset from the start of the segment to the memory starting location and checking this value against the limit. As with the page table, part of the segment table can be stored in associative memory for faster access. When segmentation and paging are both provided, there may be two TLB tables, one for each. When both are provided, the translation process performs its mapping in two steps. First, the segment table is used to determine the location of the pages that make up the segment. Then, the page table locates the desired frame. Since the programmer establishes the segments, segmentation is less invisible to the programmer than paging, even though during operation it is still invisible. This provides a few advantages to the programmer, stemming from the fact that each segment can be treated independently. This means that a particular segment could be shared among different programs, for example. Nonetheless, segmentation is harder to operate and maintain than paging and has rapidly fallen out of favor as a virtual storage technique.

Process Separation

The use of virtual storage offers one additional benefit that should be mentioned. Under normal program execution without virtual storage, every memory access has the potential to address a portion of memory that belongs to a different process. This would violate system security and data integrity; for example, a program in a partitioned memory could access data belonging to another process simply by overflowing an array. Prior to virtual storage memory management, this was a difficult problem. It was necessary to implement memory access limits for each process in hardware, because there is no way for operating system software to check every attempted memory access while a program is executing. With virtual storage, every memory access request points to a logical address, not a physical one. Since the logical address is within the space of the process itself, the translation process assures that it is not possible to point to a physical address belonging to another process, unless the page tables have been set up intentionally to share frames between the processes. Thus, virtual storage provides simple, effective separation protection between processes.

18.8 SECONDARY STORAGE SCHEDULING

On a busy system, it is common to have a number of disk requests pending at any given time. The operating system software will attempt to process these requests in a way that enhances the performance of the system. As you might expect by now, there are several different disk scheduling algorithms in use.

First-Come, First-Served Scheduling

First-come, first-served (FCFS) scheduling is the simplest algorithm. As requests arrive, they are placed in a queue and are satisfied in order. Although this may seem like a fair algorithm, its inefficiency may result in poorer service to every request in the queue. The problem is that seek time on a disk is long and somewhat proportional to the distance that the head has to move. With FCFS, one can expect the head to move all over the disk to satisfy requests. It would be preferable to use an algorithm that minimizes seek distances.

This would suggest processing requests that are on nearby tracks first. The other algorithms in use attempt to do so.

Shortest Distance First Scheduling

The **shortest distance first (SDF) scheduling** algorithm looks at all the requests in the queue and processes the one nearest to the current location of the head. This algorithm suffers from the possibility of **indefinite postponement.** If the head is near the middle track on the disk, a request near the edge of the disk may never get serviced if requests continue to join the queue.

Scan Scheduling

The **scan scheduling** algorithm attempts to satisfy the limitation of SDF scheduling. The head scans back and forth across the disk surface, processing requests as it goes. Although this method is fairer than SDF, it suffers from a different limitation, namely, that blocks near the middle tracks are processed twice as often as blocks near the edge. To see this more clearly, consider the diagram in Figure 18.24. Consider the head moving smoothly back and forth across the disk at a constant speed. The diagram shows the time at which the head crosses various tracks. Note that the middle track is crossed in both directions, at about equal intervals. Tracks near either the inside or outside track, however, are crossed twice in quick succession. Then there is a long interval in which they are not touched. A

FIGURE 18.24

Scan Scheduling Algorithm

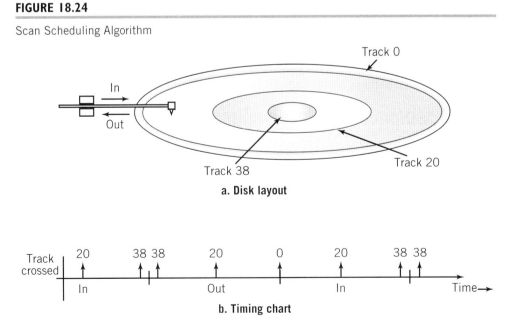

a. Disk layout

b. Timing chart

track at the very edge, inside or outside, is touched only once for every two times that a track in the middle is touched.

N-STEP C-SCAN Scheduling

Two changes improve the ***n*-step c-scan scheduling algorithm.** One is to cycle in only one direction, then return to the other end before accessing blocks again. This assures that each block is treated equally, even though a bit of time is wasted returning the head to its original position. The other change is to maintain two separate queues. Once the head has started to traverse the disk, it will read only blocks that were already waiting when the traverse started. This prevents block requests that are just ahead of the head from jumping into the queue. Instead, such a block would be placed in the alternate queue to wait for the next pass. This approach is fairer to requests that have already been waiting. Practically, there is no reason to move the head beyond the last block sought, and reversal will take place at that time. Some writers refer to this as c-look scheduling.

Figure 18.25 compares the head movement for different scheduling algorithms. These drawings, based on an example and drawings by Silberschatz et al. [SILB08], assume a disk queue containing blocks in tracks 98, 183, 37, 122, 14, 124, 65, and 67. The head starts at track 53.

18.9 NETWORK OPERATING SYSTEM SERVICES

To take advantage of networking, the operating system must include services that support networking and provide the features offered by networking capability. These services include implementation of network software protocols, augmentation of the file system to support the transfer and use of files from other locations, remote login capability, and additional utilities and tools. Modern operating systems include networking facilities as part of the base system.

OS Protocol Support and Other Services

The operating system implements the protocols that are required for network communication and provides a variety of additional services to the user and to application programs. Most operating systems recognize and support a number of different protocols. This contributes to open system connectivity, since the network can then pass packets with less concern for the protocols available on the network stations. In addition to standard communication protocol support, the operating system commonly provides some or all of the following services:

- File services transfer programs and data files from one computer on the network to another. Network file services require that identification of the network node occur ahead of the file manager in the operating system hierarchy. This allows file requests to be directed to the appropriate file manager. Local requests are passed on to the local file manager; other requests go to the network for service by the file manager on the machine where the file resides. This concept is shown in Figure 18.26.

FIGURE 18.25

Comparison of Different Disk Algorithms

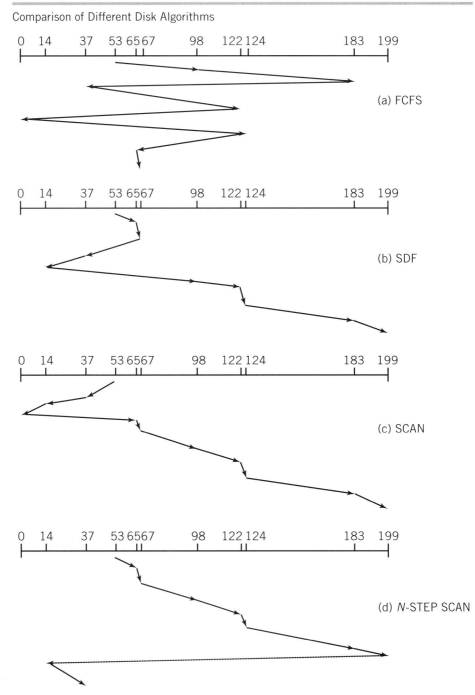

Source: A. Silberschatz, J. Peterson, P. Galvin, *Operating Systems Concepts*, 5/e. © 1998 by John Wiley & Sons, Inc. Reprinted by permission of John Wiley & Sons, Inc.

FIGURE 18.26

The Access for a Networked Operating System

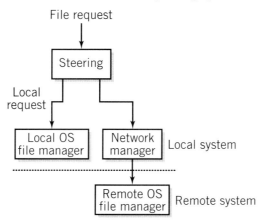

- Some file services require a logical name for the machine to be included on network file requests. For example, Windows assigns pseudodrive letters to file systems accessible through the network. To the user, a file might reside on drive "M:". Although this system is simple, it has one potential shortcoming: different computers on the network might access the same drive by different letters if care isn't taken to prevent this situation. This can make it difficult for users to find their network-based files when they move between computers. Other systems allow the network administrator to assign names to each machine. Many Bentley University machines, for example, are named after Greek gods. To access a file on the "zeus" computer, the user types "zeus:" ahead of the file path name.

- Some operating systems provide transparent access to files on the network. On these systems, network files are mounted to the file system in such a way that network files simply appear in the directory structure like any other file. The operating system uses whatever method is appropriate, local or network, to access the requested files. The user need not know the actual location of the file.

- Print services work similarly to file services. Print requests are redirected by the operating system to the network station that manages the requested printer. This allows users to share expensive printer resources.

- Other peripherals and facilities can also be managed as network services. System-intensive operations, such as database services, can be processed on large computers with the capability and then passed over the network to other computers. This technique places the processing burden on the system that is most qualified to handle it and has the additional benefit of making the data available wherever it is needed.

- Web services accept requests from the network connections and return answers in the form of HTML files, image files, and more. Frequently, Web pages require data processing on the server to prepare dynamically created pages. Operating system scripts and servers are often used for this purpose. The common gateway interface (CGI) protocol provides a standard connection between the Web server and the scripts and operating system services.

- Messaging services allow users and application programs to pass messages from one to another. The most familiar application of messaging services is e-mail and chat facilities. The network operating system not only passes these messages, it also formats them for display on different systems.

- Application program interface services allow a program to access network services. Some network operating systems also provide access to services on remote machines that might not be available locally. These services are called **remote procedure calls (RPCs)**. RPCs can be used to implement distributed computing.

- Security and network management services provide security across the network and allow users to manage and control the network from computers on the network. These services also include protection against data loss that can occur when multiple computers access data simultaneously.

- Remote processing services allow a user or application to log in to another system on the network and use its facilities for processing. Thus, the processing workload can be distributed among computers on the network, and users have access to remote computers from their own system. The most familiar services of this type are probably *telnet*, and *SSH*.

When considered together, the network services provided by a powerful network operating system transform a user's computer into a **distributed system.** Tanenbaum [TAN95] defines a distributed system as follows:

> A distributed system is a collection of independent computers that appear to the users of the system as a single computer.

Network operating systems are characterized by the distribution of control that they provide. **Client-server systems** centralize control in the server computer. Client computers have their network access limited to services provided by the server(s). Novell NetWare is an example of a client-server system. The operating system software on the server can communicate with every computer on the network, but client software communicates only with the server. In contrast, **peer-to-peer network software** permits communication between any two computers on the network, within security constraints, of course.

18.10 OTHER OPERATING SYSTEM ISSUES

There are many challenges in the design of an operating system. In this section we make a few comments about one of the more interesting operating system issues, deadlock.

Deadlock

It is not unusual for more than one process to need the same computer resource. If the resource is capable of handling multiple concurrent requests, then there is no problem. However, some resources can operate with only one process at a time. A printer is one example. If one process is printing, it is not acceptable to allow other processes access to the printer at that time.

When one process has a resource that another process needs to proceed, and the other process has a resource that the first process needs, then both are waiting for an event that can never occur, namely, the release by the other process of the needed resource. This situation can be extended to any number of processes, arranged in a circle.

This situation is called **deadlock**, and it is not unfamiliar to you in other forms. The most familiar example is the automobile gridlock situation depicted in Figure 18.27. Each vehicle is waiting for the one to its right to move, but of course no one can move.

In a computer system, deadlock is a serious problem. Much theoretical study has been done on deadlock. This has resulted in three basic ways in which deadlock is managed. These are **deadlock prevention**, **deadlock avoidance**, and **deadlock detection and recovery**.

Deadlock prevention is the safest method; however, it also has the most severe effect on system performance. Deadlock prevention works by eliminating in general any condition that could create a deadlock. It is equivalent to closing one of the streets.

Deadlock avoidance provides a somewhat weaker form of protection. It works by continually monitoring the resource requirements, looking for situations in which a deadlock potential exists and then not allowing that situation to occur. If the fourth car is not allowed into the street because there are three other cars already in the intersection, that is deadlock avoidance. In a computer system, the equivalent would be a refusal by the operating system to allocate a resource because doing so would have a potential to cause deadlock.

FIGURE 18.27

A Familiar Deadlock Situation

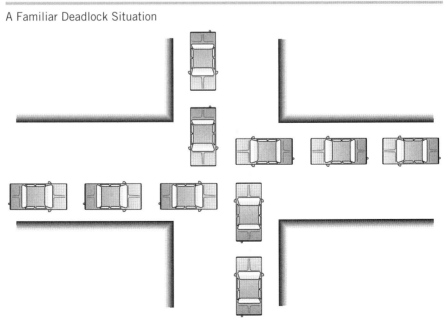

Deadlock detection and recovery is the simplest method to implement, but the most costly when things go wrong. This methodology allows deadlocks to occur. The operating system monitors the resources. If everything stops, it assumes that a deadlock has occurred. It may take some time to notice the condition, time that is lost to productive system work. Recovery techniques include terminating processes and preempting resources. Terminated processes must be rerun. Much work could be lost and require re-creation. Deadlock recovery is generally considered the least satisfactory solution. To drivers too!

Other Issues

There are other issues that must be considered in the design of an operating system. Operating systems require a method for communication between processes. In some systems, interprocess communication may be as simple as sharing variables in a special pool or sending semaphore messages that indicate completion of a task. In others, there may be a complex message passing arrangement, with mailboxes set up for each process. Interprocess communication has increased in importance over the past few years, due to the desire to move data and program execution more easily from one application to another.

One form of communication that is sometimes very important is the ability to synchronize processes with each other. Two or more processes may be cooperating on the solution of a complex problem, and one may be dependent on the solution provided by another. Furthermore, both may be required to access the same data, the order and timing in which access takes place can be critical, and these conditions can affect the overall results. This requires a solution to the problem of **process synchronization**.

As a simple example, consider an address card file shared by you and your roommate or partner. A friend calls to tell you that she has moved and to give you her new phone number. You place a new card with this information in the card file box. Meanwhile, your roommate has taken the old card from the box and has used it to write a letter. He returns to the box, sees the new card, figures that it must be obsolete, and so throws it away and replaces it with the original. The new data is now lost. Similar situations can occur with data being shared by more than one process.

As another simple example, consider two processes, with the goal to produce the result c, where process 1 solves the program statement

$$a = a + b$$

with initial values $a = 2$ and $b = 3$.

The second process solves the statement

$$c = a + 5$$

where the value of a is to be taken from the first process.

Clearly, it is important that the first process complete before the value of a is used by process 2. If process 2 looks at the value of a too early, the result, c, will be $2 + 5 = 7$. The correct value is $5 + 5 = 10$. The solutions to the problems of interprocess communication and process synchronization are beyond the scope of this textbook. They are both difficult and interesting. Various books, such as Stallings [STAL08], Silberschatz et al. [SILB08], and Tanenbaum [TAN07], discuss these issues at length.

18.11 VIRTUAL MACHINES

From Chapter 11, you're aware that it is possible to combine the processing power of a number of computers to form a cluster that acts as a single, more powerful computer. The inverse is also true. It is possible to use a powerful computer to simulate a number of smaller computers. The process for doing so is called **virtualization**. The individual simulations that result are called **virtual machines**. Each virtual machine has its own access to the hardware resources of the host machine and an operating system that operates as a **guest** of the host machine. On a desktop or laptop computer, the user interface for each virtual machine typically appears in a separate GUI window on a display. A user can switch from one to another simply by clicking in a different window.

The use of virtualization has increased rapidly in volume and importance in recent years. There are a number of factors that account for this:

- Although computer hardware is relatively inexpensive to purchase, the overhead costs—software, networking, power consumption, space requirements, and support costs of various kinds—make the overall cost of ownership of each additional machine a significant burden.

- Modern computers generally have processing capability far in excess of usage or need.

- The development of virtualization technology has reached the state that even small computers can be virtualized easily, effectively, and securely, with complete isolation between virtual machines operating on the same host. Recent virtualization software and hardware also supports a wider range of different operating systems.

The obvious application for virtual machines is the ability to consolidate servers by operating multiple servers on the same hardware platform, but there are a number of other useful purposes as well:

- A server can be set up to create a separate virtual machine for each client. This protects the underlying system and other clients from malware and other client-generated problems.

- A system analyst can evaluate software on a virtual machine without concern for its behavior. If the software crashes or damages the operating system, the analyst can simply kill the virtual machine without damage to the underlying system or any other virtual machine that is running on the host.

- A software developer or Web developer can test his software on different operating systems, with different configurations, all running on the same host. For example, a database specialist can test changes to the database without affecting the production system and then place them into production easily and efficiently.

- A user can operate in a **sandbox**. A sandbox is a user environment in which all activity is confined to the sandbox itself. A virtual machine is a sandbox. For example, a user can access dangerous resources on the Internet for testing a system against malware safely. Malware loaded into a virtual machine disappears when the virtual machine is closed. The sandbox is also useful for Web research, where the safety of the Web sites accessed is not assured.

Virtualization creates an important illusion. The virtualization mechanism makes it appear that each virtual machine has the computer system entirely to itself. It allocates physical resources on a shared basis, processes on different machines can communicate with each other using built-in networking protocols, and there is a common set of interrupt routines, controlled by the virtualization software. In effect, each virtual machine offers an exact duplicate of the system hardware, providing the appearance of multiple machines, each the equivalent of a separate, fully configured system. The virtual machines can execute any operating system software that is compatible with the hardware. Each virtual machine supports its own operating system, isolated both from the actual hardware and from other virtual machines. The virtual machine mechanism is invisible to the software executing on a virtual machine.

As an example, the IBM z/VM operating system simulates multiple copies of all the hardware resources of the IBM mainframe computer, registers, program counter, interrupts, I/O, and all. This allows the system to load and run one or more operating systems on top of z/VM, including even other copies of z/VM. The loaded operating systems each think that they are interacting with the hardware, but actually they are interacting with z/VM. Using virtualization, an IBM mainframe can support hundreds of virtual Linux machines simultaneously.

Figure 18.28 shows the basic design of virtualization. An additional layer called a **hypervisor** separates one or more operating systems from the hardware. The hypervisor may consist of software or a mixture of software and hardware, if the CPU provides hardware virtualization support. Most recent CPUs do so. There are two basic types of hypervisors.

- A *native*, or *type 1*, hypervisor is software that interfaces directly with the computer hardware. The hypervisor provides required software drivers, manages interrupts, and directs the results to the correct results of its work to the proper virtual machine. To the operating system or systems, the hypervisor looks like a

FIGURE 18.28

Virtual Machine Configuration

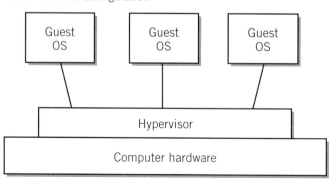

hardware interface. One way to implement a type 1 hypervisor is to use the facilities of a stripped-down operating system.

- A *hosted* or *type 2* hypervisor is software that runs as a program on a standard operating system. Some operating systems routinely provide hypervisor software as part of the standard package. Guest operating systems then run on top of the hypervisor.

SUMMARY AND REVIEW

An operating system is quite complex internally. This chapter has considered some of the more important components of the operating system in some detail. We began by looking at the critical components of a simple multitasking system, particularly scheduling and memory management.

Turning our attention to more general multitasking systems, we discussed the concepts of processes and threads. We showed you how the operating system creates and manages processes, including description of the standard process states. Threads are important in current systems, and we discussed threads as simplified processes, without the overhead.

Next, we introduced the two, and sometimes three, types of CPU scheduling. We described the difference between preemptive and nonpreemptive multitasking, described the different objectives that can be used to measure performance, and introduced several CPU dispatching algorithms, comparing the way in which these met different objectives.

The focus of memory management is to load programs in such a way as to enhance system performance. We briefly discussed the shortcomings of partitioning methods as a way to introduce virtual storage. The emphasis in this chapter is on the symbiosis between the hardware and the operating system to provide a memory management technique that addresses many of the shortcomings of other memory management techniques. The virtual storage methodology eliminates the requirement that the sum of programs to be loaded as a whole must fit all at once into available memory; instead, the active parts of each program are sufficient. It allows each program to exist in the same virtual memory space. It allows programs to be loaded anywhere in memory, and noncontiguously. And it eliminates the need for relocation procedures.

We explained the page fault procedure and discussed several page replacement algorithms. We considered the number of pages that are required to execute a program successfully and efficiently, and we considered the problem of thrashing.

Next, we discussed the algorithms used for secondary storage. Following that, we presented the operating system components that support networking. We next introduced briefly the issues of deadlock, process synchronization, and interprocess communication. These issues are representative of some of the more complex problems that must be faced by operating system designers and administrators. Finally, we introduced the concept of a virtual machine. We explained why virtualization is so important, explained how it's used, and showed how it works. The VM operating system provides virtual machines that can be treated as independent machines, each with its own operating system, applications, and users.

FOR FURTHER READING

Any of the references mentioned in the For Further Reading section of Chapter 15 also address the topics in this chapter. If you have become intrigued by operating systems and would like to know more, there are a large number of interesting problems and algorithms with intriguing names like "the dining philosophers problem." We have only barely touched upon the surface of operating system design and operation, especially in the areas of deadlock, process synchronization, and interprocess communication. We highly recommend the textbooks by Deitel [DEIT03], Tanenbaum [TAN07], Silberschatz, et al. [SILB08], and Stallings [STAL08] for thorough and detailed treatment of these and other topics. Information about network and distributed operating systems can be found in Tanenbaum [TAN/WOOD06, TAN/VANS06] and in most recent operating systems and networking texts. See the For Further Reading section in Chapter 13 for additional references.

Virtualization is currently a hot topic. Much information, including readable introductions, can be found at the vmware.com, xen.org, and sun.com websites. There are also numerous books and magazine articles on virtualization. Some of these are listed in the references at the back of this book.

KEY CONCEPTS AND TERMS

associative memory	dynamic address	internal fragmentation
backing store	translation (DAT)	job
Belady's anomaly	dynamic priority	job steps
best-fit algorithm	scheduling	largest-fit algorithm
blocked state	event	least recently used (LRU)
blocking	event-driven program	page replacement
child process	external fragmentation	algorithm
client-server system	first-come, first-served	local page replacement
clock page replacement	(FCFS) disk scheduling	locked frame
algorithm	first-fit algorithm	miss
cloning	first-in, first-out (FIFO)	multilevel feedback queue
concept of locality	fixed partitioning	algorithm
cooperating processes	forking	n-step c-scan scheduling
deadlock	fragmentation	algorithm
deadlock avoidance	frame (memory)	nonpreemptive systems
deadlock detection and	global page replacement	not used recently (NUR)
recovery	guest	page replacement
deadlock prevention	high-level (long-term)	algorithm
demand paging	scheduler	offset
dirty bit	hit	page fault (trap)
dispatcher	hypervisor	page swapping
dispatching	indefinite postponement	page replacement algorithm
distributed system	independent processes	page table

paging
parent process
peer-to-peer network
    software
preemptive systems
prepaging
priority scheduling
process
process control block
    (PCB)
process identifier
    (PID)
process state
process synchronization
ready state
remote procedure call
    (RPC)
response time

resumption
roll-out, roll-in
round robin
running state
sandbox
scan disk scheduling
segmentation
segment table
shortest job first (SJF)
shortest distance first (SDF)
    disk scheduling
spawning
starvation
suspended state
swap file
swap out
swap space
swapping

system process
task
thrashing
thread
time-out
translation lookaside buffer
    (TLB)
turnaround time
user-level thread
user process
variable partitioning
virtualization
virtual machine (VM)
virtual memory
virtual storage
wake-up
working set
worst-fit algorithm

READING REVIEW QUESTIONS

18.1   What is the fundamental purpose of any operating system? What is the role of the file manager? What other basic functions must the operating system be able to perform?

18.2   Where is the first stage of a bootstrap loader for a computer stored? What tasks does it perform?

18.3   How does a process differ from a program?

18.4   What are user processes? What are system processes?

18.5   What are the major items found in a *process control block*?

18.6   Draw and label the process state diagram used for dispatching work to the CPU. Explain each state and the role of each connector.

18.7   Explain the purpose of a *spawning* operation. What is the result when the spawning operation is complete?

18.8   What features characterize threads? How are threads used?

18.9   What is an *event-driven* program?

18.10 What are the potential difficulties that can occur when nonpreemptive dispatching is used in an interactive system?

18.11 Explain how the *shortest job first* algorithm can result in starvation.

18.12 Explain the *first-in-first-out* dispatch algorithm. Discuss the advantages and disadvantages of this algorithm. Is this a preemptive or nonpreemptive algorithm?

18.13 UNIX systems use a dynamic priority algorithm where the priority is based on the ratio of CPU time to the total time a process has been in the system. Explain how this reduces to *round robin* in the absence of any I/O.

18.14   What is the basic problem that memory management is supposed to solve? What is the shortcoming of memory partitioning as a solution?

18.15   What is a *page* in virtual storage? What is the relationship between a program and pages?

18.16   What is a *frame* in virtual storage? What is the relationship between a frame and physical memory?

18.17   What are the contents of a page table? Explain how a page table relates pages and frames.

18.18   Explain how page translation makes it possible to execute a program that is stored in memory noncontiguously.

18.19   Virtual storage makes it possible to execute a program that is larger than the available amount of memory. What obvious characteristic of program code makes this possible?

18.20   A program's page table is shown in Figure 18Q.1. Assume that each page is 4 KB in size. (4 KB = 12 bits). The instruction currently being executed is to load data from location $5E24_{16}$. Where is the data located in physical memory?

18.21   Explain the concept of a *working set*.

18.22   Describe the process that takes place when a *page fault* occurs? What happens if there are no frames available when a page fault occurs?

18.23   The *not used recently* page replacement algorithm stores two bits with each page to determine a page that is suitable for replacement. What does each bit represent? Which combination of bits makes a page the most desirable for replacement? Justify your answer. What combination would be second best?

18.24   Explain *thrashing*.

18.25   Describe at least three network services offered by most operating systems in addition to protocol services.

18.26   Explain *deadlock*. What are the three possible ways that an operating system can handle the issue of deadlock?

FIGURE 18Q.1

Page	Frame
0	2A
1	2B
2	5
3	17
4	18
5	2E
6	1F

18.27   State at least three advantages that result from the use of virtual machines.

18.28   Describe the tasks that are performed by a *hypervisor*.

EXERCISES

18.1   Describe, in step-by-step form, the procedure that the operating system would use to switch from one user to another in a multiuser time sharing system.

18.2   What values would you expect to find in the process state entry in a process control block? What purpose is served by the program counter and register save areas in a process control block? (Note that the program counter entry in a PCB is <u>not</u> the same as the program counter!)

18.3   Describe what occurs when a user types a keystroke on a terminal connected to a multitasking system. Does the system respond differently for a preemptive or nonpreemptive system? Why or why not? If the response is different, *how* is it different?

18.4   Discuss the steps that take place when a process is moved (a) from ready state to running state, (b) from running state to blocked state, (c) from running state to ready state, and (d) from blocked state to ready state.

18.5   Why is there no path on the process diagram from blocked state to running state?

18.6   Earlier versions of Windows used an essentially nonpreemptive dispatching technique that Microsoft called "cooperative multitasking." In cooperative multitasking, each program was expected to voluntarily give up the CPU periodically to give other processes a chance to execute. Discuss. What potential difficulties can this method cause?

18.7   A VSOS (very simple operating system) uses a very simple approach to scheduling. Scheduling is done on a straight round-robin basis, where each job is given a time quantum sufficient to complete very short jobs. Upon completion by a job, another job is admitted to the system and immediately given one quantum. Thereafter, it enters the round-robin queue. Consider the scheduling objectives given in the text. Discuss the VSOS scheduling approach in terms of these objectives.

18.8   Discuss the shortest-job-first scheduling method in terms of the various objectives given in the text.

18.9   The multilevel feedback queue scheduling method looks like FIFO at the upper levels and like round robin at the lowest level, yet it frequently behaves better than either in terms of the performance objectives mentioned in the text. Why is this so?

18.10   What is the risk that can result from the mixed nonpreemptive-preemptive scheduling system taken by Linux, as discussed in the text?

18.11   There are a number of different factors, both hardware and OS software, that affect the operating speed of a virtual storage system. Explain carefully each of the factors and its resulting impact on system performance.

18.12   In the memory management schemes used in earlier operating systems, it was necessary to modify the addresses of most programs when they were loaded into memory because they were usually not loaded into memory starting at location 0. The OS program loader was assigned this task, which was called *program relocation*. Why is program relocation unnecessary when virtual storage is used for memory management?

18.13   What kind of fragmentation would you find in virtual storage? Is this a serious problem? Justify your answer. Discuss the relationship between fragmentation and page size.

18.14   The CPU scheduling algorithm (in UNIX) is a simple priority algorithm. The priority for a process is computed as the ratio of the CPU time actually used by the process to the real time that has passed. The lower the figure, the higher the priority. Priorities are recalculated every tenth of a second.

  a.   What kind of jobs are favored by this type of algorithm?

  b.   If there is no I/O being performed, this algorithm reduces to a round-robin algorithm. Explain.

  c.   Discuss this algorithm in terms of the scheduling objectives given in the text.

18.15   Develop an example that explains thrashing clearly.

18.16   Figure 18.E1 shows that, for a given process, the page fault rate in a virtual storage system increases as the page size is increased and then decreases to 0 as the page size approaches P, the size of the process. Explain the various parts of the curve.

FIGURE 18.E1

18.17   Assume that you have a program to run on a Little Man-type computer that provides virtual storage paging. Each page holds ten locations (in other words, one digit). The system can support up to one hundred pages of memory. As Figure 18.E2 shows, your program is sixty-five instructions long. The available frames in physical memory are also shown in the diagram. All blocked-in areas are already occupied by other programs that are sharing the use of the Little Man.

  a.   Create a starting page table for your program. Assume that your program will start executing at its location 0.

  b.   Suppose a page fault occurs in your program. The OS has to decide whether to swap out one of your older pages, or one of somebody else's pages. Which strategy is less likely to cause thrashing? Why?

FIGURE 18.E2

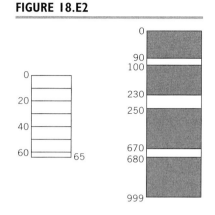

18.18   Show in a drawing similar to Figure 18.18 how two different programs with the same logical address space can be transformed by virtual storage into independent parts of physical memory.

18.19   Show in a drawing similar to Figure 18.18 how two different programs with the same logical address space can be transformed by virtual storage partially into the same part of physical memory and partially into independent parts of physical memory. Assume that the two programs use the same program code, located from logical addresses 0 to 100, and that they each have their own data region, located from logical addresses 101 to 165.

18.20   Explain why the installation of additional physical memory in a virtual memory system often results in substantial improvement in overall system performance.

18.21   You may have noticed a number of similarities between virtual storage paging and cache memory paging. One major difference, of course, is that main memory is much faster than disk access.

　　　　Consider the applicability and performance of the various paging algorithms in a memory caching system, and discuss the advantages and disadvantages of each.

18.22   Explain why page sharing can reduce the number of page faults that occur in a virtual storage system.

18.23   Explain deadlocking.

18.24   The manual for a popular operating system points out that the number of concurrent users on the system can be increased if the users are sharing programs, such as editors, mail readers, or compilers. What characteristics of virtual storage make this possible?

18.25   [courtesy of W. Wong] Assume that a program is to be executed on a computer with virtual storage. The machine supports 10,000 words of logical memory overall, broken into pages of 100 words each. This particular machine contains 400 physical memory locations. Suppose that the machine starts to execute a program. The page table is initially empty, and is filled as necessary. Suppose that the program references the following sequence of memory locations:

> **start** 951, 952, 4730, 955, 2217, 3663, 2217, 4785, 957, 2401, 959, 2496, 3510, 962 **end**

a.   Indicate each of the points where page faults occur.

b.   Show the page table at the end of the sequence for each of the following demand page replacement algorithms:

   i.   first in first out

  ii.   least recently used

 iii.   least frequently used (using FIFO as a tie breaker)

18.26   Explain the working set concept. What is the relationship between the working set concept and the principle of locality?

18.27   Why is the working set concept much more effective if it is implemented dynamically, that is, recalculated while a process is executing?

18.28   What are the differences, trade-offs, advantages, and disadvantages between an OS that implements deadlock prevention versus deadlock avoidance versus deadlock detection and recovery?

18.29   A system status report for a virtual storage operating system shows that between 2 p.m. and 4 p.m. CPU usage and I/O usage both climbed steadily. At 4 p.m., the I/O usage reached 100 percent, but continued to increase. After 4 p.m., the CPU usage, however, dropped off dramatically. What is the explanation for this behavior?

18.30   Discuss the impact of virtual storage on the design of an operating system. Consider the tasks that must be performed, the various methods of performing those tasks, and the resulting effect on system performance.

18.31   Create a page table that meets the translation requirements of Figure 18.E3. Assume a page size of 10.

FIGURE 18.E3

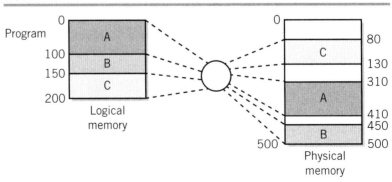

18.32 What is a real-time system? Discuss the impact of a real-time system on the design of the operating systems, paying particular note to the various components and algorithms to be used.

18.33 The designer of a new operating system to be used especially for real-time applications has proposed the use of virtual storage memory management so that the system can handle programs too large to fit in the limited memory space sometimes provided on real-time systems. What are the implications of this decision in terms of the way that virtual storage works?

18.34 Consider the operation of a jukebox. Each table has a jukebox terminal where customers can feed coins to play songs (50 cents apiece, three for a dollar). Prior to the iPod era, the queue to hear your songs in a busy restaurant could be quite long, sometimes longer than the average dining time, in fact.

   Discuss the various disk scheduling algorithms as methods of selecting the order in which to play the requested songs. Be sure to consider the advantages and disadvantages of each method in terms of fairness, probability that each diner will get to hear their songs, ease of implementation, and any other important issues that you feel should be considered. You might note that multiple diners would sometimes request the same song.

18.35 Tanenbaum notes that the problem of scheduling an elevator in a tall building is similar to that of scheduling a disk arm. Requests come in continuously, calling the elevator to floors at random. One difference is that once inside, riders request that the elevator move to a different floor. Discuss the various disk scheduling algorithms as options for scheduling the elevator in terms of fairness, service, and ease of implementation.

18.36 Discuss possible tape scheduling algorithms for a tape controller. Assume that files are stored contiguously on tape. What effect would noncontiguous, linked files have on your algorithm?

18.37 Explain the bootstrap procedure for a diskless workstation.

18.38 Discuss the various trade-offs and decisions involved in task dispatching and the options and methods used for implementing those trade-offs and decisions.

18.39 Discuss the network features and services provided in an operating system. Which services are mandatory? Why?

18.40 Consider the operation of an OS dispatcher on a computer with multiple cores operating under symmetric multiprocessing. Assuming that there are more processes being executed than there are cores, the dispatcher is responsible for maximizing the work load by keeping every core as busy as possible. In addition to the usual dispatch criteria and algorithms, there are two options for selecting in which core a process is to execute. The first option is to allow a process to execute in any core that is available each time it is selected to run; with this option, a process might execute in several different cores during its run. The second option is to require that the process run in the same core each time it is selected.

   a. What are the advantages of the first option?
   b. What are the advantages of the second option? (Hint: consider the interaction between a process and the cache memory that is assigned to each core.)

BIBLIOGRAPHY

A

Abel, P. *IBM PC Assembly Language and Programming,* 5th ed. Englewood Cliffs, NJ: Prentice Hall, 2001.

Adobe Systems, Inc., Staff. *PDF Reference, 6th ed., Version 7.1.* www.adobe.com/devnet/acrobat/pdfs/pdf_reference_1-7.pdf, 2006.

——. *PostScript Language Program Design* ("The Green Book"). Reading, MA: Addison-Wesley, 1993.

——. *PostScript Language Reference Manual,* 3rd ed. ("The Red Book"). Reading, MA: Addison-Wesley, 1999.

——. *PostScript Language Tutorial and Cookbook* ("The Blue Book"). Reading, MA: Addison-Wesley, 1985.

Aho, A. V., M. S. Lam, R. Sethi, and J. D. Ullman. *Compilers, Principles, Techniques, and Tools,* 2nd ed. Reading, MA: Addison-Wesley, 2006.

Aken, B. R., Jr. "Large Systems and Enterprise System Architecture," *IBM Systems Journal,* Vol. 28, no. 1 (1989), pp. 4–13.

Alpert, D., and D. Avnon. "Architecture of the Pentium Microprocessor," *IEEE Micro,* Vol. 13, no. 3 (June 1993), pp. 11–21.

Anderson, D. *FireWire System Architecture: IEEE 1394,* 2nd ed. Richardson, TX: Mindshare, Addison-Wesley, 1998.

——. *Universal System Bus System Architecture,* 2nd ed. Richardson, TX: Mindshare, Addison-Wesley, 2001.

—— and T. Shanley. *PCI System Architecture,* 4th ed. PC Systems Architecture Series. Richardson, TX: Mindshare, Addison-Wesley, 1999.

——, R. Budruk, and T. Shanley. *PCI Express System Architecture,* PC Systems Architecture Series. Richardson, TX: Mindshare, Addison-Wesley, 2003.

—— and T. Shanley. *Pentium Processor System Architecture,* PC System Architecture Series, Volume 5. Richardson, TX: Mindshare, 1995.

Arevolo, A., et al. *Programming the Cell Broadband Engine Architecture, Examples and Best Practices: Part 1: Introduction to the Cell Broadband Engine Architecture,* www.redbooks.ibm.com (Aug. 8, 2008).

Armitage, G. *Quality of Service in IP Networks.* Indianapolis, IN: Sams Publishing, 2000.

Atkinson, T. D., U. O. Gagliardi, G. Raviola, and H. S. Schwenk, Jr. "Modern Central Processor Architecture," *Proceedings of the IEEE,* Vol. 63, no. 6 (June 1975), pp. 863–870.

AT&T Bell Laboratories. *Unix System Readings and Applications,* Volumes I and II. Englewood Cliffs, NJ: Prentice Hall, 1987.

B

Bach, M. *The Design of the Unix Operating System.* Englewood Cliffs, NJ: Prentice Hall, 1990.

Bacon, J. *Concurrent Systems, Operating Systems, Database and Distributed Systems: An Integrated Approach*, 2nd ed. Reading, MA: Addison-Wesley, 1998.

Bailes, G., and R. Riser. *The IBM 370, Computer Organization and Assembly Language.* St. Louis: West, 1987.

Bambara, R. J., and H. F. Cervone. *MVS and UNIX: A Survival Handbook for Users, Developers, and Managers.* New York: McGraw-Hill, 1998.

Barfield, L. *The User Interface, Concepts and Design.* Reading, MA: Addison-Wesley, 2004.

Barroso, L. A., J. Dean, and U. Holzle, "Web Search for a Planet: The Google Cluster Architecture," *IEEE Micro*, Vol. 23, Issue 2 (March 2003), pp. 22–28.

Beck, M., H. Bohme, M. Dziadzka, U. Kunitz, R. Magnus, and D. Verworner. *Linux Kernel Programming,* 3rd ed. Reading, MA: Addison-Wesley, 2002.

Becker, M. C., M. S. Allen, C. R. Moore, J. S. Muhich, and D. P. Tuttle. "The PowerPC 601 Microprocessor," *IEEE Micro,* Vol. 13, no. 5 (October 1993), pp. 54–67.

——. *Beowulf Introduction & Overview.* www.Beowulf.org/intro.html.

Berstis, V. *Fundamentals of Grid Computing*, www.redbooks.ibm.com, 2002.

Bhatt, A. V. "Creating a PCI Express Interconnect," *Intel White Paper,* www.pcisig.com/specifications/pciexpress/resources/PCI_Express_White_Paper.pdf.

Bielski, L. "Got Grid?," *J. of ABA Banking,* (December 2002), p. 43.

Biggerstaff, T. J. *Systems Software Tools.* Englewood Cliffs, NJ: Prentice Hall, 1986.

Boggs, D., et al., "The Microarchitecture of the Intel Pentium 4 Processor on 90 nm Technology," *Intel Technical J,* Vol. 8, no. 1, (2004), pp. 1–17.

Bovet, D., and M. Cosati. *Understanding the Linux Kernel*, 3rd ed., Sebastopol, CA: O'Reilly & Assoc., 2006.

Brendel, J. C., H. Sprang, and J. Quade. "Going Virtual, A Practical Look at Virtualization," *Linux Pro*, no. 90, (May 2008), pp. 21–25.

Brewer, E. "Clustering: Multiply and Conquer," *Data Communications,* Vol. 26, 9 (July 1997), p. 89.

Brey, B. *The Intel Microprocessors*, 8th ed. Englewood Cliffs, NJ: Pearson Education, 2008.

Brookshear, J. G. *Computer Science, An Overview*, 10th ed. Menlo Park, CA: Benjamin Cummings, 2008.

Brown, G. D. *System 390 JCL,* 4th ed. New York: John Wiley & Sons, 1998.

Brumbaugh, L. J. *VSAM, Architecture, Theory, and Applications.* New York: McGraw-Hill, 1993.

Burgess, B., N. Ullah, P. Van Overen, and D. Ogden. "The PowerPC 603 Microprocessor," *Comm. of the ACM,* Vol. 37, no. 6 (June 1994), pp. 34–41.

Burke, P. H. "IBM ES/9000 Series: First Looks," *Datapro,* Computer System Series: Systems 3937. New York: McGraw-Hill, May 1993.

Buyya, R. *High Performance Cluster Computing: Architecture and Systems, Vol. 1.* Upper Saddle River, NJ: Prentice Hall, 1999.

C

Calta, S. A., J. A. deVeer, E. Loizides, and R. N. Strangwayes. "Enterprise Systems Connection (ESCON) Architecture—System Overview," *IBM J. of Research and Development,* Vol. 36, no. 4 (July 1992), pp. 535–552.

Card, R., E. Dumas, and F. Mevel. *The Linux Kernel Book.* New York: John Wiley & Sons, 1998.

——. *Cell Broadband Engine Architecture*, version 1.02, www-01.ibm.com/chips/techlib/techlib .nsf/techdocs, October, 2007.

Chen, T., R. Raghavan, J. Dale, and E. Iwata, "Cell Broadband Engine Architecture and its First Implementation," www-128.ibm.com/developerworks/power/library/pa-cellperf.

Cheswick, W. R., S. M. Bellovin, and A. D. Rubin. *Firewalls and Internet Security: Repelling the Wily Hacker,* 2nd ed., Boston, MA: Addison-Wesley, 2003.

Chevance, R. J. *Server Architectures: Multiprocessors, Clusters, Parallel Systems, Web Servers,* Burlington, MA: Elsevier Digital Press, 2005.

Christian, K., and S. Richter. *The UNIX Operating System,* 3rd ed. New York: John Wiley & Sons, 1994.

Colwell, R. P., and R. L. Steck. "A 0.6 μm BiCMOS Processor with Dynamic Execution," *Digest of Technical Papers, IEEE International Solid State Circuits Conference*, Vol 38, (February 1995), San Francisco, CA.

Comer, D. E. *Computer Networks and Internets with Internet Applications*, 4th ed., Englewood Cliffs, NJ: Prentice Hall, 2003.

——. *Internetworking with TCP/IP*, Volume 1, *Principles, Protocols, and Architecture*, 5th ed. Englewood Cliffs, NJ: Prentice Hall, 2005.

——. "Special Issue on ATM Networking," *Comm. of the ACM,* Vol. 38, no. 2 (February 1995), pp. 28–109.

Cormier, R. L., R. J. Dugan, and R. R. Guyette. "System/370 Extended Architecture: The Channel Subsystem," *IBM J. of Research and Development,* Vol. 27, no. 3 (May 1983), pp. 206–217.

Cortada, J. W. *Historical Dictionary of Data Processing,* Volume 1, *Biographies,* Volume 2, *Organizations,* Volume 3, *Technology*. Westport, CT: Greenwood Press, 1987.

Cowart, R., and B. Knittel. *Using Microsoft Windows Vista*, Indianapolis, IN: Que, 2006.

Cox, K., and D. Walker. *User Interface Design,* 2nd ed. New York: Simon & Schuster, 1993.

Crawford, C. H., D. M. Dias, A. K. Iyenger, M. Novaes, and L. Zhang. "Commercial Applications of Grid Computing," *IBM Research Report*, RC22702, January 22, 2003.

D

Davidson, J., and R. Vaughn. "The Effect of Instruction Set Complexity on Program Size and Performance," *Proceedings, Second International Conference on Architectural Support for Programming Languages and Operating Systems*, October 1987, Palo Alto, CA.

Davis, W., and T. M. Rajkumar. *Operating Systems, A Systematic View*, 6th ed. Redwood City, CA: Benjamin Cummings, 2004.

Decker, R., and S. Hirshfield. *The Analytical Engine, An Introduction to Computer Science Using The Internet.*, 2nd ed. Boston, MA: PWS, 2003.

Deitel, H. *Operating Systems*, 3rd ed. Reading, MA: Addison-Wesley, 2003.

Denning, P. J. "Virtual Memory," *Computer Surveys,* Vol. 2 (September 1970), pp. 153–189.

Dershem, H. L., and M. J. Jipping. *Programming Languages, Structures and Models.* Boston, MA: PWS Publishing, 1993.

Diefendorff, K. "History of the PowerPC Architecture," *Comm. of the ACM,* Vol. 37, no. 6 (June 1994), pp. 28–33.

——, R. Oehler, and R. Hochsprung. "Evolution of the PowerPC Architecture," *IEEE Micro,* Vol. 14, no. 2 (April 1994), pp. 34–49.

Dijkstra, E. W. "The Structure of the T. H. E. Multiprogramming System," *Comm. of the ACM,* Vol. 11, no. 5 (May 1968), pp. 341–346.

——. *Domain Name Industry Brief*, Vol. 5, Issue 3, www.verisign.com/static/043939.pdf.

Donovan, J. J. *Systems Programming.* New York: McGraw-Hill, 1972.

DuCharme, B. *The Operating Systems Handbook, UNIX, Open VMS, OS/400, VM, MVS.* New York: McGraw-Hill, 1994.

Dumas, M. B., and M. Schwartz. *Principles of Computer Networks and Communications*, Upper Saddle River, NJ: Pearson Education, 2009.

E

Elliott, J. C., and M. W. Sachs. "The IBM Enterprise Systems Connection (ESCON) Architecture," *IBM J. of Research and Development*, Vol. 36, no. 4 (July 1992), pp. 577–592.

F

Feng, W., M. Warren, and E. Weigle. "The Bladed Beowulf: A Cost-Effective Alternative to Traditional Beowulfs," *Proceedings of the Int'l Conf. on Parallel Processing*, IEEE Press, 2002.

Ferguson, P., and G. Huston. *Quality of Service: Delivering QoS on the Internet and in Corporate Networks.* Secaucus, NJ: John Wiley & Sons, 1998.

Fiedler, D. "The Unix Tutorial, Part 2: Unix as an Application-Programs Base," *Byte,* Vol. 8, no. 9 (September 1983), pp. 257–278.

——. "The Unix Tutorial, Part 1: An Introduction to Features and Facilities," *Byte,* Vol. 8, no. 8 (August 1983), pp. 188–219.

Finnie, S., and P. Gralla. "Hands On: A Hard Look at Windows Vista," *Computerworld Networking [online]*, (November 13, 2006).

Fisher, C. N., and R. J. LeBlanc, Jr. *Crafting a Compiler.* Redwood City, CA: Benjamin Cummings, 1988.

Fitzgerald, J., and A. Dennis. *Business Data Communications and Networking*, 9th ed. Secaucus, NJ: John Wiley & Sons, 2007.

Flanagan, J. R., T. A. Gregg, and D. F. Casper. "The IBM Enterprise Systems Connection (ESCON) Channel—A Versatile Building Block," *IBM J. of Research and Development*, Vol. 36, no. 4 (July, 1992), pp. 617–632.

Flores, I. *The Logic of Computer Arithmetic.* Englewood Cliffs, NJ: Prentice Hall, 1963.

Folk, M. J., and B. Zoellick. *File Structures*, 2nd ed. Reading, MA: Addison-Wesley, 1992.

Forouzan, B. A. *Data Communications and Networking*, 4th ed., New York: McGraw-Hill, 2007.

Fountain, D. "The Pentium: More RISC than CISC," *Byte,* Vol. 18, no. 10 (September 1993), p. 195.

Fraser, B. "Understanding Digital RAW Capture," white paper: www.adobe.com/digitalimag/pdfs/understanding_digital_rawcapture.pdf, September 4, 2004.

G

Galitz, W. *The Essential Guide to User Interface Design: An Introduction to GUI Design Principles and Techniques*, Secaucus. NJ: John Wiley & Sons, 1997.

Gentzsch, W. "DOT-COMing the Grid: Using Grids for Business," *Sun Microsystems*, www.sun.com.

Georgiou, C. J., T. A. Larsen, P. W. Oakhill, and B. Salimi. "The IBM Enterprise Systems Connection (ESCON) Director: A Dynamic Switch for 200Mb/s Fiber Optic Links," *IBM J. of Research and Development*, Vol. 36, no. 4 (July 1992), pp. 593–616.

Ghemawat, S., H. Gobioff, and S-T. Leung. "The Google File System," *19th ACM Symposium on Operating Systems Principles*, Lake George, NY: 2003.

Gibson, D. H., and G. S. Rao. "Design of the IBM System/390 Computer Family for Numerically Intensive Applications: An Overview for Engineers and Scientists," *IBM J. of Research and Development,* Vol. 36, no. 4 (July 1992), pp. 695–712.

Gifford, D., and A. Spector. "Case Study: IBM's System/360-370 Architecture," *Comm. of the ACM,* Vol. 30, no. 4 (April 1987), pp. 292–297ff.

Glass, G., and K. Ables. *Linux for Programmers and Users, A Complete Guide.* Englewood Cliffs, NJ: Prentice Hall, 2006.

Gochman, S., A. Mendelson, A. Naveh, and E. Rotem. "Introduction to Intel Core Duo Processor Architecture," *Intel Technical J.,* Vol 10, no. 2, (May 2006), pp. 89–97.

Goldberg, D. "What Every Computer Scientist Should Know about Floating Point Arithmetic," *ACM Computing Surveys,* Vol. 23, no. 1 (March 1991), pp. 5–48.

Goodman, J., and K. Miller. *A Programmer's View of Computer Architecture, with Assembly Language Examples from the MIPS RISC Architecture.* Philadelphia: W. B. Saunders, 1993.

Grosch, H. R. J. "The Way It Was: 1957, A Vintage Year," *Datamation,* (September 1977), pp. 75–78.

Grosshans, D. *File Systems: Design and Implementation.* Englewood Cliffs, NJ: Prentice Hall, 1986.

Gschwind, M., H. P. Hofstee, B. Flochs, M. Hopkins, Y. Watanabe, and T. Yamazaki. "Synergistic Processing in Cell's Multicore Architecture," *IEEE Micro,* (March-April 2006), pp. 10–24. (Available at www.research.ibm.com/people/m/mikes/papers/2006_ieeemicro.pdf.)

Gustavson, D. "Computer Buses—A Tutorial," *IEEE Micro,* Vol. 4, no. 4 (August 1984), pp. 7–22.

H

Halfhill, T. R. "Intel's P6," *Byte,* Vol. 20, no. 4 (April 1995), pp. 42–58.

——. "AMD vs. Superman," *Byte,* Vol. 19, no. 11 (November 1994), pp. 95–104.

——. "80X86 Wars," *Byte,* Vol. 19, no. 6 (June 1994), pp. 74–88.

Halsall, F. *Data Communications, Computer Networks, and OSI,* 4th ed. Reading, MA: Addison-Wesley, 1996.

Hartmann, D. "Introduction to Quality of Service, White Paper," globalknowledge.com, at www.findwhitepapers.com, 2004.

Hatfield, D. J., and J. Gerald. "Program Restructuring for Virtual Memory," *IBM Systems Journal,* Vol. 10, no. 3 (1971), p. 189ff.

Hayes, J. P. *Computer Architecture and Organization,* 3rd ed., New York: McGraw-Hill, 2002.

Heath, S. *PowerPC, A Practical Companion.* Oxford: Butterworth Heinemann, 1994.

Henle, R. A., and B. W. Kuvshinoff. *Desktop Computers.* Oxford: Oxford University Press, 1992.

Hennessy, J. L., and D. A. Patterson. *Computer Architecture, A Quantitative Approach,* 4th ed. San Francisco: Morgan Kaufmann, 2006.

Hill, M. D. "A Case for Direct-Mapped Caches," *IEEE Computer,* Vol. 21, no. 12 (December 1988), pp. 25–40.

Hofstee, H. P. "Introduction to the Cell Broadband Engine," www.ibm.com/developerworks/pow/cell/docs_articles.html, May 2005.

Hopkins, M. E. "A Perspective on the 801/Reduced Instruction Set Computer," *IBM Systems Journal,* Vol. 26, no. 1 (1987), pp. 107–121.

Hoskins, J. *IBM System/390,* 3rd ed. New York: John Wiley & Sons, 1994.

——and B. Frank. *Exploring Eserver zSeries and S/390 Servers,* 7th ed. Gulf Breeze, FL: Maximum Press, 2001.

I

———. *IBM eServer zSeries 900 and z/OS Reference Guide.* Armonk, NY: IBM Corp., 2002.

———. *IBM System/370 Principles of Operation,* 9th ed. Armonk, NY: IBM Corp., 1981.

———. *IBM System x and IBM BladeCenter Servers and the IBM Systems Agenda for On Demand Business*, IBM Systems and Technology Group XSWD1616-USEN-03, (May 2006).

———. *IBM System z/10 Enterprise Class Mainframe Server Specification Summary*, www-03.ibm.com/systems/zhardware/z10ec/specification.html, 2008.

———. *IBM System z/10 Enterprise Class Reference Guide*, www-03.ibm.com/systems/z/hardware/z10ec/specifications.html, 2008.

———. *IBM z/Architecture Principles of Operation,* Armonk, NY: IBM Corp., 2001.

IBM Corporation. *The PowerPC Architecture,* 2nd ed. San Francisco: Morgan Kaufmann, May 1994.

———. "The Informal Report from the RFC 1149 Event," *Bergen Linux Users' Group*, www.blog.linux.no/rfc1149/writeup.html.

Intel Corporation. *IA-64 Architecture Manual, Vols. 1–4*, Mt. Prospect, IL: Intel, 2002.

———. *Microprocessors,* Volume II. Mt. Prospect, IL: Intel, 1991.

———. *Internetworking Technology Handbook*, www.cisco.com/en/US/docs/internetworking/technology/handbook/QoS.html, 2009.

Irvine, K. R. *Assembly Language for the Intel-Based Computers*, 5th ed. Englewood Cliffs, NJ: Prentice Hall, 2006.

J

Jacobs, B., M. Brown, K. Fukui, and N. Trivedi. *Introduction to Grid Computing*, www.redbooks.ibm.com, 2005.

Janossy, J. G., and S. Samuels. *CICS/ESA Primer.* New York: John Wiley & Sons, 1995.

Johnson, R. H. *MVS, Concepts and Facilities.* New York: Intertext, McGraw-Hill, 1989.

Jones, O. *Introduction to the X Window System.* Englewood Cliffs, NJ: Prentice Hall, 2000.

Joseph, J., and C. Fellenstein. *Grid Computing*. Armonk, NY: IBM Press, 2004.

K

Kane, G., and J. Heinrich. *MIPS RISC Architecture*, 2nd ed. Englewood Cliffs, NJ: Prentice Hall, 1992.

Kay, D. C., and J. R. Levine. *Graphics File Formats*, 2nd ed. New York: Windcrest/McGraw-Hill, 1995.

Kendall, G. W. "Inside the PCI Local Bus," *Byte,* Vol. 19, no. 2 (February 1994), pp. 177–180.

Kim, B. G., and P. Wang. "ATM Network: Goals and Challenges," *Comm. of the ACM*, Vol. 38, no. 2, February 1995, pp. 39–44.

———. "Examining the Peer-to-Peer Connectivity and Multiple Network Support of Chicago," *Microsoft Systems Journal,* Vol. 9, no. 11 (November 1994), pp. 15–32.

King, G. M., D. M. Dias, and P. S. Yu. "Cluster Architectures and S/390 Parallel Sysplex Scalability," *IBM System J.,* Vol. 36, no. 2 (1997), pp. 221–241.

Kirk, D. S. *The MVS Primer.* Boston, MA: QED, 1992.

Knuth, D. *The Art of Computer Programming,* Volume 2, *Seminumerical Algorithms*, 3rd ed. Reading, MA: Addison-Wesley, 1997.

Korpela, E., D. Werthimer, D. Anderson, J. Cobb., and M. Lebofsky. "SETI@Home: Massively Distributed Computing for SETI," Computing in Science and Engineering, Vol. 3, #1 (2001), pp. 78–83.

———. *Unicode Explained*. Sebastopol, CA: O'Reilly & Assoc., 2006.

Kulisch, U., and W. Maranker. *Computer Arithmetic in Theory and Practice.* New York: Academic Press, 1981.

Kurose, J. F., and K. W. Ross. *Computer Networking: A Top Down Approach*, 4th ed., Boston, MA: Pearson Education, 2008.

L

Lan, R., F. Yang, and S. Zheng. "Financial Service Innovation Based on Grid Computing," *Proc. of the International Conference on Services Systems and Services Management*, Vol. 2, Nos. 13–15 (June 2005), pp. 1081–1084.

Laszlo, E. *The Systems View of the World: A Holistic Vision for Our Time*, 2nd. ed. Cresskill, NJ: Hampton Press, 1996.

Lehrer, T. *That Was the Year That Was* (recording). Originally released 1965, reissued on CD, Reprise 6179.

Lewin, M. H. *Logic Design and Computer Organization.* Reading, MA: Addison-Wesley, 1983.

Liaw, M. "Reading GIF Files," *Dr. Dobb's Journal,* Vol. 20, no. 2 (February 1995), pp. 56–60ff.

Lipschutz, S. *Essential Computer Mathematics,* Schaum's Outline Series in Computers. New York: McGraw-Hill, 1982.

Liptay, J. S. "Design of the IBM Enterprises System/9000 High-End Processor," *IBM J. of Research and Development,* Vol. 36, no. 4 (July 1992), pp. 713–732.

Livadas, P. *File Structures: Theory and Practice.* Englewood Cliffs, NJ: Prentice Hall, 1990.

M

Mano, M. M., and M. D. Celetti. *Digital Design*, 4th ed. Englewood Cliffs, NJ: Prentice Hall, 2007.

Mansfield, N. *The Joy of X: An Overview of the X Window System.* Reading, MA: Addison-Wesley, 1993.

Marcus, A., N. Smilonich, and L. Thompson. *The Cross-GUI Handbook for Multiplatform User Interface Design.* Reading, MA: Addison-Wesley, 1995.

Markoff, J. "David Gelernter's Romance with Linda," *The New York Times*, Business Section, January 19, 1992, pp. 1ff.

Marsan, C. D. "Grid Vendors Target Corporate Applications," *Network World*, Framingham, MA, January 27, 2003.

McDowell, S., and M. Seger. *USB Explained.* Englewood Cliffs, NJ: Prentice Hall, 1999.

McHoes, A. M., and I. M. Flynn. *Understanding Operating Systems*, 5th ed. Florence, KY: Wadsworth Publishing, 2008.

McIlroy, M. D., E. N. Pinson, and B. A. Tague. "UNIX Time-Sharing System: Foreword," *Bell System Technical Journal,* Vol. 57, no. 6 (July–August 1978), pp. ix–xiv, reprinted in *UNIX System: Reading and Applications,* Volume 1. Englewood Cliffs, NJ: Prentice Hall, 1987.

Messmer, H. *The Indispensable PC Hardware Book*, 4th ed. Reading, MA: Addison-Wesley, 2001.

Methvin, D. "An Architecture Redefined," *PC Tech Journal,* Vol. 5, no. 8 (August 1987), pp. 58–70.

Meyer, J., and T. Downing. *Java Virtual Machine,* Sebastopol, CA: O'Reilly & Assoc., 1997.

Microsoft Corporation. *Microsoft Windows 2000 Resource Kit.* Redmond, WA: Microsoft Press, 2000.

Miller, M. A. *Internetworking: A Guide to Network Communications, LAN to LAN; LAN to WAN,* 2nd ed. New York: M&T Books/MIS Press, 1995.

——. *The 68000 Family, Architecture Programming and Applications,* 2nd ed. Columbus, OH: Charles E. Merrill, 1992.

Mollenhoff, C. R. *Atanasoff, Forgotten Father of the Computer.* Ames: Iowa State University Press, 1988.

Moore, C. R., and R. C. Stanphill. "The PowerPC Alliance," *Comm. of the ACM,* Vol. 37, no. 6 (June 1994), pp. 25–27.

Moore, S. K. "Winner: Multimedia Monster," www.spectrum.ieee.org/jan06/2609/.

Mueller, S. *Upgrading and Repairing PCs,* 18th ed., Indianapolis, IN: Que, 2008.

Murdocca, M., and V. Heuring. *Computer Architecture and Organization, An Integrated Approach.* Secaucus, NJ: John Wiley & Sons, 2007.

Murray, J. D., and W. van Ryper. *Encyclopedia of Graphics File Formats,* 2nd ed. Sebastopol, CA: O'Reilly & Assoc., 1996.

N

Newmarch, J. "Stream Control Transmission Protocol (SCTP) Associations," *Linux Journal,* (October 2007), pp. 74–75.

Nich, J., C. Vaill, and H. Zhong. "Virtual-Time Round-Robins: An O(1) Proportional Share Scheduler," *Proc. of the 2001 USENIX Annual Tech. Conf*. June, 2001.

Nick, J. M., B. B. Moore, J.-Y. Chung, and N. S. Bowen. "S/390 Cluster Technology: Parallel Sysplex," *IBM System J.,* Vol. 36, no. 2 (1997), pp. 172–201.

——, J.-Y. Chung, and N. S. Bowen. "Overview of IBM S/390 Parallel Sysplex—A Commercial Parallel Processing System," *Proc. of the IEEE International Parallel Processing Symposium,* Hawaii, 1996, pp. 488–495.

——. *NVidia GeForce 8800 GPU Architecture Overview,* NVidia Technical Brief TB-02787-001, v0.9, (Nov. 2006).

P

Paceley, L. *"Intel P6 Technology."* Mt. Prospect, IL: Intel, 1995.

Padega, A. "System/370 Extended Architecture: Design Considerations," *IBM J. of Research and Development,* Vol. 27, no. 3 (May 1983), pp. 193–202.

Panko, R. *Business Data Networks and Telecommunications,* 7th ed. Upper Saddle River NJ: Pearson Education, 2009.

Parker, T., K. Siyan, and K. Siyan. *TCP/IP Unleashed,* 3rd ed. Indianapolis, IN: Sams, 2002.

Patterson, D. A., and J. L. Hennessy. *Computer Organization and Design, The Hardware/Software Interface,* 3rd ed. revised. San Francisco: Morgan Kaufmann, 2007.

—— and R. S. Piepho. "RISC Assessment: A High-Level Language Experiment," *Proc. 9th Annual Symp. on Comp. Arch,* Austin, 1982, pp. 3–8.

—— and C. H. Sequin. "RISC I: A Reduced Instruction Set VLSI Computer," *Proc. 8th Annual Symp. on Comp. Arch,* Minneapolis, MN, 1981, pp. 443–457.

——. *PCI to PCI Bridge Architecture Specification,* Revision 1.0, PCI Special Interest Group, April 5, 1994.

——. *PCI Local Bus Specification,* Production Version, Version 2, PCI Special Interest Group, 1993.

——. *PDF Primer White Paper,* www.pdf-tools.com/public/downloads/whitepapers/whitepaper-pdfprimer.pdf, 2005.

Pfister, G. F. *In Search of Clusters,* 2nd ed. Upper Saddle River, NJ: Prentice Hall, 1998.

Pietrek, M. "Stepping Up to 32 Bits: Chicago's Process, Thread, and Memory Management," *Microsoft Systems Journal,* Vol. 9, no. 8 (August 1994), pp. 13–26.

Plambeck, K. E. *PowerPC Architecture.* Austin, TX: IBM, 1993.

——. *PowerPC 601, RISC Microprocessor User's Manual,* Item MPC601UM/AD, Revision 1. Phoenix, AZ: Motorola, 1993.

——. "Concepts of Enterprise Systems Architecture/370," *IBM Systems Journal,* Vol. 28, no. 1 (1989), pp. 39–57.

Pogue, D. *Mac OS X, Leopard The Missing Manual.* Sebastopol, CA: O'Reilly & Assoc., 2007.

Prasad, N. S., and J. Savit. *IBM Mainframes,* 2nd ed. New York: McGraw-Hill, 1994.

Q

Quercia, V., and T. O'Reilly. *X Windows System User's Guide,* Volume 3. Sebastopol, CA: O'Reilly & Assoc., 1993.

R

Rao, G. S., T. A. Gregg, C. A. Price, C. L. Rao, and S. J. Repka. "IBM S/390 Parallel Enterprise Servers G3 and G4," *IBM J. of Research and Development,* Vol. 41, no. 4 &5 (1997), pp. 397–404.

Reiss, L., and J. Radin. *X Window Inside and Out.* New York: Osborne McGraw-Hill, 1992.

——. RFC 1149 [see Waitzman, D.].

Richter, J. *Advanced Windows,* 3rd ed. Redmond,WA: Microsoft Press, 1997.

Ridge, D., D. Becker, P. Merkey, and T. Sterling, "Beowulf: Harnessing the Power of Parallelism in a Pile of PCs," *Proc. of IEEE Aerospace Conference*, Vol. 2, pp. 79–91, 1997.

Rimmer, S. *Bit-Mapped Graphics,* 2nd ed. New York: Windcrest/McGraw-Hill, 1993.

Ritchie, D. M. "The Evolution of the UNIX Time-Sharing System," *AT&T Bell System Technical Journal,* Vol. 63, no. 8 (October 1984), pp. 1–17,   reprinted in *UNIX System: Reading and Applications,* Volume II. Englewood Cliffs, NJ: Prentice Hall, 1987.

Robb, D. "Plugging into Computing Power Grids," *Computerworld,* (Apr. 22, 2002), pp. 48–49.

Rochester, J. B., and J. Gantz. *The Naked Computer: A Layperson's Almanac of Computer Lore, Wizardry, Personalities, Memorabilia, World Records, Mind Blowers, and Tomfoolery.* New York: William A. Morrow, 1983.

Rosch, W. *Hardware Bible*, 6th ed. Indianapolis, IN: Que, 2003.

Rosen, K. H., R. R. Rosinski, and J. M. Farber. *Unix System V Release 4: An Introduction for New and Experienced Users.* New York: Osborne McGraw-Hill, 1990.

Rosen, S. "Programming Systems and Languages, A Historical Survey," *Proc. of the Spring Joint Computer Conference*, Vol. 24, AFIPS, 1964, pp. 1–14.

Russinovich, M., and D. A. Solomon. *Microsoft Windows Internals*, 4th ed. Redmond, WA: Microsoft Press, 2005.

Ryan, B. "Inside the Pentium," *Byte,* Vol. 18, no. 6 (May 1993), pp. 102–104.

——. "RISC Drives PowerPC," *Byte,* Vol. 18, no. 9 (August 1993), pp. 79–90.

S

Samson, S. L. *MVS Performance Management: OS/390 Edition, SP Version 5.* New York: McGraw-Hill, 1997.

Sargent, M., III, and R. L. Shoemaker. *The Personal Computer from the Inside Out,* 3rd ed. Reading, MA: Addison-Wesley, 1995.

Scalzi, C. A., A. G. Ganek, and R. J. Schmalz. "Enterprise Systems Architecture/370: An Architecture for Multiple Virtual Space Access and Authorization," *IBM Systems Journal,* Vol. 28, no. 1 (1989), pp. 15–37.

Schmerken, I. "Girding for Grid," *Wall Street and Technology*, New York: March 12, 2003. (At www.wallstreetandtech.com/story/wst200303031250005.)

Schulke, M. H., and L. J. Rose. "IBM ES/9000 Series," *Datapro*, Computer System Series: Systems 3938. New York: McGraw-Hill, January 1993.

Schurmann, T. "Virtues of the Virtual," *Linux Pro*, no. 83, (Oct 2007), pp. 21–25ff.

Senturia, S., and B. Wedlock. *Electronic Circuits and Applications*. New York: John Wiley & Sons, 1975.

Shanley, T. *The Unabridged Pentium 4: IA32 Processor Genealogy*, PC Systems Architecture Series. Richardson, TX: Mindshare, Addison-Wesley, 2004.

——. *PowerPC System Architecture*, PC Systems Architecture Series, Volume 7. Richardson, TX: Mindshare, 1994.

Sharp, A., Y. Rogers and J. Preece. *Interaction Design: Beyond Human Computer Interactions*, Secaucus, NJ: John Wiley & Sons, 2007.

Silberschatz, A., G. Gagne, and P. Galvin. *Operating System Concepts*, 8th ed. Secaucus, NJ: John Wiley & Sons, 2008.

Smith, A. J. "Cache Memories," *Computing Surveys*, Vol. 14, no. 3 (September 1982), pp. 473–530.

Smith, R. *Learning Postscript, A Visual Approach*. Berkeley, CA: Peachpit Press, 1990.

——. *Linux Power Tools*, Somerset, NJ: Sybex: Wiley, 2003.

Smith, R. M., and P. Yeh. "Integrated Cryptographic Facility of the Enterprise Systems Architecture/390: Design Considerations," *IBM J. of Research and Development*, Vol. 36, no. 4 (July 1992), pp. 683–694.

Sobell, M. G. *A Practical Guide to Linux Commands, Editors, and Shell Programming*. Redwood City, CA: Benjamin Cummings, 2005.

Solomon, D. A. *Inside Windows NT*, 2nd ed. Redmond,WA: Microsoft Press, 1998.

Spaniol, O. *Computer Arithmetic*. New York: John Wiley & Sons, 1981.

Stallings, W. *Computer Organization and Architecture*, 7th ed. Indianapolis, IN: Macmillan, 2005.

——. *Business Data Communications*, 6th ed. Upper Saddle River, NJ: Pearson Education, 2009.

——. *Operating Systems*, 6th ed. Indianapolis, IN: Macmillan, 2008.

——. *Data and Computer Communications*, 8th ed. Indianapolis, IN: Macmillan, 2006.

——. *Local and Metropolitan Networks*, 6th ed. Upper Saddle River, NJ: Prentice Hall, 2000.

Stamper, D. A. *Business Data Communications*, 6th ed. Redwood City, CA: Benjamin Cummings, 2002.

Stoddard, S. D. *Principles of Assembler Language Programming for the IBM 370*. New York: McGraw-Hill, 1985.

Stumpf, R. V., and L. C. Teague. *Object-Oriented Sysems Analysis and Design with UML*. Upper Saddle River, NJ: Prentice Hall, 2005.

Suko, R. W. "MVS, A History of IBM's Most Powerful and Reliable Operating System," www.os390-mvs.freesurf.fr/mvshist.htm, April 26, 1993.

Sullivan, J. W., and S. W. Tyler, eds. *Intelligent User Interfaces*. New York, NY: ACM Press, 1991.

Swartzlander, E. E., ed. *Computer Arithmetic*, Volumes I and II. Piscataway, NJ: IEEE Computer Society Press, 1990.

——, ed. *Computer Design Development: Principal Papers*. Indianapolis, IN: Hayden, 1976.

T

Tabak, D. *Advanced Microprocessors*, 2nd ed. New York: McGraw-Hill, 1995.

Tanenbaum, A. S., and M. Van Steen. *Distributed Systems: Principles and Paradigms.* Englewood Cliffs, NJ: Prentice Hall, 2006.

——. *Modern Operating Systems,* 3rd ed. Englewood Cliffs, NJ: Prentice Hall, 2007.

——. *Structured Computer Organization,* 5th ed. Englewood Cliffs, NJ: Prentice Hall, 2005.

——and A. Woodhull. *Operating Systems, Design and Implementation,* 3rd ed. Englewood Cliffs, NJ: Prentice Hall, 2006.

Tate, J., F. Lucchese, and R. Moore. *Introduction to Storage Area Networks,* ibm.com/redbooks, 2006.

Taylor, J. *DVD Demystified.* New York: McGraw-Hill, 1998.

Teufel, B. *Organization of Programming Languages.* Wien: Springer-Verlag, 1991.

Thompson, T. "Power PC Performs for Less," *Byte,* Vol. 18, no. 9 (August 1993), pp. 56–74.

——and B. Ryan. "PowerPC 620 Soars," *Byte,* Vol. 19, no. 11 (November 1994), pp. 113–120.

Thorne, M. *A Tour of the P6 Microarchitecture, February 1995.* Mt. Prospect, IL: Intel, 1995.

Tidwell, J. *Designing Interfaces: Patterns for Effective Interaction Design.* Sebastopol, CA: O'Reilly & Assoc., 2006.

Treu, S. *User Interface Design, A Structured Approach.* New York: Plenum Press, 1994.

Tufte, F. R. *Envisioning Information.* Cheshire, CT: Graphics Press, 1990.

Turner, D., "Apple's iPhone. An Inside Look at a Sensation," *Technology Review,* Vol. 110, no. 5 (Sept 2007), pp. 30–31.

U

Ullman, J. D. *Fundamental Concepts of Programming Systems.* Reading, MA: Addison-Wesley, 1976.

The Unicode Consortium. *The Unicode Standard, Version 5.0.* Reading, MA: Addison-Wesley, 2007.

V

Vacca, J. R. "Taking the RISC out of Servers," *Computerworld,* Vol. 29, no. 25 (June 19, 1995), p. 99.

Vahalia, U. *Unix Internals: The New Frontier.* Englewood Cliffs, NJ: Prentice Hall, 1996.

Valacich, J. S., J. F. George, and J. A. Hoffer. *Essential of Systems Analysis and Design,* 3rd ed., Englewood Cliffs, NJ: Prentice Hall, 2007.

Various authors. *X Window System,* set of volumes. Sebastopol, CA: O'Reilly & Assoc.

Vetter, R. J. "ATM Concepts, Architectures, and Protocols," *Comm. of the ACM,* Vol. 38, no. 2 (February 1995), pp. 30–38.

W

Waitzman, D. "A Standard for the Transmission of IP Datagrams on Avian Carriers," RFC 1149, www.ietf.org/rfc/rfc1149.txt, (April 1, 1990).

Wakerly, J. F. *Digital Design, Principles and Practices,* 4th ed. Englewood Cliffs, NJ: Prentice Hall, 2005.

Waldrop, M. M. "Grid Computing Could Put the Planet's Information Processing Power on Tap," *Technology Review,* (May 2002), pp. 31–37.

Warford, J. S. *Computer Systems,* 3rd ed. Sudbury, MA: Jones & Bartlett, 2005.

Wayner, P. "SPARC Strikes Back," *Byte,* Vol. 19, no. 11 (November 1994), pp. 105–112.

Weiderhold, G. *File Organization for Data Base Design.* New York: McGraw-Hill, 1987.

Weinschenk, S., P. Jamar, and S. C. Yeo. *GUI Design Essentials.* Secaucus, NJ: John Wiley & Sons, 1997.

Weizer, N. "A History of Operating Systems," *Datamation,* (January 1961), pp. 118–126.

White, R. *How Computers Work*, 8th ed. Emeryville, CA: Que, 2005.

Wilkes, M. V. "The Best Way to Design an Automatic Calculating Machine," *Report of the Manchester University Inaugural Conference*. Manchester University Electrical Engineering Department, pp. 16–18, 1951, reprinted in [SWAR76, pp. 266–270].

Williams, D. E., and J. Garcia. *Virtualization with Xen*. Burlington, MA: Syngress Publishing, 2007.

——. www.jayeckles.com/research/gridpc.

Y

Yau, S. S. ed. "50 Years of Computing," *Computer,* Vol. 29, no. 10 (1996), pp. 24–111.

Young, J. L. *The Insider's Guide to Power PC Computing.* Indianapolis, IN: Que, 1994.

INDEX

abacus, 24
abnormal event interrupt, 291–292
absolute path name, 576
abstraction, 45–46
access control list (ACL), 521, 584
access point, 405, 469
access restrictions, physical and
   logical, 439–440
accumulator, 202
active matrix LCD, 329
active window, 531
acyclic-graph directory, 577–581
address field, 229
addressing, instruction, 229–234
addressing, network, 396–398
Address Resolution Protocol (ARP),
   434–435
advanced intelligent format (AIT),
   322
Aiken, Howard H., 25
AIT (advanced intelligent format),
   322
algorithm, 612–613
alias, 579
alphanumeric character data,
   100–109
      alternative sources of
         alphanumeric input, 107–108
      codes used in, 100–106
      conversion between character
         and number, 100
      keyboard input, 106–107
alphanumeric codes, 100–106
alphanumeric data, 100
ALU (arithmetic logic unit), 14, 200
American National Standards
   Institute (ANSI), 101
amplifier, 459
amplitude, 452
amplitude modulation, 457
amplitude shift keying (ASK), 449,
   457

analog, 381
analog (signal), 450
      conversion to digital
         (digitizing), 119–120, 451, 463
      transmission, 450–460, 466–468
analytical engine, 24–25
Andreessen, Max, 34
ANSI (American National Standards
   Institute), 101
API (application program interface),
   17, 487, 524
Apple Macintosh, 31, 528–532
      application, 51
      application architecture, 51
      application layer of TCP/IP,
         389–390, 395–398, 423–424
      application program interface
         (API), 17, 487, 524
      architecture. *See also* system
         architecture
      client-server, 51–55
      defined, 45
      n-tier, 54
      peer-to-peer, 56–57
      three-tier, 54, 56
      two-tier, 53
arithmetic instructions, 221–222
arithmetic/logic unit (ALU), 14, 200
arithmetic shift instruction, 223
ARPANET, 34
ASCII, 101–105, 334
ASK (amplitude shift keying), 449,
   457
associated application, 531
association, 553
associative memory, 630
Asynchronous Transfer Mode
   (ATM), 382, 414, 441
asynchronous transmission, 461
Atanasoff, John V., 25
Atanasoff-Berry Computer (ABC),
   25–26

ATM (Asynchronous Transfer
   Mode), 382, 414, 441
A-to-D converter, 119–120, 464
attenuation, 458
attributes (file), 567–568, 573, 574
audio data, 119–123
authoritative domain name server,
   425–426
average seek time, 313

Babbage, Charles, 24–25
backbone networks, 407–408
backing store, 624
backplane, 351
bandwidth, 380, 454
bar code readers, 107–108
base(s), 69. *See also* number base
basic input/output system (BIOS),
   492
batch processing, 486
batch program, 527, 528
batch system commands, 527–528
BAT file, 490
BCD (binary-coded decimal),
   139–141
Belady's anomaly, 628
Beowulf cluster, 362–363
Berners-Lee, Sir Tim, 34
Berry, Clifford, 25
best-effort delivery service, 393
best-fit algorithm, 616
best-fit strategy, 563
binary arithmetic, 69
binary-coded decimal (BCD),
   139–141
binary-decimal conversion, 79,
   167–168
binary-hexadecimal conversion,
   81–83
binary number, 69
binary-octal conversion, 82–83

binary point, 84
binary representation, 143, 147–149,
    151–155, 165–168
bit, 69
bit manipulation instructions, 222
bitmap, free space management, 569
bitmap, image, 109–112
bitmapped fonts, 328
bit rate, 380
bit vectors, 569
blade, 362
blister technology, 320–321
block (of data), 551
block (disk), 311–315
block coding, 462
blocked state, 605
blocking, 606
Boggs, David, 34
Boole, George, 25
Boolean data, 126
Boolean logic, 25, 222
booting, 599
boot record, 600
bootstrap, 599–601
bootstrapping, 484
Bourne shell start-up, 542
branch dependencies, 255
branch history table, 256
branch instruction processing,
    255–256
broadcast bus, 216
broadcast in hub-based Ethernet, 404
buffer, 282
bundled twisted pair, 466
burst, 352
bus, 15, 214–218, 349–350
        architecture, 354–356
bus interface bridge, 201
bus interfaces, 350–352
bus protocol, 218
bus topology, 401–402
Byron, Augusta Ada, 24
byte, 15
byte stream, 377

cable, 216
cache controller, 259
cache line, 259
cache memory, 210, 259–263
cameras, digital and video, 119, 335
campus area network, 411
card image, 540

carriers, 457
Carrier Sense Multiple Access with
    Collision Detection (CSMA/CD),
    405, 435
carry flag, 153
cathode ray tube (CRT), 329–330
CAV (constant angular velocity), 311
CD-ROM, 319–321
CD storage allocation, 570
Cell Broadband Engine processor,
    268
cell processor block diagram, 268
central processing unit (CPU), 13,
    200. *See also* CPU-memory-I/O
    architectures
        architectures, 242–246
        dispatching, 605, 610–615
        features and enhancements,
            246–256
        model for improved
            performance, 249–253,
            263–265
        scheduling, 608–610
channel (I/O), 15
channel, communication. *See*
    communication channel
channel architectures, 357–358
channel control word, 357
channel program, 299
channel subsystem, 357
char data, 126
checksum, 600
child process, 604
chips, 346
circuit, 466
circuit switching, 382
CLI (command line interface), 524,
    525–527
click to focus, 530
client-server (model), 51–52
client-server architecture, 51–55,
    371–372, 373–376, 536–539
client-server system, 638
clock, 247, 253, 495
clock page replacement algorithm,
    629
cloning, 604
cluster, 360–363, 553
        Beowulf, 362–363
        classification and configuration,
            360–362
        overview of, 360
CLV (constant linear velocity), 312

coaxial cable, 466
codecs, 465
code morphing layer, 245
cold boot, 601
collating sequence, 105
collision, 435, 561
command execution services,
    489–490
command language, 528, 539–542
        elements of, 541–542
        start-up sequence files, 542
command line interface (CLI), 489,
    524, 525–527
command shell, 542
commodity-off-the-shelf (COTS),
    362–363
Common Gateway Interface (CGI),
    54
common look and feel, 516
Common Object Request Broker
    Architecture (CORBA), 523
communication, 2, 18
        history of, 33–34
communication channel, 18,
    376–381
        data transmission directionality,
            381
        medium, 380–381
        model of, 448
        multi-link channel, 449
        number of connections, 381
        topology, 399–402
communication channel technology,
    446–471
        introduction to, 447–450
        routing, 382–386
        signaling technology, 450–465
        transmission media and
            signaling methods, 466–468
        wireless networking, 468–471
communications support services,
    496–497
compaction, 563
complement, 144
complementary arithmetic, 143–155
complementary numbers, 154–155
completion signal, 289–290
computer system architecture,
        bus architecture, 354–356
        channel architecture, 357–358
        history of, 23–24
                communication, networks,
                    and the Internet, 33–34

early work, 24–25
hardware, 25–28
operating systems, 28–33
computer systems. *See also* modern
computer systems
architecture of, 2–3. *See also*
computer system architecture,
history of
components of. *See* computer
systems, components of
description of, general, 18–20
embedded, 5
layout of, simplified, 11
operations of, basic, 12
overview of, 3
protocols, 9, 21–22
selecting, 7–8
standards, 20–21
virtualization and, concept of, 20
computer systems, components of, 2,
9–13, 346–353
communication, 18
hardware, 13–16
software, 16–17
concept of locality, 626–627
concurrent processing, 483
conflict of resources in superscalar
processing, 256
connectionless service, 391
connection-oriented service, 391
constant angular velocity (CAV), 311
constant linear velocity (CLV), 312
context, 286
context switching, 495
contiguous storage allocation,
562–563
control codes, 105–106
control dependency, 244
controls, 531
control statements, 489
control unit (CU), 14, 200
conversational systems, 486
conversions. *See* number conversions
cooperating processes, 603
CORBA (Common Object Request
Broker Architecture), 523
corona wire, 332
COTS (commodity-off-the-shelf),
362–363
country-code top-level domain name
server (ccTLD), 425
CP/M (Control Program for
Microcomputers), 32

CPU architectures, 242–246
overview of, 242–243
traditional modern, 243–244
VLIW and EPIC, 244–246
CPU block diagram, 263–265
CPU bound process, 495
CPU features and enhancements,
246–256
fetch-execute cycle timing
issues, 247–249
scalar processor organization,
253–254
superscalar processor
organization, 253–256
CPU-memory-I/O architectures,
198–233
basic components of, 349
buses, 214–218
components of CPU, 200–201
fetch-execute instruction cycle,
211–214
instructions, classification of,
218–229
instruction word formats,
229–230
instruction word requirements
and constraints, 230–233
memory unit, 204–211
registers, concept of, 201–204
CPU scheduling, 608–610
cross-interleaved Reed-Solomon
error correcting code, 319
CRT (cathode ray tube), 329–330
C-shell script, 542
CSMA/CA protocol, 470
CSMA/CD (Carrier Sense Multiple
Access with Collision Detection),
405, 435
CSNet, 34
CTSS operating system, 30
cycle, directory, 579
cycle, instruction, 189–192
cylinder, disk, 311

daisy chaining, 293
dangling link, 578–579
DASDs (direct access storage
devices), 310
DAT (dynamic address translation),
620–622
data, 2, 66–176
data communications, 373–474

addressing, 396–398
channel characteristics, general,
378–381
messages, 377
OSI network model, 395–396
packet routing, 382–386
packets, 377–378
standards, 415–416
TCP/IP network model,
387–395
data compression, 123–124
data deck, 29
data dependency, 244, 255
data formats, 96–128
alphanumeric character data,
100–109
audio data, 119–123
data compression, 123–124
general considerations, 97–100
image data, 109–119
internal computer data format,
125–128
page description languages,
124–125
datagram switching, 383
data integrity protection, 521
data link layer, 393–394, 435–437
data movement instructions, 219–221
data security and integrity protection,
521
data sharing operations, 521–522
data streaming, 322
DCOM (Distributed Component
Object Model), 523
deadlock, 638–640
deadlock avoidance, 639
deadlock detection and recovery,
639–640
deadlock prevention, 639
decimal-binary conversion, 79
decimal point, 84
decomposition, 44
defragmentation (defragging), 563
demand paging, 626
demodulation, 381, 457
desktop, 528, 531–533, 576
detector, 457
device card, 302
device controller, 283, 302
device driver, 287, 354
DHCP (Dynamic Host Configuration
Protocol), 433–434
differentiated service (DS) field, 438

DiffServ capable nodes, 438
digital cameras, 119
digital signal, 450
diminished radix complementary representation, 144
direct access storage devices (DASDs), 310
direct memory access (DMA), 297–300
directory, 555
directory structure, 573–581
    acyclic-graph directories, 577–581
    file attributes, 573, 574
    single-layer directory system, 574–575
    tree-structured directories, 575–577
dirty bit, 628
discrete signal, 450
disk. *See* magnetic disk; optical disk
disk arrays, 317–318
disk cache, 263
disk commands, 520
disk controller, 283
diskless workstation, 485
dispatcher, 608
dispatching, 494, 605, 610–615
    nonpreemptive, 612–613
    objectives, 611
    operating system, 493–496
    preemptive, 495–496, 613–615
displays, 322–330
    CRT, 329–330
    LCD, 328–329
    OLED, 330
display server, 536
Distributed Component Object Model (DCOM), 523
distributed computing, 19, 49–57
Distributed Computing Environment (DCE), 508
distributed system, 507–508, 638
DMA (direct memory access), 297–300
DNS root server, 425
dock, 531
Domain Name System (DNS), 397, 424–425
    directory services, 424–428
    local server, 426–428
    root server, 425

dot matrix printers, 330
double indirect block pointers, 566
drag-and-drop, 531
DRAM (dynamic RAM), 210, 257
drive arrays, 317–318
DSL access multiplexer, 448–449, 465
DVD, 320
DVD storage allocation, 570
dye sublimation printer, 333
Dynabook project, 31
dynamic address translation (DAT), 620–622
Dynamic Host Configuration Protocol (DHCP), 433–434
dynamic priority scheduling, 614–615
dynamic RAM (DRAM), 210, 257

EBCDIC, 101–105
Eckert, J. Presper, 26
edge, 409
edge router, 409
EDVAC, 27
EEPROM (electronically erasable programmable ROM), 211
electrically based media, 466–467
electromagnetic wave, 455–457, 467–468
electronically erasable programmable ROM (EEPROM), 211
electronic signatures, 439
e-mail, 33, 34
embedded computer systems, 5
embedded control system, 507
encoders, 334
encryption, 440
end-around carry, 147
Englebart, Doug, 31
ENIAC (Electronic Numerical Integrator and Computer), 26–27
enumerated data, 126
environment, system, 43
environmental variable, 576
EPIC (explicitly parallel instruction computer), 243, 244–246
Ethernet, 34, 403
    hub-based, 404, 436–437
    IEEE standards, 403, 416
    switched, 437
    tiered, 407
    wireless, 405–406, 468

Ethernet and TCP/IP networking, 422–442
    application layer, 423–424
    data link layer, 435–437
    DHCP, 433–434
    domain name system directory services, 424–428
    IP addresses, 431–433
    IP operation, 434–435
    network layer, 430–431
    network security, 438–440
    protocols, alternative, 440–442
    quality of service, 437–438
    TCP and transport layer, 429–430
event, 607
event-driven program, 487, 607
exception, 292
excess-N notation, 158
execution protection, 584
execution unit, 251
    multiple, parallel, 253
    pipelining, 251–253
explicitly parallel instruction computer (EPIC), 243, 244–246
explicit source address, 230
exponent, 155
exponential notation, 156
external event, 288–289
external fragmentation, 616
extranet, 411

failover, 360
fail-safe operation, 497
FAT (file allocation table), 564–565
fault-tolerant computers, 317
FCFS (first-come, first-served) disk scheduling, 633–634
FDDI bus, 402
FDM (frequency division multiplexing), 450
fetch-execute instruction cycle, 189–192, 211–214, 247–249, 343
fetch unit, 249–251
fiber-optic cable, 467
fibre channel, 583
fields, 550
FIFO (first-in, first-out), dispatch algorithm, 612
FIFO (first-in, first-out), page replacement, 628

file access methods, 560–562
    indexed, 561–562
    random, 560–561
    sequential, 560
file allocation table (FAT), 564–565
file attributes, 567–568, 573, 574
file commands, 519–520
file extension, 552
file management, 490–491, 548–586
    directory structure, 573–581
    file access methods, 560–562
    file protection, 584–585
    journaling file systems, 585–586
    logical and physical view of files, 549–554
    network file access, 581–582
    operations, 557–558
    partitions, 572
    physical file storage, 562–570
    storage area networks, 582–583
    storage pool, 573
    system, 490–491, 554–559, 570–573
    volumes, 572–573
file manager, 554–555
file protection, 584–585
file server, 309
file storage, physical, 562–570
    CD, DVD, and flash drive allocation, 570
    contiguous storage allocation, 562–563
    free space management, 568–569
    indexed allocation, 566–568
    noncontiguous storage allocation, 564–565
    tape allocation, 569–570
filtering, 455
Finder, 533
FireWire, 354
first-come, first-served (FCFS) disk scheduling, 633–634
first-fit algorithm, 616
first-fit strategy, 563
first-in, first-out (FIFO), 612
fixed partitioning, 616
flag, 203
flash drive storage allocation, 570
flash memory, 210, 310
float data, 126

floating point calculations, 163–165
    addition and subtraction, 163–164
    multiplication and division, 164–165
floating point format, 157–159
    IEEE 754, 166–167
    normalization, 159
    single-precision, 166–167
floating point in the computer, 165–167
floating point numbers, 137, 159–161
flow dependencies, 255
fonts, 117, 328
forking, process, 604
formatting disks, 315
form image, 550
FORTRAN Monitor System (FMS), 29
fractional conversion, 83–89
fractional numbers
    representation and conversion of, 83–89
fragment (packet), 393
fragmentation, 616
frame (memory), 618–620
frame (packets at data link layer), 393
Frame Relay, 410, 414, 441–442
free space bitmap, 569
free space management, 568–569
frequency (sine wave), 452–457
frequency division multiplexing (FDM), 450, 458
frequency shift keying (FSK), 457
front side bus (FSB), 350
ftp (file transfer protocol), 581
full-duplex channel, 381
full-duplex line, 216
fusing system, 332

gadget, 528
Gates, Bill, 209
gateway, 383–384
Gelernter, David, 364
General Motors Research Laboratories, 29
general-purpose register, 202–204, 219–221, 229–230, 231, 256
GIF (Graphics Interchange Format), 21, 112–114
global page replacement, 627–628
glyphs, 117

Google, 58–61
graphical input using pointing devices, 119
graphical objects, 109
graphical user interface (GUI), 31, 489, 524, 528–533
graphics cards, 302
Graphics Interchange Format (GIF), 112–114
graphics tablet, 334
grid computing, 363–364
ground line, 216
groups, 521, 584
guest in virtual machines, 641
GUI (graphical user interface), 31, 489, 524, 528–533
guided media, 466
guided medium, 380–381

half-duplex channel, 381
half-duplex line, 216
handshaking, 429
hard-coded link, 579
hard disk drive, 311–318
hardware, 2, 13–16
    history of, 25–28
    implementation, 269
hashing, 561
hazard, 255
helical scan cartridge, 322
Hertz (Hz), 452
hexadecimal-binary conversion, 81–83
hexadecimal number, 69, 81
hexadecimal point, 84
hidden node condition, 469–470
hierarchical configuration, 502–503
hierarchical directory, 575
high-level (long-term) scheduler, 494, 608–610
high-performance computing, 363–364
hit, 259, 630
hit ratio, 259
Holographic Disk (HVD), 318
hop, 412
hosts, 376
hot carrier injection, 210
HTML (HyperText Markup Language), 21, 125
HTTP (HyperText Transfer Protocol), 9, 21–22, 374–375

hub, 354, 404
hub-based Ethernet, 404, 407, 436–437
HVD (Holographic Disk), 318
HyperText Markup Language (HTML), 125
HyperText Transfer Protocol (HTTP), 9, 21–22, 374–375
hyperthreading, 267
hypervisor, 642

IANA (Internet Assigned Numbers Authority), 416
IAS, 27
IBM 701 computer, 29
IBM OS/360, 30, 32
IBM PC, first, 28, 32
IBM System/360, 30
IBM zOS, 527–528, 539
IBM zSeries
    I/O channel architecture, 357–358
    numbers stored in BCD format, 140–141
    processing an interrupt in, 296
    program-accessible registers in, 204
    table of interrupts for, 293
IBSYS, 29
ICANN (Internet Corporation for Assigned Names and Numbers), 416
icons, 518, 530
IEEE, 416
    Computer Society, 166
    Ethernet standards, 403, 416
    754 standard formats, 166–167
    1394 bus, 354
IETF (Internet Engineering Task Force), 416
image data, 109–119. *See also* displays
    bitmap images, 110–114
    image and video input, 118–119
    object images, 114–117
    representing characters as images, 117
    video images, 117–118
image scanning, 118–119, 335
impact printer, 330
implicit source address, 230
indefinite postponement, 611, 634
independent processes, 603

index block, 566
indexed sequential access method (ISAM), 562
indexed storage allocation, 562, 564
Initial Program Load (IPL), 484
inkjet printer, 330, 332–333
i-node, 566
input, 13
input/output (I/O), 276–302. *See also* CPU-memory-I/O architectures
    channel, 15
    characteristics of typical devices, 278–283
    device commands, 520
    direct memory access, 297–300
    interrupts, 285–297
    modules, 300–302
    programmed, 284–285
    services, 491–492
input/output (I/O) bound, 495
input/output (I/O) system architectures, 353–359
    channel, 299, 357–358
    I/O bus, 354–357
    peripherals, 306–341, 354
input-process-output (IPO) model, 10, 12
Institute for Electrical and Electronics Engineers. *See* IEEE
instruction cycle, 189–192, 211–214, 247–249
instruction pointer, 201
instruction register (IR), 202, 212
instruction reordering, 252–256
instructions, classification of, 218–229
    arithmetic instructions, 221–222
    bit manipulation instructions, 222
    Boolean logic instructions, 222
    data movement instructions, 219–221
    multiple data instructions, 228–229
    program control instructions, 224–225
    shift and rotate instructions, 223–224
    single operand manipulation instructions, 222
    stack instructions, 225–227

instruction set architecture (ISA), 242
instruction sets, 244–245
    IBM mainframe, 233
    Little Man Computer, 183–189
    68000, 220
    Sun SPARC, 233
instruction unit, 252
instruction word formats, 229–230
instruction word requirements and constraints, 230–233
integer data, 126
integer numbers, 137
integer representation. *See* signed integers, representations for
integers, unsigned, 138
integrated circuit, 28, 346
Intel 8008 microprocessor, 28
interactive systems, 486
interblock gap, 315
interface, I/O, 278–283, 297–298, 300–302, 349, 352–359
interface system, 43–44
interface unit, 14–15
interlace, 324
internal computer data format, 125–128
internal fragmentation, 616
internal operating system, 592–643
    CPU dispatching, 605, 610–615
    CPU scheduling, 608–610
    issues, other, 638–640
    loading and execution operations, 607–608
    memory management, 615–617
    network operating system services, 635–638
    processes, 601–606
    requirements, fundamental, 594–599
    secondary storage scheduling, 633–635
    start-up using bootstrap, 599–601
    threads, 606–607
    virtual machines, 641–643
    virtual storage, 617–633
International Organization for Standardization (ISO), 416
International Telecommunications Union Telecommunications Group (ITU-T), 416
Internet
    history of, 33–34

Internet Assigned Numbers Authority (IANA), 416
Internet backbone, 412–414
Internet Corporation for Assigned Names and Numbers (ICANN), 416
Internet Engineering Task Force (IETF), 416
Internet Service Provider (ISP), 409
interprocess message servicing, 492–493
interrupt handler, 287
interrupt lines, 286
interrupt routine, 287
interrupts, 285–297
    as abnormal event indicator, 291–292
    as completion signal, 289–290
    as external event notifier, 288–289
    as means of allocating CPU time, 290–291
    multiple, prioritization and, 293–297
    page fault, 624
    servicing, 285–288
    software, 292–293
interrupt service, 285–288
interuser communication, 521–522
intranet, 55–56, 408, 516
inversion bit in 1's complement arithmetic, 147
I/O. *See* input/output (I/O)
IP address, 397, 424–425, 431–433
IP datagram, 392
IPL (Initial Program Load), 17, 599
IP operation, 434–435
IRQ (interrupt request), 286, 501
ISA (instruction set architecture), 242
ISO (International Organization for Standardization), 416
isochronous data transfer, 355
ISP (Internet Service Provider), 409
ITU-T (International Telecommunications Union Telecommunications Group), 416

Jacquard, Joseph Marie, 24
Java Virtual Machine (JVM), 20
JCL (Job Control Language), 30, 489, 539–540
jitter, packet, 437–438
job, 486, 539, 602

job control cards, 539
Job Control Language (JCL), 30, 489, 539–540
Jobs, Steve, 31
job steps, 602
Joint Photographers Expert Group (JPEG format), 114
journaling file system, 491, 585–586
JPEG format (Joint Photographers Expert Group), 21, 114

Kay, Alan, 31
kernel, 17, 484–485, 502–505
kernel mode, 502
key field, 552
keyword operand, 526

label-switched router, 441
LAN (local area network), 402–407
lane, 352–353
large frames, 320
largest-fit algorithm, 616
laser printer, 330, 331–332
latency time, 314
launch, 531
layered configuration, 502
layer 3 switches, 393
LCD (liquid crystal display), 328–329
LDAP (Lightweight Directory Access Protocol), 581
least frequently used algorithm, 628
least recently used (LRU) algorithm, 260, 628
left shift, 77
letterpress printing, 331
light pen, 334
Lightweight Directory Access Protocol (LDAP), 581
line (bus), 215
linear memory addressing, 192
linear recording cartridge, 321–322
linked list, 569
linked storage allocation, 562, 564
links, channel, 378
links, directory, 577
Linux, 32
liquid crystal display (LCD), 328–329
Little Man Computer (LMC), 180–192
    computer architectures and, 192
    instruction cycle, 189–192
    instruction set, extended, 186–189

    layout of, 181–183
    mnemonic instruction codes, 187–189
    operation of, 183–185
    program example, 185–186
loading and execution operations, 607–608
local area network (LAN), 402–407
local DNS server, 426–428
local domains, 425
locality of reference, 261, 626–627
local page replacement, 627
locked frame, 628
locking, 579
logical addresses (TCP/IP), 397
logical addresses (virtual storage), 620–622
logical connection, 20, 391
logical file, 549–554
logical link control sublayer, 394
logical register, 256
logical shift, 223
logical topology, 402
loosely coupled system, 359
lossless data compression, 123–124
lossy data compression, 123, 124
LRU (least recently used) algorithm, 260, 628

MAC (medium access control), 336, 394
MAC address, 336, 398, 435
Macintosh OS X, 32, 528–532
Madnick, Stuart, 181
magnetic disks, 311–318
magnetic stripe readers, 108
magnetic tape, 321–322
mainframe computers, 19–20. *See also* IBM+
majority logic, 317
MAN (metropolitan area network), 409–411
Manchester encoding, 462
mantissa, 156, 157
Mark I, 25
mask, 432
maskable interrupts, 295
Master Control Program (MCP), 30
master file table (MFT), 567
master-slave multiprocessing, 267
Mauchly, John W., 26
medium-access control (MAC), 336, 394

medium, communication, 380–381
memory, 13, 200, 204–211. *See also*
   CPU-memory-I/O architectures
      cache, 210, 259–263
      flash, 210, 310
      frame, 618–620
      nonvolatile, 209
      partitioning, 615–617
      primary, 308–309
      solid state, 310
      virtual, 617–633
      volatile, 209
memory address, 229
memory address register (MAR), 202,
   204–208
memory buffer, 556
memory data register (MDR), 202,
   204–208
memory enhancements, 256–263
      cache memory, 259–263
      memory interleaving, 258–259
      wide path memory access,
         257–258
memory interleaving, 258–259
memory management, 493, 615–617
memory management unit, 201,
   204–211
      memory capacity, 208–209
      memory characteristics and
         implementation, primary,
         209–211
      operation of memory, 204–208
memory partitioning, 615–617
menu bar, 528
mesh network, 400–401
mesh point, 406
message, 377
metadata, 98, 111–112
Metcalfe, Robert, 34
metropolitan area network (MAN),
   409–411
MFT (master file table), 567
microkernel configuration, 502,
   504–505
microwaves, 467
middleware, 55
MIDI format, 121
miniature operating system
   (MINOS), 596–599
minicomputers, 19–20
MINOS (miniature operating
   system), 596–599

mirrored array, 317
miss, 259, 630
mixed number conversion, 89
mnemonics, 187–189
model for improved CPU
   performance, 249–253
      execution unit, 251
      fetch unit, 249–251
      multiple, parallel execution
         units, 253
      pipelining, 251–253
modem, 18, 465
modern computer systems, 342–364
      blocks and interconnections of,
         345–353, 359
      clusters, 360–363
      high-performance computing,
         363–364
      I/O system architectures,
         353–359
.MOD format, 120
modifier, operand, 526
modulation, 381, 457–458, 463–464
modulus, 146
monitor, display, *See* displays
monitor, operating system, 488
monolithic configuration (operating
   system), 502–503
Mosaic, 34
motherboard, 351
mount, 572
mount a device, 520
mounted tape, 321
mount point, 572
mouse, 334
mouse focus, 530
MP3, 21, 121, 122–123
MPEG-2, 21, 118
MPEG-4, 21, 118
MPLS (Multi-Protocol Label
   Switching), 440–441
MS-DOS, 32
multicomputer system, 359
multicore processors, 265
MULTICS (Multiplexed Information
   and Computing Service), 30–31
multidrop bus, 216
multilevel feedback queue algorithm,
   613–614
multimedia devices, 335
multiple data instructions, 228–229
multiplex, 218

multiplexing, 450
multiple zone recording, 313
multipoint bus, 216
multiprocessor systems, 265–268
multiprogramming, 483, 596–599
Multi-Protocol Label Switching
   (MPLS), 440–441
multitasking, 483, 596–599
multiuser system, 483

.NET, 523
network access point (NAP), 414–415
network communication devices,
   335–336
networking, wireless, 468–471
network interface card (NIC), 18,
   335–336
network interface controller (NIC),
   302, 394
network interface unit (NIU)
   controller, 335–336
network layer in Ethernet and
   TCP/IP networking, 430–431
network layer of TCP/IP, 392–393
network propagation delay, 437
networks, 371–471
      backbone, 407–408
      history of, 33–34
      Internet backbones and the
         Internet, 412, 414
      local area networks, 402–407
      metropolitan area networks,
         409–411
      networking, impact of, 372–373
      operating system services,
         635–638
      piconets, 414–415
      support services, 496–497
      topology, 399–402
      wide area networks, 411–412,
         413–414
network security, 438–440
      access restrictions, physical and
         logical, 439–440
      categories of, 438–439
      encryption, 440
network topology, 399–400
Neumann, John von, 26–27
NFS (Network File System), 581
NIC (network interface card), 18,
   302, 335–336, 394
9's decimal representation, 144–147

NIU (network interface unit) controller, 335–336
nodes, 360, 376
noise, 458–460, 464, 466
noncontiguous storage allocation, 564–565
nonpreemptive dispatch, 495–496, 612–613
   first-in, first-out, 612
   priority scheduling, 613
   shortest job first, 612–613
nonpreemptive systems, 606
nonresident attributes, 568
nonresident commands, 489
nonvolatile memory, 209
normalization, floating point, 159–161
not used recently (NUR) algorithm, 628–629
NSFNet, 34
n-step c-scan scheduling, 635
NT File System (NTFS), 567
n-tier architecture, 54
number base
   performing arithmetic in different, 74–77
   related, 81–83
   shifting a number in, 77
number conversions
   alternative conversion method, 79–81
   between base 10 and base 2, 167–168
   binary-decimal, 79
   binary-hexadecimal, 81–83
   binary-octal, 82–83
   fractional, 83–89
   mixed number, 89
numbers. *See also* fractional numbers; real numbers
   binary, 69
   complementary, 154–155
   counting in different bases, 70–74
   floating point, 137, 159–161
   hexadecimal, 69, 81
   integer, 137
   vs. numeric characters, 100
   octal, 69
   as physical representation, 70
   port, 397
numerical data, representations, 136–169

programming considerations, 168–169
real numbers, 155–168
for signed integers, 141–155
for unsigned binary/binary-coded decimals, 138
numeric characters *vs.* numbers, 100
NUR (not used recently) algorithm, 628–629
n-way interleaving, 258

object or vector image, 109, 114–117
octal-binary conversion, 82–83
octal number, 69
octet, IP address, 397
off-line storage, 309
offset addressing, 620
offset printing, 331
OLED (organic light-emitting diode) display, 330
1's complement representation, 141, 147–149
online storage, 309
op code, 183–185
open architectures, 351
open computing, 19
Open Systems Interconnection Reference Model (OSI), 387, 395–396
operand(s)
   fields, 230
   keyword, 526
   positional, 526
   in program execution, 518
   single operand manipulation instructions, 222
operating system (OS), 16–17, 478–643. *See also* Linux; UNIX; OS X; Windows, IBM z/OS
   API, 17, 487, 524
   concept of, 481–488
   file management, 490–491
   history of, 28–33
   input/output services, 481–492
   internal. *See* internal operating system
   kernel, 17, 502–505
   memory management, 493
   network and communications support services, 496–497

organization, 502–505
process control management, 492–493
program execution, 518–519
program services, 523–524
requirements, fundamental, 594–599
scheduling and dispatch, 493–496
secondary storage management, 496
security and protection services, 497–498
system administration support, 498–502
types of, 505–509
user interface and command execution services, 489–490
operating system (OS), user view of, 514–543
   command and script languages, 539–542
   introduction, 515–516
   services to programs, 542–543
   user functions and program services, 518–524
   user interface, purpose of, 516–518
   user interface, types of, 524–536
   X Window and other graphics display methodologies, 536–539
optical character recognition (OCR), 107
optical disk storage, 318–321
organic light-emitting diode (OLED) display, 330
organization
   CPU, 242–246, 253–256
   defined, 242
   in operating systems, 502–505
   in superscalar processing, 253–256
OSI (Open Systems Interconnection Reference Model), 387, 395–396
OS X, 32, 528–532
outline fonts, 328
out-of-order processing, 255
output, 13
overflow, 147–149, 561
owner (file protection), 584

packed decimal format, 140–141
packet, 377–378
packetization, 390
packet routing, 382–386, 394–395
packet sniffing, 439
packet switching, 383
page (virtual storage), 618, 620–621
page description languages, 124–125
page fault (trap), 624–626
page replacement algorithm,
    627–629
        first-in, first-out, 628
        least frequently used, 628
        least recently used, 628
        not used recently, 628–629
        second chance, 629
page sharing, 627
page swapping, 625
page table, 620–621
page table implementation, 630–632
paging, 618, 620–623
palette, 112
palette table, 323
PANs (piconets), 414–415
parallel bus, 216
parallel port, 354
parent process, 604
parked (disk position), 313
partition, 572
partitioning, memory, 615–617
Pascal, Blaise, 24
passive matrix LCD, 329
path, 576
pathname, 575–581
path variable, 525
PCB (process control block),
    286, 603
PCI-Express/PCI bus, 351–353
PCL print command, 331
PDF (Portable Document Format),
    21, 125
peer, 387
peer-to-peer architecture, 56–57
peer-to-peer network software, 638
period, sine wave, 452
peripherals, 306–336
        defined, 307
        displays, 322–330
        I/O architecture, 354
        magnetic disks, 311–318
        magnetic tape, 321–322
        network communication
            devices, 335–336

optical disk storage, 318–321
printers, 330–333
solid state memory, 310
storage, hierarchy of, 308–310
user input devices, 333–335
permanent virtual circuits, 442
personal area network (PAN),
    414–415
personal computers, 14, 19–20
phase, sine wave, 453
phase shift keying (PSK), 457
phonemes, 108–109
phosphors, 329
physical address, 398
physical layer of TCP/IP, 394–395
physical topology, 402
physical view, 549–554
piconets (PANs), 414–415
PID (process identifier), 603
pipelining, 249, 251–253
pixel aspect ratio, 111
pixels, 110–111, 322–323
plug-and-play, 492
plug-ins, 125
pointing devices, graphical input
    using, 119, 333–335, 530
point of presence, 409
point-to-point bus, 216
polling, 286, 293
port, 31, 216
Portable Document Format (PDF),
    21, 125
port address, 397
port number, 397, 429
positional operand, 526
PostScript language, 115–117, 331
preemptive dispatch algorithms,
    495–496, 613–615
        dynamic priority recalculation,
            614–615
        multilevel feedback queues,
            613–614
        round robin, 613, 614
preemptive systems, 606
prepaging, 626
presentation layer of OSI network
    model, 396
primary memory, 308–309
primary storage, 15
printers
        dot matrix, 330
        dye sublimation, 333
        impact, 330

inkjet, 330, 332–333
laser, 330, 331–332
thermal wax transfer, 333
priority in multiple interrupts,
    294–295
priority scheduling, 613
private virtual circuits, 412
privileged instruction, 219, 292
process, 601–606
        child, 604
        cooperating, 603
        creation, 604–605
        independent, 603
        states, 604, 605–606
        system, 604
        user, 604
process control block (PCB), 286, 603
process control management,
    492–493
process identifier (PID), 603
process state, 604, 605–606
process synchronization, 640
program control instructions,
    224–225
program counter (PC), 200–201
program counter register, 202
program execution, 518–519
programmed I/O, 284–285
programmer, 7
programming considerations,
    168–169
program services, 523–524. *See also*
    user functions and program
    services; API
Program Status Word (PSW), 204,
    295–297
program-visible register, 202
progressive scan display, 325
Project MAC, 30
proprietary format, 99
protocols, alternative, 440–442
        ATM, 441
        Frame Relay, 441–442
        MPLS, 440–441
        SONET/SDH, 441
protocols and standards, 20–22
protocol stack, 387
protocol suite, 22, 387
protocol support, 635–638
PSW (Program Status Word), 204,
    295–297
public key–private key cryptography,
    440

public switched telephone network (PSTN), 411–412
pulse amplitude modulation (PAM), 464
pulse code modulation, 463–464

Quality of Service (QoS), 437–438
quantum, 291

radian, 453
Radio Frequency Identification (RFID), 108
radio signals/waves, 451
radix point, 84, 155
RAID (redundant array of inexpensive disks), 317–318
RAM (random access memory), 15, 209–211
random access files, 552
random access memory (RAM), 15, 209–211
raster image, 109–112, 569
raster scan, 324
raw format, 119
read-only memory (ROM), 17, 211
read protection, 584
ready state, 605
real data, 126
real numbers, 137, 155–168
    conversion between base 10 and base 2, 167–168
    exponential notation, review of, 155–156
    floating point calculations, 163–165
    floating point format, 157–159
    floating point in the computer, 165–167
    normalization and formatting of floating point numbers, 159–161
    programming example, 162
real-time system, 289, 507
records, 550
red, green, and blue (RGB), 323–324
redundant array of inexpensive disks (RAID), 317–318
register alias table, 256
register file, 202
registers, 201–203
relative access files, 552, 561
relative pathname, 576

reliable-delivery service, 391
Remote Procedure Call (RPC), 523, 638
rename register, 256
rendering, 117
rendering engine, 117
repeaters, 464
replication, 426
requests for comments (RFCs), 416
resident commands, 489
resolution (of domain name), 426–428
resolution (of screen), 112, 322–323
response time, 611–612
resumption, 606
rewind, 557, 560
RFID (radio frequency identification), 108
RGB (red, green, and blue), 323–324
right-of-way access, 409
right shift, 77
ring topology, 402
Ritchie, Dennis, 31
roll-out, roll-in, 606
ROM (read-only memory), 17, 211
rotate operation, 223
rotational delay, 314
rotational latency time, 314
round robin, 613, 614
route, 383
router, 383–385
    edge, 409
    label-switched, 441
routing, 382–386
RPC (Remote Procedure Call), 523, 638
running state, 605
runs, 568

SAIT (super-AIT) cartridge, 322
SAN (storage area network), 582–583
sandbox, 641–642
scalar processing, 253–254
scan codes, 106–107, 333
scan disk scheduling, 634–635
scanners, 335
scheduling, 493–496, 605, 608–615
screen, 528
scripting language, 517
script language, 539–542
    elements of, 541–542
    start-up sequence files, 542
scripts, 528

SCSI (Small Computer System Interface), 354, 390
SDH (Synchronous Digital Hierarchy), 441
second chance page replacement, 629
secondary storage, 309
secondary storage management, 496
secondary storage scheduling, 633–635
    first-come, first served scheduling, 633–634
    n-step c-scan scheduling, 635
    scan scheduling, 634–635
    shortest distance first scheduling, 634
sectors, 311
security
    access restrictions, physical and logical, 439–440
    categories of, 438–439
    data integrity protection and, 521
    encryption, 440
    network, 438–440
    operating system, 497–498
seek, 560
seek time, 309, 313
segmentation, 618, 632–633
segments, 391
segment table, 633–634
self-synchronization, 462
separator symbol, pathname, 576
sequential access, 560
sequential files, 552
Serial Advanced Technology Attachment (SATA), 22, 354
serial bus, 216
serial port, 354
server, 309. *See also* client-server+
service provider (SP), 409
service request, 487
services
    command execution, 489–490
    communications support, 496–497
    connectionless, 391
    connection-oriented, 391
    DNS directory services, 424–428
    input/output (I/O), 491–492
    operating system, 635–638
    to programs, 542–543. *See also* user functions and program services; API

servicing the interrupt, 286–288
shadow mask, 329
shards, 61
shared-disk, 360–362
shared-nothing, 360–361
shared server, 52
Share Operating System (SOS), 29–30
shell, command, 484
shell scripts, 489–490, 528, 540–541
shift and rotate instructions, 223–224
shift operation, 223
shortcut to file, 579
shortest distance first (SDF) disk scheduling, 634
shortest job first (SJF), 612–613
shredder software, 569
signal, 450–451
signaling technology, 447–465
    analog signaling, 451–460
    digital signaling, 460–465
    modems and codecs, 465
    transmission media and signaling methods, 466–468
signal-to-noise ratio, 466
sign-and-magnitude representation, 141, 142–143
signed integers, representations for, 141–155
    complementary numbers, summary of, 154–155
    diminished radix complementary representation, 144
    9's decimal representation, 144–147
    1's complement representation, 141, 147–149
    other bases, 153–154
    overflow and carry conditions, 153
    sign-and-magnitude representation, 141, 142–143
    10's complement representation, 150–151
    2's complement representation, 141, 151–153
SIMD (Single Instruction, Multiple Data) instructions, 228–229
simplex channel, 381
simplex line, 216
simultaneous thread multiprocessing (STM), 267

sine wave, 452–454
single indirect block pointers, 566
single-layer directory system, 574–575
single operand manipulation instructions, 222
single-precision floating point format, 166–167
Small Computer System Interface (SCSI), 354, 390
socket, 389, 429
software, 2, 16–17
    interrupt, 292–293
    peer-to-peer, 638
    shredder, 569
solid-state drives, 310
solid state memory, 310
SONET (Synchronous Optical Network), 441
spawning, 604
spectrum, electromagnetic, 454–456
speculative execution, 256
SRAM (static RAM), 210
stack instructions, 225–227
stack, memory, 225–226
stack pointer, 226
stack, protocol, 387
stall time, 261
standards, 20–21, 415–416
star topology, 402
start-up
    sequence files, 542
    using bootstrap, 599–601
starvation, 610, 611
static RAM (SRAM), 210
statistical TDM, 464
status register, 203
STM (simultaneous thread multiprocessing), 267
storage. See also file storage, physical; virtual storage
    hierarchy of, 308–310
    linked storage allocation, 562, 564
    logical storage elements, 259
    off-line, 309
    online, 309
    optical disk, 318–321
    secondary, management of, 496
    secondary, scheduling of, 633–635
storage area network (SAN), 582–583

storage pool, 573
stored program concept, 16, 26, 192
stream, character, 107
Stream Control Transmission Protocol (SCTP), 392
streaming (video), 118
striped array, 317–318
subchannel, 357
subdirectories, 575
submit (a job), 29
subnet, 432
subroutine call and return, 224
subsystem, 44
suite (protocol), 22, 387
super-AIT (SAIT) cartridge, 322
supercomputing, 363–364
superscalar processing
    branch instruction processing, 255–256
    conflict of resources, 256
    organization, 253–256, 263–265
    out-of-order processing, 255
    vs. scalar processing, 253–254
supervisor, 488
support chips, 346
suspended state, 606
swap file, 606, 624
swap out, 608
swapping, 608
swap space, 624
switch, 526
switched Ethernet, 405, 407, 437
symmetrical multiprocessing (SMP), 267
symmetric key cryptography, 440
synchronization, 603
Synchronous Digital Hierarchy (SDH), 441
Synchronous Optical Network (SONET), 441
synergy, 344
sysgen, 500–502
system
    abstractions of, 45–46
    architecture. See system architecture
    components of, 43–47
    concept of, general, 40
    e-business, 45
    environment, 43
    home network, typical, 42
    interface, 43–44

inventory control, flow diagram of, 41
plumbing, diagram of, 41
representation of, general, 44, 46–47
solar, 42
subsystems, 44
system administration support, 498–502
system administrator (sysadmin), 8, 498–500
system analyst, 7
system architecture, 38–62
defined, 45
of distributed processing systems, 49–57
example of (Google), 58–61
role of, 57–58
top-down approach and, 49
system bus, 349–353
system generation (sysgen), 500–502
system languages, 487–488
system manager, 8, 488
system process, 604
systems architect, 7
system scalability, 497
system status information, 522–523

table image, 550
tag, memory, 259
talk facilities, 33
tape allocation, 569–570
task, 602
task bar, 528
TCP (Transmission Control Protocol), 391, 429–430
TCP/IP, 22, 34, 387–395. *See also* Ethernet and TCP/IP networking operation of, 388, 423–425
TCP/IP layers, 388–395
application layer, 389–390
data link layer, 393–394
network layer, 392–393
physical layer, 394–395
transport layer, 390–392
TCP layer in Ethernet and TCP/IP networking, 429–430
TDM (time division multiplexing), 450
10's complement representation, 150–151
text messaging, 33

text mode display, 326–328
thermal wax transfer printer, 333
thin client, 485
Thompson, Ken, 31
thrashing, 629–630
threads, 256, 493, 606–607
three-tier architecture, 54, 56
thumb drives, 310
tiered Ethernet, 407
tightly coupled systems, 265–268, 359
time division multiplexing (TDM), 450, 464
time-out, 606
time sharing, 495
time-slicing, 495
title bar, 528
TLB (translation lookaside buffer), 630
Tomlinson, Ray, 33
toner, 332
top-down approach, 49
top-level domains, 425
touch screen, 334–335
track (disk), 311
transfer time, 314–315
translation lookaside buffer (TLB), 630
Transmission Control Protocol (TCP), 391, 429–430
Transmission Control Protocol/Internet Protocol. *See* TCP/IP
transmission media and signaling methods, 380, 403, 466–468
transport layer of TCP/IP, 390–392, 429–430
trap, 292
tree-structured directory, 575–577
triple indirect block pointers, 566
true color, 323
turnaround time, 613
twisted pair, 403, 466
2's complement representation, 141, 151–153
two-tier architecture, 53

UDF (Universal Data Format), 570
underflow, 158
unguided medium, 380, 468
Unicode, 21, 101–105
UNIVAC I, 26
Universal Data Format (UDF), 570

Universal Serial Bus (USB), 354
universe, 584
UNIX/Linux systems
file commands, 520, 525–527, 558
organization, 489, 566–567, 573, 579–580
security and data integrity protection, 521, 584–585
shell scripts, 540–541
start-up sequence files, 542
X Window, 534, 539
unmount a device, 520
unsigned integers, 138
untwisted pair, 403, 466
Usenet news, 34
user, defined, 7
User Datagram Protocol (UDP), 391
user datagrams, 391
user functions and program services, 518–524
disk and other I/O device commands, 520
file commands, 519–520
interuser communication and data sharing operations, 521–522
program execution, 518–519
program services, 523–524
security and data integrity protection, 521
system status information, 522–523
user input devices, 333–335
keyboards, 333–334
multimedia devices, 335
pointing devices, 334–335
scanners, 335
user interface, 524–536
batch system commands, 527–528
command execution services, 489–490
command line interface, 524, 525–527
graphical user interfaces, 528–533
purpose of, 516–518
trade-offs in, 533–536
user-level thread, 607
username@hostname format, 33
user process, 604
user-visible register, 202

vacuum tubes, 27
variable cards, 25
variable partitioning, 616
vectored interrupt, 293
vector images, 109
vector scan, 325
very-large-scale integrated circuit
    (VLSI), 346
very long instruction word (VLIW),
    243, 244–246
video cameras, 119
virtual, 20
virtual circuit, 382
virtual circuit identifier, 441
virtual computer, 345
virtual file systems, 570
virtualization, 20, 345, 641
virtual local area network, 408
virtual machine (VM), 20, 641–643
virtual memory. *See v*irtual storage
virtual private network (VPN), 497
virtual storage, 292, 493, 617–633
    concept of, 623–624
    concept of locality, 626–627
    dynamic address translation,
        620–623
    frames, 618–620
    overview of, 617–618
    page faults, 624–626
    page replacement algorithms,
        627–629
    pages, 618, 620–623
    page sharing, 627
    page table implementation,
        630–632
    process separation, 633
    segmentation, 632–633

thrashing, 629–630
    working sets, 627
VLIW (very long instruction word),
    243, 244–246
.VOC format, 121
voice input, 108–109
volatile memory, 209
volume, 531, 572–573
volume table of contents, 572
von Neumann, John, 192
von Neumann architecture, 27, 192

wake-up, 606
WAN (wide area network), 411–412,
    413–414
warm boot, 601
waveform, 450–459
wavelength, 452
wavelength division multiplexing
    (WDM), 458
.WAV format, 121–122
Web-based computing, 55–56
Web services designer, 8
well-known port, 397–398
what-you-see-is-what-you-get
    (WYSIWYG) output, 326
wide area network (WAN), 411–412,
    413–414
wide path memory access, 257–258
widget, 528
Wi-Fi, 405–406, 468–471
wild cards, 527, 558
WiMAX, 468
window, 517
Windows PowerShell, 490
Windows Scripting Host, 490

Windows Vista, 32
Windows XP, 32
wired media, 466–467
wireless Ethernet, 405–406, 468
wireless networking, 468–471
word, 15
working directory, 576
working set, 627
workstations, 19–20
World Wide Web, 34
WORM (write-once-read-
    many-times) disks, 320–321
worst-fit algorithm, 616
wraparound, 146
write back, 261
write-once-read-many-times
    (WORM) disks, 320–321
write protection, 584
write through, 261
WYSIWYG
    (what-you-see-is-what-you-get)
    output, 326

x86 CPU family of computers, 28
Xerox PARC (Palo Alto Research
    Center), 31, 34
XML (Extensible Markup Language),
    21
X Window, 534, 536–539

ZBR (zone bit recording), 313
Z-CAV (zone-CAV recording), 313
zone bit recording (ZBR), 313
zone-CAV recording (Z-CAV), 313
zOS, 527–528, 539
Zuse, Conrad, 25